# THE LIFE OF JAMGON KONGTRUL THE GREAT

# The Life of
# Jamgon Kongtrul the Great

Alexander Gardner

SNOW LION
BOULDER
2019

FRONTISPIECE: Painting of Jamgon Kongtrul with hand- and footprints kept in eastern Tibet. Photograph by Matthieu Ricard/Shechen Archives.

Snow Lion
An imprint of Shambhala Publications, Inc.
4720 Walnut Street
Boulder, Colorado 80301
www.shambhala.com

9 8 7 6 5 4 3 2 1

First Edition
Printed in the United States of America

♾ This edition is printed on acid-free paper that meets the American National Standards Institute z39.48 Standard.
♻ Shambhala Publications makes every effort to print on recycled paper. For more information please visit www.shambhala.com.

Snow Lion is distributed worldwide by Penguin Random House, Inc., and its subsidiaries.

LIBRARY OF CONGRESS CATALOGING-IN-PUBLICATION DATA

Names: Gardner, Alexander, author.
Title: The life of Jamgon Kongtrul the Great/Alexander Gardner.
Description: First edition. | Boulder: Snow Lion, 2019. |
Includes bibliographical references and index.
Identifiers: LCCN 2018030207 | ISBN 9781611804218 (hardcover: alk. paper)
Subjects: LCSH: Kong-sprul Blo-gros-mtha'-yas, 1813–1899. |
Lamas—China—Tibet Autonomous Region—Biography. |
Buddhism—China—Tibet Autonomous Region—History.
Classification: LCC BQ968.O57 G37 2019 | DDC 294.3/923092 [B]—dc23
LC record available at https://lccn.loc.gov/2018030207

# Contents

*Part Three: Deaths*

# PREFACE

In the middle of January 1879, an elderly Tibetan monk named Jamgon Kongtrul went on an arduous hike in search of a cave. Kongtrul was then known across the Tibetan Plateau as a collector and propagator of scores of religious traditions, and as a skilled ritual specialist and a man of great learning. The sixty-six-year-old lama and his companion tied rope ladders to rocks, scaled cliffs by clinging to roots and vines, and arrived at a spacious cave high on the central peak of a ridge shaped like a lotus hat. Inside they found a formation which Kongtrul declared to be a naturally arising statue of Padmasambhava, the Precious Guru revered by Tibetans as the man who imbued their landscape with Buddhism. They named nearby overhangs "the cave of the religious companion" and "the long-life cave." Inside these three caves Jamgon Kongtrul found physical evidence of Padmasambhava's long-ago activity there—footprints, small images, and miraculous substances. Pocketing these, he descended the ridge in the midst of a furious wind.

The climb was the culmination of an effort to locate a site that would firmly embed Padmasambhava in a place dear to Jamgon Kongtrul—Ronggyab, the "small hidden valley" where he was born, a place of undulating flower-strewn meadows and thickly forested slopes. He had spent the majority of his life elsewhere, always moving, walking or riding horses across the region known as Kham. His peregrinations took him from one valley to another, where he would sleep for a night or months at a time in great monasteries, small temples, or cold mountain caves, performing rituals and giving basic Buddhist instruction to increasingly large crowds. He sanctified dozens of places—announcing the presence of Padmasambhava and other deities—built monuments and temples, and established ritual programs. He possessed the ability to find the Buddha wherever he placed his feet.

Finding statues and sacred substances in a cave above his home valley was but one moment in the career of a man who spent his life with his feet on the ground, a ground that was rich in miracles and inspiration— "treasure" in Tibetan parlance—but the ground all the same. For a man who explained profound theories of consciousness and the nature of reality,

Jamgon Kongtrul did not live in the abstract. Everything he did was firmly within a tradition, an institution, and most importantly, a place. Jamgon Kongtrul is famous now in Tibet and the West for seeking out a dizzying amount of scripture, publishing it in vast collections, and transmitting it all to future generations of Tibetan Buddhists. His collections of sacred literature, like the retreat schedule he created for his hermitage at Tsādra Rinchen Drak, were nothing less than practical applications of the Buddha's message of nonduality. For Jamgon Kongtrul the scriptures were not so much timeless abstractions as they were lived practices in places where people tended animals and harvested grain. His reverence for the scriptures of Buddhist India was matched by his faith that the Buddha's message of liberation from suffering and compassion for all beings was being revealed in his own land—that the Buddha's teachings were, in fact, always appearing around him. Kongtrul did all of this with an ecumenical attitude and heartfelt appreciation for the diversity of Tibetan doctrinal and ritual systems—the extent of which has rarely been seen elsewhere.

Western scholars and devotees fill libraries with biographies of Christian and Jewish saints and religious leaders. The best of these accounts tell the story of the life of such individuals in a way that shows their inspiration while allowing for the lived reality of the person, their struggles, and their humanity to shine through. The worst depict the subject as perfectly formed at birth, untainted by the concerns of the communities around them. After over a hundred years of Buddhist and Tibetan Studies in the West, biographies of Tibetans in English and other European languages continue to treat their subjects less as people and more as archetypes. This book is the first full-length biography of Jamgon Kongtrul written in English, and it joins a mere handful of historical biographies of Tibetans, chief among them David Jackson's biography of the Third Dezhung Rinpoche and Donald Lopez's biography of Gendun Chopel.[1] That said, there are scores of sketches of Kongtrul's life, beginning with Gene Smith's famous 1970 essay which has been widely copied.[2] Elio Guarisco's twenty-page biography in his introduction to *Myriad Worlds* is original and well worth reading.[3] I hope this book will not be the last word on Kongtrul, as there are many unanswered questions and many fascinating issues about his life left to be explored. A literary biography, which surveys his compositions and traces the development of his thinking, would be a great contribution. We still await full biographies of his key collaborators, Khyentse Wangpo and Chokgyur Lingpa, who both feature prominently in this book.

Jamgon Kongtrul kept a detailed diary that was published in Tibetan and translated into English in 2003 by Richard Barron.[4] It is a fascinating first-person account of his activities, and I encourage readers to consult it. It serves as the primary source for this book, but I do not approach it uncritically. Barron gave his translation the title *The Autobiography of Jamgon Kongtrul*, but the work is almost entirely a record of events rather than a fully crafted autobiography. Outside of the section of his youth, there is little sense of narrative arc. Still, Kongtrul was, like most people, concerned about how his peers and posterity would view him, and he edited and framed his narrative accordingly. Kongtrul was perpetually creating, producing, and redefining, even if he was forced by social convention and literary norms to present himself as a passive receiver of commands, advice, and the fully crafted works of others. He could not acknowledge his active role in his own endeavors without risking accusations of egotism, and so he credits the inspiration or command for almost everything he did to his colleagues. He made inevitable errors, occasionally inserting information at points in the work that is anachronistic, misleading, or simply confused.

I have also relied on the biographical literature of his colleagues and the historical and self-reflective information found in Kongtrul's famous collections of his and other people's writings which are known as the "Five Treasuries": the Treasury of Kagyu Tantra, the Treasury of Revelations, the Treasury of Knowledge, the Treasury of Instructions, and the Treasury of the Expansive. The last of these, sometimes simply referred to as his Collected Works, is less frequently but more awkwardly known as the Treasury of the Uncommon. The Treasury of Revelations contains hundreds of Kongtrul's own compositions, the colophons for which contain valuable information about when and where he wrote. And of course these five great collections, the full corpus of his literary activity, offer insight into his beliefs, prejudices, and goals. I do not claim to have read it all; Kongtrul himself knew that few human beings could ever read all that he wrote or collected. I have done my best to favor storytelling over lists of texts and transmissions, but Kongtrul's life would not be what it was without the constant swirl of literature, and his biography would be thin without tracking his engagement with the books. Western scholarship and translations of Kongtrul's work have also been invaluable, and I stand humbled before master translators such as Guarisco, Barron, Sarah Harding, Elizabeth Callahan, Ngawang Zangpo, Ken McLeod, and many others who have done us all a great service by bringing Kongtrul's writings into English.[5] Andreas

Doctor's research into the life and revelations of Chokgyur Lingpa has also been of great use.[6] Unless otherwise noted, all translations in this book are my own.

I first read this material as a graduate student at the University of Michigan under the guidance of Donald Lopez, a scholar who can craft a sentence like no one else. Don models for all of us how to write about beloved topics with a critical eye. For many years after, I was fortunate to work for and then share an office with Gene Smith at the Tibetan Buddhist Resource Center (TBRC, now BDRC). Gene had an endless fascination with the comings and goings of Tibetans and loved to gossip about the long dead. I absorbed what little I could from him and his exceptional staff. I have also shared space with Himalayan Art Resources and have been able to rely on Jeff Watt's astonishing knowledge of Tibetan deities and ritual systems. I am grateful to Shelley and Donald Rubin for employing me for close to a decade and allowing me to develop the Treasury of Lives, a project I hope continues to promote biographies in the spread and study of Tibetan Buddhism. I am grateful to the editors at the Treasury, Catherine Tsuji and Tenzin Dickyi, for keeping the project running while I wrote this book. Other key web-based resources are Tsadra Foundation's searchable catalog of the Treasury of Revelations, not to mention their many other web projects and publications. Good friends and respected elders have graciously responded to an unending stream of questions and some even read drafts, and I thank them as well: Annabella Pitkin, Kate Wylie, Elizabeth Callahan, Sarah Harding, Sarah Jacoby, José Cabezón, Jann Ronis, Michael Sheehy, Jacob Dalton, Andrew Quintman, and Benjamin Bogin. This book began at the invitation of Kurtis Schaeffer, albeit for another context; Nikko Odiseos and Casey Kemp gracefully guided this book through publication, and Alex Catanese copyedited with a fine eye. It's fair to say that the book would not exist without the help of all these people. I take sole responsibility for any errors.

I dedicate this book to my parents, Betsy and Larry—a nurse and a teacher—who taught me the value of compassion and curiosity.

## A NOTE ON TRANSLATION AND DATES

In this book I use a system of phonetics developed in collaboration with TBRC and the Rubin Museum of Art. It is intended primarily for English readers and so dispenses with any accents, and it aspires to readability. The system acknowledges popular forms that do not conform to the principles which, with a list of exceptions, can be accessed at the Treasury of Lives website. Sanskrit titles of deities and scriptures are given with diacritical marks, but Tibetan place names that use Sanskrit letters are not. I have translated all the names of Tibetan books, but have left proper names untranslated. Tibetan transliterations for all names, titles, and terms are given in the glossary.

Kongtrul dated events in his diary according to a lunar calendar in a sixty-year cycle derived by combining twelve animals with five elements. Because such dates—"new moon of the monkey month in the Iron Hare Year" and the like—have no meaning to modern readers, I have translated them into those corresponding to the Western calendar, making use of the excellent online charts of the late Edward Henning.[7] Kongtrul followed the Tsurpu tradition of calendrical calculation, as opposed to the more familiar, at least in the West, Pukpa system. He composed a textbook on it, a *Compendium of Practical Astronomy*, which Edward Henning makes use of. None of the dates in this book are verified against a second source, and Kongtrul makes several mistakes in his diary that I was able to catch—it is of course likely that there were others I missed. Moreover, Kongtrul gives several dates that Henning records as having been omitted from the given year's calendar. For these reasons, I offer the dates in this book only as close approximates and provide the Tibetan date in the notes.

# PART ONE
# TRAINING

# KHAM

Ronggyab is a small valley to the northeast of the city of Derge, near the edge of the ancient kingdom of Ling, where the folk hero Gesar is said to have been active. In Kongtrul's day it was under the administration of the Derge Kingdom, one of the largest and most independent of the many polities of the eastern Tibetan Plateau, or Kham.[1] One of three traditional regions of the Tibetan cultural region, Kham is a vast area of deep river valleys, high mountain ridges, and open grasslands. Located west of the Sichuan Basin of China, east of the Lhasa-administered territories of Tibet, and south of the wide plains of Amdo (Qinghai), for centuries Kham had been viewed by the international power centers of Beijing and Lhasa as a border region. For most of its history the region was ruled not from far-away imperial centers but by local kingdoms or monastic estates. Rulers in Lhasa and Beijing competed for influence and control of the region, pursuing a slate of shifting policies of accommodation, in which local kings or leaders of monastic estates enjoyed imperial titles and hosted Tibetan representatives, but, to various degrees, maintained local autonomy. Kham was a relatively wealthy region, thanks largely to the lucrative trade between Tibet and China, which, in the absence of actual political control, provided the two powers with their primary means of establishing a presence. The religion, culture, and language of the region are Tibetan, but for the people of Kham, "Tibet" denoted the places ruled by Lhasa. Kongtrul himself referred to "Tibet" (Bod) as somewhere to go to from Kham.

Among the many kingdoms and monastic estates of Kham, Derge—located at the geographical center of Kham—was the most successful in maintaining actual independence. Derge's ecumenical support for multiple religious traditions provided a foundation for rich cultural exchange, bringing scholars from across Tibet to teach and study, and producing some of the greatest thinkers and ritual specialists in Tibetan history. The kingdom spanned the upper reaches of the Yangtse River, known in Tibetan as the

Drichu, with open fertile valleys such as Mesho and Terlung (also known as Tinglung) in the east, the high nomadic plains of Yilhung in the north, and dense pine forests in the south. Derge traced its history back to the seventh century, to an imperial Tibetan minister named Gar Tongtsen, whose great-grandson settled in the Drichu Valley in the early ninth century. The family upheld Nyingma and Bon practices until the thirteenth century, when the patriarch Sonam Rinchen served as an attendant to Pakpa Lodro Gyeltsen, then chaplain to Kublai Khan, the emperor of the new Yuan Dynasty in China. In return for his service, following the Yuan conquest of Tibet, Sonam Rinchen was given an estate in south-central Kham called Samar. Pakpa, later passing through the region, complimented it as a place of "four accomplishments and ten virtues"—*de zhi ge chu*, the first and third syllables of which contracted to Derge and was taken as the name of the family.

In the fourteenth century the head of the thirty-first generation the family, Botar, moved north and established today's Derge city. Botar married his daughter into the royal family of Ling, the kingdom that then controlled most of the region. According to legend, her father offered Botar as much land as he could plow in a day. Botar yoked two yak hybrids and plowed in a straight line, cleverly securing a sizeable dowry. Botar's descendent Jampa Puntsok, of the family's thirty-seventh generation, expanded the kingdom's territory through military campaigns against neighboring kingdoms in the 1630s. In 1639 the Khoshut Mongol leader and fierce Geluk partisan Gushri Khan invaded Tibet at the invitation of Geluk leaders in Lhasa.[2] On his way through Kham, Gushri attacked the Bon kingdom of Beri to the east of Derge, and Jampa Puntsok sent men to help. For his role in the conquest, Gushri rewarded Jampa Puntsok with extensive new territory.

The details of Jampa Puntsok's aid to Gushri have not yet been explored; nor is it known why Gushri would tolerate and reward a Sakya family while on a decidedly sectarian campaign, one which resulted in the forced conversion of non-Geluk institutions in Tibet and suppression of teachings critical of Geluk doctrine. Jampa Puntsok had by then built the royal monastery in Derge, Lhundrubteng, also known as Gonchen, establishing it as a Sakya institution. Gonchen is considered a branch of Ngor Monastery in Tibet, and since the seventeenth century retired abbots routinely traveled from there to Derge to serve as court chaplains and to funnel donations back to Ngor. Perhaps Jampa Puntsok's willingness to participate in the religious crusade against Bon would have impressed Gushri. In any case, the Mongol invasion was a great boon to Derge, and the family's supporting role, real or imagined, in the establishment of the Geluk dominance in Tibet was remembered for centuries. The Fifth Dalai Lama, himself a practitioner of Nyingma teachings, cosponsored with the Derge royal family the construction of two Nyingma monasteries in Derge, Dzogchen and Pelyul. Derge later, again, earned the Lhasa government's gratitude when it gave safe haven to the young and not-yet-enthroned Seventh Dalai Lama in 1714.

In the eighteenth century the ruler of Derge's forty-first generation, Tenpa Tsering, considerably increased Derge's territory. The Manchu Qing Dynasty in China followed a strategy toward territories on its borders of granting imperial titles to local rulers, who would accept nominal Chinese sovereignty with few, if any, obligations. Tenpa Tsering was the first king to accept Qing titles and patronage—in 1728 he received the title of "Pacification Commissioner of Derge" and became "Goodwill Commissioner" in 1733. He greatly expanded the royal monastery and established the Derge Printing House. Built around a preexisting temple begun by his predecessor around 1721, the printing house was designed to store thousands of printing blocks that had already been carved in Derge and to prepare for the carving of printing blocks for the new edition of the Tibetan Buddhist canon that Tenpa Tsering was sponsoring.[3]

Substantial financing for the printing of the first section of the canon, the Kangyur—the translated words of the Buddha—came from Beijing, which ordered the Sichuan governor general to send 180,000 standard measures of silver, or *tael*, and to distribute copies across Tibet and Mongolia.[4] The great Kagyu scholar Situ Paṇchen Chokyi Jungne, the Eighth Tai Situ of Pelpung Monastery,[5] supervised the production of the Kangyur, and a decade after it was finished a Sakya scholar based at Gonchen, Zhuchen Tsultrim Rinchen, was tasked with editing the Tengyur, the second section of the Tibetan canon, which contains the translations of the main Indian and Tibetan commentaries. These were only the largest of many works printed at Derge, as scores of additional collections and compositions by Tibetans continued to be carved and printed for distribution across Tibet. The Kangyur and Tengyur together required upwards of two hundred thousand printing blocks, and a single printing would thus require about a hundred thousand individual pieces of paper. The Kangyur alone was printed 1,500 times between 1733, when it was completed, and 1744, when the Tengyur was finished. This required printing some 11,000 pages a day—all by hand. With the completion of the Tengyur, this number increased by more than threefold. The cost of such endeavors was enormous, a reflection not simply of the wealth of the kingdom, but the extent to which that wealth was directed toward religious endeavors.

The production of the canon under the supervision of lamas from the Kagyu and Sakya traditions exemplified the ecumenical culture of Derge. The royal monastery may have been Sakya, but the family designated five additional monasteries to provide chaplains. Four of these were Nyingma: Katok, Dzogchen, Pelyul, and Zhechen. The fifth, Pelpung, founded by the royal chaplain Situ Chokyi Jungne, was Kagyu. Each performed rituals for the royal family and court on occasions of significance for the kingdom. There was certainly competition and tension between the different traditions, but a balance of power was maintained, allowing Sakya, Nyingma, and Kagyu institutions to flourish side by side, as lamas would regularly meet to teach and learn from each other. The pre-Buddhist Bon tradition also had a presence, though it appears to have never had royal support. The Geluk tradition, so dominant in central Tibet and areas surrounding Derge, was essentially absent from the kingdom.

Derge was not without sectarian tension. In 1788 Tenpa Tsering's son Sawang Kunga Dega Zangpo traveled to Tibet with his wife, Tsewang Lhamo, a daughter of the Garje aristocratic family. There the royal couple met and became disciples of Jigme Lingpa, one of the era's most charismatic and influential Nyingma lamas.[6] Soon after their return, Sawang passed away and Tsewang Lhamo took the throne as queen on behalf of her four-year-old son, Tsewang Dorje Rigdzin.[7] There was precedence for this: when Sawang had been just seven years old, his father had died, and his aunt, a nun named Yangchen Dolma, had served as regent for about ten years. During Tsewang Lhamo's rule, she supported an expansion of Nyingma activity in Derge. Hailing from a Nyingma family, she was deeply devoted to Jigme Lingpa and his disciples, including the First Dodrubchen and his disciple Jigme Gyelwai Nyugu of Dzogchen Monastery, and Getse Paṇḍita of Katok Monastery. Under their supervision she sponsored the printing of several major collections of Nyingma scripture, including the Collected Nyingma Tantras and the Collected Works of Jigme Lingpa. She also promoted Nyingma icons in the royal monasteries, installing a large statue of Padmasambhava in the Yudruk Chapel at Gonchen in 1801.

Tsewang Lhamo's evident favoritism toward Nyingma lamas and her increased attention to Nyingma monasteries seems to have inspired or exacerbated some sectarian tensions between the Sakya and Nyingma. The Nyingma had never before been the main beneficiary of royal support, and

Tsewang Lhamo's interests were perceived as a threat to Sakya leadership in the kingdom's government institutions, at least in the printing house and in the royal monastery. Getse Paṇḍita, in his 1797 catalogue of the Collected Nyingma Tantras, felt the need to include a lengthy defense of the Nyingma tradition against criticisms leveled by members of the Sakya and other traditions. But the spirit of ecumenicalism prevailed, and the Nyingma scriptural collections were produced at the same level of quality as the Kangyur and Tengyur before them.[8]

The queen proved to be a less capable political ruler than she was a religious patron. In 1796 and again in 1806, Derge lost armed conflicts with its neighbors. The first, a war with Ling, required Qing military assistance. When bandits from Golok and Sershul later harassed the northern edges of the kingdom, Derge initially relied on a nomadic tribe to repel the invaders, but that tribe also rebelled, requiring another Manchu intervention. The Qing Empire in China had by then begun its two-centuries-long decline. As Western powers carved up its coastline and colonial territories rebelled, it would be less and less capable of involving itself in the region's affairs. No doubt by this point the Sakya aristocracy was relieved to mark the adulthood of Tsewang Lhamo's son, and by 1808 Tsewang Dorje Rigdzin was enthroned as both king of Derge and abbot of Lhundrubteng. Tsewang Lhamo lived out the remainder of her years in the comfort of royal palaces, dying in 1812.[9]

The following year, on December third, 1813, the tenth day of the tenth month of the female Water Bird Year of the fourteenth sexagenary cycle, Jamgon Kongtrul was born in Ronggyab.[10]

# 2

## BIRTH, YOUTH, AND EARLY EDUCATION

### 1813–1829

Jamgon Kongtrul's mother was named Tashi Tso. She was a gentle, good-natured woman, generous and devout. She was from a well-connected family, with at least one brother in government service. Kongtrul was devoted to her. After leaving home he returned several times to visit her, and in 1843 she came to live with Kongtrul at his retreat center, where she kept house for him. Over the course of her life, she recited the six-syllable mantra of Avalokiteśvara—*oṃ maṇi padme hūṃ*—one hundred fifty million times.[1] Tashi Tso lived a good long life, passing away in 1867.[2] Assuming she was about twenty when Kongtrul was born, she lived well into her seventies. Assuming again that she started her mantra accumulation at the age of about fifty, when she went to live with her son, she would have averaged about 17,000 mantras a day. This is theoretically possible if she spent three minutes on a full circuit of her rosary of 108 beads and recited for eight hours a day, 360 days a year.

During her pregnancy with Kongtrul, Tashi Tso reported several auspicious dreams. These included a vulture arriving from the northwest to roost in her home shrine room and another in which an important person gave her a silk brocade and a rosary made of conch shell. Vultures and conch both carry auspicious symbolism in Tibet, the first for a connection with the *ḍākinī*—a class of female deities associated with wisdom—the second being a sign of wealth and royalty. Tashi Tso enjoyed an easy pregnancy, without suffering from illness or exhaustion, maintaining a healthy glow throughout. The birth, which Kongtrul reports was without complication, would likely have occurred at the family's house with the aid of village women. Traditional Tibetan births involve a fair amount of butter, in the form of cakes that have been blessed and as melted butter for the mother to ease the delivery. Butter would also have been rubbed on the infant's nose and head.

Kongtrul added that he would not nurse for his first week and had to be sustained with melted butter.[3]

At the time of Kongtrul's birth, Tashi Tso was married to a lay Bon practitioner named Sonam Pel. This man, according to Kongtrul, was not his biological father; Kongtrul names him his foster father.[4] He made his living as an artisan, and he was at least somewhat literate, as he was diligent in his prayers and recitations and he taught Kongtrul and other boys their letters. A skilled meditator, he had completed the preliminary practices of generating the mind of enlightenment, taking refuge, confessing fault, *maṇḍala* offering, prostrations, and guru yoga. His practice, Kongtrul reported, had provided him with some insight into the nature of mind. He was a stern disciplinarian, keeping Kongtrul on a strict schedule of study and, typical of Tibetan fathers, beating Kongtrul at the smallest infraction. The family was not wealthy, but neither were they poor. Until Kongtrul was born they had been childless, and he remained their only child. The extended family included uncles and aunts, and several maternal relatives would enter his life in later decades. The household also included at least one grandfather who lived until Kongtrul was a young boy. This man was known by the nickname Ata, an abbreviation of Tashi with the affectionate prefix of "A."

Kongtrul claimed that his biological father was a Bon lama named Khyungpo Lama Yungdrung Tendzin.[5] Despite Tashi Tso's marriage to Sonam Pel, Khyungpo Lama's role in fathering Kongtrul may have been publicly known; Kongtrul certainly made no effort to hide it in the diary. It is difficult to fully understand how this came to be, and Kongtrul does not explain. It was not uncommon for single women in Tibet to become mothers, and it was not unheard of for the father to be a lama or even a monk, given the inconsistent enforcement in Tibetan monasteries of the celibacy vows. Depending on circumstances such as ordination status and rank in the monastery, the man might or might not accept paternity and support the child. But Tashi Tso was married to Sonam Pel when Kongtrul was born; even if she was pregnant at the time of the marriage, her husband would surely have assumed paternity. Lamas routinely aided childless parents through ritual means—blessings, empowerments, or prayer. Had the pregnancy been the result of an illicit affair, or worse, a rape, the lama's parentage surely would not have been made public knowledge. A childless couple would be unlikely to request a lama to impregnate the wife—and publicize the arrangement—and Kongtrul does not offer this explanation. Tibetans commonly practice polyandry, with two brothers marrying the same woman in order to preserve patrimony. But Kongtrul does not identify his two fathers as brothers or relations of any kind. Nor does it appear that Khyungpo Lama had partnered with Tashi Tso intentionally to produce an heir for himself, in spite of her marriage, as Kongtrul was not brought into Khyungpo Lama's household. If his parentage had been an embarrassment, Kongtrul could have easily erased it from his diary by the time he stopped writing in 1895; sufficient time would have passed to provide distance from any living witness. Instead, Kongtrul describes growing up with both fathers in his life, grateful for a kind and gentle man to counterbalance Sonam Pel's beatings.

Khyungpo Lama Yungdrung Tendzin was a member of the Khyungpo clan, an important family lineage of the Bon tradition. Kongtrul took pride in this Khyungpo heritage despite his later ambivalence regarding Bon, filling a page of his diary with the legend of the clan's supernatural origins. He later composed multiple prayers to the Khyungpo lineage holders.[6] Kongtrul would eventually establish a strong affiliation with the Shangpa Kagyu tradition that was established by Khyungpo Neljor, a member of the same clan, whom he would claim as a previous life. One can speculate that Kongtrul embellished—and possibly invented—his Khyungpo heritage in order to emphasize his right to assume the mantle of the Shangpa Kagyu tradition.

Bon is the religious tradition that continues to observe elements of doctrine, rituals, and mythology that existed in Tibet before the advent of Buddhism.[7] When Buddhism was brought into Tibet in the seventh century, many court priests were hostile to the foreign religion and attempted to prevent it from receiving royal patronage. Buddhist propaganda describes crimes committed by these priests against Buddhist teachers and speaks of gallant subjugation of indigenous deities by Buddhist ritualists. Over the succeeding centuries Bon and Tibetan Buddhism borrowed heavily from each other, with Buddhism adopting many native Tibetan characteristics and practices, and Bon absorbing Buddhist vocabulary and practices. Mutual influence has not led to peaceful coexistence, however, and there has been considerable persecution of the Bon by Buddhist communities. The Bon tradition, originally a lay religion, "reformed" in later centuries, leading to the establishment of monasteries and an increase in institutional Buddhist characteristics. The Bon and the Nyingma, the holders of the earliest traditions of Tibetan Buddhism, both share a reverence for Padmasambhava, a penchant for revealing scripture, and a fondness for the tantric teaching of Dzogchen, yet it is a mistake to overemphasize their similarities and overlook their significant differences.

Several other Bon lamas were present in Kongtrul's infancy. When he was three years old, Sonam Lodro, the abbot of Menri Monastery, the main Bon institution in Tibet, passed through Ronggyab. Kongtrul's parents requested a blessing for their son, and Sonam Lodro performed a *tonsure* ceremony—essentially a blessing in which he cut a few locks of the child's hair. He gave the boy the name Tendzin Yungdrung, which became the name by which he was known in his youth—he did not record the name his parents had used until that point, if he had one. Tendzin is a common Tibetan name, meaning "holder of the teachings"; Yungdrung is the Tibetan word for swastika, an important Bon symbol. It was a solid Bon name. A second prominent Bon lama based at the ancient Tarde Hermitage in Ronggyab gave a prophecy to Kongtrul's family. This man, whose name was Tokden Yungdrung Puntsok—*tokden* is a title meaning "possessed of realization"—was reputed to have gained the power of clairvoyance through his purity and yogic practices. He told them that Kongtrul had the status of a bodhisattva, meaning he had, in a past life, vowed to attain enlightenment for the benefit of all beings, and that he had been blessed—"struck by the radiance"—by Padmasambhava. Yungdrung Puntsok predicted that Kongtrul would become famous but that around his thirtieth year he would suffer great obstacles.[8]

In the years leading up to Kongtrul's birth, Ronggyab had repeatedly suffered from the environmental calamities of hail and frost, common dangers of high altitude agriculture which could quickly destroy a year's crop of barley in minutes. Apparently, following Jamgon Kongtrul's birth, these misfortunes subsided, and farmers enjoyed abundant harvests for twelve years straight. Whether or not this beneficial turn was a result of his coming into the world, as Kongtrul seems to imply in his diary, such an increase in agricultural output likely resulted in greater employment for Sonam Pel, whose livelihood as an artisan would have depended on the landowners of the valley having surpluses. Kongtrul apparently was never sent out to bring in additional income and was able to spend his childhood playing and studying. According to his account, his play was not like that of other children. He makes no mention of chasing other boys or making forts in the hills or any other activity typical of childhood. Instead, he claims that he cared only to dress up in monk's clothing and make believe that he was a lama, performing rituals for his playmates. He pretended to give empowerments, make *torma*—ritual offering cakes—out of dirt, and perform offering ceremonies modeled after smoke offering rites to local protector deities.[9]

Such descriptions of a lama's childhood are typical in Tibetan biographical literature, which unfortunately too often turns human exemplars of Buddhist achievement into one-dimensional saints. The requirements of Buddhist-inflected humility prevented Kongtrul from representing himself as too extraordinary in his reminiscences of his youth, yet he continued with claims of an early religious awareness: as soon as he could speak, he uttered ornate religious phrases, and at age four he came across a meditation manual for the Buddhist deity White Mañjuśrī and was able to repeat the prayers after hearing them recited only once.[10] The association with Mañjuśrī, the bodhisattva of wisdom, is made here to emphasize Kongtrul's intelligence. Convention demanded humility, but there would also be an expectation of signs of greatness; Kongtrul was writing for an audience that would have been shocked into disbelief to find a description of the great man developing out of an ordinary child. He could neither boast nor depict himself as a typical child. Nevertheless, there is no reason to believe that in his youth Kongtrul was not, in fact, extraordinary, as many children who go on to do great things are.

Sonam Pel took charge of Kongtrul's education. In the spring of his fifth year his father taught him the Tibetan alphabet, which Kongtrul learned quickly, if without much enthusiasm. Only when he was eight did he develop a substantial interest in learning, and by age ten he had copied out numerous volumes of scripture. Among these were descriptions of the nature of mind that inspired him to long for a teacher to guide him and that engendered faith in the deities and the great lamas of the past. In particular, he was drawn to Padmasambhava, and as his devotion grew he yearned to meet lamas who embodied the Precious Guru. He even boasted to his friends that he himself was an emanation of Padmasambhava, a bold—if somewhat childish—statement to make. And he cultivated a powerful ethical sensibility, expressed in a fear of the hells that Tibetan teachers use to frighten people away from negative actions. Nightmares of these hells would wake him from sleep. In one, he was traveling in a hell with his grandfather, who, because he was reciting prayers, was allowed by the Lord of Death to proceed to enlightenment, his consciousness shooting off as a white ball of light. Kongtrul was left behind, afraid, doomed to travel through additional hell realms alone.[11]

Kongtrul's other, more enjoyable dreams and visions expressed a longing to undertake the religious life. He claimed to have had his first religious vision not long after his naming ceremony at the age of three. At sunrise while he was sitting on a relative's lap, he saw a person who seemed to be a renunciate coming across a field in the east. The figure was carrying a victory banner that was entirely surrounded by flames. When he asked who it was, he was told there was no one there. He later dreamed that a resplendent lama flew across the sky from the northwest to the southeast, landed in his village, and spoke several prophetic phrases. The lama gave him some lovely things and then left. In another dream he was visited by a famous prognosticator named Moma Kunshe Tingpo, who used a cord and knot method to make positive, if cryptic, predictions. Included in this was the line "From the east, where the sun rises, an ant will come carrying a red flower." Kongtrul's later interpretation of the dream was that he was destined to travel eastward to Zhechen and Pelpung Monasteries; the first was where he would initially train as a monk and the second was his home for most of his life.[12]

Kongtrul studied with his fathers and Tarde Tokden until he was about sixteen years old. Sonam Pel, as mentioned, was strict. When Kongtrul was practicing reading and writing, or was engaging in rituals, he was required to sit still, without allowing himself to be distracted. If he lost control and exhibited even the slightest distraction, his father would beat him. He was not allowed to play outside unless given permission to do so. His father would also harangue him with stories of greedy boys who did not study but instead engaged in feckless behavior such as drinking, stealing, or lying, and who were ostracized from their communities as a result. He would scold Kongtrul and the other boys he taught, telling them they too would end up like this unless they minded him. The scoldings were hurtful and discouraged Kongtrul at the time. Yet later in life he looked back and appreciated the intention behind his foster father's stern discipline, even crediting him for instilling in him ethical standards that served him well in life.[13]

Khyungpo Lama was also involved in his education, but he was kind and affectionate, and Kongtrul was always glad to be with him. Every day Khyungpo Lama would teach Kongtrul iconography—an important part of a young lama's education, given the expansive pantheon of Tibetan deities. Unfortunately, this gentle guide passed away when Kongtrul was only seven years old, around the year 1820. In his place, Yungdrung Puntsok and the monks of Tarde Monastery gave him religious instruction. Starting around the time he was eight or nine, he would attend the assemblies and the public readings. He could memorize chants after hearing them only a few times, and after observing ceremonies he could flawlessly perform rituals, make torma, arrange offerings, or play the drums and cymbals. In this way he came to serve as a ritual assistant to the community and to prepare and perform rituals on his own. Later in life Kongtrul claimed to have little inclination toward Bon save for the peaceful and wrathful Padmasambhava teachings of Mishik Dorje, an eighteenth century Bon mystic. In any case, his activities at the monastery led his playmates to tease him that he was a little monk.[14]

Tarde Tokden gave Kongtrul an oral transmission for the practice of Pelden Lhamo, an ancient Tibetan deity that had been assimilated into Buddhism as a form of the Indian deity Śrīdevi and came to serve as a patron saint of Buddhist Tibet and the personal protector of the Dalai Lamas. She is popular as well in the Bon tradition, where she is generally known as Sipai Gyelmo, or Queen of the Universe, and employed as both a meditational deity and a protector of the teachings. She is wrathful, with three faces and six hands holding various weapons that serve to cut through illusions and destroy the three poisons (greed, ignorance, and anger) that keep beings tethered to saṃsāric existence. This was Kongtrul's first initiation into a formal tantric practice, and he spent some time with it. After performing the basic rite and some additional related rituals, he had some experiences that he understood to indicate that he was successful. Among these was a dream in which a female gave him four or five sheathless knives, which he took as a sign that he was beginning to develop insight; the blades cut through dualistic thinking, which is the hallmark of ignorance.[15]

Later, around the age of fifteen, he dreamed of both Padmasambhava and the Queen of the Universe appearing together, the imagery of which was drawn from the life story of Padmasambhava. Before coming to Tibet from India, Padmasambhava is said to have spent time in the kingdom of Zahor, a region which is now Himachal Pradesh, to the northwest of Nepal. The king of Zahor initially welcomed him, but when the Guru began to practice sexual yoga with a royal princess named Mandarava, the outraged king had the couple burned alive. Padmasambhava transformed the pyre into a lake—now said to be Lake Rewalsar—and rested comfortably on a lotus floating in the air. The king, realizing his folly, offered Padmasambhava his kingdom, including his robes and the five-petaled lotus hat that contains multiple layers of symbolism. The outfit became a standard iconographic form of Padmasambhava known as Loden Chokse, and it was this form that Kongtrul saw, surrounded by a circle of orange light, brilliant like the sun. From him emerged a ball of light the size of a flat round brass charm Tibetans customarily wore on their belts called a mirror, a few inches in diameter. This struck Kongtrul, and he fell into a faint. When he regained consciousness, still in his dream, there were a few women who said to him, "Now, look into the sky. The Queen of the Universe, with a hundred heads and a thousand arms has come." With confidence in the face of such splendor, Kongtrul gazed up and saw the sky was full of rainbows, in the midst of which was a vague figure. He then awoke.[16]

From an early age Kongtrul put great stock in the interpretation of his dreams. He claims to have been able to lucid dream after hearing of the practice from his playmates—that is, he could become aware that he was dreaming and manipulate events. Kongtrul filled his diary with his dreams, positive and negative, in various degrees of detail depending on how significant he found them to be. In cases of prophetic dreams, he supplied the future events they predicted, one of the surest pieces of evidence that he edited his diary before publication. The dreams were not consistent throughout his life. He claims to have never bothered to fully master lucid dreaming in his youth and to have lost the ability. The frequency and vividness of his dreams faded in the late 1840s, something that he ascribed to the moral contamination of handling monastic property; he also claimed that he simply became too busy to record them.[17]

Around his tenth year Kongtrul heard that a lama was giving transference instructions based on the collection known as Secret Treasury of the Ḍākinī and he went to receive them.[18] Transference, or *powa*, is the practice of ejecting consciousness, either one's own or that of another, and transferring it to a new and better location. It is most frequently performed as a funeral ritual but is also commonly practiced early in religious training, an initial step in mastering techniques of manipulating the subtle body. The sign of accomplishment, in both the living and the dead, is an opening in the fontanel—the spot at the top of the head where the three plates of the skull meet—out of which consciousness is believed to depart the body. After three days of successful practice, liquid should ooze from a newly opened aperture, such that a stalk of grass can be inserted. In the case of a funeral, the skull is examined after cremation or the consumption of the corpse by vultures, a funeral practice known as sky burial.[19]

Kongtrul continued to learn about iconography. He drafted images of Buddha Vairocana and of the different forms of Padmasambhava, and he sought out monks from the nearby Karma Kagyu monastery of Namgyel Ling to teach him the iconography of Bernakchen, the central Karma Kagyu form of the Buddhist deity Mahākāla and the personal protective deity of the Karmapa incarnations. In his diary he described experiencing delight on first hearing the name of that buddha, which he had probably come across during his earlier study of iconography. He also studied medicine. In traditional Tibetan educational style, Kongtrul memorized some of the foundational texts of the Tibetan medical tradition, such as *Discourse on Pulse Diagnosis and Urinalysis*, and he worked with a doctor named Karma Puntsok to recognize medicinal herbs.[20]

In the spring of Kongtrul's fourteenth year, 1826 or 1827, his grandfather died. Ata had recited close to two hundred million mantras during his life and was skilled, Kongtrul wrote, at maintaining his mind in its natural lucid state. On the day of his funeral, there was a clear sky in which white light spread from east to west in a way that reminded Kongtrul of the dream visit to the hell realms with his grandfather, suggesting to him that his grandfather had attained liberation. Toward the end of his life, Ata had begun a series of "expanded vastness" rituals. This rite, in which the one hundred buddhas of the Bon tradition are invoked, is performed to cultivate merit and to prepare oneself for death. It is also a common part of a funeral. Ata had intended to complete one hundred repetitions but had only been able to accomplish eighty, and Kongtrul promised to make up the difference. He was unable to do so, however, as he was soon forced to leave his valley. His relatively easy life was coming to an end—a consequence of political turmoil in Derge.[21]

Derge in the early nineteenth century was governed by a fairly decentralized political system concerned primarily with land management and trade. Under the ruling family there were three ranks of hereditary aristocratic families, and the kingdom was divided into twenty-five districts, each controlled by a titled official of the first rank, known as a chieftain. Four representatives of these districts, together with a treasurer, a secretary, and a steward in charge of food and offerings, comprised the highest bureaucratic body in the capital. The second rank of aristocratic officials administered the thirty-three counties, or *dzong*, each headed by a county headman appointed either by the chieftains or the king. The third rank of officials were eighty village representatives who could be either appointed or hereditary. These officials were in charge of organizing the tax for the support of traveling officials. While the ruling family controlled the bulk of cultivated and grazing land, the aristocracy and monasteries were also granted substantial land holdings and both accumulated and controlled considerable wealth. Both could lease their land to individual families in return for direct payments or for a fixed or flexible percentage of the harvest. They could also demand that their tenants provide labor for public projects. Thus while the administrative system of Derge was centralized, power—mainly in terms of control of the land and the rights to collect taxes—was distributed among the aristocracy. The system nicely mirrored the religious patronage of the royal family, a system in which the Sakya was heavily favored, but institutions belonging to other traditions also enjoyed patronage and influence. The aristocratic families intermarried, forming multiple vectors of allegiances. Monastic leadership was often drawn from the aristocratic families via education or the institution of identifying reincarnated lamas, or *tulku*, meaning that secular and clerical power frequently intermingled.[22]

In 1826 the king of Derge, Tsewang Dorje Rigdzin, retired from the throne to focus on religious activities. He took full ordination at the royal monastery, Lhundrubteng. His eldest son, Damtsik Dorje, was only fifteen at the time, but he presumably took the throne, surrounded by ministers drawn from the aristocracy and chaplains from the major monasteries. Kongtrul's family had some connections to the local aristocracy through both his maternal relatives and Khyungpo Lama. Several years earlier the chieftain of Den Chode County, a man by the affectionate name of Amgon—probably properly named Gonpo—had come to Ronggyab with an unnamed Derge official. These two had a kinship affiliation with Khyungpo Lama, and they presented Kongtrul with a silk monk shawl and teased him to his great delight, saying "now you are a lama."[23]

Since the time of Tsewang Lhamo's reign, the power of the chieftains had been on the rise; with a fifteen-year-old now on the throne, the opportunity to more closely control their territory further increased. The chieftains of the area closest to the Drichu, which included Kongtrul's own valley of Ronggyab in Den Chode County in the Chode District, imposed such excessive demands on the people that according to Kongtrul close to a third of the region's families were driven to destitution. While Kongtrul's maternal uncle was at the time well off, he had enemies, and his family was soon swept into a lengthy and bloody conflict. Kongtrul explained that enemies of his uncle set out to ruin him and steal his property. More people became involved, including a person from the household of a Derge minister, who seems to have suffered some insult or injury. The minister's retribution was considerable and appears to have included the local monasteries. At the end of the year, just at the start of the *gutor* ceremonies—rites of propitiation to the protective deities performed in the last days of one year to ensure prosperity in the next—the local monks and laypeople killed the minister and his representatives, inciting yet more reprisals from the relatives of the slain men. Kongtrul reports that all families in the valley, high and low, were ruined. Kongtrul's father Sonam Pel was imprisoned at the Chode Palace.[24] It is not clear what his living situation was there, who was responsible for his upkeep, and whether he ever returned to Ronggyab.

Conditions in Ronggyab remained so dire that Kongtrul's mother urged her son to leave her and enter a monastery, promising that she would care for herself. Kongtrul refused to abandon her; although there is reason to believe she owned at least one small piece of land and had other family members, it is possible that he feared leaving her without protection. It may also have been that he had nowhere to go; there would have been no monastery willing to accept him, coming as he would have without financial support, and the life of a destitute itinerant yogi begging for food apparently did not appeal to him. Nevertheless, not long after, in the spring of Kongtrul's sixteenth year, his mother did for him what he considers a kindness comparable to giving him his life: she sent him to Chode to care for his father.[25] In doing so he left his childhood home, the first step in the life of a religious renunciate. Had Kongtrul previously entertained any expectation of marrying and raising a family in Ronggyab, that life was now shown to be a path of violence and suffering. His childhood fascination with the trappings of the religious life, and the faith he had cultivated in Padmasambhava and other deities, now blossomed into the focus of his life.

At Chode, Kongtrul was able to continue his education under the supervision of a monk from Chamdo Jampa Ling, a major Geluk monastic center in western Kham. The monk was a chant master, responsible for leading the community in public prayers, and Kongtrul spent the spring and summer copying texts and reciting prayers. The monk was also a statue maker, which probably explains his employment so far from his community. He was able to teach Kongtrul iconography and painting in the Menri tradition of Tibetan religious art. Kongtrul was an eager and attentive servant. He was also a willing and obedient aid to whomever needed assistance. His humility and gentle disposition earned him the affection and kindness of the Chode Palace community, and he soon came to the attention of Tsepel, the chieftain of Chode and a member of the aristocratic Khangsar clan.

Tsepel was also a fully ordained monk in the Drukpa Kagyu tradition, although apparently he did not belong to any particular monastery in the region. Ordination would not necessarily preclude him from government service. On the contrary, in a land without public education and low levels of literacy, the monasteries were the training ground for government officials. At the time, Tsepel was in need of a secretary, and Kongtrul served him in that capacity for the second half of the summer of 1829. Kongtrul affectionately referred to the man in his diary as the "Old Chieftain."[26]

Tsepel brought Kongtrul on an administrative tour that took them to the summer encampment of the Derge royal court in Rudam. These were regions to the north of the Derge capital, on high meadows among snowy peaks where the alpine lakes remained ice-covered well into summer. Jigme Losel, a lama from Zhechen Monastery who had been a student of Jigme Lingpa, was there at the time. Zhechen, which lay nearby, had been founded a hundred years earlier under royal charter and with the support of the Fifth Dalai Lama. It was one of four major Nyingma monasteries in Derge and one of the five monasteries that sent chaplains to the Derge court. Jigme Losel asked Kongtrul to explain Bon history to him, and he listened with attention as Kongtrul spoke on the liturgies and legends of the tradition. The lama was impressed. He praised Kongtrul to Tsepel for having a clear intellect and for being well-spoken. Tsepel informed the lama that because Kongtrul was so clever he had been thinking of sending him to advance his studies but was unsure which field to point him toward. Jigme Losel suggested he put the question to Zhechen Wontrul Gyurme Tutob Namgyel, then the leading lama of Zhechen Monastery. In the meantime, Tsepel arranged for books on various topics to be made for Kongtrul at the printing houses at Derge and Pelpung Monastery.[27]

At the end of summer, the Khangsar chieftain gave Kongtrul a letter of introduction to Zhechen Wontrul and provisions for several months, including a horse and two sets of clothing. With an escort Kongtrul then set off from Rutok to the hermitage at Zhechen Monastery. On the day he arrived, a large snow fell, an auspicious symbol for a meeting of great significance.[28]

# 3

## Zhechen

### 1829–1833

Jamgon Kongtrul lived at Zhechen Monastery for three years, from the end of 1829 to the beginning of 1833.[1] He received his first significant Buddhist instruction there, and more importantly, he met his first teacher, whom he loved like a father and remembered tenderly his entire life. Zhechen Wontrul Gyurme Tutob Namgyel was forty-two years old when Kongtrul came to him in the late fall of 1829. Born in southern Kham in 1787, he was educated at many of the major Nyingma monasteries, including Katok, where he studied for five years under the Getse Paṇḍita, and at Mindroling in central Tibet, where he studied for three years under the sixth throne holder, Gyurme Pema Wanggyel. Only then did he arrive at Zhechen, where he remained for the rest of his life. He was a master of Tibetan grammar, a passion for which he passed on to Kongtrul. He was a junior incarnation at Zhechen at a time when the monastery had several prominent incarnations, including two who were his teachers: the Third Zhechen Rabjam and the Second Zhechen Gyeltsab.[2]

Recognition as a reincarnation was a strategy used by monastic communities to give status to promising young men. By giving a child the identity of a deceased master of the tradition, the community prevented young men from being called into government service or enticed away by another monastery. It was not necessary for the identity to belong to a man of great renown; "Wontrul" means "reincarnated nephew." Gyurme Tutob Namgyel had been given the identity of a man named Tokden Sanggye Rabten, a nephew of a Drubwang Pema Gyeltsen. These two lamas of Zhechen were sufficiently well known at the time to provide the needed tether to Zhechen, but they are known to history solely through their connection to the man who inherited their charisma.

On meeting the young Bon practitioner then named Tendzin Yungdrung, Zhechen Wontrul blessed him by putting his hand upon his head.

He put Kongtrul in the care of an old lama from the Zhechen retreat center named Orgyen Peljor.[3] Kongtrul likely put his bedding in the lama's log cabin, where he would have assumed responsibility for keeping the coals warm and the tea hot. Zhechen Monastery is built on the edge of a narrow north-south running valley, with most of the monastic structures on the western hillside. Like other monasteries in Kham, it is a collection of small, two-storey rectangular houses surrounding a central temple, all made of pounded earth and logs harvested from the surrounding pine forests. The ground floor of the residences were often no more than crawl spaces, backed up as they were against the sloping walls of the valley. They were for storage of firewood and other supplies, with a ladder by which one ascends to the living quarters. Inside the second floor would be one or two rooms for sleeping and studying and another with a clay wood stove to cook and make the charcoal that warmed the house in small braziers. A small closet with a slit on the floor served as a toilet; waste collected in a bin on the ground floor until full, after which it would be used for agriculture. Walls were rough wood, possibly whitewashed and decorated to the degree to which the owner could afford. Light was by window; candle or oil lamps were used at night if one had the means to purchase them.

Wontrul began his instruction with divination, using the Chinese system known as Mother, Child, Foe, or Friend. This intricate system uses black and white pebbles to determine the combined effects of five elements (wood, fire, metal, earth, and water).[4] Kongtrul comprehended it after only one explanation, and as a result they quickly moved on to grammar and poetics. Here they initially used the manual called the *Kavyadarśa*, a seventh-century Indian poetics manual written by the poet Daṇḍin and translated in the thirteenth century by Shong Lotsāwa Dorje Gyeltsen. Wontrul would teach Kongtrul during the day, in either long or short sessions as needed, and Kongtrul would spend the evenings memorizing the texts, memorization being a standard foundation for study in Tibet. Kongtrul would also review commentaries at night and returned to Wontrul the next day to be tested on his memorization and comprehension. The method of studying was not easy, but Kongtrul was diligent, and Wontrul was pleased by his progress.

Kongtrul had at this point received no Buddhist doctrinal instruction, only iconography, astrology, and grammar. While he could memorize the texts and recite them to Wontrul when asked, he lacked a basic understanding of Buddhist terminology and concepts. Wontrul thus gave him a glossary called *Ocean of Enumerations* and advised him to memorize it. The work, by a Nyingma scholar from Nyarong named Nyakla Pema Rigdzin, gave Kongtrul familiarity with the words but not their meaning, and to help him decipher it he went to Gyurme Tendzin, a learned lama who had studied at Mindroling Monastery under Trinle Chodron, the daughter of the fifth throne holder of Mindroling and sister to the eighth throne holder, Yishin Wanggyel. Kongtrul himself would study with both brother and sister in January 1858 (see chapter 17). Although it was difficult for him, and Kongtrul had some doubts that he would succeed, he passed his exam on the *Kavyadarśa*.[5]

Zhechen Wontrul's instruction continued with the two classics of Tibetan grammar, *Thirty Verses* and *Guide to Signs*, both said to have been composed by the man believed responsible for creating the Tibetan alphabet in the seventh century, Tonmi Sambhoṭa. Wontrul was by then considered to have been his reincarnation, a particularly Tibetan form of praise for a person who effectively embodies the accomplishments of a past saint. Kongtrul memorized these two works, and afterwards he and Wontrul examined his understanding. Wontrul also taught Kongtrul additional Sanskrit grammar using the three systems of grammar as defined by Tibetans.[6] First is the three-volume Candrapa, based on Candragomin's *Candravyākaraṇa*, with the related two volumes of *Amarakoṣa*, the earliest surviving Sanskrit thesaurus, written by Amarasiṃha possibly as early as the sixth century C.E. Second is the Kalapa, based on a text by Iśvaravarman. The third, the Sārasvata, is based on a group of translations made by the seventeenth-century Jonang master Tāranātha and others. The central text of this system is the *Sārasvatavyākaraṇa* by Anubhūtisvarūpācārya, who lived in the thirteenth or fourteenth century. Years later, in 1837, when he was at Karma Gon teaching the Fourteenth Karmapa, Kongtrul composed an introduction to grammar based on his notes from these teachings (see chapter 7). This is published in his Collected Works under the title *Sea of Enjoyment*.

In early 1830 Zhechen Wontrul gave Jamgon Kongtrul his first Buddhist initiation. This was an authorization ceremony to practice White Mañjuśrī, the deity Kongtrul reported expressing interest in at age four. Zhechen Wontrul taught from the tradition of the twelfth-century Kashmiri tantric master Mati Paṇchen.[7] This master was a teacher to Śākyaśrībhadra, who was invited to Tibet at the end of his life by Lotsāwa Rinchen Sengge, the initiator of the Tropu Kagyu tradition. Mati Paṇchen's presentation of White Mañjuśrī was eventually adopted by all traditions of Tibetan Buddhism. The bodhisattva is depicted emerging from an ocean of nectar, surrounded by playful animals, and sitting on a lotus with his legs crossed. His body is youthful, white in color, adorned with silks, his long hair tied in five knots. His right hand is at his right knee, palm out in the gesture of generosity. His left hand is in front of him, holding a lotus stalk, which blossoms at his left shoulder and carries a volume of Prajñāpāramitā scriptures. The authorization Wontrul gave was permission to practice an "approach," an early-stage tantric rite in which one supplicates the deity with mantras and prayers.

The next transmission was *Mañjuśrīnāmasamgīti*. This early Indian tantra, a propitiation to multiple forms of Mañjuśrī, was first translated into Tibetan in the eighth century as part of the first transmission of Buddhism to Tibet. Following the one hundred fifty-year period in which no new Indian scriptures were brought to Tibet, it was translated again in the eleventh century, during the second stage of diffusion of Buddhism. It is a common initial tantra for Tibetan Buddhist practitioners as it offers relatively simple techniques of engaging with the deity as well as lengthy descriptions of his many forms and his maṇḍala, or cosmic realm. The evening Kongtrul received the transmission he dreamed that a full moon rose into the center of a clear sky, a visual sign of the quality and fervor of his inspiration. For some time after, he recited both the White Mañjuśrī and the *Mañjuśrīnāmasamgīti* daily.[8] Mañjuśrī remained a valued deity for Kongtrul but did not become a primary bodhisattva in his personal pantheon, ceding pride of place in 1841 to Avalokiteśvara, the bodhisattva of compassion.

In the summer of 1830, Kongtrul fell ill, afflicted with an unnamed malady. To counter the effects, Wontrul gave him a blessing of Black Hayagrīva and granted permission for a practice of the One Hundred Peaceful and Wrathful Deities.[9] Both are standard treatments for the sick, a means of marshaling potent forces to good effect. Hayagrīva, a form of Avalokiteśvara, is depicted in wrathful form, standing, one hand raised and wielding a sword with which to sever enemies, the other holding a hook with which to snare the dead. He has blood-covered fangs, eyes wide and menacing, his body draped in skins. His wrath is understood to be directed against causes of illness, and so he is frequently called on to heal the sick. The Nyingma tradition has two main groupings of deities: the Peaceful and Wrathful, and the Eight Commands. The One Hundred Peaceful and Wrathful Deities are a single grouping of forty-two peaceful and fifty-eight wrathful deities, commonly said to have originated in the *Guhyagarbha Tantra*. Each correspond to a separate element of a person. In meditation practice, this maṇḍala, with all one hundred deities, is visualized at one's heart center and then expanded to cultivate the understanding of the fundamental sameness of the buddhas and oneself. The technique is said to aid a person after death, as the deities each manifest at the moment the corresponding elements of the mind and body dissolve. Recognizing oneself as those deities is said to provide a singularly opportune moment to attain enlightenment. Short of that, reciting the liturgy is useful in cases of illness in that it guides one's awareness to supercede physical illness and restore a body to health.

Kongtrul, who had previously studied herbal medicine, makes no mention of other treatments for his illness, if there were any. Aside from his practice of Mañjuśrī and the Peaceful and Wrathful Deities, he spent most of 1830 on grammar, memorizing texts in the evenings and being examined in the mornings.[10]

In the spring of 1831, Zhechen Wontrul was called away to the Dzonggo Monastery, the recently established royal religious center of the nearby kingdom of Ling, and in his absence Kongtrul turned to several Zhechen lamas for additional teachings. First, from Gyurme Tenpel, a monk of the monastery who had dedicated his life to retreat, he requested empowerments for two tantric cycles—Mahākaruṇika: Gathering of Sugatas, and Union of All Rare and Precious Jewels. The first is a revelation by one of the founders of Mindroling Monastery, Terdak Lingpa, focused on a form of Avalokiteśvara. The second is a hugely popular revelation focused on Padmasambhava by the seventeenth-century mystic Jatson Nyingpo. Both became central liturgies for his personal practice and keystones of his textual collections.[11]

The earlier "permission" ritual Kongtrul received allowed him to practice supplications to a deity.[12] Scholars have suggested that the "approach" practice represents an early stage of Tantra that developed from basic Indian sacrifice rites. Here, a supplicant would create an altar, invite the deity to appear in the sky above, make offerings and request boons, and then request the deity to depart. Visualization practice in Buddhism is no mere intellectual exercise—the presence of the deity is taken as fact. As the rituals developed in India, around the early eighth century this became internalized. The supplicant's own body was visualized as the altar, and the deity was invited to merge with him or her. The deity's maṇḍala, no longer external, was visualized within the body of the practitioner. These practices came to be classified as Yoga Tantra, while the earlier form of worship was classified as Kriyā Tantra.

A second major historical development of Tantra, dating to around the ninth century, is known as the Mahāyoga Tantra in Nyingma or as Anuttarayoga Tantra in the other traditions. Tantras such as the Guhyagarbha and Guhyasamāja offered a wide range of new yogic techniques to manipulate the practitioner's subtle body—the complex metaphysical system of channels and disks (cakra) through which consciousness is believed to flow. Tantra as a social movement in India was by nature transgressive, using the muck of existence to force the mind and body into buddhahood. Sexual practices were a main element of these Mahāyoga techniques, with intercourse between a male and female practitioner being both a symbolic and literal means of accomplishing elevated states of perception.

These advanced practices, formulated in ritual manuals known as sādhana, require a more elaborate ritual of initiation which is called an empowerment, or abhiṣeka. This empowerment has been likened to the coronation of a king or even to baptism. In early versions the initiate might be bathed, dressed, adorned, anointed, and given objects to hold, all methods for transforming him or her into a suitable vessel for the deity to inhabit and to sit in the center of the maṇḍala and receive offerings. In theory, the empowerment recreates for the disciple the accomplishment of the guru, who must enter into the proper meditative state before the bestowal. With the increased complexity of the Mahāyoga Tantra subtle-body practices, however, yet more stages of empowerment became necessary, and four levels of empowerment eventually became the norm. The first of these is the vase, or water empowerment, which evokes the royal benediction and roughly corresponds to Yoga Tantra considerations. The guru, having entered the state of meditation prescribed by the desired tantric system, places a vase on the practitioner's head. The second, the secret empowerment, requires that the teacher have intercourse with a consort, enter into an advanced mental state, and place a drop of their combined sexual fluid on the tongue of the disciple. The third empowerment has the disciple himself join in sexual union with the consort—the techniques had become so specialized that the disciple would need to perform them in the guru's presence for guidance. The fourth empowerment was the guru's verbal affirmation that the performance had been done properly.

As one would imagine, all four of these empowerments have been sanitized for monastic communities, and a consort is rarely, if ever, actually present. In some cases the sex act is visualized and in others it is completely elided, and the four are given with objects symbolic of the stated intent of the four levels. The first purifies the defilements and impurities of the body. The second purifies speech. The third, known as the "wisdom" empowerment, purifies mind. The fourth, the "word" empowerment, purifies any remaining karmic obscurations. Tibetan Buddhist tantric theory further classifies the basic Yoga Tantra practices of visualizing oneself as the deity as creation stage practice. The subtle-body techniques of the Mahāyoga/Anuttarayoga Tantras are classified as completion stage. A full tantric system combines both of these in sequence, with the practitioner first mastering visualization and then engaging in subtle-body yoga. The first two empowerments are said to authorize these two categories of practice. In the Nyingma tradition, a third stage, known as Dzogchen, or Great Completion, is added, in which the disciple merges his or her mind with primordial wisdom. This, at least in the Nyingma tradition, is authorized by the third and fourth empowerment. During his time at Zhechen, Kongtrul began his lifelong practice of Dzogchen.

Empowerments are generally given together with a "reading transmission" of the entire liturgy and an "instruction" on its meaning and method for practice. The reading transmission is likely a relic of Indian oral tradition; when texts were not written, recitation was a crucial means of preservation. In Tibet the ritual serves little practical function; it is done at lightning speed and is literally unintelligible. In a religious system that values secrecy and restricted access to its literature, the ritual provides students with authorization to read the text. Much of Tibetan literature includes warnings against reading without proper transmission, promising all sorts of karmic retributions should the injunction be disregarded. The instruction consists of the lama explicating the semantic meaning of the text as it is understood by the tradition. Socially these three rituals of initiation insert the recipient in an established community, symbolically placing the disciple in the center of his or her own maṇḍala that is, in fact, part of a larger network.

Following the empowerments, Gyurme Tenpel gave Kongtrul what is commonly called a "pointing-out instruction." This is a method of using rhetorical tricks, posing questions, and making suggestions that guides the disciple to an experience of enlightenment, in which for a brief moment one perceives the nonduality of mind and phenomena. Kongtrul recorded that the lama used a mirror as a prop for the ceremony. Gyurme Tenpel also gave Kongtrul a reading transmission and a training manual for alchemical techniques, specifically for transmuting substances for medicinal purposes. These rites were from the Northern Treasures tradition, a set of revelations from the fourteenth century that form the core set of teachings of Dorje Drak Monastery, one of the main Nyingma monasteries of central Tibet. Kongtrul practiced this for seven days, during which time he had a vision one afternoon of a massive tree, the top of which was lost to sight. Spiraling upward about the tree was a marvelous bird which appeared to be a phoenix.[13]

Kongtrul's second teacher in Zhechen Wontrul's absence was Kunzang Sang-ngak, a lama working in the protective deity temple. This lama taught him the three vows, a category of instruction that covers the three divisions of the Buddhist teachings as understood by Tibetans: Hīnayāna, Mahāyāna, and Vajrayāna.[14] "Hīnayāna" refers to the earliest strata of Buddhist teachings, the sole surviving school of which is the Theravāda, the dominant Buddhist tradition of South and Southeast Asia. "Hīnayāna" means "Lesser Vehicle," a pejorative term used only by adherents to the self-styled "Mahāyāna," or "Greater Vehicle." "Vajrayāna" is another term for Tantric Buddhism. Tibetans received all three at the same time and have always combined elements from each. In both early and later developments of Buddhism, there is an emotional aspect to ignorance and wisdom and to the path: even as early Buddhist doctrine advocates for a rejection of attachment to the world and its inhabitants, compassion and love have always been understood to be potent methods for realizing no-self and, later, emptiness. Love and compassion—the will that others experience well-being and do not experience suffering, respectively—are understood to break the attachment to the self and thereby free the mind to realize the fundamental nonduality of self and other. Buddhist meditations such as Tonglen, or "giving and taking," and the Chod, or "severance" practices, in which one visualizes offering one's own body to other beings, are widely performed techniques to cultivate love, compassion, and generosity. Devotion to a deity or teacher is another method for the practitioner to use the power of emotion to lessen his or her attachment to self. Kongtrul would come to deeply love three people over the course of his long life: his two teachers Zhechen Wontrul and Situ Pema Nyinje, and his friend Jamyang Khyentse Wangpo.

A study of the three vows is a study of the full span of Buddhist teachings as available in Tibet and a model of an ecumenical approach, in that the author of such a treatise is forced to explain all disparate and contradictory teachings of the Buddha. Theologians engage an interpretive strategy of "relative" and "definitive" teachings, the first being taught by the Buddha for those not yet ready to engage with the advanced practices and doctrines which describe reality as it actually is. The Buddha, Mahāyāna theorists are fond of stating, taught with a technique known as "skillful means," or *upāya*, and is said to have taught 84,000 different doctrines, each designed to respond to the need of the listener. No Tibetan scholar would ever reject as spurious any Buddhist teaching transmitted from India, but oceans of ink have been employed to argue which teaching is definitive and which is provisional. Zhechen Wontrul himself also later taught Kongtrul the three vows using one of the most famous compositions on the topic, *Ascertaining the Three Vows* by the sixteenth-century Nyingma exegete Ngari Paṇchen Pema Wanggyel.[15]

Kunzang Sang-ngak also introduced Kongtrul to a practice that would inform his entire life's work: pilgrimage. In pilgrimage one walks toward the Buddha hoping to find evidence of his presence in the destination; in a religion conceived of as a path, the correlation between pilgrimage routes and the pursuit of enlightenment is hard to miss. That year—the Iron Hare, from early 1831 to 1832—at a pilgrimage destination called Sengge Namdzong to the west of Zhechen, near the famous temple of Longtang Dolma, meritorious activity was said to be magnified a thousandfold. Such an event was typical of places of pilgrimage, usually falling on a date corresponding to a particular animal of the Tibetan zodiac and thus occurring every twelve years. Kunzang Sang-ngak proposed to Kongtrul that the two of them go and circumambulate the mountain.[16] Circumambulation is one of the most popular religious practices in Tibet. People walk around funeral reliquaries (*stūpas*), temples, entire monasteries, and mountains. Buddhists walk clockwise, Bon followers walk counterclockwise. It is a means of showing respect to a sacred place, of earning merit, and of receiving the blessings of the site. The practice can be interpreted as communally demarcating sacred from profane, a way for individuals and groups to affirm a shared belief in the power that a specific place possesses and which is unavailable elsewhere.

The two would have needed several days to arrive at Sengge Namdzong, and probably one or two to walk the full circuit, which they did without incident. At the end, however, as they were descending from the north, heavy snow blocked their way. During the afternoon, after spending a day without food, they were struggling to get up a small valley. They found shelter near a large boulder, where Kongtrul's companion instructed him in meditation, saying, "When one is exhausted, worn down by hunger and thirst, and one settles into meditative equipoise on the nature of a moment of awareness, that, and nothing else, is the nature of mind." They sat in proper posture, their legs crossed, their backs straight, and cultivated this awareness.[17] This was perhaps Kongtrul's first experience in meditative absorption, recognizing his mind free of any preconceptions or intellectual projections. Indeed, he lacked at the time the proper Buddhist terminology to describe his experience and did not feel bereft because of it. Scores of words exist to describe what he gained sitting beside that boulder, and he later learned them all. Yet the impression that moment of meditation made on him, the moment of resting in the nature of mind, lasted his entire life. The vital role Sengge Namdzong played in the map of his life was later reflected in a list Kongtrul composed of the major power places in Kham; it was to be one of the eight sites that guide beings through enlightened activity, specifically, as it had Kongtrul, through wrath.[18]

Kongtrul received teachings from several additional lamas at Zhechen. The first, Gyurme Tendzin, taught him the Seven Treasuries of the great fourteenth-century scholar Longchenpa Drime Wozer.[19] Longchenpa was a student of the Third Karmapa, Rangjung Dorje, of the Sakya patriarch Lama Dampa Sonam Gyeltsen, and of the Nyingma mystic Kumārāja. He spent several years at the monastic college at the Kadam monastery Sangpu Neutok training in the philosophical traditions of India before spending the major part of his life meditating in caves in southern Tibet and Bhutan. Longchenpa is famous for having systematized the many disparate streams of Dzogchen teachings. For some five hundred years before him, teachers had promoted doctrines and practices that were allegedly based on material brought to Tibet in the seventh and eighth centuries but which also had considerable native and Chinese influences. Tantras said to be translations from India and copious new materials being revealed in Tibet developed shared ideas and used shared terminology, but until Longchenpa these lacked a single organizing structure. They were "Nyingma," meaning "ancient," only because they did not belong to any of the "Sarma," or "new," traditions then developing, such as the Sakya, Kagyu, or Geluk. Longchenpa applied contemporary scholastic frameworks to the received Nyingma doctrine, of which Dzogchen is the heart. Longchenpa's writing is famous for its clarity and sophistication and remains widely read in Tibetan monastic colleges.[20] Kongtrul studied them as often as he could, reading into the evening any time he could fuel a lamp.

Zhechen Wontrul sent Kongtrul to Lama Pema Kelzang to train in calligraphy, and to the chant master Gyurme Chodar to learn the proportions for drawing deities and handwriting. Two other lamas gave him tantric empowerments. Another teacher was Kunzang Sonam, an accomplished practitioner, who gave Kongtrul the empowerments for Vajrasattva and Amitāyus in the form of the Innermost Heart of Immortality, a longevity practice in the Mindroling tradition. Vajrasattva is a buddha of purification and Amitāyus is the buddha of long life. The lama also gave him a ritual called a "life-force entrustment" for Black Hayagrīva. This ritual is generally performed for worldly protector deities, not for buddhas such as Hayagrīva. It is most common in traditions stemming from revelations, which often introduce a new form of a deity for which the adherents might not feel an obligation to employ the full scale of the Indian ritual system. A retreatant named Samten gave him the empowerment for an Avalokiteśvara revelation of Guru Chowang, the Gathering of the Great Heart, which Samten had practiced so extensively that he had completed 115 million recitations of the six-syllable mantra.[21]

Around the turn of spring to summer, in 1831, Kongtrul developed a greater interest in Jatson Nyingpo's Union of All Rare and Precious Jewels, which he had received that spring. He ceased his practice of the Peaceful and Wrathful Deities and focused now on this.[22] Nyingma sacred literature is divided into two primary categories. The first of these is "Spoken Word," or *kama*, which refers to all teachings that were classified as having been translated from an Indic language. The spoken word teachings were first collected in the seventeenth century by Terdak Lingpa and greatly expanded in the twentieth century by Dudjom Rinpoche.

The second category, "Treasure" or *terma*, refers to all scripture that is identified as having been revealed inside of Tibet. According to legend, Padmasambhava concealed scores of teachings across the Tibetan landscape and placed keys to their recovery in the minds of his disciples. Future incarnations of those men and women were fated to discover the treasures and disseminate them to the public. The earliest revelations were recovered from imperial-era temples, such as Samye or Zha Temple, but soon visionaries were finding inspiration in caves and sacred mountains, places where Padmasambhava was said to have physically visited and left his blessing. Tibetans argue that because all treasure literature was first taught by Padmasambhava or another Indian saint such as Vairocana, they are authentic Indian scriptures and therefore legitimate Buddhist teachings. The treasure label further allowed the charismatic men and women who produced them to evade the unseemly taint of egoism; treasure revealers are understood to be vessels for the word of the Buddha, not authors setting forth their own ideas. Scriptures come, legend has it, fully formed from Padmasambhava; the revealer need only transcribe it.[23] The Jatson Nyingpo revelation was Kongtrul's first involvement with a liturgical cycle that was presented as treasure. While each treasure revealer's work is customarily published in distinct editions, Kongtrul's Treasury of Revelations stands as the dominant collection of the material.

Some Tibetan critics have dismissed treasures as fraudulent, but the practice is almost universally accepted in Tibet.[24] Why this is the case is not difficult to understand, even for the Western mind. Only seven years after Kongtrul took up the Union of All Rare and Precious Jewels, Ralph Waldo Emerson, writing at a time when hundreds of men and women were revealing Christian scriptures from the soil of North America, famously warned a group of Harvard undergraduates to not dismiss ongoing revelation, observing that "Men have come to speak of the revelation as somewhat long ago given and done, as if God were dead."[25] If Tibetans could accept that the Buddha and his representatives were present in the landscape, then it is easy to expect them to keep teaching. Kongtrul fully embraced treasure literature, never doubting the possibility of revelation even as he carefully evaluated each treasure revealer's work. Although he was not blind to the realities of abuse and deception, he was enraptured by the brilliance of the creative minds at work, the beauty of the literature, and the profundity of the divine inspiration it represented.

Kongtrul soon after had two dreams that he attributed to the practice and which tell us a great deal about the state of his mind. His confidence was growing, his earlier anxiety calmed, and he was hopeful that his practice and training would yield results. In the first dream he experienced himself as Guru Drakpo, a wrathful form of Padmasambhava. In his right hand he held a *vajra* scepter—an ancient symbol of power and enlightened activity. In his left hand he held a *kīla* dagger, a symbol of subjugation, similar to a stake. With the unshakable confidence that comes from an unwavering identification with a deity, he pierced the head of a haughty evil female with his kīla, utterly obliterating her. Kongtrul felt that this dream signified that the harmful influence of *gyel* and *sen* demons—two types of malicious Tibetan spirits—was no longer an issue, for the woman represented the demons and in the form of the wrathful guru he had vanquished them.[26]

For a young heterosexual man embarking on a life of celibacy, vanquishing female "demons" is a psychic necessity.

A second dream occurred on the evening of a feast offering from Union of All Rare and Precious Jewels. Tantric systems such as this contain multiple elements of both public and private rituals. A feast—*gaṇacakra* in Sanskrit—is a symbolic banquet performed to accumulate merit, to which the deities are invited to come as honored guests, bestowing their blessings to the community in exchange for the offerings. Kongtrul saw in the mountains surrounding him many naturally occurring images of Padmasambhava and other deities, as well as multiple signs of treasure and treasure doors.[27] At eighteen Kongtrul could already look around at the landscape and see the possibilities. He could see that the ground was fertile and he felt confident that he would draw forth something of great value.

In the late fall of 1831, Kongtrul was reunited with Khangsar Tsepel, who brought him to a gathering of officials at Rudam, not far from Zhechen, near Dzogchen Monastery. While there, he had a dream of Padmasambhava in which many women were reciting the Spontaneous Accomplishment of Goals, a supplication to the Guru that was revealed by the eighteenth-century mystic Tsasum Lingpa. Kongtrul joined them in prayer and saw Padmasambhava in the eastern sky, a white buddha figure in his crown. The following day, he was inspired to ask a lama from Zhechen named Pelden Chogyel to give him a transmission of the Seven-Line Prayer.[28] This short supplication to Padmasambhava was revealed by Guru Chowang in the thirteenth century and became one of the most widely recited prayers in Tibet. It reads:

> HŪṂ! In the north-west borders of the land of Oḍḍiyāna
> Sitting atop a blossoming lotus,
> Having attained extraordinary supreme enlightenment
> You are renowned as the Lotus-born,
> Surrounded by many hosts of ḍākinīs.
> Grant me your blessings so I too,
> Following in your footsteps, may be free!
> *guru padma siddhi hūṃ*

The Seven-Line Prayer became a major focus for Kongtrul in his later years, and he eventually revealed his own system for its practice, a treasure titled Seven-Line Guru Sādhana. Kongtrul does not record how he served the Old Chieftain at the time, but he must have done it well, as his patron's interest in him continued to grow.

Back at Zhechen, Kongtrul continued to study with Zhechen Wontrul. They worked on grammar—which went smoothly—and the meter systems for composing poetry. Kongtrul tried his hand at composing a few lines of verse, his first foray into writing. Wontrul also taught him some arithmetic, and it was at this time that he taught Kongtrul Ngari Panchen's Three Vows treatise. At the time, Zhechen Wontrul was accumulating one hundred million recitations of the mantra from Mahākaruṇika: Gathering of Sugatas. Kongtrul served as an assistant during the related ceremonies, as would be expected of a young disciple in the midst of his training. This would have been an opportunity to learn the intricacies of ritual performance and chanting. Kongtrul himself was personally reciting the Innermost Heart of Immortality for about three weeks.[29]

The Tibetan custom for calculating one's age gives children a year at birth and adds a year at each New Year. Thus, by Tibetan reckoning, on February 2, 1832, the first day of the lunar new year, Kongtrul, who was born on December 3, 1813, turned twenty. This was the appropriate age for full monastic vows, and Zhechen Wontrul ordered Kongtrul to be ordained. At twenty years old Kongtrul was probably at his full height. We do not know what that was. We do not know whether he had a beard, if his forehead was high, or if his ears were flat against his skull. Tulku Urgyen Rinpoche's grandmother, who had met Kongtrul as a young girl, recalled that he was of average height with a prominent nose, "very straight and square."[30] There are no photographs of him, and all paintings of him are done in a style that cared little for individual characteristics. One of these, however, from when he was in his sixth decade, has prints of his hands. His fingers are long and crooked, almost as though arthritic (see p. ii).[31] Judging by his hands, we can presume he was probably tall, like many men of his region, possibly close to six feet. At Zhechen he would have kept his head shaved and dressed the same as other monks, in a dark maroon, many-folded skirt tied around his waist with a belt. On his torso he would have worn a yellow sleeveless vest in the summer or a long-sleeved shirt in cold weather, possibly with a jacket lined with lambskin over which he would wrap a maroon shawl. His shoes would have been felt boots with colored patches around the ankle, the toes slightly curled upwards.

At his residence, using the "lower" system of the Mūlasarvāstivādin precepts traditionally used in Nyingma ceremonies, Zhechen Wontrul gave monastic ordination to Kongtrul and two other young men.[32] Kongtrul treasured this ordination, a formal inclusion into a community of people dedicated to a religious life. He must have been encouraged by Zhechen Wontrul; the invitation to take vows was clear evidence that he was welcomed and valued by the eminent teacher. Ordination ceremonies form a bond among those involved; fellow initiates become like siblings, and preceptors become akin to parents. Kongtrul took the vows seriously, motivated by a real affection and devotion toward Zhechen Wontrul and by faith in buddhas and bodhisattvas.

Zhechen Wontrul had by now become for Kongtrul a beloved lama, a Tibetan word that loosely translates the Sanskrit "guru." In Tantric Buddhism the guru is the surrogate for the Buddha himself, teaching the path to liberation he himself has already successfully traversed. The disciple, particularly one who is ordained and living in a monastic setting, engages in a form of transference, in which affection that might otherwise be directed at parents and lovers is cultivated for the guru. To cultivate this emotional bond disciples regularly practice guru yoga, one of the basic tantric rituals, which intentionally blurs the line between the revered teacher and the Buddha such that the full weight of one's love for parent, lover, friend, teacher, and Buddha are merged. Needless to say, guru devotion can be dangerous, and Kongtrul and many others since have written lengthy warnings about avoiding unqualified teachers.[33]

The ordination ceremony was followed by a series of teachings and empowerments. Wontrul first gave Kongtrul, the Third Zhechen Gyeltsab (who was born around 1817), and Lama Pema Kelzang detailed instructions on the three basic monastic ceremonies—the summer retreat, the confession of infractions, and the fortnightly reaffirmation of vows. He followed this with a reading transmission of 103 volumes of the Kangyur. Wontrul read for fifty days, beginning, as was customary, with the *Bhadrakalpikasūtra*, known in English as the *Fortunate Eon Sūtra*, the first text in the Tibetan canon, which describes the thousands of buddhas who preceded and who will follow Śākyamuni Buddha. Kongtrul records that on the day the reading began snowflakes shaped like flowers fell and covered the ground in a white carpet. Wontrul next gave the first ten volumes or so of the Tengyur, the Derge edition of which is in 213 volumes.[34]

Zhechen Wontrul, Kongtrul, Gyeltsab, and Pema Kelzang then moved from the monastic residence to Wontrul's hermitage where they completed the transmission of the Tengyur. Wontrul followed with the classics of the

Nyingma tradition. This started with the Collected Nyingma Tantras, the Derge edition of which is in twenty-six volumes. This collection contains tantras central to the Nyingma tradition, such as the Vajrakīla scriptures. Vajrakīla is the central deity of the Nyingma tradition and is equally popular in the Sakya, having been passed down through the Sakya's ruling family from the days of the Tibetan Empire. The standard editions of the Tibetan Buddhist canon, however, were assembled by men who considered Nyingma scriptures to be apocryphal and they therefore excluded them. In the twelfth century, the great scholar Sakya Paṇḍita dealt with this issue by finding a Sanskrit version of the *Vajrakīla Tantra* in Sakya Monastery's library. Nyingma scholars, less beholden to the norms of the New Translation traditions, created an alternative canon for their own tantras. The Derge edition of the Collected Nyingma Tantras runs twenty-six volumes.[35]

Zhechen Wontrul also taught other early Nyingma works, all foundational texts for the development of the cult of Padmasambhava. They read the two volumes of the *Collected Instructions on the Mantra*, a revisionist history of the Tibetan Empire that has multiple authors, including the twelfth-century mystic Nyangrel Nyima Wozer, who also wrote the best-known hagiographies of Padmasambhava. Next, they read the *Chronicles of Padmasambhava* and the *Five Chronicles*, two early hagiographies of Padmasambhava that were discovered as treasure by the fourteenth-century mystic Orgyen Lingpa.[36]

They continued the reading transmissions with the writings of early masters of the Nyingma, Kagyu, and Jonang traditions, some of which provided Kongtrul with his initial introduction to doctrines that would form the core of his own thinking. These began with the compositions of Longchenpa, including his Seven Treasuries and the Resting at Ease Trilogy (which are his commentaries on Dzogchen) and various additional works. Next was *Mountain Doctrine, Ocean of Certainty* by Dolpopa Sherab Gyeltsen. This thirteenth-century work is a foundation of the Jonang tradition. After that was *Profound Inner Principles* by the Third Karmapa, Rangjung Dorje. This was followed by the eighteen volumes of United Intent of the Gurus, a revelation by the fourteenth-century master Sanggye Lingpa, and the nine volumes of Jigme Lingpa's compositions and revelations, including his famous Heart Essence of the Vast Expanse revelations, still one of the most widely practiced Dzogchen liturgical cycles.[37]

Zhechen Wontrul gave Kongtrul and the other young men three significant tantric empowerments. First was Eight Commands: Gathering of

Sugatas, a revelation by Nyangrel Nyima Wozer. Second was Karma Lingpa's *Self-Liberated Mind of the Peaceful and Wrathful Deities*, one of the main Nyingma liturgies on the techniques to prepare for death and the *bardo*, the intervening period between one's death and one's next rebirth. Third was *Excellent Vase of Bounty*, a collection of liturgies for the deities of the Nyingma tradition. This was compiled by Terdak Lingpa Gyurme Dorje and Lochen Dharmaśrī, the brothers who founded Mindroling Monastery in the seventeenth century. Wontrul gave the basic empowerments for these three cycles as well as the reading transmission for the explanatory materials. He encouraged them with the advice: "Do not forget these. Who knows which of you will benefit the Buddhist teachings."[38]

The Eight Commands: Gathering of Sugatas would later become one of Kongtrul's primary practices. The grouping of deities was created by Nyangrel Nyima Wozer in the twelfth century with this revelation. It consists of five Mahāyoga tantric buddhas that are each the subject of individual liturgical traditions, with some variations in membership: Yamāri or Yamāntaka, Hayagrīva, Saṃpuṭa or Yangdak Heruka, Vajrāmṛta or Cakrasaṃvara, and Vajrakīla, together with three worldly protectors that may have existed in Tibet before the advent of Buddhism: Mamo Botang, Jikten Choto, and Mopa Drakngak. The grouping proved popular and was later reformulated and expanded, first by the man who claimed to be Nyangrel's reincarnation—Guru Chowang—and later by the great fourteenth-century initiator of the Northern Treasures tradition, Rigdzin Godemchen.[39]

While at Zhechen, Kongtrul composed his first ritual manuals, a mending and a thread-cross ransom liturgy to the deity Pelden Lhamo. He had encountered this deity several years earlier back in his home village when the Bon teacher Tarde Tokden Yungdrung Puntsok had given him the transmission. A mending rite is a form of appeasement, a way to make up for deficiencies in one's commitments to a deity. A ransom, often made with a kind of god's-eye thread cross, is done to exorcise negative spirits. Kongtrul reported that he wrote these because environmental signs were ominous that spring, with several instances of lightning striking nearby and other portends of harm. He also wrote a sādhana and related rituals for the wrathful Buddhist deity Vajradaṇḍa and a set of indigenous deities called the Three Wild Tsen Brothers. These, like many other worldly protectors in Tibet, are said to have been subjugated by Padmasambhava during his time in Tibet and made to swear oaths to serve the new religion. Kongtrul gave his compositions to Zhechen Wontrul, who complimented them, commenting that they revealed an admirable scope of vision. He asked for the transmission so that he might practice them, which was high praise indeed, and he even reported back that he experienced positive results. He told Kongtrul that the Pelden Lhamo practice would be good for curing disease in people and cattle and that the Vajradaṇḍa practice would ease the obscurations caused by breaking a *samaya*—the contract a student makes with his or her guru to practice particular transmitted teachings.[40] Wontrul's comments were prophetic; several years later, in response to bullying by his peers at a new monastery, Kongtrul would burn the compositions in an effort to conform to a new community, only to reconstruct them in order to cure himself of an illness and reaffirm his Nyingma heritage (see chapter 10).

In three years at Zhechen, Kongtrul had won the praise and affection of an influential Nyingma master and was well positioned to thrive at Zhechen. Many years later he claimed that while he was there he saw indications in the surrounding landscape of treasures that he might reveal. That is, he recognized the signs that Padmasambhava had concealed teachings meant for him to extract and disseminate. Kongtrul did not act on these signs. This could have been because he was still young, immersed in training, and not ready to risk claiming the status of a treasure revealer. Such a claim would be difficult for any man or woman to make, given the arrogance of the assertion that Padmasambhava had, over a thousand years earlier, placed material in the soil meant specifically for oneself. Self-described "treasure revealers" were routinely derided for their self-importance, and many were rejected outright by the religious institutions they needed for the distribution of their revelations. Few young men who felt the presence of Padmasambhava in his surroundings would rush to announce it. Kongtrul perhaps believed he had time to complete his Nyingma education and attain the backing he would need to embark on a career of revelation. The treasure signs indicated that Kongtrul saw great potential for his life at Zhechen. He was loved and supported, and he was sure in ability to take good advantage of his opportunities. He forever felt a wistful sorrow that it was not to be.[41]

# 4

## PELPUNG

### 1833–1834

Despite having taken full ordination and having developed a close relationship with an influential lama of the monastery, Kongtrul's status at Zhechen was nevertheless uncertain. A life in a monastery was hardly removed from the material concerns of daily life. A monastic vocation was one that was fully a part of the local economy; rare was the individual who was able to disappear into the mountains to meditate. Monks in Tibetan monasteries relied on the financial support of family or patrons, and many had to perform rituals for the public in exchange for money or goods. Monastery kitchens would occasionally provide communal meals, but for the most part each monk was responsible for his own lodging, meals, and materials. They might occasionally receive a salary for participating in communal ceremonies that were sponsored by a donor or supported by the monastery's land holdings. Monks would also go on alms tours—a tradition that dates back to the Buddha himself—walking the nearby valleys and returning to their home regions to collect whatever food and other necessities could be spared by subsistence farmers. When needed, monks would help their families with the harvest, care of animals, or construction projects. Nor were teachings free for monks—students were expected to make offerings to lamas in exchange for empowerments and instruction. Kongtrul, at age twenty, with no family wealth, was no different from his peers. He relied entirely on the patronage of Khangsar Tsepel and the kindness of Zhechen Wontrul, who, by taking him as a favored disciple, probably fed him and possibly exempted him from certain fees.

The Old Chieftain, Khangsar Tsepel, a Drukpa Kagyu monk, had sent Kongtrul to Zhechen on the advice of a Nyingma lama he met at a Derge summer encampment, but he appears to have had no personal connection to the monastery. Instead, it seems his interests lay elsewhere, at Pelpung, where, at the beginning of 1833, he offered a new monastic residence hall.

Pelpung Tubten Chokhor Ling was the major Karma Kagyu monastery in Derge and one of the largest monasteries in Kham. It had been established in the late 1720s by the Eighth Tai Situ, Chokyi Jungne, popularly known as Situ Paṇchen, who moved his seat there from Karma Gon in the nearby kingdom of Nangchen, on the western side of the Drichu River. The move was the result, at least in part, of the recent submission of Lhasa to the Manchu rulers in Beijing and the absorption of Tibet into the Qing Empire. In 1725, everything to the west of the Drichu came under Tibetan administration at a time of fierce sectarian suppression of the non-Geluk traditions. Even in far-off Nangchen, the impact of Geluk chauvinism would have been felt, and a lama with wide-ranging interests such as Situ would understandably be looking for more supportive environments. Situ Paṇchen and the previous Situ incarnations had long served as chaplains to the Derge royal family. In 1726, Situ, one of the greatest artists in Tibetan history, created one of his masterpieces, a set of paintings of the eight bodhisattvas, and offered them to the Derge King Tenpa Tsering together with a request to establish a monastery in the kingdom.[1]

The Eighth Situ built a massive temple on a bluff above a narrow valley thickly forested with pine, roughly two days walk from the Derge capital. A Drigung Kagyu monastery had previously stood on the site, founded in the twelfth century by a man named Jangchub Lingpa, who was a disciple of Jikten Gonpo, the founder of the Drigung Kagyu tradition. Situ quickly became indispensable to the king and was responsible for the editing of the Kangyur at the new Derge Printing House. Pelpung remained a favored institution in the kingdom until the end of Derge's independence. A large and influential monastery such as Pelpung would continually be in need of new patrons, and it would appear that certain lamas at Pelpung had targeted the Old Chieftain.

In the early spring of 1833, Khangsar Tsepel, whom Kongtrul remembered with gentle gratitude his entire life, informed Kongtrul that he would need to join him on a trip to Pelpung to supervise the construction of the dormitory. It is not clear from Kongtrul's account in what capacity he was to serve Tsepel on the trip and in two subsequent official meetings with the royal family, but it was apparent that he was not going to be returning to Zhechen. The grief that the twenty-year-old suffered at being made to leave never faded; late in life he would recall the transfer with bitterness. He was manifestly happy at Zhechen during the years he resided there and cherished his colleagues and teachers, particularly Zhechen Wontrul. When

Kongtrul went to take his leave of his first master, prostrating to express his devotion, he was overcome with sorrow. Zhechen Wontrul gave him a silk robe that he himself had worn, a pair of ritual vases, and a benediction. The words he used are lost to us; Kongtrul only recorded that it contained the phrase "Yonten Gyatso," meaning "Ocean of Qualities." His parting advice was "Always focus your mind, cultivate mindfulness, and do not fall into sectarianism."[2] Kongtrul would briefly forget this last part, but his emergence from his struggle with sectarianism would result in giving Tibet one of its greatest exemplars of ecumenicalism.

The Old Chieftain brought Kongtrul first to his residence in Chode and then to Pelpung. The day they arrived a spring snow fell. This was followed by a warm day, which Kongtrul optimistically took as an auspicious omen. They went before an influential tulku of the monastery, Karma Tekchok Tenpel, and offered prostrations. At the time, there were two incarnation lines at Pelpung with the title of Wontrul, and as Karma Tekchok Tenpel was the elder of the two, Kongtrul referred to him as Wongen, "Old Wontrul." He was the reincarnation of a brother of the Eighth Tai Situ, possibly the brother named Won Wanggi Dorje. The current Tai Situ incarnation, the Ninth, Pema Nyinje, was then in Tibet fetching the younger Wontrul, Karma Drubgyu Tendzin Trinle, also known as the Third Jewon Chowang Tulku, the rebirth of a nephew of the Twelfth Karmapa, Jangchub Dorje, and a member of the Tromge clan of lower Derge. It was a quick introduction. Khangsar Tsepel soon went off to supervise the construction while Kongtrul sat with a lama named Tashi Gyel to learn how to draw astrological charts, relying on a manual known as *Complete Collection of Essentials*.[3]

Monasteries in Tibet relied on income from agricultural property and donations. Since the time of the Buddha, the teachings have always been given in exchange for goods and services; it is a Western misconception that the Buddhist teachings were ever given freely. On the contrary, in both India and Tibet, the Dharma was a valuable commodity that fetched a high price, and the historical record is replete with examples of monks and nuns owning property and using their wealth to purchase teachings and transmissions as well as of disciples paying astronomical fees to receive instruction from their gurus. The religion operates on an economy of merit—"good karma"—in which clerics and laypeople are mutually dependent. The faithful need merit to earn better lives in the future; if they are religious practitioners, they need merit to activate the blessings of the buddhas and the protections of the gods. Clerics renounce the world to traverse the path to enlightenment, a pursuit that transforms them into suitable recipients of offerings by lay people, who earn merit by their donations. That merit is quantifiable according to intention and ability—a destitute old woman offering a single coin with a pure heart is said to earn more merit than a self-interested rich man giving a sack of gold. Not that a monk would refuse the rich man's gold; in Tibet the early Indian monastic code against clerics owning property was almost entirely unobserved, as it likely was back in the Buddha's own time. There were of course critiques of this practice from within the tradition itself. Kongtrul's near contemporary, Patrul Rinpoche, for example, famously mocked wealthy lamas and refused to participate in the accumulation of institutional material resources.[4] That said, since Tibetans developed massive monastic communities that stored provisions through the long winter months, they required extensive landholdings by which to support the community's infrastructure. These institutions were as financially interconnected with the economy of the region as they were hubs of ritual, renunciation, and education. The lay people accumulated merit while the monasteries and the leading lamas accumulated land and gold—wealth dedicated, at least in theory, to the propagation of Buddhism.[5]

It was perhaps Karma Tekchok Tenpel who had cultivated Khangsar Tsepel as a donor. The lama quickly took notice of Kongtrul as well and gave him a task to test his abilities: the composition of a supplication prayer in the style of "auspicious circle." In this formidable genre of verse, a grid of nine boxes is drawn and a single syllable is placed in each field. The text must be readable in each direction. Kongtrul's composition impressed Wongen, and Wongen later showed it to Situ. The elderly lama now schemed to attract the two men to his household, a wealthy and connected patron and a promising young monk.[6]

After a month or so in the late summer of 1833, the Old Chieftain left Pelpung to attend to government duties, and he brought Kongtrul with him. They left for Tsikhok, traveling through Denkhok, to the north of Derge town, to welcome the king on his return from Lhasa. Tsewang Dorje Rigdzin had gone to central Tibet the year before and was now returning with a court chaplain from Ngor Monastery, probably Tartse Khenpo Jampa Kunga Tendzin, who was then about fifty-seven years old. The Old Chieftain needed to arrange the festivities on the border of the kingdom to celebrate the king's return, and he brought Kongtrul as the scribe. There was bad news from the royal party. A member of the Khangsar clan, a man

named Pema, had died in Lhasa of smallpox, as had five of the royal attendants. There was also the problem of poor financial management, if not
embezzlement, and a large amount of the royal treasure was missing. This
all seems to have been on Khangsar Tsepel to clear up, with Kongtrul by his
side to receive first-hand administrative training. With graciousness and an
even temper, the Old Chieftain received the important lamas who had come
to greet the king, he organized the necessary rituals, and he arranged the
onward journeys. Tsepel and Kongtrul traveled with the party as far as Trao
Plain and then left for Chode Palace. From there they went to Derge town.[7]

At Lhundrubteng, Kongtrul encountered a monk named Pelden Chogyel, who requested Kongtrul write a few devotional poems on his behalf,
perhaps as a test to ascertain if Kongtrul was, in fact, as remarkable as people were beginning to think. The two monks discussed Kongtrul's predic-
ament. It would seem that although Kongtrul had been informed that he
would not be returning to Zhechen, the matter of whether he would be
placed at Pelpung was still unsettled. Kongtrul was at least hoping there
was still a chance of going elsewhere. Pelden Chogyel advised him to go live
at Pelpung and warned him about trying to get back to Zhechen. He spoke
this with the force of prophecy; he told Kongtrul that he himself had been
intended for Pelpung but that he had instead gone first to Pelyul, a major
Nyingma monastery in southern Derge, and had remained there. He told
Kongtrul to avoid this fate, the implication being that it had been a negative
experience for him.[8] The parallel is obvious—Kongtrul's destiny, Pelden
Chogyel suggested, lay at Pelpung, and he must not make the mistake of
becoming ensnared at a Nyingma monastery.

Khangsar Tsepel had left Kongtrul in Derge to make another short trip to
Pelpung. He returned with the decision made; Kongtrul was to go there and
stay for an indefinite period. In addition, he would need to take ordination
again. At this Kongtrul protested. He pointed out, no doubt with humility
and deference, that he had been trained as a Nyingma monk and that he was
unconnected to the traditions at Pelpung. Moreover, he continued, he was
already fully ordained. The Old Chieftain dismissed his concerns and went
as far as to disparage his Zhechen ordination, insisting that Kongtrul was to
take ordination in the Kagyu tradition as soon as the Ninth Situ returned
to the monastery.[9] It is reasonable to suspect Wongen had set the terms.

Wongen was then at Kyodrak Monastery, a Barom institution in Nangchen, welcoming Situ, and he used the occasion to enlist Situ in his campaign to have Kongtrul installed at Pelpung. He showed Situ Kongtrul's

grid poem and told him of his background. Situ accepted the recommendation with a typical Buddhist flourish. He responded by relating a dream he had the previous night in which the sun was shining, which he interpreted as a positive omen of Kongtrul's arrival at Pelpung, and went on to say that "the Khangsar clan has always been a beneficial and loyal patron to me. The current chief, Tsepel, has altruistic intentions and firm faith. Here again he has brought great benefit to the Buddhist teachings."[10]

Situ and his retinue arrived at Pelpung on November 12, 1833.[11] Kongtrul caught only a glimpse of him as his procession passed by. Five days later, Wongen instructed Kongtrul to join several young important incarnations who had requested ordination from Situ. Kongtrul was distraught, repeating in vain to Wongen that he was already ordained. In his diary he recorded an unusual comment made by Zhechen Wontrul during his first ordination; his guru assured him that should he need to return his vows in the future he would be able to do so. This would have been highly exceptional, as the expectation in Tibet is that ordination is for life. Unless Zhechen Wontrul had reason to suspect Kongtrul was going to leave monastic life, he would have little cause to make such a remark, and it is likely that Kongtrul scripted the exchange decades later when editing the diary. In any case, Wongen provided no time for Kongtrul to return the vows, and on November 17,[12] the sixth day of his residence at Pelpung, Kongtrul was ordained a second time.[13]

All ordinations in Tibet are given according to the Indian Mūlasarvāstivādin school of Mahāyāna Buddhism, one of multiple ordination platforms that circulated in India in the centuries of the first millennium of the Common Era. This is the reason the English term "order" cannot be used to describe the diverse Tibetan Buddhist traditions; technically they are all part of the same ordination tradition. However, Tibet maintains two separate lineages of Mūlasarvāstivādin ordination tradition, having received the transmission from India twice. The first, known as the "lower" (meaning eastern) tradition, dates to the first propagation of Buddhism in Tibet, to the ordination of the first seven Tibetans at Samye Monastery by Śāntarakṣita. It was preserved in Amdo following the collapse of the Tibetan Empire in the tenth century and the subsequent loss of imperial support of the monasteries. According to legend, a man who came to be known as Lachen Gongpa Rabsel took ordination there and later, toward the end of the tenth century, gave vows to men from central Tibet who had come seeking to restore full ordination to Tibet. These men gave birth to the

Kadampa tradition, which, after Tsongkhapa, was absorbed into the Geluk tradition. Nyingma adherents claim never to have abandoned the early ordination at all, and so technically it shares the same lineage. The "upper" (that is, western) tradition was introduced in the early thirteenth century by the Kashmiri Paṇḍita Śākyaśrībhadra and is followed by all other Tibetan Buddhist traditions.[14]

Wongen and Situ's insistence that Kongtrul take ordination a second time was a part of a strategy to keep him—and his wealthy patron—at the monastery. It was not required for him to join the monastic community of Pelpung. That is, there was no doctrinal reason for the ordination; it was purely institutional. Nor was it an example of sectarian strife per se; the contest was not between the Kagyu and Nyingma traditions but between Pelpung and the rest of the communities that might draw Kongtrul away. The Old Chieftain may have disparaged the Zhechen ordination, but he did not slight the Nyingma tradition. The disparate ordination lineages allowed Wongen to use a ceremony to help secure his desired goal of binding Kongtrul into the ranks of the monastery and to populate his institutional family with superior stock.

Even with his dependence on Khangsar Tsepel, Kongtrul was technically free to go wherever he chose. Promising monks were enticed from one monastery to another, similar to the way skilled athletes transfer from team to team. He could have left for central Tibet, or joined a band of itinerant practitioners, or simply returned to Zhechen to try to make his own way there. Zhechen Wontrul was his family, his Guru, and his protector, but even so, the lama would have been unlikely to accept a monk whose financial patron intended him to be elsewhere. Zhechen Wontrul would not easily offend a powerful aristocrat. In any case, Kongtrul was loyal to the Old Chieftain and was loath to leave his service. Kongtrul acquiesced to the ritual, but he resisted, privately, from start to finish.[15]

The ceremony took place at the meeting hall, Tashi Temple. A quorum of five fully ordained monks are required, with specific roles to play: abbot, preceptor, mentor, timekeeper, and chant leader. At Kongtrul's ordination, Situ performed the dual roles of abbot and preceptor. Wongen served as the mentor. The timekeeper was a doctor named Karma Tsepel. The chant leader was Karma Khentsun, who also gave a short explanation of the ceremony. A relative of Situ's, Karma Tokme, made up the quorum. Kongtrul did not record the names of any others. Situ gave Kongtrul the name Karma Ngawang Yonten Gyatso Trinle Kunkhyab Pelzangpo. The name is, as is the case with most Tibetan names, a string of Buddhist terms: Karma, Lord of Speech, Ocean of Qualities, All-Pervading Enlightened Activity, Glorious and Good. Kongtrul went along with it and received the three vows of layman, novice, and monk. But in his mind, he did not comply. He wrote, many years later, that thoughts of his earlier ordination prevented him from feeling that these second vows were entirely legitimate. This was in direct contrast to his description of the Zhechen ordination, about which he felt everything had occurred exactly as it should. At Pelpung he experienced no sense of transformation, no joy at being joined to a community. His antipathy to the ceremony exemplifies a lifelong ambivalence toward his sectarian identity. His Nyingma ordination was deeply felt; he was numb to his Kagyu ordination.[16] He grew into one of the greatest Karma Kagyu masters in history, yet he also embodied an ecumenicalism that seems as much born out of personal frustration as from a wildly curious intellect. As for the ordination name, a section of it became one of his most commonly used names, Yonten Gyatso. Yet in his diary Kongtrul explicitly credited Zhechen Wontrul with having given him this name first, in his farewell benediction.[17]

Several days after the ceremony, Situ summoned Kongtrul and gave him gifts and advice. These included a vajra scepter and bell set, required for anyone performing tantric rituals either in a group or privately, and a lower robe. Situ pointed to a Chinese scroll painting and said, "look there—the man of long life." Kongtrul understood this to be a blessing, but it was hardly an impressive meeting with the man who would serve as his beloved guru for the next twenty years.[18]

Nowhere does Kongtrul speak of his welcome by his peers at the monastery, and, in fact, there is sufficient evidence to suggest that he encountered some hostility from the beginning. He lived most of the rest of his life at Pelpung and was ever vigilant against claims of misappropriation of offerings—the mishandling or even theft for personal use of what had been given to the community for religious practice. It is an accusation of disloyalty, lodged against those who do not belong. He never cited an instance, but he was ever on guard. It was years before a peer befriended him or before he joined in a communal ceremony. He seems to have spent his first years at Pelpung largely isolated.

While Kongtrul spent the winter memorizing liturgies and commentaries necessary for life in a Kagyu monastery, Wongen was continuing his program of securing the young monk's fealty to Pelpung. Having moved to prevent another monastery from drawing Kongtrul away, he now attended to the risk that the Derge court might requisition Kongtrul to government service. To prevent this, he requested Situ to identify Kongtrul as an incarnation; named incarnations could not be drafted. This would have the added advantage of tightening Kongtrul's ties to Pelpung, as the identification of him as the rebirth of a lama connected to the monastery would further embed him in the community. Choosing incarnations was not a simple matter, and his took some time. In many cases the deceased's property was transferred to the new incarnation, and often the family of the chosen boy was elevated in social status and income. Rivalries could outlive individuals, and influential lamas could refuse to allow the identification of their enemies.[19]

These concerns factored in the decision regarding Kongtrul's previous identity, limiting Situ's options in selecting a previous birth for his new student. The Fourteenth Karmapa, the Eighth Pawo, and the Eighth Drukchen, all three powerful figures in the Kagyu tradition, had previously advised Situ that reincarnations of three of the previous Situ's students were not to be recognized. The men in question were named Alo Kunkhyen, Belo Tsewang Kunkyab of Zurmang, and Tamdrin Gonpo; nothing is known of them or their infractions against the tradition. The three hierarchs warned that if a man was given the name of one of these three men, not only would the monastery not be able to hold on to him but his life would be difficult. After some consideration, they decided on a student of the Eighth Situ, a lama named Kongpo Bamteng Tulku Tsoknyi Lekdrub. "Kongtrul" is an abbreviation of his title "Kongpo Bamteng Tulku," meaning the incarnation from Bamteng in Kongpo, a region in south-central Tibet.[20] For Kongtrul to reveal the artifice behind the selection of his previous incarnation speaks to how little he valued it. He was not opposed to creating links to previous lives—decades later in *Mirage of Nectar,* his "secret autobiography," he composed biographies of the famous men whom he claimed as previous incarnations. But Kongpo Bamteng Tulku would not be among them.

# 5

# EARLY KAGYU FOUNDATIONS, PART ONE

*Teachings at Karma Gon*

1834

---

For the next six years, Kongtrul received trainings befitting a named incarnation of a Kagyu institution in Kham. He forged a relationship with the Fourteenth Karmapa, an embodiment of the nonsectarian zeitgeist of Kham of which Kongtrul himself would become one of the greatest exemplars. While he was receiving a foundation of Kagyu texts and practices at Pelpung, Karma Gon, and other monasteries, he also received Nyingma, Sakya, and Jonang teachings. These, however, came almost entirely from Kagyu lamas, and Kagyu lamas repeated many transmissions and empowerments that he had received at Zhechen. The teachings and practices of non-Kagyu teachings were not problematic for the establishment as a Kagyu community member; the transmissions from non-Kagyu teachers, at least for a monk previously trained in a Nyingma monastery, apparently was. Kongtrul also established a pattern of activity that would hold for the rest of his life: near-constant giving or receiving of teachings, going into retreat, and traveling to nearby and distant places to meet with scholars and interact with the land.

In March 1834,[1] Situ gave the transmission for *Ocean of Deities*, a compilation of iconography and sādhana made by Tāranātha. Kongtrul was invited to receive this, and afterwards Situ gave Kongtrul empowerments for several longevity practices. These were given in response to a comment Wongen made to Situ suggesting that a young man of Kongtrul's promise ought to be assured of a long life. Long-life practices are common in Tibetan Buddhism, a way to marshal one's strength for extended religious activity. Situ gave him Atīśa's White Tārā and Ratna Lingpa's fifteenth-century treasure cycle focusing on Avalokiteśvara in the form of Guhyasamāja called Gathering of Secrets. Atīśa Dīpaṃkara was one of the great teachers of the second diffusion of Buddhism in Tibet. A monk from the famous northeastern Indian monastery of Vikramaśīla, he spent the later decades of his life in Tibet. White Tārā, a deity popularized by Atīśa, is one of the most widely practiced—she, Amitāyus, and Uṣṇīṣavijayā are together known as the Three Deities of Long Life. White Tārā and Gathering of Secrets both became part of Kongtrul's daily practice.[2]

Buddhism was brought into Tibet piecemeal. Tibetans would go down to India, Nepal, or Kashmir to bring back texts and techniques, or Indian masters would come to the Plateau and disseminate what they possessed. The major second-diffusion traditions developed around specific texts or teachings. The Six Yogas of Nāropā and the core Kagyu teaching of Mahāmudrā were brought by Marpa Chokyi Lodro in the eleventh century and passed to his disciple Milarepa, the famous poet-yogi. These then mingled with the new tantric systems that were beginning to circulate in Tibet around the *Cakrasaṃvara, Hevajra,* and *Guhyasamāja Tantras.* Their disciples gave rise to the Kagyu tradition. Translators such as Marpa established teaching lineages and, in some cases, institutions that lent their names to distinct religious traditions. Many translation lineages, however, were not tethered to particular institutions or traditions but were shared across communities. These included distinct approaches to deities that are credited to individuals, such as Atīśa's White Tārā.

In April 1834,[3] the sixty-year-old Tai Situ went to Karma Gon Monastery in western Kham. Wokmin Karma Gon was the first Karma Kagyu monastery, founded in 1147 by the First Karmapa, Dusum Khyenpa. It was the seat of the Situ incarnations until the Eighth Situ built Pelpung, and it likely remained under their supervision. Pema Nyinje spent the next six months at Karma Gon giving the transmission of the Kangyur to a group of young incarnations, including the Fifth Karma Chakme, the Fifth or Sixth Dzigar Choktrul (their dates are not known), and the Ninth Drukchen.[4] It was the last time Situ traveled outside of Pelpung; on his return to his seat, he remained in his residence for the last twenty years of his life. Wongen was part of Situ's entourage at Karma Gon, there to receive the same transmission as the others, and he brought Kongtrul with him.[5]

The transmission began at the end of May 1834 and ran until the end of September.[6] The young men sat in a room in an ancient temple that was cool on even the hottest days and dimly lit when clouds covered the sky. The windows lacked glass and remained open to let in light or were covered with cloth to keep out the wind and rain. In the dark rooms the eyes of gilded buddhas glowed from the light of the butter lamps, and patches of sunlight rendered the dark corners all the more impenetrable. Reading would have started as soon as there was sufficient light and continued with short breaks for tea and toilet and a noon meal. Oil lamps could extend the reading sessions into the evening. In the main temple the participants' cushions lay on a floor of pounded earth. In an upper room the floor was also pounded earth, over a layer of gravel and brushwood held up by the beams of the building. (Wooden planks were used only in later construction.) Situ would have sat on a raised throne, several feet above the rug-covered ground while everyone else sat cross-legged on the floor mats.

Kongtrul served Wongen as an attendant, sitting by him and serving his tea. But for parts of the summer, Wongen was ill with a fever, and while the elder monk was confined to his room, the Kangyur transmission was halted, providing Kongtrul with the opportunity to receive teachings and empowerments from other lamas. From the Karma Chakme tulku he received the oral transmission for *Mountain Doctrine*, a lengthy survey of the Buddhist path from the Karma Kagyu perspective by the First Karma Chakme, as well as that master's instructions on Mahākaruṇika, a form of Avalokiteśvara, the bodhisattva of compassion, who stands with eleven heads and one thousand outstretched arms, an eye on each hand. The tulku also gave him several Ratna Lingpa transmissions and empowerments, including his Peaceful and Wrathful Deities and the practices of Hayagrīva, Vajrakīla, and Yamāntaka, the wrathful form of Mañjuśrī.[7]

The Dzigar Choktrul gave Kongtrul the reading transmission for the Collected Works of Tāranātha.[8] This was a foundational transmission for Kongtrul, providing him with an early introduction to the doctrine of "other-emptiness" that would form the core of his philosophical position. In Tibetan Buddhist philosophy emptiness is either conceived of as an absolute negation or as lacking all but its own characteristics: luminosity and awareness. At the most basic level the debate is simply about whether one can describe ultimate reality in positive terms or whether one must always use the language of negation. That is, whether anything at all can be said to exist outside of our deluded perception. This debate played out between the philosophical schools of Madhyamaka, which is largely based on the writings of the Indian philosopher Nāgārjuna, and the Yogācāra, which takes as its core scriptures the Five Books of Maitreya and the commentaries by the Indian saint Asaṅga. Geluk and most Sakya lamas hold to an orthodox Madhyamaka view, while Nyingma and most Kagyu thinkers hold to some version of a fusion of the Madhyamaka and Yogācāra doctrines. For most of Tibetan history, the debate between advocates of "self-emptiness" and "other-emptiness" was not contentious and, in fact, contributed to a fertile intellectual environment. Monasteries might advance a particular position, but monks and teachers would move from institution to institution studying with teachers who could disagree with each other without danger. Various syntheses of the two views continue to be common in Tibet and, in fact, it is rare to meet a Tibetan who does not venerate most of the players in the debate, both Indian and Tibetan philosophers.

The tone of the debate changed in the mid-seventeenth century with the ascendance of the Geluk tradition, backed by the fiercely partisan Mongol armies. Doctrinal differences became the language to contest political battles, and subtle points of doctrine became sacred idols in need of protection from enemies of the faith. Geluk partisans staunchly opposed "other-emptiness" treatises, and when the Fifth Dalai Lama developed a personal grudge against the Jonang abbot and "other-emptiness" proponent Tāranātha, he was ready to permit action against him and Jonang Monastery. Following Gushri Khan's conquest of Tibet in the 1660s, Tāranātha's writings were banned and both Jonang Monastery and Tāranātha's own monastery, Takten Puntsokling, were converted to Geluk. Printing of Tāranātha's Collected Works at the nearby monastery is said to have resumed in the nineteenth century after a lama from Zhalu Monastery, Ribuk Tulku Losel Tenkyong, was able to convince authorities to allow him access. In Tibet, sectarian conflict only worsened in the eighteenth century, with successive Mongol invasions resulting in increasingly brutal repressions of non-Geluk institutions. Between 1717 and 1720 the Dzungar Mongols razed scores of Kagyu and Nyingma monasteries and murdered some of the greatest lamas of the era, including Terdak Lingpa of Mindroling. Although the Qing emperor sent in troops to restore order and the monasteries were mostly rebuilt, the spirit of ecumenicalism, at least in central Tibet, never fully recovered.[9]

Not so in Kham, where a Kagyu tulku could give a former Nyingma monk a transmission of Tāranātha's writings. These were supplemented with a triple transmission from the Ninth Drukchen of the One Hundred Instructions of the Jonang, a compilation of Jonang teachings made in the seventeenth century by the twenty-fourth abbot of Jonang, Kunga Drolchok.[10] This was the inspiration for Kongtrul's final great compilation, the Treasury of Instructions, and is included in its last volume. (This despite the Ninth Drukchen being only thirteen at the time.) Kongtrul would certainly have known of the persecution of the Jonang tradition. One can speculate that receiving the transmission of banned Jonang material at the age of twenty-one had an additional lasting effect on Kongtrul. This was his first exposure to what can be reasonably described as endangered teachings. Banned in Tibet (although preserved and continuously taught in southern Amdo), the teachings of Tāranātha, rich with expositions on "other-emptiness," were rendered inaccessible to many Tibetans and were at risk of disappearing altogether. Kongtrul would dedicate himself to collecting, editing, and disseminating such material in order that no Buddhist teachings could vanish from Tibet. He developed a lifelong commitment to the Jonang teachings; in his seventieth decade he had a vision of a stūpa that had a cleft in the southwest corner, a deficiency that would be repaired if the Jonang teachings were to be likewise restored to their former glory.[11]

The Dzigar Choktrul also gave Kongtrul the transmission for a second work of lesser, but still significant impact for Kongtrul's later career, the Four Medical Tantras. These foundational texts of the Tibetan medical tradition are religious scriptures as well as scientific ones, full of ritual instructions and religious doctrine. They are compilations of instructions and information that are said to have been first gathered by Yutok Yonten Gonpo in the ninth century and concealed as treasure. This was revealed in the eleventh century by Drapa Ngonshe and systematized by his disciple, also named Yutok Yonten Gonpo. Needless to say, the issue of authorship is complicated. Kongtrul had first engaged with this literature when he was fourteen, memorizing a few of the sections, such as the Discourse on Pulse Diagnosis and Urinalysis. Although he never practiced medicine, he dabbled in the manufacture of medicinal compounds and wrote explanations of certain medical practices.[12]

During the periods before and after the Kangyur transmission, Kongtrul received instructions from a man named Lhalung Khewang Tenpel. The lama taught Kongtrul from the works of the Third Karmapa, Rangjung Dorje. These were Profound Inner Principles, Treatise Distinguishing Ordinary Consciousness from Primordial Awareness, and Treatise on Buddha-Nature.[13] The first of these deals with tantric topics of the subtle body and yogic practices, with relating astrological material. The second and third are commentaries on the Yogācāra theories of consciousness and the doctrine of buddha-nature. There have been multiple and contradictory presentations of buddha-nature throughout the development of Indian and Tibetan Buddhism, ranging from the notion that all sentient beings possess the potential to become buddhas to the assertion that all sentient beings are by nature already perfected buddhas, their nature obscured by adventitious karmic stains. Both Indian and Tibetan philosophers concerned with the definition of ultimate reality struggled to reconcile buddha-nature with emptiness. Most Geluk and Sakya thinkers relegate buddha-nature to provisional status, meaning that it cannot be taken to be literally true. The Third Karmapa studied with Dolpopa Sherab Gyeltsen, who had trained in both Sakya and Kadam institutions and had settled at Jonang Monastery in Tsang, making it a center of "other-emptiness" thought. The Third Karmapa favored the "other-emptiness" approach, making for an easier adoption of buddha-nature as definitive. Kongtrul would return repeatedly to the Third Karmapa's trilogy of "other-emptiness" compositions, and they would become central to his intellectual development and the basis for some of his own best-known commentaries.[14] Lhalung Khewang Tenpel also taught him the Single Intent instructions from the Drigung Kagyu tradition, and he studied, with several unnamed teachers, the grammar system of the seventh-century Indian Yogācāra master Candragomin.

The Karma Chakme tulku passed away suddenly in September, bringing an abrupt and tragic end to the Kangyur transmission. Situ had read the first five sections: the Vinaya, the section on ethics; the Prajñāpāramitā, or Perfection of Wisdom section; the *Avataṃsaka Sūtra*, or *Flower Ornament Sūtra*; the Ratnakūṭa, or Jewel Heap section; and the section of remaining sūtras. The transmission ended there, without the reading of the tantric scriptures in the collection. It is possible that Situ would have continued with the remaining works but that Karma Chakme's death made it impossible, or undesirable, to continue. Summer was over, and the progress had been remarkably slow—only two years earlier Zhechen Wontrul had given the entire Kangyur to Kongtrul in just fifty days. Perhaps this was due to Wongen's illness, or perhaps it was simply the way Situ had planned the event.[15]

The tulku's death made an impression on Kongtrul. He had developed an affection for the young man, and he saw him soon after in a dream, standing before a golden throne. Kongtrul rested his head against the tulku's heart, and the tulku smiled and placed his hands on Kongtrul's shoulders, giving Kongtrul a sensation of intense warmth and well-being. He was bereft, but he made peace with the loss after sensing that the tulku would move on to a good rebirth. Situ led the funeral service on October 3, 1834.[16] They then returned to Pelpung, where Situ gave the remaining sections of the Kangyur to Wongen, Kongtrul, and others. The pace was quicker at Pelpung, and they finished within a few months.[17]

# 6

# EARLY KAGYU FOUNDATIONS, PART TWO

*Early Retreats, Dreams, and Visions*

1835–1837

By the end of 1834, a little less than two years after he had transferred to Pelpung, Kongtrul had received a second ordination in the Karma Kagyu tradition and a second transmission of the Kangyur, both from one of the greatest living Karma Kagyu masters. He had received more than half of the transmission at the very first Karma Kagyu monastery ever built. As a named incarnation he was part of a well-established Karma Kagyu institutional system, and he would spend the next several years receiving additional Kagyu teachings and transmissions to solidify his position. As he did so, he struggled to reconcile his new identity with his Nyingma heritage, as most of the teachings he held dear were transmitted a second or third time by Kagyu lamas. He was confronted with substantial suspicion by other monks at Pelpung, occupying as he did the precarious position of the convert.

Institutional and sectarian identity was always part of the Tibetan social fabric, albeit with varying degrees of weight and enforcement, and most Tibetans wove complicated tapestries of affiliations and allegiances. Clan and region also factors into Tibetan identity, often conflicting with other markers when called to the fore. At Pelpung, Kongtrul felt pressure to leave behind who he had been at Zhechen, and his regret at leaving his Nyingma monastery would stay with him his entire life. And yet he continued to receive Nyingma teachings as part of his formal education at Pelpung, and at Pelpung he put into practice some of the Nyingma teachings he had been given at Zhechen. This was Kham in the nineteenth century, and, to many, to be a member of a Karma Kagyu tradition was to embrace teachings from many sources. The Kagyu tradition had integrated Nyingma teachings as far back as the First Karmapa, who was initially a Nyingma practitioner. In this spirit, Kongtrul first tried to maintain his Nyingma heritage, but when this became untenable in the face of bullying by his Pelpung peers, he repressed it and tried to transform himself into an unadulterated Kagyu monk.

In February 1835,[1] at the beginning of the Wood Sheep Year of the Tibetan calendar, Kongtrul began a formal practice of White Mañjuśrī. He had first received initiation into the practice of White Mañjuśrī back in 1830 from Zhechen Wontrul. The practice he had received, Mati Paṇchen's, was observed by all traditions of Buddhism in Tibet, so there would have been no doctrinal reason to receive a second transmission at Pelpung. Nevertheless, it is telling that Kongtrul chose a teaching he had received at Zhechen for his first formal retreat. He had at this point only received the permission for the deity and not the full empowerment, so he performed the "approach," which is essentially an accumulation of mantra recitations. This initial phase of the practice would be done to familiarize himself with the deity and lay the foundation for a more intensive and technical practice later on. "Approach" is generally done in a retreat environment, meaning the practitioner closes him or herself off from other concerns and focuses exclusively on the rituals. Many monasteries, Pelpung among them, have separate buildings or rooms dedicated to retreat activities. Kongtrul does not mention in his diary whether this first retreat took place in a center or simply in his own room.[2]

On completing the predetermined number of recitations, Kongtrul then presented himself to the Ninth Situ and requested guidance regarding his daily practice, a primary responsibility of the guru. That he went to Situ and not Wongen reflects the direction of his devotion. Situ became, in Kongtrul's diary, "my lord and master." Wongen was only ever just Wongen. Situ told him to concentrate on White Tārā, the practice that he had given him the year before in advance of leaving for Karma Gon, and he instructed him to enter a retreat to do so. Kongtrul accordingly performed an "approach" phase practice for White Tārā in the tradition of Atīśa. While he was accumulating the mantra—oṃ tāre tuttāre ture mama ayuḥ punya jñānā puṣtiṃ kuru svāhā—he had several dreams filled with positive signs of long life and accomplishment, such as sunrises and excellent harvests and glorious stūpas the size of mountains. Stūpas can be either reliquaries and/or representations of enlightened mind. In one dream he heard voices whispering the number of years he would live, but he forgot the number on waking. He dreamed of Situ Rinpoche, in a small room, with a consort who sat apart in royal posture on a throne in a courtyard. Kongtrul felt enormous devotion to her, and touching his head to her feet he made multiple prayers, including "I pray to the mother, Yeshe Tsogyel."[3]

Situ was a fully ordained monk, and there is no record of his having engaged in consort practice with a woman. Sexual yoga, a highly controversial topic in Tibet and Tibetan Buddhism, is claimed in Tantric Buddhism to be necessary for complete enlightenment. Doctrine has it that only intercourse can untie the knots in the subtle body that prevent awareness from fully recognizing itself. According to tantric theory, consciousness flows through the human body along a network of channels, or *nāḍīs*. A central channel stretches from the crown of the head to the groin, ending either at the perineum or the tip of the penis. Side channels branch out at various places, meeting the central channel at intersections called cakras. In unenlightened beings the intersections are twisted in ways that block the flow of the vital wind on which consciousness rides. Advanced practices involving both visualization and breathing techniques manipulate this wind in order to open the channels, and a set of four visions are said to naturally arise in sequence as a result. Having mastered this, the practitioner then manipulates the *tikle*, a term probably of Tibetan origin which is sometimes translated as "elements" or "drops." These are the subtle forms of the sperm and egg from which one's life began, and they are believed to reside in the subtle body until the moment of death. Individual practices such as *tummo*, or yogic heat meditation, generate not only warmth but an experience of bliss, one that is without any attachment or ignorance, and so is identical to a realization of emptiness.[4]

Sexual yoga involves intercourse with a partner in order to maximize the flow of the tikle and completely open the knots of the subtle body. Some have also claimed that the practice purifies the stains of a broken commitment, a strategic claim for a practice that violates monastic ordination vows. In the Nyingma tradition, sexual yoga is sometimes said to be a requirement for revelation, the only method that could release the final stains that obscure access to one's allotted treasure. While some fully ordained monks claim to visualize a consort, some monks practiced with a consort in secret, earning disdain and expulsion from their community upon discovery. In general, in monastic communities, the practice was restricted to the leaders of the community who had the status to withstand social condemnation. Many Nyingma mystics, including treasure revealers, simply did not take monastic vows in the first place, but this often left them to scramble for institutional support. Contentious as it would be to allege that a highly respected monastic leader had a consort, Kongtrul's dream would have been taken as symbolic and not libelous. By identifying the woman as Yeshe Tsogyel, Padmasambhava's legendary Tibetan consort, the Situ in the dream was made the equivalent of Padmasambhava himself. Kongtrul's veneration was growing.

In the summer and autumn of 1835, Wongen gave Kongtrul and his younger peer, Wontrul Jewon Chowang Tulku, many of the primary Kagyu tantric empowerments. He gave them the reading transmission for all available editions of the major and minor Karma Kagyu maṇḍalas, liturgical texts, and rites to protective deities. Wongen also gave them empowerments and instructions on the tradition of Chod from the tradition upheld by Zurmang Monastery, a Karma Kagyu institution in northwestern Kham. It has given rise to some of the most haunting and delicate melodies in Tibetan music. It is closely related to Zhije, which was brought to Tibet by the eleventh-century Indian master Padampa Sanggye, a teacher to Machik Labdron, the originator of Chod. To Kongtrul alone, Wongen gave instructions on how to practice these systems as well as instructions on two central Kagyu meditation teachings, Mahāmudrā and the Six Yogas of Nāropā. The Mahāmudrā instruction was based on a famous trilogy of the Ninth Karmapa: *Ocean of Definitive Meaning, Mahāmudrā: Eliminating the Darkness of Ignorance*, and *Pointing Out the Dharmakāya*. Presumably, Wontrul was too young to receive these advanced materials.[5]

Kongtrul continued to have dreams in which his devotion to the Buddhist patriarchs was expressed and which included prophetic elements. One in particular from November of 1835[6] reflects the psychological adaptation to his new home. Kongtrul dreamed of coming into the presence of the Buddha, who was two stories high. He then found him circumambulating in a counterclockwise direction—the direction that the Bon tradition follows—around a structure that disappeared into the sky. A massive copper and gold stūpa appeared, and Kongtrul began to ascend the surrounding steps in the Buddhist direction. In the alcove of the vase section of the stūpa, he saw a statue of Guhyapati, the Lord of Secrets, which is a popular form of the bodhisattva of power, Vajrapāṇi. In the deity's crown was an image of the Kagyu patriarch Rechung Dorje Drakpa, who was said to have been an emanation of the bodhisattva. As Kongtrul walked around to the left side of the stūpa, it appeared to be made of clay, with a deep cavity inside. He reached his hand in and drew out many yellow scrolls of text—a standard mode of appearance of treasure literature.

The dream next took him to a hillside on which were many black tents. He said to himself "Since this is a dream, these are negative omens." Convinced then that he was the treasure revealer Mingyur Dorje, he began stamping all the tents, at which point he transformed into Dorje Drolo, a wrathful form of Padmasambhava, brandishing a kīla dagger. He went next to a gully where he encountered a terrifying figure holding a knife. He initially felt some fear, but remembering that he was Mingyur Dorje he wrested the weapon away from the fearsome being and snapped it in two. He killed the entity, hurling stones at it until its corpse was half buried in earth. Continuing on, he arrived at what looked like the mountain Uchetem, a peak above Pelpung, saw his residence, and awoke. The following day, a man from the Kardze region, Karma Nyima Wozer, arrived and gave him a volume of Dorje Drolo teachings. Not long after that, Wongen gave him the transmission and empowerment for the practice.[7]

This is a remarkable dream in many ways. It indicates the transition from Bon to Buddhist and a conviction that Nyingma practice—textual revelation—was possible within a Karma Kagyu institutional structure, symbolized by the stūpa with the image of Rechungpa. Kongtrul's Bon heritage was fading, but he continued to reach for Nyingma teachings. The presence of Mingyur Dorje as a vanquisher of demons emphasizes the role Kongtrul saw for the Nyingma practices within a Kagyu framework. Mingyur Dorje was a Nyingma treasure revealer who worked in concert with the prominent Karma Kagyu monk Karma Chakme. Their relationship was a model on which Kongtrul himself would later base his work with a young Nyingma treasure revealer named Chokgyur Lingpa. Karma Chakme was ordained and highly educated, while Mingyur Dorje was young, charismatic, and illiterate. The monk transcribed most of the boy's revelations and provided the institutional support for their propagation.

At the end of 1835 Kongtrul entered the main retreat center of Pelpung and completed the four preliminary practices of the Mahāmudrā tradition. These are refuge, Vajrasattva, maṇḍala offerings, and guru yoga. Kongtrul does not tell us whether he received transmission for the preliminary practices from Situ or Wongen, nor which liturgy he used, although it was almost certainly that of the Ninth Karmapa, whose *Chariot for Traversing the Noble Path* was the most commonly used manual. In 1841 Kongtrul would write a commentary on this titled *Torch of Certainty*, one of his earliest compositions.[8] Preliminary practices are common across all religious traditions of Tibet. They are done before advanced meditation practice and are designed to develop the proper attitude, accumulate necessary merit, and familiarize the practitioner with the basic techniques.

Each practice includes a prayer or mantra that is recited 100,000 (or more) times. The practitioner first visualizes the refuge field in the space above, which contains the lineage of masters of the tradition. Tibetans customarily perform full-body prostrations as they recite the refuge prayer. Vajrasattva is the bodhisattva of purity, and the practice is performed to purify mental obstacles to enlightenment. Maṇḍala practice increases merit through symbolic acts of generosity. One pours substances such as grain mixed with semiprecious stones onto a metal plate, representatives of the entire universe and its contents. The fourth practice, guru yoga, is fundamental to tantric practice. The guru is likened to the Buddha, in that he teaches the path to liberation. Guru yoga involves visualizing one's own lama in enlightened form alongside all the patriarchs of the lineage. The disciple fervently prays, pleading with the guru—undifferentiated from the gods and the great masters of the past—to protect and teach. The visualized guru then sends blessings and dissolves into the practitioner. The preliminary practices took Kongtrul about six months to complete. He had pleasant dreams while undertaking his guru yoga, such as finding himself in lovely green meadows filled with flowers.[9]

Kongtrul then began to put into practice the tantric cycles into which he had been initiated, during which he experienced several remarkable dreams. At the end of April or the beginning of June 1836,[10] he dedicated about a month to the approach practice of the five-deity maṇḍala of Cakrasaṃvara.[11] This is one of the most popular tantric systems in Tibet. The *Cakrasaṃvara Tantra* was likely composed in India in the eighth or ninth century, and scholars have argued that it bears a close relationship with Śaivite traditions, with the two likely developing out of a common ancestor. The buddha Cakrasaṃvara, a form of the wrathful buddha Heruka, is generally depicted as wrathful, blue in color, with four faces and twelve hands, and adorned with garlands of human skulls and tiger skins. He is often shown in sexual union with his female partner, Vajravārāhī.

After finishing the retreat, Kongtrul dreamed he entered a magnificent chamber where he found Zhechen Wontrul carrying several yellow scroll manuscripts wrapped in cloth that gave off a smell like camphor, several of which were open. Kongtrul was able to recognize that he was dreaming, and yet rather than examine the books, as one might expect, he turned his back to his previous guru and looked outside. In a sort of courtyard he saw a group of seated figures, children by the looks of them. These were the mahāsiddhas—the great tantric saints of India—among whom were Lawapa, who is credited with developing the yoga of lucid dreaming, as well as Kṛṣṇācārya and Ghaṇṭāpada. Kongtrul would later claim to be a rebirth of Kṛṣṇācārya who, with Ghaṇṭāpada, was instrumental in transmitting the Cakrasaṃvara practices. They all vanished, and Kongtrul rested in awareness of the nature of mind. This was one of the few dreams Kongtrul had of Zhechen Wontrul after leaving Zhechen, and in it he rejected the teacher and the texts he was offering to instead go outside and watch the Indian saints of the Kagyu tradition.[12]

On August 22, the tenth day of the monkey month, Kongtrul began a one-week retreat on Union of All Rare and Precious Jewels, the treasure cycle of Jatson Nyingpo that he had received from Gyurme Tenpel at Zhechen in 1831. The tenth day of every month is sacred to Padmasambhava. At this time Kongtrul simply performed the approach practices—he would request a new empowerment for the cycle from Situ Rinpoche and undertake the preliminaries seven years later, in 1843, on entering his first long-term retreat at the hermitage he would build that year above Pelpung (see chapter 11). For now he would not complete a Nyingma-derived practice. Following the week's approach practice in 1836, he performed one hundred feast offerings, during which time he composed devotional prayers.[13]

Kongtrul was moved by Union of All Rare and Precious Jewels, so much so that he had several dreams of Padmasambhava. In one he and some women venerated the master while a few young men without faith stood by. In another he found himself at the peak of a high mountain. On becoming aware he was dreaming, he decided to fly to Cāmaradvīpa, one of the four continents in traditional Buddhist cosmology and a location of Padmasambhava's pure land, the Copper-Colored Mountain. He came to a reddish-brown peak, about half of which was visible above a range of iron-like mountains that encircled it. Its summit was in clouds, its slopes clear. While Kongtrul prayed, an astonishingly large river erupted from one side, frightening him, and causing him to forget he was dreaming, at which point he woke up. In his diary Kongtrul took this dream to indicate he had erred in allowing his interest in the Kagyu tradition and his growing devotion to the Kagyu masters to obscure his commitment to Nyingma practices. He viewed this as creating an obstacle to his practice and he felt regret. He was finding himself unable to resist the pressure he was facing at Pelpung to abandon his Nyingma identity, if not his Nyingma practices.[14]

It was not only his embrace of the teachings he was receiving at Pelpung that threatened to diminish his Nyingma activities and sympathies. Apparently teachers and other monks there actively insulted the education he had received at Zhechen and criticized the short sādhana he composed to Pelden Lhamo and Vajradaṇḍa. Kongtrul never makes clear whether his bullies disparaged the Nyingma teachings in general or simply mocked his own background, but considering the degree to which Karma Kagyu monks engaged with Nyingma practices it seems probable that the insults were directed at him personally. He was cowed by the disapproval of his peers and teachers and to his later regret he burned his compositions.[15]

During the summer and fall of 1836, Kongtrul nevertheless continued to receive and practice both Nyingma and Kagyu teachings at Pelpung, and his dreams reflected the mental effort at properly integrating the two and forging a sense of self that could support both. The occasional bias against his past that he encountered likely added emotional pressure to maintain a clear separation of the systems. He was eager for the teachings he was receiving at Pelpung, and his faith in the Karma Kagyu lineage masters was true, yet even as he capitulated to social pressures he was never more than ambivalent about fully adopting a Karma Kagyu identity. Being kept under suspicion would only have exacerbated his own ambivalence. Other monks in his community were taking teachings from other traditions, but they had always been Karma Kagyu monks. They had no reason to question their institutional status; they were Kagyu monks from the start who were training in teachings given to them by their Kagyu masters. Kongtrul had begun life as a Bonpo and had become a Buddhist at a Nyingma monastery. His conversion to Karma Kagyu had not been of his own volition. He had resisted the second ordination and never gave back his Nyingma vows. His identity—and loyalty—was therefore open to suspicion by both others and himself. He attempted to prove this loyalty by burning compositions he had made at Zhechen, but he suffered for the effort.

Situ Rinpoche at the time was performing a Padmavajra treasure cycle by Yongge Mingyur Dorje, who was a close teacher of the Eighth Tai Situ, and whom Kongtrul would later claim as a previous birth. Kongtrul had started practicing Mahāmudrā and Six Yogas, but he stopped to receive the empowerment for Situ's practice together with another Yongge Mingyur Dorje revelation, a longevity practice called Integration of Means and Wisdom. At the same time, Situ gave Kongtrul and Wongen the empowerment for a major Kagyu tantric cycle, the nine-deity maṇḍala of Hevajra according to the tradition of Sarohavajra. The *Hevajra Tantra* was a later composition than the *Cakrasaṃvara*, likely composed around the late ninth or tenth century in eastern India. It was translated into Tibetan in the eleventh century by Drokmi Śākya Yeshe whose activity gave rise to the Sakya tradition; Hevajra is the basis for the Sakya's central teaching of Lamdre, literally "Path and Fruit." The tantra was also promoted by Marpa Chokyi Lodro, and it became a main tantra of the Kagyu tradition as well. Hevajra is typically depicted as blue, with eight faces, and with sixteen hands, all of which hold skull cups full of various objects or miniature figures of deities. He stands in dancing posture, embracing his consort, Nairātmyā. Situ gave the *Hevajra* using a set of manuals called the One Hundred Transmissions of Mitra.[16] This was compiled by the twelfth-century Indian master Mitrayogin while he was at Tropu Monastery at the invitation of the Tibetan translator Tropu Lotsāwa Jampa Pel and was a common textbook for Kagyu empowerment rituals. The collection would later provide inspiration for Kongtrul's Treasury of Kagyu Tantras.

Kongtrul requested from Situ the empowerment for the nine-deity maṇḍala of Jinasāgara, which he had already received the year before from Wongen. Jinasāgara is a peaceful form of Avalokiteśvara, red in color, that was brought into the Kagyu tradition by Milarepa's disciple Rechungpa Dorje Drakpa. In the seventeenth century, Terdak Lingpa, one of the founders of the Nyingma monastery Mindroling, had a vision of the deity which became popular in Karma Kagyu communities. This would seem to be the version that Kongtrul requested of Situ, and as payment for the empowerment Kongtrul presented his master with a statue of Terdak Lingpa that Zhechen Rabjam had given him.[17] Jinasāgara became a central practice for Kongtrul; as with other cycles, he preferred that his transmission come from Situ rather than Wongen.

A contemporary of Kongtrul's at Pelpung, Dabzang Tulku Karma Ngedon, who soon became a close friend and collaborator, requested from Situ the empowerment for Combined Practice of the Undying Three Roots of the Tathāgata, a sādhana concerning the guru, *yidam*—one's meditational deity—and ḍākinī revealed in the seventeenth century by Choje Lingpa. During the ceremony, Situ gave Kongtrul a secret initiation name, Pema Gargyi Wangchuk Trinle Drodul Tsel. The name means something like "Lotus Lord of Dancers, Powerful Guide of Beings through Enlightened Activity." Kongtrul would use this name in the title of his account of his past lives, and in the byline for a handful of compositions, most notably the table of contents for one of his masterworks, Treasury of Revelations. A lama named Kam Lama Tsewang Pema Norbu Tashi instructed him in the details of the practice. Kongtrul performed the preliminaries and the basic sādhana briefly, enough to feel that he had a connection with it. The same lama also gave Kongtrul three empowerments: a central Dzogchen tantra called the Tantra of Luminous Expanse, the Sky Teaching revelations of Namcho Mingyur Dorje, and the revelations of an eighteenth-century Kagyu mystic named Rolpai Dorje. Kam Lama Norbu gave instructions on the nature of mind to Kongtrul and a group of other monks. The students all individually described their meditation experiences to him. After Kongtrul met with him, Kam Lama Norbu praised him, saying "You understand well the method for cultivating awareness of the nature of mind."[18]

Perhaps due to the transmission of so many treasure cycles, Kongtrul again began to sense the possibility of revealing scripture himself. He felt the affliction of harmful spirits, the presence of goddesses, and omens regarding treasure. His dreams were filled with landscapes, both actual, such as his homeland of Ronggyab and Mindroling Monastery, and fantastical, such as Sukhāvatī, the Land of Bliss where the Buddha Amitābha resides. In his sleep he met buddhas and felt the presence of lamas, such as Terdak Lingpa, the Fifth Dalai Lama, Karma Chakme, and Mingyur Dorje, seated side by side on thrones in an old temple where the banners were threadbare. That day, Kongtrul had been reading from the biography and the collected works of Karma Chakme and had felt faith in the lama. In the dream, he was confident that in a past life he had been one of the master's students.[19]

In one dream Kongtrul assumed the role of a translator traveling to Nepal where he came across a large pile of books stored in Tibetan style— wrapped in cloth and stacked lengthwise, brocade at their ends, with the titles written on them. Kongtrul examined one and found it to be a previously unknown tantra of the Guhyasamāja cycle. The Guhyasamāja Tantra is one of the earliest tantras of the so-called Anuttarayogatantra class to which belong all the tantras that came in with the second diffusion of Buddhism to Tibet. Composed in the late eighth or early ninth century, it was the first to use overt sexual language, famously beginning with the line "Thus did I hear at one time. The Buddha was dwelling in the vaginas of the women who are the essence of the conqueror's body, speech, and mind." It was translated into Tibetan in the eleventh century by Rinchen Zangpo and the Indian scholar Śraddhākaravarman. Like Cakrasaṃvara and Hevajra, Guhyasamāja is generally depicted as blue, but unlike them he is sitting in meditation posture. He has three faces—one red, one white, and one blue—each with three eyes and six arms, and embraces his consort, Sparśavajrā. Kongtrul left the book and continued on. This dream would appear to have served as his first initiation into the Guhyasamāja maṇḍala; he does not himself mention another source, although his disciple Tashi Chopel, in the Treasury of Wish-Fulfilling Jewels, states that Wongen gave him the Guhyasamāja transmission. In either case, he had now received the three central tantras of the Kagyu tradition. As difficult as he found it to withstand the lingering suspicion of the Pelpung community, he was well on his way to a complete Kagyu education.[20]

# 7

## THE FOURTEENTH KARMAPA

### 1836–1839

Among the dreams Kongtrul had while receiving tantric empowerments in 1836 were several that related to the Karmapa. In a dream in which he died and decided to go to Sukhāvatī, after arriving at an intermediate place and hiding himself in a lotus, Kongtrul realized he was dreaming. He continued on to the Land of Bliss, where he saw a bodhi tree and the throne of Amitābha inscribed with the mantras of various deities. Thinking he ought to meet Avalokiteśvara, who, in tantric Buddhist theology is an emanation of Amitābha, he beheld the common four-armed version of the bodhisattva. Avalokiteśvara then transformed into the Karmapa. Kongtrul asked for a blessing, at which point the Karmapa told him "You must return to your own land."[1]

The Karmapas are among the highest-ranking lamas of Tibetan Buddhism, with a line of incarnations stretching back to the early days of the second propagation. The Kagyu tradition began in Tibet with the translator Marpa Chokyi Lodro, who made several trips to India for new Buddhist teachings. He is said to have studied with Nāropā, one of the Indian Mahāsiddhas, who was a disciple of Tilopā. Over the course of three visits to India, he brought back the *Hevajra, Guhyasamāja,* and *Cakrasaṃvara Tantras*, as well as the teachings of Mahāmudrā and the Six Yogas of Nāropā. He translated and taught these to numerous disciples, chief among them Milarepa, whose life story is one of the most famous of Tibet. In his youth Milarepa murdered dozens of family members in revenge for poor treatment. From regret he sought out Buddhist teachings on a path that led him to Marpa. To purify the karmic stains of his misdeeds, Marpa put Milarepa through a series of arduous ordeals, chiefly building and dismantling a several-storied tower. The tower still stands at the center of the monastic community Sekhar Gutok in southern Tibet. After finally teaching him, Marpa sent Milarepa to meditate in caves across Tibet, where he sang songs of realization for villagers and scores of disciples who gathered around him.[2] Neither Marpa nor Milarepa were ordained, but among Milarepa's chief disciples was Gampopa Sonam Rinchen, who had ordained at a Kadam monastery before he met Milarepa at age thirty-one. He never renounced his vows, but instead fused Kadam monastic scholasticism with the tantric yogic practices Marpa had brought from India. In 1121 Gampopa established the monastery Daklha Gampo, where he trained his disciples, including Dusum Khyenpa, who initiated the Karma Kagyu tradition with the establishment of Karma Gon in 1147 and Tsurpu Monastery in 1189.[3] Dusum Khyenpa was posthumously given the title of First Karmapa.

In 1836 the thirty-nine-year-old Fourteenth Karmapa, Tekchok Dorje, transferred his residence from Tsurpu to Karma Gon. His itinerary included short visits to dozens of monasteries in Kham, staying as little as a day at some, several months at others. His presence at these Kagyu institutions would have provided the majority of the residents the opportunity to receive his blessing and to make the financial and material offerings on which large monastic systems depended. The visit was also arranged so Tekchok Dorje could receive teachings from the Ninth Situ. He was already a student of Situ Rinpoche, having taken ordination from him around 1820 when Situ was traveling in central Tibet.[4]

The Fourteenth Karmapa now sent word to Situ to send a tutor to Karma Gon to work with him on grammar. Kongtrul records in his diary that the Karmapa specifically requested that Situ send him. This is possible, as travelers might have sent word to Tsurpu of the promising young monk, or Situ might have sent a letter to his student in which he mentioned Kongtrul. It seems more likely, however, that the Karmapa had simply sent a request to Situ to send someone who could instruct him, and that it was Situ who selected Kongtrul. Either way, such a summons was a great honor and was not to be ignored. Situ released Kongtrul from the retreat vows he had taken and dispatched him with a lovely blessing. Kongtrul requested a transmission of Prayer in Seven Chapters, a famous supplication to Padmasambhava that was revealed in the fourteenth century by Zangpo Drakpa. As he recited the verses, when he reached the line in chapter four—"in this way, all that appears in the field of vision . . ."—Situ paused to explain to Kongtrul that this was not simply a devotional prayer but that it was fundamentally a pointing-out instruction. The words, he told Kongtrul, were the very speech of Padmasambhava himself and were the distillation of the meaning of hundreds of thousands of instructions on the nature of mind.

The Eighth Situ, Chokyi Jungne, had used this very prayer to introduce the Thirteenth Karmapa, Dudul Dorje, to the nature of mind. The Thirteenth Karmapa in turn had given the transmission to Situ. And now Kongtrul was to meet the Fourteenth Karmapa for the first time. With this teaching Situ was placing Kongtrul in illustrious company. It was an auspicious send-off.[5]

Kongtrul traveled east to the Lhokhok region in the Khardo Valley and met the Karmapa at a place called Terton Gar—a name meaning "Treasure Revealer's Encampment." The Karmapa would have been traveling with a large entourage of servants and disciples acting as cooks, porters, scribes, and managers. Terton Gar was likely a meadow known to have easily accessible water and firewood, with enough level ground for their many tents. The Karmapa's tents, and those of other prominent people in the entourage, would have been made of silks and brocades and topped with brightly colored banners, and would have stood out among the dark woven yak-hair fabric of the servant tents. Kongtrul does not make much of the meeting in his diary—no depictions of joy, or veneration, no light snow falling or flowers blossoming for the occasion, as initial meetings with great lamas are often described. Perhaps he hesitated to attach himself to yet another prominent Kagyu lama. Instead, he wrote about a Nyingma lama he met there, Karma Namgyel, who impressed him with his *togel*, or "supreme vision," practice, one of two advanced meditative techniques in Dzogchen designed to bring a realization of nonduality. The yogi had, it seemed to Kongtrul, completely mastered the second vision of Dzogchen, which is called "Increasing Experience."[6]

Togel is paired with *trekchod*, or "breaking through solidity." Because saṃsāra and nirvāṇa are two opposite ways for perceiving the same phenomenon—ordinary beings' perceptions are flawed, but a buddha's is pure—every moment is an opportunity for enlightenment by simply seeing things as they truly are. Trekchod refers to practices that bring the mind to a realization of this nonduality. Once that view is stabilized, visions arise. Dzogchen speaks of the ultimate nature of existence—emptiness—in positive terms, primarily as a "ground" that underlies all phenomena. It is a decidedly "other-emptiness" approach. The ground has a nature, which is primordial purity. It is self-aware, possessing self-arisen primordial consciousness, and it has an inherent quality of luminosity, which is active and productive. Dzogchen togel practice is said to allow the ground to be revealed in the form of visions, understood to be the active displays of the ground's self-aware luminosity. These visions are mapped out in the literature, each described as it should arise. Kongtrul took advantage of the presence of such an accomplished practitioner to advance his own meditation of togel, which he had first taken up at Zhechen. He recorded that he attained a stable experience in the first vision, called "Direct Realization of Ultimate Nature."[7]

Continuing on toward Karma Gon, the Karmapa responded to invitations to visit monasteries along the route. These included Zurmang Namgyeltse Monastery, which was founded in the late fourteenth or early fifteenth century by Drung Mase Tokden Lodro Rinchen, a student of the Fifth Karmapa, Dezhin Shekpa. There Kongtrul enjoyed a fine view of the religious dances during a Cakrasaṃvara festival. By this time, perhaps he was beginning to be won over by the Karmapa, and he began to notice his presence in the landscape around him. He reports that on the road to Karma Gon he thought he saw the form of the First Karmapa emerging from a cliffside, his face white, wearing the black crown of the Karmapas. From a distance it was clear, but he lost the form as he drew close.[8]

The encampment arrived at the monastery in January 1837.[9] Kongtrul was installed in the Tsengye Temple—the temple dedicated to Padmasambhava's eight manifestations. There he instructed the Karmapa in the Kalapa system of Sanskrit grammar. For his student Kongtrul composed *Sea of Enjoyment*, an introduction to grammar based on his notes from the teachings by Zhechen Wontrul. In May,[10] while the Karmapa visited the Danang monastic estates, Kongtrul taught him from two Indian standards: the aforementioned *Sārasvatavyākaraṇa* and its Indian commentaries, the notes for which he gave the Karmapa toward the end of his instruction, and the *Candoratnākara*, a discourse on poetics by an eleventh-century Indian scholar named Ratnākaraśānti. Kongtrul had studied the first work with Zhechen Wontrul at the beginning of his stay at Zhechen, but it is not clear where he studied the second. The Karmapa in turn taught Kongtrul how to design the frontispiece of a composition, an art form in which the title of a text is written in Tibetan and two ornamental scripts called Lansa and Wartu.[11]

In June 1837[12] they continued to travel the surrounding area, the Gato region in northern Kham. There they went first to Nangchen Gar, a Drukpa Kagyu monastery in the kingdom of Nangchen, where they observed the tenth-day Padmasambhava ritual dances. The Karmapa performed a few ceremonies, including the famous Black Hat Ceremony.[13] According to legend, Dusum Khyenpa was given a black crown by a host of ḍākinīs, who had woven it out of their hair. This remained invisible to all but those who were highly realized. The Ming Emperor Yongle, who reigned from 1402 to 1424, is said to have been able to see the crown on the head of the Fifth Karmapa, and he had a replica made so others could see the Karmapa in his full glory as an embodiment of Avalokiteśvara. All Karmapas since then have engaged in the formal Black Hat Ceremony which consists simply of him placing the hat on his head and reciting the six-syllable mantra of Avalokiteśvara. It is a wildly popular ritual. The promise made is that the blessing is so powerful that all who witness it will attain the first level of the bodhisattva path within three subsequent lifetimes. In a society deeply concerned about future births, this is a substantial promise.

They went next to Kyodrak Monastery and then to Jorna Monastery in Rongpo. Around that time, the Karmapa's general secretary fell out of favor, and Kongtrul henceforth assumed his duties, including explaining the Black Hat Ceremony to the audiences. These would have been his first public teachings. They circumambulated the sacred mountain in Gato called Jowo Ri, during which crowds of people pressed them for the Black Hat Ceremony and other rites and blessings. They stopped at monasteries and satisfied the requests of disciples and patrons. En route to Lao Monastery, a woman carrying the corpse of her infant son begged the Karmapa to ease her grief. Kongtrul was moved by her lamentations. The scene is reminiscent of the Indian story of Kisagotami, a woman who approached the Buddha carrying the corpse of her child and begged him to return the child to life. The Buddha sent her to bring him a mustard seed from a family that had not experienced the pain of death. Searching widely and finding none, she came to understand that all who live suffer death, made peace with her loss, and was able to put down her son. Kisagotami returned to the Buddha, took ordination, and eventually attained enlightenment. Kongtrul responded to the woman's grief in a typical Tibetan fashion: he offered to investigate the migration of the boy's consciousness and gave the mother predictions of his next several lifetimes. If he was not yet able to teach her the means of liberation, at least he eased her suffering.[14]

Traveling on to Zurmang Dutsitil Monastery, the Karmapa led the enthronement of the Ninth Trungpa Tulku, Karma Tenpel. The Trungpa incarnations were the leading lamas of the monastery, which was established by the First Trungpa, Kunga Gyeltsen, in 1423. While there, Kongtrul requested empowerments and transmissions of the revelations of the treasure revealer Rolpai Dorje from his reincarnation named Pema Tenpel.[15]

The party returned to Karma Gon in time for the New Year celebrations for the Earth Dog Year, which fell on January 27, 1838. Kongtrul was enlisted to help in the preparation of medicinal pills. Kongtrul had first studied medicine when he was fourteen, when he memorized some of the texts from the Four Medical Tantras and learned to identify medicinal plants from the Karma Kagyu doctor Karma Puntsok. He had later spent part of the winter, spring, and summer of 1836 training with Pelpung's chief pharmacist, Doctor Karma Tsepel, a monk who had participated in his ordination in 1833. Karma Tsepel taught him from the first three of the Four Medical Tantras, the transmission of which Karma Chakme Tulku had given him at Karma Gon in 1834. These were the *Root Tantra*, which lays out the entire medical system in brief, the *Explanatory Tantra*, which covers the causes and classifications of illnesses and the properties of medicinal plants, and the *Instructional Tantra*, which deals with the three humors (wind, bile, and phlegm). The fourth, known simply as the *Last Tantra*, surveys diagnosis and treatments. It was a chapter of the fourth tantra that Kongtrul memorized when he was fourteen. In support of his studies, each day he performed sections of the Yutok Nyingtik, the tantric liturgical cycle that customarily accompanies medical training, which Wongen had transmitted to him.[16]

Karma Tsepel now came from Pelpung to aid in the preparation of the pills at Karma Gon—they would make black pills, a tradition unique to the Karmapa. Eight metals and eight special substances—including gold, silver, and mercury—are pulverized and refined through heat and other methods, allegedly in a way that transforms the harmful properties of the mercury and other ingredients into powerful medicine. The ability to successfully refine heavy metals was a particular skill that was in high demand in Tibet, and Kongtrul would become known across the Plateau for his ability. Following the successful manufacture of the pills, Kongtrul led a feast offering for Bhaiṣajyaguru, the Medicine Buddha, during which the community chanted the Buddha's mantra.[17]

In late June or early July of 1838,[18] the Karmapa moved his encampment to Pelpung. He had intended to depart the northeastern parts of Kham earlier, but a female relative had fallen ill, and he remained on to be with her. At Pelpung the forty-year-old Karmapa was reunited with his sixty-five-year-old master, the Ninth Situ. The two lamas joined the tenth-day religious dances. While the guru and disciple gave each other empowerments and longevity rituals, Kongtrul composed long-life prayers to them both. He offered these together with symbols of the Buddha's body, speech, and mind, and received gifts in return.[19]

After two months at Pelpung, the Karmapa continued his circuit of Kham, and Kongtrul accompanied him, but only as far as Zhechen Monastery. Back at his beloved first religious home after more than five years, he met with Zhechen Wontrul in the monastic retreat center. It was an occasion of great delight for both men. Kongtrul arranged an offering ceremony and requested a long-life empowerment. Zhechen Wontrul asked Kongtrul for the empowerment of the five-deity maṇḍala of Cakrasaṃvara, which Kongtrul performed, in an act of elegant symbolism.[20] Kongtrul was now a Kagyu lama and could bestow Kagyu transmissions to his former Nyingma teacher. He had left Zhechen unwillingly and yet had fully embraced the literature and rituals of his second home. The gift of the empowerment proved that these teachings were not out of place at Zhechen. Just as Nyingma practice made sense at Pelpung, Kagyu teachings could be practiced at a Nyingma monastery. The chance to prove this must have brought him some comfort. He would be able to move through different institutional settings without denying himself anything.

At Zhechen, Kongtrul also sought out Gyurme Tendzin, the lama who first taught him Buddhist terminology and the works of Longchenpa. Kongtrul saw in him an advanced Dzogchen practitioner, a man who was in a continual state of the third togel vision, called "Culminated Awareness." Gyurme Tendzin related a vision he had experienced that morning, in which Mahākaruṇika, the one-thousand headed and armed Avalokiteśvara, appeared. His back arms were not clearly visible. The lama reported this as a sign that there were obstacles to Kongtrul's longevity.[21]

Kongtrul then returned to Ronggyab to visit his mother. He did not note her living situation. On her behalf, and for the people of his home valley, he performed a prosperity rite to a deity he identifies as Pelchenma. This was likely a deity indigenous to Ronggyab. It was the first time Kongtrul had conducted a prosperity rite, a ritual that he would become known for. While he was in the valley, Tarde Tokden sent for him. This was the Bon lama who had recognized his potential and given him initiation into the deity Sipai Gyelmo, or Queen of the Universe. In his diary Kongtrul noted only that he gave the old lama an empowerment for the Peaceful and Wrathful Deities. He elides his connection to the lama, and he recorded no emotion at the reunion; whatever gratitude he felt for the earlier instruction he expressed only through the giving of the empowerment. Still, Kongtrul remained involved with Tarde Tokden in some fashion; after 1842 he composed a short account of the lama's reliquary titled *Gods' Melody*.[22]

Kongtrul's ambivalence around his Bon heritage is on full display in the section of his diary covering this visit, in what he chose to include and what he purposely left out. In Ronggyab he dreamed of the Queen of the Universe, to whom he gives that title together with the name Yeshe Pelmo rather than Pelden Lhamo. She appeared half emerged from the land, her lower skirts of shimmering peacock feathers covering the valley floor, her upper body reaching into the heavens. Kongtrul had received an initiation into the practice of this deity as a youth in Ronggyab and had performed the rituals. He had also composed liturgies to her while at Zhechen, albeit in a Buddhist form. Yet in relating this dream, Kongtrul disavows any personal connection to her. He states that neither in the past nor later had he ever worshipped such deities, by which he means a Bon deity; Kongtrul identified her as a goddess of the Bon Khyung clan, the clan of his biological father. In denying his engagement with Sipai Gyelmo, he was denying his active participation in Bon rituals. He was glad to be a member of the Khyungpo clan, but it seems that he was at the time uncomfortable having any more Bon heritage than that.[23]

Before returning to Pelpung at the end of 1838 or the beginning of 1839, Kongtrul visited two monasteries on behalf of Situ, Drentang and Tsedrum. Drentang Monastery had originally been the hermitage of the great eleventh-century translator Smṛtijñānakīrti, but it was later built out as a Karma Kagyu monastery by the Third Karmapa. Situ apparently asked Kongtrul to make an inventory of the place, and this is preserved in a short text in Kongtrul's Collected Works. The second of these, Tsedrum, was a center of the grammatical arts during the eighteenth century; Zhuchen Tsultrim Rinchen, the editor of the Derge Tengyur, had studied grammar there with Karma Chime Tubten Rabgye, an important grammar instructor of the era. What Situ sent him there to accomplish he does not say. Several years later Kongtrul sponsored a long-life ceremony at the monastery, an idea that proved so popular that Situ, Wongen, and other lamas put in funds to make it an annual event.[24]

# 8

# DREAMS OF THE MASTERS

## 1839–1841

For six years, from the end of 1839 to the beginning of 1846, Jamgon Kong-trul remained at Pelpung. Upon his return from Karma Gon, he gave to Situ all the gold that he had earned while on the road with the Karmapa—gold that was payment for services to the Karmapa's encampment and gold which was earned from the households and monasteries where he performed rituals. Soon after the New Year celebrations for the Earth Pig Year, which began on February 15, 1839, Kongtrul requested from Situ a ceremony to bestow the bodhisattva vows.[1] This is the second of three sets of vows an ordained Tibetan practitioner will take in his or her lifetime after the *prātimokṣa* monastic ordination that is based on early Buddhist codes. The bodhisattva vow articulates the additional aspiration of a practitioner on the Bodhisattvayāna, a synonym of the Mahāyāna that means the "vehicle of the bodhisattva." Rituals to generate this aspiration, known as *bodhicitta*—the mind to enlightenment—are common in Tibet and other Mahāyāna Buddhist cultures. The precepts include noble sentiments designed to cultivate self-lessness, such as to never put oneself first, as well as tradition-preserving promises to, for example, never disparage the Mahāyāna.

Kongtrul described the bodhisattva ordination he received from Situ only as "extensive." Part of the ordination was his receipt of yet another name: Jangchub Sempa Lodro Taye. The first two words mean "bodhisattva." Lodro Taye, which means "vast intellect," is one of the primary names by which Kongtrul is known in Tibet and a name he used frequently to sign his compositions. His dreams following the ceremony convinced him of its success—peering far into the future he observed his cremation, noting that there were images of the Buddha on his bones and relic pills in his ashes.[2]

In May 1839[3] segments of the Pelpung community performed eight repetitions of a popular fasting ritual. According to legend, a nun in India known by the name Bhikṣuṇī Śrīmati or Bhikṣuṇī Lakṣmī—Gelongma

Pelmo in Tibetan—was afflicted by leprosy and propitiated the bodhisattva Avalokiteśvara, who eventually appeared to her in the form of a figure draped in white. He gave her a vase of water with which to bathe, and in the morning—or in some versions, after some period of meditation—she found herself cured. Pelmo joyfully sang prayers to Avalokiteśvara, who reappeared and dissolved into her, establishing her on the eighth level of the bodhisattva path. He gave her instructions for a fasting ritual which incorporated tantric practices of visualizing and worshipping Avalokiteśvara in his thousand-armed form of Mahākaruṇika. Kongtrul does not record which liturgy the group used; he himself received the teaching from a lama named Karma Zhenpen Wozer and wrote two manuals for the practice. One of these was requested by Dabzang and another was requested by his disciple Khenchen Tashi Wozer, who himself wrote a manual translated in Wangchen Rinpoche's *Buddhist Fasting Practice*.[4]

The rite takes three days. On the first day participants stop eating after a noon meal. On the second day no food or drink is allowed. The fast is broken on the morning of the third day with a feast to the bodhisattva. Kongtrul does not say how long the eight cycles lasted, but a repetition of eight sessions is generally performed over seventeen days. On the first night of the first cycle, he dreamed of a visit from Sarvanivāraṇaviṣkambhin, the bodhisattva who removes obstacles. Short, with a mustache and dark skin, he said nothing, and simply took a stick and drew an image of Mahākaruṇika on the ground.[5]

During the summer Wongen gave Kongtrul empowerments for the complete treasure revelations of Jatson Nyingpo. Kongtrul had first received a Jatson Nyingpo transmission in 1831 from a lama at Zhechen, but this was repeated now for a Kagyu frame. Wongen gave him empowerments for all six volumes of the revelations, each containing a separate treasure cycle, and from that time forward Kongtrul included the first, Union of All Rare and Precious Jewels, as part of his daily practice. He considered this the beginning of a formal daily regime. Before this point he had performed the Mahāmudrā preliminaries, the sādhana of Cakrasaṃvara and Vajravārāhī, the prayers to the protective deities, and the typical water offering that Tibetans make each morning in seven bowls on their personal shrines. Other than the last two, these were not rituals that were intended to continue for one's entire life. From this point on, when he had sufficient time, he would perform the complete sādhana from the cycle, and, when he was pressed for time, he would perform the three forms of Padmasambhava (peaceful, wrathful, and as the ḍākinī named Siṁhamukhā, the lion-faced goddess) and the condensed daily sādhana.[6]

The transmission and empowerment for the six volumes went well. One night during the empowerment for Vajra of Meteoric Iron Long Life Sādhana, the second of Jatson Nyingpo's revelations, Kongtrul dreamed that the sun and the moon arose in the sky together, and when he directed his meditative gaze toward them, expansive togel visions appeared. Later that year he dreamed of the treasure revealer Rolpai Dorje, who told Kongtrul that he would be the custodian of his treasures and that he would spread the revelations of Jatson Nyingpo. In 1840 Kongtrul requested the transmission of Jatson Nyingpo's revelations a third time, from a Lama Ngawang Lodro, who was at Pelpung in the entourage of the Eighth Pawo incarnation, Tsukla Chokyi Gyelpo. Kongtrul identifies this lama only as a descendent of a teacher named Tenpa Dargye; perhaps Ngawang Lodro possessed a variant transmission line that descended through his ancestor, a man who must have held some significance to Kongtrul but whose name is lost to history.[7]

The quality of a transmission is judged according to the reliability of its lineage. If there was reason to doubt the integrity of the lineage, the entire system could, theoretically, collapse. Thus multiple descents were desirable. They thickened the chord linking Kongtrul to the source—be that the Buddha himself or a deity or saint. Kongtrul was never satisfied with a single transmission of a teaching and would request each alternative lineage he encountered. He was a collector, and multiple transmission lines would come with variants in the instruction, which Kongtrul could compare.

During this year, with his preliminaries completed and his approach accumulations behind him, Kongtrul progressed to the next step in tantric practice, the creation stage. Kongtrul's dreams for the next several years gave him reason to believe that his meditation was effective. He saw himself taking the form of Dorje Drolo and Hayagrīva and vanquishing demons. He met buddhas and great lamas such as Marpa Lotsāwa and the great linguist Zhalu Chokyong Zangpo and received their teachings or blessings. Zhalu Chokyong Zangpo, for example, gave him Indian manuscripts for three unnamed tantras. Karma Chakme, in the form of a jolly old monk, told Kongtrul about his past lives. And one night, in a magnificent temple-like cave complex, he met a lama named Dorje who was a reincarnation of Vairocana, the eighth-century translator and contemporary of Padmasambhava. Later in life, as his status rose, Kongtrul claimed Vairocana as one of his previous lives; this lama named Dorje was thus either an earlier or future birth.[8]

During a period in which he was engaged in multiple longevity practices, Kongtrul recorded several vivid dreams of dying. In each he is sent back with a prophecy that he would discover treasure. In one dream he traveled again to Sukhāvatī, where he encountered Wongen. His teacher told him that it was not yet time for him to pass and that three lifetimes hence he would be named Dorje and reveal treasure. Another dream reveals some anxiety regarding the practices he was doing at the time. The dream, which unfolded in four distinct episodes, was significant enough for him to give its exact date—October 15, 1839.[9] The dream began with a sensation of dying, and Kongtrul felt terribly sad. His dream-self thought, "In happy times I went through the motions of reciting and meditating, but it never really hit the mark. So now that I've died, there's nothing to help me. I wasn't able to liberate in the first stage of the bardo, and I won't be able to liberate in the second. Now I'm in the 'Bardo of Becoming,' about to take rebirth, so I had better not be distracted." For emphasis Kongtrul stamped his foot, but it made no mark, further convincing him that he was already dead.[10]

In the dream's second episode Kongtrul found himself on the Cāmaradvīpa continent. He prayed to Situ, who appeared and faded away twice before remaining. Kongtrul attempted to eject his consciousness and merge it with the simulacrum of Situ but was unable to do so, as the image of Situ was not sufficiently stable. He reprimanded himself for not adequately mastering the creation stage and tried again, using the Sky Teachings. Although this time he felt his consciousness separate from his body, he was not sure if it merged properly. Situ, placing his hand on Kongtrul's head, said, "that will do" and vanished.[11]

The third episode began with the appearance of a small Indian youth. Kongtrul took him by the hand and asked him why he had come. The boy replied with a cryptic aspirational prophecy: "I have come because you have not yet fulfilled Padmasambhava's command. As a result, you will need to take rebirth once more in a place called Sok Zamkha. The two of us will meet when you have reached the age of six or seven. You will be ordinary, without a lama or tulku title, but as soon as we meet you will remember your previous lives, and you will be able to benefit beings." Kongtrul agreed to this, but then a woman who he understood to be Yeshe Tsogyel appeared and declared, "You must take rebirth in Lhokhok—Padmasambhava has already commanded it." At these and other remarks, Kongtrul became severely disappointed.[12]

The fourth and final episode of the dream began with him reflecting on the practices he had done and the twenty-odd years he had lived thus far. Other people appeared, friends of his, whom Kongtrul took to be guides, and he felt he ought to join them on their travels. But he asked to wait a bit, for he had something to ask Padmasambhava. The group was suddenly at the Palace of Lotus Light, in Padmasambhava's pure land, inside which was a person dressed as a tantric practitioner and the woman from the preceding episode—these were Padmasambhava and his consort Yeshe Tsogyel. Kongtrul made three prostrations in a state of extreme distress and kneeled before them. He recounted his life story from birth through the present, lamenting that while he may not have benefited others, not only had Padmasambhava sent obstacles to his longevity but he had not provided Kongtrul with a prophecy as to his destined revelations. Kongtrul was prepared to complain further, but they interrupted him. A well-dressed woman began to say things such as "Make use of your life! In this life you will accomplish great things! A prophecy came when you were seven or eight. You received your treasure inventory at age thirteen and started revealing treasure at age twenty; eventually you will reveal twenty-five treasures." At that Kongtrul knew it was time to return, and he awoke.[13]

Kongtrul redoubled his effort. He continued his medical training over the summer of 1839, working with Doctor Karma Tsepel from the monastery's pharmacy and Karma Tsewang Rabten, a doctor whom he does not otherwise identify. He received from them precise instructions on the fourth medical tantra, which covers diagnosis and treatment. This included how to administer medicine and how to identify medicinal plants. He continued his training with these two doctors off and on for the next three years. At Situ's orders he also studied medicine with Wongen, a doctor named Karma Chowang from Golok, and with the steward of Pelpung, Tashi Chopel. He also progressed in his study of grammar that year. He immersed himself in the Eighth Situ's commentary on Candragomin's *Candravyākaraṇa*, which he had first read at Zhechen. He then moved on to Sabzang Mati Panchen's commentary on the Kalapa system of grammar. Sabzang was a famous student of Dolpopa's, not to be confused with the Kashmiri Mati Panchen. Kongtrul was not satisfied with his progress in grammar, feeling that there was little benefit from his efforts, either in Sanskrit or in Tibetan grammar. He notes that Wongen was a capable teacher in this topic, and he was learning a great deal with him, but Wongen's death in the following year ended that opportunity.[14]

Sometime in the summer or fall of 1839, he again studied the Third Karmapa's three treatises: *Profound Inner Principles, Treatise Distinguishing Ordinary Consciousness from Primordial Awareness,* and *Treatise on Buddha-Nature.* His instructors this time were two lamas from the Kardze-Nyarong region to the east of Derge named Karma Nyima Wozer and Sherab Gyeltsen. The former lama had given him Dorje Drolo texts several years earlier. A Lama Karma Ngedon tutored him on the fine points of the treatises. The identity of this teacher, from Pangpuk, an ancient Karma Kagyu monastery in Litang, is unclear. Because he shares a name with Dabzang Tulku, the two have been confused in sources. Kongtrul would later have a student named Karma Ngedon, but this is likely yet a third person, probably the man who became known as Mendongpa after he founded Mendong Hermitage.[15]

A yogi named Karma Norbu, a lama from Ringu Monastery (a Karma Kagyu institution in Derge founded in the fifteenth century by the Seventh Karmapa) gave Kongtrul his first transmission of the Shangpa Kagyu teachings in the spring of 1840. Kongtrul identified this lama as a reincarnation of Mokchokpa Rinchen Tsondru, a disciple of Khyungpo Neljor, the founder of the Shangpa Kagyu. This is a lineage of Mahāmudrā teachings that did not pass through Marpa Lotsāwa and thus is distinct from all other Kagyu traditions. Whereas Marpa received his transmission from Nāropā (at least according to legend), Khyungpo Neljor is said to have studied with Niguma, who may have been Nāropā's sister. Thus, where Marpa Kagyu traditions practice the Six Yogas of Nāropā, the Shangpa Kagyu practice the Six Yogas of Niguma.[16]

Like Kongtrul, Khyungpo Neljor was born to a Bon family and initially trained in Nyingma traditions before adopting Kagyu practices. He built a monastery called Zhang Zhong in the Shang Valley, which gave its name to the teaching tradition. Yet he is said to have sworn his disciple to transmit the teachings to only a single disciple for the next seven generations, and so disciples did not spread outward and establish branch monasteries or increase the stature of Zhang Zhong. Because the holders of the tradition did not succeed in building institutions to maintain the tradition independently, the Shangpa transmissions survived only because they were taken up by other institutionalized traditions. Jonang writers such as Tāranātha and Kunga Drolchok, the twenty-fourth abbot of Jonang Monastery, adopted many Shangpa teachings and wrote extensive commentaries on the material. The Shangpa tradition would have an increasing appeal for Kongtrul and he would write Khyungpo Neljor into the record of his past lives. This interest might have been behind his claim to have been the biological son of Khyungpo Lama of Ronggyab; this way Khyungpo Lama became both an ancestor and a previous life. He would eventually claim Shangpa affiliation for his two hermitages, distancing them from the Karma Kagyu monastery that was always an uncomfortable residence.

Karma Norbu told Kongtrul that he was giving an abridged version of the Shangpa corpus, for, he said, "Practice is what is most important. There's no need for explanations and multiple instruction manuals. If you practice, then it will be fine to give you the extensive version over time." Kongtrul would receive the extensive version from him in 1842, while in his first retreat at his hermitage. He was always willing to practice, but for him that did not preclude holding out for the extensive version of anything.[17]

The visit of the Eighth Pawo in 1840 was likely a fairly grand event. The Pawo line was among the highest incarnations of the Karma Kagyu tradition. The Second Pawo, Tsukla Trengwa, stands as one of the greatest Tibetan historians of the premodern era. Since the time of the Fifth Pawo, the line had been based at Nenang Monastery near Tsurpu. The Eighth Pawo gave Kongtrul the reading transmission for the two-volume collection of Indian sources of the Mahāmudrā teachings. Kongtrul later included some of these, such as Naropā's *Concise Words on Mahāmudrā* and Maitripa's *Ten Stanzas on Suchness*, in his monumental collection of Buddhist instructional texts, Treasury of Instructions. The Pawo also gave Kongtrul transmissions and empowerments for treasures of the Mindroling tradition and revealers such as Choje Lingpa and Ratna Lingpa. The Ratna Lingpa empowerments may have included Unsurpassed Innermost Vajrakīla, which became one of Kongtrul's main practices, and which he also may have received earlier from the Karma Chakme tulku in 1834. Kongtrul viewed the experience positively—he dreamed one night of Pawo scooping up handfuls of long-life pills and giving them to him and two other monks; Kongtrul received the greater share.[18]

The more Kongtrul practiced the teachings he received, the more confidence he developed in his meditation and his future successes. He dreamed he served porridge to an assembly of arhats, the legendary disciples of the Buddha, and that he would next be serving them nectar. He dreamed he flew through the air, spontaneously reciting a poem on the meaning of

Chod. He recalled the opening verse: "From beginningless time until now my mind has not recognized its own nature," and the closing line: "May I cut the root of grasping to duality." When Kongtrul set back down on earth, still dreaming, he wrote out all twenty-three two-line verses and brought them to Situ, who was delighted and told him it should be published. Kongtrul does not record whether he managed to remember it and write down the verses after he awoke.[19]

Other dreams were more prophetic. At the beginning of 1840, Kongtrul dreamed of Kam Lama Norbu, the man who had first given him pointing-out instructions and who had complimented his accomplishments in meditation. In his dream Kongtrul placed a beautiful golden crown of the five buddha families on his own head, took in his hand a golden vajra scepter, and danced down a steep staircase. At the foot of the stairs was Kam Lama Norbu, looking fine. The lama said: "Although you have seen the nature of your mind, that alone will not be enough to eliminate delusions. While you are walking, rely on mindfulness. While you are sitting, rely on mindfulness. When you are eating, or drinking—any activity you do—rely again and again on mindfulness and you will be ready for both sleep and death." What appears to be a gentle instruction on how to comport the mind in all activities was, for Kongtrul, also a premonition of the lama's death, as Kam Lama died soon after. The morning of the cremation, he dreamed of the deceased teacher in the center of a reliquary wearing a white crown of the five buddha families, bone ornaments, and riding a white mule. A host of women wearing white brocade robes and playing trumpets were escorting him into the sky.[20]

Wongen continued to transmit Kagyu and Nyingma teachings to Kongtrul. On May 1, 1840,[21] Wongen gave him a life-force entrustment. In this case the deity was a form of Yamāntaka named Molten Metal Poison Face. This was likely from a cycle by Gyazhang Trom Dorje Bar, a ninth-century treasure revealer. Oddly, Wongen told him soon after not to do the practice. It seems that, in a dream, Wongen had discovered that if Kongtrul were to recite the mantra of Yamāntaka—a wrathful form of Mañjuśrī—it would be a powerful offense, and his ability to benefit people would be impaired. Kongtrul did not follow Wongen's advice and, in fact, immediately engaged in the practice with Situ's blessing. He did wait, however, until 1891, when he was almost eighty, to formally take it up in a retreat setting. Molten Metal Poison Face apparently seduced him from the start; he reported that it helped him clear up an eye disease he had earlier contracted. This would only be temporarily—it was to be an affliction that would cause him years of trouble.[22]

In midsummer, 1840,[23] at the monastery's meditation center, Wongen gave the complete empowerments for the One Hundred Transmissions of Mitra to Kongtrul, Dabzang Tulku, and five other young monks. The series of empowerments took two months, after which Wongen gave Kongtrul the transmissions for several other practices: Karma Lingpa's Peaceful and Wrathful Deities, which he had previously received from Zhechen Wontrul; Mingyur Dorje's Sky Teachings together with commentary by Karma Chakme; and the Heart Essence of Yutok, which Kongtrul had been reciting in conjunction with his medical training.[24]

Several months later, Kongtrul took it upon himself to revise a lineage prayer for the transmission of a longevity practice called Averting Untimely Death, adding the names of several Indian siddhas. The work was part of a treasure cycle of Lhatsun Namkha Jigme, who is credited with spreading the Karma Kagyu tradition to Sikkim. Kongtrul showed this to Situ, who was no doubt delighted to see the extent to which Kongtrul was himself expanding the Karma Kagyu transmission line. Situ expressed his approval with the empowerment for a previously unknown cycle of Mañjuśrī Yamāntaka. During the ceremony, Kongtrul experienced a vision in which Situ was the bodhisattva himself, dark blue, with five faces: blue in the center, green on both sides, red above, and then another above that, which was white. He held weapons in his eight hands and was ornamented with garlands of teeth. There were black magicians all around, and to crush them Kongtrul visualized himself as Molten Iron Poison Face Yamāntaka—the form of the deity Wongen had told him not to engage. At that point an eighteenth-century Nyingma charismatic named Rigdzin Tamdrin Gonpo appeared, smiling and radiant, and Kongtrul had the conviction that all the world's gods and spirits were bound into servitude. As the sun rose in a clear sky, with white clouds gently drifting in the breeze and a glittering rain falling, Kongtrul was sure that he would surmount any obstacles. Wongen's warning was easily set aside when Situ himself was involved.[25]

By this time in his life, Kongtrul was not simply studying and practicing. He had also begun to involve himself in the publishing of books and the organization of the scriptures. In early 1839 he had proofread the woodblocks for Karma Chakme's Four Armed Mahākāla rituals. He spent two summers around this time proofing the blocks for the Integration of Means and Wisdom and a set of Dorje Drolo liturgies for Situ Rinpoche.[26] In late

1840 Situ sent him to the library in the Tongdrol Temple at Pelpung to organize the books. He found them in a complete jumble, the scriptures of all traditions piled on top of each other with no coherent structure. Wongen suggested dividing them by tradition, something Kongtrul spent several days accomplishing. While on the project he dreamed of the famous Mañjuśrī statue at Tsurpu, in front of which sat the eminent Sanskrit translator Sonam Gyatso, preaching. The master was expounding on the many reasons to be clear on the difference between Buddhist traditions.[27] This lesson Kongtrul took to heart. He would spend much of his career repeating his 1840 library work on a grand scale, reverently taking up the teachings of all the traditions of Tibet, carefully evaluating them—each one separate and complete in itself—and placing them carefully alongside each other.

## 9

# KHYENTSE WANGPO AND THE DEATHS OF WONGEN AND THE OLD CHIEFTAIN

### 1840–1842

In early 1840 a young lama named Jamyang Khyentse Wangpo crossed the Hak Pass that separated Pelpung from the Sakya monastery of Dzongsar to request teachings from Kongtrul.[1] Khyentse Wangpo would become Kongtrul's closest collaborator and lifelong dear friend. The two lamas inspired each other, swapped teachings, and visited each other in their dreams. They nurtured a real and lasting affection for each other that was born the moment they met. For nearly sixty years they delighted on meeting, expressing the strength of their feelings through gifts, praises, and ritual. Khyentse was one of the most prolific treasure revealers in Tibetan history. Tradition claims that, as a reincarnation of the eighth-century Tibetan king Trisong Detsen, who was the patron and recipient of all Padmasambhava's teachings, he had innate access to every treasure hidden in Tibet. He was therefore uniquely qualified to evaluate and authenticate other people's revelations, as well as to warn them away from the dangerous game of extracting scriptures and objects from the landscape. And like Kongtrul he was a prodigious collector and compiler of teaching traditions, reviving broken lineages through visionary experiences and, with his disciple Loter Wangpo, publishing collections of scriptures that rivaled those created by Kongtrul. Depicted in devotional literature as gentle and generous, oral history adds stories of a severe temper and a wicked sense of humor.

Premodern Tibetans such as Kongtrul viewed history similarly to premodern Europeans: as a record of things that happened rather than a steady march toward better times. There was no notion that society was improving or changing in any way. Kongtrul and his community had no knowledge of moveable type, water-powered lumber mills, railroads, steam engines, or any of the other industrial inventions that were then spreading across many parts of the world, some of which were not all that far from them. People in Tibet were living much as they had for the previous thousand years. As Buddhists they understood that there was a potential for all beings to reach enlightenment, but this was not a guarantee—the scriptures offer no prediction of a future of universal buddhahood in which all beings abide in a radically new state entirely free from suffering. Instead, Buddhist cosmology describes grand cycles of creation and collapse, and in Kongtrul and Khyentse's lifetime things were thought to be in a period of decay, as the teaching of the Buddha of the current age was fading from knowledge. Individuals such as Khyentse Wangpo, who were bulwarks against the growing darkness, were described as "a flash of lightning in the forbidding gloom of this degenerate age." Kongtrul compared Khyentse to mercury, which even when dropped on the ground does not become tainted by dust.[2] In his diary Kongtrul consistently refers to his friend in glowing terms, praising him repeatedly, and referring to him with exalted titles such as "my lord guru" and "my precious and omniscient master."

Khyentse was seven years Kongtrul's junior. He was born on July 11, 1820, the first day of the sixth month of the Iron Dragon Year. Kongtrul reports that there were miracles during his conception, gestation, and birth. These included his placenta being wrapped around his body at birth, like the robes of a monk. A meticulous chronicler of his own life, Kongtrul bemoaned Khyentse's failure to keep a diary, complaining, as he recorded the rumors about his birth, that there were "no actual records to confirm such things." His family was wealthy and well connected, based in the Terlung Valley, to the east of Pelpung—his father was a court official, and his paternal uncle was an incarnate lama, the Second Moktsa Tulku at Katok Monastery. Beginning at the age of three, Khyentse was given attention by the forty-seventh abbot of Ngor Ewaṃ Choden, Tartse Khenpo Jampa Kunga Tendzin. Ngor, in central Tibet, is one of the three minor branches of the Sakya tradition, alongside the Tsar and the Dzongpa, based at Dar Drangmoche and Gongkar Chode, respectively. When Khyentse was twelve, Jampa Kunga Tendzin identified him as the reincarnation of his uncle Tartse Khenpo Jampa Namkha Chime, who had been the forty-fourth abbot of Ngor. Khyentse's father refused to allow the lama to take his son to Ngor, however. This provided the opportunity for him to train initially in Nyingma traditions at Katok and at Zhechen, and many of the most prominent Nyingma teachers of the day came to Khyentse's family estate to bestow empowerments on him, including Jigme Gyelwai Nyugu, a disciple of Jigme Lingpa. At Zhechen, only a few years after Kongtrul had left for Pelpung, Zhechen Wontrul taught him the Māyājāla literature, which are the foundation texts for the Dzogchen teachings.[3]

When the two met for the first time, Khyentse was on the eve of his first trip to central Tibet, where he would take ordination at Mindroling and study at Ngor for three years. Khyentse went to Pelpung twice before leaving for Tibet. At this point in his career, Kongtrul was known only for being able to offer instruction in Sanskrit, and it seems the two only looked at texts relating to Candragomin's grammar. If any other topics came up, Kongtrul does not mention them. Khyentse, Kongtrul reported, treated him with considerable respect.[4]

Kongtrul himself was still immersed in his own studies. In October 1840[5] Dabzang Tulku insisted that Kongtrul study the rituals of the United Intent of the Gurus, specifically the section called "Liberation Through Seeing." Kongtrul had received the reading transmission for this extensive treasure cycle from Zhechen Wontrul back in 1833. The United Intent of the Gurus, discovered by Sanggye Lingpa in 1364, was adopted by the Karma Kagyu tradition from the very beginning. Sanggye Lingpa had been a disciple of the Fourth Karmapa, Rolpai Dorje, and the Karmapa received the treasure cycle almost as soon as its revealer had completed it. It was valued so highly in the tradition that the Fifth Karmapa is said to have brought a copy of it to Nanjing in 1407 as a gift for the Chinese Yongle emperor of the Ming Dynasty. It is considered one of the most inclusive treasure cycles, with complete liturgies for all three classes of Nyingma tantra (Mahāyoga, Anuyoga, and Atiyoga) as well as Mahāmudrā and Chod practices, powa instructions, and advice from Padmasambhava to Yeshe Tsogyel, among other things. Kongtrul, who referred to it as "unequalled by any other treasure cycle," would return to the United Intent of the Gurus his entire career, using its liturgies for public rituals time and again. He would include forty-five liturgies for it in the Treasury of Revelations.[6]

Kongtrul studied now with a lama from the aristocratic Garje family named Pema Sang-ngak Tendzin, going over the United Intent of the Gurus drubchen and mending rituals as well as other sections.[7] These two public rites in particular would become central to his professional activity as he grew into a ritual specialist in high demand across Kham. The drubchen is an intensive public ritual that lasts from one to two weeks. Like a sādhana—the word is literally "great sādhana"—it involves invoking deities with offerings, elaborate ritual dances, and prayers and mantras, which, in this case, are communally recited continuously day and night within a closed boundary. Mending rites are also publicly performed, offering a means for an entire community to reaffirm obligations and vows.

His dreams during the training were of great treasure revealers sitting at the head of a monastic assembly expounding the Dharma and of himself performing a smoke offering to the protectors and raising white silk banners above a monastery full of golden reliquaries. Confident of his right to act as a lama, on October 17, 1840,[8] Kongtrul took four people into a retreat setting to perform the approach for parts of United Intent of the Gurus, including the "Liberation Through Seeing" section. During the retreat, Kongtrul had a dream visit with Karma Chakme, who gave him further instructions on the cycle, clarifying difficult points. Dreamtime instructions such as this would continue to be a useful means of sorting through the complex liturgical material he was studying and practicing.[9]

Lama Sang-ngak also initiated Kongtrul into the Ratna Lingpa tradition of Black Hayagrīva using a life-force entrustment, and Kongtrul afterward dedicated some time to the recitation of the associated mantra. In his dreams he perceived himself as a deity subjugating demons. It would seem that Kongtrul was not satisfied with the absence of a proper empowerment liturgy; he composed one for the treasure cycle and included it in Treasury of Revelations.[10]

Through the end of 1840 and into the new year, Kongtrul continued to maintain an increased schedule of practice. In the winter he entered a retreat on the approach practice of Bernakchen. This was the first Buddhist deity Kongtrul had encountered and the first he had learned to draw when he was a child in Ronggyab. It did not start out well; Kongtrul was agitated and anxious. But by the end he was experiencing signs of success that accorded to the liturgies. In his dreams he joined Padmasambhava, Śāntarakṣita, and King Trisong Detsen in a discussion on translation.[11]

Kongtrul began to come into his own as a lama in the early 1840s, already into his third decade. He gave bodhisattva vows to a group of seventeen young men on March 7, 1841,[12] after which he dreamed that he and his new disciples raised a tall pole hung with prayer flags and a victory banner at the top. Kongtrul took this as a sign that he would bestow the vows on many occasions. Kongtrul also took charge of rituals for the monastic community. At the end of May or the beginning of June,[13] Wongen tasked him and a few other monks to perform a "circle" rite for the well-being of the saṅgha, or monastic community. In his dreams he found himself in Lhasa amidst a large assembly of monks reciting from the *Prātimokṣa Sūtra*, the main source for the monastic codes, preparing to distribute offerings.[14]

In the spring of 1841,[15] Kongtrul went for the first time to the estate of the Jadra clan. This was an aristocratic family, one of several dozen from which Derge court officials were recruited. Kongtrul apparently served them well, as they became lifelong sponsors. He first performed a basic ceremony to evaluate conditions and diagnosed disturbances from curses and the activity of a *gyelpo* demon, which he promptly dispatched. He had positive indications from a prosperity rite; after he "bound the entrance to prosperity," a large amount of barley abruptly fell into the chest in which he had placed a relic box. Kongtrul claimed that the family's wealth increased in the wake of his visit. The following year he paid a visit to the Alo Dilgo clan, another aristocratic family that was a major patron of Dzongsar; into this family Jamyang Khyentse Wangpo's reincarnation, Dilgo Khyentse Rinpoche, would be born in 1910. Kongtrul performed a peaceful and wrathful ritual for them over several days, during which his dreams were full of encounters with the local protector gods and conversations about travels to India, suggesting a comparison of the Alo Dilgo estates with the large princely estates of the Indian patrons of the Buddha, something that was sure to have been well received.[16]

Wongen brought Kongtrul, Dabzang, and five or six other monks to Pelpung's retreat center in late summer 1841[17] and gave them the complete empowerments and instructions for United Intent of the Gurus. Until then, Kongtrul had been operating with only the reading transmission, which permitted the approach practice but not the performance of the full sādhana. He now was fully initiated; he marked this moment with a dream in which Situ Rinpoche—not Wongen, who had given him the empowerment—was seated on a high throne bestowing on him a benediction. Lest one think he was developing an improper pride, Situ was resplendent in new robes, while Kongtrul was in a threadbare shawl, albeit with gold threading.[18]

Dabzang Tulku, continuing his enthusiasm for United Intent of the Gurus, insisted that they perform a *mendrub* ritual from the cycle. A mendrub, literally "accomplishment of medicine," is a complex consecration ritual that is often done in conjunction with the drubchen ritual so that the resulting medicinal substances are imbued with the blessing of both rituals. It is a tradition based on the Four Tantras and wrapped around the deities Vajrāmṛta, sometimes one of the Eight Command deities, and the

Medicine Buddha Bhaiṣajyaguru, with other deities also included. It is also rooted in a Tibetan fascination with alchemical processes, the transformation of polluted substances into the stuff of enlightenment. A mendrub ritual lasts between one and two weeks. Kongtrul's dedication to the mendrub practice is evident in his inclusion of thirteen different mendrub liturgical cycles in his Treasury of Revelations, spanning two and a half volumes of the collection. The young lamas—about twenty-five of them—gathered substances as they were able from the monastery's pharmacy with the aid of Doctor Karma Tsepel, who sent the needed tools. They set up the retreat boundary—the edge of the ritual enclosure—in late October, with formal permission from Situ and with Wongen presiding.[19]

Kongtrul recorded several dreams that came during the ceremony. The Ninth Karmapa gave him verse instructions on Mahāmudrā; a doctor named Samten, who was a relative of Situ Rinpoche, stood beside medicinal shrubs and explained many things about medicine to him; three naked women stood before him covering their genitals with their hands; the treasure revealer Choje Lingpa discussed mendrub rituals with him. Not all dreams were pleasant. In one Wongen split open Kongtrul's skull with a sword, splashing his brains everywhere. A sword is a common symbol of wisdom, wielded to cut through dualistic thinking, such as the bodhisattva Mañjuśrī wields in his right hand. The violence of Kongtrul's dream does not appear to represent this, however. Rather than an act of enlightenment by a beloved teacher, it seems more representative of physical brutality by a hostile force, and Kongtrul does not suggest that he understood it any other way.[20]

He next turned to the practice of Vajrakīla, one of the central deities of the Nyingma tradition. He began a three-month retreat on the deity on December 2, 1841,[21] and ended it around the start of the new lunar year, early February 1842.[22] Vajrakīla is generally depicted in one of two forms: One form is black, with three faces, six hands, and four legs, with wide outstretched wings; the other form has the same upper body but with a kīla dagger in place of the lower body. The deity is cultivated to subjugate enemies and overcome obstacles to one's practice. Obstacles—karmic stains from past misdeeds that have clouded the mind or blocked subtle levels of consciousness—are, in Tantra, symbolically presented as demonic enemies that can be destroyed through wrathful deity practice. Tibetans also saw demons in mundane affairs, to be blamed for crop failures or illnesses. But an enemy might also be an actual human being, such as a competitor for patronage or disciples. Famous examples of Tibetans who commanded their meditational deities to harm or even murder people include Milarepa and the highly competitive eleventh-century Ra Lotsāwa Zhonnu Pel, who infamously assassinated Marpa's son Darma Dode. Black magic being generally frowned upon, the practice is most commonly done as a preventative measure, designed to ward off harmful events.[23]

Kongtrul did not record which ritual system he relied on for this Vajrakīla retreat, but it was likely Ratna Lingpa's Unsurpassed Innermost Vajrakīla cycle. He had previously received several Vajrakīla transmissions as part of larger collections, such as Ratna Lingpa's Peaceful and Wrathful Deities, which he received from the Fifth Karma Chakme in 1834 at Karma Gon, and the Eight Commands: Gathering of Sugatas liturgy of Nyangrel Nyima Wozer, the transmission for which he received from Zhechen Wontrul in 1832. Kongtrul would henceforth perform an annual year-end Vajrakīla retreat to repel harm, although the liturgies would change over the years. Kongtrul would receive the transmissions for multiple Vajrakīla cycles by the end of his life; there are close to one hundred Vajrakīla texts in the Treasury of Revelations by twelve different treasure revealers.

His dreams during the three-month retreat included several devotional episodes featuring Situ Rinpoche and the Fourteenth Karmapa, and a vision of a mountain surrounded by the worldly protective deities, headed by the Karma Kagyu protector Lord of Rakṣa with a Garland of Skulls. One morning at dawn, he practiced lucid dreaming. Finding himself outside a building where Situ was staying, he decided to circumambulate. On the path, he encountered a woman whom he recognized as a ḍākinī, who had a delighted manner about her. Kongtrul joined with her in sexual intercourse, and by doing so he had a stable experience of all four Dzogchen visions. This was to be only the first of several sexual dreams Kongtrul felt warranted recording. Soon after the Vajrakīla retreat ended, he dreamed of a woman with a single eye in the middle of her forehead, an eye which reflected the surroundings like a mirror. They conversed, and she transformed into a beautiful woman. Kongtrul and the now attractive woman joined together in sexual congress, sitting in the center of a room with four doors. Two figures emanated from them and moved toward the entrances, representing two of the four trainings of a tantric yogi: pacifying and enriching. The other two, magnetizing and wrathful, did not have time to manifest before the dream began to fade. On April 11, 1842,[24] immediately afterwards, Kongtrul fell ill. It was something akin to an asthma attack, and it lasted a full month.[25] This illness was a major life event and will be discussed in the next chapter.

Toward the end of the year, Kongtrul began to focus on Avalokiteśvara in earnest, decreasing his attention to Mañjuśrī. He had received transmissions for both deities from multiple lamas. White Mañjuśrī and the *Mañjuśrīnāmasamgīti* were his earliest Buddhist practices, and he first received an Avalokiteśvara transmission in 1831. In late 1841 he gave to students for the first time the authorization for a Mañjuśrī practice in the lineage of Padampa Sanggye, the eleventh-century Indian master who brought the Zhije tradition to Tibet. No sooner had he given the transmission than he had a dream in which Karma Chakme told him not to rely on Mañjuśrī, but to instead put his faith in Avalokiteśvara. Kongtrul followed this advice, and Avalokiteśvara became a far more important deity to him. Kongtrul would later come to be known by an epithet of Mañjuśrī, Mañjunātha—"Jamgon" in Tibetan. It was a mark of respect for his intellectual accomplishments rather than an identification with the bodhisattva.[26]

In the Water Tiger Year, which began on February 11, 1842, both the Old Chieftain and Wongen passed away. The Chieftain died on March 6, 1842.[27] He had fallen ill a month earlier, and Kongtrul had attempted a cure, although he does not describe the methods he used. When it became clear that death was near, Kongtrul read to him the instructions for the bardo, and he placed amulets at various places on his body. Kongtrul was affected. He wrote:

> The Old Chieftain maintained the purity of his bhikṣu vows, which had been given to him by the omniscient Eighth Drukchen, Kunzik Chokyi Nangwa. He revered Lord Pema Nyinje and other lamas. He never interrupted or decreased the quantity of his prayers and recitations, and undertook several intensive retreats. The religious objects he sponsored and the merit he accumulated were vast, and whatever wealth he had he put to use for the Dharma. He never fell into major sin, such as taking lives. At the time of his death, his demeanor was so positive that I cannot imagine he has had anything but a good rebirth. He cared for me even more than my own mother and father.

Four weeks after his death, Kongtrul performed a commemorative service of the United Intent of the Guru mending and purification rituals.

Signs at the time pointed to the Old Chieftain having settled into a peaceful place. Kongtrul never again named an individual patron, referring to his benefactors only collectively by their clan name.[28]

Wongen died on January 29, 1843.[29] A dream of Kongtrul's back in March of 1840,[30] while Wongen was ill, had, to Kongtrul's mind, predicted the old lama's imminent death. It was not complimentary. In it, the moon, during a lunar eclipse, illuminated the sky. Kongtrul remarked that the light was improbably bright and wondered aloud what sort of light a fully liberated moon would bring. In Tibetan mythology lunar eclipses are caused by a demon named Rahu eating the moon. Getting free from a demon is a metaphor for liberation, thus Kongtrul's choice of words here: the moon is to be "liberated." A few ladies heard him and answered, "If the moon were liberated, we would know. Now, it will be difficult for it to be liberated." The dream suggests that Kongtrul did not view Wongen as an enlightened being and did not expect the man to attain liberation upon his death.[31] It is a remarkable insult to a man who taught him. About half a year before Wongen's death, he had another dream in which his teacher appeared and performed an ablution using the Six Perfections, a basic grouping of Mahāyāna doctrine (ethics, diligence, patience, generosity, meditation, and wisdom). Wongen made an error in his recitation, saying "I, who have departed, offer this bathing." Kongtrul corrected this to "I bathe the fortunate one." The elderly lama became embarrassed and walked off, but Kongtrul pursued him, and Wongen then performed the ritual with a copper basin.[32]

It is exceedingly unconventional for a student to correct a lama. Regardless of whether the student is factually correct, given the reverence in which the guru is held, the breach in protocol would be shocking. Moreover, to suggest Wongen did not liberate upon death would insult his memory and his disciples. Wongen was a respected lama of the monastery, and following his death Kongtrul performed a week-long mending ritual from the United Intent of the Gurus in his honor, albeit at the request of Situ Rinpoche.[33] Yet Kongtrul was ambivalent, and his veneration was thin. Kongtrul wrote no eulogy for him as he did for the Old Chieftain. Wongen was his teacher, the source of many valued transmissions. He brought Kongtrul to Pelpung and ensured that he was firmly ensconced in the institution. Yet whatever gratitude Kongtrul felt around coming to Pelpung was directed toward Situ. He blamed Wongen for stealing him away from Zhechen and from Zhechen Wontrul. That was a wound Kongtrul felt deeply all his life, and he never forgave Wongen for it.

# 10

## AGE THIRTY

### 1842

When Kongtrul was nine years old, Tarde Tokden Yungdrung Puntsok, had told his grandfather that around Kongtrul's thirtieth year he would encounter a great obstacle. Tarde Tokden was the first man outside his family to give him religious instructions, and Kongtrul respected him. He considered the prophecy meaningful enough to include it in his account of his childhood.[1] In his diary entries of this thirtieth year, Kongtrul implied that a respiratory ailment he experienced starting on April 11, 1842,[2] was the obstacle Tarde Tokden had foretold. It was so severe that for the entire month he was convinced he was going to die. Kongtrul ascribed the illness to his turning away from his Nyingma training and his attempt to conform to Karma Kagyu orthodoxy.[3] At Pelpung he had come under the influence of a fundamentalist faction that remained a malignant presence for most of his life, punishing him severely decades later when he eventually engaged in treasure discovery. In 1842 the force of their condemnation and his concurrent shame at his sense of betrayal of Zhechen Wontrul literally made him ill. Many years later, describing the initial years of his education at Pelpung in his secret autobiography, *Mirage of Nectar*, Kongtrul complained that he was then so occupied with Karma Kagyu training that he was forced to neglect his predestined treasure revelations. He had been pressured by lamas and patrons and bullied by his peers to reject all things Nyingma, and he had acquiesced to the point of burning books. After beginning the Kagyu preliminary practices, he had dreamed of turning away from Zhechen Wontrul and woke in a state of sorrow and regret for his infidelity to his Nyingma heritage.[4]

Even if the curriculum at Pelpung included teachings from Nyingma, Jonang, and other traditions, this did not mean that Kongtrul—Bon by birth and Nyingma by early ordination and training—was safe to practice them without suspicion. Ecumenicalism was not unprecedented, but neither

was it common, certainly not by a dependent monk such as Kongtrul, just
thirty years old and not in possession of an institution or an estate on which
to base his activity and authority. Kongtrul had already or would eventually repeat every empowerment that Zhechen Wontrul and other Nyingma
lamas gave him, receiving each from a Kagyu lama before practicing them.
This was the case even if the tradition was definitively Nyingma, such as the
Mindroling Jinasāgara practice. He would practice Nyingma teachings, but
he would do so in a Kagyu lineage. Even his worship of Padmasambhava
was framed in a Kagyu context; in 1845, after participating in a tenth-day
Padmasambhava ceremony on July 14,[5] he remarked that while he believed
such Nyingma ceremonies were effective, due to his broken samaya—his
having turned away from Nyingma practice—he was unable to fully receive
the blessings.[6] For decades he would rely on his treasure-revealing colleagues
Chokgyur Lingpa and Khyentse Wangpo for messages from the Guru; it
was many years before Kongtrul was comfortable communicating directly
with Padmasambhava.

Kongtrul believed his thirtieth-year illness to have been caused by his
attempt to suppress his Nyingma heritage. The orthodox faction was wrong
to pressure him, but he was mistaken in submitting to them. He cured
himself with a reassertion of Nyingma practices and by subtly but firmly
separating himself from the Pelpung monastic community. In his diary
he describes how, immediately after he regained his health, he practiced a
torma ritual to the goddess Parṇaśavarī from the Sky Teachings of Mingyur
Dorje and a longevity practice from Gathering of Secrets, the Ratna Lingpa
cycle that would ever after be part of his daily practice. Parṇaśavarī is an
Indian folk goddess of healing who appears in a number of treasure cycles.
In a dream that occurred during these practices, he received a message from
an unnamed lama in the form of a small scroll of paper. The message read
"If you pray fervently to Padmasambhava, he should, in his compassion,
clear the three junctures in your life in which major obstacles will arise. As
a result, you should be able to live for more than seventy years." His dream
self knew that every night he had been passionately reciting a supplication
prayer called Clearing Obstacles to the Path, that at times he felt that Padmasambhava and a host of deities were, in fact, removing obstacles, and that
the sky was filled with dākinīs and vidyādharas—a type of winged diety
associated with wisdom—who told him, "If you have the ability to pray,
you need no other method. His compassion will completely embrace you."
Kongtrul believed that he needed Nyingma practices to be safe.[7]

In *Mirage of Nectar*, written at the end of his life, he described the cure explicitly as an affirmation of Nyingma practices. He began to mend, he reports, only after sponsoring a set of thirteen paintings of deities from United Intent of the Guru. Yet this was not enough to fully recover; he needed to reconnect not simply with Nyingma traditions but with the person he was at Zhechen. Kongtrul had begun to practice the cycle, but he had received the transmission a second time from Wongen, and so it was within a Karma Kagyu context. Kongtrul needed an unadulterated Nyingma response. The story he tells in this later narrative has Khyentse Wangpo, who he had only recently met, inform him that he, Kongtrul, needed to perform a mending and a ransom liturgy to the deity Pelden Lhamo, a goddess whose Bon form he had recently denied having a connection. These were the very liturgies that he had written at Zhechen and that he had later burned. Kongtrul reinforced this diagnosis with a dream in which a student of his named Karma Nyima Wozer told him he would never recover from his illness unless he worshipped Pelden Lhamo using the liturgies he had composed at Zhechen. Because he had destroyed these, in their place he composed *Complete Spontaneous Fulfillment of Wishes: An Invocation to the Gracious Goddess*. This liturgy for the worship of Pelden Lhamo was published and is preserved in his Collected Writings. After reciting this a few times, he fully recovered.[8]

Kongtrul never fully made peace with the move from Zhechen to Pelpung, and the early shock and ambivalence hardened to late-life bitterness. It was a trauma that haunted him throughout his life, sufficiently to be blamed for an illness almost seventy years after his recovery. He was pressured to conform to a sectarian identity he did not choose and which he resisted. And yet he embraced all that came with it: the teachings, the lineage lamas, and the support that Pelpung and other Kagyu institutions afforded him. Being a Kagyu lama permitted a wide engagement with Nyingma teachings and practices, and once he freed himself from the orthodox faction which disapproved of his expansive interests he would go on to explore and immerse himself in many other traditions. He was cured of this thirtieth-year illness only when he rejected orthodoxy and embraced an ecumenicalism that fit the ideals, if not the reality, of the Karma Kagyu tradition. He would be a Kagyu monk who practiced many teachings from as many traditions as he was able to encounter. If that made him unwelcome at Pelpung, so be it.

Kongtrul dealt with all of this psychological turmoil by going into retreat. To find his place in the world and his community, he resolved to first withdraw into seclusion and immerse himself in the teachings that inspired him. He later wrote that "disillusioned with the world, I only desire to reside in a virtuous secluded place where a juniper forest grows, where the mountain birds sing in undulating melodies, and where I can rest my mind in meditative absorption."[9] Unsafe at Pelpung, this had to happen elsewhere, and he found a place just far enough away to assert a separation.

By 1842 Kongtrul had established himself as one of the main disciples of Pelpung's leading master. Situ had guided his education and had connected him with the Fourteenth Karmapa and with an important benefactor, the Jadra family. Although Wongen was by far his primary instructor, he would pass away the year Kongtrul began his retreat, and Kongtrul never again mentioned him in his diary. He had received the transmissions and empowerments he needed for the practices that would dominate his meditation sessions for the rest of his life. He had trained in medicine and grammar, had begun to compose—already in 1842 he reported that he had been writing biographies of Pelpung lamas[10]—and had dipped his toes into scriptural organization and publication by editing and proofreading multiple volumes of scriptures. Entering a lengthy retreat allowed him to put into practice that which he had received in his first decades of studies. It also gave him an opportunity to reflect back on his life to date and to make sense of who he was in the world. Not long after he moved into his retreat hut, he composed a short autobiographical statement, which he inserted into his diary.

In 116 lines of verse, Kongtrul's autobiographical reflections run for about four pages in the woodblock edition of his diary. More than anything it is an expression of his values and outlook. After supplicating Padmasambhava, the protector deities, and his guru Situ Pema Nyinje, Kongtrul repeats basic Tibetan Buddhist themes of being fortunate to have been born a human being and to have encountered the Buddhist teachings. This is followed with standard self-effacing statements, such as his character being driven by the ten nonvirtues (greed, ignorance, untruthfulness, and so forth) and his confidence being comparable to the child of a barren woman—meaning he had none at all. He concludes that he is "not in anyway possessed of the qualities of a saint, but is rather a fraud who camouflages the ordinary to make it seem holy." Kongtrul was clearly trying to make poetry, and there is some elegance in his verse, with alliteration and some rare descriptions of the natural world.[11]

The required expressions of gratitude and humility completed, he made his earliest statement of the ecumenical attitude for which he is deservedly famous:

> Thanks to the power of the three roots [the guru, the yidam, and the
>     ḍākinī],
> from an early age my mind was inclined toward virtue.
> Casting off [my] Bon [heritage], I entered the door of the Buddhist
>     teachings.
> These days, I am not comfortable in my practice in view and action,
> and I aspire to follow those of yore.
> I have read many treatises that are not in themselves sectarian
> and examined many biographies of the wise and accomplished ones.
> I cannot endure to even look at the books
> of partisans who arrogantly chase after fame.
> Declaring "this is good" and "that is bad" is the way of fools.
> Knowing this, I have tasted without partiality the innermost parts of
>     the enlightened intent of the old and new schools.
> I cultivate a pure view regarding all the teachings of the Victorious
>     One [i.e., the Buddha];
> rejecting [any part] of the Dharma would be a burden I could not
>     bear.

Kongtrul was "not comfortable" in his practice at Pelpung. He was grateful for his education and training but justifiably disgusted with his treatment and appalled at the distrust and prejudices he endured. In the midst of the hostility, he recognized the hazards of dualistic thinking, of accepting or rejecting aspects of the Buddha's teachings that might appear challenging or unfamiliar. His solution—to not only embrace Karma Kagyu ecumenicalism but expand it—was not simply a way to continue to engage in the traditions he knew; impartiality for him was the heart of the Buddha's teaching on nonduality.[12]

He continued his confessional with a series of common affirmations of what he believed to be the heart of religious practice, expressed in familiar pairings: simplicity and study are more honest than public ceremonies; the scriptures themselves are more immediate than the commentaries; the welfare of others is more important than his own. This is the characterization, long established in Tibetan literature, of the pure yogi who forgoes society and its pratfalls, rejects scholasticism and the words of the established teacher to connect directly with the words of the Buddha, and serves all beings with abject humility. Rather than chase fame, the holy yogin would rather live as a dog, roaming the hills freely and anonymously. Kongtrul adds "I dream of staying always in an empty cave in an empty valley where I shall die while in meditative equipoise."[13]

Kongtrul then moved on to voice the sort of confidence that he claimed earlier not to possess. He admitted to an incomplete education and to a lack of experience with meditation, but he harbored no doubts about the validity of the teachings or the traditions that sustain them. In this he was not false in his modesty; Kongtrul did not train in a scholastic center in which he would have memorized the Indian classics of Mahāyāna literature. His education was almost entirely tantric. He knew, he confessed, that he had more to study and more to practice, and he was resolute in his intention to do so, without any prejudices: "Having understood the secret of the Buddha's genius, I lack the foolishness to selfishly advance my own opinions, saying 'this is true and all else is ignorance.'" He was determined to not waste a moment of his retreat, to not fall into distraction or bickering with companions, and to vigilantly remember that each day might be his last. He concluded with some satisfaction: "Just as a bird about to fly is quickly taken aloft by the wind, these preparations for going into solitude are the supreme method for accomplishing the chosen deity."[14]

Situated as it is in a literary tradition that permits few innovations or radical departures in ideological expression, Kongtrul's confessional contains no ideas that another idealistic young lama might not voice. Ecumenicalism, humility, and intense commitment to practice, are all found across traditions and throughout Tibetan history. The values he aspired to embody were those he was taught in books and lectures and through the model of his teachers. Still, the seeds of his famous ecumenicalism are there, in his struggle to overcome the biases of his community and to make sense of the multiple traditions to which he was gaining exposure. Kongtrul's coming-of-age was a challenge of organization as much as a philosophical consideration of nondual perception.

Looking back on the piece many decades later, Kongtrul bemoaned his failure to avoid the distractions of life in public service. He falsely claimed that he was never again able to remove himself from the world, but had to work ceaselessly for kings, patrons, disciples, communities, and for the future of Buddhism.[15] Surely he already knew this would be the case; it was true that his retreats were brief, limited to weeks or months at a time, and that he was indeed pressed into service. A man called across Kham to teach the Karmapa is not one who can vanish into a remote cave. He would visit many caves in his life, but he went to consecrate and build them out for the benefit of others, and for the most part he would reside in none of them for more than a few weeks. Yet in many other aspects of his declared goals he was successful, and what was written as aspirational can, with caution, be taken as descriptive. He never adopted the easily-mocked lifestyle of a high lama, surrounded by servants and luxuries. Nor did he abandon his commitment to venerate all the Buddha's teachings. Kongtrul recognized that nondualism in practice meant not declaring "this is good" or "that is bad"; it meant a nonjudgmental and nonexclusive approach to the full span of religious teachings he would encounter. This allowed him to produce the ecumenical collections of Tibetan sacred literature that made him famous. He would never burden himself with the weight of rejecting any part of the Dharma.

# 11

# Kongtrul's Retreat at Dechen Wosel Ling
## 1842–1846

Kongtrul chose as the site of his hermitage a rock outcropping on a steep slope, on the opposite side of the ridge from Pelpung. One has to walk up for several hours behind Pelpung before crossing over and down into thick pine forest. He was not the first to build there; Jangchub Lingpa had constructed a hermitage there in the thirteenth-century. At the site of Kongtrul's hermitage, Jangchub Lingpa vanquished *nāgas* and a *tsen* named Macho Gapa, whom he bound as a protector of Buddhism and renamed Dorje Dzongmar. Nāgas are subterranean serpent deities who control water and can cause diseases such as leprosy; tsen are an ancient class of Tibetan malicious deities. He built residences for practitioners at the site, which he named Pel Jangchub Ling, but, like his monastery, this was abandoned when the Sakya Khon family took power in Tibet and the Drigung tradition lost influence. Kongtrul's history jumps then to the time of the Eighth Situ, who had a vision of the Indian saint Asaṅga there. He connects several of the Situ's disciples to the place as well: his predecessor Bamteng Tulku Tsoknyi Lekdrub meditated there and claimed to have also done so in a previous life; Karma Dudul Gyelpo and Rigdzin Dorje Drakpa, who were involved in setting up Pelpung's retreat center, both asserted that the central cliff was sacred to Mahākaruṇika; and Karma Tenpai Rabgye buried a treasure vase at the peak of the site and had visions confirming the presence of the buddhas. Someone, possibly one of these men or another lama, had constructed a retreat hut, but it fell into disuse and decay after the brother of the Eighth Situ, Won Wanggi Dorje, built the retreat center at Pelpung. Kongtrul also stretched this history back into mythological time, asserting that Songtsen Gampo and Padmasambhava and many other saints practiced there.[1]

By the time Kongtrul decided to survey the site in the late autumn of 1842, there was nothing but a bare trace of the buildings. Time had nearly erased the path. On his way up the ridge with a companion, not knowing the route, he followed a vulture that had flown from below. On the far side of the ridge, the bird flew eastward, and as Kongtrul watched his flight his gaze settled on the site of the old hermitage. In the bird's honor he named the route Vulture-Face Path. Arriving there, he performed a smoke offering—a rite that was a typical first step in establishing a connection to a place. It acknowledges the presence of local deities and asks for their grace. Kongtrul had a sense that the rite was successful and that a connection was forged.[2]

He returned later with several monks and together they raised a new building of two rooms, making use of old walls that were still standing. This became the "main level" of the hermitage around which middle and lower rings of residences were eventually constructed. Situ had reluctantly given Kongtrul permission to spend three years in meditation, apparently only in response to his thirtieth year illness—for this reason Kongtrul later declared the near-death experience a blessing—and in preparation he sold all his possessions to commission the support objects necessary for his practice. The set of paintings depicting the maṇḍala and deities of United Intent of the Gurus—eleven paintings, according to the diary—served as the symbol of enlightened body. These were the same paintings that many decades later he claimed to have commissioned in order to cure himself from his thirtieth-year illness. The Buddha's speech was represented by a volume of the *Aṣṭasāhasrikā Prajñāpāramitā Sūtra*, written in gold ink. One thousand *tsatsa*—small stūpa-shaped votive offerings—were the symbol of enlightened mind. Kongtrul requested from Situ the empowerment for Jatson Nyingpo's Union of All Rare and Precious Jewels, which he had earlier received in 1831 at Zhechen from Gyurme Tenpel. This was in keeping with his program of repeating from a Kagyu lama all received Nyingma transmissions and may have been Situ's condition for the retreat. Situ also gave the hermitage a name: Kunzang Dechen Wosel Ling, which means something like Land of All Good Luminous Great Delight.[3]

Kongtrul later explained what the site offered the practitioner:

> This place has all the positive geomantic features as described in Indian and Chinese scriptures that are shared by people of all levels of perceptions. There are no swamps. Nor are there precipices, scree fields, or brambles. It is isolated from wicked nonhuman entities and savage flesh-eating animals, and evil beings such as snakes and the like do not inhabit the surrounding areas. There

are no extremes of altitude so one is not impaired by excessive heat or cold, and in both summer and winter the environment is lovely and quite exhilarating. The majestic cliffs are draped in garlands of white, red, and blue plants, and ornamented with forests of various types of trees and pleasing carpets of meadow. Many kinds of powerful good-tasting and exceptional medicinal plants grow here. The ridges around are straight and true. Clear and cool water cascades in enchanting melodies, flowing from all sides to come together in the middle.

All of the fine qualities have particular value for the practitioner, Kongtrul explained: the dense forests are places to develop tranquility; insight develops in the high places where one's awareness becomes clear; realization arises where the great masters of the past meditated.[4]

Kongtrul's dreams as he set off for this paradise were mostly positive. He saw himself giving an empowerment to a large assembly and found himself in a room where the Fourteenth Karmapa sat on a throne, surrounded by paintings of his previous incarnations. Someone, possibly a Karmapa, said, "the mind has been described in the scriptures by the noble ones," which Kongtrul took to be significant. Yet Kongtrul was also apprehensive and saw many signs of death. He had repeated dreams of many women gathering in crowds—escorts that accompany the dead to the bardo. In response he performed a ritual to cheat death. Mortality was forever a constant concern. Throughout his life Kongtrul saw signs of it everywhere and regularly performed rituals to avert death and lengthen his life span.[5]

Aside from his religious supports, Kongtrul initially had only a small amount of *tsampa*, the roasted barley flour that is mixed with tea and kneaded in the hand, and a brick of Chinese tea leaves. Fortunately, Situ sent up butter.[6] Tibetans take their tea with butter and salt rather than milk and sugar as in India or straight as in China. When preparing tsampa, they may add an additional piece of butter to the mix if they can, an important source of fat in the arid climate of the plateau. Another staple of the traditional Tibetan diet is dried meat. Flesh is cut from yak, sheep, or goat and hung to dry with salt and spices or simply left on the bone to be cut with a knife and eaten directly. Dried cheese in various forms made from the milk of the yak-cow hybrid, called a *dzo* in Tibetan, is also a common staple for nomads and hermits alike. Unfortunately, in none of his autobiographical writings does Kongtrul ever describe a meal.

The Jadra clan also committed to providing for him during the years he was in retreat. Kongtrul was not alone—one other monk joined him, although in what capacity Kongtrul does not say. Most likely he was there as an attendant, assisting with rituals and fetching water, and Kongtrul would probably have had to provide for him. Kongtrul declined to receive his share of the monastic donations and his salary for his service to the Situ estate while in retreat, anxious about being accused of taking for himself what belonged to the community he was, in effect, leaving behind. This was to be a perennial concern of his, and he would never be comfortable handling monastic property. It was not a sealed retreat—Kongtrul would leave several times to receive teachings and participate in ceremonies at the monastery. Nevertheless, the retreat, such as it was, lasted about three years and seven months, beginning on October 19, 1842,[7] and ending, after several interruptions, around March 1846.[8]

The retreat commenced with the preliminary practices for Jatson Nyingpo's Union of All Rare and Precious Jewels. During the preliminaries his dreams were uniformly positive: Tsewang Norbu, the eighteenth-century reformer of Katok Monastery and teacher of the Eighth Situ, grasped Kongtrul's hand as he was about to fall over an icy precipice; finding himself in a hell realm, he practiced Tonglen meditation to cultivate compassion for all the beings there. This lovely practice was developed by the early Kadam masters. One visualizes taking on the suffering of others with each inhale. With each exhale, one sends joy and protection. Kongtrul records that during the guru yoga from the preliminaries he advanced in his understanding of the nature of mind.[9]

During the winter solstice, Kongtrul began the custom that he would maintain for the rest of his life: a one-week year-end Vajrakīla approach and an exorcism rite. This was accompanied by a dream in which he saw the bodhisattva in the center of a magnificent temple with his retinue surrounding him. The Jonang master Tāranātha then appeared and, placing a vajra scepter on Kongtrul's head, recited the deity's mantra. Kongtrul followed this with a week-long Tārā approach session, reciting her mantra, during which he dreamed of a Tārā statue in the famous Longtang Dolma Temple near Lhasa, which came to life and blessed him.[10]

Kongtrul started the Water Hare Year, which began on January 31, 1843, with a mending ritual from United Intent of the Gurus in Wongen's memory. This was the rite commissioned by Situ, who sent up the material supports for the week's ceremony. Kongtrul makes a point of informing his reader that the idea—and the resources—for the ceremony were not his.[11]

At some point in the late spring or summer, a devastating earthquake struck northern Kham, impacting the region to the north and east from Derge. Pelpung and the retreat center were not harmed, but Kongtrul's home valley was heavily damaged. As a consequence, Kongtrul's mother, Tashi Tso, came to stay with him, and she remained at the hermitage until she passed away nearly twenty-five years later in 1867.[12] Kongtrul rarely mentions her in his diary, only referring to her existence in his diary three times, but he cared for her deeply and was grateful to her. Not mentioning her was more a reflection of basic Tibetan attitudes; women were simply not valued highly enough to note their presence. As she recited her Avalokiteśvara mantra, she took care of Kongtrul's daily needs. Kongtrul would have few attendants or servants in his life and would rely primarily on his mother, and later, a niece, for basic household service. At this point the hermitage was just a simple, pounded-earth structure shared by all in residence. His mother would have fetched water from one of the several streams that ran through the site, collected wood for the cooking fire, and prepared meals.

Two teaching sessions pulled him out of retreat in the second half of 1843. The first, in summer, was when Lama Karma Norbu came up to the hermitage and completed his transmission of the Shangpa Kagyu teachings. This included the empowerment for the five-deity maṇḍala of Cakrasaṃvara, for the Six Yogas of Niguma based on his own compositions— the abridged version of which he had given back in 1840—and for the precepts for the protective deity Mahākāla Who Clears Obstacles. This six-armed form of Mahākāla is the particular protective deity of the Shangpa teachings, and Kongtrul thereafter adopted him as his personal protector.[13]

Karma Norbu taught Kongtrul three classic Tibetan compositions from the commentarial tradition of Tāranātha. The first was *Amulet Box of Mahāmudrā*, which is so titled because, after receiving it in India, Khyungpo Neljor inserted scrolls on which the three essential points were written into an amulet box which he wore around his neck. The second and third are classic Kadam teachings: *Stages of the Path of the Three Kinds of Beings* by Sharawa Yonten Drak and *Seven-Point Mind Training* by Atīśa. Kongtrul saw this lama once more, at Situ Rinpoche's residence. At that time—Kongtrul did not identify when—the lama spoke of his own meditative experiences, admonished Kongtrul to practice unerringly, and promised that the two would meet again in Kechara, the pure land of Vajrayoginī.[14]

Kongtrul developed his hermitage as a Shangpa institution as he would later do with his second hermitage, Dzongsho Deshek Dupai Podrang. Neither he nor his disciples left an explanation for this decision in writing. The great twentieth-century lama Kalu Rinpoche, who was said to be Kongtrul's reincarnation and who served for several decades as the retreat master at the hermitage in the early twentieth century, gave an apocryphal account, which is repeated by Ngawang Zangpo in his *Jamgon Kongtrul's Retreat Manual*. Kalu Rinpoche had Kongtrul learn that Karma Norbu was at Pelpung and break his retreat to go request teachings from him. The lama ignored him. Mortified, and sure that the icy reception was because of his own shortcomings, Kongtrul spent the night contemplating his own failings and practicing purification meditation. In the midst of his meditation, he had the inspiration to promise Karma Norbu to establish his hermitage as a center of Shangpa teachings as a way to atone for his miscellaneous and unidentified faults. When he again approached Karma Norbu the next day, before he could speak, the lama preemptively replied "Good idea!" and promised to return again to give him the full transmissions.[15] This story directly contradicts Kongtrul's own record of events and reduces a remarkable decision to a desire, born out of insecurity, to please a lama with whom he was not close.

A more plausible explanation would point to Kongtrul's sense of being an outsider at Pelpung. He was likely drawn to the Shangpa for the same reasons he was drawn to the Jonang: they were rare, underrepresented, and in a way outliers in a religious landscape of established institutions. It gave him an opportunity to occupy a space that was neither Nyingma nor Karma Kagyu but which accommodated all the teachings just the same. The Shangpa tradition was also largely unclaimed. There would be no hierarchs to demand allegiance to an orthodoxy or to otherwise direct his activities. He would rest comfortably in an amorphous religious tradition, one that was recognized and established but one in which he would be beholden to few restrictions.

A second interruption required that he again return to Pelpung. Lama Karma Wosel Gyurme, a Pelpung lama who had studied with Jonang lamas in Dzamtang, Amdo, had returned and would be teaching. Karma Wosel Gyurme had studied with Ngawang Chopel, Drubwang Lhundrub Gyatso, and others, from whom he received the complete transmission of Tāranātha's Collected Works. He was preparing to pass on this transmission at Pelpung, and Kongtrul accordingly spent about three months at the

monastery, from the end of September to December 1843,[16] alongside Dabzang Tulku and eight other monks. For this, his second transmission of the
collection, Kongtrul did not indicate the edition given, but he did note that
they covered only about five or six volumes of the master's compositions.
Karma Wosel Gyurme also gave the empowerment for most of the tantric
systems Tāranātha wrote about, chief among them the *Kālacakra Tantra*.
This tantra, the very last to be translated into Tibetan, formed the core
teachings of the Jonang tradition and is also particularly important in the
Sakya and Geluk traditions. It is the primary source of Tibetan astrology;
its translation in 1026 initiated the Tibetan calendar.[17]

On returning to the hermitage in late December, Kongtrul picked up
where he left off in his meditation, the outer sādhana of Union of All Rare
and Precious Jewels. He received a short handwritten note from Situ that
contained a single verse:

> In the forest hermitage of Kun[zang] De[chen Wosel] Ling
> An omniscient lord of men has mastered the three solitudes.
> May you be victorious in your battle against the four māras.[18]

To master the three solitudes means the rejection of unenlightened activity
by body, speech, and mind. The four māras are the personification of all that
is wrong with saṃsāra. They are the demon of the karmic stains, the demon
of death, the demon of existence, and the god of pleasure who attempted
to prevent the Buddha from attaining enlightenment by sending first his
beautiful daughters to seduce him and then warrior sons to scare him off.
The sādhana classifications of "outer," "inner," and "secret" correspond to the
three tantric classes of Yoga, Mahāyoga, and Atiyoga Tantra.

Over the first six months of the Wood Dragon Year, which began on February 19, 1844, Kongtrul practiced the inner sādhana of Union of All Rare
and Precious Jewels. More than a dozen famous historical lamas visited him
in his dreams. These included Tāranātha; Jampa Bum, a twelfth-century
lama of Katok; the Second Karmapa; the Seventh Karmapa together with
the Fourth Zhamar and the Eighth Situ; the Eleventh Karmapa together
with the Fifth Tsurpu Gyeltsab and the Fourth Situ; Padampa Sanggye;
Ra Lotsāwa; and the Tenth Karmapa together with the Fourth Tsurpu
Gyeltsab and Sanggye Nyenpa, a "crazy yogi" who studied with the Seventh
Karmapa. The dream visits were consistently positive experiences. In some
the lamas gave him something, or he offered them prayers or prostrations.

Most were simply appearances that affirmed for Kongtrul that he was advancing in his practice and that he would be in good company. In 1844, when he was about halfway through the inner sādhana, he reflected on his meditation, recalling a comment of Jatson Nyingpo's disciple Tsele Natsok Rangdrol:

> He came to understand that the natural state of mind is inconceivable, beyond mental fabrications, unconcerned with any need to refute or affirm anything at all. Uncontrived and left to itself, it simply recognizes things as they are. This was not an intellectual understanding but a conviction from the depths of my experience. In all my previous meditations and annual rituals and any "resting in nonconceptual state," none of it had taken me past an intellectual understanding, and I only ever had a partial confidence in a view that was free from elaboration and was sky-like. When I would cultivate my own mind's fundamental emptiness, my creation stage visualizations were rarely clear. When the creation stage visualizations were clear, I would think "there probably is some nature of mind," but even that was superficial. Now, with a conviction that the mind and appearances are empty simultaneously, by simply placing my attention on clear appearances, they arise in their true state. I need not seek for them elsewhere.[19]

On completion of the inner sādhana, Kongtrul went down to Pelpung to consult with Situ Rinpoche. It is customary for a student to discuss meditative experiences with the lama, to ensure that the rituals were done properly and to confirm that the experiences conformed to tradition, either as described in the manuals or as passed down orally. In Buddhism no one expects to have a novel meditative experience, one that has not been described and dissected by saints of the past. The Tibetan Buddhist path to enlightenment has been mapped out in exquisite detail, and creativity in one's meditation is warned against as deviation from the pursuit of liberation. Pleasing visions not sanctioned by tradition could be the work of demons, or worse, innovation. One has to do it the same way as the lama did it, first by studying the manuals and then by putting the theory into practice. In Kongtrul's description of his realization above, he mocks himself for his initial inability to move beyond an intellectual understanding, arriving at an experience of the truths he had studied only after performing the Padmasambhava sādhana and recalling some inspiring words of a skilled teacher.[20]

While at Pelpung, Kongtrul participated in a community exorcism ritual known as a "blade ransom" at the Vajrakīla Temple. They made the preparations during the second half of September 1844[21] and performed the ceremony in early October[22] with Dabzang Tulku and fifteen other monks. Back in retreat, over the remaining three months of the Wood Dragon Year, Kongtrul finished the remaining sādhana from Union of All Rare and Precious Jewels: the secret sādhana, which was the guru yoga; the extra-secret sādhana, which focuses on Siṁhamukhā; and the longevity sādhana. He finished the lunar year with a fire ritual to increase the four activities and with his customary Vajrakīla exorcism. At the start of the Wood Snake Year, on February 7, 1845, Kongtrul began the practices of United Intent of the Gurus, starting with the mending rite and, concurrently, the nine-deity maṇḍala of Jinasāgara in the Mindroling tradition. A dream of Terdak Lingpa during his practice later in the year included a ritual of the four empowerments directly from the master and an invitation to visit Mindroling, where Terdak Lingpa promised he was still present. Kongtrul would accept the invitation in early 1858 during a trip to Tibet (see chapter 17).[23]

In March[24] Kongtrul's practice was interrupted by a summons from Dabzang Tulku. Dabzang had requested the empowerment of Nyangrel Nyima Wozer's Eight Commands: Gathering of Sugatas from the Garwang incarnation of Zurmang Monastery, who was visiting Pelpung, and he wanted Kongtrul to attend. The Garwang incarnation line stems from Drung Mase, the founder of the monastery. This cycle was also on Kongtrul's mind at the beginning of his retreat—in 1843, while he was practicing the guru yoga from United Intent of the Gurus, he had dreamed that the Fourth Karma Chakme incarnation, Tendzin Trinle, had given him the complete empowerment and transmission for the cycle. In the dream all nine maṇḍalas were laid out in a square grid, with the deities of each in their proper places. Kongtrul recorded feeling a particular affinity for the deities of the Lotus family, headed by Hayagrīva. It is this category, belonging to enlightened speech, to which Avalokiteśvara belongs. Counting this dream, the 1845 empowerment from Garwang was thus the third time Kongtrul received the Eight Commands. Dabzang then made arrangements for a combined drubchen and mendrub ceremony while Kongtrul returned to his hermitage to engage with the peaceful and wrathful deity rituals from the cycle. He returned in April to join Dabzang in the ceremony, with thirty other monks.[25]

Back at his hermitage he began the outer sādhana of the Jinasāgara cycle, breaking on May 14 to observe the eighth day of the fourth month—a day sacred to the Medicine Buddha—and perform a two-day fasting ritual. In June[26] he was interrupted yet again, called down to Pelpung this time by Wontrul, to receive teachings from Situ Rinpoche on the second of the Four Medical Tantras. He stayed down at the monastery to participate in the tenth-day Padmasambhava ceremonies on July 14 and then returned to the hermitage where the Medicine Buddha appeared in a dream. In an astonishing expression of Kongtrul's self-confidence, Bhaiṣajyaguru placed his hand on his head and gave him a prophecy of his future buddhahood. In Buddhist cosmology buddhas appear continually, each in his or her own pure land and only after thousands of lifetimes of traversing the path. The journey commences with a prophecy from a buddha. Such a prophecy includes the name of the cosmological eon, a period of about four billion years—our current eon is named Bhadrakalpa, the Auspicious Eon—in which the enlightenment will occur, and the name by which the buddha-to-be will be known. According to the Medicine Buddha, Kongtrul would attain buddhahood in an eon called Star-Like, and will be known as the Tathāgata Paripūraṇa Cakravartin, the Buddha Completely Perfect Universal Emperor.[27]

Kongtrul's dreams continued to include sexual yoga. In September 1845 he dreamed of a wisdom ḍākinī appearing as a flesh-eating ḍākinī with a human woman's body who gave him an experience of unending great bliss. This was a remarkable dream. Ḍākinīs represent a feminine—and unpredictable—principle of enlightenment, and they regularly show up to aid in treasure revelation. But the word is also a euphemism for sexual partner, and sexual yoga is a practice that produces states of meditative bliss. Kongtrul's phrasing almost certainly was intended to communicate that he had intercourse with the ḍākinī who appeared with a woman's body. Kongtrul does not reveal the result of the union. Did he conceive of the knots in his subtle body being loosened so he could experience visions and reveal treasure? Sexual yoga was also done to cure a man's illness or dispel a man's major life obstacles, but Kongtrul does not report any physical troubles in association with the dream; his thirtieth-year illness had already passed, and, in fact, he had fallen ill directly after the first sex dream, although he made no hint of a causal connection. He mentions no particular result or significance for this dream; the night's experience is simply included in a long list of dreams.[28]

Dabzang Tulku went up to the hermitage in late October or early November[29] to assist in the rituals for the nine maṇḍalas of United Intent of the Gurus. They would have used an extensive liturgy deceptively titled Quick Method for Accomplishing the Two Principles of the Maṇḍala Rite, which runs nearly two hundred folio sides. Kongtrul does not record how many days it took them to complete the ceremonies. At the end of the lunar year, in January 1846, he dedicated a month to the approach practice of the deity Kurukullā in the tradition of Karma Chakme. Kurukullā is a late Indian Buddhist deity that is often associated either with Tārā or Hevajra. She is most commonly red, with one face having three eyes and fangs, and with four arms holding hooks and other weapons. She also wears tiger skins and a necklace of freshly severed heads and dances on corpses. Kongtrul later wrote a liturgy for the worship of this deity, which is included in his Collected Works under the title *Iron Hook of Subjugation: A Sādhana and Mending for the Bhagavān Kurukullā*. The time spent on such macabre visualizations, combined with fervent prayers to Gampopa, led Kongtrul to a dream in which he took for himself a gruesome yet highly auspicious blessing. Having come across pieces of Gampopa and Longchenpa's bodies, he took small pieces of each and ate them, saving the rest for later.[30]

Kongtrul then resumed the Jinasāgara practice, beginning the inner sādhana in February 1846. This was not an easy practice, and Kongtrul ascribed several bouts of illness to it. Measles was then spreading through the region, and Kongtrul contracted it immediately following the inner sādhana. On his recovery, he was about to begin the secret sādhana but was afflicted with severe dysentery that brought him close to death. When he regained his health, he performed the remaining ceremonies—including the feasts and other offerings—as best as his resources allowed. He was then required to perform some small ritual on others' behalf—he does not tell us whose—and as a result came down with a throat ailment. Jinasāgara practice, Kongtrul decided, was hazardous.[31]

He brought his three-year retreat to a close with a three-week longevity practice, starting around the beginning of March 1846. The liturgy was Jatson Nyingpo's Vajra of Meteoric Iron Long Life Sādhana, and he performed all three levels: outer, inner, and secret. Following the meditations, he and several students made long-life amulets and pills based on Jatson Nyingpo's instructions.[32] About to reenter the world, Kongtrul would need his strength for the years of service, teaching, and ritual activity ahead.

# PART TWO
# COLLABORATIONS

# 12

# GYARONG AND KUNTRUL

## 1846–1848

Toward the end of Kongtrul's retreat, he received orders from the Ninth Situ to travel in the Gyarong region "for the good of the teachings and the monastery." The expedition had three apparent goals: to help with the administration of Shubha, a Pelpung branch monastery in Gyarong; to pacify or eliminate a rogue Pelpung lama who was causing trouble in Golok; and to solicit donations for the monastery. Gyarong had been a primarily Bon region until a combined Qing-Lhasa expedition in the late eighteenth century had conquered its independent kingdoms and converted many of its institutions to the Geluk tradition. Other Bon monasteries succumbed over the centuries to conversion to other Buddhist traditions. It is not clear from Kongtrul's diary whether this was a prestigious assignment. Kongtrul would spend two years in the Gyarong and Golok regions, both dangerous places, infamous for banditry and other violence. Did Situ send him there because he was skilled, or because he was still relatively low-ranking? Kongtrul would earn high praise for simply returning alive.[1]

In preparation for his departure, Situ gave Kongtrul an entrustment empowerment for Bernakchen, the Kagyu guardian deity that Kongtrul had taken as his personal protector. Kongtrul had already received permission to practice liturgies to the god and had performed the approach practice in 1840; the ceremony at this time was to fortify him with the deity's protection on his journey. Situ also gave Kongtrul a lengthy audience, no doubt outlining the goals of the journey and giving instruction on interacting with the patrons and the public. Situ's staff made all the necessary arrangements for his expedition and supplied all the material goods he would need, such as tents, horses, and porters, as well as religious items. These were not given to Kongtrul but lent, meaning he would need to return or replace them using whatever funds he raised personally. He was gifted with only a few articles of clothing from Situ and from his patrons the Jadra clan. Kongtrul was clearly going out as an employee of the monastery, and he would be responsible for the safe return of its property. This created some anxiety for him, and he was soon complaining about illnesses and negative dreams caused by improper handling of monastic property, a constant concern. Kongtrul would have certainly kept a ledger of donations received, but he did not include any of the information in his diary. They departed Pelpung on July 20, 1846.[2]

The Pelpung delegation—Kongtrul does not tell us how many were with him—traveled east past Dzongsar in the Mesho Valley, on through the Terlung Valley, and then north over a pass to the sacred lake Yilhung Lhatso. They stopped at Zhechen, where Kongtrul visited with Zhechen Wontrul. He records only that he offered prostrations and requested the lama's blessing. Perhaps while on official Pelpung business, traveling with a contingent of Pelpung monks and servants, Kongtrul did not feel comfortable exchanging transmissions with his beloved teacher. After Zhechen they crossed the Dzachu River near Parka. Kongtrul was told that the region had recently suffered flash floods "with surging vermillion-colored water such as had never been seen before." Kongtrul was unsure how to interpret the phenomenon, but he did not consider it to be positive. At Datal they were met by their first official hosts, the ruler of Gyiling, who had come to escort them through Nyikhok to their nomadic encampments in Golok. Kongtrul performed ceremonies and "satisfied the wishes"—a phrase he would use repeatedly—of all the people who gathered to see him, chief among them being the family of the Gyiling chieftain.[3]

Aside from the anxiety over custodianship of monastic property, Kongtrul was otherwise optimistic about the expedition. Protector deities visited him in his dreams for most of the trip. As they passed into the Do region, a central valley of Golok, at Do Rulak he dreamed of a bearded man carrying the tools of a smith who said to him "I have come to escort you. Follow after me while I go ahead." Kongtrul took this to be the local guardian deity, Tangyak the Smith, whose mountain abode they reached the next day. There, a human escort met them, a group of monks in full ceremonial regalia of yellow robes from Yutok Namgyel Ling, a small Karma Kagyu monastery converted from a Bon institution by the Eighth Situ. Kongtrul gave the empowerments and reading transmissions for the six volumes of Jatson Nyingpo treasures to a Lama Tenpel Dodon and otherwise served the monastic community and its patrons. While there he dreamed of a casket in which Bernakchen sat, radiantly smiling and twisting to the right, albeit with a slightly dirty left cheek—a sign of coming trouble.[4]

They stopped next at Dzamtang, a major monastic center of the Jonang tradition that dates back to the fifteenth century. Three main monasteries are there—Choje, Tsangwa, and Tsechu—with multiple smaller centers spread across the valley. This was the community where Lama Karma Wosel Gyurme, for whose teachings Kongtrul had interrupted his retreat for three months in 1843, had received Jonang instructions and transmissions. They were welcomed in high style by the lamas and monks, who staged a formal procession in their honor.[5] Such a procession would involve two lines of monks in yellow ceremonial robes through which the visitor would enter the monastic compounds. The hosts would hold colorful banners and blow conches and various types of horns, alerting all resident humans and gods to the arrival of honored guests. Kongtrul gave the empowerment for Atīśa's Sarvavid Vairocana at Choje and Tsangchung and the empowerment for Guhyasamāja Mañjuvajra at Tsangchen. On his return from Gyarong, he stayed longer and requested several teachings and transmissions, but he received none during this initial stay. Presumably, he was in a hurry to arrive in Gyarong to attend to his official business, and focused as he was on his fundraising endeavors, he would need to act in the capacity as a master, not a disciple. Disciples receive teachings and make offerings; masters give teachings and receive donations.

They finally arrived in Gyarong and were met by an escort from Dzong-gak who was sent by the local chieftain. At Sokmo, then a regional capital, they stayed at a palace named Karsho, where Kongtrul explored an impressive library of Bon texts. He seemed to feel the books were well taken care of; he reported seeing signs that protector deities were watching over them. Between Sokmo and Trochu, they had to cross a pass named Potsolo, where severe weather made the going difficult. They were welcomed warmly on the far side, at a village named Otoda, and then by a procession from their ultimate destination, Shubha Monastery. Kongtrul was installed in the apartment of the monastery's head, Choje Tendzin Dondrub, and remained there for several months.[6]

Major monasteries such as Pelpung often had branch monasteries in neighboring or even far-flung regions. The relationship might have been forged by sharing a common founder or when a larger monastery assumes control of operations at an existing smaller institution. Often they are established by lamas trained at the main monastery whose reputations and activities have grown large enough to build an institution around. Branch monasteries observe the same ritual calendar and liturgical curricula as the primary monastery, and monks and teachers regularly move between them. They are generally financially linked as well, with the branch monasteries funneling donations to the primary one. The many branches of the Kagyu tradition are based around the monasteries established by the traditions' founders. Drigung Kagyu began when Jikten Gonpo established Drigung Monastery; Taklung Kagyu began when Taklung Tangpa Tashi Pel built Taklung Monastery in the twelfth century. The size and strength of the Kagyu branches is a reflection of how many branch monasteries were built—how many students the founders taught and sent out into the world. The so-called Tselpa Kagyu did not grow beyond the original monastery of Tsel Gungtang despite the renown of Zhang Tsondru Drakpa, whereas the Drukpa, Drigung, and Karma Kagyu traditions spread broadly and birthed new monasteries. The relationship between a main monastery and a branch is not always clear; Pelpung was a center to itself and was not a branch of Situ's original monastery, Karma Gon, which functions independently in some ways and also as a branch of both Tsurpu and Pelpung.

Kongtrul investigated a legal complaint against the monastery at Shubha and prepared a petition to the district government in Sokmo. The litigation, regarding some property, was between the monastery's leader, Tendzin Dondrub, and a relation of a powerful regional minister named Daro Takkyab. Despite Kongtrul's best effort, the case was decided in the other party's favor. Kongtrul lost the case, but he laid the blame on the defendant, Tendzin Dondrub, whom he faulted for refusing to abide by earlier agreements. The government's ruling came only after he left Shubha, when he was again in the regional capital at Sokmo. The abbot's lawsuit was only part of the monastery's troubles. It faced financial trouble and needed administrative reorganization. While at Shubha, Kongtrul performed public ceremonies to draw donations and sent some of his own people to collect additional donations for the monastery.[7] As part of his reform efforts, he composed new monastic regulations for the monastery, *Opening the Eye of Discrimination*.

The legal and administrative troubles infiltrated his dreams and his perception of the place, appearing as negative omens in the landscape. The year was ending, so his annual Vajrakīla recitations were timely. He also dedicated a month to an approach practice to Tārā, followed by a week on Kurukullā. All three deities are commonly called on to deflect harm and promote well-being. Positive dreams, such as seeing a splendid statue of Tārā, mixed with the ominous elements. He was visited by an old woman who warned him of coming threats he would face before arriving home safely. He did well to take the warning seriously.[8]

Kongtrul maintained his meditative practices while on the road, spending most of late February 1847 on the sādhana of a Jatson Nyingpo revelation called Avalokiteśvara, the Spontaneous Liberator of the Lower Realms. Kongtrul later composed five liturgies for this cycle for the Treasury of Revelations, including an inner and an outer sādhana. Kongtrul recited the long mantra one hundred thousand times, and he also performed prostrations and maṇḍala offerings. His dreams, populated by various deities, the Twelfth Karmapa, and Rigdzin Tsewang Norbu, were of redemption and protection. The bodhisattvas Ākāśagarbha, Nivāraṇaviṣkambhin, and Kṣitigarbha erased the burden of broken samaya. Twice he escaped hell. In one dream Avalokiteśvara appeared in sexual union with his consort. As he began giving the secret empowerment, the bodhisattva cryptically remarked, "Avalokiteśvara is the master of livestock." The joined deities then transformed into an eight-year-old boy, who told Kongtrul "earlier, when you had obstacles to your longevity, it was the practice of Union of All Rare and Precious Jewels that delivered you. See that you continue to perform the practice."[9]

He wrapped up his activity at Shubha in May or June 1847[10] with a public authorization ceremony and a consecration of a new meeting hall, after which he packed up all the donations he had collected and departed. While crossing again over the Potsolo Pass, Kongtrul dreamed of having a conversation with the two guardian deities of the place. They appeared to him as monk brothers in Mongolian robes. Kongtrul transformed himself into Hayagrīva in the Ratna Lingpa system—the transmission he had received from the Karma Chakme tulku in 1834. With the sword in his right hand he touched their heads and they bowed to him in reverence. He admonished them to maintain the lay vows his dream-self knew that Padmasambhava and the Second Karmapa had each given them, and they swore to do so. Kongtrul asked what their physical emanations were like. They told him, "There are many: including a white man on a black horse, a yellow man on a yellow horse, a red man on a red horse, and a black man on a black horse." On waking, Kongtrul had the impression that these gods were the paternal deities of the Khangsar clan, the clan of his patron, the Old Chieftain Tsepel.[11]

After concluding his work on the court case at Sokmo, the Pelpung contingent continued to Namgyel Monastery in Dzonggak—not to be confused with the Yutok Namgyel Monastery in Golok where they had stopped over the year before and would soon visit again. During a lengthy sojourn there, Kongtrul engaged in an unnamed chanting practice, and he also participated in the feast and mending rite from the United Intent of the Gurus for the offering ceremony of the twenty-fifth day of the lunar month—he does not say which—a day that is auspicious to Cakrasaṃvara and other tantric deities. Kongtrul also practiced the sādhana and made an amulet of enlightened speech from the same cycle.[12]

While still back at Shubha, in addition to dreaming of enemies and other ominous portents, Kongtrul had been told by several fortune-tellers that he would soon face a threat by an adversary equal in status to him. In response, Kongtrul performed rituals in the protective deity temple to dispel the threat. That adversary was Kuntrul—an abbreviation for a title and name that is lost to history. A rogue incarnate Pelpung lama, the origin of his antagonism toward Pelpung is unknown. Gene Smith added Shumidhur to his title in reference to the name of the place where Kongtrul and Kuntrul first encountered each other.[13] For background on the conflict there is only one passage in Kongtrul's diary, which is too ambiguous to even read clearly: "during the legal contest between Kuntrul and / of the House of Khampa [and Pelpung?] the court / monastery chamberlain suddenly decided Kuntrul needed to have a title, causing considerable troubles afterwards."[14] From this fragment we know that the boy had been hastily named at Pelpung in a failed resolution to a conflict. Kongtrul's phrasing makes it unclear who was in conflict with whom, to which side Kuntrul belonged, and which institution's official made the tulku designation. Did the monastery's leaders try to keep the boy against the wishes of his family? Officials at Pelpung could not have forced him to stay at the monastery without their consent, even with a tulku title. If the family—or their feudal lord—wished the boy to go into government service, they could have rejected the title. Perhaps the dispute was something entirely unrelated, and the title was offered as part of a package to end the conflict. Whatever the circumstances, Kuntrul turned out to be a disappointment and a malcontent, and he bore a grudge against Pelpung. Situ seems to have banished him from the monastery, after which he went to live in the Sertar region of Golok where he ingratiated himself with the local chieftain, serving him as chaplain and dreaming of revenge.[15]

One evening, Kongtrul dreamed of the local god Daro Lhagyel who pointed to a mountain in the distance and said that Kuntrul had appeared in a place near the capital of Bhu and was practicing black magic. A few days later they stopped at a place called Shumidhur, on the outskirts of Bhu, where they indeed found Kuntrul with a band of thugs ready to attack. Kuntrul's mischief forced them to remain there for several months. The narrative of the events in Kongtrul's diary is slightly suspicious. He wrote that Kuntrul sent a letter boasting that he had convinced the Bhu chieftain to send men to kill him and that he, Kuntrul, had bribed local townspeople to participate in the plan. It is hard to believe Kuntrul would give away his advantage unless he was hoping for a negotiated settlement and was not, in fact, eager to murder Kongtrul. However, as Kongtrul depicts the episode, Kuntrul's motive was revenge against Pelpung, and as Kongtrul was an official representative of the monastery, he was the target for violence. As a result, Kongtrul and his party chose to lay low. They performed a series of rituals intended to deflect harm, propitiating protective deities such as *ging* spirits and Tārā. Kongtrul never doubted the effectiveness of such activities; his reliance on supernatural forces and the rituals that enlist them was absolute, and he found evidence of success all around him. For example, one day hail fell for hours, but their camp was not harmed. During the delay Kongtrul showed his abilities as a lama; he gave a group of monks from nearby Jonang monasteries the empowerment for the Kālacakra, the instructions for the associated yogic practices called the Six Unions, and empowerments for Vajrabhairava, one of the main tantric buddhas of the second propagation.[16]

Eventually, the Sertar chieftain's militia attacked the Pelpung camp. Kongtrul's companions defended themselves, and two Sertar men were killed. Whether the two came into the camp alone or as part of a larger force we do not know. Kongtrul identified the dead as a man who had sworn to kill him and a nobleman in service to the Sertar chieftain. Their deaths reflected badly on Kuntrul, who had no doubt promised that his ritual acumen would protect the soldiers. How the two men "suddenly died" goes unexplained in Kongtrul's diary, but the implication is that Kongtrul himself was involved and took credit; his statement that "Kuntrul was unable to protect them" reads like the boast of a victor in a deadly contest of black magic. If this was Kongtrul's intentions, then we are supposed to understand that he and his companions did not passively escape harm; they vanquished their enemy. Following the violence, Kongtrul learned from scouts and communications with Dzamtang that the Sertar chieftain had placed the major part of his men in ambush, ready to attack the Pelpung delegation once they set out on the road. These Sertar forces must have outnumbered the Pelpung men, for upon learning of the ambush, most of Kongtrul's companions fled into hiding. With the help of some escorts from the Dzamtang monasteries, including a prominent teacher, Kongtrul and about six other men managed to make it to Dzamtang. There they met Kuntrul. As he was there with only a few men, and Kongtrul was now backed by a large monastic community, Kuntrul was forced to depart. If they exchanged words, they are lost to history. The remainder of Kongtrul's party eventually made their way to the monasteries; none were harmed.[17]

In spite of the violence and the threats on his life, Kongtrul took the opportunity of being at Dzamtang to receive teachings from Ngawang Chopel, the teacher to his Jonang instructor at Pelpung, Lama Karma Wosel Gyurme. Ngawang Chopel gave Kongtrul detailed instructions on the ritual practices of the Six Unions. Dzamtang was the first Jonang monastery that Kongtrul was able to visit, and his time there heightened his commitment to Jonang teachings. From other lamas at Dzamtang, he received instructions on the approach practice for the oral tradition of Vajrabhairava. It was likely during this soujourn at Dzamtang that Kongtrul wrote a short text on "other-emptiness," *Light Rays of the Stainless Vajra Moon*. The text is a synthesis of "other-emptiness" theory with Mahāmudrā, a topic of interest for Kagyu scholars since at least the days of the Third Karmapa. Ngawang Chopel was famous for his "other-emptiness" exegesis, and Kongtrul's composition shows the influence of Jonang teachings.[18]

To shore up his supernatural supporters for his onward journey Kongtrul spent three days worshipping the protective deities of the region at a large temple built by a lama named Peljor Zangpo. In his dreams Kongtrul saw Vajra Pañjaranātha, a form of Mahākāla popular in the Sakya tradition, and the deity Rangjung Gyelmo, a form of Mahākālī, the female Mahākāla and consort to Kongtrul's own protector, Bernakchen. She had four arms, was riding a red mule with a human head strapped behind the saddle, and was about three stories high. The appearance in his dreams of such powerful protectors was a comfort in the face of continuing violence.[19]

A large escort from Do met Kongtrul at Dzamtang and accompanied him to Yutok Namgyel Monastery. This was another safe place, where Kongtrul was able to give and receive teachings while waiting for additional help to proceed to Pelpung. He taught the Third Karmapa's *Profound Inner Principles* for the first time and gave the transmission for the preliminary practices of Mahāmudrā. Kongtrul practiced *Four Sessions of Guru Yoga* by the Eighth Karmapa, Mikyo Dorje, a central practice of the Karma Kagyu tradition, and a related Chod practice. He included the short ritual manual for this practice in the Treasury of Instructions. The Eighth Karmapa visited him in his dreams, accompanied by his colleague the Fourth Drukchen, Pema Karpo. In the dream the Eighth Karmapa recited the entire practice, during which the Fourth Drukchen dissolved into the Karmapa, and the Karmapa transformed into Situ Pema Nyinje, who completed the prayers. Both Padampa Sanggye and Machik Labdron appeared in the sky, and Kongtrul drank from nectar that flowed from Padampa Sanggye's fingers, delighting in its sweetness.[20] Kongtrul wrote at least two texts while there: a one-folio- side praise to the monastery, *Splendid Roar That Completely Vanquishes the Gyelyang Demon*, and a manual for making offerings to local protector deities titled *A Cloud of Pleasures*.

Justifiably concerned about the road ahead, Kongtrul sent a letter to a fortune-teller in Gyiling named Tashi Gyatso to ask which ceremonies he should do to ensure a safe journey. A contingent from the government would be coming to escort him, but he needed ritual aid. The psychic responded that Kongtrul ought to perform an enemy-defeating Mahākāla ritual, and so Kongtrul and four others who had all previously recited the necessary preliminary practices dedicated seven days to doing so. Kongtrul also participated in the end-of-year gutor ceremony, and finished the lunar year with an exorcism rite and a fire offering to the protective deities.[21]

Kongtrul received a message from Kuntrul in February 1848[22] requesting a meeting to discuss their conflict. Both sides in the dispute, Kuntrul's allies from Sertar and Kongtrul and his allies from Do, met at a small valley in Do. After several days of arbitration, the elders of the two factions came to an agreement. Kuntrul was given some horses and gemstones and was satisfied. This ended a conflict that had caused the death of at least two men. Whatever the originating cause of the dispute between Do and Sertar, and between Kuntrul and Pelpung, it had been settled by local tribal council, as was typical of justice in the region, at a cost of a few horses and jewels.[23]

Kongtrul returned to Pelpung via Gyiling and Tsabtsa, a large Karma Kagyu monastery in Lingtsang. At Zhechen he had an audience with Wontrul, to whom he made offerings and was was now able to receive several empowerments, including Guru Chowang's Vajrakīla cycle and Embodiment of the Guru's Secrets. He arrived in Pelpung in March 1848.[24] He handed over all donations that he had collected, returned the monastic property to the administrators, and made a report to Situ. Situ was satisfied with Kongtrul's mixed results. Not a single man in the expedition had lost his life. He had not succeeded in the legal case at Shubha, but he had cleaned up the monastery's administrative issues and he had managed to pacify Kuntrul, who had been menacing Karma Kagyu monasteries in Golok. And presumably he had brought back a respectable amount of offerings. Kongtrul was congratulated by others at Pelpung for surviving the expedition. Kongtrul gave Situ a piece of gold that had been given to him by a lama named Tetsa, and he requested the Kālacakra empowerment and instructions on the Six Unions to place a Kagyu frame around the Jonang teachings he had received. He then went to his hermitage to see his mother and lay his head on his own bed. He celebrated being home by performing an approach practice to Tārā.[25]

# 13

# The Language of Love and Power

*Khyentse, Dabzang, and the King of Derge*

1848–1853

Kongtrul returned from Gyarong with an increased stature and a reputation for successful service. The failure of the lawsuit at Shubha Monastery was not his but belonged to that monastery's leader, Choje Tendzin Dondrub; he made a point of this. Kongtrul dispelled the obstacle caused by Kuntrul, he returned from a perilous land intact, and he proved himself a capable administrator. The result of these victories was that he became a lama in demand; he was someone who could enlist the aid of the guardian deities, vanquish foes, and survive violent attacks. For the rest of his life, he would be called to replicate these deeds for governments, wealthy patrons, and monastic communities. Now age thirty-five, he had also established himself as a holder of many ritual systems critical to the operation of religious and social institutions. In tantric Tibet, where Buddhism was the language of the realm, kings, lamas, and wealthy landowners all required transmissions of the Buddhist teachings; rituals were part of the religious capital for political leaders, and as such these leaders sponsored rituals to benefit their realms and to promote and display their power. Transmission lineages flowed through every social relationship and functioned as a vast network of social connections. The more transmissions a lama could master, the greater his worth to the network. An empowerment linked the giver and the receiver to all who came before and would come after, an endless chain in an endless web of connections. Kings, merchants, and monks all navigated this web, exchanging transmissions and wealth each according to their role and ability.

Transmissions were not easily received and they involved considerable logistical and financial burdens. They also required engagement in the practices; before one could assume authority to pass them on, one had to master them oneself, often at great cost in time and money. The act of transmission included instructions for the system's many rituals and expositions in the underlying doctrines, all of which needed to be comprehended and enacted. Kongtrul's innate curiosity toward all teachings and ritual systems combined with his sympathy for the marginalized and underappreciated and his diligence and willingness to perform countless hours of rituals led him to possess a mastery that was rivaled only by his close friend Khyentse Wangpo. Over the next several decades, their participation in this religious economy would only increase.

There was a cost of the greater employment, to being pressed into service of so many patrons and religious hierarchs and to the continual search for more lineages to join. Kongtrul had few opportunities to spend an extended period of time in meditation retreat, and he was almost constantly on the road. Disciples began to attach themselves to him, and their presence cost money. Later in life he bitterly complained of the demands on his time and the resulting increase in mental agitation and negative emotions that derailed the progress he had made in his meditation. The more he was employed by those in power, the more material wealth he was required to manage, and he blamed the mental stains from this for obstructing his visions and meditative experiences. Kongtrul was driven to pursue his goals and yet compelled to see the material and social support they required as causes of contamination. He delighted in the work but resented the responsibilities, the near-constant summonses from government and patrons and lamas of status. Unless, that is, those summonses came from Dzongsar and his friend Khyentse Wangpo.

When Kongtrul returned from his three-year journey in Gyarong, Jamyang Khyentse Wangpo was in mourning for one of his two elder brothers. Gyurme Dondrub, who had also been a monk, had gone to central Tibet to study, but he had fallen ill and passed away there. The death caused a tear in the fabric of Khyentse's life that his friendship with Kongtrul mended. According to Kongtrul, his own safe return from Gyarong in early 1848 eased Khyentse's grief. He wrote him, in Kongtrul's paraphrasing: "Now that you have come back, I am glad almost to the point of forgetting my grief. I need to come now and receive the complete empowerments for the tantras of the Jonang tradition."[1] The emotional distress is in no way out of place beside a request to bestow a substantial empowerment. Every recorded expression of Kongtrul and Khyentse's friendship is entirely in religious terms. A transmission, particularly one-to-one, between a master and a disciple or between colleagues of equal status was a means of forging and deepening bonds, more precious than a gift of gold or cloth, and far more intimate. Lineal bonds were bonds of affection as much as they were the framework of social structures.

Rituals were a means of being together. Kongtrul's love for Zhechen Wontrul and the Ninth Situ was forged from their care for him, and their bestowal of teachings was how they expressed their love. This is why the first time Kongtrul saw Zhechen Wontrul after leaving Zhechen he both gave and received a transmission. Kongtrul and Khyentse would trade scores of teachings. They did so in service of their interest to preserve and promote the full spectrum of Buddhist traditions in Tibet, but they also did so to express and increase their mutual admiration and affection. Brokenhearted at the death of his elder brother, Khyentse wrote to Kongtrul that he needed the comfort of a friend, using the language that was available: that he simply had to come and receive a transmission.

Kongtrul welcomed Khyentse in the very residence that his patron, Khangsar Tsepel, had constructed at Pelpung, a building known as the Khangsar Monk's House. A sizable group of monks, lamas, and tulkus gathered for the transmission. Kongtrul gave all tantras relating to the Jonang tradition that he had by then received, such as the Kālacakra, relying on the writings of Tāranātha. He also gave the sādhana and the maṇḍala transmissions, instruction on the Six Unions, the seven maṇḍalas of the Ngok tradition according to the manuals written by Karma Chakme, and the blessing ceremonies and instruction for the Six Yogas of Niguma according to the Jonang tradition. The Ngok tradition was a branch of the Kagyu that stemmed from Marpa Lotsāwa's student and Milarepa's fellow student Ngokton Choku Dorje.[2] Khyentse Wangpo would later urge Kongtrul to use this collection to create what was to be the first of his great literary works, the Treasury of Kagyu Tantra.

Kongtrul returned to his hermitage and performed several repetitions of the one hundred feast offerings from United Intent of the Gurus, and, with Dabzang Tulku, he requested and received yet again the complete empowerment for the cycle, this time from Lama Sang-ngak, with whom he and Dabzang had studied the manuals in 1840. Starting some time in September 1848, he spent three months practicing the treasure cycle Profound Path, Jewel of the Mind by Choje Lingpa, which he returned to again for several weeks in February the following year. He composed, most likely at that period, two liturgies for the mendrub and drubchen rituals and a fire offering for the cycle, which are included in his Collected Works, although the cycle is not in the Treasury of Revelations.[3]

Whatever Kongtrul was bringing in by bestowing empowerments he was just as quickly spending on rituals and the upkeep of his hermitage, and in December 1848[4] he ran out of money. He was also in the process of publishing all thirteen volumes of United Intent of the Gurus, something for which he first began fundraising when he was at Tsabtsa Monastery on his return from Gyarong. His disciples, who were also his servants and dependents, encouraged him to make an alms tour, and so, at the end of 1848, he set out, borrowing pack mules and horses from the Jadra clan. Crossing eastward over the gentle Hak Pass, Kongtrul would have descended into the fertile Mesho Valley, with its twisting agricultural land and its river filled with glacial melt from the sacred peak of Dopu Pemajong. Just around a bend in the river, up the valley from where the path reaches the valley floor, is Dzongsar Monastery. Its temples and monastic quarters appear stacked on top of each other high on the southeast face of a ridge that juts out suddenly into the fields of barley. The administrators of Dzongsar Monastery and the Dzongsar regional chieftain both made donations after receiving empowerments and authorizations. This was his first visit to Khyentse Wangpo's monastery, but Khyentse was not there, having traveled to Tibet soon after their second meeting at Pelpung. He was welcomed particularly warmly by the chieftain of Mesho, whose influence paved the way for additional support from other monasteries and villages in the Terlung and Dramtso Valleys, where he performed rituals for monastic and lay communities in exchange for grain and other goods. Kongtrul was back at his hermitage in February to perform his year-end Vajrakīla rituals and continue with his Profound Path, Jewel of the Mind practices.[5]

The Earth Bird Year, from February 23, 1849, to February 12, 1850, was an "obstacle year," for Kongtrul. These are years sharing the same animal sign as one's birth year, in which dangers of illness and death are thought to be particularly acute. The third such year in a man's life is considered the single most astrologically perilous in his life (women have different astrological concerns). Kongtrul dedicated three months of the year to the various longevity practices that were part of his ritual repertoire: the outer sādhana of Gathering of Secrets, called Consummate Profundity, and White Tārā. He was not particularly anxious, and he dreamed of Padmasambhava telling him that his life span was sure to run at least forty-four more years. (He would live another fifty-one.) For meritorious deeds he had the publication of the complete United Intent of the Gurus, a project that had begun in earnest on May 28, 1848,[6] when two scribes began copying out the text in preparation of carving the printing blocks, and now picked up steam in the summer of 1849 with the employment of additional men. This was his first substantial publication, and it required that he compose several liturgies for inclusion as well as attentively edit the text to correct errors.[7] The woodblocks, one rectangular board of hand-carved raised backwards letters for each page, were completed the following year, in the summer of 1850. The final step was to have wooden covers made for each volume, slightly larger than the printed pages, and cloth to wrap each volume tightly. Unfortunately, there is no record of where the production took place or where the blocks were stored. Pelpung had an active printing house, but the only surviving woodblock print of the cycle is from blocks that were reportedly housed at Garje Monastery in southern Derge and which were destroyed in the Cultural Revolution. The cycle was included in the Treasury of Revelations, but new blocks were carved as were blocks for all texts in that collection.

During the autumn of 1849, Kongtrul assisted Situ with the consecration of a new statue, supervising the preparation of the mantras to place inside. Dabzang Tulku and the Fourth Zhechen Rabjam, Garwang Chokyi Gyeltsen, came for the consecration ceremony, which lasted two days. Situ then moved to the Upper Ling section of the monastery where Dabzang resided and gave them transmissions and instructions, after which Situ expressed a desire for a new residence for himself at the meditation center. To raise money for this, Kongtrul set out on yet another alms tour, this time targeting the Dzingkhok Valley. His enduring devotion to Situ trumped any inclination to stay close to home during an astrologically perilous period. To reach Dzingkhok he would have passed through Mesho and the Terlung Valley and then crossed over a small ridge to the south. He returned in late January 1850[8] to perform his Vajrakīla rites at year's end. Kongtrul had successfully avoided the pitfalls of his obstacle year.[9]

Most of 1850 was given over to teaching grammar to young lamas. For three months, from mid-April to mid-June,[10] he taught Candragomin to a group of students that included an unidentified lama named Sotrul. He taught the same subject to the First Gyatrul Rinpoche, Pema Do-ngak Tendzin, over a period of about a year, and medicine and astrology to a lama

Pema Lekdrub. Gyatrul, later the seventh throne holder of Pelyul Monastery, was one of the few grammar students who impressed Kongtrul; Kongtrul eventually gave him a title in honor of his successful studies and taught him multiple other topics. Kongtrul and Situ together with Chime Tulku, a nephew of the Seventh Sanggye Nyenpa, gave Gyatrul his ordination in the summer of 1851. As Kongtrul taught he also wrote, composing the needed ritual manuals for United Intent of the Gurus edition and an "auspicious circle" poem in praise of Padmasambhava at Situ Rinpoche's request, among other things.[11]

Kongtrul also received a number of new teachings in 1850. A Tendzin Tulku from Zurmang Monastery was at Pelpung in early 1850 to give the empowerment for Integration of Means and Wisdom, for which Kongtrul joined. He would have known the liturgies well, not only having already received and practiced them, but he also proofread the printing blocks for it ten years earlier. The tulku gave the transmission for a number of other practices connected to Bernakchen and his consort and the empowerments for Rolpai Dorje's Lake and Rock treasure revelations, which together run about five volumes. Kongtrul in turn taught the Zurmang tulku the Five Books of Maitreya, central Indian Yogācāra scriptures. Later in the year, the head of Nyidzong, a Drigung Kagyu monastery in southwestern Amdo, came to receive the Single Intent teachings from him, which he had received from Lhalung Khewang Tenpel in 1834 at Karma Gon. He finished the year with his usual Vajrakīla rites and a practice for the Shangpa Kagyu protector known as Swift Acting Wisdom Protector, a form of the Six-Armed Mahākāla, which he presumably received from Lama Karma Norbu in 1843; while doing the practice he had a vision of a radiant Karma Norbu in the sky in front of him.[12]

With a growing host of patrons, Kongtrul expanded his annual meditation program to serve their interests. He spent three weeks in early 1850 on Gathering of Secrets under the sponsorship of the Jadra clan. Kongtrul soon added the Sokmo and Nera families of the Mesho Valley to his list of patrons, further evidence of his growing social status.[13] Sponsors of rituals share the merit, and the value is evaluated on the strengths of the agent; the prayers of a prominent lama are worth more than those of a novice. Patrons naturally direct their resources to the men who can offer them a healthy return on their investment, and Kongtrul's services were by now seen as desirable goods. These aristocratic families were already patrons of Khyentse Wangpo, who surely would have been instrumental in making the introduction. In the future, when he was at Dzongsar, he would spend a few days with one of the families performing rituals to promote their prosperity.

Kongtrul's renown also brought him to the attention of the Derge government. He complained in his diary that in 1851 he was ordered multiple times to perform ceremonies at the capital. He may have bemoaned this service for the distraction from his practice, but he was consistently proud of it, noting the value he brought the government and the successful effects of his work. The first call came in the spring of 1851 to bless the birth of a new prince in the family. Kongtrul does not tell us which prince, only that he was a "young" one. Tsewang Dorje Rigdzin, who, if he was still alive, would have been about sixty-five years old, had abdicated back in 1823 after the birth of his last son and had taken robes at the monastery. Damtsik Dorje, born in 1811, was then the nominal head of state. Tsewang Dorje Rigdzin's two younger sons were Tsewang Puntsok Tenkyong, born in 1822, and Tsewang Dorje Dradul, born in 1823. Damtsik Dorje had two sons, Pelden Chime Takpai Dorje and an unnamed younger brother. The prince here was almost certainly Pelden Chime Takpai Dorje, who would later be enthroned as king. His brother was likely born in 1853.[14]

Kongtrul did not record what his orders were in Derge, only that he was summoned to perform a number of ceremonies and that he accomplished them all in proper order. In June 1851[15] Lama Karma Ngedon from Pangpuk Monastery in Litang, with whom he had studied in 1839, passed along a request for Kongtrul to prepare astrological charts for a new prince in Derge, certainly Chime Takpai Dorje. Kongtrul drew the charts using a handbook called *Melodious Rain of White Lapis* and manuals of Chinese astrology. He was then summoned to the capital.[16]

Derge town is laid out at the confluence of two valleys. The royal monastery, Lhundrubteng, also known as Gonchen, is in the smaller east-west valley, the last building before the start of the farmland that rings the base of the surrounding ridge. In Kongtrul's day the royal palace stood to the west of Gonchen, flanked on the other side by the printing house, with the town a short distance below, wrapped around the small Tangtong Gyelpo Temple. The town now edges up against the printing house, and a school stands on the site of the palace. Monastic residences line the valley walls on either side of the monastery and the printing house, which is made of logs and pounded dirt and painted with the grey, red, and white stripes typical of a Sakya monastery. At Lhundrubteng, Kongtrul performed ceremonies to dispel the evil inflicted on the community by earth spirits, to ensure good fortune for the newborn, and to give blessings in the form of empowerments to the royal family.[17]

Kongtrul was back in Derge in the summer of 1852 helping with the construction of a new meditation center at the monastery. This was at the order of a young prince, again unnamed, but in this case it was likely one of Damtsik Dorje's younger brothers. Kongtrul dispelled obstacles caused by earth spirits and performed prosperity rites, and using the religious objects there he practiced the sādhanas of liberation through touch and sight from United Intent of the Gurus. Later in the year, the royal family came to Pelpung to observe ritual dances, and on that occasion Kongtrul gave them three days of empowerments. These included the One Hundred Peaceful and Wrathful Deities, a Vairocana and Amitāyus empowerment for Damtsik Dorje's son, and several authorizations for his younger brothers.[18]

At Pelpung, Dabzang Tulku was then continuing his own building project, begun the year before, in the Upper Ling section of the monastery, and he requested Kongtrul's assistance. Dabzang was an important collaborator and peer of Kongtrul's and a protector of sorts as well, as his status was far more institutionally secure and financially stable than Kongtrul's. Nothing is known of his life save for what is found in the biographies of his colleagues; there appears to be no biography of the man himself. Kongtrul answered all of Dabzang's summonses and willingly participated in any of Dabzang's projects without an expression of complaint. Dabzang seems to have revered Kongtrul, and his requests for Kongtrul's presence were unending. The ardor does not appear to have been fully reciprocated. In Kongtrul's diary Dabzang is only ever simply named Dabzang Tulku. There is interest and collegiality, even some affection, but absent are the expressions of love that surround Khyentse Wangpo. In the late fall of 1851, the two had exchanged several transmissions, with Kongtrul giving Dabzang and his students the reading transmission for Longchenpa's Seven Treasuries and Dabzang giving Kongtrul the empowerments for a Mindroling tradition called Noble Wish Granting Vase. The two then requested Nyingma teachings from a lama named Gonpo Tulku, who in turn requested Jonang transmissions from Kongtrul. Dabzang completed his residence in the middle of 1852, and Kongtrul helped him consecrate it. In return, Dabzang gave Kongtrul the empowerment for the Amitābha practice revealed by Taksham Nuden Dorje.[19]

Khyentse Wangpo had returned from Tibet in early 1852, and Kongtrul sent over a painting of the one hundred mahāsiddhas, a grouping of

Indian tantric saints that is especially venerated in the Kagyu tradition. Khyentse sent back a bronze statue of Vajrakīla that had been revealed as treasure by Kunkyong Lingpa with the message that the statue would be a boon in clearing obstacles to their collaborative work. Several months later, when Kongtrul was in Mesho at the request of the Sokmo clan performing funeral rites for them, he gave Khyentse Wangpo the transmission for Source of Jewels, the Collected Sādhanas of the Jonang Tradition, a collection made by Tāranātha. Khyentse was joined by Donyon Tulku of Katok Monastery and about twenty other monks. Khyentse reciprocated with a set of Tāranātha's Collected Works and a "regent" statue—a statue of Padmasambhava said to be made by the Guru's own hand and concealed as treasure. There are dozens if not hundreds of such statues in Tibet; this one had been revealed by Dorje Lingpa. Kongtrul also requested the empowerment for a Guru Chowang Avalokiteśvara treasure cycle called Stirring the Depths of Saṃsāra. This would become a regular practice for him.[20]

Back at Pelpung, at Situ Rinpoche's request, Kongtrul gave the Six Yogas of Niguma to a group of monks at the meditation center and the blessings of the one hundred mahāsiddhas to a few lamas from Trokyab Monastery in Gyarong at Situ's residence.[21] That Kongtrul was requested by the head of the monastery to give the central Shangpa Kagyu teachings to monks at Pelpung indicates how slight the separation in affiliation really was between Pelpung and his hermitage and between the Karma Kagyu and the Shangpa Kagyu.

Khyentse Wangpo went to Pelpung in late August 1852[22] at Kongtrul and Dabzang's invitation and passed about two months at Dabzang's residence giving a series of empowerments, most of which he had received while training at Mindroling Monastery. The list reveals an impressive breadth of genre and tradition, with teachings from all of the "eight chariots of accomplishment" categories, Kongtrul's favored doxography of Tibetan Buddhism that he would employ in several of his greatest compositions. Kongtrul would pass on most of these teachings numerous times. They began with Nyingma teachings such as *Innermost Heart Drop of the Guru*, Longchenpa's commentary on the Heart Essence of Vimalamitra Dzogchen teachings, and the complete treasure revelations of the Mindroling tradition. Next was the Book of Kadam, which is a collection of teachings of Atīśa and early Kadam masters, and instructions on the Sixteen Drops and other Kadam teachings. Shangpa Kagyu was next; these were the Twenty-five Scriptural

Teachings of Niguma, instructions of various forms of six-armed Mahākāla, and the instructions of Sukhasiddhi, another Indian female contemporary of Niguma who was said to have taught Khyungpo Neljor. Marpa Kagyu teachings consisted of compositions by Dakpo Tashi Namgyel on Mahāmudrā and the Six Yogas of Nāropā. Following these were Zhije teachings of Lochen Dharmaśrī and Chod teachings of Tangtong Gyelpo. The Sakya tradition was represented by Kurukullā instructions and related subtle body and transference practice from the Tsarpa branch. Then more Kadam teachings—Gyelse Tokme Zangpo's *Seven-Point Mind Training*—and finally a blessing for the collected mantras of Guhyasamāja, Cakrasaṃvara, and Vajrabhairava.[23]

Kongtrul reveled in these teachings. He dreamed of meeting Padmasambhava, of finding relics of Tsele Natsok Rangdrol, and of giving empowerments to people while taking the form of Vajravārāhī. He carefully recorded the name of each teaching, grouped by tradition. More and more Kongtrul was coming to the understanding that a fully educated, fully engaged religious practitioner was one who could embrace all the traditions, each according to its own system. In contrast, Kongtrul compared lamas who judged or refused to engage with other traditions to a yak who is afraid of his own tail.[24]

Khyentse was Kongtrul's model of respect for the integrity of the diverse traditions with which they engaged, Buddhist or Bon. As he wrote of him:

> He was forever humble, never arrogant or wrathful in the slightest, ever abiding in the manner of someone who has abandoned everything; he had a singularly amazing expansive mind. The lord condemned no tenet system, practicing them with pure vision and without sectarianism, and without mixing them together.[25]

Kongtrul credited Khyentse with both inspiring him and for saving him from falling onto a narrow sectarian path. Before he began to work with Khyentse, Kongtrul self-deprecatingly wrote in his diary that he had lacked the intellectual ability to carry a wide array of teachings. With Khyentse at his side, an unbiased faith in all the Buddha's teachings grew and he was able to pursue them all without partiality.[26]

Khyentse also gave Kongtrul and the group the empowerments, transmission, and instruction of his recently completed Compendium of Sādhana. This was a fourteen-volume set of Sakya sādhanas that he first began working on when he was staying at Sakya Monastery in the late 1840s. As Kongtrul would do in his own collections, Khyentse composed liturgies for practices where they were lacking, drawing as needed from Kagyu or Geluk traditions. This was the second time that Khyentse had given the transmission, having given it once before in Tsang where he had done the work. It was a primary model for Kongtrul's own scriptural collections. Kongtrul followed Khyentse back to Dzongsar in November 1852[27] to exchange yet more transmissions. Khyentse gave Kongtrul primarily Nyingma teachings, including Dzogchen cycles and the *Guhyagarbha Tantra*—a Nyingma tantra which Kongtrul had not received before—based on his own commentaries and those of Rongdzom Chokyi Zangpo and Yungton Dorje Pelwa, two early Nyingma exegetes. Khyentse had received these Dzogchen transmissions during his time at Mindroling. Afterward, Khyentse journeyed again to Tibet and Kongtrul returned to Pelpung.[28]

In response to a summons by a prince of Derge, Kongtrul returned to Gonchen in January 1853 to consecrate the new meditation center and dispel obstacles. At that time, Kongtrul performed seven days of a Vajrakīla rite and a "liberation on sight" sādhana from United Intent of the Gurus to consecrate the objects. He was not the leader of the consecration ritual, however. This fell to a lama named Dzipu Khenpo, of whom Kongtrul appears to have had a low opinion; he reports that there were disturbing signs when Dzipu performed the rite.[29]

On returning home in February 1853,[30] Wontrul Rinpoche taught him how to perform the annual vase ceremony using a liturgy from Ratna Lingpa's Gathering of Secrets. The vase ceremony was a major community event at Pelpung, and Kongtrul would be enlisted to participate for decades. The ritual involves the consecration of a vase and pills through the combined efforts of the monastic community and the population of the surrounding villagers, who collectively chant mantras and then receive the blessings. During the training and the performance the next month, Kongtrul composed a lengthy manual for just such a public ritual, *Lion's Roar of Brahmā*. At the start of the Water Ox Year, Kongtrul and Dabzang led the ceremony, acting as "vajra king" and "regent," respectively. If he was nervous about this first performance of an important public ritual in front of a large crowd, he felt confident that he did well; all signs, he reported, pointed to its success. He spent the spring on the longevity practices of Drubpai Gyelmo, a twelfth-century Indian female saint who was a teacher to Rechungpa. He did so at the behest of some patrons, performing the entire cycle from the preliminary practices up through the development stage.[31] He was now a leading lama in his monastery and in his region.

# 14

# PAST LIVES REVEALED, THE DEATH OF SITU, AND THE ORIGIN OF THE TREASURY OF KAGYU TANTRA

## 1853–1855

When Jamgon Kongtrul had given the transmission for the Ngok maṇḍala in 1848, Jamyang Khyentse Wangpo had decided that the manuals by Karma Chakme that Kongtrul had used were in need of being replaced.[1] Khyentse had gone to Tibet after the transmission and remained there for three years. According to Kongtrul, while in Tibet Khyentse had decided that Kongtrul should take on the project of writing new manuals and he had several experiences to confirm this. First, while visiting the seat of the Ngok tradition, Zhung Treshing, Khyentse had received a prophecy that Kongtrul was the right person to write out the Ngok maṇḍalas. Soon after, while visiting Zhalu, an ancient Sakya monastery in the Tsang region of central Tibet, a lama Khyentse only identified as Choktrul had told Khyentse that he had been tasked by a teacher of his, a hermit who was said to be a reincarnation of Marpa himself, to find someone to compose manuals for the tantric teachings of Marpa. Choktrul had been unable to find a disciple capable of accomplishing the project, and he asked Khyentse to assign someone. Khyentse thus wrote to Kongtrul from Tibet: "Although the power of the lineage of the Ngok tantras is intact, the manuals written by Karma Chakme are insufficient for performing the rituals. You must compose a set of manuals that gives instructions for each of these rites."[2] Kongtrul also relates that, upon his return, Khyentse spoke to Dabzang and the Fourth Zhechen Rabjam about the project, and they also urged Kongtrul to undertake it. Now, in 1853, Khyentse again pressed Kongtrul on the subject.[3]

By tracing the inception of this monumental project back to the instigation of a reincarnation of Marpa, and having other lamas also insist on his taking up the task, Kongtrul was almost certainly protecting himself from potential accusations of hubris. The task was not a small one; he would need to write instructions pertaining to the rituals for thirteen separate mandalas—there are over a hundred separate liturgical texts in the six volumes of the completed work. Yet this is the work that Kongtrul delighted in: he would be able to revise the entire corpus of Kagyu tantric literature, establishing new standards for generations. It also provided an opportunity for him to establish some needed credentials. In his narrative of the birth of the project, Kongtrul pleads, somewhat disingenuously, his lack of qualifications: "I did not know of the quality of my previous or future incarnations or the strength of my aspirations; this task might be harmful to my life span, possibly blocking my progress to liberation, or even detrimental to Buddhism. I therefore had put it off. Now that it was unavoidable, I needed to muster my resolve."[4] This set forth a flurry of exchanges in which "the quality" of his previous lives were charted in order to establish his right to take on the project, which he named the Treasury of Kagyu Tantra at the end of the summer of 1854.

Although Tibetans, like most residents of a Buddhist-dominant society, took reincarnation for granted, few would have the audacity to question who they were in a previous life, much less consider that they were anyone of importance; an anonymous Indian from ancient times maybe, but not a famous lama. While Kongtrul was already a titled incarnation, the originating life—Kongpo Bamteng Tulku, a student of the Eighth Situ— brought little esteem and no resources to Kongtrul.[5] He felt the need for a much larger corpus of past lives to underwrite his growing authority. Narratives of a person's past lives belonged to a genre restricted to the highest of Tibetan lamas, as only those of considerable accomplishment or potential would have the social status to claim the mantle of the saints of the past. In the *Mirage of Nectar*, Kongtrul filled several pages at the start dissembling about how he would never have thought to assert such things but for the assurances of the Ninth Situ, the Fourteenth Karmapa, Khyentse Wangpo, and Dabzang Tulku.[6] A lama's record of past lives was always a collaborative effort, constructed by the subject's teachers, disciples, and colleagues to bolster prestige and affirm credentials. Kongtrul was by no means a passive beneficiary of the process; as he made clear in his diary, he initiated the process by requesting Dabzang and Khyentse to investigate his past lives for him.

Dabzang Tulku received the first of Kongtrul's requests to examine his past lives. To prepare an answer, Dabzang set aside his Jinasāgara practice and took up a three-week practice from Ratna Lingpa's Gathering of Secrets.

As he was assembling the substances needed for the investigation and was about to proceed (Kongtrul does not tell us of his method), Dabzang had three dreams that were significant for Kongtrul. In the first, Dabzang was reading a biography in which the subject's past lives were discussed and came to the passage "He will be supreme among the line of these fourteen lives." The passage was annotated with the words "this is important." Dabzang next dreamed of seeing a square field in which four figures of Padmasambhava each stood in one of the cardinal directions holding a plow. In the four intermediate points, four women stood holding sacks of grain. All around a large crowd had gathered, and Dabzang asked a girl what was happening. She told him "This is Rigdzin Terdak Lingpa founding Mindroling Monastery. He has blessed the earth by meditating on Padmasambhava for a week." At this point Dabzang was convinced that Kongtrul was the reincarnation of Terdak Lingpa, who was known to have fourteen famous previous lives. A third dream expresses the esteem in which Dabzang held Kongtrul: he found Kongtrul at the top of a high tower on the peak of a mountain gazing at the sky and writing with his finger in the air. In reference to the third dream, Kongtrul explained to Dabzang that whenever he composed something, he always consulted the gods before he put pen to paper.[7]

The association with Terdak Lingpa appealed to Kongtrul. Many of his personal practices were in the Mindroling tradition, and the man was an attractive model for Kongtrul's own life. Terdak Lingpa was a prolific treasure revealer and institution builder and he had, at least as described by Kongtrul, an ecumenical approach to the Buddhist teachings. In the short biography Kongtrul composed of Terdak Lingpa in his account of his own past lives, Kongtrul praises him for "revitalizing the teachings of minor lineages such as the Jonang, Shangpa Kagyu, Zhije, Chod, and Bodong," and as a prolific author of scores of ritual manuals for his own and other masters' revelations. Moreover, Terdak Lingpa came with an already-established line of prior births—including the fourteen most recent and most prominent—from Indian saints through the likes of Padmasambhava's disciple Vairocana, Sakya Paṇḍita, Longchenpa, and Tāranātha.[8] Kongtrul had his own dreams of being the next in line after Terdak Lingpa, although by the conventions of humility he had to present the matter as "unresolved."[9]

Kongtrul then turned to Khyentse, who first assured him by relating a vision he had of the Sanskrit word *udaya*. Udaya translates as "rising" and "flourishing," and Khyentse took it to be a sign that Kongtrul's writings would clearly explain the teachings and have wide appeal. Khyentse next had a dream involving figures crucial to the restoration of Buddhism following the so-called dark period when Buddhism lost Tibetan imperial support. In it he went into his residence and found a book on his shrine. An unidentified person told him that it was an account of Yonten Gyatso's past lives. Thinking he ought to examine it closely, he opened it to the back and found that it was a biography of Lume Tsultrim Sherab. "That's not Yonten Gyatso—that's Lume!" someone, possibly Khyentse, exclaimed. "They are one and the same" came a reply. Khyentse read on, through Lume's past lives. Among them were the monk Vairocana, including an account of how he caused the Tibetan queen Margyenma to come down with leprosy, a story which would become significant several years later.[10] Lume was the leader of the ten men from central Tibet who went to Amdo in the eleventh century to restore monastic ordination. On their return they went to Samye and were offered its keys and returned the monastery to its magnificence. According to legend, Lume declined to take responsibility for the treasury, however, a detail Kongtrul includes in his sketch of him in *Mirage of Nectar*, where he has Lume state that it would be "unacceptable for him to be contaminated by taking possession of the place"—a clear echo of Kongtrul's lifelong concern with the appearance of financial impropriety. All the same, Lume accepted responsibility for restoring the monastery and sent disciples to establish religious institutions across Tibet and fill their libraries with books. The appeal to Kongtrul was obvious.[11]

Khyentse had an additional dream, which he related in extensive detail, pointing to yet another of Kongtrul's past lives. In it he was traveling with attendants to the Zabbulung Valley in central Tibet. At a town called Neda, they stopped over at a home where Khyentse was treated with proper esteem. When asked where they were going, they replied, "To Zabbulung, the valley of treasures." Rain started and Khyentse's companions became concerned, but he eased their anxieties and they soon reached a nomadic encampment about halfway up the valley, where everyone came running to receive Khyentse's blessing. The people told them they still had far to go, so Khyentse and his attendants stayed with the nomads for the night. Their hosts told them that at sunrise a lama would come, one who was extremely strict about cleanliness. Khyentse therefore told his monks to be mindful of this and spent the evening meditating. In the morning, they continued on and arrived at a place known as Deshek Dupai Podrang, the Palace Where the Sugatas Gather. Kongtrul would later use this same name for his second hermitage above the Dzinkhok Valley. Aside a boulder, as though protecting himself from rain, sat Trengpo Terton Sherab Wozer, a stout yogi with a topknot, wearing monastic robes and a few tantric ornaments. The yogi said, "How auspicious that you have come! Let us go reveal treasure!" With great joy Khyentse went to the boulder out of which they removed a scroll of paper. Suddenly, the yogi transformed into Kongtrul, who said, "you are the custodian of this yellow scroll, so I will now give you the transmission." Kongtrul read the scroll aloud; it seemed to him to be a section of Trengpo Terton's chief revelation, the Sphere of Liberation, dealing with increasing wisdom and obtaining perfect memory.[12]

Trengpo Terton brought several key figures into Kongtrul's chain of lives, including another link to Vairocana the translator: Khyungpo Neljor, the founder of the Shangpa Kagyu; Lama Zhang Yudrakpa, who started the Tselpa Kagyu tradition; and the great translator Rinchen Zangpo. The man himself was apparently not so vital, as Kongtrul neglected to include a sketch of his life in *Mirage of Nectar*. His entry in *One Hundred Treasure Revealers*, a masterpiece written in 1886 that fills half of the first volume of the Treasury of Revelations, is only four folio sides long. This was apparently enough to bring his previous lives into Kongtrul's chain of incarnations. With these three carefully chosen past lives—Terdak Lingpa, Lume, and Trengpo Terton—Kongtrul now had dozens of famous men behind him and his Kagyu tantras project.[13]

In the midst of the attention to Kongtrul's past lives a tragedy befell Kongtrul in his current life: Situ Rinpoche passed away. The great lama had fallen ill in late May or early June 1853 and breathed his last on June 13th or 14th.[14] In one of their final meetings, Situ had filled a fine jade bowl with food and offered it to Kongtrul, an act that Kongtrul later interpreted as a transmission of blessing. Situ knew he was dying and he dictated his will to Dabzang Tulku and Wontrul; Kongtrul was a devoted disciple, but he was all the same lower in status than his two colleagues and was not brought into close quarters in Situ's final days. His colleagues summoned him the day after Situ's passing to serve as scribe as they repeated Situ's instructions for his funeral, and Kongtrul, recognized for his administrative skill, was charged with drafting the needed documents. The funeral ceremony was performed at the Lhasar Temple of the meditation center with a liturgy from Heart Essence of Vajrasattva, a revelation of Taksham Nuden Dorje. Lhasar, where Situ had long resided, was the site of the Eighth Situ's reliquary and Pema Nyinje's would be installed there beside it. On the twenty-first day following the death, Kongtrul, Lama Sang-ngak, and a group of other monks performed the mending rite from United Intent of the Gurus at Lhasar.[15]

Kongtrul remembered Situ as the future buddha Maitreya in person, a man whose physical presence was commanding, and whose teaching was so potent that, Kongtrul relates, he once had a meditative experience known as the "unity of bliss and emptiness" while listening to him preach. The death caused a significant rift in the community and, Kongtrul relates, in the surrounding landscape: on the day of his passing there were tremors as though an earthquake struck. Kongtrul visited his dead master in his dreams, seeing him radiant, sitting on a throne near a lake surrounded by snow mountains. He took this to be a sign of Situ's rebirth by the shores of Lake Namtso in central Tibet. He now reconceived of his tantra compendium project as a memorial to the Ninth Situ. Dabzang and Wontrul had earlier both urged him to expand the work to include other tantric systems taught by Marpa; Wontrul told him that since Situ "was widely considered a reincarnation of Marpa, whose main deities were Hevajra and Guhyasamāja, these rites cannot be omitted" from the project. Thus, while the Ngok maṇḍala remained the core of the collection, the work expanded to include additional tantric systems "with the principal intention of commemorating" the Ninth Tai Situ.[16]

Kongtrul began with the *Hevajra Tantra* sādhana and maṇḍala rituals. Situ had owned books on the subject by Trukhang Lotsāwa Sonam Gyatso and Rinchen Zangpo, but as the oral transmission line for these had been lost, Kongtrul, following common custom, could not use them. Tibetans take lineage seriously, enough to exclude a tradition if no one could be located who had received the transmission from a lineage holder. Once interrupted, the line was lost, unless, that is, someone received the transmission in a vision, something Khyentse Wangpo was particularly skilled at doing. At least in the Nyingma tradition, a desired teaching was rarely, if ever, actually abandoned. Here Kongtrul probably preferred to work with other texts. He chose a manual by the Fourth Zhamar, Chodrak Yeshe, and several by Tāranātha that "were like cast gold." Fortunately, at the end of the forty-nine day mourning period, the Sixth Traleb Rinpoche came to Pelpung and was able to give Kongtrul the transmission for the Fourth Zhamar's manual. The texts by the Fourth Zhamar and Tāranātha thus served as the core of his project; any Tāranātha transmissions Kongtrul was lacking he would receive several months later from Lama Karma Wosel Gyurme.[17]

In September 1853[18] Situ's reliquary was complete, and the salt that had been used to preserve the body until cremation and the top of his skull which had survived the fire intact were placed inside. For two days Kongtrul and others consecrated the tomb using the rituals of the Vimalaraśmi and Vimaloṣṇīṣa, two early Indian Tantric systems commonly used in the consecration of stūpas. Dabzang had left for Karma Gon by this point, and Kongtrul soon left for the Terlung Valley to spend several months in retreat in a cave named Dagam Wangpuk, on the side of a mountain there called Riwo Wangzhu. Kongtrul does not record what inspired him to go, only that conditions were ripe for him to practice there and to compose a gazetteer for the region, although no such composition exists in his Collected Works. Not having an especially high rank at this point, and now bereft of his primary champion at the monastery, Kongtrul may have decided to remove himself from Pelpung during this period of inevitable power struggle so as to avoid those unnamed monks who objected to his actvities. He was joined at the cave by several more companionable monks, and together they performed his customary year-end Vajrakīla and other rites, to which he had added the Six-Armed Mahākāla from the Shangpa Kagyu tradition. After this he spent a period practicing the mending rite of United Intent of the Gurus.[19]

Back at Pelpung in April 1854,[20] Kongtrul joined Wontrul in leading the monastery's vase consecration ceremony. A monk in the assembly came down with measles, but as no one else became infected, Kongtrul diagnosed the case as having been brought on by the force of the ritual, certain practices being thought to stir up karmic propensities that otherwise lay dormant. The monk, it seems, due to past deeds, was destined to contract measles. Following the ceremony Wontrul and the others went to Alo Peljor, a Karma Kagyu monastery on the route between Pelpung and Derge, while Kongtrul went to the monastery meditation center and received additional Tāranātha transmissions from Lama Karma Wosel Gyurme. These included some Kālacakra, Hevajra, Cakrasaṃvara, and Yamāntaka transmissions. Kongtrul offered him a payment, "as much as was necessary," for the services. On May 1, 1854,[21] he presided over a large public performance of a White Tārā ritual, the liturgy for which he had recently arranged. Over the next few months, he dropped in and out of the ceremonies commemorating Situ, such as the ones for Hevajra—for which he served as vajra master—Guhyasamāja, and Mahāmāya. In the Lhasar Temple, he joined a seven-day United Intent of the Gurus mending rite with twelve other monks and also attended ceremonies venerating the Peaceful and Wrathful Deities in the tradition of Jatson Nyingpo. Since Dabzang was at Karma Gon, Kongtrul also had to instruct the residents of the retreat center on their rituals. He then returned to his hermitage.[22]

Kongtrul continued to expand his corpus of past lives. In a dream that spring, he was Rigdzin Tsewang Norbu serving Tāranātha, who was preparing to grant him a major empowerment. Kongtrul took this to be an indication that he was the rebirth of Tāranātha's close disciple Yeshe Gyatso, whom Tsewang Norbu had claimed as a past life. As he developed this theory in later years, he would assert that Tāranātha and Yeshe Gyatso had identical realization and were part of the same mind, thereby allowing him to further claim to be virtually identical to Tāranātha.[23]

In the summer of 1854, Kongtrul continued to work on the Kagyu tantra project, his efforts now part of the memorial services for his guru. In June[24] he gave the Hevajra empowerments and taught several of the tantras that make up the collection—including the Hevajra, Mahāmāya, and Guhyasamāja—to the Pelpung community. Up at his hermitage, he composed liturgies for the sādhana, maṇḍala, fire, and other rituals along with instructions for the completion stage practices, authorization rites, and propitiation to the guardian deities. The Ngok maṇḍala forms the core of the compilation, to which he added six additional systems. The six volumes of the completed collection were divided into two traditional categories: "father tantra" and "mother tantra." Father tantras are generally said to emphasize the subtle body and the secret empowerment. Mother tantras, also known as yoginī tantras, are said to emphasize wisdom. In the mother section are Hevajra, Cakrasaṃvara, Mahāmāya, Vajracatuḥpīṭha, and Buddhakapāla. The father section has Guhyasamāja, *Mañjuśrīnāmasamgīti*, Yamāntaka and Vajrabhairava, and Vajrapāṇi. He also included liturgies, both old and newly composed, for Vajrasattva, Green Tārā, and other deities, and several Nyingma/Sakya tantric traditions as well: Vajrakīla, Samyak, Yamāntaka, and Vajravidāraṇa. Only at this point, in the late summer of 1854, did Kongtrul give it the name by which it is known: Treasury of Kagyu Tantra.[25]

A series of dreams of the Kagyu patriarchs and deities that occurred soon after the completion of the Treasury of Kagyu Tantra reflect his pleasure with the work, although curiously, the Ninth Situ, to whom he was now dedicating the work, was not among his nocturnal visitors. The following year Kongtrul performed one hundred offerings to the deity Dhūmāvatī, investing her as the protector of the collection.[26] Although Kongtrul considered it complete, he would continue to work on it for decades, adding liturgies and instructions right up through to the 1880s. In 1870 he would compose commentaries on three works of the Third Karmapa, Rangjung Dorje, which he had been studying for many years: *Profound Inner Principles*, *Treatise Distinguishing Ordinary Consciousness from Primordial Awareness*, and *Treatise on Buddha-Nature*, and he added these to the collection. He gave the complete empowerments of the collection seven times. Unfortunately, he did not record when the blocks were carved. Five volumes were prepared at some point at Pelpung, and an expanded edition of eight volumes was published by Dilgo Khyentse in Bhutan in 1982.

In the midst of compiling the Treasury of Kagyu Tantra, while he was teaching at the summer retreat center, Kongtrul wrote a short guide to Lojong, or mind training. The book, *An Easy Introduction for the Challenged*, is a short explication on *Seven-Point Mind Training*, a Kadam teaching by Chekhawa Yeshe Dorje that is practiced in all Buddhist traditions in Tibet. On the evening he began writing, he dreamed he ate a piece of Vairocana's heart that had been revealed as treasure by the Katok lama Rigdzin Dudul Dorje and distributed pieces to others to their delight. It would seem that in the pursuit of his past lives he found himself ingesting his own body, a perfect metaphor for taking ownership of the earlier men's identities. Kongtrul's composition also proved to be appealing to students, and he later included it in his Treasury of Instructions. Two disciples named Karma Tutob and Karma Tabkhe Namdrol requested the composition; neither of these men are mentioned elsewhere. Kongtrul also mentions that a Lama Karma Ngedon urged him to write, and while this was likely Dabzang Tulku, it could have been one of three men in his life who shared that name.[27]

In the wake of Situ's death, Kongtrul turned even more to Khyentse Wangpo, to whom he began referring as his "precious omniscient guru." In late October or early November 1854,[28] Kongtrul went to Dzongsar to meet with him. Khyentse gave him over a dozen empowerments, including the Sakya tradition of Vakrakīla—in the form of Vajravidāraṇa—to help with an eye ailment that was troubling him that year and a treasure of Tashi Tobgyel called United Families of the Three Kāyas. Khyentse's student Ngawang Lekdrub was there from Ngor, and from the two of them Kongtrul received several additional empowerments. Kongtrul reciprocated with Guru Chowang's Embodiment of the Guru's Secrets revelation, which he had received from Wontrul in February 1848. During his time at Dzongsar,

Kongtrul met with Situ in a dream. Situ gave him the full transmission of all his compositions and ordained him as their trustee. Situ had now given him everything and Kongtrul was free to move on.[29]

After the visit, Kongtrul responded to invitations from his patrons in Mesho—the Sokmo and Puma families—and raised funds there and in the Terlung Valley. He then returned to his hermitage to perform his annual Vajrakīla rites. Khyentse had instructed him to add the sixty-deity mandala of Vajrabhairava to his annual program. During this practice, Kongtrul dreamed he was Hayagrīva obliterating *gyelpo* demons and that he subjugated three women he assumed were *senmo* demons. The three surrendered to him their "life-force syllables"—*ni na ra ra hūm ra*—and he named them Dorje Pelmo Tsel, Dorje Wangdrub Tsel, and Dorje Yeshe Tsel.[30]

While in Mesho or Terlung, Kongtrul had another dream that pointed to yet another past life. This time he was visited by Tangtong Gyelpo, stout and radiant, alongside another yogi. Kongtrul prostrated to the two of them, at which point Tangtong Gyelpo began to tell him about his past lives: "In the past, when Padmasambhava was giving United Intent of the Gurus at the meditation spot at Samye Chimpu, you were Ngenlam Gyelwa Chokyang, whose secret name was Pelgyi Nyingpo Lodro Drime Tsel. I was your assistant Lhabu Donyo De." Tangtong Gyelpo went on to explain that the two of them had been connected in all lifetimes since, and he described how in each of those lifetimes Kongtrul had as part of his name the words *pel*, meaning "glorious" or "auspicious" and *lodro*, meaning "intelligence." The dream was as much an expression of the bond between Kongtrul and Khyentse as it was part of the development of Kongtrul's narrative of past lives; Khyentse Wangpo was, Kongtrul reports, an emanation of Tangtong Gyelpo. The two had been together for hundreds of lifetimes.[31]

To visit with Khyentse Wangpo, particularly at an emotionally trying time after the loss of his guru, was, for Kongtrul, to be inspired. He departed Dzongsar with a renewed dedication to the ecumenical approach he so aspired to embody. He felt his biases and attachments to tradition had softened. He was humbled by Khyentse's example, seeing in him the perfect exemplar of all that he valued, to the point of feeling a sort of ecstatic reverence. With Situ gone, Khyentse would become more than a friend, he would become Kongtrul's "lord guru" and "precious omniscient lord." Perhaps wary of appearances, he included two passages from Indian scripture to support his growing devotion of Khyentse. From the Vinaya: "Rely on worthy people like a vine clings to a sāla tree and you will be embraced by the glory of their excellence." The second, from the *Sūtra on the Questions of the King of the Nāgas*, reads:

> O King of the Nāgas, there are two actions that for a bodhisattva are the work of Māra, the devil. What are they? Not revering the guru, and boasting of oneself in arrogance. The bodhisattva completely abandons these two acts of Māra.[32]

Kongtrul observed both clauses of the second admonition. He could not be accused of boasting of his grand project, for, he maintained, it was not his idea and he resisted taking it on. His colleagues celebrated his illustrious past lives; he had only asked them to check to make sure he had the necessary merit to accept the commission. He certainly could not be accused of not revering his guru. He dedicated the work to Situ Pema Nyinje, and he adored Khyentse Wangpo; it would be a sin to feel anything less.

# 15

# CHOKGYUR LINGPA

## 1853–1855

Soon after the Ninth Situ passed away, Kongtrul began to experience trouble with his eyes. It became so severe that he woke one morning to find that he could not open his eyelids. His speech, he reported, was slurred, and his mind dulled. For seven days Kongtrul practiced an Avalokiteśvara revelation of Nyangrel Nyima Wozer for clearing up one's vision. He had some improvement after the end of the week, apparently thinking enough of the practice to later include it in the Treasury of Revelations. But the relief was only temporary, and for the next few years he would relapse. At times he was unable to look at bright light, and the pain would be such that he would wrap his eyes in dark cloth for several days. Kongtrul initially ascribed the cause to the influence of nāgas.[1] His recent identification as a reincarnation of the eighth-century Tibetan monk named Vairocana, however, offered the potential for yet another diagnosis. In early 1853 an enterprising and charismatic young man from Nangchen had arrived in Derge to establish his credentials. Kongtrul had been drawn to him, yet wary, and he made the young man wait two years before he and Khyentse Wangpo invested him with the name Chokgyur Lingpa and the authority to promote his revelations. Once suitably empowered, the brilliant treasure revealer would take credit for curing Kongtrul of his disease.

Chokgyur Lingpa slipped into Pelpung in February 1853, noticed by hardly anyone. No one even seems to have remembered his actual name—Kongtrul records it as Norbu Tendzin in the *One Hundred Treasure Revealers*, while most biographies of him have it as Konchok Tendzin.[2] Chokgyur Lingpa was born in the Nangchen region, to the northwest of Derge, in 1829, on either July 11th or November 6th.[3] His family's clan name was Kyasu. He entered the Taklung Kagyu monastery of Pelme as a young man and was given his novice vows by the Eighth Pawo, Tsukla Chokyi Gyelpo—no doubt in a group ceremony—but he soon moved to the Drukpa Kagyu monastery in the capital of the kingdom, Nangchen Gar. He claims to have begun having visions at age thirteen, and at Nangchen Gar he announced to his monastic community that he would soon reveal treasure, something his teachers denied him permission to do. This earned him the nickname by which Kongtrul first knew him—Kyater, short for Kyasu Terton. The epithet has the tone of "the so-called treasure revealer of the Kyasu clan." Treasure revealers who have earned legitimacy are given proper names.[4]

The life of a treasure revealer in traditional Tibet does not appear to have been an easy one. While the vocation brought renown to those who succeeded, it also engendered scorn and suspicion—the accusation of fraud and vanity was never far behind any mystic. It is a career option available to the uneducated, untrained, and unaligned, to charismatic men and women who lacked access or the inclination to join the monastic institutions of Tibet. Treasure revealers are said to be called by the Guru, forced by destiny rather than setting out on the path by their own volition. Their ambition always should, in theory, be sublimated to the service of religion. Chokgyur Lingpa's relentless pursuit of legitimacy through the affirmation and acceptance of Kongtrul and Khyentse was by no means the only venue for success; other revealers might gather disciples around them through the force of their charisma and build enduring communities at fixed locations with grand temples, as happened with the great Nyingma monasteries of Mindroling and Dorje Drak. By partnering with Kongtrul and Khyentse, however, Chokgyur Lingpa gained not only credibility but access to two men who would be able to translate his inspiration into some of the most beloved Tibetan liturgical literature of recent centuries. Although he would eventually establish two small communities of his own, his collaboration with the two young Kagyu and Sakya lamas ensured that his treasures would be prized by the widest possible audience.

In his early twenties Chokgyur Lingpa took a consort, a woman named Dechen Chodron, with whom he had two children. Both may have been born before he arrived at Pelpung, if not soon after. Tibetan hagiographical literature about men rarely includes information about wives and children, so unfortunately there is little information about her other than that she was the sister of one of Chokgyur Lingpa's main disciples, Barwai Dorje. Tulku Urgyen Rinpoche's grandmother described "Degah," as she was known, as a fierce lady, fond of an occasional drink, and able to hold her own against Chokgyur Lingpa.[5] He also adds that Khyentse Wangpo treated her with considerable respect. It is not known for certain when their relationship began or when their two children were born. Kongtrul mentions her only in the colophon to his *Auspiciously Curling Tune*.[6] She was a practitioner who remained part of the community well past Chokgyur Lingpa's death and lived at least until 1874 when she requested Kongtrul compose his famous *Light of Wisdom*, his commentary on Chokling's treasure called *Stages of the Path of the Wisdom Essence*.[7]

Another woman, a niece of Jamyang Khyentse Wangpo, became Chokgyur Lingpa's partner and gave birth to a third child. Although her name is nowhere recorded in Chokgyur Lingpa's considerable biographical material, there is good reason to think she was named Tsultrim Pelmo, a woman from Drachen.[8] Kongtrul devotes considerable space to a description of her funeral, which he did only for relatives or people dear to him. He described her as a woman of faith, skilled at drawing and reciting, and as someone who experienced visions of deities such as Amitābha and completed the preliminary practices of Union of All Rare and Precious Jewels. He added that she served Chokgyur Lingpa as a sexual consort at times, when he was sanctifying new treasure sites and during feast offerings. When she fell ill—a result of a broken samaya—Kongtrul attempted unsuccessfully to cure her through rituals and recitations. After her death he dedicated his practice to her once a week for seven weeks, at significant points in her journey through the bardo, and he added practices to his ritual calendar to benefit her. Kongtrul dreamed of her, gaining confidence that he had helped her perceive reality while in the bardo and that he had helped her gain entrance to the Palace of Lotus Light, Padmasambhava's residence in his pure land. Khyentse later had a vision in which a ḍākinī told him that because of the samaya infraction Tsultrim Pelmo had initially been reborn as a low woman in a charnel ground—legendary places in India where corpses were discarded and tantric magicians gathered to display their skills. Due to Kongtrul's interventions, he explained, she had then gone to a pure land, with greatly reduced obscurations and advances on the path to liberation. Khyentse Wangpo had an additional vision about her subsequent lives. All of this befits a person of status, either aristocrat, revered lama, or relative.[9]

Chokgyur Lingpa had three children with his two consorts. Degah gave birth to his first son, known as Wangchuk Dorje and Tsewang Drakpa, who died at the age of twenty-seven. Dechen also gave birth to a daughter named Konchok Peldron, who lived into her seventies and had four sons of her own, all of whom taught their grandfather's revelations (Konchok Peldron's fourth son was the reincarnation of her brother Wangchuk Dorje).

Chokling's second son, the child of his second consort, was Tsewang Norbu who, like all of Chokling's descendants, became a member of the practitioner communities he founded.[10]

Although some accounts of his life claim that Chokgyur Lingpa had been expelled from Nangchen Gar when, due to a vision, he altered the steps during a religious dance—literally dancing to a different beat—his sexual relationship and children were more likely the reasons. A young man claiming to be a treasure revealer would almost certainly practice sexual yoga with a consort in order to perform preparations alleged to be necessary to reveal treasure, and Chokgyur Lingpa claimed to have revealed several major treasure cycles before arriving at Pelpung, which the lamas in Nangchen refused to allow him to organize and teach. Chokling would have probably left Nangchen with some relief, unable to gain recognition in an unwelcoming environment. Assuming the relationship began before his arrival at Pelpung, it is unlikely that he would have brought his consort with him to the monastery, particularly at a time when he was seeking acceptance of his revelations. Regardless of when his children were born, knowledge of Chokgyur Lingpa's sexual relationships with women would have factored into his reputation, providing the necessary allure of highest yoga practice and at the same time earning him scorn from monastics. He was not warmly welcomed at Pelpung; it would be years before he earned the trust and respect of his colleagues there.[11]

Chokgyur Lingpa went to Pelpung claiming to have in his possession a treasure called Lotus Crest which contained a prophecy that positioned him as Lhase Muruk Tsenpo, a son of the Tibetan emperor Trisong Detsen, both of whom were disciples of Padmasambhava. The prophecy states that in a later life, at the age of twenty-five, Lhase would meet the future buddha Maitreya embodied in a person named Pema Nyinje at a place called Pelri on the eastern bank of the Golden River. Chokgyur Lingpa was twenty-five when he arrived at Pelpung, which lays to the east of the Dri River, known in Derge histories as the Golden River Sands, where he met Situ Pema Nyinje, who was believed to be the embodiment of Maitreya. It was an audacious entrance—an unknown man from another kingdom announcing that his arrival was foretold by Padmasambhava himself—if not unprecedented. Treasure revealers throughout Tibetan history have had to put their charisma on full display in order to make themselves known. Chokgyur Lingpa gained an audience with Situ, presented him with the prophecy, and asserted that he must give him an empowerment for a Vajrakīla practice called "Smiling Powerful Vajra," a part of the Lotus Crest revelation. Situ was not impressed and declined to accept it. Yet he gave Chokgyur Lingpa the opportunity to go into retreat and perform the liturgy himself. Kongtrul wrote thirty years later in *One Hundred Treasure Revealers* that Situ did afterwards accept the blessing from the retreat and was pleased with it, but this is unlikely. Situ knew he was dying and would have been wary of accepting a blessing from a strange young man of suspect character.[12]

Four months after Chokgyur Lingpa's arrival, Situ passed away, and the young man turned his attention to Kongtrul and Dabzang, who responded with ambivalence. Kongtrul and Dabzang would have recognized the young man's enormous potential, but they needed time to evaluate him. According to a biography Khyentse Wangpo wrote of him, Chokgyur Lingpa received bodhisattva vows from Dabzang on July 10, 1853,[13] and tantric vows from Kongtrul on July 30.[14] Kongtrul made no record of the vows; if he did indeed bestow them, it was likely as part of a group ceremony. The same was surely the case for Dabzang, who did not warm to Chokgyur Lingpa until 1856. The vows were both probably part of the community's services around Situ's death. In the autumn of 1853, Chokgyur Lingpa spent a month in a longevity retreat for Kongtrul's benefit. He brought him the retreat substances afterwards and reported that there had been positive signs. Kongtrul records that he too had good dreams on the night Chokgyur Lingpa came to him, such as a rising moon, donning new robes, and finding a cache of treasure. Yet he had his doubts. For half a year Chokgyur Lingpa had already pressed both him and Dabzang to affirm his legitimacy as a treasure revealer and accept his revelations, and neither were yet willing to do so. Kongtrul wrote in his diary:

> Chokgyur Lingpa had been persistent in seeking acceptance from Dabzang Tulku, who had looked into it while Situ was alive but had decided nothing. We certainly could not drop the matter. He requested I make an examination, and yet I too could not arrive at a decision. That being the case, Dabzang decided that we ought not give him a treasure-revealer name, just refer to him as Kyasu Lama, and avoid the risks of exchanging empowerments.

Thus Kongtrul, as Situ likely had before him, declined to accept the blessing of Chokgyur Lingpa's practice. Nor did they exchange any transmissions or empowerments.[15]

Dependent on Kongtrul and still in a probationary period, Chokgyur Lingpa had little means of support. When Kongtrul was setting off to begin his three-month retreat at Dagam Wangpuk in the late fall of 1853, as described in the last chapter, Chokgyur Lingpa announced that he intended to make an alms tour of the Terlung Valley. Kongtrul generously gifted him some provisions: two sets of clothing, some *katas*—the ubiquitous Tibetan greeting scarves—and paper and ink. The last gift suggests that Chokgyur Lingpa was able to read and write, although later hagiographies have suggested that he was illiterate, as will be discussed below. Dagam Wangpuk, of course, is located in the Terlung Valley. Chokling followed Kongtrul there, stopping off at Dzongsar where, on October 10, 1953,[16] he received a transmission of a Terdak Lingpa Vajrakīla revelation called the Innermost Secret Kīla Razor as part of a group ceremony. Chokgyur Lingpa may not have yet attained much status, but, at least according to his own account of his time in the cave, he was hardly confined to the shadows; while drunkenly haranguing a pious monk named Karma Tsepel, he had a vision of Vimalamitra, the eighth-century Indian monk who was Padmasambhava's contemporary— and Kongtrul's prior incarnation—at which point he received the revelation known as Vimalamitra Guru Sādhana. Kongtrul, however, nowhere made mention of Chokgyur Lingpa's presence at the cave.[17]

Chokgyur Lingpa did not direct his efforts at Kongtrul alone. Khyentse Wangpo by then had earned the reputation as a master of treasure literature, and any aspiring treasure revealer would reasonably hope to gain his attention. At the end of 1854, Chokgyur Lingpa begged Kongtrul for a letter of introduction to Khyentse Wangpo. The Nera family, one of Kongtrul's patrons in Mesho, had sent a request to Kongtrul to come there and perform an Eight Commands ritual. Kongtrul decided to send Chokgyur Lingpa in his stead and supplied him with a letter to Khyentse Wangpo, thereby killing two birds with one stone. The letter expressed his favorable, if guarded opinion of the young man; he thought well enough of him to supply him for the alms tour, send him in his stead to his patrons, and furnish a letter to Khyentse, but he was not yet ready to accept him without the backing of Khyentse Wangpo:

> This one has a good foundation and such; no matter how you look at him, he is like no other. It is possible he might be a treasure revealer, as he himself claims. He has a treasure teaching called Lotus Crest, but he has produced no decent documenta-

tion, and he has no forms of compositions at all. I respectfully request you look into the matter.[18]

It is from this passage that later biographies surmised that Chokgyur Lingpa was illiterate. Tibetan is an infamously vague language; the phrase I read as "has no forms of compositions at all" others have read "is unable to read or write." Orgyen Tobgyal, for example, paraphrased the passage as "[Chokgyur Lingpa] is quite uneducated and couldn't even write a letter himself." Chokgyur Lingpa may have depended on Kongtrul and Khyentse Wangpo to expand and enhance his revelations to a far greater degree than he would have been able to do himself, but there is no reason to think he was unable to write; numerous colophons, written in the first person and crediting Chokgyur Lingpa with the extraction *and* the transcription, would indicate otherwise.[19]

With this letter of introduction, Chokgyur Lingpa returned to Dzongsar in late December 1854 or early January 1855,[20] and this time he got individual attention, receiving multiple empowerments over the course of a month. Khyentse quickly recognized the ardent young man's exceptional qualities. He recorded that during a life-force authorization rite for the Dzogchen protector Ekajaṭī, Chokgyur Lingpa had a vision of the goddess, who told him "If you two, master and disciple, remain together for three years, I shall grant you a great boon!" Khyentse, the master, interpreted this as a prophecy pertaining to Three Sections of Dzogchen that the two of them would reveal on December 30, 1857,[21] at Pema Shelpuk Cave above Dzongsar. Khyentse was clearly ready to work with him.[22]

Kongtrul's ambivalent letter had opened a critical door at Dzongsar, and now, with Khyentse Wangpo's backing, Chokgyur Lingpa returned to Pelpung to cement his connection to Dabzang, who was willing to receive an empowerment, and Kongtrul, who was now willing—albeit in a group setting and amidst much other activity—to bestow an empowerment on the young treasure revealer. In late May or early June 1855,[23] Kongtrul presided over the annual vase consecration ceremony and acted as vajra master for the Hevajra commemoration rites for Situ. A Lama Karso came to Pelpung and gave Kongtrul several wrathful deity transmissions, including the Molten Metal Poison Face Yamāntaka of the Drigung tradition, which he had received years earlier from Wongen. During this time Lama Sangngak gave Kongtrul several Ratna Lingpa empowerments, and Dabzang, who had gone to Karma Gon in 1853 and only just returned, gave Kongtrul a Ngari Paṇchen Pema Wanggyel treasure called Gathering of Wisdom Holders. Kongtrul gave Dabzang the transmissions for the working version of the Treasury of Kagyu Tantra, and at this point he gave Chokgyur Lingpa—whom he still named Kyater—the empowerment for the Sakya tradition of Vajrakīla. The empowerment was not for Chokgyur Lingpa alone. Several lamas and monks had come from Dzamtang and pleaded with Kongtrul to compose a history of Tāranātha's writings on the Sakya and Jonang Vajrakīla teachings. He obliged them with *Lunar Crystal Mirror: The Texts and Tradition of Vajrakīla, the Conqueror of Māra*, which can be found in his Collected Works. The Dzamtang contingent would have received empowerments before they headed off with the book, and Chokgyur Lingpa likely joined this group. Kongtrul was cautiously allowing meaningful contact between himself and Chokgyur Lingpa.[24]

Chokgyur Lingpa was back at Dzongsar in October 1855[25] for another round of empowerments from Khyentse Wangpo. It had been two years since he first passed through Mesho and attended a public empowerment at Dzongsar, and it had been a year since his second meeting with Khyentse. On this occasion Khyentse taught him Mahāmudrā and gave him Sakya Vajrakīla transmissions. He was not yet ready to write out revelations, however. For this, Khyentse first sent Chokgyur Lingpa to Pelpung to receive from Kongtrul the empowerment for the *Māyājāla Tantra*. This scripture is one of the main Indian tantras in the Nyingma canon closely related to the *Guhyagarbha Tantra*, and it was needed, it seems, to form a foundation for the first of Chokgyur Lingpa's major treasure cycles. Kongtrul, with direct instructions from Khyentse, acquiesced, giving the Peaceful and Wrathful Deities empowerment and an explanation of the tantra to Chokling and a few others. The group performed related rituals, such as the torma and the feast offerings. Kongtrul was not yet ready to receive an empowerment in exchange; he requested only an ablution and blessing from the Drukpa Kagyu tradition of five ablution deities, something any decently trained Drukpa Kagyu monk would know.[26]

After Chokling had left, Kongtrul invited Lama Sang-ngak to the hermitage and received from him a number of major empowerments, including one of the most important Nyingma scriptures, the *Sūtra That Gathers All Intentions*, using the manuals of the fourteenth-century master Nyelpa Delek. He also received a Dzogchen text called *Eighteen Meanings of A*, whatever remaining empowerments for Stirring the Depths of Saṃsāra that he had not received from Khyentse Wangpo in 1852, and the revelations of Zhikpo Lingpa and the great Bhutanese treasure revealer Pema Lingpa, such as United Intent of Samantabhadra and others. Kongtrul's eyes were bothering him again, and he rested by reciting liturgies from United Intent of the Gurus and other cycles.[27]

Meanwhile, Chokgyur Lingpa was back in Dzongsar and he and Khyentse had begun to transcribe a treasure, Dispelling All Obstacles, identical versions of which they each claimed to have revealed. Chokgyur Lingpa is said to have extracted, on October 7, 1848,[28] the first section of this famous cycle from a cliff above his birthplace. According to legend, he had been sworn to secrecy by the protector deities. Khyentse Wangpo is said to have received it some time before the meeting in 1855 as a "mind treasure"—a type of revelation that appears fully formed in the mind of the mystic. Another way of explaining this, which Kongtrul did many decades later in *Mirage of Nectar*, was that the highly literate and brilliant Khyentse Wangpo organized and properly formatted the revelation, which Chokgyur Lingpa had been unable to do. Kongtrul depicts Khyentse Wangpo as generally skeptical of self-proclaimed treasure revealers, warning them against taking their visions seriously. He would tell them that most likely they were suffering from hubris and other wind disorders. It had taken three years for Khyentse to accept Chokgyur Lingpa, three years of testing him in ritual performance and on the basis of the content of his visionary experiences. Once earned, that support never flagged, although Kongtrul did, toward the end of their collaboration, seem to grow weary of the young man's extravagant method of the revelation.[29]

Treasure revelations are said to appear when there is need, when the available ritual cycles are no longer able to meet the demands of the era. Similar to other forms of literature, each generation produces a corpus that speaks the language and reflects the mood and concerns of the era better, it is said, than those that came before. Khyentse and Kongtrul both were dedicated to the propagation of the traditions they held dear, but they also embraced new versions and new arrangements of ritual systems. Providing practitioners and the public with ritual systems that suited their needs was a primary strategy, and Khyentse must have seen value in Chokgyur Lingpa and in the young man's presentation of long-standing ritual systems.

Dispelling All Obstacles cycle is based on the *Māyājāla Tantra*, about which Khyentse had sent Chokling to Pelpung to receive teachings from Kongtrul in preparation for the task of writing out the various components. It contains a lengthy root tantra, titled *Wish-Fulfilling Essence Manual of*

*Oral Instructions*, and practices for Amitāyus, Avalokiteśvara, and Padmasambhava. It also contains practices for the twelve manifestations of Padmasambhava, a group that was invented with this treasure, as well as liturgies for the propitiation of ḍākinīs and protective deities. It became one of Chokgyur Lingpa's most successful revelations, expanded over the years through additional revelations, and both Kongtrul and Khyentse composed liturgies for its eventual publication in ten volumes and for its inclusion in Treasury of Revelations. As part of the writing of the cycle, Khyentse gave the man his treasure name: Orgyen Drodul Chokgyur Dechen Zhikpo Lingpa, commonly shortened to Chokgyur Lingpa. He was now an authorized treasure revealer, and in his diary Kongtrul henceforth honored him with that name.[30]

Chokgyur Lingpa then returned to Pelpung where Kongtrul asked to receive the blessing of the revelation. Chokgyur Lingpa's reply is perhaps suggestive of a bit of irritation at being made to wait so long for Kongtrul to affirm his authenticity: "In the past there was a need for me to offer this to you, but you never spoke to me about it. Moreover, as you are, in fact, my lama, I did not dare to presume to offer. Now it is urgent that I give the transmission." Chokgyur Lingpa was finally able to offer transmissions to Kongtrul, but the testing was not over. Kongtrul instructed Chokgyur Lingpa to begin with the longevity empowerment from Union of All Rare and Precious Jewels, a work that he knew well and would serve as an easy evaluation tool. Chokling succeeded, and so he next gave Kongtrul the transmission for his Vimalamitra Guru Yoga he had received at Dagam Wangpuk in 1853. Chokgyur Lingpa then gave Kongtrul the four empowerments for Dispelling All Obstacles together with the body, speech, and mind empowerments. Kongtrul was clearly impressed, remarking in his diary that Chokgyur Lingpa performed the service without the use of a written text, using a "regent" statue as a support. The fruit of Chokling's fecundity, of his ability to extemporaneously give voice to the teachings of Padmasambhava, would over the next fifteen years be translated into written form by two of the greatest editors and authors of treasure literature in Tibetan history. His Collected Treasures are published in thirty-nine of forty volumes and continue to be some of the most popular cycles in Tibetan Buddhist communities today.[31]

Whatever doubts Kongtrul might still have harbored as to the nature and origin of the cycle were addressed by a lengthy account of how Chokling had revealed the treasure. Such a narrative is a key part of a treasure revelation, serving to place a historical frame around the literature, not unlike the standard frame around Buddhist scriptures that are said to have been taught by the Buddha. Sūtras and Tantras begin with the famous phrase "Thus did I hear at one time" and proceed to name the place of the teaching and the prominent members of the audience. This frame informs all readers that the material within is legitimate *buddhavācana*, the true words of the Buddha. Treasure literature is likewise presented with specific narrative keys: the teacher, a prophecy, the time and place of revelation, and the name of the revealer. While most major treasure cycles contain a discrete treasure history, individual texts within the cycle might also have amended to them brief accounts of their production. These do not always conform with each other or with accounts found in biographies and other sources. The treasures of Chokgyur Lingpa have, in some instances, four or five separate origin stories that differ substantially. For some of the revelation events, Chokgyur Lingpa, Kongtrul, and Khyentse were all present, and each left descriptions that vary from each other in significant ways. After the great treasure revealer's death, Khyentse Wangpo organized his revelations into thirty-seven separate "caskets," each with the crucial elements of the treasure narrative frame. Yet his was not the final word on the matter, and Chokling's reincarnation Konchok Gyurme included all available versions of the extraction narratives in his massive biography of his predecessor. Time, place, and method of extraction are all crucial elements of a treasure and yet were rarely fixed, changing across different accounts of the same revelation as the spark of inspiration was translated into root texts and liturgies.

Kongtrul credited the empowerment of Dispelling All Obstacles for helping to cure his eye ailment, and Chokgyur Lingpa's skillful diagnosis added weight to Kongtrul's claim to be the reincarnation of the controversial imperial-era monk Vairocana. One of the first Tibetans to become ordained, Vairocana was also perhaps the first Tibetan to claim enlightenment and thus the authority to teach. In his era Buddhism was new in Tibet and the Tibetans were still relying on teachers from India, and, to some degree, China—societies where the authenticity of the teachers was unquestioned and the possibility of enlightenment was believed to be real. Tibetans were then still disinclined to consider that one of their own had the potential to equal the revered foreigners. As a result, in part, of his audacious claim to be enlightened, Vairocana was at one point banished from Tibet, but before this happened he was involved in a bedroom intrigue with a wife of King Trisong Detsen named Margyenma. Legend has it that the queen had attempted to seduce the monk, who spurned her. In revenge she attempted to murder him with an infection of leprosy. This would have been accomplished by giving him an object tainted with the blood or excrement of a victim of the disease. Vairocana avoided the infection and returned the object to the queen, who fell ill. Although Vairocana had escaped the disease, he defiled his karmic stream with an act of harming another person. The result, Chokling explained to Kongtrul, was that all subsequent incarnations of Vairocana were fated to suffer from leprosy in the eye. His prescription: "Recite and practice the Vajradaṇḍa sādhana from the Dispelling All Obstacles and you will definitely be cured."[32]

Chokgyur Lingpa then left for Nangchen. Kongtrul's dreams were mixed. He saw flowers and singing cuckoos and found a skull cup and pieces of turquoise. In one dream Chokgyur Lingpa told him "You are the custodian of the third empowerment." He also dreamed that Situ Pema Nyinje, smiling on him, gave him an ablution of Vajravidāraṇa, a deity of purification. There were negative dreams as well, in which he ate mud mixed with manure and vomited, causing him nausea during the day. As usual, in his diary he took this as a sign that he had sinned in his handling of donations, his standard interpretation for negative omens. Yet Kongtrul credited Chokgyur Lingpa's Vajradaṇḍa transmission with curing his eyes. After Khyentse Wangpo gave him the texts for the practice, Kongtrul added it to his daily schedule. His eyes, he claimed, never again bothered him to the same degree. His confidence in Chokling was thus cemented; in his diary he wrote, "As a result of this, I developed faith in the great treasure revealer's words and in his treasure teachings, so different from what generally comes out of the dirt and rocks!"[33]

# 16

# The Birth of the Treasury of Revelations, the Discovery of Dzongsho Deshek Dupai Podrang Hermitage, and the First Opening of Tsādra Rinchen Drak

### 1855–1857

Tibetans have produced a dizzying amount of treasure literature. Already by Kongtrul's time most of these were threatened by obscurity. Revealed scripture competed with the vast amount of liturgical traditions received from India, and few of them ever gained widespread popularity. A new treasure cycle would also need to compete first with the cycles that preceded its revelation and later with those that followed it. New revelations continually supplanted the old, emphasizing different deities and revising common practices for new generations. During the summer solstice of 1855, while practicing the approach to White Tārā in the Dudul Dorje tradition, Kongtrul decided to begin a project he had been considering for some time: a collection of liturgies of lesser-known treasures. He recorded the genesis of the concept in his diary:

> I considered taking up a project I earlier contemplated to gather together many of the old, minor but significant treasures I had received over the years, thinking that it would go some distance toward supporting their transmission. Even in those cycles there are minor practices of some benefit. Now I thought to include these in a comprehensive collection of the empowerments for the rare and lesser transmissions of some of the renowned treasure revealers.[1]

With this fairly modest initial idea, Kongtrul would ultimately produce the Treasury of Revelations, a collection that was published in his lifetime in sixty volumes; a modern expanded edition contains one hundred eleven.

Treasure revelation was not only in service of the production of literature, however. Lost in the discussions of whether treasures are "legitimate" or not is a recognition that treasure extraction is a highly choreographed and often exceptionally physical activity. It is a ritual that, like many others, is enacted to effect a change in the world or, at least, a community's perception of it. Even as Kongtrul, Chokgyur Lingpa, and Khyentse Wangpo would amass scores of volumes of texts, they also used their treasure activity to sanctify places dear to them and, in at least one case, pass messages to Padmasambhava.

Kongtrul had by now been receiving empowerments and transmissions for over twenty years—from the obscure and the nearly abandoned to those that were widely popular. Each contained some beauty in language or phrasing, each had at least a taste of inspiration. Kongtrul recorded every transmission he received—his disciple Nesar Khenpo Karma Tashi Chopel compiled these notes into a two-volume, eight-hundred-page account of each lineage titled *Treasury of Wish-Fulfilling Jewels*[2]—and he sought out what he heard of and had not yet received; he was constitutionally unable to bear the thought of any of them vanishing forever. Kongtrul also understood the power of printing. Most treasure revelations had never been published but instead circulated in manuscript copies. Something beautiful, a teaching that might guide a person to a more ethical, more enlightened existence, could vanish in a fire or become a nest for mice. Printing blocks could ensure wide distribution and a much more secure future. Kongtrul positioned himself as a link in scores of transmission chains, preserving those lineages at least for another generation by his own activity. By publishing the texts, the ephemeral spark that was otherwise passed on using hand-written copies of manuals was fixed in wood, in volumes that have been printed almost continually and that have circulated around the world.

He brought the idea to Khyentse Wangpo, who enthusiastically approved of the idea and gave him four volumes of treasure that he himself had already collected, apparently motivated by a similar idea. Khyentse added: "Ideally, in order to fulfill your aspirations, it should also have the guru sādhana, Dzogchen teachings, and Avalokiteśvara practices of the great treasure revealers." Ever deferential to his friend and colleague, Kongtrul begged Khyentse to decide for him which cycles to include and in which order. At least this is the narrative he presented in his diary—Kongtrul ultimately made all the decisions, even as he declined to take credit for initiating such a monumental endeavor without considerable deference to another lama.[3]

In preparation for the project, Kongtrul spent the rest of the year in meditation. Following the initial recitations and the supplication prayers he was aware of positive signs, and he moved on to the inner, outer, and secret practices of Jatson Nyingpo's Vajra of Meteoric Iron Long Life Sādhana together with the rituals for making pills. During this time he dreamed of seeing relic pills of Vimalamitra, Yeshe Tsogyel, and Shelkharza Dorje Tso—one of Yeshe Tsogyel's female students—and a fourth pill that had been worn by Padmasambhava around his neck. He finished the Jatson Nyingpo practice on February 13, 1856,[4] and then dedicated a week to Mañjuśrī and to blessing pills. Kongtrul was eager to start his new project: he dreamed of seeing the sun and moon rise, and of sitting on a throne, wearing formal robes and reading a book written in silver ink. The working title for the first few years was Garland of Treasures. Not until 1862 did it take the name of Treasury of Revelations. Kongtrul would compose close to eight hundred separate liturgies for the Treasury of Revelations—for smoke offerings, exorcism rites, visualization practices, and a number of other rituals that are typically part of a treasure cycle.[5]

Coming out of retreat in early 1856, Kongtrul's inclination to collect empowerments and transmissions had now been given new meaning. He was no longer collecting them for personal practice and to pass them on to his own disciples; he now was collecting them in order to publish and distribute texts for their long-term propagation and for the benefit of communities beyond his own. He henceforth considerably increased his reception of revelations. He requested several treasure traditions from a Lama Dampa at the retreat center, and they invited Tokden Samten Tendzin, a lama from Ji, who gave half a dozen more. Kongtrul left for Mesho to perform a prosperity rite at Jelo, after which he met with Khyentse and exchanged additional transmissions.[6]

While at Dzongsar, Khyentse tasked him with composing liturgies for Dispelling All Obstacles, and in response he dreamed that Chokgyur Lingpa revealed a wish-fulfilling vase, from which Kongtrul requested a blessing and which was full of pills to be distributed. Kongtrul wrote in his diary that the following day he "came into the presence" of some Dispelling All Obstacles teachings, which he wrote down when he arrived home. This might mean that Khyentse gave them to him before he left, or that he received the sections of the revelation in his dream. Back at the hermitage, Kongtrul enlisted three copyists to begin transcribing treasures he had received to date.[7]

For the rest of 1856, Kongtrul sought out and received transmissions, interrupted only by his institutional obligations. It would be a project-driven program of activity he would maintain for decades. Kongtrul was liberal in his reception of transmissions, though less so in his selection for the compilation. Assuming Kongtrul observed the stricture against reading ritual texts without first receiving the empowerment and transmission, in order to evaluate a cycle for inclusion he needed first to find a lineage holder to give him the necessary authorization. He did not include everything he received. In May Kongtrul supervised the vase consecration and a Hevajra ceremony at Pelpung and attended the community's Guhyasamāja and Mahāmāyā rites. Again, at Dzongsar, he gave a Jinasāgara offering ritual in honor of the recently deceased Ngari Lama, an appointed officer of the monastery. While there he exchanged transmissions and empowerments with Khyentse. A Lama Pewang at Dzongsar gave him Choje Lingpa's Cycle on Red Jambhala and Fierce Lama: The Mother Khrodhakāli, both of which Kongtrul included in the Treasury of Revelations. Back at Pelpung, Lama Sang-ngak gave Kongtrul and Khyentse the Namcho cycle of White and Black Khrodhakāli. Empowerments come with a requirement of practice; there is generally a minimum set of rites and time commitments one must vow to observe. Kongtrul spent time at his hermitage satisfying these before returning to Pelpung for yet more empowerments from a hermit named Ritrul Dargye Gyatso.[8]

It was around this time that Kongtrul received word that the rebirth of Situ Pema Nyinje had been found in Tibet. This was Pema Kunzang, a man with whom Kongtrul would have a disastrous relationship. Kongtrul would leave for Tibet the following year to bring him back to the monastery. Overjoyed that his beloved teacher had returned, Kongtrul perceived miracles at Lhasar Temple, events such as doors opening and closing by themselves. To celebrate he prepared a combined drubchen and mendrub ceremony at Lhasar and invited Khyentse Wangpo to participate. Khyentse arrived on June 27[9] and the two dedicated sixteen days to the ritual. They then exchanged empowerments, with Kongtrul receiving from Khyentse a treasure of Choje Lingpa that he put into the Treasury of Revelations: a longevity practice called Short Lineage of Tangtong Gyelpo that Unites Pure Vision, Spoken Word, and Treasure. Before heading up to his hermitage, Kongtrul received additional empowerments and teachings from Lama Sang-ngak and a teacher named Guru Nātha, a Sanskrit version of the Tibetan Lama Gonpo, or "lama protector." On returning to his hermitage, Kongtrul performed a smoke offering and worked on new compositions, likely either liturgies for Dispelling All Obstacles or for other cycles in the Treasury of Revelations. He was then in the process of editing and correcting the work of the scribes and gathering the resources for the publication of the ten volumes then completed.[10]

He continued to seek out new teachings and new lineages of teachings he had already received, strengthening his confidence in his right to possess and preserve them. On August 27[11] Khyentse Wangpo came to Pelpung to give the reading transmission for the full thirteen volumes of United Intent of the Gurus as well as the main Peaceful and Wrathful Deities cycles. About twenty lamas gathered afterward, and Kongtrul gave them a series of empowerments, primarily Jonang, as well as his recently finished edition of Eight Commands: Perfection of Secrets, a treasure revelation of Guru Chowang for which Kongtrul wrote three of the nine liturgies included in the Treasury of Revelations. He had already given the transmission to Khyentse Wangpo earlier that year. Khyentse remained with Kongtrul and gave him the bodhisattva vows according to the Mindroling Madhyamaka tradition as well as the Yogācāra tradition using manuals he himself had composed. Khyentse offered him a transmission for a Jonang teaching that Kongtrul had received earlier, One Hundred Instructions of the Jonang by Kunga Drolchok, as well as the Kālacakra Tantra and its main commentary, the Vimalaprabhā, in the Zhalu tradition, and more than twenty other transmissions from multiple traditions—Sakya, Drukpa Kagyu, Taklung Kagyu, and Bodong. Khyentse also gave him three days of Lamdre teachings using the manual called A Full Clarification of the Hidden Meaning, written in 1347 by Lama Dampa Sonam Gyeltsen. During all of this, Kongtrul had dreams of flowers in bloom, of people handing him statues of Padmasambhava, and of prostrating to Ngorchen Kunga Zangpo, the founder of Ngor Monastery, who sat on a throne, his upper body in the form of Hevajra.[12]

Khyentse was invited by a person named Gyelse Mingyur to Tsenri Dorje Drak, a Nyingma monastery in southern Derge on the western bank of the Drichu. Kongtrul accompanied him, and there he received from him yet more transmissions, including Heart Drop of the Ḍākinī Expanse and Peaceful and Wrathful: Compendium of Teachings, both revealed by Pema

Dechen Lingpa, whom Kongtrul counted among his previous lives. Both of these Pema Dechen Lingpa revelations are represented in the Treasury of Revelations. Kongtrul gave a transmission for a Guhyajñāna practice, probably from the Terdak Lingpa revelation Mahākaruṇika: Gathering of Sugatas, which is in the Treasury of Revelations and for which Kongtrul wrote the daily practice manual. Khyentse also transmitted the complete treasures of Zhikpo Lingpa and of Longsel Nyingpo, both of whom are well represented in the compilation. Kongtrul received further transmissions from a Lama Pema, including the Vajrakīla tradition of Rongzom Chokyi Zangpo, a translator of the second propagation era who was one of the first men to collect the Vajrakīla teachings, and Trengpo Terton's Collected Works. Lama Karma Ngedon from Litang was also there, and he gave Kongtrul several Sakya teachings that Khyentse Wangpo had not had the time to transmit.[13]

On his return to his hermitage in the autumn of 1856, Kongtrul performed some of his annual rites and was asked by the head of the Situ estate to help with a winter alms tour to raise funds in anticipation of the Tenth Situ's eventual transfer to Pelpung. They set out through Alo and Tsetsa and camped their first night in Ngulkhar. In his diary entry about these few days, he included a dream that he met the two treasure revealers Ngari Paṇchen Pema Wanggyel and Dudul Dorje, and that in the upper part of the valley was Lambaka, a sacred Himalayan mountain related to Devīkoṭa, a key location in the tantric geography of India. Kongtrul frequently recorded dreams in his diary intended to foreshadow coming events; this dream anticipates both the discovery of his second hermitage site and the naming of his main hermitage, discussed below. They camped next at Sholhak in Rakchab, where he dreamed that Longsel Nyingpo showed him statues of the Eight Command deities and some relics he had revealed but had reconcealed. The next day Kongtrul asked people in the valley whether there was a treasure site nearby. Would the locals have noticed the presence of protector deities? Were there stories of peculiar occurrences nearby? No one could provide any useful information.[14]

The following night they camped at a place on the far side of the pass between the Terlung and the Dzingkhok valleys, a spot on the southern face of a ridge surrounded by several shear granite columns where the route over the pass seems to be cut through a wall of stone. Kongtrul had traversed the same route in 1849 on an earlier alms tour without recording any impressions of the place. Camping there now in 1856, Kongtrul dreamed Situ Pema Nyinje showed him a mountain shaped like Yeshe Tsogyel riding a peacock, with caves inside of which were statues of deities. The next morning he claimed he saw letters written on the cliffs. The dream and the magically appearing letters were enough for Kongtrul to conclude that the place was an "abode"—a place imbued with the presence of a deity or a saint—and thus worth developing. He had found the location of his second hermitage.[15]

According to the norms of Tibetan religious geography, abodes need human intervention in order to be accessed; they need to be "opened" so they can function as a conduit between the faithful and the deity or saint's ongoing presence. Openings can employ any combination of rituals that interact with the deities of the place and generally include both offerings to gain favor and subjugation rites to assert dominance. Practices dedicated to familiar Buddhist deities further serve to absorb the place into mainstream religious activity, situating the buddhas and bodhisattvas alongside the local protectors. Once opened the abode is suitable for religious practices such as meditation retreats and pilgrimage. Identification of key features— primarily places where deities or saints performed specific activities or which embody objects and relics of the saints—lays out a geography of sanctity for the practitioner and the itinerary for the visit. Pilgrims to a Tibetan sacred place will arrive seeking to encounter traces of the Buddha and his representatives; they will traverse a predetermined path with identified stations and proscribed activities, one that almost always includes a circumambulation route that serves as a demarcation line between the extraordinary and the everyday landscapes that surround it. In the Nyingma and Kagyu traditions, treasure revelation was a key component of the opening process, as it provides proof that Padmasambhava had visited the site and had left behind his blessing. Kongtrul used all these techniques to open Dzongsho on his return from the fundraising tour in Dzingkhok on December 7, 1856.[16]

The first day was dedicated to rituals. Kongtrul and his companions performed one hundred feast offerings according to Union of All Rare and Precious Jewels and then one hundred fire offerings and "gift of the body" rituals. That night Kongtrul dreamed of meeting Jatson Nyingpo, seated in a temple surrounded by iron mountains and protector deities. The saint gave him some relic pills that liberate on being eaten, and, declaring "there is a military threat in the east that you must repel," he rode a black horse eastward. With this dream Kongtrul was likely foreshadowing the coming threat of Nyake Gonpo Namgyel, a warlord who was then conquering the districts in Nyarong, to the east, and who would within a decade overrun most of Kham.[17]

The following day Kongtrul went to the "peak" of the place, by which he meant the top of the highest cliff, and performed an exorcism rite using the female deity Siṃhamukhā. He then scouted most of the caves—little more than indentations in the cliffs—where he found gypsum and vermillion and what he identified in his diary as "nourishing earthen pills made with medicinal waters which Padmasambhava had used when he performed an effigy ritual there." Decades later, in *Mirage of Nectar*, he clarified his description: the pills themselves were medicinal, they brought liberation upon being eaten, and Padmasambhava had made them when performing a ritual involving a human corpse. He would later name the indentation where he found the pills the "Hayagrīva Cave." These were the first physical evidence of Padmasambhava's presence, and identifying them was Kongtrul's first foray into the business of extracting treasure. White rhododendron were blooming, and the sky was filled with rainbow light, an auspicious and beautiful, if fairly common meteorological phenomenon in Tibet where ice crystals frequently amass in the lower atmosphere and refract sunlight. The next morning, when they set off for the Terlung Valley at sunrise, an overwhelmingly brilliant white light illuminated them, snowflakes fell as though they were flower petals, and swirling rainbow-colored lights danced across their paths. They toured the villages of Mesho and Terlung and then returned to Pelpung.[18]

Why, at the end of 1856, did Kongtrul want to open Dzongsho? It would be ten years before he fully developed the new site and another twenty before he would give it a name, Dzongsho Deshek Dupai Podrang, the Dzongsho Palace Where the Sugatas Gather. His hermitage near Pelpung was comfortable and secure, and he would focus the majority of his institution-building there. At the time, his relationships with the leadership of Pelpung—Dabzang Tulku, Wontrul, and the steward of the Situ estate—were still robust. He was participating in community rituals, many of which he led. Still, his continuing reference in his diary to ongoing concerns about his reputation—his anxiety over being perceived as mismanaging monastic donations—are a reminder that there were members of the community that opposed his activities. In later years, conflicts at Pelpung would cause Kunzang Dechen Wosel Ling to feel too close to the monastery, and Kongtrul would take refuge at Dzongsar, but for the next ten years he was comfortable there. Yet other than making some simple smoke offerings, he had never formally opened the site of his first hermitage. The retreat center had a name given it by Situ, but the ground itself had never been sanctified or even named. Having dedicated a day opening Dzongsho inspired Kongtrul to now do so.

On his arrival at Pelpung, Kongtrul received a command that took precedence. Wontrul ordered him to go to Tibet to bring the Tenth Situ to Pelpung. He would need time to make preparations for a departure the following year. Immediately on receiving the assignment, to eliminate potential supernatural obstacles to the journey, he spent a day in each of the protector temples participating in the ongoing rituals there. He then went up to his hermitage and performed the approach practice for Union of the Families of the Three Immortal Kāyas, a treasure revelation relating to Amitāyus by Trengpo Terton Sherab Wozer of the Northern Treasures tradition.[19]

He was then occupied with obligations to his friends. Chokgyur Lingpa had returned from Nangchen the month before, and on December 30, 1856,[20] he and Khyentse Wangpo had opened Pema Shelpuk, a cave in the Dzamnang Valley, high above Dzongsar, near the Sidu Pass into the Rongme Valley. Pema Shelpuk, or Lotus Crystal Cave, would become a primary treasure site for Khyentse Wangpo. The cave is in a granite chimney jutting from the center of a spacious eastward-facing bowl. The two of them extracted two treasures there, including Three Sections of Dzogchen. This was the cycle that Khyentse later associated with the vision Chokling experienced three years earlier during the life-entrustment ceremony at Dzongsar. The revelation was public, meaning that people had been invited to witness and even participate in the event, and as many as twenty-five people joined the rituals and possibly several hundred more came to watch. It was quite a show by most accounts.[21]

Legend has it that the cave was then popularly known as the "Ghost Cave" due to all the fearsome spirits said to haunt it. When word got out that Khyentse and Chokling would be revealing treasure there, people were eager to watch them battle the ghosts, not fully convinced that Chokling, at least, would avoid being devoured. No one would have worried about Khyentse Wangpo, feared as he was by men and ghosts alike. Chokling apparently announced that the treasure protectors were under a weighty injunction not to release the treasure, and these beings, to drive people away, brought up a driving wind and rain. The two lamas boldly faced down the treasure protectors and the hostile spirits that occupied the site, performing offering feasts and subjugation rites and proclaiming their command over the place. Some accounts have Chokgyur flying to the roof of the cave—roughly five meters at its highest—to extract the yellow scrolls. The second treasure was a reliquary of Garab Dorje, a mythological lineage holder of the Dzogchen teachings, which Chokling extracted from the hillside to the southeast of the cave on January 5, 1857.[22] Khyentse reported that in preparation for the second extraction Chokling had performed a mendrub ritual, during which a summer-like warmth pervaded the ridge even though it was the depth of winter. Before leaving they laid out a circumambulation route that included a marker for the Garab Dorje revelation and for several springs that flowed with medicinal waters.[23]

Kongtrul was informed of the event by a messenger sent to Pelpung to announce Chokgyur Lingpa's pending arrival. He prepared to receive the new treasure by performing feasts and torma offerings, noting in his diary the gale winds that Pema Shelpuk's protectors had brought forth. Chokgyur Lingpa crossed the Ha Pass between Mesho and Pelpung and was welcomed in high style; the monks hung banners and blew conches, and they performed a smoke offering in his honor while an auspicious gentle snow fell. It was a considerable contrast from his earlier visits. Kongtrul was now eager to take Chokgyur Lingpa seriously and to participate in the writing of his ongoing revelations.[24] Textual treasures are said to come on small scrolls of yellow paper, written in a cryptic script that only the revealer is able to read, often with the aid of ḍākinīs. A single line of this might unlock—for the revealer—volumes of scripture. Once decoded, the text is either transcribed by the revealer or is dictated to a scribe. Of the one hundred twenty-four texts in Three Sections of Dzogchen in the Treasury of Revelations, Kongtrul wrote out at least eight of them. Khyentse Wangpo wrote no fewer than forty-six. Chokgyur Lingpa is identified by name as having transcribed twenty-two.

With ritual preparations for the Tibet trip already completed, and the transcription of Chokgyur Lingpa's third major revelation underway, Kongtrul returned to the opening of the site of his hermitage. He was in a strong place. His dreams were of living to the age of eighty and of discovering Yamāntaka treasures. He had identified a second hermitage site and had revealed his first treasure substances. Kongtrul finally permitted Chokling to give him the transmission of the Lotus Crest revelation.

Chokling gave this together with two sections of Seven Profound Cycles that he had revealed the previous year at Karma Gon with Dabzang and the Fourteenth Karmapa. Kongtrul recorded the names of these as Stirring the Depths and Longevity Lord Yamāntaka, the second of which Chokling had declared was destined for Kongtrul personally. The Seven Profound Cycles is extensive, with preliminary practices and inner, outer, and secret sādhanas pertaining to seven topics: the Māyājāla Tantra, Viśuddha, Hayagrīva, Mañjuśrī Yamāntaka, Kīlaya, Mamo, and the Three Roots of guru, deva, and ḍākinī.[25]

At the conclusion of these transmissions, Kongtrul made a request of Chokling: "In the past there was no opportunity for me to ask this; now the time has come. Please put together a gazetteer for the site of my hermitage." Chokling responded with a remarkable assertion, one that would impact the religious landscape of Kham ever after, and which would provide both himself and Kongtrul with an enormous amount of geographical work: "Because this is one of the twenty-five great abodes of Kham, there is a gazetteer for it concealed as treasure; there is no need to compose one." This was Chokgyur Lingpa's announcement of his next revelation: *A Brief Inventory of the Great Abodes of Tibet Composed by Padmasambhava, the Wise One of Oḍḍiyāna.* Kongtrul's hermitage site was but one of many abodes in Kham included on the list.[26]

This gazetteer is a work of remarkable intelligence, one that remakes the landscape of Kham in the image of Chokgyur Lingpa's own treasure activity. It provides a list of forty-two places according to the schema of enlightened body, speech, mind, activities, and qualities. Each of these five has a main place and then five subsidiary sites according to the same divisions: for example, Kongtrul's hermitage site is the mind-aspect of enlightened qualities. To this list of thirty, there are four "exceptional places" and eight places that guide beings through enlightened activity; the mountain in Kongtrul's home valley of Ronggyab would in 1867 be labeled the site which leads beings via the activity of the Lotus Family. Chokling used this gazetteer to strengthen his standing and the legitimacy of his treasures. He included all places where he had revealed treasure alongside long-established sacred places such as Longtang Dolma. The effect was to elevate his treasure sites the ranks of well-known local abodes, as the glory of each would, in the shared geography, be distributed across locations. Treasures extracted in any of these locations would be more likely to be taken seriously. Chokling ensured his patrons' cooperation by including their own sites of activity on the list: in addition to Kongtrul's hermitage site, Pema Shelpuk is the speech-aspect of enlightened qualities, and Riwo Wangzhu—the mountain where Dagam Wangpuk is located—is the place that guides beings through enlightened power. Chokling wisely left many slots unnamed; it was only 1857, and he had many more treasures still to reveal.[27]

Before Chokgyur Lingpa could obtain this fascinating text and proceed with the opening of the hermitage site, however, he and Kongtrul had some preparations to take care of. Chokling first gave Kongtrul a curious object that he claimed to have revealed at a place called Yelpuk: an image of the protector goddess Blazing Fire that he said had been carved by Nāgārjuna out of a black stone from the famous Indian Buddhist burial ground of Śītavana. Chokling requested something to replace it, and Kongtrul selected an ancient regent statue. This was perhaps the statue Khyentse Wangpo had given him back in 1852, the only such statue he recorded possessing up until that point.[28]

Treasure inventories—lists of forthcoming revelations that were themselves concealed—and treasure caches were appearing to Chokgyur Lingpa in increasing quantities. Kongtrul took advantage of this time of abundant production to nudge Chokgyur Lingpa into assisting him with the Treasury of Revelations. As he had previously requested of Khyentse, he now solicited Chokling for advice on which cycles would be suitable to include in the collection. Kongtrul could not have hoped for—or composed—a better response than the one which, according to Kongtrul's own account, Chokgyur Lingpa gave him: the younger man declined to offer his own opinion and instead asserted that "in periods such as these when I am meeting Guru Rinpoche in person, it is the perfect opportunity to ask him such questions; I will remember to put the matter to him and will not forget his responses." At the height of his career, Chokgyur Lingpa could convincingly converse with Padmasambhava.[29]

Chokling then set out up valley from Pelpung to the Jadra estates in Pamay. There, at a place called Pawopuk Wangchen Drak, he performed feast and mending rituals, and on February 26, 1857,[30] the first day of the Fire Serpent Year, he revealed the list of the great abodes. He then returned to Kongtrul's hermitage, the yellow scrolls in hand. The two men made offerings to the treasure protectors, and Kongtrul asked whether he had made inquiries to Padmasambhava about the Treasury of Revelations. Chokling said that he had indeed made inquiries and that he had received many lines of verse about the matter. Kongtrul records that he only wrote out a few fragments of these: "The main gist appeared to be that I had received an edict to the effect that, based on the force of my karmic propensity and aspirations, I was permitted to include whatever I wished to."[31]

Kongtrul had initially relied on Khyentse's authority in deciding which cycles to include in the Treasury of Revelations. As the project proceeded, having practiced treasure revelation himself, his confidence grew in his own authority to make his own decisions. Yet Tibetans shy away from bold personal statements of abilities and privileges. Authority is generally reflected in the repeated words of praise by one's peers or in the figure of deities who manifest to declare a person's worth and rights. Khyentse had not told Kongtrul he was qualified to decide for himself which cycles to include in the Treasury of Revelations, so Kongtrul turned to someone who would, an even higher power: Padmasambhava. To do that he needed a credible messenger, and when Chokgyur Lingpa presented himself as preparing to speak to Padmasambhava, Kongtrul saw the opportunity. Treasure revealers are mediums; they reach one hand into the supernatural and draw something out into the other side. Kongtrul would continue to rely on Khyentse for advice, but he now had the word of Padmasambhava that he could include whatever he wanted to.

Kongtrul was not shy about demanding revelations where he felt the collection was lacking. In early 1863 he pressured Chokgyur Lingpa to decode a sādhana from a revelation at Sengchen Namdrak, southwest of Derge, that included a treasure cycle titled *Six Scrolls of Pure Dharma* and a hagiography of Padmasambhava entitled *Garland of Jewels*. With the text and its transmission in hand, Kongtrul was able to insert it into the Vajrasattva section of the Treasury of Revelations, and he composed a manual to compliment it, for, he wrote, "it is unsuitable for a sādhana to be without an associated empowerment manual." They evidently composed further texts from the revelation, as additional liturgies for it are found in Chokling's Collected Revelations, and they performed the feasts and the mending and supplication rites from the cycle, but Kongtrul used only these two in the Treasury of Revelations.[32]

There was still the opening of the hermitage site to complete. The hermitage had a name, Kunzang Dechen Wosel, but the site itself still lacked one, and for this Kongtrul turned to two experiences of the past year. The first naturally involved Khyentse Wangpo. The previous year, when the two had been supervising the combined drubchen and mendrub rituals at Lhasar Temple in preparation for the arrival of the Tenth Situ, Khyentse and several students had performed a longevity ceremony on Kongtrul's behalf. As part of this, Khyentse gave a short exposition on the five auspicious circumstances required for success in religious practice: the Dharma, the teacher, the place, the time, and the assembly. In describing the place, Khyentse apparently heard a voice saying "this excellent abode is the third Devīkoṭa, the wisdom eye at the uppermost point of the central nāḍī." The remark had stayed with Kongtrul as he later passed through Dzongsho, suggested by his dream in which a voice told him to look for a place connected to Lambaka, as described above. Now Kongtrul decided that the "third Devīkoṭa" was the location of his hermitage.[33]

The development of Indian Tantra not only interiorized the rite of sacrifice; it also mapped on the human body an intricate geography of the known world that was further charted onto the body's system of channels and discs. The *Cakrasaṃvara Tantra*, one of the main sources for this geography, sets forth a system of twenty-four *pīṭhas*—geographic points—associated with the buddha Cakrasaṃvara's defeat of the demon Bhairava. The geographic locations became religious sites in India, and when the Tantras were brought to Tibet so too was the geography. Scholars have made much of the penchant in Tibet for identifying mountains with Indian deities and their maṇḍalas or pure lands, noting that the practice speaks both to the Tibetan assimilation of Buddhism and the multiple techniques available for proponents of particular places to establish and popularize the sites. The Kagyu were particularly active in this, importing the entire Cakrasaṃvara maṇḍala, with its twenty-four pīṭhas and eight cemeteries arrayed around the perimeter. A large Himalayan massif was in this way identified as both Devīkoṭa and Cārita, transliterated into Tibetan as Tsāri, and saints such as Milarepa went there to further sanctify the place with their practice.[34]

Tibetans understand these abodes to be the residence of a deity, be that a fully enlightened buddha, a regional protector god, or a local guardian spirit. Pre-Buddhist Tibetans understood their landscape to be inhabited by all sorts of noncorporeal entities. Many of these, though not all, were absorbed into the Buddhist pantheon. Because deities can be said to reside in any location—a cave, a grove of trees, a lake, an oddly-shaped rock, and so forth—abodes are by no means limited to locations as grand as mountains. An abode might also be a place that was visited by buddhas or saints and imbued with their blessings. By visiting these sites, the pilgrim can partake in these blessings, which permeate the objects of the site. The common Tibetan terms for pilgrimage, "tour the abode" or "encounter the abode," invoke this aspect of the term, the act of connecting physically with the divine. Moreover, a cave site or mountain will often be described as having the ability to multiply exponentially the merit of any religious activity done there, such as prostrations or the counting of mantras, particularly at astrologically auspicious times. While Buddhist doctrine teaches that all of existence is in actuality a pure land, the unenlightened do not perceive this, and abodes, more heavily imbued with the buddha's presence, are places that a practitioner can more easily shake off deluded perception. Over the course of the next fifteen years, Kongtrul, Chokling, and Khyentse Wangpo would develop the site of Kongtrul's personal hermitage into a central abode in the geography of Kham.

Kongtrul and Chokling began in earnest to open the site of the hermitage, which Kongtrul now referred to as Tsādra Rinchen Drak—The Jeweled Cliff Similar to Tsāri—on February 28, 1857.[35] It did not start well. They began with the Mindroling longevity ceremony Innermost Heart of Immortality in order to establish their presence, made a smoke offering and a golden libation—a common offering of beer or tea mixed with grains— and then performed an extensive ritual to bind the gods and spirits to an oath. This was their announcement to the resident supernatural beings that they would henceforth command the place. Chokgyur Lingpa had a vision of the Nyingma protector deity Ekajaṭī and fell into a faint. He was able to recover only after Kongtrul placed a special seal of Padmasambhava on his forehead. The fainting spell had apparently allowed him to commune with Padmasambhava, for when his mind cleared he identified all the important features of the site. The following day a terrific wind arose as they surveyed the central part of the place and investigated other unidentified obstacles to their progress. This led them both to conclude that the time was not yet ripe to open the site. Or, as Kongtrul later wrote in his pilgrimage guide, "the opening of particularly powerful places does not come easily." The site, the faithful were to understand, was so powerful that even the combined efforts of Kongtrul, Khyentse Wangpo, and Chokgyur Lingpa could not open it on their first try.[36]

Leaving off the opening for the time being, they turned to the revelation of the regional gazetteer, descending to Situ's residence to decode the scrolls. The work provided the first description of Tsādra Rinchen Drak:

> Regarding the eminent site of the mind-aspect of the enlightened quality, on a glorious mountain like a standing elephant, in the

Tibetan Dokham region called Dri, is Devīkoṭa Tsādra Rinchen Drak, a site in the manner of the nine Śrī Herukas. The Lotus Practice Cave is like a blossoming flower. The cliff has self-arisen peaceful and wrathful [deities] and is the site, in the form of a crescent moon, of the practice of the vidyādhara of the enlightened mind, Namkhai Nyingpo. Desiring an eminent site for practice, I one-pointedly practiced here. Concealed elsewhere is the site which was blessed by my crown ornament, Vimalamitra. The mantra protector of the place is Bhaṭayi. In a nearby cave is the site where I, Orgyen [Padmasambhava] myself practiced. While there, the mind vidyādhara Hūṁkara came, and they conversed for three days. There is a self-arisen statue of myself, the master, and clearly [evident] signs of the wisdom body; [the site] is in possession of those sorts of amazing things.[37]

Kongtrul had requested a proper gazetteer, but Chokling had instead given him this. It was a start, but it was not enough. Almost every element of this description would be expanded over the next half decade, first in Chokling's treasure gazetteer for Tsādra when it finally came two years later, and eventually by Kongtrul's own pilgrimage guide, *Music from the Ocean of the Mind*, a work written in 1864 that is packed with such enormous detail that nearly every rock one might pass is described as a buddha in physical form.

Khyentse and Chokling together left Pelpung for Derge to perform a medical sādhana, presumably for the royal family. On February 3, 1857,[38] they also opened an abode there, Dri Nyendong. This site is number twenty-one in the gazetteer, the site of the body-aspect of the buddha qualities. It is a small mountain that is visible from the royal palace and is considered a protector of the kingdom—a wise choice for his gazetteer. As part of its consecration, Chokgyur Lingpa revealed a treasure with the title of Heart Essence of Mañjuśrīmitra, although it seems to have never been put into writing. From Derge, Chokling sent word that Kongtrul and Wontrul were needed at their next destination in what appears to have been a tour of the sites in the gazetteer of abodes. This was Sengchen Namdrak, Sky Cliff of the Great Lion, the twenty-fourth on the list, the activities-aspect of the enlightened qualities. Kongtrul and Wontrul arrived there from Pelpung on February 8, 1857,[39] with a retinue of several other monks, a day or possibly two before Khyentse and Chokling came. At the peak of the site, a cave named Pema Shelpuk, they performed a Vajravārāhī feast offering, a thousand feast offerings of Vajrasattva, smoke offerings, and other consecration-related rituals in preparation for the large public revelation events that were to come. Khyentse and Chokling arrived either that day or on the following day.[40]

Chokgyur Lingpa was at this point in his most prolific period, revealing not only extensive liturgical cycles but also physical objects such as relics, statues, and medicinal substances. The records of his extractions provide narratives of ritual extravagance and abundant treasure production with little historical coherence. Kongtrul, Khyentse, and Chokling all wrote accounts of the days at Sengchen Namdrak, each with their own specific agenda; none agree on the content or the dates of the extraction events. Chokling's autobiography states that all events happened on one day, February 8, and is the most exuberant, extolling the miraculous abundance of treasure. Khyentse Wangpo, who attempted to systematize all of Chokgyur Lingpa's treasures into thirty-seven separate and distinct revelations, was primarily interested in the basic treasure frame and mostly dispensed with additional detail. He has events occur over a full week, from February 8 to February 16.[41] Kongtrul placed them at the site for five days, from February 8 to February 14.[42] For his purposes it was sufficient to note that he was at the abode with Khyentse Wangpo and Chokling, that he assisted in writing out treasure scripture, and that Chokling gave the transmissions for the cycles that were eventually deemed to be the products. Chokgyur Lingpa's treasures were of great value to Kongtrul, and he included several of them in the Treasury of Revelations.[43]

On Chokling and Khyentse's arrival, the group identified the Secret Padmasambhava Cave at the peak of the site and continued their rituals there. Kongtrul reported that rainbows and vultures filled the sky and that Chokling told them that these were ḍākinīs and vidyādharas. In his account of the first day of their activities, Khyentse listed the title of a single treasure cycle, Heart Essence of Yeshe Tsogyel, which was never written down, and a guide to further treasure. Chokgyur Lingpa, in his autobiography, gives an extensive list of extracted objects:

> While everyone was watching, I revealed, from inside the cliff, amṛta and medicinal waters for earth illnesses, which still flow today. I also revealed the undergarment from Padmasambhava's own body, his brocade cloak, his hat, a wheel of Vajrapāṇī that liberates on sight, pieces of the Buddha's robes, Yeshe Tsogyel's

earrings made of indranīla [sapphire], ruby, emerald, and the like, fine gold and Jambhu-River gold in a small pouch, clothes from Trisong Detsen, Yeshe Tsogyel, Mandharava, and so forth, robes of Vairocana, ornaments from Vajrasattva made from all sorts of desirable objects, a Padmasambhava representative statue made with his blood, many kinds of sacred objects, medicinal amulet boxes, and a seal of Padmasambhava. As for the treasure teachings, manifest there was an Anuyoga Dharma cycle comprising six volumes of pure Dharma of sealed secrets and six prophecies. The revealed treasure also included about one measure of camphor, which the crowd scrambled to obtain. Also written there was a list of a place called Drakri Rinchentsek. In addition, from Dzi Pema Shelpuk, I revealed the cycle titled Śāntarakṣita's Robes and life-extension substances. I also received some jewels from the area around there.[44]

Kongtrul, in his diary, only mentions the revelation of a statue of Padmasambhava and distributes other items mentioned by Chokling to subsequent days.[45]

As Kongtrul recounted, after taking out all that he could from the peak, Chokling recommended the group move their camp up the ridge to a place called Sengpu, which he claimed was the center of the abode. They remained there three days, during which the group continued their ritual activities in support of Chokgyur Lingpa's ongoing revelations. They were joined there by the young king of Derge, Damtsik Dorje, who had come to witness the revelations at the head of a growing crowd of onlookers. Here, Kongtrul clarified, was where Chokgyur Lingpa's copious extractions occurred, with texts, medicine, and relics appearing seemingly from every direction. Several scriptural treasures produced from the revelations connected to these events were written out for inclusion in the Treasury of Revelations under the titles Ocean of Dharma That Embodies All Teachings, Vajra Array Great Transmission, and a Vajrasattva cycle called Six Scrolls of Profound Dharma. More medicinal substances apparently caused a minor stampede when Chokling distributed them among the crowd. On the banks of the Tsechu River, Chokling gave a final empowerment for a form of Padmasambhava, Great Bliss Guru. Kongtrul, having served as witness and ritual master of ceremonies, returned to Pelpung to begin his voyage to Tibet.[46]

# 17

# TIBET

## 1857–1859

On August 12, 1857,[1] Jamgon Kongtrul left Pelpung for Tibet. He was making the long and difficult trip on Wontrul Rinpoche's orders to escort the Tenth Situ, then about three years old, to Pelpung. The preparations took months to complete. Pack animals had to be secured, tents and provisions gathered, and rituals performed to ensure success. Kongtrul also had to send messages to the government in Lhasa and to Tsurpu Monastery, where the Situ incarnation was then living and where Kongtrul would base himself while in Tibet. Permission from the government to take an incarnate lama out of Tibet was required. He would need to negotiate the release not only with the government in Lhasa but also with the administrators of Tsang province (where the boy had been born) and Tashilhunpo Monastery, to which the boy's family belonged. Kongtrul was anxious, and his dreams were agitated and ominous. Ever a believer in the prophetic power of dreams, the mention of the negative dreams was a foreshadowing of the poisonous relationship he would have with this Situ incarnation.[2] Kongtrul had a second task in Tibet, which was to bring the newly decoded sections of Seven Profound Cycles to the Karmapa and to practice them in Tibet. The Karmapa had participated in this revelation but had left Kham before much of the material was written.

At Pelpung, Kongtrul had institutional responsibilities to perform before he left. In the spring of 1857, after returning from the treasure revelation activities at Sengchen Namdrak, he gave the bodhisattva vows, Kālacakra empowerments, and teachings at the monastery's meditation center. He participated in the monastery's annual vase ceremony, during which time he gave public empowerments. In early July[3] he consecrated Tārā statues Wontrul had commissioned in Situ's residence, performing two days of a Cakrasaṃvara rite and three days of a Tārā rite. To ready himself and his entourage for the voyage, he performed an approach practice for the Lord of Life from Seven Profound Cycles. The deity is a form of Yamāntaka, the wrathful form of Mañjuśrī. On July 2[4] he sent the men who would be traveling with him to the sacred peaks above Pelpung—Kardzin and Uchetem—to supplicate the gods there.[5]

Kongtrul himself went to Dzongsar to meet with Khyentse Wangpo. Khyentse gave him his recently revealed Heart Essence of Chetsun, which came to him as a "memory treasure," and is considered Khyentse's primary Dzogchen revelation. In contrast to a mind treasure, which is said to have been placed in the mind by Padmasambhava, a memory treasure is one that was revealed in a previous lifetime and then recalled. According to the origin story, in the eleventh century, Dangma Lhungyel, the caretaker of the Zha Temple to the northeast of Lhasa, discovered seventeen Dzogchen tantras, which he claimed had been hidden there in the eighth century by Nyang Tingdzin Zangpo, a disciple of Vimalamitra, the Indian translator and contemporary of Padmasambhava. Dangma Lhungyel transmitted the teachings, then supposedly known as Heart Essence of Vimalamitra, to Chetsun Sengge Wangchuk. Jamyang Khyentse Wangpo announced that he was a reincarnation of Chetsun and thus able to remember the teachings, which he named not after himself but the man who last heard it. Khyentse gave Kongtrul two additional treasures of his: Heart Essence of Siṃhamukhā and Heart Essence of Vairocana. Khyentse also transmitted the Yangdak section from Chokgyur Lingpa's Seven Profound Cycles.[6]

Khyentse had toured central Tibet twice, from 1840 to 1843 and again from 1848 to 1851, and he would write a famous guidebook which has been translated into Western languages several times, most recently by Matthew Akester as *Jamyang Khyentse Wangpo's Guide to Central Tibet.*[7] Kongtrul never mentions this work, and it is reasonable to assume it was not yet written in 1857 when Kongtrul set out for Tibet. Khyentse did speak to Kongtrul about the places he had visited, describing their important features and how Kongtrul could reach them. Khyentse then gave him gifts and sent him off. Kongtrul left for Tibet immediately afterward.[8] Kongtrul himself was no travel writer. He would visit dozens of famous places but would neglect to include any identifying details beyond the name of the place—no historical information, no physical description or remarks on what he saw.

Kongtrul would not have set out on such an important and potentially perilous journey without first visiting Khyentse Wangpo; all the empowerments provided the opportunity for intimate contact before a long separation. Despite all the recent collaboration, Kongtrul seemed to be much less concerned about securing an interview with Chokgyur Lingpa. The group went in stages to the Nangchen region, where Kongtrul knew Chokling was then in retreat at Wokmin Karma near Karma Gon. This was where Chokling revealed Seven Profound Cycles, and it is site number three in the gazetteer of abodes, the speech-aspect of enlightened body. Kongtrul sent a message to Chokling, presumably letting the younger man know that he was in the area. The messenger returned with an urgent request for Kongtrul to meet with him, but Kongtrul declined, citing his duties with his entourage and his disinclination to make a detour. Kongtrul continued on, satisfying the wishes of people in the places where he camped with rituals and empowerments. In the meantime, Chokling broke his retreat and made his way quickly, traversing the distance in only six days and meeting him in Gyama Tseldo. There was a clear hierarchy to their relationship that Chokgyur Lingpa had tested and which Kongtrul refused to disregard. Chokling explained himself by flamboyantly telling Kongtrul that "had the present opportunity to connect been lost, it was certain that in the future nothing would come out well." They stayed together for five days. Chokling gave Kongtrul additional empowerments from Seven Profound Cycles that he had by then completed, and he gave Kongtrul instructions for its propagation. Chokling had enough invested in Kongtrul's transport of Seven Profound Cycles that he was forced to move quickly when he found Kongtrul unwilling to alter his route.[9]

Kongtrul's party joined a contingent from the Derge government and others who were then traveling to Tibet. Kongtrul offered his ritual services, performing a smoke offering on the combined encampment's behalf, and offered his advice for how to proceed. Combining companies, even diverse groupings of monastics, government officials, and traders, was practical in an era of widespread banditry. They reached Tsurpu on November 18, 1857,[10] three months after setting out from Pelpung. Their arrival was celebrated with a procession and a feast.[11]

Kongtrul stayed at Tsurpu for less than two weeks. On November 23, the seventh day of the tenth month—a date selected for its astrological characteristics—Kongtrul had an audience with the Fourteenth Karmapa at the monastery's main temple. The two had not met since Kongtrul had toured Kham with the Kagyu patriarch over twenty years earlier. During their meeting the Karmapa requested Kongtrul give him an account of Chokgyur Lingpa's treasure activities. During the revelation of Seven Profound Cycles, the Karmapa and Chokling had constructed a narrative of their relationship in which Chokgyur Lingpa was the predestined treasure revealer in service of the Karmapa. Chokgyur Lingpa had by then or would soon announce his famous vision of twenty-one Karmapa incarnations, including seven who would follow the Fourteenth. Kongtrul was able to describe the revelations of the past year, having been present for most of them, as well as the decoding of Seven Profound Cycles, and the Karmapa was extremely pleased by the report. The audience was also the first meeting Kongtrul had with the chosen reincarnation of his beloved teacher. He would call the boy Kuzhab, meaning something akin to Your Excellency or Venerable One.[12]

Four days later, on November 27,[13] the Karmapa performed the black hat ceremony, and he gave the Tenth Situ an official benediction by bestowing on him the red hat of his own incarnation line. On November 30[14] Kongtrul gave the Karmapa empowerments from Chokling's treasures that he had not yet received, including those hastily transmitted when Chokling waylaid him on his journey to Tibet. The two performed a feast offering on December 1,[15] and Kongtrul requested a copy of a prophecy the Karmapa had received. If this was Chokling's prophecy of the twenty-one Karmapas, Kongtrul does not say.[16]

Kongtrul then left the majority of his entourage at Tsurpu and headed off on a tour of central Tibet with about five students as companions. They first went southeast, down the Tolung Valley to Lhasa. Kongtrul needed the permission of the Tibetan government to begin negotiations for the release of the Situ incarnation, but it appears he was not able to meet with any representatives at the time. He and his companions instead spent the time they had on pilgrimage. In Lhasa they worshipped the famous Jowo Mañjuvajra Buddha image in the Lhasa Cathedral and the Jowo Yishin Norbu Buddha statue in the Ramoche Temple, each of which are said to have been brought to Tibet in the seventh century by the queens of King Songtsen Gampo. They visited the Potala, the massive palace built on a ridge in Lhasa by the Fifth Dalai Lama, and then Chakpo Ri, the famous medical center on the ridge opposite the Potala. Crossing Lhasa's Kyichu River, they turned east and stopped at Tsel Gungtang, the monastery founded by Zhang Yudrakpa in the twelfth century. This was the starting point for the trek south to the Drakyul Valley on the north bank of the Yarlung Tsangpo River, known as the Brahmaputra when it reaches India. At Drak Yongdzong, a massive Padmasambhava cave complex near the head of the valley, Kongtrul dedicated five days to the sādhana of the Yamāntaka cycle from Seven Profound

Cycles as well as to feast and fulfilment rites. This subsection of Seven Profound Cycles is particularly well filled out in the Treasury of Revelations, with fifteen separate liturgies, half of which were written by Kongtrul.[17]

The vast main cave has a wide mouth and a ceiling some fifteen meters high, with plenty of natural light, comfortably accommodating many days of practice. After five days Kongtrul and his students ventured to the inner sanctum of the complex, the Tsogyel Cave. One reaches it by climbing a ladder to a small opening to the left of the main cave and pulling oneself up through a tight chimney of limestone worn to a high polish over the centuries by pilgrims' bodies sliding against the walls. A bridge over a deep and sudden chasm brings one to the small oval chamber, likened to the womb of Yeshe Tsogyel. Tiny fragments of white limestone cover the floor, prized as relics of the saint. There Kongtrul and his companions performed one hundred feast offerings.[18]

Walking south toward the Yarlung Tsangpo, they stopped at Tsogyel Lhatso, a small pond said to be the life lake of Yeshe Tsogyel—that is, the storehouse of her life's essence—and the Khardo stūpa, which marks the spot of her birth (Khardo was Tsogyel's clan name). They turned east at the river and continued to Samye, Tibet's first monastery, about ten kilometers downriver. Kongtrul and his companions visited all the temples to make prostrations, and, on the winter solstice, in the Dudul Ngakpaling Temple, they performed a Vajrakīla exorcism ritual from Seven Profound Cycles. He continued the project of planting the cycle in Tibet by performing a three-day group torma ritual to White Amitāyus—from the Three Root Profound Life section of the cycle—at the Yamalung Hermitage, a Padmasambhava site up the valley from Samye. Some monks from Mindroling Monastery were there, and they offered him a performance of the Innermost Heart of Immortality longevity ritual. On December 26, 1857,[19] now back at Samye, Kongtrul performed one hundred feast offerings from Dispelling All Obstacles in the Yuzhel Shrine on the second floor of the main temple. On his descent to the ground floor, Kongtrul spied a doorway on his right and went in, seeing for the first time the famous "Looks Like Me" statue of Padmasambhava. Legend has it that it was consecrated by the saint himself, who, during the ceremony, commented on the resemblance. Kongtrul found the face to be brilliant white, almost radiant. This was not a positive thing—Kongtrul viewed the statue a few more times and ultimately paid for the face to be gilded, providing the proper golden hue Kongtrul had expected.[20]

Just to the north of Samye is the famous cave hermitage complex Chimpu, a practice site of numerous Tibetan luminaries, including the Third Karmapa and Jigme Lingpa, who had visions there of traveling to Nepal to receive Heart Essence of the Vast Expanse from ḍākinīs. In the main cave, Kongtrul dedicated three days to the approach and accomplishment practices of Hayagrīva from Seven Profound Cycles. In the Drakmar Keutsang Cave, where Padmasambhava is said to have practiced, the group performed one hundred feast offerings using the liturgies from Gathering of Sugatas and United Intent of the Gurus. They made a feast offering in the Flower Cave using Khyentse Wangpo's treasure Heart Essence of Chetsun. Leaving Samye, they went next to Tsetang, about twenty kilometers to the east on the south side of the river. They made a quick visit to Tranduk, an ancient temple south of town that predates both the Lhasa Cathedral and Samye and which by Kongtrul's time had been converted to the Geluk tradition. They also saw some sacred items such as the clay statue of "The Panchen" near the marketplace of Dramda.[21]

Members of Kongtrul's group needed to be back at Tsurpu by the end of the lunar year, less than two months away, and so by now they were in a hurry to reach their ultimate destination: Mindroling. They passed over the opportunity to visit the other sacred sites of the Yarlung Valley and turned west, going up river for about fifty kilometers before turning down the Drapchi Valley to the monastery. Kongtrul and his companions were welcomed warmly and with considerable hospitality. They were put up in a small house next to the residence of the head of the monastery, the eighth throne holder, Yishin Wanggyel. Kongtrul had a long list of teachings he wished to receive from multiple masters at the monastery, most of which he would later include in the Treasury of Revelations. Yishin Wanggyel gave him all the Nyingma Spoken Word transmissions he had not previously received, the empowerment for the Innermost Heart of Immortality, and the entrustment for several protective deities. Trinle Chodron, Yishin Wanggyel's sister and an important teacher to Khyentse Wangpo, gave him a dozen transmissions—repeating some volumes of Nyingma spoken-word scriptures—and several treasure cycles. In return for these, Kongtrul offered empowerments for multiple Dzogchen teachings, including the Yangdak Heruka and White Amitāyus sections of Seven Profound Cycles, the first of which Chokling had entrusted personally to him.[22]

The company left Mindroling on February 6, 1858,[23] and arrived at Tsurpu on the twelfth of the same month,[24] on the eve of the new lunar year. They had retraced the same route they had used before, this time stopping on the way to visit Drapa Ngonshe's monastery of Dratang, which is not far from Mindroling. At Tsurpu, Kongtrul participated in the annual ceremonies marking the end of one year and the start of the other, the Earth Horse Year. He introduced rituals from Chokgyur Lingpa's revelations, including the torma exorcism rite of the Lord of Life from Seven Profound Cycles.[25]

With the ceremonies complete, Kongtrul set off again to meet with government officials to secure the release of the Tenth Situ. In Lhasa he viewed the pageantry of the annual Monlam, a prayer festival that was initiated by Tsongkhapa in 1409, during which monks from the three major Geluk monasteries surrounding the city gather at the Jokhang for about a week of rituals. Kongtrul was able to meet with the head of state, the Third Reting Rinpoche, Ngawang Yeshe Tsultrim Gyeltsen, at the Potala Palace, to whom he prostrated and offered gifts. The Twelfth Dalai Lama, Trinle Gyatso, was at the time only two years old. Kongtrul next met with the influential minister Shedra Wangchuk Gyelpo and petitioned successfully for permission to bring the Situ incarnation and his parents back to Kham. Whether or not Kongtrul made cash payments to the Tibetan government he does not say; the offerings to the Reting regent might have fulfilled this requirement.[26]

Kongtrul was not merely some petitioner from an outlying region but a lama of some reputation who was on official business from a major monastery in Kham. He was therefore, possibly in exchange for his own request, pressed into government service. He would spend the next two months touring the region once again to perform rituals for the benefit of the Tibetan state. This began before he left Lhasa. A Nyungne Lama, whom Kongtrul does not otherwise identify, sponsored a thousand feast offerings in a small chamber outside of the Padmasambhava Cave in the bowels of the Potala Palace's foundation. Kongtrul chose to use the Dispelling All Obstacles. He also performed the thousandfold offering ceremony before the main statue of Śākyamuni, and offered ornamentations and gold in all of the temples of the palace. Kongtrul gave empowerments and teachings to Nyungne Lama and several ministers, aristocrats, and *geshes*—highly educated Geluk monks—at their request. He did not record what they had requested.[27]

In the second half of March 1858,[28] Kongtrul set off on yet another circuit of religious sites in central Tibet, revisiting some he had seen several months prior and stopping at places he was earlier forced to miss. His travel arrange-

ments this time were made by the Tibetan government, and the entire delegation from Pelpung traveled with him. Where the earlier trip was personal
and undertaken on a tight budget, this one was comfortable. They traveled
to Samye first, via Dechen and over the Gokar Pass, the customary route
for government representatives. At the pass they met the Ninth Drukchen,
Mingyur Wanggyel, who was then on his way to Tsurpu. Both delighted
in the unexpected reunion—Kongtrul had taught him at Karma Gon in
1834—but they did not tarry to exchange teachings or empowerments.
Most of Kongtrul's company proceeded to Samye directly, but he stopped
over at Yamalung to practice the White Amitāyus from Seven Profound
Cycles. A group of monks were there performing ongoing rites for the benefit of the government, and Kongtrul gave them empowerments. On the way
to Samye, he stopped in at Drakmar Drinzang, the birthplace of Trisong
Detsen. At Samye, in the Yuzhel Shrine, Kongtrul again performed feast
offerings from Dispelling All Obstacles. He made further offerings and
feast celebrations in the other temples of the monastery and made prayers
for the well-being of Tibet and Kham in the Āryapalo Temple, the monastery's earliest building. During this visit he climbed Hepo Ri, the low but
steep ridge that hangs over Samye. It was from the peak of this ridge that
Padmasambhava is said to have subjugated the gods of Tibet and forced
them to serve as protectors of the new religion. Kongtrul mimicked the
iconic deed with his own performance, ritually reminding the gods and
spirits of their oaths.[29]

With the Yarlung Valley as their destination, they went up to Chimpu,
where Kongtrul headed a large feast offering. They then went to the east
to Tashi Dokha, a hermitage of Tsongkhapa, to Densatil, which was Pakmodrupa's seat, and to Zangri Khangmar, a meditation cave complex developed by Machik Labdron, performing feast offerings at each place. Circling
westward along the Tsangpo River, the company arrived at the Yarlung
Valley, passing the Tsechu Bumpa stūpa that marks the entrance to the
valley. Their first stop was the temple on Gangpo Ri, the hill above Tsetang
Monastery, where he performed a feast and bound the gods and spirits to
their oaths. At Tranduk, Kongtrul gave gold, ornaments, and performed
the thousandfold offering ceremony and an extended feast in the Padmasambhava shrine room. At Sheldrak, on the far side of the valley, Kongtrul
and about thirty monks spent a week performing a drubchen and mendrub
ritual from the Peaceful and Wrathful Magical Display section of Seven
Profound Cycles.[30]

While there, Kongtrul encountered a person who held the lineage for the "mandate" of the Embodiment of the Secret Ḍākinī, a revelation of Jomo Menmo, who was the main consort of Guru Chowang, and he requested the transmision. This cycle has thirty-eight liturgies in the Treasury of Revelations, eight of which Kongtrul composed. This cycle is said to have not been transmitted by Jomo Menmo herself but only "rediscovered" (in Tibetan parlance) by Khyentse Wangpo through a visionary encounter with the saint. That is, though credited to her, she herself never taught it, and the teaching only came into the world when Khyentse acquired it. Khyentse would frequently use this structure for his treasures, setting up an original revealer for his own revelations. Kongtrul repeats this particular assertion twice, in his biography of Khyentse Wangpo and in his *One Hundred Treasure Revealers*, both of which he composed decades after his visit to Sheldrak and after he had received the revelation's transmission from Khyentse.[31] Nowhere does Kongtrul remark on the contradiction between this later narrative and his meeting with a lineage holder.

The group proceeded in turn to Yumbu Lagang, said to be the first palace built in Tibet, and to the other two of the three major stūpas of the valley: Takchen Bumpa and Gontang Bumpa, making offerings at each. On the slopes of Mount Yarlha Shampo, the abode of the protector deity of the same name, Kongtrul performed the ransom rites from Truly Perfected King, a section of Seven Profound Cycles. They toured the tombs of the ancient kings in Chonggye, at the head of the valley, and then continued south.[32]

The company's next destination was Mawochok, a monastery far to the south that was the seat of Nyangrel Nyima Wozer, the self-proclaimed reincarnation of Guru Chowang, and then on to Sekhar Gutok, the site of Milarepa's tower. Their route took them along the western shore of Drigu Lake, and they would have also passed Tsering Jong, the seat of Jigme Lingpa, but Kongtrul does not record stopping there. His interest in the wildly popular Heart Essence of the Vast Expanse was minimal; he included only eighteen texts from the cycle in the Treasury of Revelations, four of which he wrote (there are over a hundred texts of Heart Essence of the Vast Expanse in Jigme Lingpa's Collected Works). Perhaps a cycle that he was not at liberty to rework did not appeal to him. The company continued southward into the Lhokha region, stopping at a number of sites: Benpa Chakdor, a famous temple to Vajrapāṇi; Guru Lhakhang, the seat of Pema Lingpa's incarnation line; and the famous statue of Vairocana at the

Khoting Lhakhang on the border of Bhutan. Along the way they performed feasts from Guru Chowang's Eight Commands cycle. They spent five days in the Chakpuchen Cave, a major Padmasambhava site, practicing the Yangdak Heruka section of Seven Profound Cycles. Kongtrul reports stopping at two places between Kharchu and Sekhar which he names Lhamokhar and Pelgyi Pukring. The first is a Tibetan rendering of Devīkoṭa and thus suggests the great pilgrimage mountain of Tsāri, to which his hermitage was associated. Tsāri, however, is hundreds of kilometers to the east of Kharchu. The second, Pukring, is a small nunnery in the region.[33]

At Sekhar they performed feast offerings in the presence of the image of Marpa and again at the Nyanya Lungten Cave. Turning north to return to Tsurpu, they passed along the east shore of Pemaling Lake and arrived at Lhalung, stopping at Lhayak Guru Lhakhang, Guru Chowang's seat. They continued through the Yamdrok region and the vast Yamdrok Lake to Chakzam Chuwori Monastery, near the site of Tangtong Gyelpo's famous iron bridge across the Yarlung Tsangpo River. At such an important crossroad, Kongtrul and his companions performed rituals to bind the gods and spirits to the protection of Buddhism and the well-being of Tibet. On Sinpo Ri, the ridge at the confluence of the Lhasa Kyichu and the Tsangpo Rivers, Kongtrul offered a further feast and visited the famous statue of Cakrasaṃvara in the thirteenth-century Sakya temple there. They then crossed back to the south bank of the Tsangpo and went east to the small temple of Zhung Treshing to see the relic kept there said to be the skull of Marpa. This was Kongtrul's final pilgrimage destination in Tibet. They crossed the river again, went over the Jela Pass and up the Kyichu, and arrived at Lhasa. There Kongtrul reported to the government that he had performed the rituals they had commissioned.[34]

Kongtrul's official tasks were now complete. He had secured permission to bring the Situ incarnation to Pelpung and had fulfilled the obligations put on him by the Tibetan government in exchange. He returned to Tsurpu on June 4, 1858,[35] arriving in time to observe the tenth-day dances. Perhaps exhausted by two back-to-back tours of central Tibet, Kongtrul spent the next month in personal retreat at Pema Khyungdzong, a cave in the cliffs above the monastery that was a practice site of the Second and Third Karmapas. Kongtrul spent his time on the White Amitāyus from Seven Profound Cycles, dedicating that practice to the long life of the Fourteenth Karmapa, and on Vajradaṇḍa, the form of Vajrapaṇi he had long been personally interested in. It was the Vajradaṇḍa section of Dispelling All Obstacles that Chokling had prescribed to him to cure his eye disease; perhaps his eyes were bothering him again.[36]

On June 19[37] the Karmapa summoned him from the cave, and Kongtrul went to where he and his retinue were camped for the summer to transmit the revelations of Chokgyur Lingpa. Kongtrul first gave the Karmapa the empowerment of the White Amitāyus, fresh from his practice, and prepared to continue with extensive transmissions on the 21st.[38] The Ninth Drukchen was still there, but he initially declined to take part, not yet trusting Chokgyur Lingpa's work. The Karmapa had suffered poor eyesight since returning from Kham, and the Drukchen apparently suspected Chokling's treasures were the cause. The Fourteenth Karmapa and Kongtrul had both already struggled through their reticence to accept Chokling, but the Drukchen as yet had not. On the eve of the ceremonies, however, the Drukchen had several dreams which satisfied his doubts, and so he joined the Karmapa and about twenty others in receiving the complete Dispelling All Obstacles transmission. Kongtrul further soothed the Drukchen's anxiety with the promise that the hierarch was the fated custodian of the Lord of Life cycle. The elderly Eighth Pawo and the Tenth Situ participated, despite the Situ being only a few years old. Kongtrul gave the Lord of Life section of Seven Profound Cycles to the Karmapa, the Drukchen, and to the Chowang Tulku. This person was the rebirth of Guru Chowang, the line having initiated only in the seventeenth century with the recognition of a nephew of the Ninth Karmapa. Returning to the monastery, Kongtrul gave additional transmissions to the Karmapa and Wontrul, who had come to Tibet: the Magical Display and the Stirring the Depths sections of Seven Profound Cycles, as well as Choje Lingpa's revelation Vajrakīla Essence of Mind, for which Kongtrul composed the daily practice in the Treasury of Revelations. Also while at Tsurpu, Kongtrul gave Chokling empowerments to the Ninth Tsurpu Gyeltsab incarnation. With the completion of all these transmissions, Kongtrul reported in his diary, he fulfilled Chokgyur Lingpa's instructions.[39]

The Eighth Pawo invited the Situ incarnation to his seat at Nenang Monastery, a few kilometers down the valley from Tsurpu. Kongtrul accompanied the child, and while there gave the Pawo the Vajrakīla empowerments from Seven Profound Cycles. Kongtrul took the opportunity to receive, from a man he names only as Rigdzin Tulku, Kagyu and Nyingma empowerments that the lama had received from the previous Pawo. Returning to Tsurpu having fulfilled all his responsibilities, Kongtrul finally took time to tour the sights of the monastery. He visited a meditation cave of the First Karmapa and the famous statue of Śākyamuni Buddha known as the Ornament of the World, a twenty-meter bronze commissioned by the Third Karmapa.[40]

During the summer of 1858, Kongtrul began to prepare for the return to Kham. He consulted with astrologers to select the best day for departing and performed smoke offerings and other rituals to ensure his party's safety. He left via Lhasa in order to bid a final farewell to government officials and to the Buddha statues in the Cathedral and Ramoche. The Third Reting gave them an audience, sending them off with silks from the government treasury to offer Chokgyur Lingpa.[41]

Kongtrul and his several companions made their way from Lhasa by way of Drak Yerpa to the northeast of the city, and then turned northwest into the Penyul Valley and proceeded north to Taklung and then northeast to Reting Monastery. At Sangzhung, on the northern route, they were met by the remaining Pelpung contingent which had taken the main route through Yangpachen and Damchukha. At nearby Tashi Umatang, the Derge government escort joined them, together with Wontrul. Further north, at Nakchu, they reunited with the Karmapa, who was also traveling east with a large entourage. The Tenth Situ and his family, including a brother who would also be raised as a lama, were possibly with the Karmapa's party, but the parents might also have remained home and may never have seen their son again. Their progress was repeatedly delayed by the faithful requesting teachings and the black hat ceremony. Rivers swollen by summer rain also slowed their journey. At some point en route, the treasure revealer Chogyel Dorje arranged to meet with Kongtrul and transmitted to him all his treasures. Two of his cycles are in the Treasury of Revelations: Azure Wrathful Guru and the Orgyen Jambhala. Kongtrul and Chogyel Dorje spent three days performing the Yongge Mingyur Dorje longevity ritual called Integration of Means and Wisdom to celebrate their meeting, and Kongtrul performed an additional longevity ritual for the Situ incarnation.[42]

Passing as quickly as possible through the Zurmang region—the Karmapa apparently had decided to accompany Kongtrul and the Tenth Situ all the way to Pelpung before making his way to his own monastery—they crossed the Drichu River and arrived at Tsagye Plain, to the north of Derge. There a delegation from the government welcomed them. Kongtrul found himself ashamed of his appearance. He wrote that he was "dressed like a poor government servant" and was extremely distraught that this was the

way he presented himself to be greeted by the government. Ever the pessi-
mist regarding his personal stature, Kongtrul took this as an omen that his
strength and authority had peaked and would henceforth wane. The remark
was possibly meant to be prophetic, a hint of how his fortunes at Pelpung
would change for the worse with the arrival of the Tenth Situ.[43]

The child was already showing signs of instability. The journey seems to
have exhausted him, and his mood was foul and unpredictable. He objected
to the weather, and became increasingly agitated as they neared the monastery. He may simply have missed home. They reached Pelpung on November
16, 1858,[44] to a large celebration. Kongtrul took his leave and ascended to his
hermitage and to his mother, whom he found in good health. He hoped to
spend the remainder of the year there, practicing his customary annual rites
of Vajrakīla and Tārā, but before the Earth Sheep Year could start he was
summoned to Derge by Chokgyur Lingpa and Khyentse Wangpo to begin
long decades of government service.[45]

18

## GOVERNMENT SERVICE,
## THE CONTINUED OPENING OF TSĀDRA,
## AND THE TENTH SITU'S
## ENTHRONEMENT

1858–1860

Chokgyur Lingpa flourished during the decade of 1856 to 1866. Of the thirty-seven caches into which Khyentse Wangpo organized his revelations, thirty-three date to this period, and almost all of these were produced with the assistance of Kongtrul. While Kongtrul was in Tibet, Chokling had stayed in Nangchen, but at the end of 1858 he was back in Derge offering his services to the government. To the east, Gonpo Namgyel, a chieftain of the Nyarong Valley, had been conquering neighboring territories, and the leadership of Derge was alarmed. In November Chokling had fallen ill at Trao Plain, near the capital, with something like blood poisoning, and Khyentse had gone to cure him, after which the two of them continued to Derge to perform the rituals for the protection of the state. Kongtrul was back less than two months before they summoned him to participate. He was now a lama of stature, one who negotiated with the government in Lhasa and who would be expected to help guide the next generation of leaders at Pelpung. As he supervised the production of an astonishing amount of treasure literature, he was continually called to serve government and monastery officials.[1]

In January 1859, during the last month of the Earth Horse Year, Chokling and Khyentse were in Dokhoma, a spot outside the city where in the early eighteenth-century King Sonam Puntsok had constructed a stūpa. They were performing drubchen rituals and exorcisms using wrathful deities from the Eight Commands—rituals intended to protect the kingdom—as was fitting for the end of a lunar year and especially needed in times of increased danger. Chokling was there with his wife and children.[2] By this point he had most likely sired all three of his children with his two consorts, and the children would have then been only a few years old. Although sexual yoga is not supposed to result in pregnancy—in a successful performance the man theoretically draws his semen back into his own body—children are often an unintended, if not an entirely unpredictable, consequence of the practice. The presence of children in a treasure revealer's entourage often sparks criticism, either from questioning the treasure revealer's intentions or his yogic abilities. Yet the children's presence also attests to the sexual yoga, even if they are not the intended result, and they are for this reason not concealed from the public. Kongtrul and Khyentse were both reputed to be able to speak with deities, but there were still things that only a sexually active layman could do. Chokgyur Lingpa was now an established treasure revealer and secure enough to bring his family to his public performances.[3]

Khyentse gave a lecture that Kongtrul found "marvelous," but the rituals did not go well, as indicated by a violent wind that rose when they cast the torma. Chokling was forced to perform additional exorcism rituals for several days, and Kongtrul did so himself, using Union of All Rare and Precious Jewels and Atīśa's system of Vajrabhairava. The ground sufficiently cleared of dangers, Kongtrul then gave the complete empowerments for the Nyingma spoken-word scriptures, an event that would have taken many weeks. There to receive the empowerments were Khyentse, Chokling, and the queen and princes of Derge. These were Choying Zangmo, the widow of Damtsik Dorje, and her two sons, Pelden Chime Takpai Dorje and his unnamed brother who was then about ten years old. His mother was acting as head of state in the capacity of a regent. Pelden Chime Takpai Dorje would not be enthroned until after the defeat of Gonpo Namgyel in 1865.[4]

Following the ceremonies, Chokgyur Lingpa informed the Derge court that he had received a prophecy indicating that for the benefit of religion and the state the government should construct a new temple at Tro Maṇḍala, to the northeast of the city on the route to Dzogchen Monastery and the northern districts of the kingdom. The temple was apparently to be classified as Nyingma. In the first days of the Fire Sheep Year, which began on February 3, 1859,[5] Kongtrul, Khyentse, and Chokling went to Tro Maṇḍala to survey possible spots for the construction. The omens on their departure were not good; an unwelcomed snow called "stages of white, red, and black" fell, and there were other phenomena that Kongtrul interpreted as negative indications.[6]

Chokling's proposal to the government came at a time when Derge's sovereignty was threatened by the slow rise of Gonpo Namgyel. What began in the 1840s as a personal feud between rival families had by the late 1850s developed into a regional war. By 1859 Gonpo Namgyel had conquered all of the Nyarong Valley and parts of neighboring regions, and the leaders of Derge and of its many monasteries had reason to fear invasion. Rituals to repel harm and new constructions designed to ensure public welfare were not undertaken in the abstract. Khyentse described the need for the new temple at Tro Maṇḍala in these terms: "If a temple with just four columns and an image of Maitreya were to be built now, it will ensure that the turmoil of Nyake will not come here." Kongtrul, Khyentse, and Chokling accordingly performed rituals to ready the selected site for construction. They performed feast offerings to the gods, Khyentse gave a sermon on the topic of tantra to plant Buddhism at the site, and they concealed a treasure vase as a means of earning the favor of the local deities. Chokgyur Lingpa made gifts to the royal family, including a "regent" statue of Padmasambhava that he claimed to have revealed as treasure, and in response he received their promise of support for the new temple. The three then went together to Tsādra.

Chokgyur Lingpa had not sufficiently won over the leadership of Gonchen Monastery, however, which opposed the temple construction. In his diary Kongtrul accused the Sakya Gonchen community of excessive attachment to their sectarian affiliation. The queen's patronage might have reminded ministers and aristocrats of Queen Tsewang Lhamo's Nyingma sympathies a half century earlier. Chokgyur Lingpa complained that the monastic treasurer, Tashi Gyatso, blocked the disbursement of funds out of a belief that government support for the Nyingma temple would threaten its commitment to the Sakya monasteries.[7] The new temple was never built, although many decades later, in 1886, after a nearby ancient monastery burned down—one which had originally been Bon and had been converted to Sakya—Khyentse arranged for it to be rebuilt on the spot Chokling had selected. It continued to operate as a Sakya monastery.[8]

Kongtrul, Khyentse, and Chokling took the opportunity of being together to exchange new teachings. Khyentse gave them Heart Drop of the Venerable Goddess of Immortality, which he is said to have received in a vision in January 1855[9] and kept secret until recently. He had already given the initial transmission to Chokgyur Lingpa and now gave the full cycle to both men. Kongtrul ultimately adopted this popular long-life White Tārā revelation as one of his main longevity practices. Chokling gave Kongtrul his recent revelation, Mahākaruṇika: Dredging the Pit of Cyclic Existence, and the three men also transcribed the liturgies for Chokling's Wish-Fulfilling

Jewel of the Guru's Intent. Chokling dictated, and Kongtrul and Khyentse both acted as scribes. The Fourteenth Karmapa himself joined them, and he wrote out a one-page offering liturgy. It may have been around this time that the Karmapa and Khyentse together composed a supplication prayer to Kongtrul's past lives, Melodious Āḍambara Drum.[10]

The three lamas returned to Derge to perform more rituals for the state. Khyentse Wangpo spent two weeks transmitting the *Sūtra That Gathers All Intentions*, including performing the extensive drubchen and mendrub rituals. In the palace, Chokling installed a statue of Vaiśravaṇa, the guardian deity of the north and a god of wealth. Kongtrul performed a ransom ceremony for the princes, a rite of protection for their vitality. They then parted ways and Kongtrul returned to his hermitage. Dabzang Tulku had returned from Karma Gon and requested the empowerments for all of Jatson Nyingpo's revelations, and various other petitioners came through requesting teachings.[11]

While Kongtrul was in Tibet, Chokgyur Lingpa had established his two religious communities in Nangchen: Neten and Tsike. Nevertheless, he continued to stay close to Kongtrul and Khyentse. He went to Tsādra soon after the ceremonies in the capital to continue to transmit and transcribe his revelations and to solidify Kongtrul's investment in his treasures. Chokling performed an extensive feast offering and made prayers to bestow on Kongtrul "the blessings of his lineage." Kongtrul found the ceremonies fruitful. He recorded that on the evening of the blessing he dreamed of Padmasambhava, who, in the form of the treasure revealer Dorje Lingpa, gave him the blessings of the teachings of the "one hundred treasure revealers." Kongtrul recorded in his diary that in the dream he recalled being a student of Dorje Lingpa's and having in that lifetime received all of his teachings. He also remembered being Dungtso Repa, the fourteenth-century mystic who revealed teachings supposedly concealed by Gampopa and which form the basis of the Zurmang tradition of Mahāmudrā. With this dream, Kongtrul felt he had received the actual transmission of both men's teachings and was therefore able to include them in the Treasury of Revelations; as usual, he wrote many of the liturgies himself.[12]

This was the first instance Kongtrul recorded of reviving a teaching lineage—in this case that of Dorje Lingpa's revelations—by means of dream encounters. He nowhere indicated that he was unable to locate an acceptable master to give him the transmission, but that may well have been the case. Not long after Kongtrul dreamed of his connection to Dungtso Repa and

Dorje Lingpa, Chokling transmitted to him Khyentse's revealed version of the Embodiment of the Secret Ḍākinī. This was the cycle for which Kongtrul had previously claimed to have received the "mandate" from a living lineage holder while in Tibet. The two also continued to transcribe Chokling's treasures, completing the Wish-Fulfilling Jewel revelation. Kongtrul records that they worked on a revelation related to the form of the Six-Armed Mahākāla known as Swift Acting Wisdom Protector, the Shangpa Kagyu protector, but there is no record of Chokling having a treasure connected to this deity, so if it existed it appears to have been lost. Kongtrul would install this Shangpa Kagyu deity in a place of honor at Tsādra.[13]

Kongtrul had asked Chokgyur Lingpa for a treasure gazetteer for Tsādra two years earlier but had yet to receive it. They had still not completed the opening and needed a gazetteer to detail all the features of the place and explain the benefits and methods of practice there. At some point Kongtrul had written to Chokling repeating the request and received a prophecy in response that explained that a Vajrakīla temple would need to be constructed there before the revelation and the completion of the opening could occur. The passage, from the ḍākinī section of Three Roots, a part of Seven Profound Cycles, reads:

> Tsādra, the supreme site of enlightened mind
> Has the form of the heart's eight petals.
> It is essential, in order to open the site,
> to construct a temple to the Glorious Heruka
> in the eastern gate
> and to make images and supports for the guardians.[14]

Note that according to the earlier gazetteer of Kham, Tsādra is not the main site of enlightened mind but the mind-aspect of enlightened qualities. The eight petals of the heart refers to subtle-body theory. Chokling felt that the leadership of Pelpung ought to sponsor the temples, and he sent a message to that effect to the Situ estate. This prophecy was received well, and construction at Tsādra began quickly.[15]

Chokgyur Lingpa appears to have selected the site for the temple and scattered flowers there to prepare it. On April 12, 1859,[16] Lama Ngedon, the vajra master of Pelpung's meditation center, performed a Cakrasaṃvara "earth rite" and other rituals of preparation and renewed the vows of ten monks who had completed three-year retreats.[17] On April 17[18] Kongtrul and a few other monks performed a separate "earth rite" from the Kālacakra tradition and they buried a treasure vase. The earth rite is a ceremony to allay the negative effects of the terrestrial spirits and is done prior to breaking ground in a construction project. Kongtrul recorded in his diary that during the ceremonies witnesses saw a ring of white light surrounding the two men. Construction for the temple began in that same month. Wontrul arranged for pillars, beams, and other material for the outer structure to be sent up from Pelpung, and Kongtrul requested and received additional material for residences. A clansman of Kongtrul's named Yungdrung Tsultrim[19] donated the gilded copper roof ornament and paintings of the Buddha and the eight bodhisattvas as well as one of Vajrakīla. Kongtrul otherwise raised the money for carpentry and accepted donations of all other objects, such as door locks and pots and pans, as well as the sacred objects such as statues of the Vajrakīla and the Six-Armed Mahākāla.[20]

That same month, the fourth of the lunar calendar, Kongtrul and Chokling went down to Pelpung to participate in the annual vase ceremony. This year the liturgy used was the Hayagrīva from Seven Profound Cycles, and Chokling presided, a remarkable honor for a man who was once ignored by the community and evidence of Kongtrul's leading role there. However, the insertion of a new Nyingma treasure cycle into the Kagyu monastery's liturgical calendar may have contributed to ongoing resentment against him among more orthodox members of the community.[21]

On his return to his hermitage, Kongtrul was able to take personal time for meditation, performing the fulfillment from United Intent of the Gurus and the sādhana of approach and accomplishment for Khyentse's Heart Drop of the Venerable Goddess of Immortality. When he was done with these, Chokling returned and continued to landscape the hermitage. He selected the locations for the shrines to the protector deities and the nāgas, and he supervised their construction and the manufacture of the images and necessary amulets. He performed a feast offering, fulfillment rite, and smoke offering at Uchetem to pacify the local gods and designated particular features as naturally occurring manifestations of the Buddha. When the temple construction was complete, Chokling and Dabzang performed the consecration using the liturgy from Heart Essence of Vajrasattva's Enlightened Mind, a White Tārā fire offering, and a feast and mending ritual from Union of All Rare and Precious Jewels.[22]

After promising over two years earlier that a guidebook to Tsādra was concealed there, Chokling finally revealed it that summer. Multiple dates and narratives are given for the extraction: Kongtrul records the tenth day of the sixth month, July 9, 1859, as does the text itself in the colophon.[23] Khyentse, however, has it as the tenth day of the seventh month, September 6.[24] This could be a factor of the different systems of calculating the monkey month, but it just as easily could be that they had not yet settled on a specific time. Nor was the location of the revelation yet decided when Kongtrul wrote his diary entry. He notes it was at the Vairocana Cave, but other accounts, such as the text's colophon, have it happening at the Padmasambhava Cave. Along with the scrolls for the gazetteer, Chokgyur Lingpa produced substances for use in filling the Vajrakīla image for the new temple and Three Cycles of the Secret Heart Essence, which Kongtrul promptly assisted in decoding and which he later included in the Treasury of Revelations. With the gazetteer in hand, Chokling laid out the inner and outer circumambulation routes—meaning the route close to the core of the site and the longer route that encircles the entire domain. As part of that process, they opened a small shrine to the resident nāgas. Chokling left soon after.[25]

The treasure gazetteer provided all the description Kongtrul needed. Building on the passage in the regional gazetteer from two years earlier, it locates the place in the global geography, calling it the Vajra Citta Koṭa—Vajra Mind Palace—of the eight palaces of Cārita. It narrates lists of the saints and deities who are present and gives the time in which all deities gather there—the monkey month of the Sheep Year—when pilgrimage is encouraged. And it promised the rewards of practice there—one session of meditation being equal to a year's practice elsewhere, and the like. Kongtrul would later expand the description in his catalog of the site, All-Pervading Melody of the Pure Lands, which he wrote in 1864, but for the needs of the day it was more than sufficient.

The remainder of 1859 was dedicated to transmissions, practice, and preparations for the Fourteenth Karmapa's visit. Kongtrul surveyed the monastery and ensured that supplies were in place at the various temples and at Situ's estate, and he sent an escort to meet the Karmapa. In the meantime, he gave the full empowerments for the Shangpa Kagyu tradition to Donyon Tulku of Katok Monastery and others, and he gave the complete empowerments for Jatson Nyingpo's revelations to a lay tantrika named Tridu Behu and his students, who promised to build a retreat center for the practices. Kongtrul received Taksham Nuden Dorje's Heart Drop of Mitra from Dabzang Tulku; he included this Mahākaruṇika cycle in the

Treasury of Revelations, for which he composed an empowerment manual. His meditation during this period continued to be Heart Drop of the Venerable Goddess of Immortality, which gave him confidence that his life span could possibly reach ninety years (he died at age eighty-seven). He responded to requests of patrons and then left for Mesho and Terlung to collect the monastery's share of the year's crop. On his return he visited Khyentse at Dzongsar. The transmission they shared was the nine-deity mandala of Amitāyus. The Karmapa had by then arrived at Pelpung, and Kongtrul went to welcome him with a transmission and teaching on the Eight Commands.[26]

In February 1860, as the lunar year ended, Kongtrul moved to Bongsar, a residence at Pelpung. He practiced a Vajrasattva cycle called Sphere of Mind from Chokgyur Lingpa's Seven Profound Cycles. He was pleased with the results; he composed the manuals for the empowerment and the blessing ceremonies in the Treasury of Revelations. He instituted continual practice in the protective deity shrine room there and performed his annual end-of-year exorcism rituals.[27]

The Tenth Situ, Pema Kunzang Chogyel, was enthroned at Pelpung on February 26, 1860.[28] The ceremony lasted several days and included a lengthy speech by Kongtrul. He carefully crafted the lecture, which was later published in his Collected Works under the title *A Celebration of the Opening of One Hundred Doors to Great Wonder: A Lecture on the Mandala Offering to the Supreme Emanation of Maitreya on the Occasion of His Investiture to the Lion Throne*. We have no way of knowing how Kongtrul gave this lecture. Perhaps he read it, or perhaps he spoke from notes which were later collected and composed into the published work. It was certainly delivered in front of a large crowd, with the young Situ on a throne supported with eight carved lions, the Fourteenth Karmapa sitting beside him on a seat slightly higher. Pelpung's massive assembly hall could accommodate hundreds of monks and guests, and the hillside on which the temple is perched would have been surrounded by many hundreds more monks, nuns, and laypeople eager to partake in the blessings and participate in the festivities. Unfortunately, Kongtrul recorded few details about the ceremonies in his diary. Offerings were made from Tsurpu, Pelpung, Derge, and other centers, a communal meal followed the main ceremonies, and several lamas gave reading transmissions. Regarding his own lecture, he wrote in his diary only that he gave "an extensive lecture on mandala."[29]

The lecture was a reminder of institutional identity, designed to reinforce for the community their allegiance to the Situ incarnations and their place in the wider family of Karma Kagyu and Buddhist traditions. It is divided into three sections: the setting, an overview and praise to the lives of the Situ incarnations, and an explanation of the investiture ceremony. The first lays out the institutional stage using the categories of "five perfect conditions": the teacher, teaching, assembly, place, and time. The teacher here was the Karmapa, the head of the Karma Kagyu congregation. The teaching was Kongtrul's exposition on the lives of the previous Situ incarnations. The assembly was the community that encircles the Situ and which was defined by his activity. The place was Pelpung, his seat, and the time was the moment of the enthronement. The affirmation of these constants—Karmapa, Situ, Pelpung, and the congregation—was offered to heal the rift that the Ninth Situ's death had caused. The second chapter, on the lives of the Situ incarnations, proclaims that the young boy on the large throne was, in fact, a continuation of the Situ's activity, a return home of a being who was only briefly absent. Kongtrul in this section names all historical and mythological figures said to have been prior incarnations of the Situ line, starting in India and progressing through generations of leading Tibetans, including Marpa Chokyi Lodro and Tāranātha. Through all this, Kongtrul told his audience, Situ's activity never ceased; he simply "changed bodies." In the final section of the second chapter, Kongtrul included two prophecies regarding the Tenth Situ's birth, the first from a Karmapa, the second from Seven Profound Cycles of Chokgyur Lingpa, whom Kongtrul describes as an "indisputable and timely great treasure revealer." Kongtrul also asserts that other treasures revealed by Chokling at several different locations also attest to the boy's identity as an emanation of Padmasambhava.

The third part of the lecture is an explanation of the ritual being performed: the public investiture of the Tenth Situ on the throne of Pelpung, starting with the cultivation of the proper attitude and ending with the dedication of merit. Presumably the entire congregation participated in these activities, with Kongtrul delivering his lecture before or during the performance. The service was done according to the seven stages of a traditional sādhana: visualization of the deities, the making of offerings, confession of faults, rejoicing in positive activities, requesting teachings, asking that the teacher remain in the world, and the dedication of merit. Following this the congregation made offerings and fashioned as a vast maṇḍala; this section of the service provided the name of the lecture and explains Kongtrul's sole remark about it in the diary. The congregation visualized the full spectrum of a traditional maṇḍala offering—the entire universe symbolized in various auspicious objects.[30]

Three additional lectures followed Kongtrul's reading. They covered six foundational scriptures: Candrakīrti's *Madhyamakāvatāra*, Asaṅga's *Uttaratantra* and *Abhisamayālaṃkāra*, Vasubhandu's *Abhidharmakośa*, the *Hevajra Tantra*, and the Third Karmapa's *Profound Inner Principles*. The first three represent teachings on the fundamental Mahāyāna doctrines, while the last two cover tantric theory and practice; the *Hevajra Tantra* is considered the basis for the Mahāmudrā teachings. Kongtrul unfortunately does not tell us who gave the three lectures or how the three speakers divided the subjects.[31]

The ceremony continued the following day with a banquet during which Kongtrul delivered another lecture, this time on the *Guhyagarbha Tantra*, the foundational Indian scripture for the Dzogchen teachings. The Karmapa followed with the reading transmission for the Collected Works of the First Karmapa and the Second Zhamar, after which Kongtrul gave the reading transmission of the Dharma Ocean of Precepts, a treasure of Orgyen Lingpa which is one of the main Eight Commands cycles. He also gave the reading transmission for the Eighth Karmapa's composition on the Vinaya, *Great Commentary on Discipline*. The meditation center's vajra master Karma Ngedon and other lamas requested empowerments for *Ocean of Deities* and Lightning Garland of Protective Deities: Peaceful Garland, Wrathful Garland with associated protective deities, and Chokling's Seven Profound Cycles. At this point Kongtrul begged off from continuing with the communal rites and retired to Tsādra to perform his longevity practices. His dreams were disturbing him.[32]

The Fourteenth Karmapa remained at Pelpung for some time. In May 1860 Kongtrul gave him the empowerments and transmissions for his Treasury of the Kagyu Tantras. This was the first transmission of the seven-year-old collection. The Karmapa presided over the annual vase ceremony in May, and in late June, with a retinue of some fifty people, he went up to Tsādra. Khyentse Wangpo also came and bestowed his Heart Drop of the Venerable Goddess of Immortality. The contents of the Vajrakīla Temple were installed and the lamas dedicated eight days, from June 21 to June 28,[33] to a long-life drubchen and mendrub ritual using United Intent of the Guru. They then consecrated the objects as, Kongtrul wrote, the wisdom deities entered the temple and icons and "flowers of virtue came down like rain."

Then, in October, a group of fifteen monks, ten of whom had mastered the three trainings of ethics, meditation, and wisdom, and which included the young Tenth Situ, used a Cakrasaṃvara liturgy composed by the Ninth Karmapa to further consecrate the religious objects over two days. Kongtrul organized additional consecration ceremonies over the next two years: on April 18, 1861,[34] Khyentse Wangpo performed extensive rites from multiple traditions, and in the spring of 1863 Kongtrul himself spent ten days with a group of monks. The site was now fully opened and consecrated and ready for a dramatic expansion.[35]

# 19

# THE FIRST THREE-YEAR RETREAT AT TSĀDRA

*Rimay Part One*

1860–1862

By 1860 Nyake Gonpo Namgyel had conquered all of Nyarong and was expanding into neighboring territories. He had become a man whose summons would be heeded by even the most revered lamas. In early July[1] he sent word to Pelpung requesting the presence of the Fourteenth Karmapa and the Tenth Situ, newly enthroned but not yet six years old. Kongtrul was also called alongside his more prominent masters.[2] It was the first of many episodes of Kongtrul's involvement in the growing conflict which would soon consume the entire region. Before the war came to him, however, he would initiate a formal retreat community at Tsādra and compose his greatest work, the Treasury of Knowledge, two milestones in the expression of the ecumenicalism for which he is so revered.

Upon receiving the summons, the lamas left immediately and met the warlord and his family in Drangdil in the Ase region of Upper Nyarong. The occasion was the death of Gonpo Namgyel's grandson, Pelchen, the son of Chime Gonpo. The young man had apparently died from smallpox, possibly contracted during a failed siege of Litang in the late 1850s; the defenders supposedly threw bags of snuff mixed with the blood and excrement of smallpox victims into the Nyarong forces, spreading the disease among them and forcing a temporary retreat. The lamas were invited to participate in the forty-nine day funeral observances, although it is not clear from the diary whether they were tasked with organizing the entire ritual program. Nyakla Pema Dudul, a prominent lama of the Nyarong valley who was Gonpo Namgyel's main guru, surely presided. During the event Pema Dudul received teachings from the Fourteenth Karmapa and gave the Karmapa empowerments from his own treasure revelations. Kongtrul only states that the Karmapa presided over the cremation and performed the famous black hat ceremony, and that as part of the service they gave some authorization rites. The Karmapa apparently flattered the warlord with a prediction that the boy would be reborn human and able to practice Buddhism.[3]

On their return from Nyarong, the lamas detoured north to the Ter-lung Valley and they stopped at Dagam Wangpuk where Jamyang Khyentse Wangpo was in residence. Inside the large cavern—a temple building was at some point constructed inside it—the lamas together celebrated an extensive feast offering. The entire entourage would have been able to sit inside for the ceremony, enjoying natural light and the fine view across the valley. This was likely the first opportunity for Khyentse to transmit his revelations to the Karmapa, and he gave him three. The first was Heart Essence of the Tamer of Beings: Mahākaruṇika Cittaviśramaṇa, which he had revealed at Samye in 1848 and which Kongtrul included in the Treasury of Revelations. Khyentse also transmitted Heart Essence of Chetsun and Heart Essence of the Lake Born. After the feasts and the transmissions were concluded, Kongtrul and the Karmapa left Khyentse in the cave. Kongtrul went directly to Tsādra, and the Karmapa went to Pelpung.[4]

With an eye to establishing a program of formal group retreat, in August, 1860,[5] Kongtrul prepared the hermitage for a visit from the Karmapa.[6] Kongtrul had been teaching widely for over a decade and was by then known as a master of scores of teaching transmissions that he distributed widely through ritual activity and publishing. He had received transmissions in all of the Buddhist traditions of Tibet, and he was intent on drawing them all forward. He was forty-seven years old. He had disciples, and he had his own personal retreat center that he had been developing for a dozen years, building temples and residences and inviting his famous colleagues to perform rituals. The opening activities had stretched over a decade, concluding only the year before with Chokling's revelation of the gazetteer and Secret Essence, his twenty-fifth treasure revelation. A formalized retreat program for his disciples was not in any way an expected outcome of this activity. It was, in fact, a bold move, one which would raise his profile and influence in the religious landscape of Kham, in that he would be training scores of young teachers in the ecumenical approach he would champion. It was potentially risky as well; Pelpung had a retreat center with an already-established program of three-year, three-fortnight retreats to train lamas, and Kongtrul had been providing instruction there for some time. The retreat center at Tsādra would not be an extension of that but would be a separate institution, identified as Shangpa Kagyu but where all Buddhist traditions would be taught. In his years of developing his own retreat hermitage and now a retreat community with a distinct ritual program and curriculum of study, it would not have been unreasonable for monks at Pelpung to suspect Kongtrul of pursuing his own goals and of building a community with himself at the center, rather than working for the common good of Pelpung Monastery. Over the next forty years he would initiate nine retreat cycles at Tsādra.[7]

Tibetans had been going to the mountains to practice meditation for well over a thousand years, both singularly or in small groups. They were sent by their teachers, or they made their own way. Tibetans delight in stories of hermits who survived on next to nothing, relying on a yogic technique known as "extracting the essence" to extend the nutrient value of scarce provisions. Milarepa famously turned green from eating only nettles, his body covered in the fine silky hair that signals severe malnutrition. Sitting in a cave was arduous. They are cold, lonely, and frightening. Once established by the practice of a famous hermit, however, a cave would continue to be occupied and its residents might be able to expect regular provisions from nearby villagers, nomads, or from pilgrims passing through. Many cave and remote retreat locations across Tibet developed into centers of teaching and practice, as hermits attracted disciples and patrons built residences and temples inside or around the original cave. Some of these hermitages became associated with monasteries or developed into monasteries in their own right, with their own annual ritual calendars and programs of study.[8]

Monasteries often established dedicated retreat centers for their monks to gain expertise in the rituals of the tradition, both the group ceremonies and the advanced meditative techniques. For the most part, however, both hermitages and monastic retreat centers were places without fixed or mandated periods of residency. Monks (or lay people in the case of communities of tantric practitioners) would join for as long as they liked, caught in the orbit of a particular teacher or tasked with specific duties. Nor did all inmates of hermitages or monastic retreat centers spend their days in meditation—most, in fact, were serving the teachers or the hermits by cooking, cleaning, gathering water and firewood, or attending to the physical components of the rituals.

Jamgon Kongtrul intended to establish a fixed program of training and practice to which retreatants would commit to completing. It was to last three years and three fortnights, during which the inmates would neither leave the retreat enclosure nor lay eyes on anyone not also participating in the retreat. On completion the residents would depart, and a new class would enter. He supervised nine retreat cycles, running the center almost continually until only a few years before his death in 1899. This model became the standard across Kagyu and Nyingma institutions and was replicated in European and North American centers in the late twentieth century.[9]

Kongtrul explained the time frame of three-year, three-fortnight retreats in the Treasury of Knowledge, which he composed during the first retreat. The calculation is based on the *Kālacakra Tantra*'s presentation of "wind" and on the number of breaths a person takes in a lifetime. In tantric cosmology, wind is the vehicle for consciousness and, typical of Tantra, is understood to be nondual, the basis of both ordinary and enlightened perception, or pristine awareness. Most of the wind that courses through our existence is karmic, the stuff of saṃsāra, but a portion of the day's breaths is pristine awareness. In a given day, a person is said to take 21,600 breaths, which means 7,776,000 each lunar year of 360 days, or 7,884,000 every solar year of 365 days. Of the day's breaths, 675 are said to be moments of pristine awareness. An ideal human lifetime is said to be one hundred years, during which 777,600,000 breaths will occur calculating by the lunar year, and 788,400,000 per solar year. During a lifetime, Kongtrul explains, "the total time taken by the movements of pristine awareness wind equals three years and three fortnights. If, during that period, one were to transform all karmic wind into pristine awareness wind, one would attain enlightenment." He quotes the *Kālacakra Tantra* to confirm this: "the state of the vajra holder is attained in three years and three fortnights."[10]

On August 3[11] Kongtrul began to employ artisans in the outfitting of the Vajrakīla temple he had built the previous year on Chokgyur Lingpa's recommendation. Four monks assisted him with the preparation of the temple and its statues, readying it for the Karmapa's visit when they would be consecrated. They filled the statues of the wrathful deities, building out their internal symbolic bodies with central axes and special substances at the five main cakras (forehead, throat, chest, navel, and anus) and placing inside mantra-inscribed paper and other materials. The Karmapa arrived on September 23.[12] The two lamas greeted each other formally, the Karmapa giving blessings and Kongtrul wishing the Karmapa good health. The Karmapa, being the senior lama, gave the first transmissions: Heart Essence of the Lake Born, which Khyentse Wangpo had only months before given to both of them, and the Sādhana of the Guru's Intent: Wish-Fulfilling Jewel. That Kongtrul received this Chokling treasure from the Karmapa rather than from the treasure revealer himself reflects how close the Karmapa and Chokling had become.[13]

Work continued on the Vajrakīla Temple and the associated protector temple. On October 12[14] Kongtrul and his attendants performed rituals for the protective deities and began constructing a statue of the Shangpa Kagyu deity Swift Acting Wisdom Protector. Along with the other customary substances, Kongtrul placed inside another, smaller statue of the deity that had been revealed as treasure by Chokgyur Lingpa the year before. All preparations were complete by November 19,[15] with statues of Kālacakra, Vajrakumāra, and the principal wrathful deities of United Intent of the Guru in the protector temple. Kongtrul paid the artisans, gave them katas and a small banquet, and sent them away. Wontrul and the Tenth Situ came to preside over the two-day consecration ceremony together with fifteen monks, using a ritual based on the *Cakrasaṃvara Tantra*. Kongtrul thanked them all with another banquet.[16]

The Vajrakīla and protector temples completed, Kongtrul had one last task to perform before requesting permission and funding from Situ's estate to initiate the retreat program: he needed to obtain the approval of Khyentse Wangpo. Kongtrul might be taking more credit for his own ideas than he had earlier, but he could not present himself as being so arrogant as to think of launching such a significant project without a guru's imprimatur. He wrote in his diary with customary feigned humility: "[I thought] it would be beneficial to establish a meditation center at the temple here, but because I could not know what would come with the passing of time, I requested my precious lord at Dzongsar to investigate what would become of efforts to build a retreat center." Khyentse responded with a dream and a vision; the first confirmed Kongtrul as a venerable teacher and the second predicted a radiant future for the hermitage and the blessing of the local government protector deity. The first came the night before Khyentse received Kongtrul's request. Khyentse had dreamed of Vimalamitra—a proxy for Kongtrul—standing in front of him in a halo of light. The master gave him extensive instructions on methods starting with the transference of consciousness at the moment of death, helping Khyentse to comprehend points that he had previously not understood. In the vision, Khyentse found himself on a high slope as the sun was rising and snow was falling in crystals of rainbow light. He entered the residence of a local protector, whom he understood to be Dri

Nyendong, the guardian of Derge. Inside was a treasury of representations of body, speech, and mind—statues, books, and stūpas—as well as other objects. The deity told Khyentse he could take whatever he liked. Khyentse selected an octagonal crystal about a cubit long, on the sides of which were carved images of the peaceful deities from the Vajradhātu maṇḍala. Khyentse placed it on his shoulder—a symbol of veneration and commitment to uphold the tradition of worship—and experienced tremendous happiness. As soon as he thought that he ought to share the crystal with others, he lost it and felt faint. He immediately found a second, smaller crystal, which he could carry in his hand, and awoke. Tsādra's resplendence would be grand but manageable, its impact portable for those who entered its curriculum.[17]

With confirmation from Khyentse Wangpo, Kongtrul next approached the Situ estate for funding. In the peculiar Tibetan custom of financial exchange, Kongtrul offered Wontrul Rinpoche four pieces of gold and silver as seed funding, an offering intended to spur a greater outflow of financial support from the estate. The request was approved and seven men were selected: five to undertake the retreat, one to serve as the vajra master, and one to perform the rituals to the guardian deities. The vajra master was the leader of the community, responsible for supervising the activity and instructing the members in method and doctrine. He managed the finances and the resources for the group and acted as custodian for the retreat buildings. He was also the disciplinarian, correcting mistakes and imposing punishments where necessary. The lama of the protector temple had several main functions, chief among them the propitiation of the hermitage's protector deity, Swift Acting Wisdom Protector. The statue of this deity took pride of place in the protector temple, which is named Cool Grove after the Śītavana charnel ground of this particular form of Mahākāla. The protector lama is charged with leaving the retreat buildings twice a year: during the fifth month to perform feast offerings in the six distinct sacred spots at Tsādra. The lama was joined by a long-term resident of the hermitage whose job was to perform longevity rites to commemorate Chokgyur Lingpa's 1859 Tsādra revelations. He went out again in order to manage the nāgas during the fourth lunar month, when they are said to appear at the small shrine Kongtrul and Chokling built to honor them.[18]

When the seven men had gathered, Kongtrul calculated the astrologically auspicious date to begin the retreat, which he unfortunately neglected to record. They began with rituals to ensure success and clear away obstacles. These included the Tārā maṇḍala, supplications to the protective deities of all traditions, and Chokling's Vajrakīla Secret Essence, one of the three sections of Secret Essence revelation Chokling brought forth at Tsādra in 1859. Thus, they began their three-year, three-fortnight program.[19]

Although Kongtrul did not invent the three-year, three-fortnight time frame, he did break new ground by incorporating an ecumenical curriculum in a single retreat. Other Tibetan three-year, three-fortnight retreats focus on the cultivation of a single deity within a single tradition; Kongtrul's was dedicated to a program that drew from all religious systems, from seven of the "eight chariots of accomplishment." Kongtrul curiously left out Lamdre, the main teaching of the Sakya tradition. To rectify this, during the first year of the retreat, Khyentse Wangpo came and gave the retreatants a lengthy series of Sakya empowerments.

The doxography of eight chariots of accomplishment was first developed by Trengpo Terton in the sixteenth century, whom Kongtrul claimed as a previous life. It is an alternative to the more familiar division of Tibetan Buddhism as four major traditions—Nyingma, Sakya, Kagyu, and Geluk—which appears to have been formulated by Chinese observers and organized somewhat poorly by hat color. The eight chariot schema allows for Buddhist traditions in Tibet that did not develop around monastic institutions, or which were practiced across institutional communities. The Nyingma, Sakya, Marpa Kagyu, and Geluk are four of the eight, but they are characterized more by their central teaching than their monastic identities: Dzogchen, Lamdre, Mahāmudrā and the Six Yogas of Nāropā, and Lamrim and Lojong, respectively. Alongside these are the Shangpa Kagyu, with its Mahāmudrā and the Six Yogas of Niguma, as well as Jordruk, Zhije/Chod, and Orgyen Nyendrub. The Jordruk refers to the six yogas of the Kālacakra tradition. Orgyen Nyendrub are tantric teachings—*nyendrub* means "approach and accomplishment"—organized by Orgyenpa Rinchen Pel, who traveled to the Oḍḍiyāna region of India in the thirteenth century.[20]

Kongtrul laid out a dense ritual calendar and composed the codes of conduct. It began with a series of empowerments, after which the first five months were dedicated to the preliminary practices based on the Ninth Karmapa's manual *Chariot for Traversing the Noble Path*. Students needed to also consult Gampopa's *Jewel Ornament of Liberation*, the Ninth Karmapa's *Ocean of Certainty*, and Tāranātha's *Stages of the Path for the Three Types of Individuals*. According to Ngawang Zangpo, two of Kongtrul's own compositions were likely recommended to the retreatants during this initial period: his *Torch of Certainty* and *An Easy Introduction for the Challenged*.

Retreatants dedicated the next fifteen months to Shangpa Kagyu practices, beginning with the practices of the deities of the Five Tantras, a configuration of the deities of the Guhyasamāja, Mahāmāyā, Hevajra, Cakrasamvara, and Vajrabhairava Tantras. This was followed by the Six Yogas of Niguma, *Amulet Box of Mahāmudrā*, and other Shangpa practices. The next six months were dedicated to Kālacakra. In Kongtrul's *Illuminating Morality*, a manual for the hermitage, the sole mention of texts for this segment of the retreat is Tāranātha's *Meaningful to Behold*. Nyingma practices filled the final year of the retreat. These are primarily the creation stage practices of Vajrasattva and Yangdak Heruka, done in three months, and the completion stage of Dzogchen, which takes up the remaining nine months. The Vajrasattva is based on Terdak Lingpa's treasures, whereas the Yangdak is from the So tradition based on translations from Indian originals said to have been made by Namkhai Nyingpo in the eighth century. The Dzogchen is drawn from both revelation and received scriptures and is based on Longchenpa's systematization of the Nyingtik teachings. A rigorous set of daily practices was mandated. Retreatants were expected to perform offering and supplication rites, Chod practices, and practices from Chokling's Secret Essence.[21]

The rituals of commemoration and worship that were observed monthly and annually, while primarily Kagyu, also express the ecumenical spirit of the retreat. The Kagyu patriarchs Marpa, Milarepa, Gampopa, the Third Karmapa, and the Eighth and Ninth Situ are honored. Padmasambhava, Terdak Lingpa, and Longchenpa from the Nyingma tradition, Dolpopa and Tāranātha from the Jonang, and Khyungpo Neljor from the Shangpa Kagyu are also given commemorative days. The seventh day of the month is for Padmasambhava. Tārā is worshiped on the eighth day of every month in the tradition of Atiśa. The tenth day is for celebrating feasts using liturgies from various treasure revealers. The fifteenth days (the full moon) are for Kālacakra rituals in the Jonang tradition. The twenty-fifth day is for Shangpa Kagyu rituals. The twenty-ninth day is dedicated to Swift Acting Wisdom Protector. And the thirtieth days (the new moon) are dedicated to Yangdak. All of these days employ a variety of liturgies from multiple traditions.[22]

Kongtrul acknowledged the unconventionality of the ecumenical curriculum—and responded to critics of the approach—in his *All-Pervading Melody of the Pure Lands*, written in 1864. He was not shy about insulting his critics, scorning those who doubted whether students could manage a program that draws on more than one tradition and includes a variety of practices. Such naysayers, he sarcastically implied, were of lesser capacity and lacked vision:

> It might seem that putting one's efforts into the creation and completion phases of a single tradition during a three years and three fortnights period is the way to zero in on the essentials. But then, it might also seem that not having so many elaborate prayers and recitations would be easier for dullards and lazies.[23]

Those who complain about too many teachings would also probably prefer fewer rituals in general, and rare is the Tibetan who would advocate for that. Anyone who understands the value of intricate rituals should therefore also appreciate the value of an eclectic approach. In Tibet, more is almost always better. It could easily have been real critics whom Kongtrul was referring to in a later passage, the unnamed esteemed religious leaders who, due to the decline of the Dharma in the world, have limited scope of vision. "These people," he continues, "only concern themselves with the study, meditation, teaching, and propagation of their own traditions, without endeavoring to learn from others. Even if they dabble in another tradition, they do not involve themselves in the maintenance or spread of its lineage, and so while their own established traditions flourish like an excellent harvest, superior and distinguished practice lineages are disappearing."[24]

All teachers, Kongtrul believed, have a responsibility not only to learn from the many religious traditions around them but to engage with them and ensure their survival.

Kongtrul did not claim originality in his eclectic approach. Continuing his defense, he held up his own Karma Kagyu tradition as an example of syncretism and named the patriarchs on whose shoulders he intended to stand. Gampopa himself famously united the Kadam tradition of his early training with the esoteric teachings he received from Milarepa, and *Stages of the Path of the Three Kinds of Beings* by the Kadam master Sharawa Yonten Drak remains fundamental for Kagyu practice. The Second and Third Karmapas famously "made the streams of Gampopa's lineage and the Nyingma flow together." The Third Karmapa had a vision of Vimalamitra and taught what he received as the Heart Essence of the Karmapas, and Karmapas since have accepted custodianship of many treasure revelations, integrating them into their teaching. The Second Karmapa received the transmission for the Six Unions teachings of the Kālacakra and for Zhije and Chod, the Fourth Karmapa embraced the Shangpa teachings, and at some point Orgyenpa's Three Vajra teachings entered the tradition.[25] These are classified as separate traditions in the doxography of the eight chariots of accomplishment, and all have flourished in Karma Kagyu institutions. The Third Karmapa, the Seventh Karmapa, the Second Zhamar, the First Tsurpu Gyeltsab, the Eighth Zhamar, the Eighth Tai Situ, and others "not only studied whatever religious tradition could be found in Tibet, but they also, while serving as heads of their own tradition, propagated, without sectarianism, these systems of theory and practice. In this they were of inconceivable benefit to Buddhism."[26]

The great masters of the Karma Kagyu tradition embraced ecumenicalism, and Kongtrul's critics were therefore wrong to take him to task for doing the same. He was expressing a noble ideal of great pedigree. Yet he was defending himself against members of his own community for putting this idea into practice. Kongtrul's ecumenicalism came up against real parochialism and strong sectarian partisanship at Pelpung. We do not know who spoke out against him, but outside of his own disciples and a few powerful protectors, Kongtrul's vision was not shared. In contemporary Tibetan Buddhist communities, Kongtrul's ecumenicalism is what he is remembered for embodying. Yet it seems to have caused him further isolation in his own community.

Kongtrul unfortunately recorded very little about who the first retreatants were other than Khenchen Tashi Wozer. He gave neither their names nor the reasons they were selected—or volunteered—to join the retreat. We know that they did not come empty-handed; although Kongtrul provided for "the necessary materials for the ceremonies and the protector temple, and all needed empowerments, transmissions, and instructions," the retreatants needed to come with a considerable amount of their own supplies.[27] This included food and tea and a long list of books, which Kongtrul admonished "would be pointless not to gather," as most were then in print.[28] Based on contemporary retreats, life in the hermitage was not easy. Inmates would practice upwards of twenty hours a day, with only one or two days off a year, and had to sleep sitting up. Retreatants were also responsible for communal expenses; each year they would collectively donate two bricks of tea to purchase whitewash for the retreat building and juniper from the Alo Peljor Valley.

The list of texts mandated in *Illuminating Morality* is yet another testament to Kongtrul's ecumenical approach. While it is primarily Shangpa Kagyu, Karma Kagyu, and Nyingma, it includes representations from seven of the eight chariots of accomplishment. Kongtrul also required an extensive list of books for support in meditation. These books alone would have been a considerable expense for the retreatants; the books that were not then in print would have been copied by hand before the retreat began. They were, however, forbidden to bring additional books into the retreat. Kongtrul admonished them:

> For those who are new to all this, when entering retreat, they may bring with them only those texts specified as one, with the exception of books which explain the three vows; any study of the other topics is strictly forbidden. Although study, reflection, and training are generally considered crucial, when meditation is the primary focus, if there are many sources of discursive thought, there will be obstacles to the meditative experiences. One period of effective meditation is more valuable than a lifetime of study and reflection, so one should persevere with one's meditation.[29]

The retreat schedule was designed for Kongtrul to be able to come and go as he needed. The retreatants were not the only residents of Tsādra; Kongtrul's mother and, later, a niece lived there with him, as did attendants and other students. He was able to remain at the hermitage for only the first months of the year. By the end of 1860, he was called to Derge to perform Vajrakīla rituals, petition the protective deities in the Vaiśravaṇa Temple, and celebrate a smoke offering to curry favor with the local spirits. He gave empowerments to Prince Chime Takpai Dorje and his mother, Choying Zangmo, and performed an exorcism and other similar rites. He was back at Tsādra by January 6, 1861,[30] to join the Swift Acting Wisdom Protector ritual that finished the lunar year in the retreat.[31]

On February 13, 1862,[32] the retreatants were successfully tested on their accomplishments in tummo, the practice that raises the temperature of the body. Each retreatant would stand outside with a damp cotton sheet draped over his body and dry it with body heat alone.[33] The retreat ended in May 1864.[34]

# 20

# THE TREASURY OF KNOWLEDGE

*Rimay Part Two*

1861

Between 1861 and 1867, a period that included the first three-year, three-fortnight retreat at Tsādra and the culmination of the Nyarong War, Kongtrul composed several major works, including what is arguably his greatest, the Treasury of Knowledge. This survey of Buddhist history and doctrine as it existed in Tibet, comprised of a root verse and autocommentary, fills three volumes in the original Tibetan. Where the retreat program was his institutional expression of his ecumenical view, the Treasury of Knowledge is its single best literary articulation.

In his diary Kongtrul recorded that in early 1862 Dabzang Tulku asked him to compose a treatise on the three vows, for which he, Dabzang, would compose a commentary. Treatises on such topics were frequently composed in such a format: a "root" text in verse, which is typically much condensed due to the restraints of the format, followed with a commentary either by the author or a colleague that elucidates the meaning. It was not a commission that interested Kongtrul; he remarked that "pretty much everyone has a treatise on the three vows," and he suggested instead that he compose a treatise "that addressed all the classifications of knowledge" which would "be of benefit to those who had not studied much." Taking this as his focus, between meditation sessions Kongtrul composed a text in verse on the three trainings—ethics, meditation, and wisdom. He gave it the title *Encompassing All Knowledge*. As was his habit, later in the year he showed the finished work to Khyentse Wangpo, who was impressed, remarking "It is certain that this has been accomplished through the strength of the lama's blessings and from the opening of your nāḍīs by the ḍākinī." And, further: "You must compose an autocommentary for it." This simple command allowed Kongtrul to credit Khyentse Wangpo for the decision to undertake the autocommentary. The root verses are the work of a mature, confident scholar, one who needed little encouragement to write a summary of the entire span of human knowledge available in nineteenth-century Tibet. It was an astonishing display of vision and ability and possibly too close to hubris than Kongtrul was comfortable permitting himself; his ambition was therefore concealed by the commission from Khyentse.[1]

Kongtrul composed the bulk of the autocommentary in the spring and summer of 1863[2] with the financial support of Tashi Wozer. This young monk had just completed the first three-year retreat and would be one of Kongtrul's closest disciples in the last decades of his life. Kongtrul continued to work on it in the first half of 1864 and either completed it at that time or soon after.[3]

As a piece of literature, the Treasury of Knowledge can be related to the genre of "religious history," and yet it is so much more. It is divided into ten sections, starting with Buddhist cosmology and continuing through the three main divisions of Buddhism to culminate with Dzogchen. It includes sections on ethics, on the secular subjects of study such as poetics and art, and includes a lengthy section describing the eight chariots of accomplishment. Though commonly described as being a treatment of traditional Tibetan topics of study, the work is just as much a history of Buddhism, outlining its development from the early teachings of the Buddha and the differentiation of the doctrine into the various schools of thought, and then giving a survey of the doctrines of the various divisions of Buddhism in Tibet.[4]

The work is divided into four books with four sections each. Only in Book Four, Section Four are the secular topics covered, including such things as grammar, medicine, and poetics, the subjects of Kongtrul's earliest Buddhist training. Book One is dedicated to Buddhist cosmology. The historical frame is dominant in Book Two, which deals with the Buddha's life, and Books Three and Four, on the spread of the teachings. In Book Four, Section Three, Kongtrul surveys the eight chariots. Book Five (on ethics), Six and Seven (on wisdom), and Eight (on meditation) make up the promised "three trainings." Books Nine and Ten deal with the paths and results of these trainings, with Dzogchen being presented last, as the final, and highest, attainment. Not all of the work is original—Kongtrul lifted long passages from the works of some of his favorite authors, such as Buton Rinchen Drub and Tāranātha, and made extensive use of Śākya Chokden's unique presentation of "other-emptiness." Plagiarism of this sort is not uncommon, especially in a treatise of this breadth and length, and indeed much of Kongtrul's other compositions were likewise lifted verbatim from the work of other authors.[5]

The Treasury of Knowledge presents the vast content of the Buddhist teachings chronologically and also hierarchically. The work is not simply a catalogue of teachings. It is a doxography, presenting each subject of Buddhist knowledge in turn—that is, beginning with the organization of the world, it culminates with its transcendence. Tibetan fixation on doxography was a result of the astonishingly large amount in Indian material they imported over several hundred years. Nothing Indian was rejected, but every scripture and each doctrine and practice were placed in relation to one another in degrees of proximity to the ultimate truth, however that was understood by the author. The overriding notion was that all paths lead to enlightenment, but some were not complete in themselves and by necessity flowed into more advanced routes. Kongtrul had a dream about this common metaphor back in 1845 while in retreat for the first time at the hermitage. He saw a valley full of flowers with a hill in the center, on which all the Buddhist paths were laid out. Someone appeared to explain to him the hierarchy of beings and approaches: ordained people were better than gods and so forth, all of which arose from the understanding of the four noble truths.[6] Nor were all paths appropriate for all people. Buddhist soteriology describes three different types of people: those of superior, middling, and lesser capacity. One's abilities are based on karmic achievement over the many lifetimes one has been pursuing enlightenment, and one is tasked with finding the appropriate path to pursue during one's current life—that is, if one is eligible for religious practice at all; most people are said to be suited only for the life of the householder—working and bearing children and otherwise maintaining society.

Kongtrul's own opinion regarding what is the highest path—meaning the most effective—is evident within the historical and topical outline and in his granting certain topics extensive attention and denying comparable space to others. As Gene Smith pointed out, the "special intention" of the Treasury of Knowledge was "to stress the virtues of the Dzogchen *atiyoga* approach of the Nyingma" tradition.[7] Not only does the entire work conclude with a discussion of the Dzogchen completion stage of tantric practice, but also most books likewise conclude with a discussion of it. Dzogchen, we are to understand, is the highest teaching, the final development of the Buddhist doctrine and the most effective path to liberation for those with the capacity to pursue it. It was Kongtrul's own path.

Kongtrul would later employ the same eight chariot structure in the Treasury of Advice, where it serves as the outline for the entire work, and again in a short undated composition titled *Necklace of Clear Understanding: A Brief Non-Sectarian Religious History*. Here it is not Nyingma that is emphasized but the "other-emptiness" philosophical position. All religious traditions of Tibet are given respect, but Kongtrul organizes the great thinkers of the past in a way as to argue that, for the most part, "other-emptiness" has been the dominant view. This work, like the Treasury of Knowledge, begins with the Buddha and the development of Buddhism in India as it is understood by Tibetans: the three turnings of the wheel—Hīnayāna, Mahāyāna, and Vajrayāna. He frames Indian Buddhism very much in terms of "self-emptiness" and "other-emptiness," the first being the teachings of the disciples of Nāgārjuna and the second that of Asaṅga, which Kongtrul describes as "definitive Madhyamaka."[8]

In the *Necklace of Clear Understanding*, Kongtrul describes Tibet before the advent of Buddhism as dominated by Bon, defined as a ritual system that deals with worldly concerns. The Buddhist kings, identified as emanations of buddhas and bodhisattvas, brought in Buddhism, which was propagated by Padmasambhava and his disciples. Padmasambhava concealed treasures throughout Tibet, which are revealed by the reincarnations of the kings and the disciples. Kongtrul returns to Bon to include it in the list of valid traditions; the tradition undergoes a reformation in which the negative aspects were outlawed and "divination, astrology, the reading of omens and the reading of fortunes, and so forth—those things which are of benefit to beings—were largely left as they were," as were the scriptures that taught transcendence, all of which were allowed to be propagated as Bon.[9]

The *Necklace* next turns to the New Translation (*Sarma*) traditions initiated by Atīśa and Rinchen Zangpo. These translators and their disciples established the Kadam tradition, which, Kongtrul asserts, has been fully absorbed into the Kagyu, Geluk, and Sakya, save for at Reting Monastery. During this time, Śākyaśrībhadra came to Tibet and initiated the "upper" transmission of the Vinaya observed by the Kagyu and Sakya. The many branches of the Kagyu tradition then are listed, each stemming from a disciple of Marpa, Gampopa, or Pakmodrupa, with the Karma Kamtsang branch receiving the most attention. This is followed by the Shangpa Kagyu, the teachings of which were absorbed into the Kagyu, Geluk and Jonang, and the Sakya with its subdivisions into Ngor, Tsar, and Gongkar. Zhije and Chod come next, initiated by Padampa Sanggye and Machik Labdron. Kongtrul then leaves off the eight chariot schema and gives space to the

Jonang tradition of Dolpopa and Tāranātha, who promoted "the great lion's roar" of "other-emptiness." Tsongkhapa and his disciples, the founders of the major Geluk monasteries, follow, after which Kongtrul describes the Bon treasure tradition. Kongtrul is explicit here that Bon is a valid tradition:

> These are some of the manifestations of the inconceivable methods of Padmasambhava and his twenty-five disciples for taming beings. By giving these teachings the name "Bon" there is [nonetheless] no conflict with the four seals that signify the teachings of the Buddha regarding the view and practice; it is a definite teaching on the path and the ultimate goal.[10]

Having listed all the men and women who initiated and led the religious traditions of Tibet, Kongtrul concludes with a survey of who upheld the "other-emptiness" position. It is a remarkable list, one that surely would have surprised more than a few of its readers with the inclusion of Dolpopa beside the great Kagyu patriarchs:

> The view and conduct of the learned adepts of the secret mantra Nyingma school, such as the omniscient Longchenpa Drime Wozer and other followers of Padmasambhava; the learned adepts of the four major and eight minor Kagyu, from the followers of Marpa, Milarepa, and Gampopa Dakpo Lhaje to the all-seeing religious advisor for the entire doctrine, Situ Panchen Chokyi Jungne; Sachen Kunga Nyingpo and [the Sakya line of] uncle and nephews, Zilung Panchen Śākya Chokden, Bodong Panchen Chokle Namgyel, and particularly the all-knowing buddha of the three times, the great Dolpopa, whose teaching was clarified by Jetsun Chenpo Tāranātha, and the other great beings in the transmission line of the Jonangpa, [their view] was the "other-emptiness" Madhyamaka alone; though there are particularities in their method of explanation, the differences are minor.[11]

With this list, Kongtrul was announcing that contrary to hundreds of years of Kagyu exegesis there is not a substantial difference between the "other-emptiness" theory of the Jonang tradition and that of the Kagyu.

He goes on to state that the opposing side is not itself a united front—Kongtrul asserted that there are substantial differences among the philosophical positions of the great proponents of "self-emptiness," such as Buton Rinchen Drub, the Eighth Karmapa, Pema Karpo, and Tsongkhapa. Here Kongtrul is certainly correct—there is quite a bit of space between the views of the Eighth Karmapa and Tsongkhapa. Kongtrul oversimplified their positions—Tsongkhapa was ardently opposed to "other-emptiness," to such a degree that his opponents accused him of nihilism, but both the Eighth Karmapa and Pema Karpo were less interested in choosing a side of the debate than in finding a reconciliation between the two, and their inclusion on a list of opponents to "other-emptiness" would have raised questions. His motive here for emphasizing differences among those who adhered to "self-emptiness" was to explain how theorists whom he otherwise admired could be part of the opposing camp. That is, the great Pema Karpo might have advocated for "self-emptiness," but that did not make him identical to Tsongkhapa.[12]

The *Necklace* is one of only two Kongtrul compositions that uses the term "*rimay*" in its title; the other is his diary. The word can be translated as "nonsectarian," "nonpartisan," or "ecumenical." Like the retreat program and the Treasury of Knowledge, the work expresses an expansive and inclusive vision of religion: all religious traditions known to Kongtrul are affirmed as valid methods in the pursuit of liberation. Only certain elements of the Bon tradition were to be rejected, as they had (allegedly) been back in imperial times by the bodhisattva kings. Kongtrul engages in neither polemics nor apologetics and neither denigrates nor defends any tradition. Yet this does not mean that he viewed all traditions and all practices equally or of equal value for all practitioners. Kongtrul was a Kagyu monk, and the Kagyu tradition receives the greatest space in the work, followed by the Nyingma. This is similar to his presentation of the "self-emptiness" and "other-emptiness" debate. While many prominent scholars held fast to one side, other scholars argued that the two were poles in dualistic thinking, akin to the eternalism and nihilism between which the Buddha preached a middle way. Kongtrul lionized "other-emptiness" because his view was primarily formed by Tantra and the affirmative language of meditation. Thus, the "other-emptiness" position is unequivocally presented as the highest view, and those who taught it were lions of Buddhist history. Yet he recognized the practical value of Nāgārjuna's language of negation in helping the student develop an understanding of emptiness and thereby shed attachment to delusions. In the spirit of previous efforts to reconcile Madhyamaka and Yogācāra, Kongtrul found value in both positions and so rejected neither.

As with Christian ecumenicalism in the West, Kongtrul's rimay view is not a synthesis of all traditions as if they all taught some universal truth and the differences between them could be discarded, or as though religion were a buffet from which to spoon especially appealing morsels and arrange however one likes on one's own individual plate. Kongtrul rejoiced in the differences, and he was adamant that each tradition and each lineage be maintained as a distinct stream. Each practice preserves its own sectarian identity—Dzogchen is always Nyingma, Lamdre is always Sakya, and Mahāmudrā, save for the independent Geluk tradition that Kongtrul briefly mentions at the end of *Necklace of Clear Understanding*, is always Kagyu. Nor was Kongtrul in any way calling for a new tradition or a synthesis of multiple traditions. He was not a Gampopa or a Tsongkhapa or a Dolpopa, whose presentations of the path and methods to pursue enlightenment gave students a framework on which to establish new and distinct traditions. There is no indication in any of Kongtrul's writing or activity that either he or his students ever considered his work anything but the continuation of the institutional framework in which he operated, one which was comfortable with exploration across the sectarian divisions of Tibetan religion. Kongtrul's rimay is an attitude by which one approaches religious practice and teachings. It is how one is supposed to view the full span of Buddhist teachings.

Kongtrul never mentioned *Necklace of Clear Understanding* in his diary, and so we do not know when he wrote or published it or why—no one is credited with requesting it. He frequently mentions the Treasury of Knowledge, however, as was befitting a work of such monumental importance. Kongtrul no doubt knew the value of the work. Yet due to the chaos of the Nyarong War he was not able to teach it for over two years following its completion. He first mentions teaching it in the summer of 1866 to a lama from Ngor Monastery named Ngawang Rinchen and a few others, reading the text in full and explaining it as he went.[13] He used the root verses later that year to teach a group of lamas and monks at the Situ residence. In August or September 1871[14] he taught it at Pelpung's summer retreat, and in late November or early December 1873[15] he taught it at Pelpung to a group of officials and incarnations, including Dongkham Tulku Ngawang Damcho Gyatso from Drayab and Sertal Lhatse Tulku. It also became a required text at the Tsādra retreats.

In 1875 Kongtrul taught the text to a group and for the first time indicated that it was leaving his control to be taught by others:

> My venerable lama Jamyang Khyentse, Khangsar Khen Rinpoche Ngawang Sonam Gyeltsen, and other lamas, in all about twenty tulkus and colleagues, received the transmission for the Treasury of Knowledge, both the root text and commentary with additional explanation, which took about ten days. After it was done, we recited the dedication prayer and benediction. Khyentse praised it effusively, calling it a timeless treatise and instructing the representatives of each monastery to propagate it at their own seats, which they promised to do. Khangsar Khen Rinpoche said he would propagate it at Ngor, and so forth. I am uncertain whether they followed through.[16]

Kongtrul was being disingenuous. He knew well that the men who were increasingly seeking him out to receive the transmission were bringing newly printed copies of the book and transmitting it forward. Wontrul Rinpoche, who passed away in 1873, left funds for the printing, and Kongtrul reports that he requested the Derge royal family to sponsor the printing as well.[17] Thus, in early 1875 the Pelpung steward Pelek took up the task, publishing first the three-volume Treasury of Knowledge and beginning the lengthy process of preparing the blocks for the Treasury of Revelations. Kongtrul taught it at least on two other occasions after the printing: in August 1881[18] at Dzongsar, and again on April 26, 1888,[19] when he taught the first four books to the Fifteenth Karmapa at Pelpung.

# 21

## THE NYARONG WAR

### 1862–1866

---

Gonpo Namgyel, the chieftain of Middle Nyarong, first invaded his nearest neighbor, Lower Nyarong, in 1847 and soon after started harassing nearby Drango and other bordering regions. The chieftain of Middle Nyarong, known also as Nyake Amgon and various derogatories such as "the demon of Nyarong," was heir to a fairly long line of chieftains, born into a family that nursed several generations worth of grudges against their neighbors. Nyarong itself was a cauldron of banditry; groups of young men from the region periodically raided Qing military garrisons stationed along the tea and horse trade route, amassing a store of weapons with which they would successfully defend themselves against Qing reprisals. Twice in the early eighteenth century Qing troops had attempted to suppress the valley, and twice they were forced back. Gonpo Namgyel's father, Norbu Tsering, likewise repelled a Qing campaign in 1812. In that skirmish the neighboring territory of Drango joined the Manchu forces and earned enduring enmity of the Nyake family, which ultimately erupted as the Nyarong War.[1]

During his lifetime the people of Kham viewed Gonpo Namgyel as either a bloodthirsty demon or a magnificent leader, depending on which side of the conflict they were on. He was a brilliant strategist and a master at forging loyalties and alliances. He murdered lamas and monks and displayed the heads of opposing soldiers on spikes. He was said to fatten infants with milk and throw them off the walls of his fortress for sport. In the century and a half since the war's end, he has been transformed into a local hero both by Tibetans bemoaning Chinese rule and by Chinese Communists in search of a Tibetan who made himself an enemy of Lhasa. Chinese and Western scholars have lumped Gonpo Namgyel in with late-era border region rebellions against the Qing, yet in her exhaustively researched study of the war, scholar Yudru Tsomo argues convincingly against such narratives. Such uprisings along the borders of the Qing Empire were in reaction to excessive taxation or administrative corruption. In the first half of the nineteenth century, there was no Qing administration in Nyarong or elsewhere in Kham—what little presence the Manchu rulers of China had in the region was understood to be concerned solely with the tea trade and communications with Lhasa. Titles granted to rulers of the many municipalities of Kham were ceremonial and known to be so. Instead, Tsomo documents, the motivations behind Nyake Amgon's conquests were personal, based on seeking retribution for past insults and on the desire for power and wealth. There was no external power against which Nyarong rebelled, only neighbors to be conquered.

In 1848, as Kongtrul was returning from Gyarong, the leaders of Derge and other polities in Kham, concerned about the unification of Upper, Middle, and Lower Nyarong and Gonpo Namgyel's incursions into Drango, participated in a failed campaign to push him back in Middle Nyarong. In the wake of that campaign, Derge king Damtsik Dorje joined with others in Kham to send a petition to the Qing administration in Sichuan asking that the Qing Empire send a force into Nyarong to protect mutual interests. In 1849 the Qing army, led by Qi Shan, the governor of Sichuan, with soldiers requisitioned from various localities in Kham, marched on Nyarong and was defeated. A repeatedly victorious Gonpo Namgyel, with no serious opposition, spent the decade of the 1850s consolidating conquered territories and expanding to the south. He took Litang in the early 1860s after several attempts, during one of which his grandson contracted smallpox and died. This was the young man in whose funeral the Fourteenth Karmapa, the Tenth Situ, and Kongtrul participated in July 1860, as described in chapter 19.

The people of Kham, for the most part, dreaded Gonpo Namgyel. Yet they had no great love for the Qing forces who attempted to drive him back into Nyarong, as villagers were forced to billet soldiers and young men were requisitioned to fight. Tibetan troops, when they came in 1863, were generally greeted with relief, yet they looted towns and monasteries and so came to be viewed with similar ambivalence. Kongtrul himself expresses no overt loyalties beyond those to his colleagues, his institutions, and his patrons in Derge. Nowhere does he indicate any awareness of being, even nominally, a subject of Beijing, or of his homeland being a field of contest between China and Tibet. His opinion on the conflict changed substantially as more and more of his sponsors and friends suffered from its effects. Yet nowhere does he condemn any side. He had already ministered Gonpo Namgyel, and he would serve the Tibetan war effort before the war ended. He was careful not to advocate openly for either side, but only bemoan the violence and destruction wrought by all. Once the war came to Derge, he was emphatic that he had not chosen to get involved. Ever casting himself as a passive player, at the same time he was not shy in boasting of the benefits of his service, be it to Pelpung, Derge, or the Tibetan army. This last service he took pains to justify.

According to Kongtrul, the Derge royal family feared invasion by the beginning of 1862. Following his chronology, Kongtrul was summoned to Derge in March or April 1862,[2] when Queen Choying Zangmo and her two sons were preparing to flee the capital. The government summoned Khyentse Wangpo to perform rituals to protect the kingdom and the royal family, but Khyentse had been ill for some time. Kongtrul had spent several days attempting to cure him from afar with rituals such as "turning back the escort," longevity sādhanas, and a thread-cross rite to the Tenma goddesses. He went to Dzongsar to offer a longevity ceremony and several empowerments and reading transmissions, which he does not name other than to note that Khyentse "had not already received them." Khyentse returned the favor with reading transmissions of several printed works of Vilāsavajra, an eighth-century Indian author of tantric commentaries. The illness enabled Khyentse to decline the summons from Derge, and Kongtrul was called in his stead. He did not want to go, and described the order in negative terms, writing that "there was no way to avoid going" and adding that there were extremely negative omens on the journey over.[3]

Kongtrul resided in Derge for about a month, attended by three disciples. They set themselves up in the Vaiśravaṇa Temple at Gonchen and spent the first weeks on rites to restore the kingdom's well-being. He gave the two princes empowerments from Dispelling All Obstacles, which he later felt eased their journey when they were taken prisoner by the Nyarong army. He dreamed that four victory banners sent by the central Tibetan government were placed on a temple roof, one in each of the four cardinal directions, together with a large red seal. Kongtrul later interpreted this dream to portend the arrival of the Tibetan army. In his diary he also inserted other prophetic dreams he had in earlier years, which he now also considered to be omens of the coming violence: in one he saw a large field lying fallow; in another he was summoned to Derge only to find he recognized no one. He was told that soldiers were stationed in the monastery, and he saw the royal palace in ruins.[4]

At the end of the month, the chamberlain excused him, explaining that the kingdom no longer had the financial means to support his rituals. He returned to Pelpung in May 1862[5] in time to lead the annual vase ceremony. By this point Derge had sent troops into battle and had suffered the conquest and defection of outlying territories, with the consequence of reduced tribute coming to the capital. It was another deadly blow to the kingdom in an era when central power had been in decline; as local chieftains grew stronger, they most likely reduced their payments to the throne as well. Derge would never recover.[6]

In the early summer of 1862, Kongtrul built a stūpa at the Lhasar Temple at Pelpung in accordance with the instructions of Chokgyur Lingpa, who had a bit of a predilection for dictating where stūpa and temples ought to be built. With his disciples he consecrated the ground with a ritual of the two Vimala, repeating the ceremony again to prepare the icons that would fill the edifice, which featured an image of the deity Cittaviśramaṇa that liberated on sight. The liturgy they used was from Khyentse Wangpo's treasure, Heart Essence of the Tamer of Beings: Mahākaruṇika Cittaviśramaṇa. Back at his hermitage—the first retreat was still in session—Kongtrul began a series of exorcism and pacification rituals that would occupy him for most of the remaining months of the year. He also put time into the Treasury of Revelations; it was at this point, he wrote in his diary, that he began organizing the various manuals, empowerment rites, and instructions for the treasure cycles he had collected and written, and it was at this point that he settled on the collection's final name.[7]

Kongtrul remained involved in the ritual administration of Pelpung. Two years earlier the Fourteenth Karmapa had pressed Wontrul to honor the Ninth Situ's wishes that Pelpung institute the tradition of an annual summer retreat, an early requirement of Buddhist ordained communities that Tibetans inconsistently observe. In 1862 Kongtrul supervised the first such retreat at the Lhasar Temple. This entailed writing the necessary manuals and training the chant master, a man named Rinchen. Remaining at the monastery, he instituted an annual rite at the Vajrakīla Temple at the Situ estate. The temple itself had been built by the Eighth Situ on the advice of Rigdzin Tsewang Norbu, who had prophesied of dire times for the community. The temple would, he predicted, suppress the demonic forces that would otherwise plague the region. The Eighth Situ had built it according to instructions and provided that a lama always be in residence performing rituals. Chokgyur Lingpa later determined that an annual Vajrakīla drubchen ritual was necessary to protect the community, and Wontrul agreed to fund it. Thus, in early October 1862,[8] Kongtrul trained a chant master and a shrine keeper in the rituals associated with both mundane and transcendent matters—the defense of life and property and the pursuit of enlightenment. The drubchen ritual began on October 7.[9] Kongtrul served as vajra master, supervising about forty monks who chanted in shifts, first propitiating the enlightened deity and then the worldly protector. A separate group of five monks prepared the blade exorcism, and on the 22nd[10] they planted the kīla dagger and drove back the harmful influences. The next day they performed the ritual to accept the accomplishment of the ceremony, a concise empowerment, and an extensive feast. The ceremonies came to an end on October 23[11] and Kongtrul returned to his hermitage. After the war, Chokgyur Lingpa was eager to point to this ritual for saving Pelpung from destruction. Chokling himself sat out the war in a retreat in far-off Wokmin Karma.[12]

Despite the war, Kongtrul continued his activities. In early November 1862[13] Kongtrul received several transmissions of Mati Panchen teachings from Lama Sang-ngak. He dedicated some time to Khyentse Wangpo's Tārā revelations called Heart Essence of the Noble Deathless One, and from late November until the beginning of February 1863,[14] he performed the approach and accomplishment for Khyentse's Heart Essence of the Tamer of Beings: Mahākaruṇika Cittaviśramaṇa. The indications were positive— he dreamed he was given a piece of Nyangrel Nyima Wozer's embalmed body, some of which he ate and the rest he distributed to others. In early February he rejoined the three-year retreat for the propitiation of the protector deities, participating in the fabrication of new offering tormas, and he trained the protector temple lama in a new thread-cross rite to Bernakchen before ending the lunar year with his personal rites to his protector. Kongtrul began the new lunar year, which he incorrectly recorded as the Iron Pig Year—it was the Water Pig Year—with an empowerment of Union of All Rare and Precious Jewels for the nine-year-old Tenth Situ. He also gave him Choje Lingpa's Vajrakīla and Vajravidāraṇa.[15]

In late 1862 Gonpo Namgyel mounted a full-scale invasion of Derge. Territories of the kingdom that bordered Nyarong, such as Tromtar, had already been taken with little resistance. Three divisions moved on the capital: cavalries came down from the north via Yilhung and Rudam, from the south via Tromtar and Pelyul, and through Pewar and Pelpung. These reached the city in January 1863. A middle division, without horses, marched from Kandze through Mesho, arriving later. When the Nyarong forces from the north reached a village on the outskirts of the capital called Ngulpulung, Gonpo Namgyel sent a message to the government announcing his

intentions. The queen and her two young sons fled south to their palace at
Dokhoma but were captured there. Gonpo Namgyel stationed troops to
hold the royal family and to build a new fortress called Sokmo Podrang.
Kongtrul and Khyentse Wangpo were naturally distraught to see combat-
ants march past their monasteries, and they sent messages back and forth
to comfort each other. The head of the Garje aristocratic family died at
this time, possibly in the fighting, and Kongtrul was called to perform rituals, although he does not record where precisely he went to do them.[16]
Many Derge aristocrats fled to Lhasa, where they successfully petitioned the
Tibetan government to intervene. Lhasa, eager to regain a foothold in the
east, needed little encouragement to send an army to Kham.

Around this time another death occurred that demanded Kongtrul's
attention: the consort of Chokgyur Lingpa's named Tsultrim Pelmo from
Drachen, who may have been the niece of Khyentse Wangpo and the mother
of Chokling's second son (see chapter 13). As befitting her status as a relative
of Khyentse Wangpo and consort of Chokgyur Lingpa, Kongtrul added rituals for her benefit to his daily program, marking the weeks she would spend
in the bardo and added a liturgy on her behalf called Firelight to his annual
United Intent of the Gurus recitation. Kongtrul's dreams and Khyentse's
visions confirmed that she had reached Padmasambhava's Palace of Lotus
Light at the center of his pure land, the Copper-Colored Mountain. Kongtrul arranged for one hundred thousand Akṣobhya tsatsas to be produced
and for the construction of a stūpa, which he consecrated.[17]

Gonpo Namgyel took the Queen Choying Zangmo and her sons
to Nyarong as hostages at the end of March or early April.[18] This was a
standard strategy he employed when conquering hostile territory; he sent
politically and religiously important individuals to Nyarong, housing his
unwilling guests in his fortresses and palaces. Kongtrul wrote that he was
frantic with worry. He and Khyentse both could perform rituals but could
do little more. The next month the middle division of the Nyarong army
reached Mesho and assaulted Dzongsar Monastery, although the extent of
the damage is not clear. The people of Mesho had attempted to repel the
Nyarong army, and the monastery was burned in retaliation. According to
several accounts, Khyentse Wangpo was able to bribe Gonpo Namgyel's
generals to allow the community to remove books and statues before the
army set the monastery on fire on May 2, 1863.[19] Kongtrul did not mention
the episode in his diary; Khyentse remains absent from the diary until late
1866. To aid his patrons in the valley, Kongtrul performed a supplication

to the Peaceful and Wrathful Deities, the mitigating effects of which were felt, he reported, by those "with faith and a samaya connection" with him. Despite the war, he continued to supervise the three-year retreat at Tsādra, writing at this time the new manual for the Vajrasattva rites and working on the autocommentary to the Treasury of Knowledge.[20]

The warlord also took as hostages leading lamas from many of the region's monasteries. Wontrul Rinpoche was among them, and in his absence Kongtrul was needed to lead the 1863 summer retreat at Pelpung, which thirteen lamas joined. There are many accounts of Gonpo Namgyel's treatment of lamas, from fawning patronage to brutal and violent atrocities. He lavishly patronized three Nyingma monasteries in Nyarong, which he is said to have compared in glory to the three famous Geluk monasteries of Lhasa: Ganden, Sera, and Drepung. Local legend at Dzogchen Monastery tells of Gonpo Namgyel asking the Fourth Dzogchen Rinpoche for a prediction of his future births. Despite warnings from his attendants, the lama gave the warlord the bad news: not only would he be going straight to hell, but should he attempt an invasion of Tibet he would not even reach Chamdo. Gonpo Namgyel was impressed by the lama's courage, and securing the lama's promise to save him from hell for at least one subsequent lifetime, he made an offering and departed. Other lamas were not so lucky. He is said to have tied lamas from Dzogchen and Katok in sacks and to have tossed them into the Dzachu River, although this is almost certainly apocryphal. He decimated Raktrul Monastery in Nyarong, but this was because the prominent Raktrul family opposed him.[21]

Other prominent lamas who were taken to Nyarong included Adzom Drukpa Pawo Dorje, the Third Drime Zhingkyong, the Tongkhor Zhabdrung,[22] the Fourth Dzogchen Ponlob, and the Second Katok Getse Tulku.[23] Kongtrul never explained why he was not himself taken to Nyarong alongside Wontrul. He wrote that there was some talk about him being included, but "thanks to the blessings of the Three Jewels" the summons never came.[24]

In September 1863[25] the Situ estate sponsored a Vajrakīla drubchen ritual as a response to the war. Kongtrul, while walking down from his hermitage to take part, experienced some sort of edema in his legs, which swelled and caused him great pain. During the ceremony, everyone seems to have become ill with a viral infection. In his diary, Kongtrul described eruptions on his skin and pain such that it was close to impossible for him to rise in the morning and attend the ceremonies. He took this all to be a reflection of the horrifying conditions under which his patrons were then suffering.

Kongtrul wished his readers to know that although he continued to avoid the immediate effects of the war, due to his empathy and his ritual service he was shouldering a portion of the tragedy. He spent the rest of the lunar year supplicating Vajrakīla and the protective deities.[26]

At the beginning of the Wood Mouse Year (in his diary Kongtrul again errs in the designation of the new year, writing Earth Bird), which began on February 8, 1864, the Tenth Situ was facing unnamed difficulties, and Kongtrul cleared them up with a few empowerments and ablutions. He does not indicate whether these were a result of the war or simply more of Situ's erratic personality coming to the fore.[27] In early 1864 the Tibetan army took Pelyul and Jomda, two territories in southern Derge on opposite sides of the Drichu. They then began a seven-month siege of Derge, which ended in November 1864. Kongtrul wrote that he had first heard news of the Tibetans coming to Derge's rescue in early 1863; "rumors abounded that the Tibetan government sent an army led by Cabinet Minister Pulungwa and others that was so large it made heaven and earth shake." It is still not clear when the Tibetan forces left Lhasa and when they arrived in Kham.[28]

The Tibetan army was under the command of Cabinet Minister Pulungwa Tsewang Dorje, assisted by General Trimon Chime Dorje, General Dokharwa Tsewang Norbu, and paymaster Punrabpa Tsering Pelden. Pulungwa assembled troops along the way, possibly amassing a force of 13,000 soldiers, professional and otherwise. They arrived in Batang by June 1863, when Qing agents there sent reports of atrocities committed by the Tibetan forces. Yudru Tsomo points out that these narratives may have been exaggerated; the Qing administration, then facing rebellions and foreign invasions across the empire, was unable and unwilling to assist the Tibetan army. The empire had more to fear from the presence of a confident Tibetan army in Kham than from Gonpo Namgyel's conquests of his neighbors. Manchu bureaucrats scrambled to explain why the Tibetans were unwelcome and why the Qing were not taking the lead on defending their (nominal) dependents in Kham.[29]

Kongtrul continued his ritual response to the war with practices from Dispelling All Obstacles. In the spring and summer, he completed the Treasury of Knowledge and continued to write manuals for the Treasury of Revelations, and the three-year retreat ended. He also wrote, in February 1864,[30] his exhaustive Tsādra catalog titled *All-Pervading Melody of the Pure Lands: A Catalog of the Buildings and Contents of the Pelpung Hermitage Kunzang Dechen Wosel Ling.* Kongtrul does not explicitly explain why he took on the subject, but it is reasonable, in light of the destruction at Dzongsar, that he wanted an inventory should the hermitage be destroyed. With Wontrul still in Nyarong, the annual vase ceremony was delayed until August.[31] The Tenth Situ had another episode, and Kongtrul again attempted a ritual cure, this time being stricken himself with some sort of illness that kept him laid up for a week. He noted in his diary that, henceforth, whenever he performed an exorcism or ablution, he would experience an agonizing case of contamination, as though he took on himself the suffering of others.[32]

Although Kongtrul had escaped being taken hostage by Nyarong, he would not avoid a summons by the Tibetans. An important local contingent of the Tibetan army appears to have been from Drayab, a kingdom in southern Kham on the western bank of the Drichu, and thus, at least nominally, under the rule of Lhasa. A leader of this army, then stationed in Ngulsib, was a prominent lama from Drayab Monastery, the Dongkham Tripa, Ngawang Damcho Gyatso. In November 1864[33] the lama fell ill and requested the services of the most skilled physician in the region. Kongtrul boasts that his name was given, and thus he was summoned. Self-aggrandizement aside, Kongtrul went in a state of great agitation. The war was not yet finished, and he feared the Nyarong forces. By then it was clear that Gonpo Namgyel was murdering cultural and political leaders who gave assistance to the Tibetan army. If Kongtrul was later caught by Nyarong troops, he would be executed. At the same time, the Tibetan army, Kongtrul wrote, was engaged in its own reprisals, punishing monasteries and lamas who had served Gonpo Namgyel, as he himself had done five years earlier. Pelpung, he feared, was a target: after the Tibetan conquest of Derge, he wrote, "territories in the region that did not submit were attacked, and as our monastery was accused, it was about to be seized." Kongtrul could easily have been exaggerating the threat to the monastery, but he did have reason to worry that he would not return from the Drayab encampment. He had little choice but to submit, and so he dealt with his anxiety in a customary way: he threw a divination to ease his mind and received positive results.[34]

At the Tibetan encampment, Kongtrul "performed some empowerments and ablutions for the Dongkham Tripa." He reported that "the foundations of the illness ran deep, so I did a divination to see whether it was better he depart or remain, and I determined it would be best if he left, which he did, via palanquin." Having dispatched the lama who had required his presence, Kongtrul was probably hopeful he too would be able to leave. Instead, he was brought before Pulungwa and ordered to perform rituals to curry favor with the protective deities. The Tibetan army was then preparing a push into Nyarong, a battle described by Kongtrul as "a situation of heartbreaking chaos, like being in the bardo." Kongtrul wrote:

> He cast divinations as to when the enemy would strike and from where they would come, and so forth. As far as I could tell, such topics are hardly covered in the manuals on divination! However, by speaking whatever came to mind, by the blessing of the Three Jewels, what I 'predicted' came to pass exactly so, and the great minister gained confidence in me. Because the Tibetan army was later victorious in battle, I was praised and honored.

Kongtrul also alleged that he "surrendered" Pelpung and all its territories to Pulungwa, naming everyone he could think of in order to place them under the general's protection. As a result, he was given a guarantee that Pelpung, its temples and territories, would not be harmed.[35]

Kongtrul was allowed to temporarily return home before the end of the war, sometime in the late autumn of 1864. Despite conditions, he had determined to begin a second three-year, three-fortnight retreat at Tsādra that winter, so he undertook to give the ten incoming monks the necessary empowerments and training. He performed his year-end Vajrakīla rites and then dedicated about five months to the inner sādhana of Dispelling All Obstacles. Kongtrul was now in a state of exultation, having survived the Tibetan service and possibly protected his community from disaster. His dreams during his retreat were full of glorious symbolism and saints and deities. In one he saw treasure scrolls belonging to Chokgyur Lingpa and decoded them. In another Bernakchen and Swift-Acting Wisdom Protector crushed his obstacles. The First Karmapa and the Ninth Situ gave him advice and instructions. Situ, however, appeared exhausted—there was clearly trouble brewing in the incarnation line. Dabzang appeared, also delighted, and Kongtrul saw himself wearing a mask of Yamāntaka. He saw the Buddha surrounded by a retinue of monks, who ordained him with the traditional phrase used to bring men into the saṅgha: "Come hither." Kongtrul was then able to join the community in its reaffirmation of their vows.[36]

How real was the threat to Pelpung? Certainly Kongtrul, Situ, and Wontrul had ministered to Gonpo Namgyel, but by that measure nearly every monastery in the region would have been at risk. Scholars have speculated that the Tibetan government was intent on seizing monasteries for conversion. This was a strategy used in the past to ensure obedience and punish recalcitrant communities, such as during the Mongol invasion in the seventeenth century and the Tibetan conquest of Gyarong in the eighteenth. It is a reasonable hypothesis, but there is no evidence that any such conversions actually took place in Kham at this time. The Tibetan army did destroy a Nyingma monastery in Nyarong, but this was in battle, and it was rebuilt as a Nyingma institution. Not a single Nyingma monastery in Nyarong was converted, and even today there is no Geluk monastery in the valley.[37] Kongtrul may have overemphasized the dangers faced by himself and Pelpung in order to allay accusations that he assisted the Tibetan army. By most accounts the Tibetans had been welcomed as liberators, but by the time Kongtrul was preparing his diary for publication, several decades after the events, the subsequent occupation of Nyarong by the Tibetans had produced a great deal of antipathy toward Lhasa.

At the war's conclusion, Lhasa demanded an indemnity from Beijing on the grounds that the region belonged to China and that the Qing court should therefore pay the Tibetan expenses. It was a shrewd move, for in place of the 200,000 tael of silver that the nearly bankrupt Qing could not afford, Lhasa accepted a counteroffer of sovereignty over Nyarong. Consequently, a governor was installed and a Tibetan army was stationed there for the next several decades. Luciano Petech, citing Chinese sources, wrote that the Tibetan victory "was marred by the indiscipline of the Tibetan troops, who inflicted much looting and violence upon the local population." The British consular officer Edward Baber, who traveled the region a decade or so after the conclusion of the conflict, described the administration of the Tibetan governor in Nyarong as brutal and exploitative, evidence that "a conqueror is not always a judicious administrator."[38] Due in large part to the Tibetan behavior, only a few decades after the war Gonpo Namgyel was on his way to being regarded as a local hero, a man who had tried to unite Kham but had been destroyed by invading Tibetans. Kongtrul's service to the Tibetans, the rituals he performed to bring about the defeat of Nyarong, and the rewards he received as a result, by the end of the century required some explanation. He thus refashioned his narrative into one in which he saved Pelpung from the Tibetans.

Starting in May 1865, Kongtrul spent about a month in Derge once again performing rituals for Pulungwa and the Tibetan army. He would continue to serve the Tibetan governors-general in Nyarong until his final years. He was also tasked with purifying Derge's sacred buildings. Yudru Tsomo describes the Nyarong occupying army in Derge as having been divided over the treatment of Gonchen and the printing house. One commander, Puyang Dramdul, initially wanted to garrison troops in the buildings but was prevented by another, more devout man named Luma. Puyang Dramdul, however, fell ill and became convinced that the cause was his opposition to the Tibetan army. He defected, and at the end of the war he was given an estate in central Tibet. Luma did not object to the destruction of houses and government buildings, including the royal palace in Changra, and facing retreat he was willing to allow the destruction of both Gonchen and the printing house. Gonpo Namgyel's son Sangdak Gonpo, however, a man even more devout than Luma, intervened to save the buildings. Kongtrul states that "During the turbulence, Lhasar Temple, the printing house, etc., had been used to house the army and had been sites of conflict. As a result, the contamination was severe, and I was instructed by Pulungwa that they needed to be reconsecrated." Perhaps it was not the Nyarong army but the Tibetan troops who desecrated the buildings; Pulungwa appears to have remained in Derge until the war concluded in July 1865. Kongtrul performed ablutions, consecration rites, feast offerings, and supplications to the protective deities. He returned to Pelpung for the annual vase ceremony and then to Tsādra to continue with rituals relating to the war.[39]

Kongtrul recorded that in June 1865[40] he and the young Situ went to the peak of Uchetem to supplicate and demand the aid of the deity. The weather was fierce at first, with wind, lightning, and hail coming at them from all directions. But by the end of the ritual the mountain was pacified and the weather was calm. Other signs pointed to a positive conclusion to the war. Down at Lhasar Temple the two performed a "reversal of wrath" rite of the Eight Commands. When they cast the torma, Kongtrul spied significant omens, and when they prepared the effigy, some participants dreamed of the enemy army's defeat. He was back in Gonchen in late July or early August[41] to attend to Pulungwa's karmic load. He spent one week releasing him from his karmic debts incurred by the war and another on longevity rites, and then he performed one hundred ablution and long-life empowerments. He responded to the requests of other ministers and aristocrats and then returned to Pelpung.[42]

Gonpo Namgyel was defeated in July 1865. (Kongtrul erroneously dates the war's conclusion to the eighth month of the Wood Ox Year—September 20 to October 19, 1865.) That spring, the Tibetan army—General Trimon leading one division and General Petsel leading another—closed in on Gonpo Namgyel at this fortress in Nyarong. According to Kongtrul, Pulungwa was also at the final battle, although other sources fail to place him there. It was at this time that Zhiwa Monastery was destroyed and all hostages were either released or liberated. General Trimon is said to have attempted a negotiation but he was rebuffed, and Gonpo Namgyel and his entire family burned to death in their fortress. There is no definitive account of who set the fire, whether it was the Tibetan troops or members of Gonpo Namgyel's family. The Queen and her two sons returned to Derge, and Wontrul came back to Pelpung. Kongtrul offered them rituals by way of welcome. Pulungwa ordered Kongtrul to perform Mahākāla rites for the capital, with a thread-cross ritual of victory. He chose to do an approach practice using the four-armed form of the bodhisattva, which has a particular association with Cakrasaṃvara and the Kagyu tradition, and in October he prepared all the materials he needed. A lama from Zhechen named Lama Donpel came and joined the ritual, at which a large number of Pelpung monks were also present. Kongtrul, ever on the lookout for transmissions, took the opportunity to request some from Lama Donpel, himself a student of Zhechen Wontrul. Kongtrul ended the year teaching grammar to a student named Lhaksam Tenpai Gyeltsen and undertaking an approach practice of Swift-Acting Wisdom Protector and other year-end rituals at the hermitage.[43]

Pulungwa left for Tibet at the turn of the Fire Tiger Year, which began on February 16, 1866. Kongtrul went to Derge for his departure and sent him off in his customary fashion, with further rituals to free him from the negative karmic effects of the war and to lengthen his life. The Derge prince was ill, so Kongtrul also performed one hundred long-life rituals for him. Pulungwa, Derge, and Pelpung all rewarded Kongtrul for his activities. The Tibetan commander gave him some nomadic pastureland down the valley from Pelpung known as Tsetru. Kongtrul is careful to note that the land was then unclaimed and that previously it had been used by whomever was able to use it; he was not, he made clear, given property stolen by the Tibetans. The Derge government gave Kongtrul unnamed gifts for the rituals he had performed for the benefit of the queen and princes during the years they were under threat or were prisoners of Nyarong. Wontrul told him:

> It was from your kind intervention that the Pelpung teachings, monastery, and surrounding area has been allowed to remain

independent and safe. In the past the Situ estate has given you nothing at all. Now we shall offer assistance; for its support, the buildings and land of Drama in Naru will be ceded to [your] hermitage for as long as it exists.[44]

Kongtrul has Situ agreeing to this inaccurate assessment of past support with a written testimonial, and he affirms that the transfer was carried out. It is a sly yet stark expression of ingratitude on Kongtrul's behalf; the Situ estate had been supporting Tsādra since the beginning, when Situ sent up butter for Kongtrul's first retreat there. Yet Kongtrul was evidently resentful and unsatisfied. Still, he was fortunate to have managed the hermitage as he had. A greater involvement by the Pelpung administration would have resulted in less independence for Kongtrul, enveloping the hermitage in the institutional structure of the monastery. Considering that within a decade he would be confronted with accusations of impropriety and expelled from Pelpung for eleven years, keeping Tsādra independent was fortuitous.

# 22

# AFTERMATH OF THE WAR, PART ONE

*Make Love Not War*

1866–1868

On March 4, 1866,[1] at Pelpung's Lhasar Temple, Kongtrul began transmitting the entire Kangyur to the Tenth Situ, then about thirteen years old. Kongtrul chose the date, he explains in the diary, because it was the day of the month commemorating the Buddha's miracles when the sun was in the Hasta lunar mansion, a particularly auspicious day of the year. Kongtrul was not able to get through much before he fell ill. He was reading the Vinaya section of the canon when he first collapsed, exhausted. A doctor named Chogyeb performed some rites for his recovery and, not one to miss an opportunity to collect a teaching, Kongtrul requested of him the transmission of several medical collections: the Ten Million Relics by Zurkharwa Nyemnyi Dorje and One Hundred Instructions of Darmo, the collected medical teachings of the Fifth Dalai Lama's personal physician, Darmo Menrampa Lobzang Chodrak. This restored him somewhat, and he continued the transmission to Situ, completing the Vinaya on April 10.[2] At this point he suspended the ritual until April 27[3] to receive transmissions from Dabzang—the Zurmang tradition of Heart Drop of the Ḍākinī—and to instruct the residents of the monastery's meditation centers. After reading the Prajñāpāramitā and other Mahāyāna sūtras, he again paused to return to Tsādra to participate in the retreat's Vajrasattva rituals. Then, on May 28[4] he was back at the monastery to continue, getting through four tantras before again falling ill. This time it was in his genitals, possibly lymphatic. He was forced to return to Tsādra, unable to ride a horse as he normally would have done. Dabzang came again to help him. He had been with Chokgyur Lingpa and was able to give Kongtrul a few new revelations as well as other forms of ritual assistance—a long-life and a "decontamination" rite. A doctor diagnosed him with a "cold bile" condition—probably jaundice and possibly related to his eye disorder—and gave him medicine. He did not return to the Kangyur transmission until late September or early October.[5]

The war was over, the royal family was back in Derge, and Kongtrul had been rewarded for his services. Yet there was a pervasive sense of unease that Kongtrul could not shake. In the five years following the war, Kongtrul was frequently ill. The war's negative effects were ongoing; Kongtrul found negative omens in temples, the landscape, and in dreams. The Tibetan government remained in Kham administering—badly—the conquered Nyarong region. Trade relations suffered, and this rippled through the region. The Tenth Situ continued to show signs of volatility. Kongtrul was halfway through his sixth decade, and most of his writing was done; three of his major works—the Treasury of Kagyu Tantra, Treasury of Revelations, and the Treasury of Knowledge—had largely been completed. He did not compile the fourth, Treasury of Instructions, until 1871. In his confusion Kongtrul turned even more to Khyentse Wangpo for guidance and comfort. It was a period of intense collaboration between the two ecumenical masters and Chokgyur Lingpa; the three worked in such unison that they are still known as "the triad of Khyentse, Kongtrul, and Chokling." It was their final years, as Chokling would be dead by the end of the decade.

When Chokgyur Lingpa returned to Derge from his monasteries in Nangchen where he had waited out the war in retreat, he immediately caught on to the mood in the region. He first gave Kongtrul the transmissions of his revelations Kongtrul had not previously received. During a medicine consecration ritual of United Intent of the Gurus at Pelpung, which began on July 7, 1866,[6] and over which he presided, Chokling fervidly told Kongtrul he must write new mendrub and drubchen liturgies and that "this year, due to all that has happened, your usual rites of service and the like will have no benefit. Instead, you will need to perform a 'festival to the heroes and heroines,'" thereby setting up a very unpleasant episode of what can only be described as sexual abuse.[7]

Chokgyur Lingpa seems to have suggested this rite to Kongtrul to prepare the way at Tsādra for a colleague of his, a man named Ngawang Rinchen. This man may have had some connection to Ngor Monastery; according to Konchok Gyurme, Chokling's biographer, he held the office of vajra master there. Ngawang Rinchen and Chokgyur Lingpa had been collaborating on rituals together in the area, and they appear to have discussed potential treasure revelations; Ngawang Rinchen let slip to Kongrul the name of a treasure that Chokling would reveal later that year.[8] He had ostensibly gone to Tsādra to transmit to Kongtrul certain treasures of Chokgyur Lingpa's, although Kongtrul does not record their names. Possibly in return for this, Kongtrul taught him and several unnamed others the Treasury of Knowledge, the first time that Kongtrul recorded teaching his newly completed composition.[9]

Almost immediately after the teachings were complete, Ngawang Rinchen pushed Kongtrul to assist him in preparing for a hero and heroine festival, the ritual Chokgyur Lingpa had advised Kongtrul to perform. Ngawang Rinchen suggested that the festival be held at Tsādra, at the spot called Dechen Pemako Lhamdo Burmo, also known as Burmo Drak and Lhamdo Burmo. This cliff was becoming a focal point at Tsādra; Kongtrul at some point composed a two-page liturgy for smoke offerings and other rituals to worship there. Chokling revealed treasure here, his sole Bon treasure, a liturgy for the worship of two Bon deities. At some point Chokling also revealed a brief gazetteer for this place, and Kongtrul would later reveal his first scriptural treasure there, United Intent of the Three Roots.[10]

Ngawang Rinchen changed his mind, however, and he suddenly returned to the hermitage building, declared that the festival had to occur there, and immediately started his preparations. And as part of those preparations Kongtrul found himself in the uncomfortable position of having to supply the lama with a young girl to complete the assembly. A feast of heroes and heroines requires an equal number of male and female practitioners to gather together at night in a suitable isolated place. After consecrating and ingesting the feast substances—meat, alcohol, etc.—the male and female pairs join in sexual union in order to generate a state of bliss and emptiness, after which they dance and sing to display their realizations.[11]

The ritual can be performed with the female roles visualized by the males, but this evidently was not what Ngawang Rinchen had in mind. He informed Kongtrul that the festival required five men and five women in attendance and that he was short one "heroine." Kongtrul responded with an offer of a niece of his, a girl from his father's side of the family whom his mother had cared for since the time the girl was a child. He does not indicate how old the girl was at the time of the festival. Kongtrul writes only that Ngawang Rinchen accepted the girl and proceeded to preside over a feast and mending rite. The man apparently took a fancy to her. On the night of the ceremony, Kongtrul relates, the lama had an extravagant dream about the girl. He claimed in his dream he saw twenty-five women, all students of Kunga Bum, the fourteenth-century female tantric adept. Five of these women had been especially blessed by the ḍākinī of the five families—buddha, vajra, lotus, jewel, and action—and the one who received the blessing of the ḍākinī of the buddha family, who was named Sanggye Tso, had been the consort of Dungtso Repa. Ngawang Rinchen claimed to be a reincarnation of Dungtso Repa and believed that Kongtrul's relative was the reincarnation of Sanggye Tso.[12]

Kongtrul appears to have initiated something with which he was not entirely comfortable. He found himself being told by Ngawang Rinchen that the girl—whom he ever after referred to by the name Ngawang Rinchen gave her, Chime Deter Rigdzin Dolma—should not marry. Were she to marry, Ngawang Rinchen claimed, the ḍākinīs might become angry and bring down their wrath, and in any case no good would come to the family into which she was sent. Kongtrul suggested that the girl therefore could become a nun, in order that no one establish a sexual relationship with her, but this was not what Ngawang Rinchen had in mind. No, he replied—it would not be good for her to have too many obligations; better that she remain a practitioner and so be available for his use. He continued to make his case for taking the girl for his own: he explained that there were twenty-five women prophesied to be his consorts, five of whom lived in the Derge region. As yet, he had been unable to meet any of them; he had encountered some women and engaged in sexual yoga with them only to discover that they were not among the fated few. This, he told Kongtrul, resulted in damage to his practice—breaches of samaya. The effect on the women he spurned goes unmentioned. Ngawang Rinchen sensed Kongtrul's hesitation. He told him he was certain that Kongtrul's young relative was one of the girls prophesied to be his and that he would be speaking to Wontrul about initiating a relationship with her. Wontrul, as Kongtrul knew too well, would be able to override any objection Kongtrul might have to the man taking his relative as a sexual consort.[13]

Ngawang Rinchen proceeded to perform a feast offering, and Kongtrul records that there were clear signs that Yeshe Tsogyel began to confer on the man the prophetic guide for the treasure United Intent of the Ḍākinīs. This is a section of Five Cycles of the Essence of the Noble Dharma that Chokgyur Lingpa and Khyentse Wangpo would reveal later in the year. (Or so Ngawang Rinchen boasted, mining previous conversations with Chokling in order to entice a potential patron.) Kongtrul, however, was not impressed. The man demanded an empowerment from *Innermost Heart Drop of the Ḍākinī* of Longchenpa, and after receiving it he left. Kongtrul never mentions him again. He ends the section in his diary with a quotation from Tāranātha on the need for the proper circumstances to practice religion:

> A single initial effort might be enough to ensure auspicious circumstances, but even auspicious circumstances are conditioned—how could they be permanent? One is pleased as long as that positive momentum does not dissipate, but when later adversity derails those auspicious circumstances, that single deed at the start was not enough. This is important, something that everyone should understand.[14]

Rare is the individual who received criticism from Jamgon Kongtrul, even as veiled as this. Ngawang Rinchen had been sent from Chokgyur Lingpa, an auspicious initial circumstance. He served as a conduit for some of Chokling's revelations, but Kongtrul did not even name them. Ngawang Rinchen's fatal move was to push Kongtrul to give him a relative who was most likely under his protection and to threaten to go over his head to keep her in a possibly nonconsensual sexual relationship. Whatever favorable conditions Ngawang Rinchen had arrived with, he squandered it all.

After finishing the Kangyur transmissions in the fall of 1866, a group of disciples requested additional transmissions of cycles pertaining to the Peaceful and Wrathful Deities, such as Karma Lingpa's works and the Lightning Garland of Protective Deitics: Peaceful Garland, Wrathful Garland. Kongtrul also gave them Yongge Mingyur Dorje's longevity practice Integration of Means and Wisdom. Chokgyur Lingpa returned and requested a few transmissions, and Kongtrul took the opportunity to give him a pared-down instruction of the Treasury of Knowledge, thus teaching the work for the second time. Chokling reciprocated with the transmission of Tincture of Molten Meteoric Iron from Seven Profound Cycles, a Yamarāja practice that Kongtrul chose not to include in the Treasury of Revelations.[15]

Soon after, Chokgyur Lingpa appeared to Kongtrul in a dream while he was practicing Vajra Sitātapatrā, a female protector deity, from October 23 to December 17.[16] Kongtrul was using the liturgy from Chokling's Three Roots revelation, a section of Seven Profound Cycles, three texts of which he included in the Treasury of Revelations. Kongtrul first dreamed of discussing his meditative accomplishments with Padampa Sanggye. At fifty-eight years old, Kongtrul had few teachers left to discuss his experiences in practice; Khyentse Wangpo and perhaps Wontrul and Dabzang were all who remained of his peers. Disciples routinely relate their experiences to their teachers, who affirm their progress and suggest additional practices, evaluating the student's accomplishment against descriptions given in the literature and against their own mastery. Without a guru to rely on, Kongtrul appears to have turned to the great saints of the past via dream interviews. In a second dream, Kongtrul had a conviction that Padmasambhava was still residing in Tibet. Going inside a temple where he expected to encounter him, he found instead Chokgyur Lingpa, to whom he prostrated with great faith, and he moved through the four stages of meditative absorption. Kongtrul also performed the Longevity Lord Yamāntaka practice from Seven Profound Cycles. He was satisfied with the practices, writing that his dreams were consistent with those of his previous practices of United Intent of the Gurus.[17]

While Kongtrul was engaged with Vajra Sitātapatrā, Khyentse Wangpo and Chokgyur Lingpa were in a valley near Dzongsar named Rongme opening caves and revealing treasure. They had spent two weeks at the site, from November 2 to November 19.[18] There are many narratives of this event, including a magnificent painting that is preserved at a monastery in Kham. The painting illustrates events on the front which are described in text on the back. Khyentse and Chokling, together with Chokgyur Lingpa's consort Dechen Chodren and at least one of his sons, as well as a crowd of observers, had arrived at Rongme directly from Pema Shelpuk, crossing the pass between the valleys directly above the cave. They descended to the valley floor and reached a prominent rocky outcrop they named Chime Karmo Taktsang, arriving there at noon on November 2 to perform smoke offerings and feasts. They attempted to open a Yeshe Tsogyel cave but were unable to do so for reasons that remained unrecorded. The next day they surveyed the site from the peak and performed additional rituals there. On the fourth[19] they opened the Padmasambhava cave and publicly extracted various objects—Khyentse later identified the textual treasure as Chokling's thirtieth revelation, the Five Cycles of the Essence of the Noble Dharma, the name of which Ngawang Rinchen had prematurely divulged several months earlier. The following day they again sought to open the Tsogyel cave. The difficulty was first in reaching the chosen site—they needed to cut a tree to make a ladder, and, according to Konchok Gyurme's later embellishments, a young monk almost perished in the attempt. Second, they apparently needed to break rock in order to access the treasure inside, a process that lasted until the night. The painting depicts the use of fire to shatter the stone.[20]

On November 6[21] prominent observers began to arrive. The first was the steward of Derge, Sonam Tobgyel, who immediately received empowerments, accompanied by an entourage made up of members of the royal family and other aristocrats, who were the guests at rituals the following day. On November 8[22] Khyentse and Chokling gave the royal family the White Tārā long-life empowerment and performed rituals to benefit the kingdom. The young prince Chime Takpai Dorje—he had not yet been enthroned—arrived on November 12.[23] Two days later they began to break the treasure seals, producing marvels such as melted gold. On the evening of the sixteenth,[24] the entire contingent stayed awake singing and dancing, "fervently calling out prayers in lovely melodies with the sound of drums resounding." Khyentse, Chokling, and the king and ministers went to one of the caves in a grand procession for a feast offering "ululating a rush of beautiful melodies."[25] This night-long orgy of singing and dancing and praying would have brought about a shared ecstatic state conducive to visionary and other forms of revelatory experiences. Indeed, Khyentse Wangpo attributed to the day after the revelry one of the more important of Chokgyur Lingpa's treasures, *Stages of the Path of the Wisdom Essence*, for which Kongtrul later composed a famous commentary, *Light of Wisdom*.

The following day, November 17, Chokling and Khyentse also discovered a vajra protruding halfway out of a cave wall, which they declared had belonged to Padmasambhava in his menacing form of Wrathful Vajra Power. The group was so overcome with faith that they rested there in a state of primordial awareness, after which they allowed the public entrance to view it. Chokling adds that he revealed additional treasure—unnamed—and gave a treasure empowerment to about three hundred people, including the king and his family.

On their descent to the valley floor two weeks earlier, Khyentse and Chokling would have noticed a glacial lake to the north, on the far side of a difficult scree field. After opening the caves at Rongme, on November 18[26] they returned to that lake, which they named Lion's Roar Turquoise Lake. Past masters had allegedly made retreat huts there by stacking flat pieces of shale from the surrounding scree field. Inside of one of these, they performed rituals and practiced togel. In their meditative state they had visions of colored banners radiating over the lake, which seemed to point to the existence of treasure. Khyentse Wangpo subjugated the lake's guardian nāga, Chokling tossed his belt into the water as though fishing for the treasure, and a rain of gold dust fell around them as a substitute for what they were about to extract. In his own narrative Chokling ends the account here after the party takes the treasure and returns to Chime Karmo Taktsang.[27]

Other sources expand the story: having cut through the ice in the center of the lake, Chokgyur Lingpa warned the others not to throw rocks, as they might harm the nāga guardian of the lake. Khyentse Wangpo roared back with "What is there to fear in a nāga? It is a worm! The so-called nāga has no primordial existence. If he is there, I want to wake him up! I do not fear nāgas! If there is a nāga, let it come here!" At this point he threw many stones into the lake. The others, however, obeying the command, refrained from throwing stones. Chokling attempted to retrieve treasure from the lake by tying his lower robes with his belt into a scoop of sorts, and he had his attendants cast it into the lake. The robes repeatedly came back empty, perhaps because he forbade the attendants from looking toward the lake, having warned that were they to gaze upon it the nāga would breathe poison on them and refuse to grant treasure. Suddenly, the lake seethed with serpents, Chokling screamed "there's a snake!" and pandemonium ensued, in the thick of which Chokling's rosary broke. Khyentse slapped Chokling on the cheek, scolding him that as Guru Rinpoche's representative he ought not cower so. In response to it all, Chokgyur Lingpa lamented, "Not only has no treasure been extracted but now I have to collect all the beads of this rosary!" Giving up on the robe, Chokling sat down on the shore, and with the statement that "this nāga needs to be tormented a little" he entered a wrathful nāga-taming samādhi of Hayagrīva. He shouted to the nāga to come, at which point a treasure chest appeared in the water and the lake and the shore overflowed with gold "like a clay pot full of provisions." Chokling withdrew the chest with his own hand, his robe sleeve ever after yellow from the gold dust. The lower robe-scoop finally produced something, coming out filled with chunks of gold. Everyone gathered the gold, and he and Khyentse Wangpo did a short treasure-substitute dance. With Khyentse claiming that it was the rocks he threw that effected the retrieval of the treasure, they returned to the encampment at the cave site below. Remaining in wrathful mode, Khyentse continued to throw stones at everyone, purifying the karmic stains of all those he struck.

Kongtrul received notice about the Rongme events shortly after his Vajra

Sitātapatrā retreat concluded. Chokling and Khyentse had moved to Dagam Wangpuk, and after Kongtrul received their summons he joined them there. Together they decoded the scrolls from Five Cycles of the Essence of the Noble Dharma as well as additional liturgies from the unendingly productive Seven Profound Cycles, including Four Dharmas of Protector of the Teachings, Great Dog, which is a deity related to Hayagrīva, and the root sādhana of Combined Precepts of Dzogchen. Not mentioned in the diary is *Stages of the Path of the Wisdom Essence*. The colophon for the text itself states that Kongtrul decoded it at Dagam, although it is entirely possible that the colophon attribution was later contrived in order to tie the text to the Rongme revelation events. As part of the process, Chokling gave Kongtrul and Khyentse the empowerments for all of these. Khyentse gave them the empowerment for Heart Drop of the Great Siddha, his mind-treasure cycle dedicated to Tangtong Gyelpo.[28]

The three went next to Khangmar Monastery, a Nyingma monastery in southern Derge, and continued with empowerments. Chokling was ablaze, presiding over mendrub and drubchen rituals, during which he brought forth "an extraordinarily splendid display of blessings." Khyentse gave an "ultimate empowerment"—the streamlined version—of the Wrathful Power, a Northern Treasures cycle. Kongtrul wrote that Khyentse used the actual yellow scrolls during the ritual, which suggests that he revealed the treasure himself, although there is no treasure cycle by that name associated with him. Khyentse also gave an extended teaching based on the treasure they had just written out, Stages of the Path of the Wisdom Essence, and also of *Stages of the Path of Secret Mantra* by Getse Paṇḍita.[29]

At the end of 1866 or in the early days of 1867, the eighteen-year-old Chime Takpai Dorje was finally enthroned as the king of Derge. Kongtrul, Khyentse, and Chokgyur Lingpa all transferred to the capital for the ceremony. Chokling gave a benediction that Kongtrul described as "very extensive," as though perhaps he spoke too long. He also performed a benediction from the Northern Treasures titled Blazing Jewel of Temporal Rule and made public the Cycle of Dependent Origination, a section of the recently revealed Three Cycles of Dzogchen. Kongtrul says nothing of his role in the ceremonies, if he had one. This is peculiar, given the extent to which he was lauded for his service during the war. Following the festivities, he returned to give teachings at the retreat centers at Tsādra and Pelpung and to perform his annual Vajrakīla rites.[30]

In March 1867[31] Kongtrul went to Dzongsho to reunite with Khyentse and Chokgyur Lingpa, as had been arranged by Chokling. They continued the writing projects begun at Dagam, finishing the Great Dog and "some secret prophetic records" of Chokling's treasures. Chokling had only one cycle left to reveal, Unified Saṃvara Buddha, which would come to him at Rudam two months later, in May 1867.[32] He also revealed gazetteers for Dzongsho and Pema Shelri, a site in the Terlung Valley, and several objects from a place called Khyungtsang Drak. The three performed a drubchen ritual for the Eight Commands: Gathering of All Sugatas, Chokling's twenty-eighth revelation, dated to May 30, 1864.[33] After this, Khyentse gave them a teaching introducing them to the five categories of a being—body, speech, mind, qualities, and activities, both ordinary and enlightened—and how they are related to the five places on the body.[34]

The three then performed a second enthronement—this one of Kongtrul. Khyentse and Chokling sat Kongtrul on a throne of rock in the hidden cave named Citta and invested him with a treasure revealer name: Chime Tennyi Yungdrung Lingpa. As part of the benediction, they gave him a longevity rite; Kongtrul does not identify which liturgy. Khyentse and Chokling evidently had decided that Kongtrul ought to participate more actively in the treasure extraction activity. For decades he had been writing liturgies for treasure cycles, and he had been assisting the two of them in decoding treasures—translating their inspiration into textual form. They now insisted that he reveal treasure himself. The three went to the Dilgo family estate to perform a mendrub ritual using their Eight Commands cycle, and then, still in the Terlung Valley, opened Pema Shelri. According to Khyentse Wangpo, Chokling produced the gazetteer in the middle of April, although the colophon of the gazetteer, *Heart of the Sun*, does not give the date of its revelation. They performed feast offerings in caves, naming them the Vairocana Crystal Light Cave and the Sacred Padmasambhava Cave, revealing treasure at each. Chokling insisted that Kongtrul also reveal something, so Kongtrul reached his arm into the Secret Padmasambhava Cave and brought out a small "treasure box" which he passed to Chokling. Reluctant still to take on the role of a treasure revealer, he does not divulge the contents. It would be some years before he allowed himself to produce any scriptural revelations.[35]

From Terlung, Kongtrul returned to Pelpung in time for the annual vase ceremony in May. It was to be a difficult summer. First Kongtrul found the Tenth Situ suffering again from sores in his mouth, a condition that had afflicted the teenager for several years. Dabzang and Chokgyur Lingpa had each attempted a ritual cure, to little effect. Now Kongtrul also undertook a cure performing a long-life ritual, a separate rite to turn back death, and a feast offering. He also performed a mamo ransom ritual for the welfare of Pelpung, and, up at Tsādra, participated in the mending rite from United Intent of the Gurus.[36]

Following the two enthronements, Kongtrul was confronted with a series of deaths of significant people. First Chokling reported that he learned of a Won Lama's passing while on his way from Dzogchen, and they readied commemorative rites. This was probably Tutob Namgyel, the First Dzogchen Wontrul. They then received the news that Dabzang had passed away. Kongtrul wrote in his diary of the death of one of his closest colleagues only that it was "sad," and makes no mention of funeral arrangements other than that it became necessary to arrange them. Chokling remained at Pelpung to supervise an unrelated drubchen ritual. Kongtrul likely would have participated, but his mother suddenly fell ill, and he gathered every lama available to help her, including the Tenth Situ and Chokling. They performed over thirteen hundred recitations of purification empowerments of Vairocana and other deities before she passed away. Khyentse Wangpo came, and he and Chokling, assisted by graduates from Tsadra's retreat center, performed the transference of consciousness. The loss of his mother deeply affected Kongtrul, and from heartfelt filial piety he declared that he sold half of his possessions to sponsor recitations and other meritorious acts to dedicate to her future births.[37]

A lama's mother often has an awkward status in monastic Tibet. Mothers, as well as fathers, are frequently depicted as obstacles to the religious life, pleading with their male offspring to carry on the family line. The great eighteenth-century itinerant monk Zhabkar Tsokdruk Rangdrol, for example, repeatedly lied to his mother when he set off to meditate in remote locations, falsely promising to return quickly. Celibate men had few women in their lives, interacting with female members of patron families or perhaps monastery servants, but rarely developing a personal bond. Kongtrul's mother had done him the great kindness of sending him into the religious life, and she came to live with him at Tsādra to keep house. Whatever longing he might have had for the love of a woman and which was not sublimated in his love for Khyentse Wangpo was probably adequately covered by his mother, whom he clearly adored.[38]

Kongtrul's mother remained with him in dreams and ritual activities for years after her death. News of her positive rebirth came in an astonishing dream of Khyentse's, which provided some comfort to Kongtrul in the summer of 1867. Kongtrul not only recorded the dream in great detail but he also included it, nearly verbatim, in his biography of Khyentse Wangpo. There was good reason for him to treasure it, as not only did it give him news of his mother but it also testified to the love he felt for and received from his friend Khyentse Wangpo. In the late summer, Khyentse was at Tsādra giving instruction on *Abhisamayālaṃkāra* according to Rongton Sheja Kunrik's system of exegesis as well as other scriptures in the Tengyur and some early Kadam teachings. They performed a drubchen ritual in the So tradition of Samyak, possibly in conjunction with the ongoing second retreat; Kongtrul rarely indicates when he engaged in the retreat schedule. Khyentse gave Kongtrul (and possibly the retreatants) a few treasure empowerments, including Dorje Lingpa's Spacious Expanse of the View. Khyentse's dream occurred the evening of the main part of the empowerment.[39]

The dream began with Khyentse seeing himself as the wife of an ordinary householder in Lhodrak who goes unnamed. The wife was named Dorje Tso. One evening the husband announced, "a lama is coming, we must ready a place for him to stay," so she swept the house and prepared a place for him to sit and sleep. A short, corpulent lama came, whom she understood to be Dorje Lingpa, a famous fourteenth-century treasure revealer. He had a small topknot and full mane of hair, and he wore a yellow upper garment. At her request, he placed his hands on her head in blessing and she served him food and drink. That evening, she went to him and the two passed the night in various modes of lovemaking—caressing, kissing, and embracing. The lama shifted in identity between Dorje Lingpa and Tāranātha, at times impossible to differentiate in the thick of the passion. At daybreak Dorje Tso reverentially served the lama a meal, after which he mounted his horse and departed, several attendants on foot beside him.[40]

The lama had left a small box on the sofa he had used, covered with silk and humming like a hive of bees. Finding it, Dorje Tso exclaimed, "the lama has left something in our house," and she carried it after him and placed it in his hands. He told her that it was his casket of treasure substances. "The fact that I left it behind," he told her, "is quite auspicious. You must keep it and care for it as though it were gold." She was concerned, conscious of being a woman and not in control of her movements or possessions; "I am utterly unable to keep it. I cannot care for it. I do not know how to do any of what you ask" she wailed. "No matter," he replied, "keep it for me, and

I will return for it." She replied, "I do not know where or when I will be going somewhere, I do not dare care for it. Please give me your blessing." At this point the lama opened the casket and removed a large yellow scroll— the kind on which revelations are written—and read what seemed to be an inventory for the treasures of Dorje Lingpa, both known and unknown texts. He closed the box and placed it on the woman's head, saying once more "Take care of this for me, and my future incarnation will return to you for it." Dorje Tso understood this to mean that she would give birth to his reincarnation, and she worried that it would not be possible given that she was already on in years, while the lama was quite young. She asked him "When will the tulku come?" He replied, "Not for about five hundred years from now."[41]

The dream next took an even more peculiar turn, shifting to an awareness of the present. Taking the casket, Dorje Tso turned toward home but then thought, "This lama is surely Padmasambhava himself. I should ask him where Kongtrul's mother has been reborn." Dorje Lingpa began to respond with "she took birth in a watery land" but was interrupted before he could continue, as Dorje Tso wailed "what kind of water place, and what should we do now?" She wept in sadness of this news of Kongtrul's mother existing as a lowly fish or some other sea creature. The lama continued: "However, things will improve for her if you do some Akṣobhya practice." With this information Dorje Tso's understanding of "the watery land" shifted, and she understood it to be a wondrous pleasure land of jeweled palaces. Here the dream ended.[42]

After Khyentse recounted this dream, he told Kongtrul that he was well aware of having been the woman Dorje Tso—the episode came in a dream but it was as much a memory as a fantasy, and it was the reason Khyentse was able to access Dorje Lingpa's treasures. Beyond the comfort the dream offered Kongtrul regarding his mother, the significance is evidently that Khyentse Wangpo, in an earlier incarnation, made love to Dorje Lingpa, and in so doing he helped him reveal his treasures. He was both an aid and an heir to those revelations. There is an additional layer of meaning in the dream. While Dorje Tso/Khyentse Wangpo made love to the lama, the lama shifted between being Dorje Lingpa and Tāranātha. Kongtrul believed himself to be a reincarnation of Terdak Lingpa, among whose previous births was Tāranātha. He also claimed to be the rebirth of Yeshe Gyatso, Tāranātha's close disciple, whose mindstream was said to have been identical to his master's. The dreamtime lovemaking was not simply between Khyentse Wangpo and Dorje Lingpa; it was between Khyentse Wangpo and Kongtrul. Kongtrul and Khyentse Wangpo would both have understood this. Khyentse was continuing to offer emotional support.[43]

Khyentse had several additional visions while at Tsādra, including a lengthy conversation with Yeshe Tsogyel in which she gave him extensive advice and prophecies, enumerated for him all the treasure revealers of the past, and urged him to complete the inventory to United Intent of the Ḍākinī. Although he reported all these, he declined to involve Kongtrul in his plans to fulfill the goddess' instructions, to Kongtrul's frustration. He would only say that it was not a beneficial time to go to the treasure encampment and that the prophecy would need to remain unfulfilled. He did, however, bring out a combined Yangdak and Vajrakīla practice that was the first part of his "oral lineage," and Khyentse and Kongtrul did perform a torma exorcism ritual together. Khyentse went down to Pelpung to give the transmission for this teaching in the winter of 1867 and then returned to Tsādra in February 1868[44] to give Kongtrul further transmissions, this time for Cakrasaṃvara and other works from the transmitted teachings of the Nyingma and from the collected writings of the great treasure revealers. Kongtrul celebrated a longevity rite and a feast offering in his honor.[45]

## 23

## AFTERMATH OF THE WAR, PART TWO

*Kongtrul's Kham Gazetteer, the Death of Chokgyur Lingpa,*

*and the Treasury of Instructions; Rimay Part Three*

1867–1871

At the end of 1866, Kongtrul spent his final weeks with Chokgyur Lingpa. The two had achieved all that they would together, and Kongtrul was somewhat weary of the young man. He was now in his midfifties, and although he was hardly slowing down in his own output, he was perhaps impatient with the near-continuous treasure revelations, each one more elaborate and public than the last. Kongtrul was a ritual specialist of unparalleled skill and demand, but his preference was for those rituals that followed defined textual instructions. If a requested ritual did not have a written form, he would provide it. Revelation activities by nature include a certain degree of magic, of an embrace of the supernatural, but Kongtrul was lukewarm toward Chokling's extravagances. Where other narratives celebrate the flying, the mystical travels, and the feats of supernatural bravado, Kongtrul does not describe revelation events beyond basic details of time, place, participants, and rituals performed. Kongtrul had no doubts regarding the authenticity of treasure, and he appreciated the physical and ritual elements of its production. But the bacchanalia did not appeal to him.

Even as Kongtrul continued to celebrate public ceremonies at a remarkable pace, he increased his literary production. Between 1867 and 1872, he produced several of his major works: commentaries to the *Uttaratantra* and the *Hevajra Tantra*, as well as the Treasury of Instructions—his fourth major collection of what would be called his "Five Treasuries." He also composed—in response to the Tibetan conquest of Nyarong—a revision of Chokling's religious gazetteer of Kham. Both his gazetteer and the Treasury of Instructions were additional examples of his ecumenicalism, the first including sites sacred to all the traditions save the Tibetan government's Geluk, and the second once again employing the schema of the eight chariots of accomplishment.

Two years after the conclusion of the Nyarong War, the Tibetan government was firmly ensconced in Kham. Kongtrul remained a willing servant to any patron, but he would have known of the Tibetans' misrule in Nyarong. It was exploitative and imperialistic, and news of it would have reached him. Kongtrul would also have been keenly aware of the steady decline of Derge. The rise in power of the kingdom's aristocratic families that had led to such suffering in Ronggyab in his youth, combined with the government's ineffectual defense of Derge during the Nyarong War, had significantly undermined the royal family's hold on power. Chime Takpai Dorje was an inadequate ruler, and his two sons, Dorje Sengge and Ngawang Jampel Rinchen, would plunge the kingdom into a civil war within two decades. Kongtrul must also have begun to understand that at his own monastery there was a similar power vacuum, as the Tenth Situ was failing to grow into a stable leader. The turbulence of the war had exacerbated divisions, and as Kongtrul looked out at the alpine meadows and forested ubacs he must have felt uneasy regarding the future of his homeland.

Kongtrul was not a politician, he was not a military strategist, nor was he an activist; he neither initiated nor advocated for a social movement. He was, in fact, quite conservative: he preserved and promoted the familiar and the already existent. He delighted in new versions of rituals produced via socially accepted methods, not new rituals. Still, Kongtrul wielded religious authority in the region, and he could employ rituals and mythologies to help shape the cultural landscape. Rituals promoting well-being, of exorcising demonic influences, of long life and prosperity, of geomancy—all had a real impact on the communities of Kham, organizing perception and the means by which people interacted with their world and each other. The religious activity of which he was a master was imbedded in all aspects of his cultural territory, and he surely understood this. He was able to alter the geography of a place, symbolically connect disparate parts of the region, and determine cultural identity through ritual means—by opening "abodes" and placing them side by side on a map. Chokgyur Lingpa had done this for the benefit of his own treasures when he revealed his 1857 gazetteer of Kham. Kongtrul would use the same platform in 1866 with his own version of the list, *A Brief Clarification of the List of the Twenty-five Great Abodes of Kham Together With Their Auxiliaries*. Chokling had left fourteen of the forty-two places on his map unidentified in order to later insert the locations of his future revelations. The result of this was that Kongtrul had some holes to fill.[1]

Kongtrul had felt the effects of the Chinese and Tibetan attempts to annex Kham, and he had suffered through an indigenous attempt at unification. The Nyarong War had been a disaster. Kongtrul offered his map as an alternative, a symbolic unification rather than a military effort, using the ecumenical tools he had at his disposal. Fragmented and borderless, for Tibetans and Chinese the Kham region had been empty space. Kongtrul's map established an indigenous cartographic reality to what had before been the mere idea of a place: Dokham, centered on Derge and stretching north into Amdo and south to Mount Kawa Karpo on the Burmese border; from Chamdo and Nangchen in the west to Dartsedo in the east, on the very edge of the Tibetan-Chinese frontier. It might not hold back armies or administrators, but it would articulate and preserve a sense of place.

With his gazetteer, Kongtrul identified twelve of fourteen unnamed slots of Chokling's list conclusively and left one, Pema Lhatse in Ronggyab, "to be determined." Among the sites he added was Dzongsho, where he had just recently been enthroned. Chokling was not concerned with the sectarian affiliations of the sites on his list—what mattered to him were the connections to his revelations and his patrons' activities. Kongtrul, however, populated the lacuna of Chokling's map with sites associated with the Nyingma, Kagyu, Sakya, and Bon traditions. One of the primary pieces of information that Kongtrul adds to the list is the name of the men who are associated with the sites, such as who opened them and who revealed treasure there. These names included many of the greats of the religious history of the region. Although a few sites are associated with only one tradition, most share a multisectarian heritage—combinations of Nyingma, Kagyu, Sakya, Chod, and Bon. The gazetteer draws the many sites together while simultaneously preserving their individual integrity to produce a united and coherent whole in the midst of diversity. Thus, where Chokling's unified landscape was largely placed in service of his authority and the legitimation of his treasures, Kongtrul's territorial creation can be seen to have benefited Kham itself: its institutions, its people, its culture.

Kongtrul's gazetteer was a geographic representation of his ecumenical view, but unlike the Treasury of Knowledge, *Necklace of Clear Understanding*, and his coming Treasury of Instructions, the map excluded any Geluk representation. Not a single site is associated with a Geluk master or institution. This was intentional, given its social function. The Geluk belonged in

Tibet and Lhasa; Kham was to be united in its diversity against a hegemonic orthodoxy. It would be too reductionistic to argue that Kongtrul developed his ecumenicalism in order to resist Geluk Lhasa, or that his ecumenicalism was somehow a response to Geluk hegemony.[2] The Geluk masters and their teachings are well represented in all of Kongtrul's surveys of Tibetan religion. They are conspicuously absent on the map, however, and for this reason it can reasonably be seen as a form of resistance. Had Lhasa not been synonymous with Geluk, and if his map was not intended to resist Tibetan incursions into Kham, he surely could have found a few Geluk places to include. Kongtrul was a man who boundlessly embraced all things and yet was still capable of responding to real events with whatever means he had available.

Exactly when he created his gazetteer is not clear. The colophon to the text states that Kongtrul finished it on February 18, 1868.[3] The description of site number eight, Pema Shelri, states that it had not yet been opened, but Kongtrul, Khyentse, and Chokling had opened a Padmasambhava cave there the previous spring, in March 1867, on their return from the enthronement at Dzongsho. Perhaps Kongtrul did not consider this the formal opening of the site, although in his diary he does give the mountain its full name. In any case, the gazetteer found a wide audience, and authors have adopted its framework for sites across Kham. Despite there being forty-two places mentioned, the rubric of twenty-five abodes became the common parlance for the system. To this day many local gazetteers and geographical descriptions of places on the list make use of their inclusion, the authors proudly proclaiming membership to the "twenty-five great abodes of Kham."

Kongtrul produced his updated version of Chokling's treasure text either immediately before or directly after his last encounter with Chokgyur Lingpa. The treasure revealer left Derge sometime after May 1867,[4] revealed his last treasure in August, and then went to Tibet for about a year. Before leaving, Chokling gave Kongtrul and Khyentse the two texts of his revelation called United Intent of the Dharma Protectors, a section of the Five Cycles of the Essence of the Noble Dharma. Kongtrul himself had written one of them, at Tsādra, and the other was decoded at Riwo Wangzhu in collaboration with Khyentse. Chokling evidently did not want to bring the manuscripts to Tibet; better to leave them—to "entrust them"—to Kongtrul (in the language of the diary) so as to ensure their inclusion in the Treasury of Revelations. Hail fell and thunder sounded from the east as soon as the exchange took place, a fairly common and, at least outside of agricultural areas, auspicious occurrence.[5]

Kongtrul and Khyentse accompanied Chokling as far as a place called Kyabche Goto, where he departed for Tibet. Here and henceforth in his diary Kongtrul literally wrote "Tibet"—*bod*—in place of *Utsang*, a term usually translated as "central Tibet." Kongtrul understood that Chokling was going from Kham to Tibet. Before departing, Chokling gave Kongtrul "some important instructions and documents," but Kongtrul opted to not carry out a single one. His work with Chokgyur Lingpa was all but done.[6]

On Chokling's return, he and Kongtrul met in Alo Peljor, where Kongtrul was performing rituals for his patrons. Chokling was as active as ever, experiencing visions of endless abodes and continuing to work on Five Cycles of the Essence of the Noble Dharma, combining the revelations into coherent systems. Chokling detoured through Chayang, where he met the Second Katok Situ incarnation, and then reunited with Kongtrul at Pelpung. The treasure revealer gave Kongtrul a final suggestion that he did accept: to open a site called Dzongchen Khampuk. On later going to the place, Kongtrul was able to identify several caves and perceived positive omens when performing a feast offering, such as a large flock of vultures coming to eat the feast and a blaze of rainbow light in the sky.[7] He wrote three texts related to the site: *Mirror of Mindfulness* and *Mirror of Faith*, both descriptions of the place, and an invocation to its deities called *Tambura of Goodness*.

Kongtrul and Chokgyur Lingpa never saw each other again. Chokgyur Lingpa died on May 1, 1870, at the age of forty.[8] In his diary Kongtrul recorded learning of the death two months later. He betrayed no emotion in response, writing only "we received the unpleasant news from Neten that the great treasure revealer had passed into the pure realms." Kongtrul was in the midst of a vase ceremony at Changra. If he paused or altered the ritual program to acknowledge Chokling's death, he did not indicate this.[9] There is a legend told by Orgyen Tobgyal in his biography of Chokgyur Lingpa that might suggest a bit more grief on Kongtrul's part:

One day the three masters decided to have a horse race and see who would win. Chokling, on a dappled horse, came first, followed by Khyentse on a dark blue horse. Kongtrül finished last and arrived crying like a child. "I am so unfortunate," he wailed. Some people said, "Jamgön Kongtrül is usually a great lama, but

he weeps when he loses a horse race." Others said it was because
he was the oldest. The real reason was they were seeing who
would first reach the Copper-Colored Mountain.[10]

Orgyen Tobgyal understands this legend to speak to Kongtrul's sadness
at the coming death of his friends, but Ngawang Zangpo and Surya Das,
who each repeat the legend, read this legend as Kongtrul bemoaning that
he was to be left alone. The story does not set Chokling's coming death
apart from Khyentse's; nowhere in the hagiographical tradition is Kongtrul
presented as grieving for Chokling.[11]

In early 1868 Kongtrul received a collection of iconography compiled by
Chim Namkha Drak called *One Hundred Gods of Nartang* (so titled despite
only describing about thirty). Soon after this he received transmissions from
Dzogchen Lingtrul of scriptures from the Tengyur and revelations such
as Ancestral Line of the Vidyādhara and Openness of Realization Tantra—both part of the Northern Treasures—and Pema Lingpa's important
Lama Jewel Ocean cycle. He had already received the first from Jetsun Pema
Trinle when he was at Mindroling. Lingtrul had come to Pelpung to join the
inaugural transmission of the Treasury of Revelations. It would be two years
until Kongtrul received additional transmissions from anyone. During the
last three and a half decades of his life, he composed, taught, and performed
rituals, but he rarely received new treasure revelations or textual traditions.
This was partly because he had already received most of what was available
and partly because he had already composed all but one of his grand collections, the creation of which drove their acquisition. The last collection, the
Treasury of Instructions, was only a few years from being written.[12]

In the spring of 1868 Kongtrul began to give the transmissions and
empowerments for the Treasury of Revelations for the first time. Khyentse
Wangpo had promised to sponsor this initial teaching and to advise on who
should be included in the group of recipients, but he was ill and was unable
to come to Pelpung, so Kongtrul was forced to preside over the ceremony
on his own. Khyentse henceforth remained in his residence at Dzongsar
until the end of his life. The event must have been widely advertised, as
participants had begun gathering at Pelpung as early as the end of March;
Kongtrul gave a group of these early arrivals teachings on the Indian scriptures pertaining to Mahāmudrā, which the Tenth Situ joined, but which
Wontrul apparently did not. This he began on April 17.[13] Then, starting

on May 31,[14] for three months he read texts and performed the empowerments for the cycles in the collection, finishing on September 1 or 2.[15] The Treasury of Revelations was not yet closed—he would add to it for several decades still. The Tenth Situ joined the ceremonies, and on their conclusion his estate sent "extensive offerings," which Kongtrul received along with donations from the other individuals. Additional funds from Pelpung came in after the steward, Pelek, received Mahāmudrā teachings at Tsādra. Kongtrul used the Chinese tael Pelek brought to support the activities at the hermitage—Kongtrul records that he earmarked eight tael for the retreatants. The second three-year retreat finished toward the end of 1868, and straightaway Kongtrul undertook all the necessary empowerments, transmissions, and instructions for the third group.[16]

The remainder of the Earth Dragon Year was challenging for Kongtrul. Wontrul had assigned him to supervise the monastery's major public rituals in the next year, and he was feeling the strain even before the ceremonies began. His duties at Tsādra were a hardship, requiring him to take time away from his practice and writing, and they put him in close contact with the faction at Pelpung that disapproved of him, which seemed to be more and more aligned with the Situ estate. Before the end of the retreat, he had performed ceremonies in recognition of his mother's death anniversary and was likely feeling her loss anew. In September 1868[17] he had gone for a rest at his patron's estate in Chayang—one of the few instances in his diary in which he acknowledged taking time to recover from the effects of his busy schedule—but on his return he was immediately inundated with the obligations of the hermitage and the monastery.[18]

From the winter solstice of 1868 to the first week of the Fire Serpent Year, in the middle of February 1869, Kongtrul had disturbing dreams and was ill. He addressed this with personal practice, performing his usual Vajrakīla rites, adding to it the Vajrakīla from Khyentse's recent "oral tradition" revelations and the outer sādhana and longevity practices from Gathering of Secrets. Wontrul, who had originally taught him this practice, joined him in March,[19] and together they performed one hundred repetitions of the longevity practices from Integration of Means and Wisdom. With these Kongtrul improved, and, now free of his commitments at Tsādra, he was able to continue composing liturgies for the Treasury of Revelations. Unfortunately, his duties at Pelpung forced him to interrupt his writing again in May. Situ led the vase ceremony in the position of vajra master, with Kongtrul managing the details. There were considerable "disturbances" which Kongtrul did not detail. After the ceremony, Kongtrul bestowed the bodhisattva vows to Situ and the inmates of the monastery retreat center and then returned to Tsādra to give the retreatants there the empowerments for United Intent of the Gurus.[20]

Kongtrul now had several months free before he was to lead Pelpung's summer retreat. He used it to compose a word-by-word commentary of the *Hevajra Tantra*. As with several of what he considered his important compositions, Kongtrul described the process and thinking behind this composition in his diary. He seemed to feel the need to justify his decision to compose a new commentary on such an important theme. He began by explaining that the available commentaries in the Kagyu tradition were not sufficiently clear or useful in teaching. The two most commonly used—*Jewel-Like Commentary on the Hevajra* by Ngok Zhedang Dorje and the Third Karmapa's *Stainless Light*—were too esoteric and too literal, respectively. Another Kagyu commentary by the Fourth Zhamar, the *Lamp That Illuminates the Essence*, was excessively based on Indian commentaries and so was not easy to understand; earlier commentaries by Ram Tsenchen or Tsak Darma Gyelpo were likewise extremely muddled. Kongtrul states that two others were perfectly fine—an apparently lost commentary by Karma Trinle and Dakpo Tashi Namgyel's *Beams of Sunlight*—and he used them as references. He wrote with the intention to "focus on the meaning of each word by clarifying the hidden and ultimate meanings of each." He titled the finished work *Opening of the Secret Invincible Vajra of Liberation*.[21]

Kongtrul taught the Hevajra commentary for the first time at the 1869 summer retreat at Pelpung. This was one of the annual tasks that had been a burden on his mind the previous winter. He also taught the *Uttaratantra* and the Third Karmapa's *Profound Inner Principles*. Despite his anxiety, it was, in a way, a fruitful assignment, for not only did Kongtrul compose the Hevajra commentary in advance of the retreat, he also composed commentaries on the other two texts soon after. His commentary on the *Uttaratantra* came first, written almost directly after the summer session. The *Uttaratantra*, properly known as the *Ratnagotravibhāga*, is a main source of buddha-nature theory. It was translated into Tibetan six separate times—although only that of Ngok Loden Sherab and the Kashmiri paṇḍit Sajjana is extant—and became one of the core texts of Tibetan monastic curricula. Kongtrul's commentary is not properly his but is almost identical to Dolpopa's commentary on the same work, with a short introduction of his own composition. In October[22] Kongtrul completed the work, which he titled *Irrepressible Lion's Roar*. Directly after finishing the book, he received a gift from Khyentse Wangpo, who had sent over a package containing representations of the eight auspicious substances. These are materials such as mustard seed and milk that are associated with major events of the Buddha's life. Ever in demand, Kongtrul was called down to Pelpung to give the empowerments and transmissions for core Dzogchen scriptures to Sertal Lhatse Tulku and his disciples.[23]

In late 1869 Kongtrul was summoned by the government of Derge to perform rites for the protection of the state. Khangsar Khenpo Ngawang Sonam Gyeltsen, until recently the abbot of Ngor Monastery, was now in Derge and requested empowerments. Kongtrul then went on an alms tour through Alo, Dzomtok, and Tsetsa to raise money for new statues. He performed rituals for patrons and the public as he went, stopping at a site called Arab. He declared this place to have the same blessing as the River Godavāri in India, on the shores of which the Buddha attained enlightenment. He was called back to Derge to deal with a malevolent entity then harassing the kingdom. It seems that other ritualists had divined that a *gongpo* spirit—a class of bewitching spirits—named Artay was responsible for a series of negative events, but no one had been able to subjugate it. Kongtrul alleges in his diary that he was called four times to the capital to do battle with the spirit, but he refused on the grounds that if other, more powerful lamas had been unable to vanquish it, he would fare no better. His false modesty—he was at the time one of the premier ritual specialists in the region—perhaps masked a sense of irritation that he had been asked to intervene only after others failed to bring results. In any case, he eventually agreed to travel to the capital and try his hand.[24]

Kongtrul arrived in Derge in April or May,[25] a day after an ominous occurrence in the Tangtong Gyelpo Temple—a butter lamp on the altar was overfilled and spilled. Starting the next day he and a group of assistants performed rituals for a week. Ten days later he suppressed and dispatched the demon, and on the following day he performed a fire offering and purifying rites. Kongtrul was pleased with his efforts and was praised by Khangsar Khenpo, who told him he dreamed that night of harmful spirits fleeing the capital. Kongtrul cautioned that although the immediate signs indicated a positive outcome, and circumstances might ease for a time, if the government were to not sponsor regular rites of suppression, the demonic forces would flare up again. The well-being of the state, he firmly believed, depended on consistent ritual activities. Before returning to Pelpung, the distressed royal family commissioned him to perform a ransom ritual to buy favor with all the other supernatural beings of the valley so as to convince them to leave the kingdom in peace. He chose a liturgy from Chokgyur Lingpa's General Assembly of Mamo. Kongtrul wrote in his diary that he performed the entire liturgical cycle, both basic and auxiliary practices, in an extensive manner. He added that of all the rituals for the public welfare this one was the finest. However, his opinion of it appears to have diminished, for it was not published—there is but a single liturgy from this cycle in Chokling's Collected Revelations, and Kongtrul did not include it in the Treasury of Revelations.[26]

Kongtrul served other patrons during the year; in July[27] he went to Changri for a vase ceremony. He attended the vase ritual at Pelpung in August[28] but was ill and could not participate. He did, however, give the group the empowerments and transmission for an unnamed Vimaloṣṇīṣa practice. A lama Karma Selje was in attendance, and Kongtrul requested of him the transmission for Collected Works of Dolpopa, a collection that he had remarkably not received before. In November[29] Kongtrul was back in the capital to prepare the ground for the arrival of a daughter of the Tibetan minister Dokharwa Tsewang Norbu, now stationed in Nyarong, who was coming to marry Chime Takpai Dorje. This was Tseten Dolkar, who would be a patron of Kongtrul's. The marriage may have been part of the peace negotiations, either a marriage alliance forced upon the kingdom or a desperate attempt by a fading royal family to remain relevant. Kongtrul composed a short description of the Derge marriage customs as a commemoration of the wedding: *A Lecture on Planting the Silken Arrow on the Occasion of the Arrival in the Kham Kingdom of Derge of the Daughter of Tibetan Minister Dokhar*.[30]

In the spring of 1870 Kongtrul began a commentary on *Profound Inner Principles*, completing it in the early summer, along with commentaries on the *Treatise Distinguishing Ordinary Consciousness from Primordial Awareness* and *Treatise on Buddha-Nature*, the Third Karmapa's three masterpieces of tantric exegesis that he had been studying and teaching for decades. He defended his decision to compose new commentaries by explaining the failings of earlier works. Regarding *Profound Inner Principles*, he felt that the Third Karmapa's auto-commentary was too dense, focused almost entirely on a few difficult points. That of the Fifth Zhamar, Konchok Yenlak, was incomplete, while other available treatises had either lost the transmission or were not of "appropriate length." He again turned to a work of the First Karma Trinle, this one titled *Illuminating Garlands of Light*, and he also read the notes from lectures by Tsurpu Jamyang (written by the translator Sonam Gyatso)[31] and the notes from lectures of the Eighth Situ (written by Tsewang Kunkhyab). Kongtrul titled his commentary *Illuminating the Profound Inner Principles.*[32]

Kongtrul taught this work together with the *Uttaratantra* and the *Hevajra Tantra* at the year's summer retreat. He was pleased with his work; in a dream, Situ Pema Nyinje placed a crystal rosary around his neck. In December[33] Kongtrul accompanied the Tenth Situ to the Drichu River, sending him off on a journey to Tibet. He then went to Chayang where he gave Dorje Rabten the transmission of the Second Zhechen Rabjam's Collected Works. Dorje Rabten, who was the tenth abbot of Dzogchen Monastery's Śrī Siṃha College, came to him as Kongtrul was at the time perhaps the only living man who held the transmission, having received it from Zhechen Wontrul. During the reading, Kongtrul became even more concerned about the Tenth Situ. He had dreams and saw omens that the Situ would face significant obstacles, including someone who appeared to be his own mother, who scolded him that this was not a good year to be traveling in Tibet. On his return to Tsādra, he performed rituals commissioned by the Situ to allay harm. In the early part of 1871, Kongtrul performed a few rituals in Dilgo for Khyentse Wangpo's sister and then was with Khyentse at Dzongsar. They exchanged transmissions, with Khyentse giving Kongtrul a revelation of Chokling's called Profound Essence of Tārā and another recent pure vision revelation of his own, Profound Essence Uniting the Families of the Three Roots.[34] The popular Green Tārā practice of Chokling's had apparently come to him in a vision of the bodhisattva while he was in Pema Shelpuk. Khyentse explained that she said "Lekso!"—"excellent!"—three times, at which point Chokling exhaled a deep breath and the mind treasure burst forth.[35]

Khyentse also gave Kongtrul a painting of Ekajaṭī. The painting was especially fine, and as Khyentse bestowed the blessing for the deity Kongtrul was overcome with awe and reverence. Feeling as though the goddess herself was present, he found himself numb and short of breath. Jamyang Khyentse Wangpo, as usual, was able to inspire such feeling in Kongtrul. With Situ still on his mind, Kongtrul asked Khyentse for a divination about the future of Pelpung. Not only did Khyentse Wangpo report that his dreams were ominous, but in a vision he saw a mountain overrun by bloodthirsty demons. The two by this point knew well that the Situ was going to be a problem.[36]

After several additional transmissions, Kongtrul discussed with Khyentse the concept of his last major works: a collection of "the most important empowerments, instructions, and advice" from the eight chariots of accomplishment he had received "so that they would not decay."[37] This was a real concern of Kongtrul's, and he repeats it twice in his explanation behind the collection that resulted, the Treasury of Instructions. He writes that it was done "despite the fact that no individual would have the opportunity to put them all into practice"—Kongtrul recognized that few individuals would be able to replicate his achievements—"in order that the advice of the lamas not be wasted." Not unlike his motivation for creating the Treasury of Revelations, Kongtrul feared that while the famous texts were widespread and in no danger, "the transmission lineage for some extremely rare teachings were on the verge of being cut." Were they to be severed, the collection would at least preserve the literature. If it was an admission that the loss of so many teachings was inevitable, Kongtrul still believed in the value of their words; for "to hear even just once the essence of the teachings on sūtra and tantra gives meaning to our human lives."[38]

The plan appealed to Khyentse, who told Kongtrul that he had himself been compiling teachings with a similar intent. He offered these to Kongtrul to combine with his own and recommended the name Treasury of Instructions. Khyentse apparently felt the need to make sure Kongtrul included sufficient Sakya teachings. Kongtrul rarely engaged with Sakya— Khyentse had to travel to Tsādra in 1861 to transmit Sakya teachings to the retreat inmates, possibly fearing that they would otherwise not receive them. Khyentse gave Kongtrul a list of teachings, wrote lineage histories for the teachings included in both this and the Treasury of Revelations, and he instructed Kongtrul to write an instruction manual for the Eight Cycles of the Path, a Sakya teaching connected to Lamdre. He also reported to Kongtrul a dream—one that Kongtrul wrote out in detail—which reiterated his desire that the Sakya teachings be properly represented in the collection. In the dream, Khyentse was in India, where he found his beloved teacher Jampa Kunga Tendzin on a throne. The lama said to him "How excellent that Kongtrul Rinpoche and you are writing on Lamdre." Khyentse replied, "my master and I have written nothing on Lamdre; we have only, starting this year, made a small collection of Lamdre empowerments, transmissions, and instructions." The lama was not deterred, and after repeating the initial statement, spoke about how the great fourteenth-century Sakya patriarch Lama Dampa Sonam Gyeltsen had intended to write an extensive instruction manual but had never done so; Kongtrul and Khyentse's project would fulfill the aspiration of that great master. The lama then gave Khyentse a volume of scripture called *Oral Lineage of Lamdre*, which Khyentse had previously not known existed (and which is not extant if it ever did). He told Khyentse to give it to Kongtrul, because, he explained, a previous life of Kongtrul's was Muchen Sanggye Rinchen, and thus he and Kongtrul were family. (Muchen had been the eighth abbot of Ngor, while Jampa Kunga Tendzin served as the forty-seventh.) The conflation of identity was somewhat convoluted: the lama explained that Muchen had given Kunga Drolchok Cakrasaṃvara, and Kunga Drolchok was reborn as Tāranātha, who was reborn as Kongtrul. Because Muchen and Kunga Drolchok were identical in realization, Kongtrul was to be considered the rebirth of all three men. There the dream ended. Khyentse's sly affirmation of Kongtrul's identity as Tāranātha in a dreamtime encouragement to include Sakya teachings into the Treasury of Instructions was a success; Lamdre comprises volumes five and six of the eighteen-volume collection.[39]

Khyentse gave Kongtrul several gifts relating to the project, chief among them twelve volumes of advice and instruction which he hoped Kongtrul would use in the collection. He also gave him a statue of Tārā he had brought back from Tibet which was believed to speak and to have belonged to Nāgārjuna. Kongtrul worked on Treasury of Instructions for the rest of his life, adding and revising right up until several years before his death. The work is what is known in English as a "reader." It is not a composition but a compilation of classic Tibetan texts of "instruction." Scholar Matthew Kapstein defines the Tibetan term for "instruction" as "the immediate, heartfelt instructions and admonitions of master to disciple concerning directly liberative insight and practice." Kongtrul chose some of the most beloved and loveliest religious writings of Tibet, few of which were actually in danger of being lost.[40]

The collection is organized according to the eight chariots of accomplishment, most of which are subdivided by common, uncommon, and pith instructions. The first two volumes are dedicated to the Nyingma, organized by the three divisions of Nyingma tantra: Mahāyoga, Anuyoga, and Atiyoga. The last of these, most commonly known as Dzogchen, is divided into the mind class, the expansive class, and the instruction class. Authors represented include Padmasambhava, Longchenpa, and Buddhaguhya. Volumes three and four are dedicated to Kadam teachings, with Atīśa's famous Lamrim and Lojong teachings, the *Bodhipathapradīpa* and the *Seven-Point Mind Training*. Kongtrul also included a Lamrim work by Tsongkhapa titled the *Three Principal Aspects of the Path* as well as various esoteric instructions. Volumes five and six are dedicated to the Lamdre teachings of the Sakya. Volumes seven through ten are Marpa Kagyu instructional texts for Mahāmudrā and the Six Yogas of Nāropā. The volumes start with the *Anāvila-tantrarāja Tantra*, the source for the Mahāmudrā teachings according to Kongtrul, followed by commentaries by most of the patriarchs of the tradition. The "uncommon" teachings are the Six Yogas, with texts by eight different early authors. The pith instruction texts include compositions by members of various branches of the Dakpo Kagyu tradition. Kongtrul uses a tree metaphor to organize the texts of the Shangpa Kagyu, which comprise volumes eleven and twelve: the root is the Six Yogas, the trunk is Mahāmudrā, the branches are the "three methods of carrying the path," the fruit is the "deathless state," and the flower is the practice of the goddess Khecarī. Authors represented include Khyungpo Neljor, Tangtong Gyelpo, Tāranātha, and Śākya Chokden. Volumes thirteen and fourteen are Zhije and Chod, including the Zurmang tradition of the practice, with texts by Lochen Darmaśrī and Nyedo Sonam Pel in addition to those by Padampa Sanggye and Machik Labdron. Volume fifteen is the Kālacakra Tantra tradition of Tāranātha and the compositions of Orgyenpa Rinchen Pel on the teaching known as the Stages of Approach and Accomplishment of the Three Vajras, said to have been given to Orgyenpa by the goddess Vajravārāhī. Volumes sixteen and seventeen are miscellaneous texts that Kongtrul felt were needed to ensure a successful transmission—he intended the collection to stand together as a whole and not be mined for individual texts by readers of parochial interests. Volume sixteen contains various blessing rites from multiple traditions, and volume seventeen is dedicated to rituals to the three deities of long life—Tārā, Amitāyus and Uṣṇīṣavijayā. The eighteenth and final volume is the *One Hundred Instructions of the Jonang,* which was the original inspiration for the collection.[41]

In transmitting the collection, Kongtrul advised that the guru begin with the final volume, then give volumes three through seventeen, and end with the Nyingma volumes. Evidently Kongtrul organized the collection chronologically, but he maintained that the Dzogchen teachings of the Nyingma were the highest and thus should conclude any transmission.

Kongtrul maintained consistently that he never rejected or demeaned any part of the Buddha's teaching. He wrote of this collection:

> In coming to know, without sectarian bias, the characteristics of each of these traditions, the lotus of my faith has blossomed without any limitations, and thus I have been untouched by the stain of rejecting any part of the Dharma.[42]

It was a position he was glad to thank Khyentse Wangpo for inspiring, and here he certainly was sincere; Khyentse gave Kongtrul the transmission for nearly every teaching included in the collection.

With the completion of the Treasury of Instructions, Kongtrul had completed four large collections: the Treasury of Kagyu Tantra, the Treasury of Knowledge, the Treasury of Revelations, and the Treasury of Instructions. All have "treasury" in their name, but they did not all originally: the root verses for the Treasury of Knowledge are titled *Encompassing All Knowledge*, and the collection of treasures was originally called a "garland," not a "treasury." To these four is traditionally added a fifth, Kongtrul's Collected Works, which is generally known by the title Treasury of the Expansive. Not surprisingly, Kongtrul gives credit to the conceptual frame of "five treasuries" to Khyentse Wangpo. In his diary he recorded a comment of Khyentse's and a vision which in his biography of Khyentse is expanded. The vision has become central to Kongtrul's legend and is repeated frequently in English publications. Yet both the comment and the vision contain anachronisms and cannot be taken at face value.

In his diary Kongtrul records the vision and comment as having occurred in April or May of 1861[43] and early 1862,[44] respectively. In the diary's account of the vision, Khyentse saw a large stūpa with four doors at the base and a fifth door in the upper section. Entering, he saw many sacred objects and countless volumes of scripture. He asked what the texts were, at which point an unnamed man told him that they were "the five treasuries" and explained at length their importance. The protector god Pehar Gyelpo then appeared to complain that although he had been charged by Padmasambhava to watch over Buddhism in Tibet, he was not receiving sufficient offerings and prayers. In a thinly veiled threat, he warned of the coming of evil times. Khyentse's interpretation of the vision was: "This is your mandate for what will be called the 'five treasuries.' You should give the compilations of treasures the name 'Treasury of Revelations.'" Regarding Pehar's comments,

Khyentse informed Kongtrul that he would henceforth need to include rites to the god in the daily rituals at the Tsādra protector shrine. Soon after, in the early months of 1862, Kongtrul changed the name of the Garland of Treasures to the Treasury of Revelations, though in recording the change he makes no mention of Khyentse's vision.[45]

According to his diary, roughly a year after the vision, Kongtrul showed Khyentse his root verses to the Treasury of Knowledge. He scripted Khyentse's response as: "This is the first of your five great treasuries, to be titled the Treasury of Knowledge."[46] The comment obviously could not have occurred after the vision as reported in the diary. By Kongtrul's chronology, Khyentse had only the year before called the Treasury of Revelations the first of the five. In any case, the Treasury of Knowledge would have at that point been the third of five, as seven years earlier Kongtrul had completed the Treasury of Kagyu Tantra. According to his diary, he named that collection a "treasury" upon finishing it.[47]

In his biography of Khyentse, Kongtrul dated Khyentse's vision to some six years later, in late 1867.[48] In his diary account of the visions, Khyentse names none of the treasuries—again, despite the fact that the Treasury of Kagyu Tantra was already nine years old. In the 1867 version of the vision, however, Khyentse names all five collections. Kongtrul has Khyentse tell him:

> The meaning of the stūpa is that you must complete what will be known as the 'five treasuries': a treasury of all common objects of knowledge [to be called] Treasury of Knowledge; a Treasury of Uncommon Mantra [comprised of] cycles of the new and old tantra; a Treasury of Revelations [for] ritual arrangements of the recent and earlier Dharma treasures; a Treasury of Instructions [collecting] the ripening and liberation instructions of the eight chariots of accomplishment, and an Uncommon Treasury for whatever earth or mind treasures you produce.[49]

In 1867 the Treasury of Instructions was still five years from being compiled. A further seeming error in this vision is that Kongtrul's fifth treasury, the Treasury of the Uncommon, is made up not of his earth and mind treasures—these are in the Treasury of Revelations—but of his miscellaneous compositions and liturgies which he chose not to insert in the Treasury of Revelations.

Regardless of when or if Khyentse experienced this vision, Kongtrul used it to attribute to Khyentse the concept of the five treasuries. His failure to properly edit his diary entries—and ensure accurate correspondence between his diary and his biography of his beloved friend—suggests an ambivalence regarding Khyentse's role in naming and evaluating Kongtrul's work. Certainly the two discussed the ideas over many months and years, and it is fair for Kongtrul to share with Khyentse some degree of credit for their genesis. Still, when Kongtrul finished the fourth treasury, he was sixty years old. He was the author of a considerable number of well-regarded treatises, the master of a retreat center, a chief ritual leader and teacher at Pelpung Monastery, and a head of ceremony for royal events. Khyentse Wangpo might continue to provide inspiration and collaboration, but Kongtrul probably wanted to decide on his own titles for his own work. Habit and enduring affection brought him to Khyentse for comment, but perhaps he by now felt he deserved more credit than he was accustomed to allowing himself.

# 24

# THE 1870s

*Revelations, Tsādra's Pilgrimage Year, and Expulsion from Pelpung*

1871–1878

By 1870 Kongtrul had graduated two three-year, three-fortnight retreats at Tsādra and was able to leave alumni to manage the ongoing programs. Dabzang Tulku, who had been instrumental in setting up the first retreat and teaching the inmates, had passed away. Chief among the new leaders at the hermitage was Khen Lama Tashi Wozer, who had completed the first retreat at Tsādra and had provided financial support for Kongtrul when he composed the Treasury of Knowledge. He had come to Pelpung at the age of eighteen from his birthplace in Alo and received from Kongtrul novice vows and the name Tashi Wozer Lodro Gyepai De, together with teachings on Ngari Paṇchen's *Three Vows* and Longchenpa's *Wish-Fulfilling Treasury*. He was only twenty-four when he joined the retreat in 1860. Dabzang Tulku gave him final ordination, either in 1856, when he would have been twenty, or in 1862, during the retreat, with the ordination name of Karma Zopa Rabten Pelzangpo.[1] In 1864, released from the retreat, Tashi Wozer met and received teachings and the bodhisattva vows from the famous itinerant lama Patrul Rinpoche (whom Kongtrul never met)[2] and further teachings from Dabzang, the Fourteenth Karmapa, Khyentse Wangpo, and Chokgyur Lingpa. He came to be recognized as a scholar and a teacher, and at some point he served as an abbot at Pelpung. Tashi Wozer also traveled with Kongtrul. In the spring of 1871, at Peljor Gang, he led a group of disciples in receiving the entire corpus of Karma Kagyu tantric empowerments and the chief cycles of Chokgyur Lingpa's revelations.[3]

With Tashi Wozer running the retreat center, Kongtrul felt able to spend extended periods of time away from Tsādra. During his seventieth decade, he continued to travel as extensively as ever, responding to invitations from aristocratic and government sponsors to perform rituals for the prosperity of their families and the welfare of the state. He initiated or participated in the opening of new abodes across Kham, and he never ceased teaching from his collections and compositions. He also revealed treasure. All the while his position at Pelpung continued to deteriorate, finally reaching a point in 1874 when he was banished for eleven and a half years.

In 1870 or 1871—Kongtrul only records that he was fifty-eight at the time—he revealed his first scriptural treasure. The extraction took place at Lhamdo Burmo, the cliff at Tsādra also known as Burmo Drak. It consisted of the first section of a treasure cycle titled United Intent of the Three Roots, which came together with a piece of the religious robe of Ānanda—the Buddha's cousin and close disciple—and undergarments of Padmasambhava's Indian teacher Humkara. Kongtrul brought the revelation to Khyentse Wangpo for consultation and assistance in putting it in the proper format.[4] Having written and edited for publication scores of treasure root texts and ritual manuals, Kongtrul was of course perfectly capable of drafting the revelation himself. He likely did so because revelation—at least for Kongtrul, Khyentse Wangpo, and Chokgyur Lingpa—was always a communal endeavor. Khyentse Wangpo and Kongtrul wrote many of Chokling's revelations while the younger man dictated; Khyentse and Chokling merged inspiration into single cycles for which they shared attribution; and Chokling passed to Kongtrul several revelations he said were destined for Kongtrul to perform and promote. Kongtrul's revelation was different only in that Chokgyur Lingpa was no longer alive to participate in its composition.

Kongtrul had been considering revealing treasure since he was a child. One of his complaints about being forced to leave Zhechen was that his potential revelations there were denied him. He continued to contemplate the practice during his difficult adjustment to Pelpung. Kongtrul was a consummate editor and compiler, revising and remaking everything he did. He copied the works of others extensively, but he put his own frame around everything he borrowed. His collections redefined the material with updated categories and standards that became normative for succeeding generations. Kongtrul made and remade and was never a passive participant, despite his best efforts to present himself as such in his diary. So too with his geomantic activities. Kongtrul only ever went on a single pilgrimage—in 1831—in which he did not in some way seek to transform the landscape. Even on his two tours of the religious sites of central Tibet he had work to do, planting Chokgyur Lingpa and the Fourteenth Karmapa's Seven Profound Cycles at almost every place he visited. Pilgrims went to abodes to receive blessings and merit; Kongtrul went to landscape. By 1870 he had spent close to two decades collecting, revising, and expanding the treasures of other men. He was ready now to produce revelations under his own name.

It fell to Khyentse to affirm that Kongtrul's first revelation was authentic, which he did via a vision of Ekajaṭī who told him that the time was right to break the seals. Khyentse next had an extensive vision of being in India and then at Pelpung, which was inhabited entirely by women. Kongtrul sat on a high throne and slowly transformed into Huṃkara, the Indian paṇḍit whose undergarments were concealed with the treasure text. Huṃkara conferred on him the empowerments for the Sublime Sādhana of the Vidyādhara, a section of United Intent of the Three Roots; the empowerment implements hung in the air, moving unaided as the ritual unfolded. The four stages of the empowerment rite itself were done quickly, however, and despite the presence of so many women, the wisdom empowerment was not given with the assistance of a female partner. In relating the vision, Khyentse told Kongtrul that his revelation was identical to Sanggye Lingpa's renowned—and extensive—United Intent of the Gurus, but that they would do well to write the new revelation as a more concise version which should be included in the Treasury of Revelations. Khyentse was able to decode six sections of the cycle when, Kongtrul reported, circumstances changed and he stopped, ending the textual production. What these "circumstances" were goes unmentioned. Most likely they decided that since Kongtrul's revelation would be an abbreviated version of the famous earlier work, the six sections were sufficient. The cycle as preserved in the Treasury of Revelations has ten texts, including a lengthy sādhana, a daily practice liturgy, and rites for a long-life empowerment. They performed the main liturgy once together when they had written all that they would, and Kongtrul "felt a sudden swelling of blissful warmth as an intense blessing coursed through" him.[5]

While decoding the cycle, Kongtrul had visionary experiences in which the empowerments were performed in full. He found himself amidst a gathering of ḍākinīs as Khyentse Wangpo dictated the contents of the yellow scroll and Kongtrul proclaimed other teachings and wrote them out. Kongtrul, singing prayers aloud, joined a group of supplicants in circumambulating a large stūpa. His body grew to the size of a mountain, from which flowed all sorts of miraculous springs. In this state he became aware of liturgies to the three roots: the guru, the meditational deity, and the ḍākinī.

When he awoke he remembered the verses, but they quickly faded, "drifting in his mind like specs of dust in a sunbeam." A few days later he experienced a vision in which he was inside a temple with Khyentse Wangpo, who appeared in the form of Padmasambhava. Kongtrul recited the daily practice to the vidyādhara and the refuge and bodhicitta practices from United Intent of the Three Roots. At this point Khyentse Wangpo as Padmasambhava gave him the four empowerments, first holding a vase to the crown of his head, next placing on Kongtrul's tongue the "bodhicitta" substance derived from his union with a consort as the secret empowerment. Kongtrul subsequently joined with the consort himself in order to generate the experience of bliss and emptiness that generates the wisdom empowerment. During these three empowerments, Khyentse Wangpo/Padmasambhava did not speak. He gave the final empowerment by taking out a crystal from his heart center and introducing Kongtrul to the nature of his mind with the words "All phenomena are primordially pure and luminous like a crystal. The radiance of their spontaneous presence manifests in all ways, like the light emanating out from this crystal." Khyentse briefly vanished, and on reappearing he gathered all protector deities and assigned them to guard Kongtrul's revelation.[6] Oral history apparently expanded this dream and transformed it into a teaching on nonduality. As told by Surya Das, Khyentse also said, "Within this illusory, phantasmagorical self-display, where is the difference between inner and outer, oneself and others?" and the passage ended with "The two masters were never again prey to the illusion of separation. Actualizing innate Buddha-mind, they together ascended the throne of Kuntuzangpo's kingdom."[7]

According to his own account in his secret autobiography, *Mirage of Nectar*, which he wrote late in life, Kongtrul would reveal treasure about thirteen times over the next few decades. Almost all of his treasures were objects—the robes of saints, medicinal substances, or statues of buddhas and bodhisattvas, but there were also eight scriptural treasures, five of which were full liturgical cycles with multiple titles that were revealed or decoded on separate occasions. These were all almost certainly produced in the late 1870s and 1880s; none of them, save for his two chief treasures—United Intent of the Three Roots and Seven-Line Guru Sādhana—are dated. Kongtrul published his treasures in the Treasury of Revelations rather than in the collection of his miscellaneous compositions, despite Khyentse's vision which stipulated that the last "treasury" should be comprised of Kongtrul's treasures.

In late March or early April 1871,[8] Kongtrul was called to Dzongsar to serve Punrabpa Tsering Pelden, now the Tibetan governor-general of Nyarong. Punrabpa was at Dzongsar to receive empowerments and blessings from Khyentse Wangpo as well as to survey estates seized by the Lhasa forces at the conclusion of the war. Kongtrul sat in on the transmissions, receiving from Khyentse Heart Essence of the Vast Expanse and Buton's tradition of the Kālacakra. At the governor-general's insistence, Kongtrul spent ten days performing longevity practices for his benefit. Kongtrul took the opportunity to ask Khyentse for Jigme Lingpa's collection of Vajrakīla scriptures that the great treasure revealer compiled as an addendum to his Collected Nyingma Tantras. It carries the title of Tantric-System Vajrakīla. This engendered a dream for Khyentse in which he was explaining how a man named Tsagyepa Dorje Sengge was able to extend his lama's life through the practice of Vajrakīla. Due to this dream, when Khyentse was preparing the empowerment for the Jigme Lingpa cycle, he had a vision of Nanam Dorje Dudjom, the disciple of Padmasambhava who, according to legend, propagated the Vajrakīla teachings. Khyentse Wangpo claimed to be his reincarnation. In the vision, Nanam Dorje Dudjom transmitted the teachings to Khyentse, bypassing both the cycle's revealer, Jigme Lingpa, and all others in between. The value in this vision was to render the transmission to Kongtrul particularly potent.[9]

Kongtrul returned to Pelpung to participate in the annual vase ceremony in late May or early June,[10] but Punrabpa quickly called him back to Dzongsar. The governor-general appears to have been a lot like other Tibetan administrators in Nyarong after the war. He was devout, patronizing the prominent lamas of the region, but he was also a foreigner in a conquered land, and he was intent on exploiting its resources for his own benefit. He planned to build a large-scale mercury-refining operation, a lucrative endeavor in a society that believed the metal to have magical medicinal qualities. He had attempted to commission Khyentse with the task, but Khyentse refused, as he did not leave his residence. Khyentse did his friend the disservice of recommending him in his place. Thus, Kongtrul traveled to Nyarong and provided the governor-general with a long list of necessary items and instructions.

Refining mercury has a long history in the Kagyu tradition, stretching back to India and running through both Karma and Drigung Kagyu branches. The Eighth Situ wrote a widely used manual on the practice, which gives instructions for selecting the astrologically appropriate times, cooking the mercury in stages with other substances, and performing the necessary mantras and visualization practices. Nyarong had been suffering a prolonged drought, and with the arrival of such a famed ritualist locals also requested that Kongtrul perform a rainmaking ceremony. In payment for his services, Punrabpa transferred ownership of a large plot of land in the Hakda area of Mesho, called Khangleb, to Tsādra. The previous owner of the land had crossed Punrabpa somehow, perhaps during the war, and the land would now pay its dividends to the hermitage; Punrabpa demanded that the Tsādra retreatants add an annual Kālacakra ceremony to "suppress the barbarians," by which he presumably meant the people of Nyarong. Kongtrul was back at Tsādra by the end of July.[11]

Punrabpa commanded Kongtrul to return to Nyarong a second time in early 1872. Kongtrul went at a leisurely pace, leaving his hermitage on March 21[12] and arriving in Nyarong only in the first week of April. He stopped first at Dzongsar to confer further with Khyentse on refining mercury. After they had exchanged empowerments and gifts—Khyentse gave Kongtrul objects that symbolized the "five principles of unending adornment," meaning a statue, text, stūpa, and a bell and double vajra symbolizing enlightened body, speech, mind, activities, and qualities—Khyentse urged Kongtrul to expand his instructions on mercury refining and to write additional manuals on topics already covered in the Treasury of Knowledge, such as the commentary on grammar called *Candoratnākara*. While at Dzongsar with Khyentse, Kongtrul dreamed of being at Ngor Monastery and visiting a statue of the goddess Khecarī in the Khangsar Khenpo Temple, and also dreamed of being in the presence of the Tenth Karmapa, Choying Dorje, who told him "I have something to give you; do not lose it."[13]

In Nyarong, Kongtrul spent several days in preparation for the refining process, beginning on April 8[14] with a smoke offering, a golden libations rite, a feast offering, and a propitiation to the protectors using liturgies from Heart Essence of Yutok. Rainbows, light rain, and other auspicious meteorological events abounded, and Kongtrul was pleased with the results of the refining as well as the manufacture of medicine from the resulting substances. During the process, he composed a step-by-step manual for the process as well as a manual for dealing with crystals. In the evenings, he dreamed of identifying the locations of treasure; Chokgyur Lingpa gave him a scroll for a cycle connected to the ḍākinīs and explained the symbols for some of them; in another dream his deceased colleague gave him a scroll on which was written four sets of "savage mantras" that would protect him from epidemics while traveling.[15]

At the conclusion of the alchemical activities, Kongtrul performed a Medicine Buddha consecration and, on the order of Punrabpa, a series of basic Buddhist initiation rites for the monastic communities of Nyarong. These were possibly part of the Tibetan administrator's program of reconstruction; a sizable percentage of the monastic population of Nyarong had fought in various battles of the war on both sides of the conflict and needed to be rehabilitated. Kongtrul essentially renewed their ordinations with bodhisattva vows and major empowerments from Gathering of Sugatas, the Kālacakra, and Heart Essence of the Vast Expanse, a favored cycle of the region if not one particularly dear to Kongtrul. Kongtrul was back at Tsādra by June,[16] having stopped first at Wopung (a Nyingma monastery in the Peltsa region of Nyarong) to give empowerments and transmissions and then at Dzongsar to visit with Khyentse Wangpo. At the beginning of 1876, Punrabpa attempted to again employ Kongtrul to refine mercury. The twenty-year-old Twelfth Dalai Lama had ordered Punrabpa to send either Khyentse or Kongtrul to him in Lhasa. The very thought of traveling to Tibet made Kongtrul unwell, and although he pleaded to be excused, Punrabpa was, according to Kongtrul, not going to accept a refusal. The sudden death of the Dalai Lama nullified the order. Although he would be visited by the two subsequent governors-general of Nyarong, he was never again commanded to go to the valley.[17]

The year of 1871, the Sheep Year, was the special year for Tsādra, the period when the benefits of the site are increased and pilgrims are invited to visit. By then Kongtrul had been developing his hermitage there for nearly thirty years. He had built temples, residences, and three circumambulation paths along which one could experience any number of miracles. Now, in the special year, Kongtrul invited the public to come partake of it. Twelve years had passed since he and Chokling had transformed Tsādra into hallowed ground, an anniversary that was to be commemorated with a month-long celebration of pilgrimage. As the 1859 *Tsādra Gazetteer* puts it: "in the Sheep Year, during the monkey month, the assembly of awareness holders, meditational deities, and ḍākinīs gathers from the ten directions and appears in this place."[18] Kongtrul believed wholeheartedly in the capacity of sacred ground to inspire faith and teach virtue. He would not have been unaware, however, of the more tangible benefits of promoting pilgrimage at his home. Pilgrimage is a lucrative activity for the temples and residents of the destination. Visitors to any type of consecrated space would be expected to make a donation of some form—butter or oil for lamps, grains or other foodstuffs, or even firewood, not to mention gold and silver. Giving in support of the Buddhist community, whether to ordained monastics or to lone hermits, is a core virtuous deed and a primary means for laypeople to earn merit; giving, as with any virtuous activity, is understood to be of greater merit at an abode than elsewhere. Pilgrimage also spreads renown, as travelers spread word of the place on their return home and among other pilgrim groups, not unlike modern tourists sharing information about their travels. Fame begets more visitors and more donations.

Kongtrul accordingly composed, in collaboration with Khyentse Wangpo, a notification for distribution across Kham that advertised the opportunity. This was the first of three; the two wrote another in 1883, and in 1895 Kongtrul wrote a third by himself.[19] The first notice summarizes the history of the opening, beginning with Khyentse Wangpo's 1856 visionary experience that provided the name of the site. They remind the readers that at any time at Tsādra "the effects of virtuous acts performed here—meditation practices, vajra feasts or other offerings, prostrations, circumambulations—whenever they are done—are multiplied one hundred thousand times." During the monkey month, as asserted in the treasure gazetteer, the deities of the original Cārita gather at Tsādra and thus the multiplication effect is dramatically increased: a single circumambulation of Tsādra's outer route will equal the merit of seven hundred million recitations of the Padmasambhava mantra, and three will equal a circumambulation of Tsāri, an arduous endeavor that normally takes at least a week. The notice promises that the statue of Tārā at the hermitage, which Khyentse had given to Kongtrul in 1870 and which was said to speak at times, will become much more potent, able to sooth a lifetime of sorrow. Moreover, the image of Avalokiteśvara that had once belonged to Nāgārjuna will be able to erase the karmic stains of the five acts of immediate retribution—deeds that the Buddha himself listed as among the heaviest of sins: killing one's mother, father, or an arhat, causing a schism in the saṅgha, and intentionally causing a tathāgata to bleed. Kongtrul's invitation to the faithful opened the place to everyone, not just renunciates and religious professionals. Buddhist merit can be exchanged for material benefits as well as advancement on the path; Kongtrul promised boons to lay people who sought greater wealth or a better position in their community. Reciting the bodhisattva's mantra in front of the statue, he promised, will increase "longevity, merit, social standing, wealth, and wisdom."[20]

The first circular is dated June 1, 1871.[21] It left little time for people to plan their visit in the sixth month, which began on July 18, suggesting that it was not distributed beyond the Derge region. Nevertheless, Kongtrul records that a throng of people came for the month to walk the circumambulation routes and supplicate the main statues. Kongtrul joined them, with Wontrul Rinpoche as his companion. He walked with the pilgrims, but, as one would expect, he expanded the route as he went, performing rituals and adding descriptions. When he and Wontrul set out, commencing their walk with golden libations and smoke offerings, a rainbow cloud spread across half the sky, moving from east to south. On the basis of a revelation of Khyentse Wangpo, Kongtrul and Wontrul searched out a spot named Pel Deu—a site, Kongtrul notes, that is not mentioned in Chokling's gazetteer—where they expected to find imprints of Padmasambhava's body. There, too, was a cave they named Tashi Pelpuk and a large, naturally occurring letter "ka," the first letter of the Tibetan alphabet.[22]

The 1871 event was a success, measuring by the number of people who attended and the fact that Kongtrul was satisfied. He wrote that "an extremely large amount of pilgrims gathered on the circumambulation route without interruption. There was no quarreling or fighting, and even those who had to carry or lead the lame and the blind were not exhausted after crossing the four ravines and eight defiles."[23]

Moreover, the crowds that came to supplicate the Tārā image were such that several days were spent just accommodating their needs. At one point during the month, Kongtrul went up to Reti Lake to perform a rainmaking ritual and caused a cloud to take the shape of a "source of phenomenon"— that is, a tetrahedron that symbolizes the ground, path, and fruition. This was seen, and then felt, by all who were present, for they became soaked by the rainstorm Kongtrul had brought down. The month did not pass without incident, however. Two of Wontrul's disciples sponsored a mendrub ritual from the United Intent of the Gurus at the hermitage's main temple. On the second day, a cymbal shattered, signifying a dark omen. Kongtrul later interpreted this to mean that there would be a coming rupture in his and Wontrul's relationship. In fact, Wontrul passed away not three years later. His death would deprive Kongtrul of his last patron at Pelpung and of perhaps the last person who might have prevented his exile.[24]

Kongtrul's geomantic activities continued into August.[25] He went up to the peak of Uchetem to activate it—to "bring down the blessing of the site"—with rituals to suppress harmful spirits, make smoke offerings, and cast a thread-cross exorcism, all using liturgies from Dispelling All Obstacles. Switching to Chokling's General Assembly of Mamo, he performed wrathful rituals for the general welfare of the kingdom, a group of three offering rites to the protector deities called the "medicine, blood, and torma," symbolizing the transformation of ordinary matter and emotions into pure substances and the mind of enlightenment. The torma sits on the shrine between two metal bowls containing the alcohol and oil that represent the medicine and blood. Coming off the success of the first monkey month pilgrimage festival, Kongtrul was apparently interested in expanding the reach of Tsādra outwards. Khyentse gave him the means with an earlier prophecy of three "associated sites." One of these, he decided, was an abode named Pema Drawa that someone—Kongtrul simply says "a requestor"—urged him to visit and "bring down the blessings." He determined that the place was sacred to a local protector deity named Lingtsa Tenkyob, whom Kongtrul pacified with a smoke offering and bound to an oath to guard over the region. Rainbows let him know his sanctification work had been successful. After laying out the circumambulation routes, he returned to Pelpung to teach at the summer retreat, offering lectures on the *Uttaratantra*, *Profound Inner Principles*, the *Hevajra Tantra*, and his Treasury of Knowledge.[26]

Kongtrul spent the remaining months of the Sheep Year in meditation, experiencing several positive indications of advancement on the path. He began with Vajrakīla, first with an approach practice from Khyentse Wangpo's revelation Crucial Point of the Oral Lineage Action Vajrakīla alone at his residence at Tsādra, and then in community for the annual rites at the Vajrakīla Temple there. He practiced Samyak in the treasure tradition of Guru Chowang. This gave him positive dreams, such as finding handfuls of the miraculous myrobalan fruit, prized for its medicinal properties. In another dream, someone explained the meaning of signs of accomplishments and told him that there was no practice more potent than United Intent of the Gurus, at which point he saw a massive statue of Padmasambhava emanating green light, into which he dissolved. Another notable dream occurred while he was undertaking Chokgyur Lingpa's Zangjangma practice from the Seven Profound Cycles, the liturgies for which he himself had written. He saw nine mahāsiddhas in India, two of which he was able to name: Vajraghaṇṭāpa and Kukkurīpa. The first of these two was in sexual union with a consort, and as Kongtrul observed the group, the other eight also joined with her. Those nine men and one woman were of course all forms of Kongtrul's own self. They appeared in his dream to facilitate nine consecutive sessions of consort practice. He may have seen himself as Indian mahāsiddhas and a lone woman, but the effects of the practice were all his: "this amazing symbolic display of wisdom," Kongtrul recorded of the dream, "engendered an understanding that I had not previously attained."[27]

In early 1872, while he and about thirty other monks performed a drubchen ritual to Samyak in the So tradition of the Spoken Word (using a new manual he had composed), Kongtrul had marvelous dreams. He dreamed of drinking rainwater flowing off a miraculous, naturally arising stūpa. Then he dreamed of sitting on the level of the stūpa which represented the "four immeasurables," or brahmavihāra—loving-kindness, compassion, empathetic joy, and equanimity—as he gave a series of empowerments to a large crowd. Kongtrul also experienced miracles while awake: during the end-of-year recitations and torma ritual, the nectar in the shrine's skull cup increased, bubbling up to the rim without spilling over, a sign of prosperity. The natural world also featured in these pleasurable dreams: he saw vast meadows of yellow summer flowers, scores of crystals jutting from the earth, and fields of abundant crops. He interpreted these dreams as pertaining to his future lives.[28]

All these dreams and miracles would suggest not only stability but a sense of flourishing. Patrons and supplicants, including some aristocrats, both lay and ordained, came to request empowerments and transmissions. In between obligations he edited drafts of commentaries. Kongtrul was at the height of his renown, a person targeted by those in search of both religious and material benefits. Yet there were also indications of coming crisis. His long-time teacher Lama Sang-ngak Tendzin suddenly passed away on January 10, 1872.[29] This elderly aristocratic lama had first taught him United Intent of the Gurus thirty years earlier as well as several other Nyingma treasure cycles over the years. If Kongtrul was affected by the death, he does not indicate it. When he received the notification, which came with an urgent request from the lama's retinue to come (perhaps to perform the funeral rites), Kongtrul declined and remained instead in retreat. The death of a teacher did not seem to impact his dreams.[30]

More troubling was the arrival of the Tenth Situ. Kongtrul had received word of his return from Tibet around September or October of 1871.[31] At that time, Kongtrul performed a ritual dedicated to a wrathful form of Padmasambhava known as Mekhyil and a grouping of nine gyelpo and senmo demons on his behalf, rites designed to dispel harm on the eve of a journey. As usual in ritual activity connected to the Tenth Situ, Kongtrul reported that negative omens appeared. The Tenth Situ returned in January or February 1872,[32] and on February 18, 1872,[33] he went to visit Kongtrul at Tsādra, bringing him a statue and performing more than one hundred recitations of the feast offering from Union of All Rare and Precious Jewels. Presumably these were in thanks for Kongtrul's ritual services while Situ was traveling. Kongtrul offered a formal tea ceremony, and on Situ's departure he immediately perceived signs of crisis. He remained on guard, dreaming of himself as the deities Lord of Life and Vajrakīla and subjugating the negativity.[34]

The period between spring 1872 and the end of 1873 was a busy time for Kongtrul in terms of serving government and patrons. Not only did he travel to Nyarong to refine mercury for the Tibetan governor-general, he also performed rituals for the Derge court, the kingdom's noble families, and religious communities. A marked increase in prominent lamas from institutions all across Kham sought him out for transmissions. Much of his activity was geomantic. In June 1872,[35] after his return from Nyarong, he was ordered by the Derge government to supervise a major mamo exorcism ceremony from Chokling's twenty-second treasure revelation, General Assembly of Mamo, in Mesho. Kongtrul found flaws the morning that the tormas were cast, the process of which delivers the effigies to the destructive spirits; he wrote that "considerable signs of obstacles arose," although he did not name them. Khyentse Wangpo then sent him up to Pema Shelpuk to bind the local spirits to oath and bring down the blessing. Here too there were signs of coming obstacles. Dropping down again to Dzongsar, he conferred the bodhisattva vows and eight bodhisattva teachings on a group of monks there and on Pema Vajra, the eighth abbot of Dzogchen Monastery's Śrī Siṃha College.[36]

Khyentse sent him on yet another geomantic mission, this time to sanctify a Bon shrine near Khyentse's birthplace known locally as the Ula Stūpa. Kongtrul reports that Khyentse had earlier revealed a gazetteer to the place, but apparently Khyentse had not yet dedicated the time to complete the opening process. They discussed what would be needed, after which Kongtrul crossed over to the Terlung Valley and rendezvoused with Changlung Tulku at Changlung Monastery. The two went together to the shrine, to a spot where three travel routes converged. They performed a smoke offering and an "utterly majestic" subjugation ritual. This was followed by a preliminary rite for longevity and prosperity and a condensed drubchen ritual based on the three principles of teaching, practice, and fruition. The Bon lamas laid out the plan for hermitages and other structures while Kongtrul identified the sacred features of the place—such as its center and peripheries and its caves and marks of divinity—and charted the circumambulation routes. Before returning to Tsādra, he served Buddhist communities at abodes in the valley, such as Dzing Trawo and Yulung Sheldrak, performing feasts at Pema Shelri and at Dagam Wangpuk.[37]

Kongtrul immediately fell into teaching a series of important lamas, giving the empowerments for the *Sūtra That Gathers All Intentions*, the Peaceful and Wrathful Magical Display section of Seven Profound Cycles, and the Dzogchen mind-section to Wontrul and Adzom Drukpa Pawo Dorje. From August 14 to October 16, 1872,[38] Kongtrul transmitted the Treasury of Revelations to a group that included Wontrul, the Second Katok Getse Tulku, and Chokgyur Lingpa's son Tsewang Norbu. This was the second occasion of the collection's transmission; the vajra master Lama Ratna read the texts while Kongtrul gave the empowerments. The Tenth Situ, who had attended the first transmission in 1869, sent up a painting of Vajrapāṇi. The attendants celebrated the conclusion with a longevity rite for Kongtrul, who graciously appreciated the gold, turquoise, crystal bowl, and vajra that was given to him as payment for the work. Wontrul, who by then considered himself too old to commit to transmitting the collection or many of its cycles, promised to see to its publication.[39]

Soon afterwards, Kongtrul traveled to the Ling region to give yet another transmission of the Treasury of Revelations. As was typical in his diary, he depicted the trip as undertaken on the orders of others. The chieftain— Kongtrul gives him the title of king—was then a powerful figure in northern Derge. He had, Kongtrul asserted, repeatedly expressed the intention to journey to Tsādra for the transmission but had been unable to do so. Kongtrul also reported that Khyentse Wangpo sent him a message that the chieftain was a faithful man who merited a visit from Kongtrul and the transmission. It would seem that Kongtrul was not entirely comfortable with the trip. Perhaps it was unseemly—excessively ambitious—for him to travel on his own initiative in order to minister to famous men.[40]

He left for Ling at the end of October,[41] planning to stop over in Ronggyab. He had received an invitation to meet Dechen Lingpa there. Both men were children of the valley. Dechen Lingpa, whom Kongtrul calls Tsewang Drakpa, and who was also known as Kundrol Sangwa Tsel, was a treasure revealer in both the Bon and Buddhist traditions. Some years before, Kongtrul had hoped to encounter the man, but he made the mistake of asking Khyentse Wangpo about him. Khyentse judged him to be an authentic treasure revealer who was too unfocused to ever amount to much, but he suggested that Kongtrul meet him all the same in order to heal a past breach of samaya. The meeting, so deflated, never occurred, and this 1872 invitation would bring the two together for the first time.[42]

Kongtrul arrived late, reaching Ronggyab only on November 4,[43] and Dechen Lingpa had by then gone to Latok Barsuma. They eventually connected at Tarde Monastery where Kongtrul sat to read over the thirteen volumes of Dechen Lingpa's revelations. Setting up a white tent at the base of the region's sacred mountain—then already covered in snow, and unreachable—Kongtrul and Dechen Lingpa performed a smoke offering, bound the local deities and spirits to protect the valley's inhabitants, and responded to requests from the monastic and lay communities. Then, for the treasure revealer, his wife, and his two children—one of whom, Gyelse Tsewang Gyurme, would grow into a teacher of considerable renown—Kongtrul bestowed the complete empowerment and transmission for Chokgyur Lingpa's Dispelling All Obstacles. This was reciprocated with a longevity empowerment as had been recommended by Khyentse Wangpo.[44]

Kongtrul would collaborate with Dechen Lingpa several times over the next few decades. Now, having made a connection and initiated a process of engagement with the sacred mountain of his birth valley, he continued to the Dzonggo region of Ling. This third transmission of the Treasury of Revelations appeared to have been only partial. Kongtrul wrote of no preparations nor mentioned any assistants, recording only several names of the many recipients—the Ling chieftain and the young Fifth Zhechen Rabjam, Pema Tekchok Tenpai Gyeltsen—and a list of additional cycles given. Not all that he transmitted were treasures, such as nine volumes of the *Nyingma Spoken Word*, the *Sūtra That Gathers All Intentions*, and Longchenpa's *Innermost Heart Drop of the Guru*. Kongtrul does not comment on why he added these texts to the already massive transmission event.[45]

From Ling, Kongtrul's presence was demanded by the chieftain of Den Chode, again for geomantic rituals. In early 1873 he traveled via Namling Monastery to arrive at Chode Palace. He was then sixty years old, and one has to imagine the emotion on returning to the site of his teenage religious awakening so many decades earlier. He arranged for three hundred treasure vases to be buried near the palace and "brought down the blessing" of the location in order to sanctify it as an abode, calling on the deities of the "three stages": universal worldly protectors, enlightened buddhas, and local spirits. As part of that process he spent five days in meditative practice. He repeated the same rituals at Drentang Monastery, teaching also to small groups and the public, and returned to Chode Palace. In the beginning of the Water Bird Year, in February 1873, he taught Mahāmudrā and gave longevity rites at area monasteries.[46]

Kongtrul had not yet completed his work in Ling. He returned first to Namling Monastery via Sengge Namdzong, the mountain where he made his first pilgrimage in 1831 and which he identified as the site which guides beings through wrath. Now a master of geomantic rites and a man who could influence a place that had so affected him earlier, he made a smoke offering, brought down the blessing, and bound the local spirits. He also performed a blessing ceremony at the nearby Longtang Dolma Temple. The weather was warm, as though it was summer. He stopped again at Namling to perform prosperity rites for his patrons and cleansing and consecration rituals in the temples. Back again at Dzonggo, the Jangtrul incarnation of Ringu Monastery (located in the valley) together with his disciples and the chieftain of Ling received a series of Kagyu teachings—Vajravārāhī, Cakrasaṃvara, Jinasāgara Avalokiteśvara, Mahāmudrā, and the Six Yogas of Nāropā. Kongtrul climbed to the roof of the palace to bind the local spirits to oath and bring down the blessings of the site.[47]

Kongtrul was traveling too much and performing too many large public rituals. Returning home through the capital in early April, a letter was delivered to him requesting his presence for ongoing ceremonies celebrating the arrival of the Khangsar Khenpo in the reception hall of the newly constructed palace. Since he was already there, he performed some rites to Vajrakīla and the local protectors and then continued on to the Chayang estate to recite prayers for that aristocratic family. At Tsādra he found several luminaries from Gato awaiting him: Rongta Tulku, Dzitang Choje, Pelkhyim Amye Orgyen Tendzin, and others were there to request teachings. Less than two months later, he was ordered by the capital to Changra to supervise a vase ritual and other means of supplicating the local spirits. He returned to Pelpung to supervise the summer retreat, teach at Pelpung's retreat center, and work on compositions for his collections. Around this time the third retreat at Tsādra completed its program, and Kongtrul installed the fourth group. In November 1873[48] Wontrul sponsored a combined drubchen and mendrub ritual in the summer retreat hall, at which Kongtrul served as vajra master. The liturgy was United Intent of the Gurus. The ceremony started beautifully, and Kongtrul's dreams were full of blessings and visits from the saints. An unidentifiable Indian mahāsiddha who was identical to Padmasambhava gave him a particularly potent empowerment. The mahāsiddha began with the vase and the secret empowerments when, suddenly, everything vanished, leaving Kongtrul in a state of pure blissful awareness. This, he explains, is the essence of the third empowerment. The dream faded, but before he fully awoke he heard a voice exclaiming:

> The fundamental state of Samantabhadra is originally pure,
> flawless like a crystal globe.
> With this bestowal of the wisdom empowerment
> may you remain undifferentiated from the primordial protector!

Despite this inspiring experience, on the afternoon that the medicines were being mixed Kongtrul suffered violent headaches and was unable to attend the service. In the evening, he dreamed of a charnel ground. Negative signs were appearing everywhere; he had overextended himself and fallen ill as a result.[49]

The Dongkham Tripa, Sertal Lhatse Tulku, and a large contingent of supplicants then arrived for instruction. Kongtrul taught Dzogchen, the *Uttaratantra*, and the root verses for the Treasury of Knowledge. Only at the end of December[50] was he able to meditate on his own, performing Khyentse's Crucial Point of the Oral Lineage Action Vajrakīla and Profound Meaning of Ati. His dreams were mixed—a massive and glorious Zurchung Sherab Drakpa giving someone a cup of barley said, "I have nothing else," in response to which a reverent Kongtrul thought, "this is a real Heruka." In another dream, in an ancient temple, he saw Songtsen Gampo's statue of Tārā draped with the forms of haughty demons. Kongtrul knew on waking that the dream was ominous: "I thought, this is an indication that my karmic stains from the misappropriation of offerings and other offenses have increased." He was deeply saddened. The return of the financial anxieties—his near-constant worry decades ago when he was a newly installed monk at Pelpung—were resurfacing. Kongtrul's status at Pelpung was increasingly tenuous.[51]

The final rupture between Kongtrul and the Pelpung community was sparked by his and Khyentse's decision to push the Tenth Situ into retreat. The twenty-year-old hierarch was adamantly opposed to the religious life. Several generations of hagiographers have transformed Pema Kunzang into something of a "crazy yogin" whose wild escapades were expressions of a higher state of consciousness. They certainly smashed convention—he stole, drank, competed in horse races, and sowed confusion and distress wherever he went. He was known in his life as "The Wild Situ," an epithet that was probably not entirely reverential. After nearly every encounter with him, Kongtrul coded his negative impressions in omens and signs of obstacles, and he often fell ill after empowerments and other rituals for the child. In all fairness the Situ had been taken from his parents at the age of three to be raised by celibate men thousands of kilometers away from his home. He was likely forced to remain indoors most of the day, memorizing scriptures and learning complex rituals. Rebirth of the Ninth Situ or not, he would have been beaten regularly. Based on recent confessionals of contemporary incarnate lamas, there was a high probability that he could have been sexually abused. He was also physically impaired, with sores breaking out on his tongue every few years, rendering him unable to speak clearly. The young man observed the duties of his office as best as he probably could, acting as a figurehead while his regents Wontrul and Dabzang guided his hands and did their best to contain his erratic behavior. Kongtrul now pressured the Situ estate to install the young man into the fourth retreat then starting up at Tsādra. It would not only provide three years of rigorous structure for the young man but would also temporarily remove a disruptive presence from the community.[52]

Kongtrul deflected the responsibility for the plan onto Khyentse Wangpo: "A directive arrived from Dzongsar Tulku Rinpoche stating that Kuzhab Rinpoche should spend some time in retreat." In the diary Kongtrul almost always refers to Khyentse Wangpo with florid honorifics such as "my precious all-seeing master" or "my lord guru," unless he needs to hold him up as the authority behind decisions, in which case he employs one of his friend's proper institutional titles. This did not work to protect him. Kongtrul first sent a letter to the Derge court requesting permission for the Situ to withdraw from public service, but this was denied. Kongtrul enlisted Wontrul to press the case, explaining their thinking, "faithful that it would ultimately be of benefit down the road." Without permission, yet confident that it would eventually be given, Kongtrul put Situ into retreat, probably at Tsādra with the fourth group, which was only then beginning its three-year program. He sent him off with Dorje Drolo empowerments, a suitable deity for a wild young man in need of subjugation.[53]

The Tenth Situ lasted only a few months. From the start he made it known that he was not willing to endure any of it. Increasingly angry, he repeatedly requested to leave the retreat. Several people accosted Kongtrul on Situ's behalf, and a large number of "bad monks" lodged accusations against him and Wontrul, about which Kongtrul fruitlessly complained in a letter, although he does not indicate whether the letter was intended for Situ or the Derge court. Kongtrul understood that the situation at Pelpung was collapsing, that a "major breakdown of samaya was about to occur." From Dzongsar, Khyentse Wangpo counseled Kongtrul to acquiesce to Situ's demands and otherwise do what he could to diffuse the conflict, but Kongtrul was unable to do so; either he was unwilling to back down or the crisis had already become unmanageable. The conflict with Situ had provided an opening for a faction of monks at Pelpung who aligned with the Situ estate and opposed Kongtrul, and this faction was now in ascent.[54]

By this point the discord had escaped even Situ's control, as prominent monks and abbots were now openly opposing Kongtrul and Wontrul's authority and spreading damaging allegations. Derge had initially declined to step in, but by early 1874[55] the Derge steward Tsering Dondrub was forced to intervene. He ruled against both sides. Kongtrul was pleased that the steward found "most of the accusations baseless" and that he jailed some of his adversaries. Kongtrul recorded this judgement as positive, yet it is telling that the steward had not exonerated Kongtrul—not all the accusations were deemed spurious. For their roles in the conflict, the two lamas were also punished. Wontrul was sent to Drentang and Kongtrul was confined to Tsādra, forbidden for the time being to enter Pelpung.[56]

Despite all that had happened, Kongtrul could not give up on the Situ. In his diary he has the young man swear that he had never himself turned against Kongtrul. The Situ had, it would appear, simply complained loudly about being put into retreat, and over the next decade the Situ tried several times to return Kongtrul to good standing at Pelpung. It was too late. The faction of Pelpung lamas that opposed Kongtrul had been able to openly accuse Kongtrul of wrongdoing, and their denunciation of him spread through the monastery.[57]

For four months, from early December 1873 through to March 1874, Kongtrul enjoyed a brief respite. Sequestered at Tsādra, he composed another of his most famous works, *Light of Wisdom*, a commentary to Chokgyur Lingpa's *Stages of the Path of the Wisdom Essence*, which he and Khyentse had revealed at Rongme Chime Karmo Taktsang. The work is a complete overview of the Nyingma path, from a basic introduction to Buddhism through to Dzogchen. According to tradition, Khyentse was so moved by Kongtrul's writing that he declared it to have the qualities of treasure—that is, divine inspiration. It became the central teaching of Chokgyur Lingpa's son Tsewang Drakpa, through whom all contemporary lineages flowed—he taught it to both the Sixteenth Karmapa and Dilgo Khyentse Rinpoche, among others.[58]

In April[59] Kongtrul went to Katok to give the Getse Tulku the sections of the Treasury of Revelations he had not previously received. With Pelpung now largely off limits, the rich intellectual activity at Katok appealed to Kongtrul, and he considered remaining there for an extended visit. He gave empowerments to other prominent lamas and toured the monastery's special sites, such as the Kumbum, a multistoried stūpa halfway up to the monastery from the valley floor that was built by the disciples of Dampa Deshek. Kongtrul circumambulated it with full body prostrations.[60]

Unfortunately, Pelpung drew him back with the terrible news that Wontrul, his last protector in the community, had passed away. Kongtrul immediately blamed the recent hostilities for causing his colleague's death. Wontrul's disciples begged Kongtrul to return to supervise the funeral and settle the deceased lama's estate. Kongtrul's pride was then deeply wounded, and he needed—at least in his diary—to be "repeatedly urged," for "there was no one else who could" perform the rites. Derge sent two officials to attend to the practical details, while Kongtrul took charge of the services and the distribution of Wontrul's property among the members of the sangha. At the end of the forty-nine-day observation period, the time in which a person's consciousness traverses the bardo, Kongtrul performed a seven-day mending rite from United Intent of the Gurus.[61]

Wontrul, as promised, had left funds for the printing of the Treasury of Revelations as well as enough to provide food and tea during rituals for fifteen hundred monks, three times over, a considerable expense. Kongtrul left this with Pelek, the Pelpung steward, for later use.[62] He joined Situ and select other monks in Wontrul's residence for a life stability rite, but the previous winter's controversy had not died down, and once again Kongtrul faced allegations that cut him deeply. Conditions there prevented him from performing the funeral rites for his colleague until the winter of 1875. By his own account, the majority of the Pelpung community "was utterly without conflict with me, yet a certain faction, perhaps due to previous actions, were against me."[63]

Nowhere does Kongtrul admit to what his enemies accused him of doing. Kongtrul was not a warm man, and he does not appear to have been beloved by the monks of Pelpung. He taught regularly and led rituals, and he likely did so in a firm and even sanctimonious manner—he was precise and likely expected all who participated to attend to the details. He seems to have loved his cat more than he did most people around him. Indeed, when the cat died in the early 1850s, he made offerings to the Ninth Situ, who guided the animal's consciousness to human rebirth—more of a funeral observance than he performed for most of the people he knew. There are lengthy passages in his diary denigrating lamas who build communities around them and live comfortably. One bears quoting at length, as it represents his own description of his life. He was loath to rely on others, and he was as suspicious of the Pelpung monks as they were of him.[64]

> I have always had rather humble needs. When staying in retreat, I am fine having no servants and so I never had even a reliable monk to help me. Later, even when my construction projects increased, I continued to live simply; save for my old mother, I had no one serving me, no one who might be called my manager as the important lamas and estates have. If a lama was better than me, he could be in charge, and I have nothing to do with base people—thieves and liars and the like. It is a sign of the sorry times we live in that I have never found anyone who is my equal, someone incapable of hypocrisy, someone stable, capable of supporting me over a long period of time. Therefore, I have made no effort to find a monk attendant; since my mother passed, I have entrusted my niece as her replacement.[65]

This confessional is as much a complaint about the quality of people around him as it is a boast of his simplicity. Whether through choice or not, by his early sixties he was not surrounded with a sufficient contingent of friendly monks to defend him from the accusations.

Chokgyur Lingpa had knowingly earlier advised Kongtrul not to pay heed to malicious gossip,[66] but the disparagement was over more serious issues than the misuse of donations and could not be ignored. Antipathy against Kongtrul had been festering at Pelpung for decades, and he knew it. Orthodox monks resented his Nyingma and other non-Kagyu activities as well as his refusal to harness his fame to promote Karma Kagyu doctrine or increase the wealth of Pelpung; Kongtrul built a seat on the far side of the ridge, and he labeled it Shangpa Kagyu. Only in his first few years at

Pelpung did he strive to remake himself into a Karma Kagyu monk. For most of the previous decades, he forged his own path. His growing fame surely only exacerbated their resentment, and the break with Situ gave his enemies the opportunity to accuse him openly.

The specific charges were almost certainly that Kongtrul was violating his monastic vow of celibacy as part of his treasure revelation activity. It is a modern invention that treasure revelation requires the practice of sexual yoga, but historically many treasure revealers did openly promote the practice as a needed preliminary for revelation. Those who did not practice sexual yoga—including Khyentse Wangpo and one of his reincarnations, Khenpo Jigme Puntsok—wrote of disappointing the deities and of being unable to retrieve all the treasures they were fated to discover. Khyentse Wangpo himself spent the last thirty years of his life confined to his chambers for reasons that are not yet known. The vast majority of treasure revealers did engage in the practice. Chokgyur Lingpa was not unique in having children. Nor was Tsādra a celibate institution; as we saw in chapter 22, Kongtrul had himself arranged for a niece to participate in a sexual ritual at his hermitage.

Nor did it seem that Kongtrul hid the fact of his (allegedly) sexual activity with a female companion. A woman probably named Tsering Chodron—Tashi Chopel, in his account of Kongtrul's death and funeral, gives her name in Sanskrit form as Āyurdharma—lived with him in the last decades of his life. Tashi Chopel identifies her as a servant to Kongtrul.[67] In his extensive research, Richard Barron interviewed the Third Dezhung Rinpoche and the Sixteenth Chagdud Tulku, both of whom confirmed that Kongtrul did indeed have a relationship with a woman. The two lamas, Barron writes, felt that the relationship was not sexual, but one in which she acted as "a muse of sorts." Barron reasonably speculates that Tsering Chodron was this woman.[68] Whether or not the relationship was sexual, Kongtrul's enemies—and the Derge steward—would have been justified in suspecting that it was.

In his diary Kongtrul defended himself with words from Khyentse Wangpo:

> Up until now you have propagated the teachings at that monastery with empowerments, transmissions, and instructions. You have trained people in ritual performance and served as vajra master for scores of diverse sādhana ceremonies from both old

and new transmission traditions. You have taught the secular subjects. You have spent long periods of time in the hermitage. After all this comes a series of vicious accusations against you. Quite frankly, the lama responsible for this should be put to death. Atīśa once said, "One should put a hundred kilometers between oneself and a place of conflict." You have many places you might go, both near and far; it would certainly be harmful for you to remain. Leave, do not set foot there again.[69]

The above defense does not address Kongtrul's innocence, only that he was owed a debt of gratitude for his service. Kongtrul did not lay out the accusations, but neither does he anywhere state that he did not do what he was accused of doing. Kongtrul was certainly aware of the moral condemnation of monks who break their vows of celibacy, for whatever reason. Years later, in his biography of Khyentse Wangpo, he recorded a dream his friend had in 1877 in which his own dear teacher Zhechen Wontrul was suffering for that very reason: "Come no closer!" Zhechen Wontrul warned Khyentse; "My excessive desire for women has caused me many ills. Syphilis has rotted my genitals. Know this stench and renounce desire!"[70] Did Kongtrul violate his vow of celibacy? Nowhere in any of his personal reflections on his career or outlook, in his own voice or placed in the voice of another, does Kongtrul address the topic. At the end of his life he could only criticize others who flaunt their vows yet fail to observe their true meaning.[71] Of Kongtrul's observance of vows, Tashi Chopel wrote merely that Kongtrul told him he never violated his primary tantric vows, the oath to obey his guru's every command.[72]

Kongtrul was enraged and deeply wounded, and after decades of hostility and a year of open conflict, he was ready to abandon Pelpung. In his diary he expressed compassion for his enemies, who, he judged, were swept away by past sins and obscurations. But having discharged his duties to his last remaining colleague there, he felt no further obligation to the monks of Pelpung. He "turned his mind away" from them and decamped for Tsādra, a location that allowed him to maintain a sense of loyalty to the Ninth Situ, proudly declaring in his diary that he did not return to the monastery for fourteen years, although in fact the exile lasted only eleven and a half years, from July 1874 to January 1886. He entered the monastery only twice during the entire period and never again served as a leading lama for the community.[73]

# 25

# ELEVEN YEARS OF EXILE

*Ronggyab, Retreat, the Seven-Line Guru Sādhana,*

*and Drubchen across Derge*

1874–1886

Kongtrul traveled, taught, and performed rituals without ceasing until the last few years of his life. Yet in his last decades the focus had changed, and not only because he was in exile from Pelpung. By 1874 he had written all his major works, and he had received almost all the teachings he would accept, save for the few new treasures that Khyentse Wangpo was still producing. He was now more than ever a ritual specialist whose services were hired by patrons for their estates and communities. He was sought out for transmissions by the greatest Nyingma, Sakya, and Kagyu lamas of his day, such as the Fifteenth Karmapa, Ju Mipam Gyatso, the Second Dezhung Rinpoche, Adzom Drukpa, and Terton Sogyel, as well as scores of others who were privileged to meet him. Few of them stayed long or came more than once. Even in his old age he had few close disciples. Most came for his collections, the impact of which was, by the end of the nineteenth century, beginning to pervade all of Tibetan Buddhism with a renewed and intentional dedication to ecumenical inquiry and practice. Even as he transmitted his collections he continued to expand and edit them for publication. Kongtrul also maintained the schedule of retreats at Tsādra and built out Dzongsho into a year-round hermitage, remaining there to meditate in near seclusion for a year and a half.

Places remained central to his activity. In the last two and a half decades of the nineteenth century, Kongtrul visited dozens of sacred sites, empowering the landscape with rituals and treasure extractions as though to mitigate the effects of the Derge kingdom's slow, tragic collapse. The more the government slid into irrelevance, the more the gods and buddhas of the land were needed to maintain stability. Over the course of two years, from

1883 to 1884, he went with an increasingly large retinue to thirteen separate sacred sites to perform drubchen rituals and feast ceremonies. He also considerably escalated his treasure-related activity in collaboration with Khyentse Wangpo and Dechen Lingpa, with whom he opened Pema Lhatse in Ronggyab in 1878. Among Kongtrul's revelations was a new system for chanting the Seven-Line Prayer to Padmasambhava, titled the Seven-Line Guru Sādhana, which he promoted widely. And he actively promoted his main treasure cycle, United Intent of the Three Roots.

Although Kongtrul never stopped thinking of Tsādra as his home, the hermitage was, in fact, not his base during the nearly twelve years of exile from Pelpung. During the period, he made multiple visits there but rarely stayed more than a few weeks to perform rituals, to work on his publications, or to manage the retreats. The fourth retreat ended in 1876, and Kongtrul spent several weeks preparing the fifth group. It was then that he composed his retreat manual titled *Illuminating Morality: Regulations for the Retreats at the Pelpung Hermitage Kunzang Dechen Wosel Ling*, a short work meant for monks entering into the program. His teaching duties to disciples outside of the retreats also required his presence at Tsādra. Before and after Wontrul's funeral there, in early 1875, while working on the blocks for the Treasury of Revelations, Kongtrul celebrated a sixteen-day drubchen and mendrub ritual of United Intent of the Gurus with Khenpo Akon of Dzogchen Monastery and Lama Pema Norbu. Katok Getse and Donyon Tulku, who had both received the Treasury or Revelations back in 1872, came to receive newly added cycles. And he gave Union of All Rare and Precious Jewels to Jamyang Gelek. This young man, a child of the illustrious Dilgo family, would join the fifth three-year retreat the following year and go on to head the Dzongsho community following Kongtrul's death. In 1876 Kongtrul returned again for his customary year-end rituals and gave Tāranātha's *Ocean of Deities* to the Tenth Situ and the Wongen reincarnation. In 1878 he gave the reincarnation of Dabzang Tulku most of the Treasury of Kagyu Tantra. Nor was Kongtrul's exile ironclad; he returned at least twice to the monastery to give needed empowerments, in 1877 and again in 1879. He did not describe his reception.[1]

Kongtrul passed the years of his exile almost entirely at Dzongsar alongside Khyentse Wangpo. By 1874 Situ Pema Nyinje, the Fourteenth Karmapa, Lama Sang-ngak, Wontrul, Dabzang, and Chokling were all dead, leaving Kongtrul even more isolated than before. The treasure revealer Dechen Lingpa occupied a similar role that Chokgyur Lingpa had previously served, collaborating with Khyentse and Kongtrul on the production of new revelations, but his work paled in comparison with Chokling's and Kongtrul did not include any in the Treasury of Revelations. Khyentse Wangpo was Kongtrul's sole remaining friend and teacher, the only man with whom Kongtrul could discuss his work, his dreams, and his meditative experiences, and he proudly recorded that Khyentse was "delighted" when Kongtrul would arrive at Dzongsar. The two continued to exchange transmissions when they met, primarily from Khyentse's revelations which were coming to him at a rapid pace via visions and dreams. Many of the liturgies for these Kongtrul wrote himself.

Khyentse also endured as a model for Kongtrul to emulate, creating the sort of atmosphere in which Kongtrul thrived: Kongtrul wrote that in July 1874,[2] on arriving at Dzongsar, he found an "ecumenical gathering of many lamas, tulkus, patrons, and their respective entourages," all there to perform a longevity rite from Gathering of Secrets for Khyentse Wangpo's benefit. Groups came to Dzongsar to see Kongtrul as well, and he taught the Treasury of Knowledge there to about twenty monks and lamas in 1875. That same year, he met the teacher Tamdrin Wangmo, who had come from Mindroling for the transmission of Union of All Rare and Precious Jewels, although Kongtrul does not write of receiving teachings from her. And at Dzongsar he first started teaching grammar to "the excellent scholar" Ju Mipam Gyatso, one of the greatest Nyingma philosophers of all time.[3]

## SERVICE TO DERGE AND OTHERS

The scandal that led to Kongtrul's expulsion from Pelpung appears to have had a negligible effect on the public's demand for his ritual services. Commissions from lamas, patrons, and the government came in without pause. Immediately after Kongtrul's arrival at Dzongsar in July, Dechen Lingpa announced a pressing need for one hundred thousand feast offerings from Khyentse Wangpo's Heart Drop of the Venerable Goddess of Immortality to be performed at various places across Derge. Kongtrul accepted the commission and, with his attendants, spent August and the first part of September 1874[4] at Dagam Wangpuk, Tashi Nyida Pelpuk Cave, Zhitro Shelpuk, and caves at Tsādra, such as Pel Deu. On returning to Dzongsar, he found the queen of Derge in residence. She requested that he perform a combined drubchen and mendrub ritual in Derge. Kongtrul accordingly went to Derge in late September, setting up in Tashi Podrang, the royal palace. The rituals were attended by other members of the royal family. When the rites were finished, he remained to consecrate several large new statues of the Buddha and Padmasambhava with the assistance of Tashi Wozer and an unnamed lama from the Tartse house of Ngor, possibly the current official representative from that monastery.[5]

Kongtrul also took the opportunity to petition Queen Tsewang Dolkhar, the daughter of General Dokharwa Tsewang Norbu, for support for the publication of the Treasury of Revelations. She responded positively despite the collapsing fortunes of the ruling family, speaking to him of her desire to support his work. The queen, for her part, continued to patronize Kongtrul as best she could. In 1876 she commissioned rituals at Dzongsar but was unable to afford the necessary supplies, and so Khyentse arranged for these to be provided. That year she also sent word that Kongtrul was needed in Derge to supervise the construction of a stūpa. She sponsored him to arrange a major combined drubchen and mendrub ritual at Dzongsar in 1877. This was attended by the Fifth Dzogchen Tulku, the Third Katok Lingtrul, Dongkham Tulku Ngawang Damcho Gyatso, and one of the rebirths of Chokgyur Lingpa—either the Neten Chokling, Ngedon Drubpai Dorje (who was born in 1873), or Tsike Chokling Konchok Gyurme—and she brought him to Derge in 1879 for yet more rituals for the benefit of the kingdom. The queen twice sent him to construct additional stūpas, first in 1877 at Alo Tsezuldo, and again in 1879 at Se Khardo. Both were extensive affairs, with government representatives and prominent lamas in attendance. Kongtrul's close disciple Tashi Wozer was instrumental in executing the details.[6]

## THE SEVEN-LINE GURU SĀDHANA

Interspersed with his service to aristocratic patrons, in the late 1870s Kongtrul slowly developed and promoted his own method of chanting the Seven-Line Prayer. He had received transmission of this famous prayer from the Zhechen lama Pelden Chogyel back in 1831, when he was on leave from the monastery and helping his patron the Old Chieftain, Khangsar Tsepel. As was his custom with his own innovations, he gave credit for the genesis for the new method to Khyentse Wangpo, even though he classified the final product as a revelation. Kongtrul wrote that Khyentse had a dream in the summer of 1876[7] in which Padmasambhava gave him an empowerment with an orange vase and told him "after one hundred thousand repetitions of the Seven-Line Prayer, Padmasambhava will descend into the practitioner." Khyentse related the dream in order to task Kongtrul with the recitation, which he agreed to do, humbly saying "You, dear lord, are continually suffused with the presence of Orgyen Pema; I cannot even hope for such a thing, but I will do the hundred thousand repetitions. May it be a cause for Padmasambhava to watch over me in the future." Kongtrul did not initially recite the prayers himself but sent word to residents of several hermitages, Tsādra chief among them, to complete the task. The community around Kongtrul would first generate merit, after which Kongtrul would personally recite the prayer in order to be able to reveal treasure. On completion of the recitations, he would come into contact with Padmasambhava and receive the transmission for a new liturgical cycle for the prayer.[8]

Over the course of 1876, Kongtrul was busy with preparations for the transmission of the Treasury of Revelations at Dzongsar that autumn. The transmission of the collection, from September to December 1876,[9] brought Gyatrul Rinpoche from Pelyul, the Third Moktsa Tulku from Katok, the Fifth Zhechen Rabjam Rinpoche, the Fourth Zhechen Gyeltsab, and Khenpo Akon from Dzogchen, among others. Following the transmission, Kongtrul spent most of the first part of 1877 in Khyentse Wangpo's chambers giving additional empowerments; he gave the Kālacakra to the Tenth Situ and Loter Wangpo. The Ninth Pawo, for whom Kongtrul had to briefly interrupt the transmission to go meet at Tsādra, came late to the ceremonies, and for him Kongtrul added his commentaries on the *Hevajra Tantra* and the *Profound Inner Principles*.[10]

In August 1877[11] Khyentse pointed Kongtrul back to the practice of the Seven-Line Prayer. Following a blessing the two gave to one of the rebirths of Chokgyur Lingpa, Khyentse sent Kongtrul to Pema Shelpuk to personally recite the prayer. This time the motivation was more specific than the protection of the Guru: Khyentse gave Kongtrul instructions on the practice and told him it was a necessary preparation for Kongtrul to reveal further sections of United Intent of the Three Roots. Kongtrul spent a week at the cave, during which he was quite sure he saw the syllable "jam" on a nearby cliff. This was the root syllable for the wealth god Jambhala, an optimistic sight. He crossed the Sidu Pass to spend another week practicing at Rongme and then returned to Dzongsar to perform a mendrub and drubchen ritual for the royal family.[12]

If the recitation of the Seven-Line Prayer was intended to generate visions of deities and signs of treasure to reveal, it appears to have succeeded. In the year and a half since he began to develop the method, Kongtrul had at least nineteen dreams or visions in which he was given treasure, saw signs of treasure, or was engaged by a ḍākinī in treasure-related activity, sexual or otherwise. These occurred while he was in retreat as well as while he was performing rituals for his patrons and students. For example, in late 1877 he dreamed of two ḍākinīs who gave him coded prophecies. Soon after, he dreamed of Terdak Lingpa and two ḍākinīs who told him of important treasure to reveal in the east; a man whom Kongtrul took to be a treasure revealer promised he would help acquire it. On waking, he was sure that Khyentse Wangpo had explained the code and had given him directions to the treasure cache. The dreams of treasure continued. While at Pema Shelri, Kongtrul had a vision in which a ḍākinī appeared, holding first a vajra and bell and then a long-life vase. He then had a vision of Milarepa. On his journey to Dzongsho in October 1877, at a place called Gyang Nepotsa, he dreamed that there were "many signs of treasure" at Dzongsho. Ultimately, the recitations bore actual results: during the first night of a retreat at Dagam Wangpuk that began on October 10, 1877.[13]

> Padmasambhava, in the form of the lord lama Khyentse Wangpo, opened a book made of yellow paper on which was written many fields of symbolic letters and explained it all to me, beginning with a method for the Seven-Line Prayer.[14]

Back at Dzongsar, in January 1878,[15] he reported his dream, and Khyentse gave him paper to write it down. In April[16] he wrote out a sādhana for the practice, expanding Guru Chowang's basic visualization and recitation practice to include the multiple forms of Padmasambhava. He gave the transmission for this new liturgy at least four times over the next decade, giving it first that same year to Khyentse Wangpo, who performed the Tsokye Dorje and Dorje Drolo forms of the Guru in November 1878.[17] Khyentse told Kongtrul that after doing the practice, he perceived the entire universe as the maṇḍala of Tsokye Dorje and felt confident in the future survival of the Buddhist teachings.[18]

The more Kongtrul practiced, the more his confidence grew in his revelations. At Pema Shelri he had a vision of Milarepa, the consummate model of the solitary meditator. He dreamed of a gathering of many women, in the midst of which he saw a combined figure of Gampopa and Jatson Nyingpo, two paragons of Kagyu and Nyingma monasticism who both revealed treasure; this amalgamated being gave him the transmission of Gampopa's *Precious Garland of the Supreme Path*. Soon after, Kongtrul dreamed of meeting the Ninth Situ and the Fourteenth Karmapa, who were both delighted to see him. "We would like to receive your treasures and many other teachings from you," they told him. Khyentse Wangpo appeared to give him a regent statue and a pile of jewels, and he saw Vajrasattva in the sky surrounded by deities. In several dreams he picked up crystals from the ground.[19]

After Khyentse told him to write down the method for the Seven-Line Prayer, Kongtrul dreamed that he donned new monastic robes and came across a pile of bamboo writing pens. A ḍākinī who resembled a woman of Tsurpu named Jetsun Namgyel—possibly a treasure companion to a Karma Kagyu lama—gave him a treasure inventory written in code on cloth tied with string and fastened with a kīla, and declared, "We two must reveal these." In early 1878 the Eighth Zhamar appeared in a dream, looking well. In another dream, Kongtrul discovered the skull of the First Sanggye Nyenpa and treasure scrolls. Kongtrul then dreamed that Khyentse Wangpo presented him with a large white conch he had recovered from Lhamdo Burmo, after which the two of them decoded a sādhana to the folk hero Gesar and transmitted it to a group of disciples. Finally, he dreamed that Lochen Dharmaśrī sent him a message with a treasure scroll, after which he was visited by a large blue woman claiming to be the Hindu goddess Kālarātri, a deity who in Buddhism represents passions to be conquered and is depicted crushed under the feet of Cakrasaṃvara and other tantric buddhas. With one leg pointing upwards, she mounted Kongtrul—"thrust herself between my thighs," he wrote—as a red woman nearby smiled on. His niece Rigdzin Dolma was also there with three other women; she gave him a large kīla dagger made of copper. As Kongtrul held up the dagger, he read a letter from Khyentse that listed treasures he was destined to discover.[20]

Kongtrul's recording of these dreams expresses the degree to which his own treasure dominated his attention in the early years of his long exile from Pelpung. Yet he neglected to fully document the actual revelations. There are four treasure cycles and three stand-alone texts credited to Kongtrul in the Treasury of Revelations. The cycles are: fifteen texts of Seven-Line Guru Sādhana; ten texts from United Intent of the Three Roots; three texts of Conquest of Poison, a Dorje Drolo practice; and nineteen texts of Seven Cycles of the Secret Essence. The four stand-alone texts are a biography of Padmasambhava titled Vajra Necklace, a biography of Vairocana titled Lotus Paradise, Profound Path in Seven Sections, and Guru's Heart Advice in Ten

Chapters. Only one of the colophons for these fifty-one texts gives the time of its discovery: a text from Seven Cycles of the Secret Essence revealed on February 25, 1893,[21] at Tsādra titled *Tambura Song of Devotion*.[22] Another text, *Initiation of the Vidyādhara* from the United Intent of the Three Roots, has a colophon that states it was written at Dzongsar on March 12, 1877,[23] but not when it was revealed. *Mirage of Nectar* contains no dates for revelations.

Kongtrul is surprisingly indifferent to the details of his own revelations. He mentions only two of his treasure revelations in his diary—United Intent of the Three Roots and the Seven-Line Guru Sādhana. These both unfolded over several years at several places, and while additional information can be gleaned from *Mirage of Nectar* and the colophons, many of the texts in the Treasury of Revelations are not assigned a place of discovery. Nowhere does Kongtrul give a full account of the revelations. Of his own revelations in the Treasury, Kongtrul names only three in *Mirage of Nectar*: United Intent of the Three Roots, Seven Cycles of the Secret Essence, and Profound Path in Seven Sections. Five additional revelations are named in *Mirage of Nectar* that do not appear in the Treasury of Revelations—Heart Drop of Vairocana, Caṇḍālī Swift Mother of Life, Vanquishing All Arrogant Ones, Mahākaruṇika: Resting At Ease, and Ocean of the Supreme Bliss Ḍākinī. Future research might locate these, if they ever existed; it is entirely possible that he encountered the inspiration but never did anything with it. Tibetan treasure revelation is nothing if not vague. Titles and origin accounts change as the texts develop, with shifting details and even attributions. Even more beguiling than textual revelations are the objects. In *Mirage of Nectar* and in his diary, Kongtrul also lists close to a dozen objects he revealed over the years. While some of these objects may have been brought out to be seen and held—there were a fair amount of Padmasambhava "regent" statues extracted as treasure—many objects on the list would have been included as symbolic connections to the person to whom they once belonged, whether Indian saint or Tibetan lineage master.[24]

Why was Kongtrul not more forthcoming about the discovery of his own treasures? After close to five decades collecting, editing, writing, and organizing treasure liturgies, he would have had a precise understanding of the elements and value of treasure histories; if he needed them, he knew how to write them. It is certainly not the case that every treasure cycle has been given a history with a specific place and time of its revelation, particularly those that were not in need of proving their authenticity. By 1870 no one would question Kongtrul's mastery of the genre or deem him lacking in expertise. Kongtrul did not need origin accounts to authenticate his treasures, and so he did not craft them. He simply recorded associated events in his diary as he would any other dream or meditative experience—first taking possession of United Intent of the Three Roots at Lhamdo Burmo and subsequent visions that produced its additional sections, and then the dream in which Padmasambhava bestowed on him the Seven-Line Guru Sādhana. He could easily have noted in the colophons of the treasure texts that at a particular place at a particular time the inspiration came to him and fashioned it into a treasure cycle, but he did not need to do so. Kongtrul's treasures did not come fully created in one moment of ecstasy, and they were, as stated already, collaborative. As he discussed them with Khyentse and, to some degree, Dechen Lingpa, he filled out the cycles with the necessary ritual manuals. They are revelations because they originated with inspiration from Padmasambhava and arose out of his own meditative practice. They are treasure because Kongtrul defined them as such.

## THE OPENING OF PEMA LHATSE

Dechen Lingpa was Kongtrul's primary partner in the field in the 1870s and 1880s. Kongtrul credited Khyentse Wangpo with assigning the younger man to the task, despite his initially considering him a mediocre treasure revealer. It is possible that Kongtrul brought about Khyentse's change of opinion, at least the way Kongtrul relates the story. Kongtrul himself was clearly ambivalent about the man's capabilities, alternately praising and disparaging him. Now that the treasures being produced were his own, perhaps he was content to collaborate with a man of decidedly lesser status, or maybe he simply had to accept him in the absence of anyone more competent. In *Mirage of Nectar* Kongtrul has it that very soon after he and Dechen Lingpa had been together in Ronggyab back in 1872, Khyentse revealed an inventory to Kongtrul's own treasures at Modrak Cliff in Lhamdo and shared it with Dechen Lingpa. This was understood by Kongtrul to be a precipitory event in his revelations of United Intent of the Three Roots, which began in 1874. The following year, Dechen Lingpa was in Dzongsar, and Kongtrul described his activities as "amazing."[25]

It would seem that Khyentse intended for Dechen Lingpa to assist Kongtrul in his treasure activities in ways that Chokgyur Lingpa once had, and according to Kongtrul's diary, Khyentse went as far as ordering Dechen Lingpa to Pema Shelri in 1875 to extract an additional inventory for treasures

Kongtrul was destined to reveal, which the three of them wrote down with additional help from Kongtrul's disciple Lhaksam Tenpai Gyeltsen. Khyentse could not accompany him to the sites of the revelation, as he, for whatever reason, did not leave his residence. Dechen Lingpa was no doubt eager to partner with the great lama. As seen above, he was, by 1877, familiar enough with Kongtrul and Khyentse to commission ritual activity. He had provided the treasure substances to insert into the stūpa at Alo Tsezuldo, and he helped plan and construct the Se Khardo stūpa two years later.[26]

In late 1878 Kongtrul accepted Dechen Lingpa's insistent invitation to return to Ronggyab. Only after, according to his diary, he received Khyentse Wangpo's consent that it would be worthwhile. The projects Kongtrul intended to undertake were significant enough that Khyentse had a vision of Lhatsen Tsangpa, a local deity, who instructed them to prepare the way by performing one hundred feasts from Khyentse's recent discovery, Trilogy of the Guru's Two Doctrines. After these were completed, Kongtrul went first to Tarde Monastery, but Dechen Lingpa was not there to meet him, a coincidental repeat of the first time Kongtrul went home to meet him in 1872 only to find him absent. Now, as he waited for him, Kongtrul set about performing rituals, using liturgies from Chokling's treasures as well as his own growing corpus of United Intent of the Three Roots. He and his attendants also performed a section of Kongtrul's Seven-Line Guru Sādhana. The treasure dreams continued; one evening a ḍākinī with lustrous hair gave him several objects as gifts, about which someone said, "you have a real connection to these things; they will become meaningful in a few years." He awoke, in a bed in his old homeland, feeling happy. He also, to his delight, received in a dream a piece of Karma Pakshi's mummified flesh, from which a white syllable emerged.[27]

Kongtrul was in the valley intent primarily on laying out its sacred geography. Ten years had passed since he published his gazetteer of Kham, in which he surmised that the site which guides beings via the Lotus Family was possibly the peak called Karyak in Ronggyab.[28] Chokling's treasure gazetteer had described the spot as a mountain called Karlung in the east of Ronggyab "in the shape of a lotus hat," on the peak of which was a cave where Padmasambhava meditated. From the cave to the valley floor was a day's journey on horseback.[29] It was on the basis of the description of the peak as a lotus hat that allowed Kongtrul the certainty that Karyak, which had such a shape, was the place. He needed to personally survey the place to be sure. Kongtrul spent two months in Ronggyab preparing for his momentous hike. While still awaiting Dechen Lingpa's return, he went to a sacred boulder which local people called White Tent and performed an extensive feast to good effect—rainbow light shimmered in the air and vultures landed nearby. When the treasure revealer returned, they performed a sādhana together using Chokgyur Lingpa's Wish-Fulfilling Jewel of the Guru's Intent as well as a smoke offering, a golden libation, and a ritual to bind the gods to serve Buddhism. Kongtrul then announced that Karyak was indeed the sacred spot described in Chokling's treasure, declaring "The site that guides beings via the Lotus Family, one of the eight sites which bring beings to enlightenment through activity, is Pema Lhatse," a name which was either already known to the valley or henceforth a new name of Karyak. With his crooked finger held before him, he pointed out a possible circumambulation route, and as he did a vulture landed nearby, attesting to the accuracy of his pronouncement. One evening soon after, he dreamed of a man giving him pieces of turquoise and coral and a garland of other jewels, which he took to be a sign of his longevity.[30]

Kongtrul was then asked to aid the Bon monastery, the place he had first received his formal religious education. He donated supplies and he appointed a man named Khardo Chonam to lead the community in finances, education, and construction. Among his donations was a piece of property to sustain the community. Nowhere does Kongtrul otherwise mention owning property in the valley. It was either donated to him by a patron or it had belonged to his family. If it was a family property that he had not previously benefited from personally, it may have been possessed by a relative who had recently died, only now passing it on to Kongtrul and thereby enabling him to gift it to the Bon monastery. Kongtrul was then called to Denkhok to supervise the funeral of a child of the Wentok clan, a leading family there. He reconnected with Dechen Lingpa in Drugu Dilkhar in Marong for more geomantic rituals. The place is sacred to Padmasambhava—he is said to have thrown stones there from the Copper-Colored Mountain. Kongtrul had a dream in which all eight forms of the Precious Guru appeared together. Tsokye Dorje was in the center, with Yeshe Tsogyel in the form of Dechen Gyelmo above him. To the Guru's right was Padmakara or Padmasambhava, with Pema Gyelpo and Loden Chokse to their right. On the Guru's left was Dorje Drolo and Sengge Dradrok, and Śākya Sengge and Nyima Wozer. In front of the group was Vairocana—a simulacrum of himself—sitting as Nyima Wozer placed his hand on his head and gave him empowerments.[31]

Only then, in late January or early February 1879,[32] did Kongtrul set about climbing Pema Lhatse, a ridge with three bare peaks like the three points of a lotus hat. Despite writing in his gazetteer ten years earlier that a man named Pangtse Pawo opened the place, in his diary Kongtrul explained that previously no one had thought to climb it in search of a meditation cave, as it was dauntingly steep. In the bitter cold, Kongtrul braved the ascent, holding on to bushes and trees and using a lengthy woven ladder. Midway up the central peak on a wide cliff face, Kongtrul found a cavern, inside of which he identified a rock formation as being a naturally occurring life-size statue of Padmasambhava. He named two additional caves, one on each side of the main site; the one on the right was to be called the Cave of the Virtuous Friend, the one on the left the Cave of Immortality. He saw prints in the rock left by the feet of Padmasambhava and both Bon and Buddhist saints. Taking a few items for blessings—Kongtrul wrote "statues and consecrated substances" but this is likely symbolic for stones—he descended. The way down was difficult. He does not indicate in his diary whether he went alone or with Dechen Lingpa and other aids. He was sixty-six years old, and it was the middle of winter.[33]

Kongtrul returned to Tsādra in early 1879 by way of several locations to which he had been summoned for ritual service. He went first to Ling and then over a pass to Nyen and on to the Khardo Valley, stopping at the Sheldrak Wodzong sacred site and the Dudul Tsepuk cave before arriving at Khardo Monastery. Dechen Lingpa had given him instructions to perform longevity practices for the Tenth Situ at Dzodong Temple there. He went next to Tsangrong to perform geomantic rituals at Tashi Tsekdong and at a Vimalamitra cave called Chime Keutsang. He received an order to proceed to Derge for a consecration ritual and a wealth-deity sādhana, stopping at Lhadrang Monastery on the way and Chayang afterwards. For a few months in early 1879, he was able to remain at Tsādra to edit liturgies for the Treasury of Revelations, but he was soon called to Dzongsar to give a series of empowerments which Khyentse Wangpo was too ill to perform.[34]

## RETREAT AT DZONGSHO

Dechen Lingpa continued to advise Kongtrul under Khyentse Wangpo's direction, at least according to Kongtrul's account in his diary. As always Kongtrul presents major activities and projects as having been determined through careful examination of external signs, dreams, and visions, and by the command or recommendation of his colleagues. From early 1880 to the summer of 1881, Kongtrul was in a sealed retreat at Dzongsho. In his diary he has Khyentse urge him to go into retreat, and he has Dechen Lingpa determine the location, removing himself, as usual, from agency in the matter. Kongtrul narrates the genesis of the retreat idea starting with two disturbing dreams Khyentse Wangpo had in the later half of 1879, soon after Kongtrul and Dechen Lingpa had built the stūpa at Se Khardo. In the first dream, Khyentse witnessed the explosion of a temple in which a statue of a combined Padmasambhava and Vairocana was housed. The statue survived the destruction, but he saw that it had been knocked to one side and feared it was damaged. In a dream that immediately followed the first, Zhechen Wontrul appeared to explain that the explosion indicated that Kongtrul would face serious difficulties the next year: "the sort of crisis lamas face when the hour of death is near." In the dream, Zhechen Wontrul explained that the following year Kongtrul would be sixty-eight, the age that Zhechen Wontrul himself had passed away, and he advised Khyentse to send Kongtrul into retreat in order to avoid a premature death. He was to remain in solitude, without teaching, and to focus on the approach and accomplishment practices of the Lotus Distillation, an unidentified liturgical cycle.[35]

Khyentse described an additional negative omen that indicated that Kongtrul should stay away from Tsādra and find another place for the retreat: it seems that when the Tenth Situ was leaving for Tibet several men in his entourage had died. Kongtrul was clearly uncomfortable at the hermitage: horrible winds that struck during a recent visit suggested to him that the local deities were unhappy, and the front part of a torma offering cake on the altar collapsed while he was supplicating the protective deities, an indication that they would not sufficiently protect him. Not only was Kongtrul's own hermitage too close to his enemies, but he appears to have needed to refrain from staying too long at most places in the region in order to avoid Pelpung lamas who might pass through. Where he would reside was the next matter to discuss, and again, Kongtrul, who certainly had reason to choose the eventual location, would not allow himself credit for the decision. According to his diary, Khyentse Wangpo put the question to Dechen Lingpa, who came to Tsādra with the results of his inquiry in February 1880 as Kongtrul was closing the fifth retreat and working with an editor on the woodblocks for the first forty volumes of the Treasury of Revelations. Dechen Lingpa announced that Dagam Wangpuk, Pema Shelpuk, and Rongme Chime Karmo Taktsang were all unsuitable locations, but he suggested that Dzongsho was viable.[36]

Kongtrul's second hermitage, which he had yet to develop properly, was to be his sole residence for the next year and a half. He had begun the construction of a temple there in 1878 and had returned to Dzongsho to supervise the project in person during the middle of 1879, but the work was apparently lagging. While there in 1879, he had dreamed of being pulled from floodwaters by Tārā and of receiving two volumes of treasure texts, the first of which resembled Longchenpa's Heart Essence writings and the second of which was a collection of treasure prophecies and histories. He and his students had also performed feasts from United Intent of the Three Roots.

In the middle of February 1880, Kongtrul set off for Dzongsho, stopping at Dzongsar for consultation with Khyentse. His friend had several new revelations to share with him: Kongtrul had a dream in which he was read a text written by Lochen Dharmaśrī. On relating the dream to Khyentse, his friend advised him that he ought not misplace even a stone should he discover it as treasure while at Dzongsar. Kongtrul arrived at Dzongsho on February 24, 1880,[37] immediately performed a smoke offering, and set up the symbolic boundaries for his retreat, which he initiated on the 27th[38] and ended in July 1881.[39]

Kongtrul wrote very little about his year of near isolation, stating simply "I performed the practices of the lama, chosen deity, and ḍākinī in proper sequence and recited many mantras for each." During the winter solstice of 1880, he performed several days' worth of Vajrakīla rites, as was his long-time custom, and then the daily sādhana from his own treasure cycle United Intent of the Three Roots. He did record several dreams, however, in which buddhas and saints appeared in marvelous palaces, and in which he received messages and blessings from Chokgyur Lingpa, Karma Chakme, and Khyentse Wangpo, who foretold of a treasure for Kongtrul to reveal at Tsādra. Kongtrul ever delighted in boasting of prophetic dreams: In one, a lama gave him a skull cup and recommended he use it as a drinking vessel; soon after, the Fifth Dzogchen Tulku visited and gave him a cup made from Vairocana's skull that had been revealed as treasure by Taksham Nuden Dorje. The dreams at the conclusion of the retreat reflect the devotion to Padmasambhava he had generated in the practice, his heart aching with affection and gratitude to the Guru's kindness. In between his meditation sessions, he composed liturgies for the Treasury of Revelations, and, perhaps inevitably, he did some teaching, as the Karma Chakme incarnation, disregarding Kongtrul's need for solitude, came for transmissions, and the Fifth Dzogchen Tulku came to receive instructions on Kongtrul's Seven-Line Guru Sādhana and to deliver the fated skull. The visits, coming after so many months of solitude, left Kongtrul in a state of confusion and agitation that lasted three nights.[40]

Kongtrul's isolation at Dzongsho was not entirely dedicated to meditation. He took the opportunity to construct a proper residence there. As he justified the work in the diary:

> The retreat residence which I had built earlier was placed right against the cliff and water flowed into it. There was not yet a temple, just this plain nomadic-style dwelling which was quite miserable. I simply had to construct a new building. A maternal relative went to the Derge king to make the case for help, and they kindly sent laborers in two divisions.[41]

Kongtrul's disciple Jamyang Gelek came to supervise the project, and the high quality of his work earned him praise from his fellow disciple Nesar Tashi Chopel in *Marvelous Gem-Like Vision*.[42] Kongtrul appreciated this disciple. He recorded that Khyentse once told him that he and Jamyang Gelek had been master and student in a previous life as well, and he commented that "the two of us certainly share a common aspiration." Construction commenced after Kongtrul was well into his retreat—he had already completed the Guru practice by the time they laid out the foundation. Kongtrul moved into two of the small caves at Dzongsho, Wangchen Puk and the Citta Sangpuk, until September 1880[43] when the new buildings were complete and as artisans began installing statues. The central image was Padmasambhava in the form of Orgyen Zahorma. These he consecrated with a Mindroling liturgy called Source that Yields Virtue and Excellence.[44]

Toward the end of the retreat, Kongtrul received a letter from the Tenth Situ instructing him to forgive his enemies at Pelpung, no doubt a necessary step toward reconciling and returning to Pelpung. The letter was preceded by a relapse of Kongtrul's long-term illness, which he had for the past several years ascribed to the negative karma of his enemies at Pelpung. Still disturbed by the affair, he refused to comply, stating that the harm done him was irreparable—for the perpetrators, not for him. The ruptures in the samaya connections between Kongtrul and his enemies had lingered too long, rendering them impossible to mend even if he wanted to do so. Kongtrul admitted to no malice toward them—a highly regarded and accomplished practitioner of Mahāyāna Buddhism, he could acknowledge no ill-will toward other people, regardless of how he felt. But he refused to forgive them—it was impossible to repair the damage they had done. The letter left him feeling nauseous. Situ sent word that he would travel to Dzongsho himself, increasing Kongtrul's anxiety to a degree that he could not meditate. This anxiety manifested physically in boils which swelled only to burst when the Situ arrived. With pus flowing from his open wounds, Kongtrul gave him transmissions, but Situ's efforts did not succeed. Not long after the conclusion of Kongtrul's retreat, he dreamed of seeing the ghost of a murdered monk who had returned to plague his community. Kongtrul transformed himself into Vajrakīla and drove the ghost away. The metaphorical weight of the pus and ghosts are hard to miss.[45]

## THIRTEEN DRUBCHEN RITUALS ACROSS DERGE

Kongtrul completed his retreat at the end of the summer of 1881 and returned to Dzongsar. Supplicants came to him there to receive blessings and transmissions, which Kongtrul gave from his practice of Seven-Line Guru Sādhana. Still enjoying the glow of the retreat, Kongtrul had visions and dreams of deities such as Ratnagarbha, Cakrasaṃvara, Hevajra, Mahāmāya, Śrīdevi, Amitāyus, and Yamarāja. For most of the following year, he gave teachings at Dzongsar and Tsādra. He gave the Treasury of Knowledge and his commentary on the Third Karmapa's *Profound Inner Principles* to the head of Dzigar Monastery and others. After his customary Vajrakīla rites at his hermitage, he returned to Dzongsar to edit the blocks for the Treasury of Instructions. The teaching continued back at Tsādra, where he gave the Treasury of Kagyu Tantra to Tartse Khenpo, a transmission that lasted from March 4 to May 9, 1882.[46] He then taught the Treasury of Revelations to an assembly of illustrious lamas: the Fifth Dzogchen Tulku, the Third Karma Kuchen of Pelyul Monastery, Adzom Drukpa, the tulku of Mingyur Dorje, and other representatives from monasteries as far as Gyarong. This transmission, the fourth Kongtrul had given for the collection, lasted from June 5 to September 13.[47]

Two weeks later, on September 27,[48] he began a transmission of the Treasury of Instructions to Tartse Khenpo and thirty others, finishing two months later on November 24.[49] Most of these were given at Dzongsho;

he was not receiving groups at Tsādra. He also received teachings; as usual, when meeting with Khyentse Wangpo, the two exchanged empowerments. Kongtrul gave Khyentse several transmissions, including Pema Dechen Lingpa's Heart Drop of the Ḍākinī Expanse. Khyentse reciprocated with some of his own recent revelations, such as Guru Cakrasaṃvara, a "rediscovered" treasure of Gyaton Pema Wangchuk, and the Hayagrīva liturgy from Liberation of All the Arrogant, a "rediscovered" treasure of Drugu Yangwang Tsel, as well as half a dozen cycles by other treasure revealers.[50]

After a solid year of teaching, Kongtrul felt uneasy. He had had some auspicious dreams, such as taking possession of one of the Fourteenth Karmapa's teeth, but he also began having ominous dreams and seeing portents of disaster in the natural world. For two nights running, while he was performing his annual end-of-year Vajrakīla rites to stave off harm, he heard the laughter of owls from far away on Rabsel Plain. Kongtrul knew this to be a sign of coming calamity, but his disciple Gelek made a remark about "the conceptual thought brought about by the cries of birds in empty valleys" which caused Kongtrul some embarrassment. It was a rare admission in his diary that he was perhaps not entirely confident of his reading of the natural world. The sense of unease, however, was real. At Dzongsar he requested a half dozen empowerments and transmissions of protectors and wrathful deities from Khyentse Wangpo, who assured him that the signs he was perceiving would not result in serious trouble. Among the transmissions was a Tārā practice titled Freedom from Fear. Khyentse and Kongtrul composed three texts of this practice for the Treasury of Revelations, crediting an otherwise unknown man named Yakchar Ngonmo as the original revealer. Both he and Khyentse were ill for most of the first half of 1883, victims of a smallpox epidemic that was slowly spreading through the region.[51]

Kongtrul dedicated the remaining months of 1883 and nearly all of 1884 to a series of thirteen drubchen rituals and feasts at sacred sites across Derge. These started small but grew to become major public ritual events. The idea for the program had come to Kongtrul first in September 1882,[52] in a vision of Padmasambhava, in his form known as Orgyen Nangsi Zilnon, Glorious Subjugator of All That Appears and Exists. Written under the Guru's throne were two lines of texts which instructed Kongtrul—for the benefit of Buddhism, other beings, and himself—to perform thirteen drubchen rituals and feasts, not by himself but with reliable companions. Several months later, at the start of the Water Sheep Year, in February 1883, Khyentse Wangpo had a vision of Sanggye Lingpa who told him and

Kongtrul to continue revealing treasure until they produce twenty-five. He also told them that in order to dispel obstacles to this activity, it was of the utmost importance that they perform thirteen drubchen rituals and feasts at sacred places.[53]

On learning of Khyentse's vision, Kongtrul was excited to have his own vision confirmed, and he wrote an account of his friend's vision. This led to the sole instance recorded by Kongtrul in his diary in which he acknowledged displeasing his friend. Khyentse scolded him:

> It is not appropriate, under any circumstances, to write out any prophecies that come now or in the future. Do not actively pursue these things—one must remain neutral. Now, since you have written them out, we need to follow through and compose a proper strategy for accomplishing all this.[54]

The reprimand was not subtle, and it reveals a rather significant difference in the two men's approach to visions and writing. Khyentse Wangpo was a prolific revealer of treasure; there are three hundred forty-seven texts in the Treasury of Revelations that name him as the revealer. Many of these, however, are classified as "rediscovered" treasures—that is, the claim is that they were initially revealed by men and women, most of whom are otherwise unknown to history, and then reconcealed awaiting Khyentse. Why Khyentse made use of this strategy has yet to be explained. He also transcribed and authored scores of additional texts for the revelations of other men, chief among them Chokgyur Lingpa and Kongtrul. Based on Kongtrul's biographical writings, Khyentse seems to have experienced visions and dreams almost continuously, in which he received transmissions, revelations, prophecies, and instructions. Yet aside from the revelations, he declined to put these in writing, and he mocked those who took such things too seriously. To put on paper a prophetic vision, Khyentse explained, was to force action toward its fulfilment. Better to hold off and let events unfold as they will. The implication is that visions are not to be treated as confirmation of one's own desires or as permission to act as one already intended. Visions are instead subtle suggestions of coming occurrences that aid in proper preparation. This was in stark contrast to Kongtrul's use of visions, which always conveniently gave him supernatural permission to pursue his agenda. Here, having written down the vision, Kongtrul had compelled them to act, and the two lamas thus wrote out a program for Kongtrul's next endeavor, listing thirteen abodes which were both undefiled and easily reached by pilgrims. When they were done, despite Khyentse's irritation at Kongtrul's forcing the issue, he gave him several pieces of silver in sponsorship of the program. Perhaps as a gesture of contrition, Kongtrul used liturgies for Khyentse's treasure revelations for seven of the thirteen services.

Kongtrul was ill immediately after he and Khyentse drafted the schedule, and he was caught up with giving transmissions of Chokgyur Lingpa's treasures to Khenpo Rinchen Dargye and the latest additions to the Treasury of Revelations to Gyatrul Tulku from Pelyul Monastery. He partially recovered his health only after soaking in the Dzumtsa and Tingtsa Hot Springs in the Terlung Valley, which eased the swelling and the intense itching from his slowly healing smallpox lesions.[55]

He began the program in midsummer 1883[56] at Dagam Wangpuk, using a liturgy from Khyentse's Heart Drop of the Venerable Goddess of Immortality. Kongtrul had not planned well enough. He and his ten companions had not brought enough supplies, and even working in shifts there were not enough participants to recite the requisite mantras in the time they had allotted. Worse, one of the monks had a psychotic episode, climbing to the top of the cliff face to throw stones at them in the middle of the night and forcing everyone into the cave. Kongtrul's jaundice flared up again leaving him feeling as though he was sitting in fire. On finishing the first event, Kongtrul returned to the hot springs. He committed himself to better screening the participants and to including a "young girl" at the feast offerings, which would somehow prevent against such things happening again. Perhaps Kongtrul brought his consort Tsering Chodron to the subsequent events and this remark was offered as a justification. Recognizing the community interest in the program, Kongtrul also planned a public empowerment at the start of the subsequent services.[57]

Between the summer of 1883 and the end of January 1884, Kongtrul completed the next seven ceremonies. The second was Rigdzin Godemchen's Ancestral Line of the Vidyādhara at Pema Shelri, to which several of Kongtrul's students joined. Third was Khyentse Wangpo's Guru Cakrasaṃvara[58] revelation at Dzum Tsangkar, attended by a Chod master from Pelpung named Lama Yonten and his disciples. Although he remained ill, Kongtrul continued the program. For the fourth drubchen ritual, they performed the Guru practice from Essence of Light,[59] another rediscovered treasure of Khyentse Wangpo, at Trawo in the Dzing Valley. Khyentse had transmitted this cycle to Kongtrul in November 1878.[60]

This completed the Guru section of the program. The fifth drubchen ritual was at Dzongsho, using Khyentse's Oceanic Gathering of Precepts.[61] The Third Moktsa Tulku from Katok joined them. On the tenth day of the month, Kongtrul dreamed of Padmasambhava giving him treasure objects. The sixth was Vajrāmṛta, another treasure of Khyentse Wangpo's.[62] This was performed at Godāwari, in a residence built inside the cave in 1876 by the Pelpung administrator Garje Drodok, who had earlier sponsored a ceremony at nearby Tashi Nenang. With the additional support, Kongtrul performed extended medicinal practices and a feast of ḍākas and ḍākinīs. Another patron, Tashi Samdrub from the Solpon clan, constructed a residence for him at Rameśvari in Atri, which served for the seventh drubchen ritual and feast, for which they performed a Jinasāgara Avalokiteśvara practice. Kongtrul did not identify the liturgy they used, but it would not have been one of Khyentse's, as there is no record of him revealing a treasure dedicated to the deity. Back in 1874, Tashi Sampel, the district's chamberlain of Rameśvari—also known as Rawe—employed Kongtrul to open the place. At that time the weather turned so bad that the sponsors reasonably questioned the benefit of the rituals and presumably Kongtrul's expertise at interacting with the local deities.[63] The rites in 1883 were an opportunity to restore confidence. With them he completed the deity section of the program. The eighth drubchen ritual was at Tashi Nenang, using Nyangrel Nyima Wozer's Khrodhakāli.[64]

For January 1884[65] Kongtrul was at Tsādra performing his customary year-end Vajrakīla rituals. On his way there, he had a prophetic dream about the Tenth Situ surrounded by death. He had narrowly avoided an encounter with some of his old enemies while at Evaṁ Monastery (where he stopped over on his way back from the seventh drubchen ritual at Rameśvari) and had an anxiety attack as a result, forcing him to lay over at Chayang for several days before he was calm enough to travel. The scandal and his expulsion was never far from his thoughts, and short visits at Tsādra agitated him even before he arrived.[66]

He was occupied at the retreat center until May 1884.[67] The sixth retreat had concluded and the seventh began, with the sponsorship of his niece Rigdzin Dolma. Two tulkus from Tsedrum Monastery came for empowerments, as did Tsewa Rinchen Namgyel, a "Zhechen Tulku" who was probably the Fourth Zhechen Gyeltsab, and his disciple Nesar Khenpo Tashi Chopel. During the four months, he was able to edit his compositions in preparation for publishing.[68]

The drubchen and feast program began again in June[69] at Pawopuk Wangchen Drak with the liturgy on the ḍākinī Mamo Ngondzok Gyelpo from Chokgyur Lingpa's Seven Profound Cycles. This was sponsored by the Tenth Situ. Forty-five people joined him for this, the ninth drubchen ritual and feast of the program, and Kongtrul set some of them on a separate ransom rite while thunder and lightning storms raged outside the cave. He returned to Tsādra for the tenth, at Lhamdo Burmo, using the liturgy of Gathering of All Ḍākinīs' Secrets,[70] a revelation of Khyentse's that he had received in 1875. The attending group had grown to fifty-five, all sponsored by the government of Derge. With this practice, he completed the ḍākinī portion of the program. Derge's interest in the series continued with the eleventh, at Rongme, where Kongtrul went after transmitting the Shangpa teachings to Tsabtsa Tulku. Kongtrul first practiced in the Dorje Apuk Cave there, after which he transferred to Munang Dorje Drakmar. The queen had sent provisions to support the ceremony. The group of about thirty-five performed Khyentse Wangpo's Hayagrīva liturgy Liberation of All the Arrogant[71] in honor of the place being the site of its origin. The twelfth was at Rongme Chime Karmo Taktsang, using a Mindroling liturgy of Vajrasattva, and the thirteenth was at Pema Shelpuk, using the Amitāyus practice from Seven Profound Cycles. During the thirteenth, his devoted disciple Khen Lama Tashi Wozer returned from a trip to Tibet, bringing Kongtrul statues of the three long-life deities, an appropriate gift for the conclusion of the longevity section of the program.[72]

The thirteen drubchen and feast ceremonies complete, Kongtrul went down the valley to Dzongsar. Here began a flurry of empowerments and transmissions as a dozen dignitaries came through to meet with him and Khyentse Wangpo. Khyentse gave Kongtrul several Nyingma empowerments, such as Nyangrel's Mahākaruṇika: Guide to Beings (a cycle he had expanded with additional revelations) and the Fifth Dalai Lama's Secret Visions, together with instructions on subtle-body practice. The regent of Riwoche, the Taklung Kagyu monastic estate north of Chamdo, came for Nyingma teachings. The Lodro Nyima Tulku of Tranggu Monastery came to Dzongsho for the Treasury of Kagyu Tantra. Terton Sogyel came for Zhikpo Lingpa's Uṣṇīṣavijayā and received Kongtrul's Seven-Line Guru Sādhana as well. Drubwang Tsoknyi came with other lamas of Nangchen to receive unnamed transmissions, and he in turn gave Kongtrul Ratna Lingpa's Enlightened Intent: Innermost Gathering. Dungtrul gave him a Barom Kagyu Cakrasaṃvara. From December 12, 1884, to February 18,

1885,[73] Kongtrul gave the Collected Nyingma Tantras to a large group at Dzongsar, including Khyentse Wangpo, after which he gave the same group all eighteen volumes of Tāranātha's Collected Works, finishing on March 24.[74]

Kongtrul returned to Tsādra on April 19[75] suffering from high blood pressure and exhaustion. Nevertheless, he gave the Kālacakra empowerment to Chokgyur Lingpa's son Tsewang Drakpa, Khardo Jamyang Drakpa, and the Kālacakra practitioners of Pelpung. The Tonpa Jetsuma came, and Kongtrul gave her Longchenpa's Wish-Fulfilling Jewel of the Guru's Unexcelled Innermost Essence. Terton Sogyel was with him; at Pel Deu the two men revealed a series of sādhanas to the eight Indian vidyādharas which were to be part of a cycle of Khyentse's called the United Commands of the Three Roots. Because Khyentse never recovered that cycle, the sādhanas acquired by Terton Sogyel and Kongtrul apparently were never put to paper.[76] Such episodes as this are common in the biographies of treasure revealers—they are glimpses, whispers, hints of ideas that rise like a melody in the minds of the lamas, easily lost if not expanded and properly shaped. That this unretrieved treasure was jointly perceived, or that it was to be amended to the liturgical cycle of yet another lama, is in no way uncommon; just as a melody is fully realized with harmonies and orchestration, a treasure cycle is almost always the work of many hands. In any case, as with so much revelation activity, the events at Pel Deu were probably intended to benefit the site rather than to produce new literature. A treasure revelation, regardless of whether anything is taken away, gives testament to the sanctity of the place of the revelation.[77]

Back at Dzongsar, in July,[78] Kongtrul transmitted Nyingma teachings from the Spoken Word and cycles which he had recently added to the Treasury of Revelations to the Fifth Dzogchen Rinpoche, Terton Sogyel, and the Second Dezhung Rinpoche. At the conclusion of these exchanges, Kongtrul used gold he had collected to construct an enlightenment stūpa at Dzongsho and to initiate the study of logic there among the residents. The Ninth Pawo and other lamas came to participate in a two-week combined drubchen and mendrub ritual using the United Intent of the Gurus.[79]

In 1885 Khyentse Wangpo experienced a series of visions and dreams that Kongtrul found significant. In the first dream, he met King Jah and Saraha. King Jah is said to have received the Mahāyoga Tantras; Saraha was an Indian mahāsiddha who is famous for his songs of enlightenment. Khyentse's visions convinced him that the two were identical, and as Kongtrul counted

King Jah as a previous birth, this meant that Kongtrul had been Saraha as well. The two gave Khyentse a teaching on sexual yoga called Cycle of Four and Forty, which appears to have existed in this vision alone. In December, while bestowing the empowerments and transmissions of Dorje Lingpa's Guru: Union of the Eight Commands, Khyentse was visited in a vision by a noblewoman of Ling named Jamyang Tsultrim Wangmo. She wore exquisite silk clothing and carried a vase of flowers the likes of which Khyentse had never before seen. She told him that they were cut from the practice site of Nāgārjunakoṇḍā, where Nāgārjuna had planted them. The blossoms had wilted, and she instructed Khyentse to use offering water from the practice of Guru: Union of the Eight Commands to revive them. Khyentse did so, at which point the noblewoman departed with the words "Āryadeva is now eight years old." Āryadeva was Nāgārjuna's closest disciple; Khyentse decided that traces of Āryadeva's great work the *Four Hundred Verses* were discernible in Kongtrul's teachings and that Kongtrul was a rebirth of Āryadeva. They therefore added Āryadeva to Melodious Āḍambara Drum, the supplication prayer to Kongtrul's previous lives that Khyentse and the Fourteenth Karmapa had composed some twenty years earlier.[80]

In the midst of these teachings and visions, Kongtrul's niece Rigdzin Dolma passed away. This was the woman whom the treasure revealer Ngawang Rinchen had attempted to take as a consort twenty years earlier, and perhaps he had been successful, as she had given birth to a boy four years later in 1871. In response to Kongtrul's request that he name her child, Khyentse Wangpo declared him to be the rebirth of the thirteenth-century Vajrabhairava master Ga Lotsāwa Namgyel Dorje and accordingly gave him the name Jamyang Namgyel Dorje. Khyentse recommended also that he study Kālacakra. Rigdzin Dolma had first become ill before the birth of her child, possibly with epilepsy; she would fall into seizures from time to time and report premonitory visions.[81] Her health never fully returned, although this did not prevent her from going on pilgrimage to Lhasa in 1879.[82] Kongtrul gave her medical treatment as best he could over the years, and when her condition worsened in 1885, he dedicated two days to peaceful and wrathful deity practices, but this had no effect. He gave her a funeral comparable to that of his mother: he sponsored prayers at the major government monasteries in Lhasa. He had ten lamas perform the transference of consciousness (led by Lama Ngondrub, the vajra master of the retreat center) and sponsored transference rituals from the heads of the major Kagyu monasteries. And he made donations to monasteries. Kongtrul led most of the ceremonies, but he left responsibility for the planning to Rigdzin Dolma's brother Tsering Dondrub.[83]

In his diary Kongtrul praised few individuals, reserving his appreciation for Khyentse Wangpo and members of his family—his foster father, his mother, and his nephew, who now supervised the funeral of his sister. Kongtrul judged his nephew to be generous in his religious offerings, conscientious and judicious in all activities, hardworking and capable, and a valuable attendant who had already served him for many years before the young woman's death as a scribe and in his building projects. The funeral ceremonies stretched over several months, during which time Kongtrul performed the approach for the Uṣṇīṣavijayā practice from Khyentse Wangpo's Heart Drop of the Venerable Goddess of Immortality for his niece's benefit, receiving positive signs. Tsering Dondrub arranged for the construction of his sister's memorial stūpa and its consecration.[84]

On the heels of his niece's death, Kongtrul received news that both Donyon Tulku and the Third Moktsa Tulku had passed away. Their estates requested Kongtrul go there to help with the funerals, but he declined, answering that he was too busy. Then, suddenly, Kongtrul received word that the Tenth Situ had died and that he was needed at Pelpung. His eleven and a half years of exile had come to an end.[85]

# Part Three

# Deaths

# 26

## TRANSMISSION, OLD AGE, AND THE DEATH OF KHYENTSE WANGPO

*Rimay Part Four*

1886–1897

---

Kongtrul learned of the Tenth Situ's passing on January 11, 1886,[1] in a letter from the Wongen incarnation. The young lama insisted that Kongtrul return to Pelpung to participate in the funeral and to take charge of the will. If there was any acknowledgement of Kongtrul's near-total absence from Pelpung over the last eleven and a half years—something along the lines of "all is forgiven and your enemies have been silenced"—Kongtrul makes no mention of it in his diary. He simply wrote that he went to the monastery on receipt of the letter.[2] Kongtrul returned to Pelpung a seventy-three-year-old man. He was then a senior lama of the Karma Kagyu tradition. The Fifteenth Karmapa, who would arrive the next year to receive teachings, was just a teenager of fifteen. The Ninth Pawo was probably around thirty years old—he would die in 1911. The Tenth Tsurpu Gyeltsab was ten. The great Ninth Drukchen, who was a teacher to so many Karma Kagyu masters, had passed away in 1883 at the age of sixty. Due to accusations of treason, there was a hundred-year gap between the death of the Tenth Zhamar in 1792 and the birth of the Eleventh in 1892, and so Kongtrul never met a Zhamar. Pelpung's other prominent incarnations had both predeceased the Tenth Situ: the Wongen Tulku who was Kongtrul's teacher had died in 1843, and his reincarnation would have been only about forty. Both Dabzang and Wontrul's reincarnations could only have been about ten years old. Kongtrul was needed at Pelpung for more than the funeral: the next generation of Karma Kagyu leadership, including the Fifteenth Karmapa, needed to be trained.

The Tenth Situ had never risen to the challenges of the office, neglecting the financial needs of the community and failing to prevent one of its greatest teachers from being driven away. It is hard to imagine that Kongtrul shed any tears over the young man. Kongtrul wrote very little about the funeral services for the Tenth Situ—only that "we spent about three days performing a commemoration ritual in front of the corpse" and reporting that the remains were cremated in the traditional manner. Otherwise he was occupied with an accounting of the Situ estate's possessions, a necessary step in determining how elaborate the funeral and reliquary could be.[3] There was, unfortunately, not much left in the coffers. The Tenth Situ was not a teacher, and without leading grand rituals or touring the region to give empowerments and transmissions he would not have been in a position to collect donations. The estate petitioned the aristocratic Garje family for financial support and sent out a group to raise funds. Over the next year, Kongtrul would occasionally stop over at the Situ residence for rituals dedicated to the promotion of the community, never more than a few days at a time. The reliquary was consecrated in May 1889.[4]

Kongtrul was immediately pressed into negotiating the release of the rebirth of his colleague Wontrul, who was born as the son of the Ninth Pawo. Money had to be raised to pay the local and possibly Tibetan government for the privilege of giving him the title. Kongtrul had to arrange for a delegation to travel to Nangchen—and probably Karma Gon, where the Pawo and his son were then staying—to pay the fees and bring the child to Pelpung. The child arrived in July, and Kongtrul enthroned him in an elaborate ceremony. The Pawo declined to leave his son in Kham, however, opting to raise and educate the boy himself at his own seat, Nenang Monastery near Tsurpu, in central Tibet. The Pawo promised to send Wontrul back to Pelpung once he had become an adult, but he apparently allowed him to travel back and forth in the meantime, as Wontrul returned to Pelpung in 1887 with the Fifteenth Karmapa.[5]

The end of Kongtrul's exile did not result in his unreserved embrace of—or by—the community. Between the departure of the Ninth Pawo through to the end of the Fire Dog Year seven months later, Kongtrul had no duties at Pelpung, and he spent his time elsewhere. Following the funeral ceremonies, Kongtrul gave a series of Kagyu and Nyingma transmissions to young Kagyu and Nyingma incarnations, but he did so at Dzongsar, not at Pelpung. He went there in early 1886[6] to give the Five Maṇḍalas of the Karma Kagyu Oral Lineage to Khyentse Wangpo, the Rolpai Dorje incarnation from Zurmang, and others. A tulku from Dzogon Monastery in Minyak (a Sakya monastery) came for the nine-deity Jinasāgara maṇḍala in the Karma Kagyu tradition as well as the Lightning Garland of Protective Deities: Peaceful Garland, Wrathful Garland. To Lhaksam Tenpai Gyeltsen, his longtime grammar student, Kongtrul taught his commentaries on the *Hevajra Tantra, Uttaratantra,* and *Profound Inner Principles.* While at Dzongsar, Kongtrul took the opportunity to receive the transmission for five of Mipam Gyatso's compositions, including his two-volume Kālacakra commentary and his famous commentary on the ninth chapter of the *Bodhicaryāvatāra.* Kongtrul then gave a Mahāmudrā transmission at Tsādra to Wongen and a tulku from Zurmang, who joined with about fifty other monks for ten days of rituals.[7]

Kongtrul went next to Alo Peljor for a massive Vajrāmṛta drubchen ritual that Tashi Wozer had organized. He gave his Seven-Line Guru Sādhana to Lama Choying of Gegyel Monastery and to the previous Dabzang Tulku's brother, whose name was Tendzin Namgyel. In October[8] he was at Dzongsho, where he had light teaching requests and was able to focus for three months on editing for publication three of his collections: the Treasury of Revelations, the Treasury of Kagyu Tantra, and the Treasury of Instructions. In January 1887 he taught again at Dzongsar, giving Union of All Rare and Precious Jewels to the twenty-year-old Third Dodrubchen, Jigme Tenpai Nyima, and *Stages of the Path of the Wisdom Essence* to the Sixth Khamtrul incarnation.[9]

It was during this time that Kongtrul wrote his *One Hundred Treasure Revealers* for the Treasury of Revelations. As one would expect, in his diary he wrote that he embarked on the project only after consulting with Khyentse Wangpo. Kongtrul's intention was to include a biography for every treasure revealer whose work he included in the Treasury of Revelations. Khyentse's help would be necessary, as he had by then revealed many treasure cycles that he claimed were "rediscovered." In this peculiar subset of revelations, a scripture is said to have been revealed and reconcealed by the initial master and then ultimately recovered by Khyentse Wangpo. The original revealers were, for the most part, previously unknown, and Kongtrul would need his friend to tell him the stories of their lives. In his biography of Khyentse, Kongtrul gave titles for some thirty credited "rediscovered treasures" which name twenty-three original revealers, all of whom are given entries in the *One Hundred Treasure Revealers.* The work is almost five hundred pages of Tibetan text, but the biographies are mostly sketches of the treasure revealers' lives (most of them running only about two pages of Tibetan script) and are merely reports on the discovery of the texts included in the Treasury. Chokling warranted sixteen pages, and Khyentse Wangpo twenty-two. Kongtrul was satisfied with his work, declaring it was superior to five or six unnamed collections of biographies of the treasure revealers.[10]

On February 3, 1887,[11] Kongtrul accompanied a welcoming party to a large meadow near Pelpung where the Fifteenth Karmapa and his entourage were camped. The air was warm and the ground still unfrozen, the skies clear. The following day they escorted the Karmapa to Pelpung, and on the 5th, in the Situ residence, Kongtrul offered the Karmapa a purification ritual and an authorization for White Tārā as a means of establishing a formal relationship. Kongtrul immediately went up to his hermitage in order to prepare personally for the tremendous amount of work facing him in the year ahead: the transmission of the entire corpus of teachings and practices of the Karma Kagyu tradition—as well as various Nyingma teachings—to the teenaged Karmapa. He did this with Vajrakīla, Vajrabhairava, and Khyentse's "rediscovered treasure" called Combined Practice of the Three Roots.[12] Kongtrul tasked six lamas from Dzamtang and dozens of others at Dzongsho to join in the recitations.[13]

The Karmapa went up to Tsādra in the first week of March 1887[14] with his sizable retinue, settling in for a two-month stay. Kongtrul began with the basics, teaching Gampopa's *Jewel Ornament of Liberation* (which surveys the entire Buddhist path from a Kagyu perspective) and worked his way through to the Treasury of Kagyu Tantra. The transmission attracted so many additional supplicants—Dabzang came up, the Khamtrul and Dzogon Jedrung, among many others—that the hermitage ran out of space, and they were forced to end the ceremonies. The group moved down to Pelpung at the end of April[15] and spent several days in front of the newly completed reliquary of the Tenth Situ, consecrating it with prayers to the bodhisattvas. As part of the ceremony, Kongtrul gave the bodhisattva vows to the Karmapa and a crowd of about a hundred other monks. The monastery's summer retreat began, with the Karmapa in attendance. Kongtrul initiated the program with a transmission of the opening sections of the Treasury of Instructions. This required a series of empowerments, culminating with elaborate Kālacakra empowerments, the most esoteric of which Kongtrul gave to the Karmapa in private on May 9, 1887.[16] Starting on May 16,[17] they sealed boundaries and performed drubchen and mendrub rituals from the Gathering of Sugatas, completing the ceremonies on May 27.[18] Following additional grand ceremonies, on May 29[19] Kongtrul excused himself and returned to Tsādra for a week's rest. In early June[20] he returned to begin two months of transmissions of the remainder of the Treasury of Instructions together with all the related empowerments.[21]

Kongtrul, the Karmapa, and the Karmapa's entourage then all moved to Dzongsho; the Karmapa was on his way to Litang and was traveling with an escort that included family members of the Litang chieftain. Kongtrul taught them all, and after they left he spent time writing liturgies. He went to Dzongsar in early December 1887.[22] Khyentse was not well, but he nevertheless gave Kongtrul more than a dozen transmissions of treasure cycles which Kongtrul had likely requested for inclusion in the Treasury of Revelations, such as Khyentse's and Chokling's Heart Essence of the Three Classes, a section of the Three Sections of Dzogchen. Khyentse ended their time together with rituals to ensure that the upcoming transmission of the Treasury of Revelations would be a success. Kongtrul then returned to Tsādra to perform his annual year-end Kīla rites. The seventh retreat was finishing its program, and Kongtrul gave the exiting group several needed empowerments as well as the Madhyamaka bodhisattva vows. It would be a full year before Kongtrul installed the eighth group of retreatants.[23]

The Karmapa had by then returned from Litang and had moved into the summer retreat residence in preparation for the transmission of the Treasury of Revelations. Kongtrul explained in his diary that the transmission necessarily begins with a drubchen ritual and an empowerment for an Eight Commands liturgy. The Karmapa had already received Nyangrel's Gathering of Sugatas at the beginning of the previous year's Treasury of Instructions transmission, so he chose Guru Chowang's Perfection of Secrets. Kongtrul closed the retreat boundary on March 12, 1888.[24] The transmission lasted five months, with several breaks, ending August 19.[25] This time Kongtrul had expert help; Lama Tashi Wozer read the texts for the transmission save for during two days of transmissions for cycles he had not yet received. Kongtrul was too old now to read aloud for five months straight. They were interrupted twice by a rare, repeating astrological event that necessitated community rituals: the conjunction of the star Delta Cancri—which the Tibetans call "Victor," one of the twenty-eight lunar mansions—and the planet Jupiter, first on April 21[26] and again on May 17.[27] During the first conjunction, Kongtrul spent half a day explaining the four opening chapters of the Treasury of Knowledge. After the second, Kongtrul went to Derge to send off members of the Derge royal family who were going to Tibet on pilgrimage with longevity rites. On his return the participants moved to Pelpung's Lhasar Temple for more comfortable accommodations.

At the conclusion of the transmission, the Karmapa offered Kongtrul feast offerings, a longevity service, and many gifts. The Karmapa then moved his encampment to Gato.[28]

Over the winter of 1888–1889, Kongtrul briefly visited both his hermitages and then went to Dzongsar to take Sky Teaching transmissions from Gyatrul Rinpoche, the abbot of Pelyul Monastery and Kongtrul's longtime disciple and friend. In exchange Kongtrul offered his Seven-Line Guru Sādhana and a handful of Karma Kagyu and Jonang transmissions. His obligations to the Fifteenth Karmapa were complete, and the two were now able to turn their attention to the issue of finding the Eleventh Situ. Kongtrul does not explain the process, but it apparently coincided with the Karmapa's trip to Litang. According to legend, the Karmapa had a vision in which he saw the child's village, his house, and guard dog tied to a tree outside. He likely selected the boy during the previous year's trip. In June a delegation of lamas and administrators from Pelpung traveled there to bring the two-year-old child to the monastery. The Karmapa planned to leave after greeting the new Situ incarnation, so while they waited for his arrival Kongtrul made his farewells. In the extravagant fashion of Tibetan lamas, this took the form of two-week-long drubchen and mendrub rituals of United Intent of the Gurus and various minor related practices, attended by the Karmapa's entire retinue. At the conclusion, Kongtrul presented the Karmapa with extensive material gifts: a statue of Tārā said to have been naturally arisen, nine tael of silver, one hundred eight bricks of tea, and more than three hundred head of domesticated animals. Kongtrul's personal wealth at this point was obviously quite substantial. He controlled multiple parcels of land near Pelpung and Dzongsar and collected donations from pilgrims and supplicants at two thriving hermitages. The two lamas also exchanged further empowerments to mark their parting; Kongtrul gave the Karmapa a Shangpa initiation and the Great Dog from the Seven Profound Cycles. Kongtrul requested a guru sādhana and the transmission for *Stainless Moonlight*, the verse account of the previous Karmapas' lives that the young Karmapa had composed, as well as a protective deity rite.[29]

When the Eleventh Situ arrived, the Karmapa and Kongtrul together performed his tonsure and enthronement ceremony, which unlike that of the Tenth is not described in the diary. The five-year-old Tenth Drukchen had at some point come to the monastery, and he received an ablution and longevity rituals alongside the new Situ. The Karmapa departed for Tibet, and Kongtrul returned to Tsādra to continue giving empowerments to the new group of retreatants. He spent several months writing the table of contents to the Treasury of Revelations, splitting his time between Tsādra and Dzongsho.[30]

Kongtrul devoted the majority of the early 1890s to the completion and transmission of his major collections. He had printings from the blocks of the Treasury of Revelations to edit—even after the blocks had been carved, small changes were still sometimes possible; if large changes were necessary, a new block would have to be made. Immediately after the Karmapa left, Kongtrul went to Dzongsho to give the most recent additions to the Treasury of Revelations to Gyatrul Rinpoche, after which he gave the Treasury of Instructions transmission, over two months, to a noblewoman of the Nak branch of the Khyungpo clan and Mahāmudrā transmissions to Tsabtsa Tulku and the retreatants there.[31] Toward the end of 1890 he wrote liturgies for the Treasury of Revelations at Dzongsho,[32] and in early 1891 he gave the Treasury of Kagyu Tantra at Tsādra to the Seventh Riwoche Jedrung, Jampa Jungne, a process that took a month and a half.[33] He was editing and composing texts for the Treasury of Instructions through to 1893, when he finally declared this and the other collections complete. In the late autumn of 1893, he wrote in his diary, "The main work of my life—the Five Treasuries, together with tables of content and lineage records—was complete. Aside from a few minor texts, nothing remained to be done, and as the blocks for these were close to completion I no longer had any worries."[34] If we can take this comment to be accurate, Kongtrul's Collected Works had already been assembled and was counted as the fifth treasury.

In between these transmissions, Kongtrul gave a wide range of other cycles from the Nyingma, Kagyu, and Jonang traditions, as well as for his own commentaries. In October 1891,[35] at Dzongsho, he gave United Intent of the Gurus to the Second Dzarka Tulku, Kunzang Namgyel, the Third Katok Situ, and others, and he gave the *Uttaratantra*, *Profound Inner Principles*, and the Heart Essence of Timeless Awareness to a retreat graduate named Tsepak.[36] He gave the Collected Nyingma Tantras at Dzongsar in the summer of 1892 to the Fourth Zhechen Gyeltsab and others.[37] As he commented in his diary in the summer of 1891, people were gathering from every direction to receive transmissions from him.[38]

While in Derge the Fifteenth Karmapa went to Dzongsar for transmissions from Jamyang Khyentse Wangpo only once, just before he left the region. Khyentse was then sixty-nine years old, and his health had been failing for many years. Back in early 1868 he had fallen ill with an affliction in his hands and feet—possibly some form of edema—and so was unable to attend that year's inaugural transmission of the Treasury of Revelations.[39] It would appear that from then on Khyentse did not leave his residence, remaining in his rooms for the last twenty-five years of his life. Kongtrul, of course, visited often, as did scores of other lamas in search of transmissions. Over the years, as the few lamas who could match their intellectual curiosity and capacity passed away, Kongtrul and Khyentse increasingly relied on each other for more than assistance in the production and publishing of scriptures. Kongtrul, who in several diary entries bemoaned his isolation and the absence of equals, also reported, in 1878, that Khyentse felt much the same:

> Khyentse Wangpo had studied with two hundred lamas in Kham and Tibet, four of whom he considered his root teachers. He told me, "If they were alive, I would have liked to have brought to them my religious realizations, but three have passed away. Now only you are left, and I have realizations I must impart to you." He then summarized his experiences in the completion stage practices, both conceptual and nonconceptual.[40]

Kongtrul complemented his friend with the assertion that he had attained the highest realization as it is explained in the scriptures:

> Through his subtle-body practice he has purified his central channel and attained mastery over the channels, winds, and tikles. He attained the realization of [the third stage] of Mahāmudrā, the "single taste," and then he perfected the Dzogchen teaching of awareness of "undifferentiated appearances."

Kongtrul, writing that he himself "had no experiences or realizations that could compare" to Khyentse's, nevertheless spoke to his friend about his own understanding. He did not record what he said to Khyentse, only that Khyentse confirmed that Kongtrul had attained the second Dzogchen vision, the "culmination of awareness," through his practice of trekchod.[41]

In several instances in his diary, Kongtrul reported Khyentse's delight at his visits, the sole individual who is allowed an emotional response to Kongtrul's presence. It mattered to Kongtrul that Khyentse was glad to see him, that his friend reciprocated so consistently Kongtrul's own affection.

Khyentse was present in almost every major event of Kongtrul's life; the pleasure the two friends took in being together must have made the challenges lighter and the projects more rewarding. Khyentse encouraged Kongtrul's good ideas, he contributed to—and in more ways than one made possible—the contents of his collections. As Kongtrul admitted in his diary, whenever he wished to include in a collection a text for which the teaching lineage had been broken, he could ask Khyentse to undertake a visionary experience to revive the line. Khyentse's commonly accepted ability to converse with deities and saints enabled him to receive a transmission directly from the source, even if that source had passed away hundreds of years earlier. Or, as Kongtrul wrote, "In cases where the texts for old treasures are extant but the line of empowerment and transmission is broken, I needed only to petition [Khyentse], and Guru Rinpoche himself would appear in the guise of the treasure revealer and bestow the transmission directly."[42]

Kongtrul recorded several instances of this service, such as in 1875 when he asked Khyentse to revive the Mamo Gangshar cycle,[43] and again in 1892 during their last visit when he asked for the revival of the Zhije initial and intermediate empowerments.[44] Khyentse, Kongtrul affirmed, could draw out an entire liturgical cycle from just a fragment of a text, adding needed ritual manuals for cycles that Kongtrul wished to include in the Treasury of Revelations. In almost all of Kongtrul's work, Khyentse Wangpo was quite literally indispensable.

Khyentse had been ill for years, and Kongtrul had done what he could, offering all sorts of rituals to protect him from harm and increase his well-being. His efforts were appreciated, as suggested by a dream Khyentse had in 1875 during a Vajrakīla transmission Kongtrul was performing: In a black nomad tent, Khyentse's mother, as she stoked a meager fire, berated him for his weaknesses and for allowing them to live in such conditions, while outside brigands shouted and waved knives. Khyentse, frightened, saw Kongtrul in the back of the tent on a throne loudly proclaiming the Vajrakīla mantra, at which point the men outside fled in terror, to Khyentse's relief.[45] But although Kongtrul could protect his friend in dreams, by the early 1890s it became increasingly clear that Khyentse Wangpo was failing. At the end of 1889, while Kongtrul stopped at Dzongsar on his way home from Dzongsho, in addition to several days' worth of transmission, Khyentse gave Kongtrul an extravagant gift, a painting of Uṣṇīṣavijayā and her thirteen-deity retinue from his Heart Drop of the Venerable Goddess of Immortality revelation. Khyentse also gave him two rather tender presents—a bell (the sort a lama holds during tantric practice) and a monk shawl.[46] Perhaps these were part of the initiation ceremony, but one can easily imagine the old man, knowing his death was approaching, picking up treasured objects close at hand and giving them to a dear friend who had stopped by to visit.

Khyentse admitted all visitors even as his health declined over 1889 and 1890. In fact, according to Kongtrul, so many people were flocking to Dzongsar that Khyentse had to stop his treasure production. But he was unable to perform many empowerments, and he occasionally tasked Kongtrul with attending to his visitors' requests. The last episode of multiple transmissions Khyentse appears to have exchanged with a visitor was in late July 1890, when the Second Dzarka Tulku came and gave Khyentse and Kongtrul half a dozen treasure cycles of Katok masters, and Khyentse reciprocated with works by Dudul Dorje and the newly compiled Collected Works of Zhechen Wontrul. The Dzarka remained for a time, receiving additional transmissions from Kongtrul at Dzongsho in the fall of 1891, but there were no more grand transmission events at Dzongsar. Khyentse was finished teaching. Kongtrul would go to Dzongsar largely to "venerate him and engage in conversation."[47]

In 1891 the ritual focus surrounding Khyentse Wangpo shifted from giving and receiving empowerments to offering rituals to lengthen his life and support his health. In March[48] Kongtrul "began to focus on the well-being of my precious lord lama." He gathered twenty students at Tsādra and performed a *drubcho* rite of White Tārā over several days and then spent a few more days on a rite to the three long-life deities, of which White Tārā was one. A drubcho is a public sādhana rite that is smaller and more concise than a drubchen ritual and which does not require twenty-four-hour recitations. The following month a group of about thirty people performed a drubchen ritual from Heart Drop of the Venerable Goddess of Immortality. Kongtrul sent his grandnephew Jamyang Namgyel Dorje to Dzongsar to perform additional rites there. He sent him with gifts, representations of the Buddha's body, speech, and mind, robes, and three tael of Chinese silver. Kongtrul commented that "at least with the material goods I could feel some satisfaction," an admission of sorts that he did not have high hopes from his rituals, despite reporting positive signs. After a month and a half teaching the Riwoche Jedrung, Kongtrul went to Dzongsar himself in the late summer. He stayed only long enough to successfully urge Khyentse to restore the transmission line for Zhije empowerments and to receive the instructions of Rongton Sheja Kunrik's tradition of Prajñāpāramitā exegesis before being called to Derge. Kongtrul was himself exhausted and, suffering from diarrhea, needed several days rest before going to Dzongsho in August for several months of teaching. In December,[49] back at Dzongsar, he found Khyentse had declined further. He performed a purification ritual called Dispelling All Contamination of Broken Samaya and responded to requests from supplicants who had come to see the failing master. Khyentse seems to have known that this would be their last meeting. He put into Kongtrul's hands nine "very special" representations of the Buddha's body, speech, and mind which were to be inserted in a reliquary stūpa—perhaps his own—and instructions on how to teach Situ, Dabzang, Wontrul, and the other tulkus at Pelpung. Kongtrul returned to Tsādra for his customary year-end Vajrakīla rituals, and he began the Water Dragon Year teaching the young tulkus of Pelpung and retreatants at both the monastery and Tsādra.[50]

Kongtrul heard from Dzongsar in early March 1892[51] that Khyentse Wangpo's status was stable. Khyentse wrote to him "You have been performing rituals to promote my well-being, and for the moment there is no danger. I should be improved by the twentieth of the second month." This proved not to be the case—if Kongtrul's efforts had previously succeeded in forestalling Khyentse's death, their efficacy was now exhausted. Very soon afterwards Kongtrul received a letter informing him that Khyentse had passed away on the morning of March 19.[52] Kongtrul immediately rode over the pass to Dzongsar, as fast as he was able to move, to make his farewells and prepare the body for cremation.[53]

On the morning of March 22[54] Kongtrul prayed to Khyentse to "arise again from the sky-like clear light"—the primordial state of pristine awareness that enlightened beings' consciousnesses inhabit—praying and supplicating until he felt some comfort. He washed Khyentse Wangpo's remains and laid symbols and amulets at key locations pertaining to the subtle body according to both Nyingma and later traditions. For five days he performed a Vajrasattva and a related guru ritual, five days in which to mourn privately before the public rituals commenced. Tartse Khenpo joined for the guru rites on the fourth day, March 25,[55] and he and Kongtrul acknowledged each other's grief by exchanging transmissions. Khyentse had been Kongtrul's primary emotional contact since the Ninth Situ had passed away. He had been Kongtrul's guru, friend, and partner in both writing and rituals. His friendship with Khyentse was a continual practice of guru yoga—Kongtrul's devotion to the enlightened qualities of Khyentse, an emotion that he cultivated in order to increase his love for the deities Khyentse embodied. It was no surprise that in Kongtrul's dreams Khyentse repeatedly took the form of the buddhas.[56]

They ended their supplication rituals on March 27[57] and released both the invited deities and the corpse. The cremation began the next day, March 28.[58] Kongtrul, Tartse Khenpo, Loter Wangpo, and the monastery's chant master each presided over a separate station at the four corners of the funeral pyre. For three days they stayed at the cremation, chanting and making offerings as the fire died down and the ashes cooled. Until the end of the third week of the seven-week mourning period, they performed the mending rite of United Intent of the Gurus, the drubcho rite of Jinasāgara, and the supplication of the Trilogy of the Guru's Two Doctrines, the second and third being Khyentse's own treasures.[59]

The rites at Dzongsar were sponsored by Khyentse's brother, Kelzang Dorje, who was steward of the monastery. Kongtrul records that Kelzang Dorje also provided ten significant objects to place inside the reliquary. Kongtrul himself offered two tael of Chinese silver to the monastery's services and an additional five Tibetan measures of silver to Khyentse's disciples personally to support their efforts. He also gave them the empowerment for the Mahāyoga tantra Sarvabuddha Samayoga and gave the three empowerments of the Heart Drop of the Venerable Goddess of Immortality to Tartse Khenpo and his disciples Loter Wangpo and the Tartse Zhabdrung.[60]

Kongtrul returned to Tsādra to continue his rituals, marking each seven-day period and ending the mourning period with a drubcho rite of the Padmavajra and a maṇḍala offering of the one hundred eight siddhas. Kongtrul had been building a stūpa at Pelpung prior to Khyentse's death, to be placed next to the reliquary of the Ninth Situ, although his motivation for this is not clear in his diary. For whatever purpose it was initially intended, it was repurposed as Khyentse's memorial. In May 1892[61] he set a group of ten people to work for about a month and a half writing prayers and mantras and rolling them tightly, and he then gathered his disciples and those of Khyentse Wangpo to install the contents and consecrate it in the early summer. The Pelpung steward, Jamyang Gelek, agreed to use monastic funds to pay for it, despite Khyentse Wangpo not being a Pelpung lama. Wongen, Wontrul, Tashi Wozer, and Lodro Zangpo, a close disciple of Khyentse's, all participated in the consecration. Wontrul had returned from Tibet at the beginning of 1892.[62]

Khyentse's death prevented Kongtrul from scaling back his own ritual activities, as he was no longer able to share with him the responsibility of training the next generation of lamas. And he continued to be tasked with rituals for the Derge court. Following the consecration of the stūpa at Pelpung, Kongtrul and a contingent of about eighty monks spent close to a month on a drubchen ritual of the Gathering of Sugatas and a mendrub ritual from Khyentse Wangpo's Vajrāmṛta cycle for the Derge queen. He taught Pelpung's young lamas at Tsādra, and with payments for the funeral services he employed other monks to continue commemorative rites to Khyentse Wangpo. He went to Dzongsho in August 1892[63] to transmit the Collected Nyingma Tantras to a host of prominent incarnations, including the Dzarka Tulku and Jamyang Tulku from Katok and the Zhechen Gyeltsab. This finishing in October, he then gave teachings on Mahāmudrā and empowerments to the Second Dezhung Rinpoche and gave Taksham Nuden Dorje's treasures to the Third Ripa Tulku. The commemorative rites continued there simultaneously, with a fresh infusion of funding from Pelyul Monastery. Kongtrul did his best to fill the void at Dzongsar, stopping there on his way home to teach Kālacakra to Mipam Gyatso and Norbu Tendzin, a close disciple of Khyentse's. Kongtrul accepted certain duties such as the consecration of new temple buildings. The Fifth Dzogchen Tulku returned from a Tibet trip and came for empowerments. And the ninth retreat began at Tsādra, requiring Kongtrul to bestow empowerments and instructions.[64]

In the midst of his mourning for Khyentse Wangpo, Kongtrul learned of more deaths. The queen of Derge, Gyatrul Rinpoche, and Dechen Lingpa all passed away. Kongtrul lost a sponsor, a cherished disciple, and a man who, despite having never quite risen to the level of a valued peer, had still been Kongtrul's colleague in his later treasure activities. Hardest of all, on December 17, 1892,[65] not even a year after his greatest and closest friend passed away, Kongtrul's beloved nephew Jamyang Namgyel Dorje died. This was the son of Rigdzin Dolma. He had fallen ill with a violent chest infection and declined rapidly, despite Kongtrul's ritual efforts. As he had with his mother and niece following their deaths, Kongtrul put all his attention to the young man's funeral. He recited the prayers and mantras and prepared the body. For three days the body remained in meditation posture with the appearance of vitality. At the moment of the transfer of consciousness, the ritual having been performed by a vajra master named Lama Dondrub, the body made the sound "yik," blood flowed out of the nostril, and its luster faded. These are all considered signs of a successful transfer of consciousness.[66]

Every seven days for the next seven weeks, Kongtrul performed the funeral rituals, inviting the Fifth Dzogchen Tulku, Loter Wangpo, Wongen, Wontrul, and others to join him. He made offerings to lamas "without sectarian considerations," although these were mainly directed to the hierarchs of the Karma and Drukpa Kagyu traditions. He made additional offerings to the three main government monasteries in Lhasa and to multiple monasteries in Kham to sponsor rituals for the deceased. The day following the cremation there was a beautiful white light in the clear morning sky and rainbows in the afternoon clouds. Kongtrul dreamed of the young man, healthy and strong, being called to the north, and he had a vision of a text in which was written a passage about the goddess Khecarī giving Jamyang Namgyel Dorje a pill and reporting that his consciousness had been liberated. These offered Kongtrul some comfort.[67]

Kongtrul bemoaned the death of his nephew in both personal terms and in relation to the world—the young man had potential, Kongtrul believed, to be a great lama, having trained and studied and meditated extensively. Kongtrul was bitter, angrily blaming the Pelpung community for the loss. He wrote, "There was reason to hope that he would make something of himself and be of benefit to the world, yet this monastery has long been the residence of evil forces, and now, due to these forces continuing on, whatever good anyone tries to accomplish for oneself or others is obstructed."[68]

Kongtrul was back at Pelpung, he was training the community's leaders, but he continued to resent his treatment, never forgiving the slander and mistreatment. He never left Pelpung and Tsādra again. He accepted commissions from the government and patrons to perform rituals, no doubt relying on his disciples to read the transmissions, carry the ritual implements, and receive the offerings, but he performed these at his home. More and more Kongtrul would have sat quietly on a high throne as his disciples moved around the room. Students at Zhechen and Dzogchen Monasteries requested his presence, but he declined both, apologizing that he was simply too old to travel there. On April 7, 1893,[69] a full year since his friend died, Kongtrul arranged a commemoration rite for Khyentse Wangpo.[70]

Two months later, as Kongtrul was giving the transmission of seven volumes of his own writings to the young lamas of Pelpung and his close disciples Tashi Wozer and Tashi Chopel, Kelzang Dorje wrote from Dzong-sar requesting that Kongtrul compose a biography of his brother Khyentse Wangpo.[71] Kongtrul did not need persuading. Writing had always been for Kongtrul a means of confronting and making peace with his world. On going into retreat at age thirty, anxious about surviving a dangerous year and establishing his place in a somewhat unwelcoming community, he had composed a biographical statement to affirm his values and stake his claim to Tsādra. Conscious of treasure literature circulating with few institutional or material supports and anxious that a corpus of the written word of the Buddha could be lost, Kongtrul wrote hundreds of new liturgies and expended enormous effort to print and distribute the works. He recorded his own activities, he composed a lengthy description and inventory of his beloved hermitage and other places, and he wrote multiple manuals for any activity he felt worth pursuing. His commemorative rituals were no doubt helpful in coming to terms with Khyentse's absence, but writing a biography would allow him to keep Khyentse close at hand and would ensure that the world would know his dear friend as Kongtrul wanted him to be remembered.

Kongtrul wrote the biography over several months. He described the process, defending his choices and the lack of substantial detail:

> I wrote the hagiography of my precious omniscient lama during the breaks in my practice. Scattering verses through the text would just be the conceit of a poet and would have no real value one way or another. Someone like myself is incapable of expressing the actual story of his life—vast and inconceivable as it was. Yet it is of real importance to do so, with as much detail as possible, if only from the point of view of what I myself witnessed. Khyentse left no diary or any such record of his activities in any given year, nor are there any attendants who have clear knowledge of his life. I based the biography on Khyentse's own verse autobiography, supplementing this with what I have learned from others without embellishing or minimizing anything. The circumstances were positive: people who had received empowerments and transmissions from Khyentse sent gifts and performed longevity rites for me. And as I was writing, Dragang Won Lama came and gave me a fine sitting mat with crossed vajras on it.[72]

Kongtrul named the work *Fabulous Grove of Uḍumbara Flowers: The Abbreviated Life Story of the Noble and Omniscient Jamyang Khyentse Wangpo Kunga Tenpai Gyeltsen.*

The biography, written without the benefit of a diary or any historical records on which to base his narrative, reads like a standard Tibetan hagiography. It is divided into the three customary sections of inner, outer, and secret, covering the general outline of his life, his religious training, and his meditative experiences, respectively, with a traditional opening section of verse praising Khyentse and then naming his previous incarnations. The outer biography is divided into eight sections covering prophecies, birth, entrance into the religious life, training, practice, teaching, virtuous activity, and death. The section on his training is by far the longest; Kongtrul asserts that Khyentse studied with one hundred fifty teachers from all Tibetan Buddhist traditions, and although the Sakya, Geluk, Nyingma, and Kagyu are highlighted and discussed at length, Kongtrul also includes mention of the remaining four of the eight chariots (Shangpa Kagyu, Zhije, Kālacakra, and Bodong). Bon is curiously absent in this section and all others, despite it being well known that Khyentse engaged with Bon teachings. The inner biography repeats some of this information, also dividing the teachings he received according to the framework of the eight chariots.

The secret biography, covering Khyentse's meditative and mystical experiences, utilizes the framework of the "seven descents" which Khyentse himself appears to have developed for his undated biography of Chokgyur Lingpa. Prior to Khyentse's formulation, the term "seven descents" referred to specific transmissions of the Nyingma tantras to Tibet by historical and semihistorical people, not modes of transmission. Khyentse's seven descents adapted the familiar Nyingma triad of spoken word, treasure revelation, and pure vision teachings and divided them into seven: spoken word, earth treasure, mind treasure, rediscovered treasure, pure vision, recollected teachings, and hearing lineage.[73]

The book overflows with Kongtrul's adoration of Khyentse, with ample praise for his erudition, ecumenicalism, and humility. But there is very little information about Khyentse Wangpo the person. Instead, there are mythical explanations for conditions only barely described. For example, Kongtrul ascribes the illness that plagued Khyentse's later decades to karma from a previous life; it seems he was once a bull and gored a wicked king in order to prevent him from persecuting Buddhist communities. The book is a catalog of Khyentse's activities and revelations, with the focus on the product rather than the process. The effect is that rather than being a biography as the genre is understood in the West, the book is more akin to an essay advocating the ecumenical approach so dear to Kongtrul. Khyentse's ecumenicalism is on display in the list of past lives, in the lengthy section on teachings in the outer biography, and in the repeated use of the eight chariots schema. Kongtrul praised Khyentse for his freedom from sectarian bias and for his ability to engage with multiple traditions without mixing them. It is a teaching, as hagiographies are meant to be, but it is a particular vision of "liberation story"—the meaning of the Tibetan term for hagiography. Here the content of the enlightenment is nothing other than ecumenicalism.[74]

For Kongtrul, Khyentse's ecumenicalism was an indication that Khyentse was a being with a superior understanding, a man able to see further and wider. Khyentse's ecumenical approach to religious traditions revealed a freedom from the saṃsāric limitations of "mine" and "yours." This is what Kongtrul meant in both his diary and the biography by referring to Khyentse as "omniscient." It is not an unusual compliment for a religious teacher, effectively drawing a comparison between the subject and the Buddha. Yet in most instances the recipient of the praise is a person learned in a single tradition, a master of a practice that has brought him to enlightenment—the freedom from extremes of existence and nonexistence, self and other. How, one might wonder, does one accomplish that nonduality when one is committed to a philosophical and institutional framework fixed in self and other—in which view, tradition, practice, and so forth, are reinforced through sectarianism? What sort of nondualism asserts that one's own path is true but that others are false? Similar to a Mahāyāna critique of early Buddhist striving for individual liberation, one might argue that the terms of the endeavor betray the goal.

Kongtrul and Khyentse came from two different religious traditions— Kongtrul was Karma Kagyu and Khyentse was Sakya. They were committed to their lineages and, in fact, do not seem to have been especially drawn to each other's primary teachings; Kongtrul evinced little personal involvement in Sakya Lamdre, and Khyentse did not appear to have practiced Kagyu Mahāmudrā. They met elsewhere—primarily in the treasure literature of Dzogchen—and they shared a commitment to valuing all the Buddha's teachings as equally valid, paired with an insatiable curiosity. Their paths were different but each encompassed the full spectrum of what was available, and they recognized in that difference the freedom from sectarianism.

Nonduality does not erase self and other. It surmounts the separation between them. Buddhists teach a doctrine of two truths—the ultimate truth of nonduality and emptiness, and the relative truth of difference and identities. The two truths are concurrent, two sides of the same coin so to speak. All phenomena—people, traditions, monasteries—exist as they are perceived and experienced. Yet all these things are in fact transitory, fabricated, and ultimately illusory, like the world drawn on water. Compassion and love operate in the relative sphere; they lead to a dissolution of self, but they require difference—a lover and a beloved. Love and compassion are said to be the sole motivation of all activities of buddhas and bodhisattvas. They act knowing that ultimately there is no actor or recipient of action; there is no real separation between friends. Khyentse was, for Kongtrul, all-knowing because he was free from the limitations of religious bias—his enlightenment was not a product of a single teaching but an effect of embracing all the teachings of the Buddha without attachment to self and other. Kongtrul loved him for this reason. Khyentse was, at all times, a Sakya monk. He was fully committed to that role, and yet reaching out beyond his Sakya identity was his compassion and his wisdom. And if this is true for Khyentse, then the same is true for Kongtrul, a Kagyu monk who strove in all ways to mirror his beloved friend's omniscience.

# 27

# THE DEATH OF KONGTRUL

*Rimay Part Five*

---

Jamgon Kongtrul died on December 29, 1899, the twenty-seventh day of the eleventh month of the Earth Pig Year.[1] He had been declining for several years. In either 1894 or 1895 he revised his diary at the request of his disciples Tashi Wozer and Tashi Chopel, organizing his notes into a coherent chronological narrative of his life. Everything we know of his last five years is from *Marvelous Gem-Like Vision*, an account of his death and funeral by Tashi Chopel.[2]

His disciple adored the old man, and he praised Kongtrul in unusually personal language at the beginning of the account: his teacher was humble, insisting repeatedly he was just an ordinary person and only occasionally admitting to realizations and visions. Kongtrul himself would have agreed with this assessment. He did not live in a halo of glory. He had a high status, but was so by virtue of being astonishingly hardworking. Those who lived close to him recognized his exceptional accomplishments, and he was famous during his life for his ritual acumen and mastery of religious traditions. But he was not universally loved or accepted, and he was not a center of a vast ecumenical community as is sometimes depicted today. Tashi Chopel described a lama who treated everyone who came to see him with equal cordiality and courteousness, if without much enthusiasm—he generally viewed such meetings as tedious. He received offerings with grace but without covetousness. He did not look down on those with low social status or up at the exalted, and he generally preferred the company of the simple and unpretentious, sharing food from his own plate with any guest. He fed the animals with food he would consecrate with mantras. He was, in his disciple's eyes, "a ruler among renunciates, a yogin disenchanted with the world, a religious being for whom all was like an illusion." It was thanks to the Ninth Situ that Tashi Chopel and the rest of the world benefited from his teachings; Kongtrul told his disciples that he had only ever wished to live as "a child of the mountains, with mist as his garments, alone with only the wild animals as companions." Situ fortunately forbade it, thrusting Kongtrul into service.[3]

Kongtrul lingered close to death for several years, recovering periodically to give empowerments and transmissions and even once to receive teachings—Tashi Wozer gave him the transmission of Rechung Hearing Lineage teachings, and Jamyang Loter Wangpo (Khyentse Wangpo's closest disciple) gave him a handful of Sakya transmissions. Kongtrul insisted that Tashi Chopel receive these as well since he knew he would not live to practice them and he did not want the transmission to fall on sterile ground. Kongtrul also composed a little—he dictated an explanation of the fragmentary *Vajrakīla Tantra* that Sakya Paṇḍita found in the library of Sakya Monastery, and in his last year he composed a supplication to Padmasambhava titled *Ambrosia from My Heart*.[4]

Kongtrul suffered physically in his last year. He had high blood pressure. Edema in his legs left him unable to walk. A rash irritated his skin. He declined food and medicine. His disciples gathered around him to perform intensive long-life ceremonies. These in a way recall the invasive life-prolonging procedures familiar in Western industrial medicine—everyone knew he would soon die, but they did what they could to keep him alive. Kongtrul allowed his students to perform the rites—torma offerings and ablutions, feasts and fire offerings to the ḍākinīs, long-life rituals—not out of fear of death but in recognition that they gave his community a socially acceptable method to manage their grief. Tashi Chopel wept as he begged Kongtrul to live longer, pleading with him that he was needed in the community, in the region, and particularly by the young Eleventh Situ. Kongtrul's disciples were not going to make the mistake Ānanda made when he neglected to ask the Buddha to live forever. But Kongtrul could not oblige.[5]

On Kongtrul's final day, Tashi Wozer asked him about his health, and Kongtrul replied he was well as he held out his rosary to bless his students. He passed away that night, sitting in meditation. As Tashi Chopel somewhat verbosely put it, "around midnight he entered a meditative equipoise like the space inside a shattered vase dissolves into the vast, all-pervading space of the immaculate and luminous *dharmakāya*." By this he meant that the essential enlightened nature of Kongtrul's mind—empty, luminous—ceased the pretense of individuality, the emptiness of his mind already undifferentiated from the fundamental emptiness of all things. Kongtrul's body remained undisturbed for three days, wrapped in his robes, a meditation hat crowning his head, "resting in the luminous space of the dharmakāya" while his students performed rituals to assist him in his transitional meditation. At midnight on the third day, a low earthquake shook the region, a sign that Kongtrul had finished his final practice.[6]

Loter Wangpo and Tashi Wozer washed the body and placed slips of dark paper with syllables written in gold ink on those places on Kongtrul's body that corresponded to the great sites of Buddhist cosmology. Amulets made of mantras and consecrated substances wrapped tightly in fabric were distributed across his corpse. They wrapped him in *Vārāṇasī*, cloth interspersed with fragrant medicinal herbs to mask the rot of death. On top of this his disciples dressed him in monastic robes and propped him up in a seated position with a five-point crown symbolizing the five buddha families of Yoga Tantra on his head and a vajra and bell in his hands. They placed him on a high throne and set out an offering feast before him, and for a week his close disciples performed rituals in his presence. Tashi Chopel describes the landscape around them appearing to join in the mourning:

> There were signs that those beings who guard virtue were overcome by the tragedy. The weather turned foul. The vitality of the valleys seemed to drain away and all became dull. Visitors saw that the lofty glaciers and cliff faces guarded by worldly protectors were wet, as though they too were weeping and bowing their heads in grief. The birds were chattering more than usual and making quite a din.[7]

The young Eleventh Situ came with an entourage to view Kongtrul's corpse, and Tsādra was opened for anyone else who wished to do so. The water used to wash his body was given to the faithful.

Tashi Chopel did not record the day of the cremation, stating only that it was "astrologically appropriate." Four groups were stationed at the pyre's four sides, led by Loter Wangpo, Tashi Wozer, Lama Dondrub— the vajra master of Tsādra who had performed the transference of consciousness of Kongtrul's nephew in 1892—and Gyelse Dechen Tulku of Dzogon Monastery. The rituals they performed, intended to aid Kongtrul in his rebirths, were from the Sakya tradition of Hevajra, Vajrasattva of Mindroling, Akṣobhya in the tradition of Atīśa, and Vairocana from an unnamed tradition. Kongtrul's bones and ashes were placed in an urn before being interred. Tashi Chopel reported that Kongtrul's heart was not burned by the fire and was placed in his reliquary.[8] On a visit to Tsādra in the late twentieth century, Canadian author Ngawang Zangpo was told that the heart was saved from the destruction of Tsādra during the Cultural Revolution and given to the Third Kongtrul in the 1970s.[9]

Kongtrul's nephew Tsering Dondrub, the steward of Tsādra, was charged with distributing Kongtrul's possessions; in the autumn of 1899 Kongtrul had tasked him with an inventory of all his possessions so as to avoid disagreements after his death. Kongtrul's personal wealth was primarily used to sponsor commemorative rites at the major Nyingma, Kagyu, and Sakya monasteries in Derge and at the smaller temples near Pelpung, as well as the large Kagyu and government monasteries in Tibet. Sumptuous gifts were sent to the Fifteenth Karmapa and the Thirteenth Dalai Lama. Tsādra was endowed with sufficient land to continue operations. At Dzongsho, Kongtrul's disciple Jamyang Gelek led the forty-nine-day observation rituals.[10]

A prince of Derge sponsored two reliquaries which were adorned with jewels. The larger was placed in Lhasar Temple to the left of the stūpa of the Ninth Situ, and the smaller was placed in Kongtrul's residence at Tsādra. Tashi Chopel named the prince Jigme Tsewang Dudul, but this is incorrect, as this prince, the grandson of Chime Takpai Dorje, was not born until 1915. The sponsor was probably his father, Dorje Sengge.[11] The stūpas were built quickly and consecrated in June 1900. Dozens of monasteries and prominent individuals sent gold and other offerings to decorate the tombs. Kongtrul's consort sponsored one hundred lamps during the nine days of funeral rites, gave crystals, turquoise, and agates for the tomb decorations, and she sponsored one hundred thousand repetitions of the *Bhadracarīpraṇidhāna*, an Indian scripture that lists the ten vows of Buddha Samantabhadra and is widely recited in Tibet. Funds were also dedicated to ensure that Kongtrul's Five Treasuries were completed and that blocks were carved at the Derge Printing House.[12]

These books were widely read during Kongtrul's life. Tashi Chopel lists three contemporary scholars who sought Kongtrul out "like bees drawn to a blooming lotus." These included the Third Reting Rinpoche, whom Kongtrul met in Lhasa. The Third Amchok Tulku, Jamyang Khyenrab Gyatso, a Geluk scholar in Amdo, praised Kongtrul as "omniscient." The Mongolian Geluk scholar Toyon Paṇḍita found Kongtrul's writings "irresistible." And the Thirteenth Dalai Lama issues a proclamation that included the phrase: "Kongtrul Yonten Gyatso Rinpoche, a learned and accomplished saint whose being is endowed with the intent of the teachings without sectarian bias, who led beings to clarity and veneration of the Buddha." The Dalai Lama also praised him as an embodiment of Mañjuśrī and urged him to return quickly. The Thirteenth Dalai Lama was both a highly educated lama and a skillful political tactician. That he would use the term "rimay"— which I translated here as "without sectarian bias"—in the above praise is evidence that Kongtrul was known during his own life for his ecumenicalism.[13] Tashi Chopel's choice of three Geluk patriarchs in Tibet, Amdo, and Mongolia not only indicates the geographic extent of Kongtrul's audience but emphasizes that his readers could be found across all Tibetan Buddhist traditions. That is, even the Geluk scholars were reading him. Of course, not all Geluk intellectuals read Kongtrul with enthusiasm. Scholars Higgins and Draszczyk speculated that the great scholar Pabongkha Dechen Nyingpo, who almost single-handedly revived the worship of Dorje Shukden, had Kongtrul in mind; Shukden's role is to protect Geluk orthodoxy from infiltration by other traditions.[14]

Many lamas before Kongtrul modeled ecumenicalism, but none before Kongtrul had made such an intentional effort to embody and promote it. He was so successful that today ecumenicalism—"rimay"—is an ideal that is universally praised even if it is not universally practiced. The Fourteenth Dalai Lama captured Kongtrul's ecumenicalism nicely in his 1993 letter that served as a forward to *Myriad Worlds*: "'sectarianism' in the sense of exclusively dedicating yourself to the study and practice of one particular school is not necessarily a negative thing. Most Tibetan lamas train this way. This is positive sectarianism. Negative sectarianism is to follow one tradition exclusively, while looking down on other traditions."[15] The Dalai Lama has made good use of Kongtrul's ecumenicalism in nearly sixty years of holding together a very diverse exile Tibetan community.

Jamgon Kongtrul spent more than half a century teaching, and as a teacher he promoted the views and practices he personally thought were the finest while never disparaging any other. In his choice of topics and texts, whether from his own compositions or those of others, he clearly promoted "other-emptiness" as the highest—that is, definitive—Madhyamaka view. He advocated Dzogchen as the highest practice, even over the Mahāmudrā of his own Kagyu tradition. The definitions of treasure revelation and presentations of teaching traditions that Kongtrul and Khyentse formulated became something akin to the orthodox positions on the topics. They composed the manuals—the instructions for transmission and practice— for the treasure cycles that became popular among the next generations of

Buddhists. The transmission of the Treasury of Revelations continues to be a major event in Kagyu, Nyingma, and Sakya communities. In his Treasury of Knowledge Kongtrul defined religious terminology for the last century of Tibetan Buddhists. He explained the origins, significance, and benefits of the entire corpus of Buddhist teachings and practices. He provided the standard manuals for tantric initiations and other rituals for the Kagyu tradition. And he determined which instructional texts were canonical for all eight teaching traditions of Tibetan Buddhism in his Treasury of Instructions. His treasuries were authoritative, widely accepted, and established the standards for all who came after. His disciples had brought them back to their home monasteries and spread their transmission even before his death.

Kongtrul was not absent from Tibet for long. Five official reincarnations were identified. The main incarnation based at Pelpung and Tsādra was the son of the Fifteenth Karmapa, a boy born in 1904 and named Khyentse Wozer. He is sometimes known as the Karse Kongtrul, "karse" meaning "son of the Karmapa." The Fifth Dzogchen Tulku chose a child born around 1901 to the aristocratic Gyangshar family and named him Konchok Tenpai Gyeltsen. He became known as the Dzogchen Kongtrul. Zhechen Monastery acquired a Kongtrul reincarnation in the person of a child named Pema Drime, also born around 1901. The child was the brother of three other incarnate lamas, including the Fourth Getse Getok, Gyurme Tubten Nyinje. He was known as the Zhechen Kongtrul and was, according to Gene Smith, the most accomplished of the first generation of Kongtrul incarnations. A fourth boy named Lodro Rabpel, also born around 1901, was identified by leaders of Dzigar Monastery and became known as the Dzigar Kongtrul. Gene Smith speculated that there was a Kongtrul reincarnation based at Katok Monastery, but he was unable to find any information about him, if he in fact existed. Khyentse Wozer lived until around 1953. His reincarnation, Lodro Chokyi Sengge, died tragically in a car accident in Sikkim in 1992. The current incarnation, Chokyi Nyima, was born in 1995. The current Dzigar Kongtrul is a well-known teacher in the West. Following the destruction of Zhechen Monastery and the relocation of the community's leadership in South Asia, the Zhechen Kongtrul incarnation line was merged with that of the Zhechen Gyeltsab in the person of the current Zhechen Rabjam Rinpoche, who was born in 1966, the grandson of Dilgo Khyentse Rinpoche.[16]

An additional reincarnation of Kongtrul who has been accepted by tradition but who was never formally enthroned was Kalu Rinpoche. This remarkable teacher was born in 1905 to a student of Kongtrul, the Thirteenth Ratak Pelzang Tulku, who Ngawang Zangpo identifies as the same person as Lama Pema Norbu, a graduate of the Tsādra retreats. He was ordained by the Eleventh Situ and trained at Pelpung, entering into the Tsādra retreat then directed by a lama named Norbu Dondrub and ultimately becoming the program's director. In 1971 the Sixteenth Karmapa sent Kalu Rinpoche to teach in the West, and Kalu moved about Europe and North America extensively until his death in 1989. Kalu Rinpoche opened over twenty centers in the West for long-term retreat and teachings, and his retreat graduates are now some of the most accomplished translators working today. In 1988 he invited many of his students to Bodh Gaya to initiate the translation of the Treasury of Knowledge, a project that Bokar Rinpoche supervised after Kalu Rinpoche's death. Translators initially lived at Kalu Rinpoche's center in West Bengal under conditions that Ngawang Zangpo, in his lengthy description of the translation's history, described as a "hardship setting."[17] The first volume, *Myriad Worlds*, was published in 1995. Subsequent volumes were published over the next two decades with the support of the Tsadra Foundation, an organization that takes its inspiration from Kongrul's remarkable training facility. The final volume came out in 2012. One gets a sense of the importance of Kalu Rinpoche's influence in bringing Kongtrul to English-speaking audiences by the frontispiece of *Myriad Worlds*: it is Kalu Rinpoche's photograph rather than an image of Kongtrul.[18] Sadly, Kalu Rinpoche shared the affliction Zhechen Wontrul confessed to Khyentse Wangpo in a dream; he was accused of sexual abuse by a longtime disciple in 1996.[19]

Contemporary Tibetan lamas such as Kalu Rinpoche, Khenpo Tsultrim Gyatso, and Ringu Tulku have transmitted Jamgon Kongtrul's compositions and ecumenical approach to Western students for decades now. Many of their students have completed three-year retreats and have become some of the best Tibetan translators and oral interpreters working today. They have translated volumes of Kongtrul's advice to practitioners at every level of the path, including classics such as *Torch of Certainty*, *The Great Path to Awakening*, and *Creation and Completion*. Translations of Kongtrul's philosophical treatises include Susan Hookam's *The Buddha Within* and Rosemary Fuch's *Buddha-Nature*—each of which translates different sections of Kongtrul's commentary on the *Uttaratantra*—and Elizabeth Callahan's *The Profound Inner Principles*, a translation of the Third Karmapa's work together with Kongtrul's commentary *Illuminating the Profound Inner*

*Principles*. Ngawang Zangpo has translated many of Kongtrul's writings about Tsādra and geography. Richard Barron deserves mention again for translating Kongtrul's diary.

Alongside these translators, E. Gene Smith and Chogyam Trungpa Rinpoche have done more than anyone to shape the Western image of Kongtrul. In his introductory essay to the 1970 edition of the Treasury of Knowledge, Gene Smith established the basic outline of Kongtrul's biography that has since been repeated in countless prefaces and introductions. He also created an intractable framework for the discussion of Kongtrul's legacy that is only recently showing signs of easing its grip. Where Tibetan authors such as Kongtrul used the adjective "rimay" to modify "teachings" or "teacher," Smith put it in front of "movement," and ever after Kongtrul has been characterized as the initiator of a religious reformation. This is the so-called "Rimay Movement." Better phrases have since been offered, such as "rimay period" (Jann Ronis) or "rimay zeitgeist" (Rachel Pang), and these and others are gaining traction in scholarship and popular writing. Smith's failure to define the "movement," followed by a long biographical sketch and literary survey, resulted in later authors confusing Kongtrul's life with the "Rimay Movement." For example, Smith described Kongtrul's interest in Sanskrit, and so authors have written of "rimay" as a return to basics, a drive to restore the primacy of Sanskrit scripture to the Buddhist tradition and thereby shed the accretions of sectarian divisions. Smith described Kongtrul's drive to preserve teachings, and so later authors wrote that a defining characteristic of "rimay" was the preservation of rare texts. Kongtrul's interest in Sanskrit and his drive to publish and propagate the myriad teachings of his era certainly informed his ecumenicalism, but these or any other aspect of his accomplishments cannot be taken as part of a call to transform Buddhism in Tibet. Kongtrul was a remarkable man in the breadth and quality of his activities, but in all things he was very firmly rooted in tradition and quite conservative in upholding long-standing customs.[20]

Four years after Smith's pioneering introduction of Kongtrul to Western readers, the brilliant Buddhist teacher Chogyam Trungpa gave a series of talks at Naropa University in Boulder, Colorado that were edited and published as *Journey Without Goal: The Tantric Wisdom of the Buddha*. In one talk Trungpa assailed what he called "spiritual materialism," here specifically the tendency to "collect" empowerments that, he said, was a "recent corruption in the presentation of [the] Vajrayāna." Trungpa explained that Kongtrul received transmissions from more than one hundred thirty-five teachers—a collection that Trungpa admired rather than scorned—which enabled him to initiate "a reformation of Buddhism in Tibet, which he called the Rime school." Trungpa continued: "The term Rime literally means 'without bias,' an 'ecumenical approach.'" This "Rime school" created a fair amount of opposition, according to Trungpa, and was attacked by those who wished to continue to receive "a succession of abhishekas [empowerments] purely as collectors' items." Trungpa had Kongtrul respond to the criticism by likening the collection of empowerments to the piling up of manure: "A pile of manure may be ripe, smelly, and fantastic, but it is still a pile of shit."[21]

Trungpa likened Kongtrul to "a jewel in a pile of manure" and presented him as a man who called out for reform:

> He saw that it was necessary to call upon the eight great traditions of Buddhism in Tibet ... and bring them together: "Let us unite; let us work together within this contemplative tradition. Let us experience this tradition for ourselves, instead of inviting hundreds of artists to build glorious shrines. Let us experience how it feels to sit on our meditation cushions and do nothing." This reintroduction of practice, which had long been forgotten, was the focus of the contemplative reformation of Tibetan Buddhism during the nineteenth century.[22]

Trungpa cast Kongtrul as not simply the founder of a "Rime school" but savior of all of the Buddhist teachings in Tibet. Tibetan Buddhism, he told his students, had grown corrupt and its religious institutions had long since lost their way, deteriorating into mere buildings and objects. Trungpa's American audience—so many members of which were then participating in their own anti-institutionalist movement—would have understood this "corruption" as "organized religion." According to Trungpa, Kongtrul spurned these hollow shells and created the "practice lineage," by which he meant a meditation teaching that did not rely on institution or tradition. Not depending on Tibetan religious structures, this practice lineage could easily be taken up by Trungpa's Western students—it was this "practice lineage," Trungpa told his students, "that we ourselves belong to."

Trungpa was speaking to an audience interested in some of the teachings of Buddhism, but which was composed of people who carried a considerable antipathy to religion. They were eager to study and meditate, but they appeared to want little to do with Tibet or the institutional and ritual structures that had engendered, nurtured, and preserved those teachings for centuries. Thus, to Smith's accurately depicted—if unfortunately phrased—nonsectarianism, Trungpa added an anti-institutional "Rime," one that had no place in corrupted Tibet and was ripe for Western adoption. Untethered by religious tradition or institution, this "practice lineage" could take any form Western students desired. No wonder we have so many definitions of what Kongtrul meant by "rimay" and why so few of them are anchored in what he actually said or did.

In the decades following Smith and Trungpa, Western authors wrote of a "Rimay movement" that used nonsectarianism to resist or rebel against orthodox institutionalism. The false dichotomy between "practice" and "institutions" has long roots in both Protestant antipathy toward Catholicism as well as Orientalist fantasies of a corrupt Asia whose insights are better preserved in the West. The anti-establishment culture of the 1960s and 1970s was ripe for a Buddhism that rejected ritual and authority and fantasized about an individualistic practice unaffiliated with any organization. As more of Kongtrul's work has been translated, and more nuanced portraits of life and activity in nineteenth-century Derge have been made, this notion of an anti-institutional, syncratic movement has begun to fade. Kongtrul's activities to preserve teaching lineages within a well-established institutional setting can be appreciated. His embrace of meditative techniques that are part of clearly defined hierarchies of authority need not be denied. And his promotion of an ecumenical inquiry and universal respect and veneration for all the teachings of the Buddha need not be cast as an attempt to tear down centuries of religious structures.

Kongtrul knew well that those structures were the framework for meditative realizations. Kongtrul believed in the Buddhism that he received from his teachers, and he was unquestionably committed to ritual. Far too many sketches of Kongtrul's lives have overlooked the centrality of ritual in his life—of the physicality of his activity as he moved across Kham performing religious rites—and instead focus entirely on the textual output. Kongtrul did not intend for his books to be read apart from the teaching traditions in which they were produced—he worried greatly that the instructions he gathered in the Treasury of Advice would be reduced to just pretty words if the lineages were cut. Kongtrul never simply handed someone a copy of a book; he gave an empowerment, a transmission, and instructions, three rituals that bind communities, that carry knowledge from person to person and generation to generation, and that reaffirm the truths and values that the community holds dear.

Kongtrul initially turned to religion in response to the traumas of his childhood. He left the Bon tradition and became a Buddhist. Because of the institutional interests of his sponsor, he was removed from his first religious home and installed in a place he loved but at which he was never fully accepted. Spending his life as an outsider of sorts gave him the gift of an expansive perspective—no single monastery or tradition had the definitive truth. All were simply following the teachings they knew, correctly delving deep into that tradition. Having been trained in three different traditions before he was twenty-five, and seeing how much overlap and similarities they all shared, he saw no reason to disparage any. The more he learned of other teaching lineages, the more he came to venerate the many paths the Buddha provided. It was an ecumenicalism that strengthened his understanding of the Buddha's central truth of nonduality. "Declaring 'this is good' and 'this is bad' is the way of fools," he wrote in 1842 at the age of thirty. Just as the doctrine of emptiness does not make everything go away—the vase that broke when he died was as real as the space within it—impartiality does not require one to abandon a particular method and to do everything at once. No more than nondual perception leads one to stop taking care of one's own body. Kongtrul's ecumenicalism was in no way a call for syncretism or a rejection of institutional structures of religion. He had a personal path and a view and he naturally taught it to others, holding it at the peak of his doxographical mountains. But that mountain had wide slopes and multiple ridges that accommodated pretty much everything. Kongtrul's impartiality was a recognition that all paths were valid in that they eventually led to liberation. Some might be quicker, some might need to lead into others. But to disparage any, to engage in negative sectarianism, was to fall into dualistic thinking. He refused to bear the burden of rejecting any part of the Buddha's teaching.

# TIMELINE

1813. Born on December 3, 1813, the tenth day of the tenth month of the Female Water Bird Year of the fourteenth sexagenary cycle

c. 1816. Three years old. Bon blessing, name Tendzin Yungdrung

c. 1820. Khyungpo Lama, father, passes away

c. 1827. Tarde Tokden gives Bon teachings

c. 1827. Studies painting and medicine for first time

1827. Grandfather, Ata, dies

c. 1829. Goes to Chode, meets Old Chieftain

1829–1833. Trains at Zhechen Monastery

1829. Receives first Buddhist teachings

1832. Receives Nyingma ordination

1833. Moves to Pelpung

1834. Receives second ordination at Pelpung and the name Karma Ngawang Yonten Gyatso Trinle Kunkhyab Pelzangpo

1836. Situ gives name Pema Gargyi Wangchuk Trinle Drodul Tsel

1837. Teaches grammar to the Fourteenth Karmapa at Karma Gon

1838. Visits Zhechen and Ronggyab

1839. Receives bodhisattva vows from Situ with the name Jangchub Sempa Lodro Taye

1840. Receives Shangpa Kagyu transmissions for the first time

1840. First meetings with Khyentse Wangpo

1842. Old Chieftain dies

1842–1846. Retreat

1843. Wongen dies

1843. Mother comes to live at Tsādra

1844. Writes *Torch of Certainty*

1846. Travels to Golok and Gyarong

1847. Gets harassed by Kuntrul

1847. Gonpo Namgyel invades lower Nyarong, initiating the Nyarong War

1848. Settles with Kuntrul and returns to Pelpung

1849. Undertakes alms round to Dzingkhok, likely first notice of Dzongsho

1851. First call to Derge

1853. Chokling comes to Pelpung

1853. Writes the Treasury of Kagyu Tantra

1853. Situ dies

1854. Writes *Great Path to Awakening*

1855. Begins the Treasury of Revelations

1857. Opens Dzongsho

1857–1858. Tibet

1859. Chokling reveals *Tsādra Gazetteer*

1860. Tenth Situ is enthroned

1860. Kongtrul, Tenth Situ, and the Fourteenth Karmapa perform funeral rituals for Gonpo Namgyel's grandson

1860. First transmission of the Treasury of Kagyu Tantra to the Fourteenth Karmapa at Tsādra

1861. First retreat begins at Tsādra

1862. Dzongsar burns in Nyarong invasion

1863. Derge falls to Gonpo Namgyel

1863. Writes most of the Treasury of Knowledge

1864. First retreat ends

1864. Lhasa invades Derge

1864. Writes *All-Pervading Melody of the Pure Lands* and *Music from the Ocean of the Mind*

1864. Completes the Treasury of Knowledge

1865. Second retreat begins at Tsādra

1865. Gonpo Namgyel is defeated and killed

1866. Gives first teachings of the Treasury of Knowledge to Ngawang Rinchen and others at Tsādra

1866. Teaches the Treasury of Knowledge to Chokling at Pelpung

1867. Mother passes away

1867. Dabzang dies (alternate date of his death is 1864[1])

1867. Treasure enthronement at Dzongsho by Khyentse and Chokling

1868. First transmission of the Treasury of Revelations at Tsādra

1868. Second retreat ends, third retreat begins

1870. Chokgyur Lingpa passes away

1871. Reveals United Intent of the Three Roots at Lhamdo Burmo

1871. Composes commentary on the Third Karmapa's *Profound Inner Principles*

1871. Teaches the Treasury of Knowledge at Pelpung summer retreat

1872. Gives transmission of the Treasury of Revelations at Tsādra

1872. Gives transmission of the Treasury of Revelations in Ling

1873. Third retreat ends, fourth retreat starts

1873. Teaches the Treasury of Knowledge at Pelpung

1873–1874. Writes *Light of Wisdom*

1874. Gives Treasury of Revelations transmission at Katok to Getse Tulku

1874. Wontrul dies

1874. Exile begins

1875. Teaches the Treasury of Knowledge at Dzongsar

1875. Treasury of Knowledge is printed

1876. Gives transmission of the Treasury of Revelations at Dzongsar

1876. Fourth retreat ends, fifth begins

1880. Fifth retreat ends, sixth begins

1880–1881. Retreat at Dzongsho

1882. Gives transmission of the Treasury of Revelations at Dzongsar

1882. Transmission of the Treasury of Instructions at Tsādra

1883–1884. Performs thirteen drubchen across Derge

1884. Sixth retreat ends, seventh begins

1885. Rigdzin Dolma passes away

1885. Tenth Situ passes away

1887. Writes *One Hundred Treasure Revealers*

1887. Gives Treasury of Kagyu Tantra (Tsādra) and the Treasury of Instructions (at Pelpung) to the Fifteenth Karmapa

1888. Seventh retreat ends

1888. Teaches the Treasury of Knowledge and gives the transmission of the Treasury of Revelations to the Fifteenth Karmapa at Pelpung

1889. Eighth retreat begins

1891. Teaches the Treasury of Kagyu Tantra at Tsādra

1892. Eighth retreat ends, ninth begins

1892. Khyentse Wangpo passes away on March 19, the twenty-first day of the second month of the Water Dragon Year

1899. Kongtrul passes away on December 29, the twenty-seventh day of the eleventh month of the Earth Pig Year

# MAPS

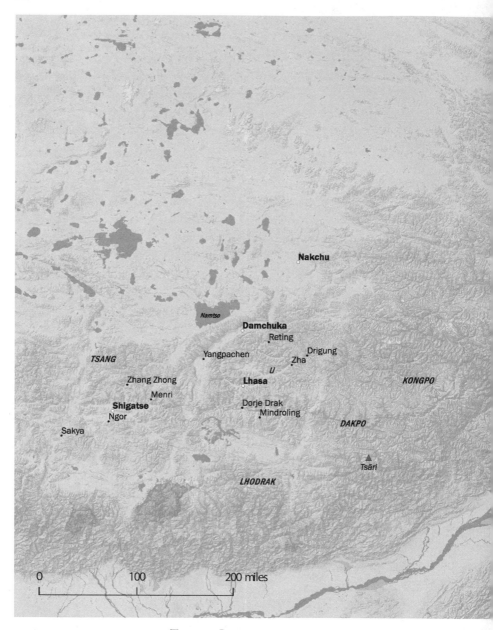

TIBETAN PLATEAU.

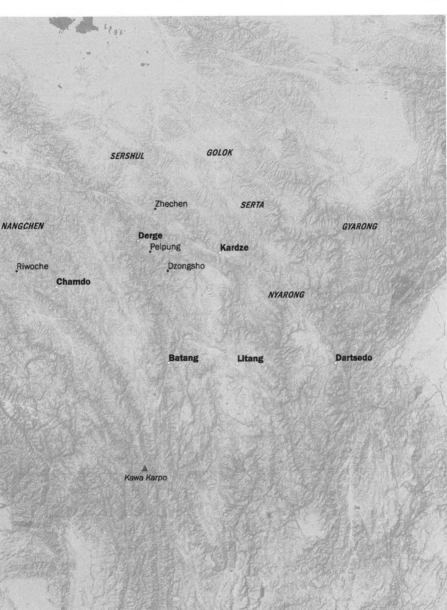

SERSHUL

GOLOK

Zhechen

SERTA

NANGCHEN

GYARONG

Derge

Pelpung

Kardze

Riwoche

Dzongsho

Chamdo

NYARONG

Batang

Litang

Dartsedo

Kawa Karpo

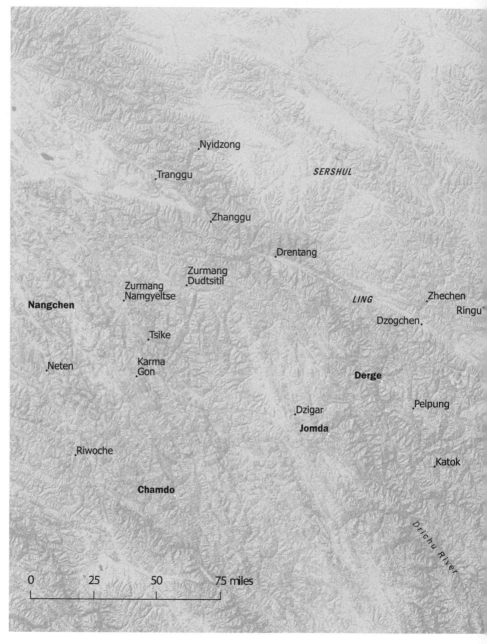

NORTHERN KHAM.

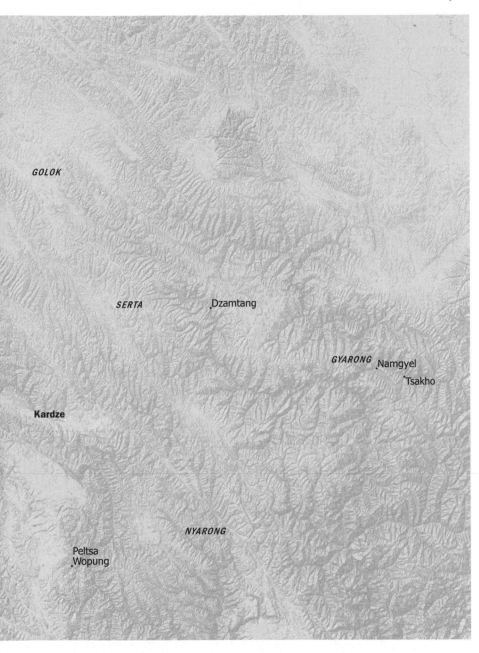

GOLOK

SERTA          Dzamtang

                              GYARONG Namgyel
                                      Tsakho

Kardze

                    NYARONG

Peltsa
Wopung

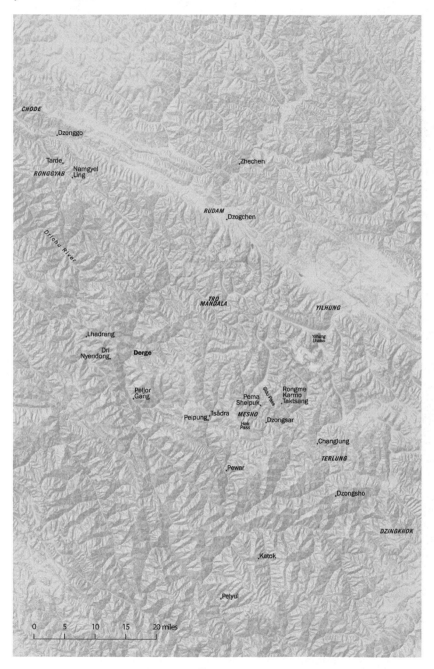

DERGE.

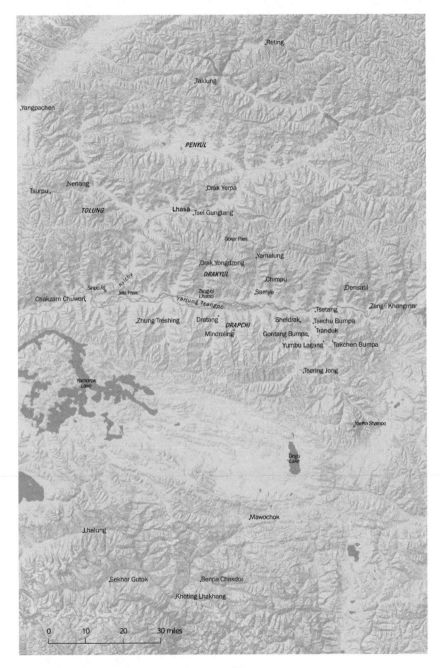

CENTRAL TIBET.

# Tibetan Orthographic Equivalents

| Phonetics | Wylie | Additional Information |
|---|---|---|
| abbot | mkhan po | |
| Adzom Drukpa Pawo Dorje | a 'dzom 'brug pa dpa' bo rdo rje | 1842–1924 |
| Alo Dilgo family | a lo mdil mgo | |
| Alo Kunkhyen | a lo kun mkhyen | |
| Alo Peljor Monastery | a lo dpal 'byor dgon | See also Peljor Gang |
| Alo Tsezuldo | a lo rtse zul mdo | |
| Third Amchok Tulku, Jamyang Khyenrab Gyatso | a mchog 03 'jam dbyangs mkhyen rab rgya mtsho | 1849–1944 |
| Amdo | a mdo | |
| Amgon | a mgon | |
| Approach practice | bsnyen | |
| Arab | a rab | |
| Artay | ar gtad | |
| Āryapalo Temple | Arya pa lo lha khang | |
| Ase region of Upper Nyarong | a bswe | |
| Ata | a bkra | |
| Atri | a khri | |
| Auspicious circle | kun bzang 'khor lo | |
| Authorization | jes gnang | |

| PHONETICS | WYLIE | ADDITIONAL INFORMATION |
|---|---|---|
| Āyurdharma | | See Tsering Chodron |
| Azure Wrathful Guru | gu ru drag po mthing ga | |
| Bardo | bar do | |
| Bardo of Becoming | srid pa'i bar do | |
| Barom Kagyu | ba' rom bka' brgyud | |
| Batang | ba' thang | |
| Barwai Dorje | bar ba'i rdo rje | 1836/9–1920 |
| Belo Tsewang Kungyab | be lo tshe dbang kun khyab | eighteenth century |
| Benpa Chakdor | ban pa phyag rdor | |
| Beri | be ri | |
| Bernakchen | ber nag can | |
| Beru Khyentse Karma Jamyang Khyentse Wozer | be ru mkhyen brtse karma 'jam dbyangs mkhyen brtse'i 'od zer | 1896–1945 |
| Bhu | bhu | |
| Black Hat Ceremony | Kongtrul only writes dbu zhwa | |
| Black Hayagrīva | rta mdrin nag po | |
| Blade ransom | dbal mdos | |
| Blazing Fire | me 'bar | |
| Bod | bod | |
| Bodhisattva vows | byang sdom | |
| Bodong | bo dong | |
| Bon | bon | |
| Bongsar | bong gsar | |

| PHONETICS | WYLIE | ADDITIONAL INFORMATION |
|---|---|---|
| Botar | bo thar | |
| Burmo Drak | bur mo brag | See Lhamdo Burmo |
| Buton Rinchen Drub | bu ston rin chen grub | 1290–1364 |
| Chakpo Ri | lcags po ri | |
| Chakpuchen Cave | lcags phur phug | |
| Chakzam Chuwori Monastery | lcags zam chu bo ri dgon | |
| Chamdo | chab mdo | |
| Chamdo Jampa Ling | chab mdo byams pa gling | |
| Changlung Monastery | lcang lung dgon | |
| Changlung Tulku Yungdrung Tenpai Gyeltsen | lcang lung sprul sku g.yung drung bstan pa'i rgyal mtshan | nineteenth century |
| Channels (nāḍīs) | rtsa | |
| Chant leader | brda sprod pa | |
| Chayang | phywa g.yang/phya g.yang | |
| Chekhawa Yeshe Dorje | mchad kha ba ye shes rdo rje | 1101–1175 |
| Chetsun Sengge Wangchuk | lce btsun seng ge dbang phyug | twelfth century |
| Chim Namkha Drak | mchims nam mkha' grags | 1210–1289 |
| Chime Deter Rigdzin Dolma | chi med bde ster rig 'dzin sgrol ma | See Rigdzin Dolma |
| Chime Gonpo | chi med mgon po | d. 1865 |
| Chime Karmo Taktsang (Rongme) | chi med dkar mo stag tshang (rong me) | |

| PHONETICS | WYLIE | ADDITIONAL INFORMATION |
|---|---|---|
| Chime Keutsang | chi med ke'u tshang | |
| Chime Tennyi Yung-drung Lingpa | chi med bstan gnyis g.yung drung gling pa | |
| Chime Tulku | chi med sprul sku | nineteenth century |
| Chod | gcod | |
| Chode District | chos sde rdzong kha | |
| Chode Palace | chos sde pho brang | |
| Chogyeb | chos rgyeb | nineteenth century |
| Chogyel Dorje | chos rgyal rdo rje | 1789–1859 |
| Choje Lingpa | chos rje gling pa | 1682–1720 |
| Choje Monastery | chos rje dgon | |
| Choje Tendzin Dondrub | chos rje bstan 'dzin don grub | nineteenth century |
| Chokgyur Lingpa/ Orgyen Chokgyur Dechen Zhikpo Lingpa | mchog 'gyur gling pa/ orgyan mchog gyur bde chen zhig po gling pa | 1829–1870 |
| Choktrul | mchog sprul | |
| Chonggye | phyongs ryas | |
| Chowang Tulku | chos dbang sprul sku | eighteenth century |
| Lama Choying | bla ma chos dbyings | eighteenth century |
| Choying Zangmo | chos dbying bzang mo | 1815–1892 |
| "Circle" rite | khor lo | |
| Circles (cakra) | khor lo | |
| Citta Sangpuk | tsitta gsang phug | |
| "cold bile" | grang mkhris | |
| Completion stage | rdzogs rim | |
| Cool Grove | bsil ba'i tshal | |

| Phonetics | Wylie | Additional Information |
|---|---|---|
| Copper-Colored Mountain | zangs mdog dpal ri | |
| Creation stage | bskyed rim | |
| Culminated Awareness | rig pa tshad phebs | |
| Dabzang Tulku Karma Ngedon | zla bzang sprul sku karma nges don | 1808–1864 |
| Dagam Wangpuk | zla gam dbang phug | |
| Daklha Gampo | dwags lha sgam po | |
| Dakpo Tashi Namgyel | dwags po bkra shis rnam rgyal | 1512/13–1587 |
| Fifth Dalai Lama, Ngawang Lobzang Gyatso | ta la'i bla ma 05 ngag dbang blo bzang rgya mtsho | 1618–1682 |
| Seventh Dalai Lama, Kelzang Gyatso | ta la'i bla ma 07 skal bzang rgya mtsho | 1708–1757 |
| Twelfth Dalai Lama, Trinle Gyatso | ta la'i bla ma 12 phrin las rgya mtsho | 1856–1875 |
| Thirteenth Dalai Lama, Tubten Gyatso | ta la'i bla ma 13 thub bstan rgya mtsho | 1876 1933 |
| Fourteenth Dalai Lama, Tendzin Gyatso | ta la'i bla ma 14 bstan 'dzin rgya mtsho | b. 1935 |
| Damchukha | dam chu kha | |
| Damtsik Dorje | dam tshig rdo rje | 1811–c. 1852 |
| Dangma Lhungyel | ldang ma lhun rgyal | eleventh century |
| Darmo Menrapa Lobzang Chodrak | dar mo sman rams pa blo bzang chos grags | 1638–1710 |
| Daro Lhagyel | da ro lha rgyal | |
| Daro Takkyab | da ro stag skyabs | |
| Dartsedo | dar rtse mdo | |

| PHONETICS | WYLIE | ADDITIONAL INFORMATION |
|---|---|---|
| Datal | zla thal | |
| Dechen | bde chen | |
| Dechen Burmo | bde chen 'bur mo | See Lhamdo Burmo |
| Dechen Chodron | bde chen chos sgron | eighteenth century |
| Dechen Gyelmo | bde chen rgyal mo | |
| Dechen Lingpa | bde chen gling pa | 1562–1593 |
| Dechen Lingpa (terton) | bde chen gling pa | 1833–1893 |
| Dechen Pemako Lhamdo Burmo | bde chen padma bkod lha mdo 'bur mo | See Lhamdo Burmo |
| Decontamination rite | grib gsal | |
| Definitive Madhyamaka | nges don dbu ma | |
| Definitive truth | nges don | |
| Dekyi Chodron | bde skyid chos sgron | See Dechen Chodron |
| Den Chode County | gdan chos sde rdzong | |
| Densatil Monastery | ldan sa mthil dgon | |
| Derge | sde dge | |
| Derge Printing House | sde dge par khang | |
| Deshek Dupai Podrang | bde gshegs 'dus pa'i pho brang | |
| de zhi ge chu | sde bzhi dge bcu | |
| Second Dezhung Rinpoche, Lungrik Nyima | sde gzhung rin po che 02 lung rig nyi ma | 1840–1898 |
| Third Dezhung Rinpoche, Kunga Tenpai Nyima | sde gzhung rin po che 03 kun dga' bstan pa'i nyi ma | 1906–1987 |
| Dilgo Khyentse Rinpoche Tashi Peljor | dil mgo mkhyen brtse bkra shis dpal 'byor | 1910–1991 |

| PHONETICS | WYLIE | ADDITIONAL INFORMATION |
|---|---|---|
| Direct realization of ultimate nature | chos nyid mngon sum | |
| Do | rdo | |
| Do Rulak | rdo'i ru lag | |
| First Dodrubchen, Jigme Trinle Wozer | rdo grub chen 01 'jigs med 'phrin las 'od zer | 1745–1821 |
| Third Dodrubchen, Jigme Tenpai Nyima | rdo grub chen 03 'jigs med bstan pa'i nyi ma | 1865–1926 |
| Dokham | mdo khams | |
| Dokharwa Tsewang Norbu | mdo mkhar ba tshe dbang nor bu | nineteenth century |
| Dokhoma | rdo kho ma | |
| Dolpopa Sherab Gyeltsen | dol po pa shes rab rgyal mtshan | 1292–1361 |
| Lama Dondrub | bla ma don grub | nineteenth century |
| Dongkham Tulku Ngawang Damcho Gyatso | gdong kaM sprul sku ngag dbang dam chos rgya mtsho | nineteenth century |
| Lama Donpel | bla ma don dpal | nineteenth century |
| Donyon Tulku (a.k.a. Dotrul) | mdo smyon sprul sku/ mdo sprul | d. 1885 |
| Dopu Pemajong | rdo phu padma ljong | |
| Dorje Apuk | rdo rje a phug | |
| Dorje Drak Monastery | rdo rje brag dgon | |
| Dorje Drak Monastery, Derge | sde dge rdo rje brag | |
| Dorje Drolo | rdo rje gro lod | |
| Dorje Dzongmar | rdo rje rdzong dmar | |
| Dorje Lingpa | rdo rje gling pa | 1346–1405 |

| PHONETICS | WYLIE | ADDITIONAL INFORMATION |
| --- | --- | --- |
| Dorje Pelmo Tsel | rdo rje dpal mo rtsal | |
| Dorje Rabten | rdo rje rab brtan | 1842–1902 |
| Dorje Sengge | rdo rje seng ge | 1877–1926 |
| Dorje Tso | rdo rje 'tsho | |
| Dorje Wangdrub Tsel | rdo rje dbang grub rtsal | |
| Dorje Yeshe Tsel | rdo rje ye shes rtsal | |
| Drachen | sbra chen | |
| Dragang Won Lama | grwa sgang dbon bla ma | nineteenth century |
| Drak Yerpa | brag yer pa | |
| Drak Yongdzong | bsgrags yongs rdzogs | |
| Drakmar Drinzang | brag dmar mgrin bzang | |
| Drakmar Keutsang Cave | brag dmar ke'u tshang | |
| Drakri Rinchentsek | brag ri rin chen brtsegs | |
| Drakyul Valley | bsgrags yul | |
| Drama | bra ma | |
| Dramda | gra mda' | |
| Dramtso | sbra mtsho | |
| Drangdil | brang dil | |
| Drapa Ngonshe | grwa pa mngon shes | 1012–1090 |
| Drapchi Valley | gra phyi | |
| Dratang Monastery | grwa thang dgon | |
| Drentang Monastery | dran thang dgon | |
| Drepung Monastery | bras spungs dgon | |
| Dri Nyendong | bri gnyen ldong | |
| Drichu River | bri chu | |

| PHONETICS | WYLIE | ADDITIONAL INFORMATION |
|---|---|---|
| Drigu Lake | gri gu mtsho | |
| Drime Kunga | dri med kun dga' | unknown |
| Third Drime Zhing-kyong Jigme Yonten Gonpo | dri med zhing skyong 03 'jigs med yon tan mgon po | died circa 1898 |
| Drubchen | sgrub chen | |
| Drubcho | sgrub mchod | |
| Drubpai Gyelmo | grub pa'i rgyal mo | twelfth century |
| Drubwang Lundrub Gyatso | grub dbang lhun grub rgya mtsho | eighteenth–nineteenth century |
| Drubwang Pema Gyeltsen | grub dbang padma rgyal mtshan | unknown |
| Drubwang Tsoknyi | grub dbang tshogs gnyis | nineteenth century |
| Drugu Yangwang Tsel | gru gu yang dbang rtsal | unknown |
| Drokmi Śākya Yeshe | brog mi ShAkya ye shes | eleventh century |
| Fourth Drukchen, Pema Karpo | brug chen 04 padma dkar po | 1527–1592 |
| Eighth Drukchen, Kunzik Chokyi Nangwa | brug chen 08 kun gzigs chos kyi snang ba | 1768–1822 |
| Ninth Drukchen, Mingyur Wanggyel | brug chen 09 mi 'gyur dbang rgyal | 1823–1883 |
| Tenth Drukchen, Mipam Chokyi Wangpo | brug chen 10 mi pham chos kyi dbang po | 1884–1930 |
| Drukpa Kagyu | brug pa bka' rgyud | |
| Drung Mase Tokden Lodro Rinchen | drung rma se rtogs ldan blo gros rin chen | b. 1386 |
| Dudjom Rinpoche Jikdrel Dorje | bdud 'joms 'jigs bral ye shes rdo rje | 1904–1987 |
| Dudul Dorje | bdud 'dul rdo rje | 1615–1672 |

| PHONETICS | WYLIE | ADDITIONAL INFORMATION |
|---|---|---|
| Dudul Ngakpaling Temple | bdud 'dul sngags pa gling lha khang | |
| Dudul Tsepuk | bdud 'dul tshe'i phuk | |
| Dungtso Repa | dung mtsho ras pa | fourteenth century |
| Dzamnang | dzam nang | |
| Dzamtang | dzam thang | |
| Second Dzarka Tulku Kunzang Namgyel | dzar ka sprul sku 02 kun bzang rnam rgyal | nineteenth century |
| Dzi Pema Shelpuk | dzi padma shel phug | |
| Fifth Dzigar Choktrul, Chokyi Nyima | dzi sgar mchog sprul 05 chos kyi nyi ma | born c. 1799 |
| Sixth Dzigar Choktrul, Ngawang Tenpai Nyima | dzi sgar mchog sprul 06 ngag dbang bstan pa'i nyi ma | nineteenth century |
| Dzigar Kongtrul Lodro Rabpel | dzi sgar kong sprul blo gros rab 'phel | c. 1901–c. 1958 |
| Dzigar Monastery | dzi sgar chos sgar | |
| Dzingkhok | dzing khog | |
| Dzipu Khenpo | dzi phu mkhan po | nineteenth century |
| Dzitang Choje | dzi thang cho rje | nineteenth century |
| Dzodong Temple | mdzod gdong lha khang | |
| Dzogchen | rdzogs chen | |
| First Dzogchen Kongtrul, Konchok Tenpai Gyeltsen | rdzogs chen kong sprul 01 dkon mchog bstan pa'i rgyal mtshan | 1901–1952 |
| Dzogchen Monastery | rdzogs chen dgon | |
| First Dzogchen Khyentse, Guru Tsewang | rdzogs chen mkhyen brtse 01 gu ru tshe dbang | 1896–1936 |
| Dzogchen Lingtrul | rdzogs chen gling sprul | nineteenth century |

| PHONETICS | WYLIE | ADDITIONAL INFORMATION |
|---|---|---|
| Fourth Dzogchen Ponlob, Jigme Choying Wosel | rdzogs chen dpon slob 04 'jigs med chos dbyings 'od gsal | nineteenth century |
| Fourth Dzogchen Rinpoche, Mingyur Namkhai Dorje | rdzogs chen 04 mi 'gyur nam mkha'i rdo rje | 1793–1870 |
| Fifth Dzogchen Rinpoche, Tubten Chokyi Dorje | rdzogs chen 05 thub bstan chos kyi rdo rje | 1872–1935 |
| First Dzogchen Wontrul, Tutob Namgyel | rdzogs chen dbon sprul 01 mthu stobs rnam rgyal | nineteenth century |
| Dzogon Monastery | mdzod dgon | |
| Dzomtok | dzom thog | |
| Dzong | rdzong | |
| Dzongchen Khampuk | rdzong chen khams phug | |
| Dzonggak | rdzong 'gag | |
| Dzonggo | rdzong mgo | |
| Dzonggo Monastery | rdzong mgo dgon | |
| Dzongsar Khyentse Chokyi Lodro | rdzong sar mkhyen brtse'i chos kyi blo gros | 1893–1959 |
| Dzongsar Monastery | rdzong sar dgon | |
| Dzongsho Deshek Dupai Podrang | rdzong shod bde gshegs 'dus pa'i pho brang | |
| Dzum Tsangkar | dzum tshang dkar | |
| Dzumtsa Hot Springs | dzum tsha | |
| Dzungar Mongol | | |
| Earth rite | sa chog | |
| Eight auspicious substances | bkra shis rdzas brgyad | |

| PHONETICS | WYLIE | ADDITIONAL INFORMATION |
|---|---|---|
| Eight chariots of accomplishment | sgrub brgyud shing rta chen po brgyad | |
| Eight Commands | sgrub pa bka' brgyad | |
| Empowerment (abhiśeka) | dbang | |
| Encounter the abode | gnas mjal | |
| Entrustment empowerment | dbang bka' | |
| Exorcism rite | gtor zlog | |
| Expanded vastness ritual | klong rgyas cho ga | |
| Expansive class of Dzogchen | klong sde | |
| Fasting ritual | smyung gnas | |
| Feast | tshogs | |
| Festival | ston mo | |
| Festival to the heroes and heroines | dpa'i bo dpa mo'i ston mo | |
| Firelight | me 'od | |
| Five Books of Maitreya | byams chos sde lnga | |
| Five Chronicles | thang yig sde lnga | |
| Five principles of unending adornment | mi zad rgyan 'khor lnga'i rten zhabs brtan gnang | |
| Five Tantras | rgyud sde lnga | |
| Five perfect conditions | phun sum tsogs lnga | |

| PHONETICS | WYLIE | ADDITIONAL INFORMATION |
|---|---|---|
| Flower Cave | me tog phug | |
| Four māras | bdud bzhi | |
| Four Medical Tantras | rgyud bzhi | |
| Four seals | bka' rtags kyi phyag rgya bzhi | |
| Four stages of meditative absorption | ting nge 'dzin gyi dbang bzhi | |
| Ga Lotsāwa Namgyel Dorje | rgwa lo tsA ba rnam rgyal rdo rje | 1203–1282 |
| Gampopa Sonam Rinchen | sgam po pa bsod nams rin chen | 1070–1153 |
| Ganden Monastery | dga' ldan dgon | |
| Ganden Podrang | dga' ldan pho brang | |
| Gangpo Ri | gang po ri | |
| Gar Tongtsen | mgar stong btsan | 590–667 |
| Garab Dorje | dga' rab rdo rje | |
| Garje | sga rje | |
| Garje Drodok | sga rje gro rdog | |
| Garje Monastery | sga rje dgon | |
| Garwang Tulku | gar dbang sprul sku | nineteenth century |
| Gato | sga stod | |
| Geluk | dge lugs | |
| Gendun Chopel | dge 'dun chos 'phel | 1903–1951 |
| Gegyel Monastery | dge rgyal dgon | |
| Gelongma Pelmo/ Bhikṣuṇī Lakṣmī/ Bhikṣuṇī Śrīmati | dge long ma dpal mo | |

| PHONETICS | WYLIE | ADDITIONAL INFORMATION |
|---|---|---|
| Gesar of Ling | gling dge sar | |
| Getse Paṇḍita Gyurme Tsewang Chokdrub | dge rtse paN Di ta 'gyur med tshe dbang mchog grub | 1761–1829 |
| Fourth Getse Getok, Gyurme Tubten Nyinje | dge rtse ge tog sprul sku 04 'gyur med thub bstan nyin byed | 1906–1942 |
| Second Katok Getse Tulku Tsewang Rig-dzin Gyatso | kaH thog dge rtse 02 tshe dbang rig 'dzin rgya mtsho | c. 1830–c. 1885 |
| Geshe | dge bshes | |
| Gift of the body | lus spgin | |
| Ging | ging | |
| Giving and taking | gtong len | |
| Godawari | go dA ba ri | |
| Gokar Pass | rgod dkar | |
| Golden libation | gser skyems | |
| Golok | gu log/mgo log | |
| Gonchen | dgon chen | See Lhundrubteng |
| Gongpo spirit | 'gong po | |
| Gonpo | mgon po | |
| Gonpo Namgyel | mgon po rnam rgyal | 1799–1865 |
| Gonpo Tulku | dgon po sprul sku | |
| Gontang Bumpa | dgon thang 'bum pa | |
| Goodwill Commissioner | xuān wèi shi | |
| Great Dog | shwa na chen mo | |
| Green Tārā | sgrol ljang | |

| Phonetics | Wylie | Additional Information |
|---|---|---|
| Guru Cakrasaṃvara | gu ru bde mchog | |
| Guru Chowang | gu ru chos dbang | 1212–1270 |
| Guru Drakpo | gu ru drag po | |
| Guru Lhakhang | gu ru lha khang | |
| Guru Nātha | gu ru nA tha | |
| guru yoga | bla ma'i rnal 'byor | |
| Gushri Khan | gu shrI bstan 'dzin chos rgyal | b. 1582 |
| Gutor | dgu gtor | |
| Gya Lotsāwa Dorje Zangpo | rgya lo tsa ba rdo rje bzang po | unknown |
| Gyama Tseldo | rgya ma mtsal mdo | |
| Gyang Nepotsa | gyang gnas po rtsa | |
| Gyangshar clan | gdung rigs gyang khar | |
| Gyarong | rgyal rong | |
| Gyarong Ngulchu (Ch: Dadu River) | rgyal rong ngul chu | |
| Gyaton Pema Wangchuk | rgya ston padma dbang phyug | unknown |
| First Gyatrul Rinpoche, Pema Do-ngak Tendzin | rgya sprul Rin po che 01 padma mdo sngags bstan 'dzin | 1830–1892 |
| Gyazhang Trom Dorje Bar | rgya zhang khrom rdo rje 'bar | |
| Gyel/gyelpo | rgyal/rgyal po | |
| Gyelse Dechen Tulku | rgyal sras bde chen sprul sku | nineteenth century |
| Gyelse Mingyur | rgyal sras mi 'gyur | nineteenth century |
| Gyelse Tokme Zangpo | rgyal sras thogs med bzang po | 1295–1369 |

| PHONETICS | WYLIE | ADDITIONAL INFORMATION |
|---|---|---|
| Gyelse Tsewang Gyurme | rgyal sras tshe dbang 'gyur med | nineteenth century |
| Gyiling | gyi ling | |
| Gyurme Chodar | gyur med chos dar | nineteenth century |
| Gyurme Dondrub (brother of Khyentse Wangpo) | gyur med don grub | nineteenth century |
| Gyurme Dondrub (teacher at Mindroling) | gyur med don grub | nineteenth century |
| Gyurme Pema Wanggyel | gyur med pad+ma dbang rgyal | seventeenth–eighteenth century |
| Gyurme Tendzin | gyur med bstan 'dzin | nineteenth century |
| Gyurme Tenpel | gyur med bstan 'phel | nineteenth century |
| | | |
| Hak Pass | hag la | |
| Hakda | hag mda | |
| Hepo Ri | he po ri | |
| Heroes and Heroines | dpa' bo dpa' mo | |
| | | |
| Increasing experience | chos nyid mngon sum | |
| Instruction | khrid | |
| Instruction class of Dzogchen | man ngag sde | |
| Invincible Wild Lion Turquoise Lake | ma pham seng rgod g.yu mtsho | |
| | | |
| Jadra | ja sbra | |
| Jamgon Kongtrul Lodro Taye | jam mgon kong sprul blo gros mtha' yas | 1813–1899 |

| PHONETICS | WYLIE | ADDITIONAL INFORMATION |
|---|---|---|
| Second Jamgon Kongtrul, Khyentse Wozer | jam mgon kong sprul 02 mkhyen brtse'i 'od zer | 1906–1953 |
| Third Jamgon Kongtrul, Lodro Chokyi Sengge | jam mgon kong sprul 03 blo gros chos kyi seng+ge | 1953–1992 |
| Fourth Jamgon Kongtrul, Chokyi Nyima | jam mgon kong sprul 04 chos kyi nyi ma | b. 1995 |
| Jampa Bum | byams pa 'bum | 1179–1252 |
| Jampa Puntsok | byams pa phun tshogs | seventeenth century |
| Jamyang Gelek (Kongtrul disciple) | jam dbyangs dge legs | nineteenth century |
| Jamyang Gelek (Pelpung steward) | jam dbyangs dge legs | nineteenth century |
| Jamyang Khyentse Chokyi Wangchuk | jam dbyangs mkhyen brtse chos kyi dbang phyug | 1893–1908 |
| Jamyang Khyentse Wangpo | jam dbyangs mkhyen brtse'i dbang po | 1820–1892 |
| Jamyang Namgyel Dorje | jam dbyangs rnam rgyal rdo rje | nineteenth century |
| Jamyang Tsultrim Wangmo | jam dbyangs tshul khrims dbang mo | unknown |
| Jamyang Tulku | jam dbyangs sprul sku | nineteenth century |
| Jangchub Lingpa | byang chub gling pa | thirteenth century |
| Jangchub Sempa Lodro Taye | byang chub sems pa blo gros mtha' yas | |
| Jangtrul | byang sprul | |
| Jatson Nyingpo | ja' tshon snying po | 1585–1656 |
| Jela Pass | bye la | |
| Jelo | bye blo | |
| Jetsun Namgyel | rje btsun rnam rgyal | unknown |

| PHONETICS | WYLIE | ADDITIONAL INFORMATION |
| --- | --- | --- |
| Third Jewon Chowang Tulku | rje dbon chos dbang sprul sku 03 | See Wontrul Karma Drubgyu Tendzin Trinle |
| Ji | lji | |
| Jigme Gyelwai Nyugu | jigs med rgyal ba'i myu gu | 1765–1842 |
| Jigme Lingpa | jigs me gling pa | 1730–1785 |
| Jigme Losel | jigs med blo gsal | eighteenth–nineteenth century |
| Jigme Tsewang Dudul | jigs med tshe dbang bdud 'dul | b. 1915 |
| Jikten Choto | jig rten mchod bstod | |
| Jikten Gonpo Rinchen Pel | jig rten mgon po rin chen dpal | 1143–1217 |
| Jomda | jo mda' | |
| Jomo Menmo | jo mo sman mo | 1248–1283 |
| Jonang | jo nang | |
| Jonang Monastery | jo nang dgon | |
| Jorna Monastery in Rongpo | rong po 'byor sna | |
| Jowo Mañjuvajra | jo bo mi bskyod rdo rje | |
| Jowo Ri | jo bo ri | |
| Jowo Yishin Norbu | jo bo yid bzhin nor bu | |
| | | |
| Kadam | bka' gdams | |
| Kagyu | bka' brgyud | |
| Kalu Rinpoche Karma Rangjung Kunkhyab | kar lu rin po che karma rang byung kun khyab | 1905–1989 |
| Kam Lama Tsewang Pema Norbu Tashi | kaM bla ma mtshedbang padma nor bu | nineteenth century |
| Kangyur | bka' 'gyur | |

| PHONETICS | WYLIE | ADDITIONAL INFORMATION |
|---|---|---|
| Kardze | dkar mdzes | |
| Kardzin | skar 'dzin | |
| Karlung | dkar lung | |
| Karma Chakme | karma chags med | 1613–1678 |
| Fourth Karma Chakme, Tendzin Trinle | karma chags med 04 bstan 'dzin 'phrin las | eighteenth–nineteenth century |
| Fifth Karma Chakme, Sang-ngak Tendzin | karma chags med 05 gsang sngags bstan 'dzin | nineteenth century |
| Karma Chime Tubten Rabgye | karma 'chi med thub bstan rab rgyas | seventeenth–eighteenth century |
| Karma Chowang | karma chos dbang | nineteenth century |
| Karma Dudul Gyelpo | karma bdud 'dul rgyal po | eighteenth century |
| Karma Gon | karma dgon | |
| Karma Khentsun | karma mkhas btsun | nineteenth century |
| Third Karma Kuchen, Orgyen Do-ngak Chokyi Nyima | karma sku chen 03 o rgyan mdo sngags chos kyi nyi ma | 1854–1906 |
| Karma Lingpa | karma gling pa | fourteenth century |
| Karma Namgyel | karma rnam rgyal | nineteenth century |
| Karma Ngawang Yonten Gyatso Trinle Kunkhyab Pelzangpo | karma ngag dbang yon tan rgya mtsho phrin las kun khyab dpal bzang po | |
| Karma Ngedon (vajra master of Tsādra) | bla ma karma nges don | nineteenth century |
| Lama Karma Ngedon of Pangpuk | spang phug bla ma karma nges don | nineteenth century |
| Karma Norbu | karma nor bu | nineteenth century |

| PHONETICS | WYLIE | ADDITIONAL INFORMATION |
|---|---|---|
| Karma Nyima Wozer (Kongtrul's teacher from Kardze) | karma nyi ma 'od zer | eighteenth–nineteenth century |
| Karma Nyima Wozer (Kongtrul's student) | karma nyi ma 'od zer | nineteenth century |
| Karma Wosel Gyurme | karma 'od gsal 'gyur med | nineteenth century |
| Karma Puntsok | karma phun tshogs | nineteenth century |
| Lama Karma Selje | bla ma karma gsal byed | nineteenth century |
| Karma Tenpai Rabgye | karma bstan pa rab rgyas | unknown |
| Karma Tabkhe Namdrol | karma thabs mkhas rnam rol | nineteenth century |
| Karma Tokme | karma thogs med | nineteenth century |
| Karma Trinle | karma 'phrin las | 1456–1539 |
| Karma Tsepel | karma tshe 'phel | nineteenth century |
| Karma Tsewang Rabten | karma tshe dbang rab bstan | nineteenth century |
| Karma Tutob | karma mthu stobs | nineteenth century |
| Karma Zhenpen Wozer | karma gzhan phan 'od zer | eighteenth–nineteenth century |
| Karma Zopa Rabten Pelzangpo | karma bzod ma rab brtan dpal bzang po | |
| First Karmapa, Dusum Khyenpa | karma pa 01 dus gsum mkhyen pa | 1110–1193 |
| Second Karmapa, Karma Pakshi | karma pa 02 karma pak+shi | 1204–1283 |
| Third Karmapa, Rangjung Dorje | karma pa 03 rang byung rdo rje | 1284–1339 |
| Fourth Karmapa, Rolpai Dorje | karma pa 04 rol pa'i rdo rje | 1340–1383 |
| Fifth Karmapa, Dezhin Shekpa | karma pa 05 de bzhin gshegs pa | 1384–1415 |

| PHONETICS | WYLIE | ADDITIONAL INFORMATION |
|---|---|---|
| Seventh Karmapa, Chodrak Gyatso | karma pa 07 chos grags rgya mtsho | 1454–1506 |
| Eighth Karmapa, Mikyo Dorje | karma pa 08 mi bskyod rdo rje | 1507–1554 |
| Ninth Karmapa, Wangchuk Dorje | karma pa 09 dbang phyug rdo rje | 1556–1503 |
| Tenth Karmapa Choying Dorje | karma pa 10 chos dbyings rdo rje | 1604–1674 |
| Eleventh Karmapa, Yeshe Dorje | karma pa 11 ye shes rdo rje | 1675–1702 |
| Twelfth Karmapa, Jangchub Dorje | karma pa 12 byang chub rdo rje | 1703–1732 |
| Thirteenth Karmapa, Dudul Dorje | karma pa 13 bdud 'dul rdo rje | 1733–1797 |
| Fourteenth Karmapa, Tekchok Dorje | karma pa 14 theg mchog rdo rje | 1798–1868 |
| Fifteenth Karmapa, Khakyab Dorje | karma pa 15 mkha' khyab rdo rje | 1870–1921 |
| Karsho | mkhar shod | |
| Karyak | dkar yag | |
| Katok Dorje Den Monastery | kaH thog rdo rje gdan dgon | |
| Second Katok Situ, Chokyi Lodro | kaH thog si tu 02 chos kyi blo gros | 1820–c. 1879 |
| Third Katok Situ, Chokyi Gyatso | kaH thog si tu 03 chos kyi rgya mtsho | 1880–1923/25 |
| Kawa Karpo | kha ba dkar po | |
| Kelzang Dorje | skal bzang rdo rje | nineteenth century |
| Kham | khams | |
| Sixth Khamtrul, Tenpai Nyima | khams sprul 06 bstan pa'i nyi ma | 1849–1907 |
| Khangleb | khang leb | |

| Phonetics | Wylie | Additional Information |
| --- | --- | --- |
| Khangsar Clan | khang gsar gdong | |
| Khangsar Khenpo Temple at Ngor | khang gsar mkhan po lha khang | |
| Khangsar Monk House | khang gsar grwa khang | |
| Khangsar Pema | khang gsar padma | nineteenth century |
| Khangsar Tsepel | khang gsar tshe 'phel | d. 1842 |
| Khardo Chonam | mkhar mdo chos rnam | nineteenth century |
| Khardo Jamyang Drakpa | mkhar mdo 'jam dbyang grags pa | nineteenth century |
| Khardo Stūpa | mkhar mdo mchod rten | |
| Khardo Valley | mkhar mdo | |
| Khen Lama Tashi Wozer Lodro Gyepai De | mkhan bla ma bkra shis 'od zer blo gros rgyas pa'i sde | See Tashi Wozer |
| Khoting Lhakhang | mkho mthing lha khang | |
| Khyungpo Clan | khyung po gdung | |
| Khyungpo Lama Yungdrung Tendzin | khyung po bla ma g.yung drung bstan 'dzin | died c. 1820 |
| Khyungpo Neljor | khyung po rnal 'byor | c. 1050–1127 |
| Khyungtsang Drak | khyung tshang grag | |
| Konchok Gyurme, the Second Tsike Chokling | rtsi ke mchog gling 02 dkon mchog 'gyur med | See Second Tsike Chokling |
| Konchok Tendzin | dkon mchog bstan 'dzin | |
| Kongpo Bamteng Tulku Tsoknyi Lekdrub | kong po bam steng sprul sku tshogs gnyis legs grub | eighteenth century |
| Kundrol Sangwa Tsel | kun grol gsang ba rtsal | See Dechen Lingpa |
| Kunga Bum | kun dga' 'bum | fifteenth century |

| PHONETICS | WYLIE | ADDITIONAL INFORMATION |
|---|---|---|
| Kunga Drolchok | kun dga' grol mchog | 1507–1565 |
| Kunkyong Lingpa | kun skyong gling pa | 1396–1477 |
| Kuntrul | kun sphrul | nineteenth century |
| Kunzang Dechen Wosel Ling | kun bzang bde chen 'od gsal gling | |
| Kunzang Sang-ngak | kun bzang gsang sngags | nineteenth century |
| Kunzang Sonam | kun bzang bsod nams | nineteenth century |
| Kuzhab | sku zhabs | |
| Kyabche Goto | skyabs che go stod | |
| Kyasu Terton | skya su gter ston | |
| Kyichu | skyid chu | |
| Kyodrak Monastery | skyo brag dgon | |
| | | |
| Lachen Gongpa Rabsel | bla chen dgongs pa rab gsal | 953–1035 |
| Lake Namtso | gnam mtsho | |
| Lake Rewalsar | padma mtsho | |
| Lama Dampa | bla ma dam pa | nineteenth century |
| Lama Dampa Sonam Gyeltsen | bla ma dam pa bsod nams rgyal mtshan | 1312–1375 |
| Lama Gonpo | bla ma mgon po | |
| Lama Pema Kelzang | bla ma padma skal bzang | nineteenth century |
| Lama Ratna | bla ma ratna | nineteenth century |
| Lama Yonten | bla ma yon tan | nineteenth century |
| Lamdre | lam 'bras | |
| Lao Monastery | la'o dgon | |

| PHONETICS | WYLIE | ADDITIONAL INFORMATION |
|---|---|---|
| Lhabu Donyo De | lha bu don yod sde | unknown |
| Lhadrang Monastery | lha 'brang dgon | |
| Lhaksam Tenpai Gyeltsen | lhag bsam bstan pa'i rgyal mtshan | nineteenth century |
| Lhalung | lha lung | |
| Lhalung Khewang Tenpel | lha lung mkhas dbang bstan 'phel | |
| Lhamdo Burmo | lha mdo 'bur mo | |
| Lhamokhar | lha mo mkhar | |
| Lhasa | lha sa | |
| Lhasa Jokhang | lha sa tsug lha khang | |
| Lhasa Monlam | lha sa smon lam | |
| Lhasar Temple | lha gsar lha khang | |
| Lhase Muruk Tsenpo | lha sras mu rug btsan po | eighth century |
| Lhatsen Tsangpa | lha btsan tshangs pa | |
| Lhatsun Namkha Jigme | lha btsun nam mkha' 'jigs med | 1597–1650 |
| Lhayak Guru Lhakhang | la yag gu ru lha khang | |
| Lhokha | lho kha | |
| Lhokhok | lho khog | |
| Lhundrubteng | lhun grub steng | |
| Life stability rite | zhabs brtan | |
| Life-force entrustment | srog gtad | |
| Life-force syllables | srog snying | |
| Ling | gling | |
| Lingtsa Tenkyob | gling tsa brten skyob | |

| PHONETICS | WYLIE | ADDITIONAL INFORMATION |
|---|---|---|
| Lion Turquoise Lake | seng ge g.yu mtsho | |
| Lion's Roar Turquoise Lake | seng ngu g.yu mtsho | |
| Litang | li thang | |
| Lochen Dharmaśrī | lo chen dharma shrI | 1654–1718 |
| Loden Chokse | blo ldan mchog sred | |
| Lodro Nyima Tulku | blo gros nyi ma sprul sku | nineteenth century |
| Lodro Zangpo | blo gros bzang po | nineteenth century |
| Lojong | blo sbyong | |
| Longchenpa Drime Wozer | klong chen pa 'dri med 'od zer | 1308–1364 |
| Longsel Nyingpo | klong gsal snying po | 1625–1692 |
| Longtang Dolma Temple | klong thang sgrol ma lha khang | |
| "Looks Like Me" statue of Padmasambhava | nga 'dra ma | |
| Lord of Life | tshe bdag | |
| Lord of Rakṣa with a Garland of Skulls | srin mgon thod phreng can | |
| Loter Wangpo | blo gter dbang po | 1847–1914 |
| Lotus hat | pad zhwa | |
| Lotus Paradise | padma dga' tshal | |
| Luma | lu'u ma | nineteenth century |
| Lume Tsultrim Sherab | klu mes tshul khrims shes rab | tenth century |
| Lunar mansion | rgyu skar | |

| PHONETICS | WYLIE | ADDITIONAL INFORMATION |
|---|---|---|
| Machik Labdron | ma gcig lab sgron | 1055–1121 |
| Macho Gapa | rma gcod ga pa | |
| Mamo | ma mo | |
| Mamo Botang | ma mo rbod gtong | |
| Mamo Ngondzok Gyelpo | ma mo mngon rdzogs rgyal po | |
| Mandate | gtad rgya | |
| Margyenma | dmar rgyan ma | |
| Marong | rma rong | |
| Marpa Chokyi Lodro | mar pa chos kyi blo gros | c. 1012–1097 |
| Mati Paṇchen | ma ti paN chen | twelfth century |
| Mawochok | smra ba cog | |
| Mekhyil | me 'khyil | |
| Mending | re skong | |
| Mendong Hermitage | sman sdong ri khrod | |
| Mendongpa Karma Ngedon | sman sdong pa karma nges don | c. 1819–1882 |
| Menri Monastery | sman ri dgon | |
| Menri painting tradition | sman ris | |
| Mentor | gsang ston pa | |
| Mesho | rman shod | |
| Milarepa | mi la ras pa | c. 1040–1123 |
| Mind class of Dzogchen | sems sde | |
| Mindroling Monastery | smin 'grol gling dgon | |
| Mingyur Dorje | mi 'gyur rdo rje | 1645–1667 |

| PHONETICS | WYLIE | ADDITIONAL INFORMATION |
| --- | --- | --- |
| (Ju) Mipam Gyatso | ('ju) mi 'pham rgya mtsho | 1846–1912 |
| Mirror | me long | |
| Mishik Dorje | mi shigs rdo rje | eighteenth century |
| Mitrayogin | mi tra tso ki | twelfth century |
| Modrak Cliff in Lhamdo | mo brag | |
| Mokchokpa Rinchen Tsondru | mog lcog pa rin chen brtson 'grus | 1110–1170 |
| Second Moktsa Tulku, Choying Dorje | rmog rtsa 02 chos dbyings rdo rje | b. 1790 |
| Third Moktsa Tulku | rmog rtsa 03 'jigs bral mthu stobs rdo rje | eighteenth–nineteenth century |
| Molten Metal Poison Face | jam dpal gshin rje'i gshed khro chu dug gdong | |
| Moma Kunshe Tingpo | mo ma kun shes thing po | nineteenth century |
| Mopa Drakngak | dmod pa drag sngags | |
| Mother, Child, Foe, or Friend | ma bu dgra grogs | |
| Muchen Sanggye Rinchen | mus chen sangs rgyas rin chen | 1450–1524 |
| Munang Dorje Drakmar | mu nang rdo rje brag dmar | |
| Nāga | klu | |
| Namgyel Ling Monastery | rnam rgyal gling dgon | |
| Namgyel Monastery | rnam rgyal dgon | |
| Namkhai Nyingpo | nam mkha'i snying po | eighth century |

| PHONETICS | WYLIE | ADDITIONAL INFORMATION |
|---|---|---|
| Namling Monastery | rnam gling dgon | |
| Nanam Dorje Dudjom | sna nam rdo rje bdud 'joms | eighth century |
| Nangchen | nang chen | |
| Nangchen Gar | nang chen sgar | |
| Naru | rna ru | |
| Nenang Monastery | gnas nang dgon | |
| Nera | gnas ra | |
| Nesar Karma Tashi Chopel/ Nesar Khenpo Tashi Chopel | gnas gsar karma bkra shis chos 'phel / gnas gsar mkhan po bkra shis chos 'phel | nineteenth century |
| Second Neten Chokling, Ngedon Drubpai Dorje | gnas brtan mchog gling 02 nges don grub pa'i rdo rje | 1873/4–1927 |
| Neten Monastery | gnas brtan dgon | |
| Ngari Lama | mnga' ris bla ma | nineteenth century |
| Ngari Paṇchen Pema Wanggyel | mnga' ris paN chen pad+ma dbang rgyal | 1487–1542 |
| Ngawang Chopel | ngag dbang chos 'phel | 1788–1865 |
| Ngawang Jampel Rinchen | ngag dbang 'jam dpal rin chen | b. 1870s, died before 1926 |
| Ngawang Lekdrub | ngag dbang legs grub | b. 1811 |
| Lama Ngawang Lodro | bla ma ngag dbang blo gros | nineteenth century |
| Ngawang Rinchen | ngag dbang rin chen | nineteenth century |
| Khangsar Khenpo Ngawang Sonam Gyeltsen | khang sar mkhan po ngag dbang bsod nams rgyal mtshan | born c. 1835 |
| Lama Ngedon | bla ma nges don | nineteenth century |
| Ngenlam Gyelwa Chokyang | ngan lam rgyal ba mchog dbyangs | eighth century |

| PHONETICS | WYLIE | ADDITIONAL INFORMATION |
|---|---|---|
| Ngok Loden Sherab | rngog blo ldan shes rab | 1059–1109 |
| Ngok Zhedang Dorje | rngog zhe sdang rdo rje | eleventh century |
| Ngokton Choku Dorje | rngog ston chos sku rdo rje | 1036–1097 |
| Lama Ngondrub | bla ma dngos grub | nineteenth century |
| Ngor Ewaṃ Choden | ngor e waM chos ldan | |
| Ngorchen Kunga Zangpo | ngor chen kun dga' bzang po | 1382–1456 |
| Ngulkhar | dngul mkhar | |
| Ngulpulung | dngul phu lung | |
| Ngulsib | rngul srib | |
| Norbu Dondrub | nor bu don grub | nineteenth–twentieth century |
| Norbu Tendzin | nor bu bstan 'dzin | |
| Norbu Tendzin (student of Khyentse) | nor bu bstan 'dzin | nineteenth century |
| Norbu Tsering | nor bu tshe ring | eighteenth century |
| Northern Treasures | byang gter | |
| Nyake Amgon Gonpo Namgyel | nyag sked a mgon mgon po rnam rgyal | See Gonpo Namgyel |
| Nyakla Pema Dudul | nyag bla padma bdud 'dul | 1816–1872 |
| Nyakla Pema Rigdzin | nyag bla padma rig 'dzin | seventeenth century |
| Nyang Tingdzin Zangpo | myang ting 'dzin bzang po | eighth century |
| Nyangrel Nyima Wozer | nyang ral nyi ma 'od zer | c. 1124–c. 1192 |
| Nyanya Lungten Cave | gnya' gnya' lung bstan phug | |
| Nyarong | nya rong | |

| PHONETICS | WYLIE | ADDITIONAL INFORMATION |
|---|---|---|
| Nyedo Sonam Pel | snye mdo ba bsod nams dpal | 1217–1277 |
| Nyelpa Delek | gnyal pa bde legs | fourteenth century |
| Nyen Valley | snyan | |
| Nyidzong Monastery | nyi rdzong dgon | |
| Nyikhok | snyi khog | |
| Nyima Wozer | nyi ma 'od zer | |
| Nyingma | rnying ma | |
| Nyungne Lama | smyung gnas bla ma | nineteenth century |
| Old Chieftain | dpon rgan | See Khangsar Tsepel |
| Orgyen Drodul Chokgyur Dechen Zhikpo Lingpa | o rgyan mchog gyur bde chen zhig po gling pa | See Chokgyur Lingpa |
| Orgyen Jambhala | o rgyan nor lha dzaM dkar tshe g.yang kha sbyor | |
| Orgyen Lingpa | o rgyan gling pa | b. 1323 |
| Orgyen Nangsi Zilnon | o rgyan snang srid zil gnon | |
| Orgyen Peljor | o rgyan dpal 'byor | nineteenth century |
| Orgyen Pema | o rgyan padma | See Padmasambhava |
| Orgyen Zahorma | o rgyan za hor ma | |
| Orgyenpa Rinchen Pel | o rgyan rin chen dpal | 1229/1230–1309 |
| Ornament of the World | thub pa 'dzam gling rgyan | |
| Other-emptiness | gzhan stong | |
| Otoda | o to dA | |

| PHONETICS | WYLIE | ADDITIONAL INFORMATION |
|---|---|---|
| Pacification Commissioner of Derge | de' er ge te an fu shi | |
| Padampa Sanggye | pa dam pa sangs rgyas | eleventh century |
| Padmakara | padma 'byung gnas | |
| Padmasambhava | padma'i byung gnas | |
| Padmavajra | pad+ma badz+ra | |
| Pakmodrupa Dorje Gyelpo | phag mo gru pa rdo rje rgyal po | 1110–1170 |
| Pakpa Lodro Gyeltsen | phags pa blo gros rgyal mtshan | 1235–1280 |
| Palace of Lotus Light | padma 'od kyi pho brang | |
| Pamay | dpa' smad | |
| Pangpuk Monastery | spang phug dgon | |
| Pangtse Pawo | spang mtshes dpa'i po | unknown |
| Parka | phar ka | |
| Patrul Rinpoche | dpal sprul o rgyan 'jigs med chos kyi dbang po | 1808–1887 |
| Second Pawo, Tsukla Trengwa | dpa' bo 02 gtsug lag 'phreng ba | 1504–1564/1566 |
| Fifth Pawo, Trinle Gyatso | dpa' bo 05 'phrin las rgya mtsho | 1649–1699 |
| Eighth Pawo, Tsukla Chokyi Gyelpo | dpa' bo 08 gtsug lag chos kyi rgyal po | b. 1782 |
| Ninth Pawo, Tsukla Nyinje | dpa' bo 09 gtsug lag nyin byed | d. 1911 |
| Pawopuk Wangchen Drak | dpa' po phug gi dbang chen brag | |
| Peaceful and wrathful deities | zhi khro | |
| Pehar Gyelpo | pe har rgyal po | |

| PHONETICS | WYLIE | ADDITIONAL INFORMATION |
|---|---|---|
| Pel | dpal | |
| Pel Deu | dpal de'u | |
| Pel Jangchub Ling | dpal byang chub gling | |
| Pelchen | dpal chen | |
| Pelchenma | dpal chen ma | |
| Pelden Chime Takpai Dorje | dpal ldan 'chi med rtag pa'i rdo rje | b. 1851? d. 1898? |
| Pelden Chogyel (teacher at Zhechen) | dpal ldan chos rgyal | nineteenth century |
| Pelden Chogyel (monk from Pelyul) | dpal ldan chos rgyal | nineteenth century |
| Pelden Lhamo | dpal ldan lha mo | |
| Pelek | gnyer pad legs | nineteenth century |
| Pelkhyim Amye Orgyen Tendzin | dpal khyim a mye o rgyan bstan 'dzin | born circa 1851 |
| Pelgyi Nyingpo Lodro Drime Tsel | dpal gyi snying po blo gros dri med rtsal | |
| Pelgyi Pukring | dpal gyi phug ring | |
| Peljor Gang | dpal 'byor sgang | |
| Peljor Zangpo | dpal 'byor bzang po | unknown |
| Pelme Monastery | dpal me | |
| Pelpung Monastery, Tubten Chokhor Ling | dpal spung dgon thub bstan chos 'khor gling | |
| Peltsa Wopung | phel tsha 'od phung dgon | |
| Pelyul Monastery | dpal yul dgon | |
| Pema | Padma | |
| Pema Dechen Lingpa | padma bde chen gling pa | 1663–1713 |

| PHONETICS | WYLIE | ADDITIONAL INFORMATION |
|---|---|---|
| Pema Drawa | padma drwa ba | |
| Pema Gargyi Wang-chuk Trinle Drodul Tsel | pad+ma gar gyi dbang phyug phrin las 'gro 'dul rtsal | |
| Pema Gyelpo | padma rgyal po | |
| Pema Khyungdzong | padma khyung rdzong | |
| Pema Lekdrub | padma legs grub | nineteenth century |
| Pemaling Lake | sgrub mtsho padma gling | |
| Pema Lingpa | padma gling pa | 1450–1521 |
| Pema Norbu | padma nor bu | nineteenth century |
| Pema Sang-ngak Tendzin | padma gsang sngags bstan 'dzin | nineteenth century |
| Pema Shelpuk | padma gshel phug | |
| Pema Shelri | padma shel ri | |
| Pema Tenpel | padma bstan 'phel | nineteenth century |
| Pema Vajra | padma rdo rje | 1807–1884 |
| Pema Yeshe | padma ye shes | nineteenth century |
| Penyul Valley | phan yul | |
| Permanently Abiding Turquoise Lake | g.yu mtsho gtan khyil | |
| Permanently Abiding Wild Lion Turquoise Lake | seng rgod g.yu mtsho gtan 'khyil | |
| Lama Pewang | bla ma pad dbang | |
| Pewar Monastery | dpe war | |
| Phoenix | tshe ring bya | |
| Pointing-out instructions | ngo sprod kyi gdams pa | |

| PHONETICS | WYLIE | ADDITIONAL INFORMATION |
|---|---|---|
| Potala | po ta la pho brang | |
| Potsolo Pass | po tsho lo | |
| Preceptor | slob dpon | |
| Preliminary practice | sngon 'gro | |
| Prosperity rite | yang skyabs / g.yangs chog | |
| Pukpa calendar system | phug pa | |
| Pulungwa Tsewang Dorje (Cabinet Minister) | phu lung ba tshe dbang rdo rje (zhabs pad) | nineteenth century |
| Punrabpa Tsering Pelden | phun rab pa tshe ring dpal ldan | nineteenth century |
| Purtsa Khenpo Akon (Konchok Wozer) | phur tsha mkhan po a dkon (dkon mchog 'od zer) | nineteenth century |
| Puyang Dramdul | phu yang dgra 'dul | |
| Ra Lotsāwa Zhonnu Pel | rwa lo tsA ba gzhon nu dpal | 1392–1481. P318 |
| Rabsel Plain | rab gsal thang | |
| Rakchab | rag chab | |
| Raktrul Monastery | rag 'phrul | |
| Ram Tsenchen | ram tsan can | twelfth century |
| Ramo Shelmen | ra mo shel sman | thirteenth century |
| Ramoche Temple | ra mo che | |
| Rangjung Gyelmo | rang byung rgyal mo | |
| Ratna Lingpa | ratna gling pa | 1403–1479 |
| Rechung Dorje Drakpa | ras chung rdo rje grags pa | 1084–1161 |

| PHONETICS | WYLIE | ADDITIONAL INFORMATION |
|---|---|---|
| Rechung Hearing Lineage | ras chung snyan brgyud | |
| Regent statue | sku tshab | |
| Reti Lake | re ti'i mtsho | |
| Reting Monastery | rwa sgreng dgon | |
| Third Reting Rinpoche, Ngawang Yeshe Tsultrim Gyeltsen | rwa sgreng 03 ngag dbang ye shes tshul khrims rgyal mtshan | 1816–1863 |
| Rigdzin Dolma | rig 'dzin sgrol ma | d. 1885 |
| Rigdzin Dorje Drakpa | rig 'dzin rdo rje brag pa | eighteenth century |
| Rigdzin Godemchen | rig 'dzin rgod ldem chen | 1337–1409 |
| Rigdzin Tamdrin Gonpo | rig 'dzin rta mgrin mgon po | eighteenth century |
| Rigdzin Tulku | rig 'dzin sprul sku | nineteenth century |
| Rinchen (Pelpung Chant Master) | rin chen (dpal spungs dbu mdzad ) | nineteenth century |
| Khenpo Rinchen Dargye | mkhan po rin chen dar rgyas | nineteenth century |
| Rinchen Zangpo | rin chen bzang po | 958–1055 |
| Ringu Monastery | ri mgul dgon | |
| Rinpung | rin spungs | |
| Third Ripa Tulku, Dondrub Gyeltsen | ri pa sprul sku 03 don grub rgyal mtshan | nineteenth century |
| Ritrul Dargye Gyatso | ri sprul dar rgyas rgya mtsho | nineteenth century |
| Riwo Wangzhu | ri bo dbang zhu | |
| Seventh Riwoche, Jedrung Jampa Jungne | ri bo che rje drung 07 byams pa'i 'byung gnas | 1856–1922 |
| Riwoche Monastery | ri bo che dgon | |

| PHONETICS | WYLIE | ADDITIONAL INFORMATION |
|---|---|---|
| Rolpai Dorje | rol pa'i rdo rje | d. 1719 |
| Rongdzom Chokyi Zangpo | rong zom chos kyi bzang po | 1042–1136 |
| Ronggyab | rong rgyab | |
| Rongme | rong me / rme / med | |
| Rongme Chime Karmo Taktsang | rong me 'chi med dkar mo stag tshang | |
| Rongta Tulku | rong mtha' sprul sku | nineteenth century |
| Rongton Sheja Kunrik | rong ston shes bya kun rigs | 1367–1449 |
| Rudam | ru dam | |
| Sabzang Mati Paṇchen Lodro Gyeltsen | sa bzang ma ti paN chen blo gros rgyal mtshan | 1294–1376 |
| Sakya | sa skya | |
| Sakya Monastery | sa skya dgon | |
| Sakya Paṇḍita Kunga Gyeltsen | sa skya paN+Di ta kun dga' rgyal mtshan | 1182–1251 |
| Śākya Sengge | ShAkya seng ge | |
| Samar | sa dmar | |
| Samaya | dam tshig | |
| Saṃpuṭa | sam pu tra | |
| Samten | bsam gtan | nineteenth century |
| Samye Chimpu | bsam yas mchims phu | |
| Samye Monastery | bsam yas dgon | |
| Sangdak Gonpo | gsang bdag mgon po | nineteenth century |
| Sanggye Lama | sangs rgyas bla ma | died circa 1080 |
| Sanggye Lingpa | sangs rgyas gling pa | 1340–1396 |

| PHONETICS | WYLIE | ADDITIONAL INFORMATION |
|---|---|---|
| Sanggye Nyenpa | sangs rgyas mnyan pa | 1445–1510 |
| Seventh Sanggye Nyenpa, Sherab Nyingpo | sangs rgyas mnyan pa 07 shes rab snying po | nineteenth century |
| Sanggye Tso | sangs rgyas 'tsho | unknown |
| Sangpu Neutok | sang phu ne'u thog | |
| Sangzhung | gsang gzhung | |
| Sarma | gsar ma | |
| Satisfied the wishes | re skong | |
| Savage mantra | sngags rgod | |
| Sawang Kunga Dega Zangpo | sa dbang kun dga' bzang po | late-eighteenth to early-nineteenth century |
| Se Khardo | gsas mkhar mdo | |
| Secret Padmasam-bhava Cave | o rgyan gsang phug | |
| Sekhar Gutok | sras dkar gu thog | |
| Self-emptiness | rang stong | |
| Sen | sen | |
| Sengchen Namdrak | seng chen nam brag | |
| Sengge Dradrok | seng ge sgra sgrogs | |
| Sengge Namdzong | seng ge gnam rdzong | |
| Senggo Yumtso | seng rgod g.yu mtsho | |
| Senmo | bsen mo | |
| Sera | se ra | |
| Sershul | ser shul | |
| Serta | gser thar | |
| Sertal Lhatse Tulku | gser thal lha rtse sprul sku | nineteenth century |

| PHONETICS | WYLIE | ADDITIONAL INFORMATION |
|---|---|---|
| Seven Descents | bka' bab bdun | |
| Shang Valley | Shang Valley | |
| Shangpa Kagyu | shangs pa bka' brgyud | |
| Sharawa Yonten Drak | sha ra ba yon tan grags | 1070–1141 |
| Shedra Wangchuk Gyelpo | bshad sgra dbang phyug rgyal po | 1795–1864 |
| Sheldrak | shel brag | |
| Shelkharza Dorje Tso | shel dkar bza' rdo rje mtsho | unknown |
| Sherab Gyeltsen | shes rab rgyal mtshan | nineteenth century |
| Shigatse | gzhis ka rtse | |
| Sholhak | sho lhag | |
| Shong Lotsāwa Dorje Gyeltsen | shong lo tsa ba rdo rje rgyal mtshan | thirteenth century |
| Shubha Monastery | shu bha 'brug dgu gling | |
| Shumidhur | shu mi dhur | |
| Sidu Pass | si du la | |
| Single Intent | dgongs gcig | |
| Sinpo Ri | srin po ri | |
| Sipai Gyelmo | srid pa'i rgyal mo | |
| Situ | si tu | See Tai Situ |
| Situ Paṇchen | si tu paN chen | See Eighth Tai Situ |
| Six Unions | sbyor drug | |
| Six Yogas of Nāropā | nA ro chos drug | |
| Six Yogas of Niguma | ni gu chos drug | |
| Sixteen Drops | thig le bcu drug | |
| Skillful means (upāya) | thabs | |

| PHONETICS | WYLIE | ADDITIONAL INFORMATION |
|---|---|---|
| Smoke offering | bsang mchod | |
| So tradition of Samyak | so lugs yang dag | |
| Sok Zamkha | sog zam kha | |
| Sokmo | sog mo | |
| Sokmo Podrang | sog mo pho brang | |
| Solpon clan | gsol dpon tshang | |
| Sonam Chopel | bsod nams chos 'phel | 1595–1658 |
| Sonam Gyatso | bsod nams rgya mtsho | nineteenth century |
| Sonam Lodro | bsold nams blo gros | 1784–1835 |
| Sonam Pel | bsod nams dpal | eighteenth–nineteenth century |
| Sonam Puntsok | bsod nams phun tshogs | eighteenth century |
| Sonam Rinchen | bsod nams rin chen | thirteenth century |
| Sonam Tobgyel | bsod nams stobs rgyal | nineteenth century |
| Sotrul | bsod sprul | nineteenth century |
| Spoken Word | bka' ma | |
| Śrī Siṃha College | shrI sing+ha bshad grwa | |
| Stages of white, red, and black | kha ba dkar dmar nag pa'i rim gsum | |
| Star-like | skar ma lta bu | |
| Swift Acting Wisdom Protector | myur mdzad mgon po | |
| Tael | Kongtrul wrote both rtil and rtel (liang) | |
| Fourth Tai Situ, Chokyi Gocha | ta'i si tu 04 chos kyi go cha | 1542–1585 |
| Eighth Tai Situ, Chokyi Jungne | ta'i si tu 08 chos kyi 'byung gnas | 1700–1774 |

| PHONETICS | WYLIE | ADDITIONAL INFORMATION |
|---|---|---|
| Ninth Tai Situ, Pema Nyinje | ta'i si tu 09 padma nyin byed | 1774–1853 |
| Tenth Tai Situ, Pema Kunzang | ta'i si tu 10 padma kun bzang | 1854–1886 |
| Eleventh Tai Situ, Pema Wangchok Gyalp | ta'i si tu 11 pad+ma dbyang mchok rgyal po | 1886–1952 |
| Takchen Bumpa | rtag spyan bum pa | |
| Taklung Monastery | stag lung dgo | |
| Taklung Tangpa Tashi Pel | stag lung thang pa bkra shis dpal | 1042–1109 |
| Taksham Nuden Dorje | stag sham nus ldan rdo rje | b. 1655 |
| Takten Puntsokling | rtag brtan phun tshogs gling | |
| Tamdrin Gonpo | rta mgrin mgon po | eighteenth century |
| Tamdrin Wangmo | rta mgrin dbang mo | born circa 1787 |
| Tangtong Gyelpo | thang stong rgyal po | 1361–1485 |
| Tangyak the Smith | thang yag mgar ba | |
| Tarde Hermitage | thar bde ri khrod | |
| Tartse Khenpo Jampa Kunga Tendzin | thar rtse mkhan po byams pa kun dga' bstan 'dzin | 1776–1862 |
| Tartse Khenpo Jampa Namkha Chime | thar rtse mkhan po byams pa nam mkha' 'chi med | 1765–1820 |
| Tartse Khenpo Jampel Zangpo | thar rtse mkhan po 'jam dpal bzang po | 1789–1864 |
| Tartse Zhabdrung Tenpai Nyima | thar rtse zhabs drung bstan pa'i nyi ma | nineteenth century |
| Tashi | bkra shis | |
| Tashi Chopel (disciple of Kongtrul) | | See Nesar Karma Tashi Chopel |

| PHONETICS | WYLIE | ADDITIONAL INFORMATION |
|---|---|---|
| Tashi Chopel (steward of Pelpung) | bkra shis chos 'phel | nineteenth century |
| Tashi Dokha | bkra shis rdo kha | |
| Tashi Gyatso | bkra shis rgya mtsho | nineteenth century |
| Tashi Gyel | bkra shis rgyal | nineteenth century |
| Tashi Nenang | bkra shis gnas nang | |
| Tashi Nyida Pelpuk Cave | bkra shis nyi zla dpal phug | |
| Tashi Pelpuk | bkra shis dpal phug | |
| Tashi Podrang | bkra shis pho brang | |
| Tashi Samdrub | bkra shis bsam grub | nineteenth century |
| Tashi Sampel | bkra shis bsam 'phel | nineteenth century |
| Tashi Temple | bkra shis lha khang | |
| Tashi Tobgyel | bkra shis stobs rgyal | 1550–1603 |
| Tashi Tso | bkra shis 'tso | d. 1867 |
| Tashi Umatang | bkra shis dbu ma thang | |
| Tashi Wobar | bkra shis 'od 'bar | |
| Tashi Wozer | bkra shis 'od zer | 1826–1910 |
| Tashilhunpo | bkra shis lhun po | |
| Tendzin Namgyel | bstan 'dzin rnam rgyal | eighteenth century |
| Tendzin Tulku | bstan 'dzin sprul sku | nineteenth century |
| Tendzin Yungdrung | bstan 'dzin g.yung drung | |
| Tengyur | bstan 'gyur | |
| Tenma Goddesses | brtan ma | |
| Tenpa Dargye | bstan pa dar gyas | unknown |
| Tenpa Tsering | bstan pa tshe ring | 1678–1738 |

| PHONETICS | WYLIE | ADDITIONAL INFORMATION |
|---|---|---|
| Lama Tenpel Dodon | bla ma bstan 'phel 'dod don | nineteenth century |
| Terdak Lingpa Gyurme Dorje | gter bdag gling pa 'gyur med rdo rje | 1646–1714 |
| Terlung Valley | gter klung/gter lhung | |
| Terton Gar | gter ston sgar | |
| Terton Sogyel Lerab Lingpa | gter ston bsod rgyal las rab gling pa | 1856–1926 |
| Thread-cross | mdos | |
| Three solitudes | dben gsum | |
| Three vows | sdom pa gsum | |
| Three Wild Tsen Brothers | btsan rgod mched gsum | |
| Tikle | thig le | |
| Time-keeper | dus go ba | |
| Tinglhung Valley | rting glung/rting lhung | See Terlung Valley |
| Tingtsa Hot Springs | rting tsha | |
| Tokden | rtogs ldan | |
| Tokden Samten Tendzin | rtogs ldan bsam gtan bstan 'dzin | nineteenth century |
| Tokden Sanggye Rabten | rtogs ldan sangs rgyas rab brtan | eighteenth century? |
| Togel | thod rgal | |
| Tolung Valley | stod lung | |
| Tongdrol Temple at Pelpung | dpal spung mthong grol lha khang | |
| Tongkhor Monastery, Amdo | a mdo stong 'khor dgon | |
| Tongkhor Monastery, Kham | khams stong 'khor dgon | |

| PHONETICS | WYLIE | ADDITIONAL INFORMATION |
|---|---|---|
| Eighth Tongkhor Zhabdrung, Ngawang Dogyu Yonten Rabgye | stong 'khor zhabs 'drung o8 ngag dbang mdo rgyud yon tan rab rgyas | 1853–1907 |
| Ninth Tongkhor Zhabdrung, Tubten Jigme Gyatso | stong 'khor zhabs 'drung o9 thub bstan 'jigs med rgya mtsho | 1820–1882 |
| Tonglen | gtong len | |
| Tonmi Sambhoṭa | thon mi sambho Ta | seventh century |
| Tonpa Jetsuma | thon pa rje btsun ma | |
| Torma | gtor ma | |
| Tour the abode | gnas skor | |
| Toyon Paṇḍita, Yeshe Dundrub Tenpai Gyaltse | tho yon paN+Dita ye shes don grub bstan pa'i rgyal mtshan | 1792–1855 |
| Sixth Traleb Rinpoche, Yeshe Nyima | khra leb o6 rin po che ye shes nyi ma | d. 1874 |
| Tranduk | khra 'brug | |
| Tranggu Monastery | khra 'gu dgon | |
| Transference | pho ba | |
| Transmission | lung | |
| Trao Plain | khra'o thang | |
| Trawo | khra bo | |
| Treasure | gter ma | |
| Trekchod | khregs chod | |
| Trengpo Terton Sherab Wozer | phreng po gter ston shes rab 'od zer. The Diary also reads 'phreng mgo/'phrang mgo | 1518–1584 |
| King Tri Songdetsen | khri srong lde'u btsan | 742–796 |

| PHONETICS | WYLIE | ADDITIONAL INFORMATION |
|---|---|---|
| Triad of Khyen-tse, Kongtrul, and Chokling | mkhyen kong mchog sde gsum | |
| Tridu Behu | khri 'du be hu | |
| Trimon Chime Dorje | khri smon 'chi med rdo rje | nineteenth century |
| Trinle Chodron | phrin las chos sgron | eighteenth–nineteenth century |
| Tro Maṇḍala Plain | khro maN+Da la thang | |
| Trochu | khro chu | |
| Trokyab Monastery | khro skyabs dgon | |
| Tromge | khrom dge | |
| Tromtar | khrom thar | |
| Tropu Kagyu | khro phu bka' brgyud | |
| Tropu Lotsāwa Jampa Pel | khro phu lo tsA ba byams pa dpal | c. 1172–c. 1236 |
| Tropu Lotsāwa Rinchen Sengge | khro phu to tsA ba rin chen seNg ge | b. 1173 |
| Tropu Monastery | khro phu dgon | |
| Trukhang Lotsāwa Sonam Gyatso | khrus khang lo tsA ba bsod nams rgya mtsho | 1424–1482 |
| First Trungpa, Kunga Gyeltsen | drung pa 01 kun dga' rgyal mtshan | fifteenth century |
| Ninth Trungpa Tulku, Karma Tenpel | drung pa 09 karma bstan 'phel | nineteenth century |
| Tsabtsa | tshab tsha | |
| Tsabtsa Tulku | tshab tsha sprul sku | nineteenth century |
| Tsādra Rinchen Drak | rtsa 'dra rin chen brag | |
| Tsagye Plain | rtsa brgyad thang | |
| Tsagyepa Dorje Sengge | rtsa brgyad pa rdo rje seng ge | |

| Phonetics | Wylie | Additional Information |
|---|---|---|
| Tsak Darma Gyelpo | rtsags dar ma rgyal po | unknown |
| Tsakho Monastery | tsa kho dgon | |
| Tsampa | rtsam pa | |
| Tsangrong | gtsang rong | |
| Tsangwa Monastery | gtsang ba dgon | |
| Tsāri | tsA ri | |
| Tsarpa | tshar pa | |
| Tsasum Lingpa | rtsa gsum gling pa | 1694–1730 |
| Tsechu Bumpa stūpa | tshes bcu 'bum pa mchod rten | |
| Tsechu Monastery | tshes bcu dgon | |
| Tsechu River | tshes chu | |
| Tsedrum Monastery | tshe b+hrUM | |
| Tsel Gungtang | tshal gung thang | |
| Tsele Natsok Rangdrol | rtse le sna tshogs rang grol | b. 1602 |
| Tselpa Kagyu | tshal pa bka' brgyud | |
| Tsen | gtsan | |
| Tsengye Temple | mtshan brgyad khang | |
| Tsenri Dorje Drak | btsan ri rdo rje brag | |
| Tsepak | tshe dpag | |
| Tsering Chodron | tshe ring chos sgron | nineteenth century |
| Tsering Dondrub (Derge steward) | tshe ring don grub | nineteenth century |
| Tsering Dondrub (brother of Rigdzin Dolma) | tshe ring don grub | nineteenth century |
| Tsering Jong | tshe ring ljongs | |

| PHONETICS | WYLIE | ADDITIONAL INFORMATION |
|---|---|---|
| Tsetang Monastery | rtse thang dgon | |
| Tseten Dolkar | tshe brtan sgrol dkar | nineteenth century |
| Tsetru | tshe phru | |
| Tsetsa | tshe tsha | |
| Tsewa Rinchen Namgyel | tshe ba rin chen rnam rgyal | nineteenth century |
| Tsewang Dorje Dradul | tshe dbang rdo rje dgra 'dul | b. 1823 |
| Tsewang Dorje Rigdzin | tshe dbang rdo rje rig 'dzin | b. 1786 |
| Tsewang Drakpa (son of Chokgyur Lingpa) | tshe dbang grags pa | nineteenth century |
| Tsewang Drakpa (terton) | tshe dbang grags pa | See Dechen Lingpa |
| Tsewang Kunkhyab | tshe dbang kun khyab | eighteenth century |
| Tsewang Lhamo | tshe dbang lha mo | d. 1812 |
| Tsewang Norbu | tshe dbang nor bu | 1698–1755 |
| Tsewang Puntsok Tenkyong | tshe dbang pun tshogs bstan skyong | b. 1822 |
| Second Tsike Chokling, Konchok Gyurme | rtsi ke mchog gling 02 dkon mchog 'gyur med | 1871–1939 |
| Tsike Monastery | rtsi ke | |
| Tsogyel Lhatso | mtsho rgyal lha mtsho | |
| Tsokye Dorje | mtsho skyes rdo rje | |
| Tsongkhapa Lobzang Drakpa | tsong kha pa blo bzang grags pa | 1357–1419 |
| Tsultrim Pelmo | tshul khrims dpal mo | nineteenth century |
| First Tsurpu Gyeltsab, Peljor Dondrub | mtshur phu rgyal tshab 01 dpal 'byor don grub | 1427–1489 |

| PHONETICS | WYLIE | ADDITIONAL INFORMATION |
|---|---|---|
| Fourth Tsurpu Gyeltsab, Drakpa Dondrub | mtshur phu rgyal tshab 04 grags pa don grub | 1550–1617 |
| Fifth Tsurpu Gyeltsab, Drakpa Choyang | mtshur phu rgyal tshab 05 grags pa mchog dbyangs | 1617–1658 |
| Ninth Tsurpu Gyeltsab, Yeshe Zangpo | mtshur phu rgyal tshab 09 ye shes bzang po | 1821–1876 |
| Tenth Tsurpu Gyeltsab, Tenpai Nyima | mtshur phu rgyal tshab 10 bstan pa'i nyi ma | 1877–1909 |
| Tsurpu Jamyang Dondrub Wozer | mtshur phu 'jam dbyangs don grub 'od zer | 1424–1482 |
| Tsurpu Monastery | mtshur phu dgon | |
| Tulku | sprul sku | |
| Tummo | gtum mo | |
| Turning back the escort | zhabs brtan sun zlog | |
| Uchetem | dbu che ltem | |
| Ula Stūpa | u la mchod rten | |
| Ultimate empowerment | don dbang | |
| Upper Ling | gling stod | |
| Upper Won | dbon stod | |
| U-Tsang | dbus gtsang | |
| Vairocana Crystal Light Cave | bai ro'i 'od gsal shel phug | |

| PHONETICS | WYLIE | ADDITIONAL INFORMATION |
|---|---|---|
| Vajra | rdo rje | |
| Vajra master | rdo rje slob dpon | |
| Wangchen Puk | dbang chen phug | |
| Wangchuk Dorje | dbang phyug rdo rje | See Tsewang Drakpa, Chokgyur Lingpa's son |
| Wentok | dban thog | |
| Wokmin Karma | og min karma | |
| Won Lama | dbon bla ma | |
| Won Wanggi Dorje | dbon dbang gi rdo rje | eighteenth century |
| Wongen Karma Tekchok Tenpel | dbon rgan karma theg mchog bstan 'phel | d. 1843 |
| Wontrul | dbon sprul | |
| Wontrul Tulku Karma Drubgyu Tendzin Trinle | dbon sprul karma sgrub brgyud bstan 'dzin phrin las | d. 1874 |
| Wrathful Power | thugs sgrub drag po rtsal | |
| Wrathful Vajra Power | rdo rje drag po rtsal | |
| Yakchar Ngonmo | g.yag phyar sngon mo | unknown |
| Yamalung Hermitage | g.ya' ma lung | |
| Yamāntaka | gshin rje gshed | |
| Yamdrok Lake | yar 'drog mtsho | |
| Yangchen Dolma | dbyangs can sgrol ma | |
| Yangpachen | yangs pa chen | |
| Mount Yarlha Shampo | yar lha sham po | |
| Yarlung Tsangpo River | yar klung tsang po | |

| PHONETICS | WYLIE | ADDITIONAL INFORMATION |
|---|---|---|
| Yelpuk | yel phuk | |
| Yeshe Gyatso | ye shes rgya mtsho | sixteenth–seventeenth century |
| Yeshe Pelmo | ye shes dpal mo | |
| Yeshe Tsogyel | ye shes mtsho rgyal | |
| Yidam | yi dam | |
| Yilhung | yid lhung | |
| Yilhung Lhatso | yid lhung lha mtsho | |
| Yishin Wanggyel | yid bzhin dbang rgyal | nineteenth century |
| Yongge Mingyur Dorje | yongs dge mi 'gyur rdo rje | 1628/41–1708 |
| Yonten Gyatso | yon tan rgya mtsho | |
| Yudruk Chapel | g.yu 'brug lha khang | |
| Yulung Sheldrak | g.yu lung shel brag | |
| Yumbu Lagang | yum bu bla sgang | |
| Yungdrung Puntsok | g.yung drung phun tshogs | late-eighteenth to mid-nineteenth century |
| Yungdrung Tsultrim | g.yung drung tshul 'khrims | nineteenth century |
| Yungton Dorje Pelwa | g.yung ston rdo rje dpal ba | 1284–1365 |
| Yutok Namgyel Ling | g.yu thog rnam rgyal gling | |
| Yutok Yonten Gonpo (the earlier) | g.yu thog yon tan mgon po snga ma | 790–833 |
| Yutok Yonten Gonpo (the later) | g.yu thog yon tan mgon po phyi ma | 1126–1202 |
| Yuzhel Shrine | bar khang g.yu zhal | |

| PHONETICS | WYLIE | ADDITIONAL INFORMATION |
|---|---|---|
| Zabbulung | zab bu klung | |
| Zahor | za hor | |
| Zangjangma | zangs byang ma | |
| Zangpo Drakpa | bzang po grags pa | fourteenth century |
| Zangri Khangmar | zangs ri mkhar dmar | |
| Zha Temple | zhwa'i lha khang | |
| Zhabkar Tsokdruk Rangdrol | zhabs dkar tshogs drug rang grol | 1781–1851 |
| Zhalu Chokyong Zangpo | zhwa lu chos skyong bzang po | 1441–1527 |
| Zhalu Monastery | zhwa lu dgon | |
| Zhalu Ribuk Tulku Losel Tenkyong | zhwa lu ri sbug sprul sku blo gsal bstan skyong | b. 1804 |
| Second Zhamar, Khacho Wangpo | zhwa dmar 02 mkha' spyod dbang po | 1350–1405 |
| Fourth Zhamar, Chokyi Drakpa | zhwa dmar 04 chos kyi grags pa | 1453–1524 |
| Fifth Zhamar, Konchok Yenlak | zhwa dmar 05 dkon mchog yan lag | 1525–1583 |
| Sixth Zhamar, Chokyi Wangchuk | zhwa dmar 06 chos kyi dbang phyug | 1584–1630 |
| Seventh Zhamar, Yeshe Nyingpo | zhwa dmar 07 ye shes snying po | 1631–1694 |
| Tenth Zhamar, Mipam Chodrub Gyatso | zhwa dmar 10 chos grub rgya mtsho | 1741–1792 |
| Zhang Tsondru Drakpa | zhang brtson 'grus grags pa | 1123–1193 |
| Zhang Zhong Monastery | zhang zhong dgon | |

| Phonetics | Wylie | Additional Information |
|---|---|---|
| Second Zhechen Gyeltsab, Pema Sanggnak Tendzin Chogyel | zhe chen rgyal tshab 02 pad+ma gsang sngags bstan 'dzin chos rgyal | 1760–1817 |
| Third Zhechen Gyeltsab, Orgyen Rangjung Dorje | zhe chen rgyal tshab 03 o rgyan rang byung rdo rje tshe dbang grub pa rtsal | born circa 1817 |
| Fourth Zhechen Gyeltsab, Pema Namgyel | zhe chen rgyal tshab 04 padma rnam rgyal | b. 1871 |
| Zhechen Monastery, Tennyi Dargye Ling | zhe chen dgon bstan gnyis dar rgyas gling | |
| Second Zhechen Rabjam, Gyurme Kunzang | zhe chen rab 'byams 02 'gyur med kun bzang rnam rgyal | 1713–1769 |
| Third Zhechen Rabjam, Rigdzin Peljor Gyatso | zhe chen rab 'byams 03 rig 'dzin dpal 'byor rgya mtsho | 1771–1807 |
| Fourth Zhechen Rabjam, Garwang Chokyi Gyeltsen | zhe chen rab 'byams 04 gar dbang chos kyi rgyal mtshan | 1811–1862 |
| Fifth Zhechen Rabjam, Pema Tekchok Tenpai Gyeltsen | zhe chen rab 'byams 05 pad+ma theg mchog bstan pa'i rgyal mtshan | 1864–1909 |
| Seventh Zhechen Rabjam, Jikme Chokyi Sengge | zhe chen rab 'byams 07 'jigs med chos kyi sengge | b. 1966 |
| Zhechen Wontrul Gyurme Tutob Namgyel | zhe chen dbon sprul 'gyur med mthu stobs rnam rgyal | 1787–c. 1855 |
| Zhije | zhi byed | |
| Zhikpo Lingpa | zhig po gling pa | 1524–1583 |
| Zhitro Shelpuk | zhi khro shel phug | |
| Zhuchen Tsultrim Rinchen | zhu chen tshul khrims rin chen | 1697–1774 |

| PHONETICS | WYLIE | ADDITIONAL INFORMATION |
|---|---|---|
| Zhung Treshing | gzhung spre'u zhing | |
| Zurchung Sherab Drakpa | zur chung shes rab grags pa | 1014–1074 |
| Zurkharwa Nyamnyi Dorje | zur mkhar ba mnyam nyid rdo rje | 1439–1475 |
| Zurmang Dutsitil Monastery | zur mang bdud rtsi mthil dgon pa | |
| Zurmang Mahāmudrā | zur mang snyan brgyud | |
| Zurmang Namgyeltse Monastery | zur mang rnam rgyal rtse dgon | |

# Notes

## Citation Abbreviations

1. Autobiography: Jamgön Kongtrul Lodrö Thayé, 2003
2. Chokling's *Kham Gazetteer*: Chokgyur Lingpa, 1982 (1857)
3. Diary: Jamgon Kongtrul, 2002a
4. Kongtrul's *Kham Gazetteer*: Kongtrul, 2005 (1868)
5. *Tsadra Gazetteer*: Chokgyur Lingpa, 1982 (1859)

## Preface

1. See Jackson 2003 and Lopez 2018.
2. See Smith 2001.
3. See Jamgon Kongtrul 1995.
4. See Jamgon Kongtrul 2003.
5. See, for example, Rangjung Dorje 2014, Jamgon Kongtrul 2002, and Jamgon Kongtrul 1987.
6. Doctor 2005. His catalog of the Collected Revelations of Chokgyur Lingpa was previously available on the Tibetan and Himalayan Library website.
7. Henning's Tsurpu calculation charts are at: http://www.kalacakra.org/calendar/tiblist2.htm.

## 1. Kham

1. For a general survey of the history of Kham, see Gardner 2003. Collections of academic articles on Kham are Epstein 2002, van Spengen and Lama Jabb 2009, and Gros 2016. Hartley 1997 remains the best survey of the Derge political structures. Kolmaš 1968 and 1988, and van der Kuijp 1988 are sources for the Derge royal genealogy.
2. Gushri Khan was lured into Kham on the pretext that the king of Beri had conspired with the king of Tsang to jointly attack the Geluk stronghold of Lhasa and put an end to the growing power of the Geluk. The Rinpung family that then ruled Tibet from their seat at Shigatse were patrons of Kagyu and Sakya institutions and supported an ecumenical religious environment in Tsang. The Geluk mastermind of Gushri's invasion of Kham, an official at the Geluk monastery of Drepung outside of Lhasa named Sonam Chopel, encouraged Gushri to bring his army into Tibet and attack Tsang, clearing the way for Geluk political supremacy.
3. On the creation of the Derge canon, see Harrison 1996, Li 1945, and Chaix 2016.

4. The *tael* was the Imperial Chinese measure of silver, usually around 35 grams, although the actual weight varied by different regions.

5. On Situ Paṇchen, see Jackson 2009.

6. On Sawang and Tsewang Lhamo's trip to Tibet, see Gyatso 1997.

7. On Tsewang Lhamo, see Ronis 2011.

8. Ronis 2011.

9. Ronis 2011.

10. Diary p. 7b.

## 2. BIRTH, YOUTH, AND EARLY EDUCATION: 1813–1829

1. Diary p. 6b.

2. Diary p. 113b.

3. Diary p. 7b.

4. Diary p. 6b. Kongtrul uses the terms *las kyi pha* and *pha yar* for "foster father."

5. Diary p. 7b.

6. Kongtrul's lineage prayer to the Khyungpo clan is *Melodious Supplication*.

7. On Bon, see Martin 1991, 1996, and 2001, Karmay 1972, and Karmay and Watt 2007.

8. Diary pp. 8a–b.

9. Diary pp. 7b–8a.

10. Diary pp. 7b–8a.

11. Diary pp. 8b–9b.

12. Diary pp. 8b–9a.

13. Diary pp. 9b–10a.

14. Diary p. 10a. Mishik Dorje's revelations are classified as "New Bon." Kongtrul declined to include any in his Treasury of Revelations. Kongtrul used the Sanskrit work *bande* for "monk."

15. Diary p. 10b.

16. Diary p. 12a.

17. Diary p. 10b.

18. Diary p. 10b.

19. For a traditional description of the transference rite, see Patrul Rinpoche 1994, Part Three.

20. Diary p. 11b.

21. Diary p. 11b.

22. Hartley 1996, Li An-che 1947.

23. Diary p. 11a. "Chieftain of Den Chode County" is a translation for *'dan chos sde'i dpon*. The name of the administrative district was Den Chode.

24. Diary pp. 12a–b.

25. Diary p. 12b. In 1872 Kongtrul donated a piece of land in the valley to Tarde Monastery. This may have come into his possession at that point through inheritance or donation, and so may have belonged to his mother; see chapter 25.

26. Diary pp. 12b–13a.

27. Diary p. 13a.
28. Diary p. 13b.

## 3. ZHECHEN: 1829–1833

1. The end of 1829 to the beginning of 1833 corresponds to the ninth month of the Earth Ox Year to the first month of the Water Snake Year.
2. Diary pp. 13a; 17a. The main biography of Zhechen Wontrul, written at the request of Jamyang Khyentse Wangpo, is Dorje Rabten 2000.
3. Diary p. 13b.
4. Diary p. 13b. For Kongtrul's description of Mother, Child, Foe, or Friend, see Jamgon Kongtrul 1995, p. 256, note 9.
5. Diary p. 13b.
6. Diary p. 13b.
7. Diary p. 14a.
8. Diary p. 14a.
9. Diary p. 14a.
10. Diary p. 14a.
11. Diary p. 14a. Kongtrul later wrote an undated manual for the approach practice of Union of All Rare and Precious Jewels titled *Lotus of Advice: A Manual for Reciting the Union of All Rare and Precious Jewels*.
12. The following discussion of empowerment rituals is drawn from Davidson 2002 and Dalton 2004.
13. Diary p. 14a.
14. Diary pp. 14b–15a.
15. Diary p. 16b. This work is translated in Ngari Panchen Pema Wangyi Gyelpo 1996.
16. Diary p. 14b.
17. Diary p. 14b.
18. See chapter 23.
19. Diary p. 15a.
20. On Longchenpa, see Hillis 2002, Butters 2006, and Jampa Mackenzie Stewart 2014.
21. Diary pp. 15b–16a, 17a. Kongtrul uses the phrase *dung phyur bco lnga*, translated as "one hundred fifteen million."
22. Diary p. 15a.
23. For studies of Tibetan treasure, see Gyatso 1992, 1993, 1994, 1996, 1998, and Doctor 2005. Tulku Thondup gives a contemporary Tibetan description of the practice. For a fascinating study of a female treasure revealer, see Jacoby 2014. On the development of the Padmasambhava myth, see Hirshberg 2016.
24. See, for example, Aris 1989.
25. Emerson 1880, p. 112
26. Diary p. 15a.
27. Diary p. 15a.
28. Diary p. 15b.
29. Diary p. 15b.

30. Tulku Urgyen Rinpoche 2005, p. 47.
31. Diary p. 16a. The painting with Kongtrul in his 60s is Himalayan Art Resources item no. 73405.
32. Diary p. 16a. Kongtrul wrote *nged grogs mched gsum* ("three of us, myself and companions") but he does not identify the two other recipients of the vows. Wontrul immediately gave extensive teachings to the Third Zhechen Gyeltsab and the teacher Pema Kelzang, which suggests they may have been Kongtrul's companions, despite the Zhechen Gyeltsab being only fifteen years old at the time; it was not unusual for recognized reincarnations to be ordained before the age of twenty. In his *Necklace of Clear Understanding*, Kongtrul gives a brief summary of the ordination lines. He nowhere recorded his ordination name.
33. For Kongtrul's own discussion of the role of the guru, see Jamgon Kongtrul 1998, chapter 1 and Jamgon Kongtrul 1999.
34. Diary p. 16b.
35. Diary p. 16b. On the Vajrakīla controversy, see Mayer 1997.
36. Diary p. 16b. Nyangrel's biography of Padmasambhava is *The Copper-Colored Mountain*. Translations include Yeshe Tsogyel 1993. For an academic study, see Hirshberg 2016. For a study of the *Collected Instructions on the Mantra*, see Kapstein 1992. Kongtrul refers to the book as *Testament of the King*.
37. Diary p. 16b.
38. Diary p. 16b.
39. On Nyangrel's Eight Commands, see Hirshberg 2016. On the grouping of deities, see Garrett 2009.
40. *Mirage of Nectar* pp. 32b–33a. The Vajradaṇḍa liturgy appears to be lost; there are two liturgies in the Treasury of Revelations to this deity written by Kongtrul, but both are part of Chokgyur Lingpa's Dispelling All Obstacles.
41. *Mirage of Nectar*, p. 32b.

## 4. PELPUNG: 1833–1834

1. Diary p. 17a. On the painting set, see Jackson 2006.
2. Diary p. 17a.
3. Diary p. 17b. On the identity of Wongen, see Ronis 2011, p. 69, note 39. Wontrul is identified as the Jewon Choktrul in multiple colophons in the Treasury of Revelations.
4. For stories of Patrul Rinpoche see Surya Das 1992. On Patrul see Schapiro 2012.
5. See Schopen 1996 for discussions of the history of monastic property in India. For a Tibetan example, see the section on Drokmi Lotsāwa in Davidson 2005, pp. 161–210.
6. Diary p. 18a.
7. Diary p. 17b. The exact identity of the Khenpo remains to be determined. The Khenpo might have been Tartse Khenpo Jampel Zangpo, who was about forty-four years old. He would also come to Kham in 1843.
8. Diary p. 18a.

9. Diary p. 18a.

10. Diary p. 18a.

11. The first day of the tenth month of the Water Serpent Year

12. The sixth day of the tenth month.

13. Diary pp. 18b, 16a.

14. Kongtrul described the ordination traditions in *Necklace of Clear Understanding*, pp. 5a–6b. See also the Treasury of Knowledge as translated in Jamgon Kongtrul 2010, pp. 243–48.

15. Diary pp. 19a–b.

16. Diary pp. 19a–b. Ngawang, an abbreviation of Ngagi Wangchuk, meaning "Lord of Speech," is the Tibetan translation of Mañjuśrī. The more common Tibetan name Jamyang/Jampayang is a translation of Mañjughoṣa, an alternate name of the bodhisattva.

17. Diary p. 17a.

18. Diary p. 19a.

19. Diary pp. 19a–b.

20. Diary p. 19b.

## 5. EARLY KAGYU FOUNDATIONS, PART ONE: TEACHINGS AT KARMA GON: 1834

1. The second month of the Wood Horse Year.

2. Diary p. 28b.

3. The third month of the Wood Horse Year.

4. Diary p. 20b. Kongtrul writes *pad dkar sprul sku*; e.g., the tulku of Pema Karpo, the Fourth Drukchen. The Treasury of Wish-Fulfilling Jewels (p. 787) confirms the identity.

5. Diary pp. 20a–b.

6. Diary p. 20a. Kongtrul recorded the date of the start of the transmission as the fifteenth day of the fourth month of the Wood Horse Year, which according to Henning was omitted. September 1834 corresponds to the eighth month of the Wood Horse Year.

7. Diary p. 20a.

8. Diary p. 20b.

9. Smith 2001, p. 250. Kongtrul writes only "The Collected Teachings, Takten Printing," which according to Michael Sheehy (private communication) is a clear reference to the Collected Works of Tāranātha. According to the Treasury of Wish-Fulfilling Jewels, Kongtrul received the collection only once, in 1843, from Karma Wosel Gyurme (p. 787; see chapter 11), and the earlier transmissions are not mentioned; nor is Ribuk Tulku. Editions of Tāranātha's Collected Works range from ten to forty-five volumes.

10. Diary p. 20b.

11. Diary p. 143b.

12. Diary p. 20a. On the Four Medical Tantras, see Garrett 2009.

13. Diary p. 20b.
14. Several recent books survey the development of buddha-nature theory in India and Tibet: Mathes 2013, Brunnhölzl 2009 and 2015, Kano 2016, and Tsering Wangchuk 2017.
15. Diary p. 20b.
16. The first day of the ninth month of the Wood Horse Year.
17. Diary p. 20b.

## 6. EARLY KAGYU FOUNDATIONS, PART TWO: EARLY RETREATS, DREAMS, AND VISIONS: 1835–1837

1. The first month of the Wood Sheep Year.
2. Diary p. 21a. Kongtrul did not receive the transmission from a Kagyu master until the Eighth Situ, Chokyi Jungne, appeared in a dream in 1880 and gave it to him; Diary p. 155a.
3. Diary pp. 21a–b.
4. On subtle-body practice, see Gyatso 1998 and Jacoby 2015.
5. Diary p. 22a.
6. The tenth month of the Wood Sheep Year.
7. Diary pp. 22a–b.
8. Diary p. 23a. *Torch of Certainty* is translated in Jamgon Kongtrul 1977. A translation of a Nyingma manual for the preliminary practices is Patrul Rinpoche 1994.
9. Diary p. 23a.
10. The third month of the Fire Monkey Year.
11. Diary p. 23a.
12. Diary p. 23a.
13. Diary p. 23b. Some of the devotional prayers may be preserved in an undated forty-page compendium in his Collected Works titled *Prayers of Supreme Devotion*.
14. Diary p. 23b
15. *Mirage of Nectar* p. 32b.
16. Diary p. 23b.
17. Diary p. 24a.
18. Diary pp. 24a–25b.
19. Diary pp. 24a–b.
20. Diary p. 25b. According to the Treasury of Wish-Fulfilling Jewels (p. 141), Kongtrul was given the Guhyasamāja by the Third Katok Lingtrul. Since this master was only born in 1850, the dream would have occurred well before the waking transmission.

## 7. THE FOURTEENTH KARMAPA: 1836–1839

1. Diary pp. 24a–b.
2. On Milarepa, see Quintman 2010 and 2013.
3. On Gampopa, see Jampa Mackenzie Stewart 2004 and Trungram Gyatrul Rinpoche Sherpa 2004. On the Karmapa incarnation line, see Lama Kunsang et al. 2012.

4. Diary p. 25b.
5. Diary p. 26a.
6. Diary p. 26a.
7. Diary p. 26a. On Dzogchen meditation, see Karmay 1988.
8. Diary p. 26b.
9. The twelfth month of the Fire Monkey Year.
10. The fourth month of the Fire Bird Year.
11. Diary p. 26b. Kongtrul later wrote (Diary p. 127a) that in 1872 Khyentse Wangpo urged him to compose a commentary to the *Candoratnākara*, but if he did it is lost.
12. The fifth month of the Fire Bird Year.
13. Diary p. 26b.
14. Diary pp. 26b–27a. The parable of Kisagotami can be found in Buddhaghoṣa 1870, pp. 98–102.
15. Diary p. 27a.
16. Diary p. 27a.
17. Diary p. 27a.
18. The fifth month of the Earth Dog Year.
19. Diary p. 27a. There are several collections of long-life prayers in Kongtrul's Treasury of the Expansive, although none are identified as having been written at Pelpung.
20. Diary pp. 27a–b.
21. Diary p. 27b.
22. Diary pp. 27b–28a. Kongtrul would compose multiple manuals for the prosperity rites. Examples are *Ear of Divine Grain* and *Rain of Virtue*, both connected to Pelchenma.
23. Diary p. 28a.
24. Diary p. 28a. The inventory of Drantang is titled *Catalog of Drentang Paṇchen Kumbum*.

## 8. Dreams of the Masters: 1839–1841

1. Diary p. 28b.
2. Diary p. 28b.
3. The fourth month of the Earth Pig Year.
4. Diary pp. 28b–29a. Kongtrul's fasting manuals are *All-Pervading Benevolence*, which was requested by Tashi Wozer and others, and *Turquoise-Trimmed Golden Reliquary*, which was requested by Dabzang and others. The Kagyu fasting lineage appears to have originated with the Sakya tradition and passed into the Kagyu with Pakmodrupa in the twelfth century. See Wangchen Rinpoche 2009 for a description of the ritual and a translation of Khenchen Tashi Wozer's manual.
5. Diary p. 28b.
6. Diary p. 29a.
7. Diary pp. 29a, 34a.
8. Diary p. 29a. On creation stage practice, see Harding 2002 and Gyatso 1998.
9. The eighth day of the ninth month of the Earth Pig Year.
10. Diary p. 30a.

11. Diary p. 30b.
12. Diary p. 31a.
13. Diary pp. 31a–b. Barron (Autobiography p. 39) reads the final exhortation as pertaining to one of Kongtrul's future lives.
14. Diary pp. 29b–30a.
15. Diary p. 30a.
16. Diary p. 30a, 33a. On Niguma, see Harding 2010. On Khyungpo Neljor, see Kapstein 1980.
17. Diary p. 33a.
18. Diary p. 33b. See Jamgön Kongtrul Lodrö Thayé 2013, p. 94 for the teachings Kongtrul received during this time that he included in the Treasury of Instructions.
19. Diary pp. 34a–b.
20. Diary pp. 32a–b.
21. The twenty-ninth day of the third month of the Iron Mouse Year.
22. Diary p. 33a, 180a. Kongtrul included the cycle by Gyazhang Trom Dorje Bar in volume 18 of the Treasury of Revelations.
23. The seventh month of the Iron Mouse Year.
24. Diary pp. 34a–b.
25. Diary p. 34b.
26. Diary p. 28b.
27. Diary p. 35a.

## 9. KHYENTSE WANGPO AND THE DEATHS OF WONGEN AND THE OLD CHIEFTAIN: 1840–1842

1. Diary p. 35b.
2. *Fabulous Grove of Uḍumbara Flowers* p. 29b.
3. *Fabulous Grove of Uḍumbara Flowers* p. 13a. Kongtrul's biography of Khyentse is translated in Jamgon Kongtrul 2012.
4. Diary p. 35b.
5. The ninth month of the Iron Mouse Year.
6. Diary pp. 35b, 38a. Kongtrul would later write a commentary to the approach and accomplishment practice of United Intent of the Gurus titled *Profound Essence of Endless Ambrosia.*
7. Diary p. 35b.
8. The twenty-second day of the ninth month of the Iron Mouse Year.
9. Diary p. 36a.
10. Diary p. 36a. Kongtrul's empowerment for Ratna Lingpa's Black Hayagrīva is *A Sliver of Enlightened Mind.*
11. Diary p. 36a.
12. The fifteenth day of the first month of the Iron Ox Year.
13. The fourth month of the Iron Ox Year.
14. Diary pp. 36b–37a.
15. The third month of the Iron Ox Year.

16. Diary pp. 37a, 40b.
17. The sixth month of the Iron Ox Year.
18. Diary p. 37b.
19. Diary p. 37b. On mendrub, see Garrett 2009.
20. Diary pp. 37b–38a.
21. The nineteenth day of the tenth month of the Iron Ox Year
22. The end of the first month of the Water Tiger Year.
23. Diary pp. 38b–39a. On Ra Lotsāwa Zhonnu Pel, see Cuevas 2015 and Davidson 2005.
24. The first day of the third month of the Iron Ox Year.
25. Diary pp. 38b–39b.
26. Diary pp. 38a–b.
27. The twenty-fifth day of the first month of the Water Tiger Year.
28. Diary p. 39a.
29. The twenty-ninth day of the twelfth month of the Water Tiger Year. Diary p. 45b.
30. The first month of the Iron Mouse Year.
31. Diary p. 32a.
32. Diary p. 44b. Barron (Autobiography p. 57) reads this last passage slightly differently.
33. Diary p. 46a.

## 10. AGE THIRTY: 1842

1. Diary p. 8b.
2. The first day of the third month of the Water Tiger Year.
3. Diary p. 39b.
4. *Mirage of Nectar* p. 32b.
5. The tenth day of the sixth month of the Wood Snake Year.
6. Diary p. 50b.
7. Diary pp. 39b–40a.
8. *Mirage of Nectar* pp. 33a–b.
9. *All-Pervading Melody of the Pure Lands* p. 8b.
10. I have not been able to identify the biographies of Pelpung lamas to which he referred.
11. Diary pp. 42a–44a.
12. Diary p. 42b.
13. Diary p. 43a.
14. Diary pp. 43b–44a.
15. Diary p. 44a.

## 11. KONGTRUL'S RETREAT AT DECHEN WOSEL LING: 1842–1846

1. *All-Pervading Melody of the Pure Lands* pp. 9a–10b, *Music from the Ocean of the Mind* pp. 11a–14b.

2. Diary p. 41b, *All-Pervading Melody of the Pure Lands* pp. 10b–11a.

3. Diary p. 41b, *Mirage of Nectar* p. 33a, *All-Pervading Melody of the Pure Lands* p. 9a.

4. *Music from the Ocean of the Mind* pp. 9b–10a.

5. Diary pp. 42a–45b.

6. Diary p. 44a.

7. The fifteenth day of the ninth month of the Water Tiger Year. Diary p. 44a.

8. "Around March 1846" corresponds to around the third month of the Fire Horse Year. Diary pp. 44a–45b.

9. Diary pp. 44a–b.

10. Diary p. 45a.

11. Diary p. 45b.

12. Diary p. 46a.

13. Diary p. 46a.

14. Diary pp. 46a–b.

15. Ngawang Zangpo 1994, p. 48.

16. The eighth month to the first day of the twelfth month of the Water Hare Year.

17. Diary p. 46b. Kongtrul wrote that for these teachings he went to *gling stod*, which Barron (Autobiography p. 59) translated as "Upper Ling Province" but which I understand to be a section of Pelpung Monastery. In other passages in the Diary it is clear that *gling stod* is Dabzang's residence at Pelpung. Examples are Diary p. 62b and p. 65a.

18. Diary p. 47.

19. Diary pp. 47a–49a.

20. Diary p. 49a.

21. The first half of the eighth month of the Wood Dragon Year.

22. The second half of the eighth month of the Wood Dragon Year.

23. Diary pp. 49b–51b.

24. The second month of the Wood Serpent Year.

25. The third month of the Wood Dragon Year. Diary pp. 46a, 49a–b.

26. The fifth month of the Wood Dragon Year

27. Diary pp. 50a–b. July 14 corresponds to the twenty-ninth day of the fifth month of the Wood Dragon Year.

28. Diary p. 52a.

29. The ninth month of the Wood Serpent Year.

30. Diary pp. 52a–b.

31. Diary p. 52b.

32. Diary p. 53a.

## 12. GYARONG AND KUNTRUL: 1846–1848

1. Diary p. 52b. For scholarship on the history of Gyarong, see Martin 1990, Greatrex 1994, and Kværne and Sperling 1993.

2. The twenty-seventh day of the fifth month of the Fire Horse Year. Diary p. 53b.

3. Diary p. 53b.

4. Diary pp. 54a–b.

5. Diary pp. 54a–b.

6. Diary p. 54b.

7. Diary pp. 55a, 57a.

8. Diary p. 55a.

9. Diary pp. 55b–56b. Kongtrul later composed five liturgies for Avalokiteśvara, the Spontaneous Liberator of the Lower Realms for the Treasury of Revelations, including an inner and an outer sādhana.

10. The fourth month of the Fire Sheep Year.

11. Diary p. 56a.

12. Diary p. 57b.

13. Smith 2001, p. 333, note 845.

14. The Tibetan for the passage is *kun sprul khams pa tshang dang rtsod 'then skabs khrims ra mgron gnyer gyis glo bur ming btags dgos byung ba la phyis bar chad chen po red song ba.* Diary p. 19b.

15. Diary p. 56a.

16. Diary pp. 57b–58b.

17. Diary p. 58b.

18. See Brunnhölzl 2014, pp. 831–53 for a translation, and pp. 324–28 for a short description.

19. Diary p. 58b.

20. Diary p. 59a. *Four Sessions of Guru Yoga* is translated in Khenpo Kharthar Rinpoche 2013. Kongtrul included the short ritual manual for *Four Sessions of Guru Yoga* in the Treasury of Instructions.

21. Diary p. 59a. Regarding "a contingent from the government," Kongtrul wrote, *'bri gnyan ldong shar gyi sgo srung dpon gyog.* Drinyendong is Derge's protector, hence my uncertain reading. Alternately, Barron (Autobiography p. 75) reasonably translates the phrase as "Drinyen Dongshar teachers and attendants."

22. The first month of the Earth Monkey Year.

23. Diary p. 60a.

24. The second month of the Earth Monkey Year.

25. Diary pp. 60a–b.

## 13. THE LANGUAGE OF LOVE AND POWER: KHYENTSE, DABZANG, AND THE KING OF DERGE: 1848–1853

1. Diary p. 61a. Khyentse Wangpo was in Tibet from 1848 to 1851, traveling with Tartse Khenpo Jampel Zangpo.

2. Diary p. 61b.

3. Diary p. 61b. The three-month retreat ended shortly before or during the eleventh month of the Earth Monkey Year. The two liturgies are the *Chest of Amṛta* and *Jeweled Comet's Tail*.

4. The eleventh month of the Earth Monkey Year.

5. Diary pp. 61b–62a.

6. The twenty-fifth day of the fourth month of the Earth Monkey Year.

7. Diary pp. 61a, 62a–b.

8. The twelfth month of the Earth Bird Year.

9. Diary p. 62b.

10. The third to the fifth month of the Iron Dog Year.

11. Diary pp. 63a–64a. This Sotrul was not Lerab Lingpa, who was not born until 1854.

12. Diary pp. 63a–b.

13. Diary pp. 63b–64b.

14. Diary p. 64a. Damtsik Dorje must have died sometime in the late 1850s as he is nowhere mentioned during the Nyarong War that devastated Derge in the early 1860s. It is curious that Kongtrul was not involved in his funeral—or, if he was, that he did not mention it in his diary. On a listing of the members of the royal family of Derge, see Kolmaš 1968 and 1988.

15. The fifth month of the Iron Pig Year.

16. Diary p. 64a.

17. Diary p. 64b.

18. Diary p. 65a.

19. Diary pp. 65a–b.

20. Diary pp. 64b–65a.

21. Diary p. 65b.

22. The seventh month of the Water Mouse Year.

23. Diary pp. 65b–66a.

24. Diary pp. 66a–67a.

25. *Fabulous Grove of Uḍumbara Flowers* p. 6a.

26. Diary p. 67a.

27. The tenth month of the Water Mouse Year.

28. Diary p. 67a.

29. Diary p. 67a.

30. The twelfth month of the Water Mouse Year.

31. Diary p. 67b.


## 14. Past Lives Revealed, the Death of Situ, and the Origin of the Treasury of Kagyu Tantra: 1853–1855

1. Diary p. 61b.

2. Diary p. 69b.

3. Diary p. 67b.

4. Diary p. 67b.

5. Ironically, in 1836 Kongtrul had a dream in which Bamteng Tulku told him he was the rebirth of someone, but Kongtrul did not remember the name. Diary p. 25a.

6. *Mirage of Nectar*, pp. 3b–5a.

7. Diary pp. 68a–b.

8. *Mirage of Nectar* p. 22a.

9. Diary p. 68b.

10. Diary p. 69a.

11. *Mirage of Nectar* p. 15b. For a more extensive account of Lume taking responsibility for Samye Monastery—but not the treasury—see Davidson 2005.

12. Diary pp. 69b-70b, *Fabulous Grove of Uḍumbara Flowers* p. 110b.

13. *One Hundred Treasure Revealers* pp. 61a–62b.

14. Kongtrul recorded the date of Situ's death as the seventh day of the fifth month of the Water Ox Year, which, according to Henning, was omitted that year.

15. Diary p. 71a.

16. Diary p. 71b.

17. Diary p. 72a.

18. The eighth month of the Water Ox Year.

19. Diary p. 72a. The Dagam retreat was from October 1853 to March 1845, the ninth month of the Water Ox Year to the second month of the Wood Tiger Year.

20. The third month of the Wood Tiger Year.

21. The fourth day of the fourth month of the Wood Tiger Year.

22. Diary pp. 73a–b.

23. Diary p. 73b.

24. The fifth month of the Wood Tiger Year.

25. Diary p. 74a.

26. Diary pp. 74a–b.

27. Diary p. 74b. The composition was translated into English by Ken McLeod as *The Great Path of Awakening*; see Jamgon Kongtrul 1987.

28. The ninth month of the Wood Tiger Year.

29. Diary p. 75a.

30. Diary pp. 75b, 76b.

31. Diary p. 75b.

32. Diary p. 76a.

## 15. CHOKGYUR LINGPA: 1853–1855

1. Diary p. 72b.

2. *One Hundred Treasure Revealers* p. 204. In his gazetteer of Kham (Kongtrul's Kham Gazetteer p. 8b), Kongtrul names him Konchok Tendzin. Norbu and Konchok are synonyms of sorts, both meaning jewel, although "norbu" lacks the supernatural splendor of the latter term.

3. Biographies disagree as to whether it was the tenth day of the sixth or tenth month of the female Earth Ox Year.

4. There is a rich corpus of biographical material on Chokgyur Lingpa. In addition to the entry in *One Hundred Treasure Revealers*, these include the *Autobiography of Chokgyur Lingpa*, a section of which is also found on the back of a painting pre-

served at Dzongsar Monastery (see chapter 22). Soon after the treasure revealer's death, Kongtrul composed *Supplication to Chokgyur Lingpa*, which Khyentse expanded as *Outline of the Supplication to Chokgyur Lingpa*. Khyentse Wangpo also wrote a hagiography that is titled *Breeze Requesting the Auspicious Tune*. Based on Khyentse's hagiography, Chokling's disciple Pema Yeshe wrote *Melody of the Fifth Auspicious Birth* at the request of the Second Neten Chokling, and he also wrote an account of Chokling's travels in Tibet called *Cuckoo's Auspicious Song*. The largest hagiography is Konchok Gyurme's *Biography of Chokgyur Lingpa*, written in 1921. The author, the Second Tsike Chokling, incorporates many of the earlier works. An invaluable English language biography is Orgyen Tobgyal Rinpoche's *The Life and Teachings of Chokgyur Lingpa*. The author is the son of the Second Tsike Chokling. Tulku Urgyen Rinpoche, Chokgyur Lingpa's great-grandson, includes many anecdotes from family lore in his autobiography, *Blazing Spendor* (See Tulku Urgyen Rinpoche 2005).

5. Both Orgyen Tobgyal (p. 26) and Tulku Urgyen Rinpoche (p. 38) also give her the name Degah. Following the vague chronology of Barwai Dorje's autobiography, Dechen Chodron's relationship with Chokling may have began around the death of the Ninth Situ in 1853 and before Chokling's discovery of Seven Profound Cycles in May 1856. See Terchen Barway Dorje 2005, p. 37.

6. Kongtrul 1982, p. 9.

7. Kongtrul 2009, p. 405.

8. Orgyen Tobgyal (p. 26) identified her as a daughter of the "Somo Tsang" clan of Derge, probably the family Kongtrul referred to as Sokmo. Hartley (p. 22) has a list of aristocratic families of Derge, including the Sokmo. Tulku Urgyen Rinpoche (p. 38) only acknowledges her existence in passing, noting Chokling's son by "another consort."

9. Diary pp. 103b–104a.

10. The first son was certainly born before 1863, the year Chokling's second consort passed away, and he died before 1892, the year Khyentse Wangpo authorized the search for his reincarnation. Orgyen Tobgyel pp. 27–31. Tsewang Norbu received transmissions from Kongtrul in 1871. Diary. p. 128b.

11. Orgyen Tobgyal p. 3, Kongchok Gyurme p. 33a, *Autobiography of Chokgyur Lingpa* p. 4a. Konchok Gyurme has Chokgyur Lingpa's mother advise him to leave Nanchen: "Later his aged mother gave him a pair of treasure revealer's boots and said 'As you are unhappy, you should go elsewhere.'"

12. The prophecy can be found in several versions in different sources and has been made part of the Lotus Crest, Chokgyur Lingpa's fourth treasure casket. It is attached somewhat awkwardly and with its own colophon, to the end of the root text of the cycle. The texts of this treasure cycle, which he claimed to have revealed in Nangchen in 1849, had yet to be transcribed, and given the variations among the different written versions, he likely recited it from memory. Different versions are found in *One Hundred Treasure Revealers*, p. 204; *Autobiography of Chokgyur Lingpa* p. 4b; Chokgyur Lingpa 1982 (1853), pp. 70a–b, *Breeze Requesting the*

*Auspicious Tune* p. 5a–b; *Melody of the Fifth Auspicious Birth* p. 9b. Situ's response is described in Tulku Urgyen Rinpoche 2005, pp. 90–91 and *One Hundred Treasure Revealers* p. 204.

13. The fourth day of the sixth month of the Water Ox Year.

14. The twenty-fifth day of the sixth month of the Water Ox Year; *Breeze Requesting the Auspicious Tune* pp. 3b–4a.

15. Diary pp. 72a–b.

16. The eighth day of the ninth month of the Water Ox Year.

17. Diary p. 73a. Orgyen Tobgyal p. 4, Konchok Gyurme p. 39b. Khyentse credited his empowerment with clearing away whatever obstacles Chokgyur Lingpa would face that year: *Breeze Requesting the Auspicious Tune* p. 4a. Khyentse records the location of the Vimalamitra visionary experience as Riwo Wangzhu, the mountain ridge where Dagam Wangpuk is located: *Breeze Requesting the Auspicious Tune* p. 11b. *Secret Path of Wisdom* p. 15b.

18. Diary 77a–77b, Konchok Gyurme p. 39b.

19. In the Diary, Kongtrul inserted his introductory letter in the section recording events of early 1855. The chronology does not make sense when compared with Khyentse's own account of his meeting Chokgyur Lingpa the previous winter. Regarding the phrase "has no forms of compositions at all" (*rtsom pa'i rigs su ni mi 'dug pa*), if one reads "*rig*" for "*rigs*," then the phrase could be read as "He has no knowledge of composition at all." Orgyen Tobgyal p. 4.

20. The eleventh month of the Wood Tiger Year. Diary p. 77b.

21. Third day of the twelfth month of the Fire Dragon Year.

22. *Breeze Requesting the Auspicious Tune* p. 4a.

23. The fourth month of the Wood Hare Year.

24. Diary pp. 76b–77b. Barron (Autobiography p. 99) misread the Diary and had Chokling give Dabzang the empowerment.

25. The ninth month of the Wood Hare Year.

26. *Breeze Requesting the Auspicious Tune* p. 5a. Diary p. 77b.

27. Diary pp. 77b–77a. On the *Sūtra That Gathers All Intentions*, see Dalton 2016.

28. The tenth day of the ninth month of the Earth Monkey Year.

29. *Breeze Requesting the Auspicious Tune* p. 6b, *Fabulous Grove of Uḍumbara Flowers* p. 93a, *Mirage of Nectar* p. 38a, Konchok Gyurme p. 49a.

30. Diary p. 78a. On Dispelling All Obstacles, see Chokling Dewey Dorje 2008.

31. Diary pp. 78a–b. Kongtrul classified the Vimalamitra revelation as a mind treasure, while Khyentse Wangpo labeled it a pure vision treasure, an important reminder of the fluid nature of the classifications of revelations. On Chokling's Collected Treasures, see Doctor 2005.

32. Diary p. 78b. The Vajradaṇḍa sādhana is found in Chokgyur Lingpa's Collected Revelations but curiously Kongtrul left it out of the Treasury of Revelations. Kongtrul's account of Vairocana and Margyenma is in *One Hundred Treasure Revealers* p. 42.

33. Diary p. 79a.

## 16. The Birth of the Treasury of Revelations, the Discovery of Dzongsho Deshek Dupai Podrang Hermitage, and the First Opening of Tsādra Rinchen Drak: 1855–1857

1. Diary p. 79a.
2. *Treasury of Wish-fulfilling Jewels* was first published at Pelpung. A modern edition was published in Beijing in 2009. See Tashi Chopel 2009.
3. Diary pp. 79a–b. Treasure cycles are categorized in two ways. The first is as Khyentse wrote: Guru, Dzogchen, and Avalokiteśvara practice. This is the overarching schema of the Treasury of Revelations. A further division of the Mahāyoga tantric liturgies is by Guru, yidam, and ḍākinī, and this is the organization of the main section of the collection: the Guru sādhana, arranged by inner, outer, and secret Padmasambhava practices; the yidam section, arranged by the categories of the Eight Commands; and the ḍākinī/dharmapāla section. These, the original core of the work, totaled some sixty-three volumes, to which an additional forty-seven volumes of ritual liturgies were amended by Dilgo Khyentse Rinpoche in the late 1970s to total one hundred eleven volumes.
4. The eighth day of the first month of the Fire Tiger Year.
5. Diary p. 79b. Kongtrul wrote that his initial preparation was a practice called Spontaneous Fulfillment of All Wishes: the Treasure Trove of Qualities. No cycle by that name appears in library records. He may have instead meant Guru Sādhana: The Treasure Trove of Qualities, a treasure of Ngari Paṇchen which is included in the Treasury of Revelations with three liturgies by Kongtrul and an explanation by Khyentse Wangpo.
6. Diary pp. 79b–80a.
7. Diary p. 80a.
8. Diary pp. 81a–b. The Namcho cycle of White and Black Khrodhakāli does not appear to be in the Treasury of Revelations.
9. The twenty-fifth day of the fifth month of the Fire Tiger Year.
10. Diary p. 81b.
11. The twenty-seventh day of the seventh month of the Fire Tiger Year.
12. Diary pp. 82b–83b.
13. Diary pp. 83b–84a. Pema Dechen Lingpa should not be confused with another treasure revealer named Dechen Lingpa who lived a century earlier. His treasures did not survive and so do not appear in the Treasury of Revelations, although Kongtrul did include him in *One Hundred Treasure Revealers*.
14. Diary p. 84a. On Lambaka and Devīkoṭa, see Huber 1990.
15. Diary p. 84b.
16. Diary p. 84b. December 7, 1856 corresponds to the tenth day of the eleventh month of the Fire Tiger Year. There is a rich scholarly literature on abodes and Tibetan sacred geography. See especially Blondeau and Steinkellner 1996, Blondeau 1998, MacDonald 1997, McKay 1998, and Huber 1990, 1994a, 1994b, 1997a, 1997b, 1999a, 1999b, and 2000.

17. Diary p. 84b. Kongtrul did not record which liturgy he used for the second and third rites. There are no "gift of the body" liturgies in Union of All Rare and Precious Jewels, but in Kongtrul's Treasury of the Expansive there is a short description of the rite, *Forest of All Delights*, which unfortunately is undated and does not state where it was written. There are four fire offering manuals in the Treasury of Revelations, one of which was written by Kongtrul, although none by Jatson Nyingpo, the man who had discovered Union of All Rare and Precious Jewels.

18. Diary pp. 84b–85a, *Mirage of Nectar* p. 36a.

19. Diary p. 85a.

20. The third day of the twelfth month of the Fire Dragon Year.

21. Diary p. 85a, *Breeze Requesting the Auspicious Tune* p. 5.

22. Tenth day of the twelfth month Fire Dragon Year.

23. *Autobiography of Chokgyur Lingpa* p. 5a, Orgyen Tobgyal p. 8, Konchok Gyurme p. 147b, *Breeze Requesting the Auspicious Tune* p. 12b.

24. Diary pp. 85a–b.

25. Diary p. 85b. Mamo are a class of indigenous female deities.

26. Diary pp. 85b–86a.

27. Chokgyur Lingpa 1982 (1857).

28. Diary p. 85b.

29. Diary pp. 85b–86a.

30. The first day of first month of the Fire Serpent Year.

31. Diary p. 86a.

32. Diary p. 104a. The manual is *Essence of Clear Light*.

33. Diary p. 82a.

34. See Huber 1990 and MacDonald 1990.

35. The third day of the first month of the Fire Serpent Year.

36. Diary pp. 86a–b, *Music from the Ocean of the Mind* pp. 14b–15b.

37. Chokling's Kham Gazetteer p. 11b.

38. The ninth day of the first month of the Fire Serpent Year.

39. The fifteenth day of the first month of the Fire Serpent Year.

40. Diary p. 86b, *Breeze Requesting the Auspicious Tune* p. 7b.

41. The twenty-second day of the first month of the Fire Serpent Year.

42. The twentieth day of the first month of the Fire Serpent Year.

43. Diary pp. 86b–87a, *Breeze Requesting the Auspicious Tune* p. 7b, *Autobiography of Chokgyur Lingpa* pp. 5b–6a, Kongchok Gyurme pp. 49b–50a.

44. *Autobiography of Chokgyur Lingpa* pp. 5b–6a.

45. Diary pp. 86b–87a.

46. Diary p. 87a.


## 17. TIBET: 1857–1859

1. The twenty-second day of the sixth month of the Fire Serpent Year.

2. Diary pp. 87a–b.

3. The second half of the fifth month of the Fire Serpent Year.

4. The eleventh day of the fifth month of the Fire Serpent Year.

5. Diary p. 87a.

6. Diary pp. 87a–b. Kongtrul appears to have made an error in his record of the teaching he received from Khyentse. There is no Heart Essence of Siṃhamukhā in Khyentse's treasures, only a Profound Oral Lineage of Siṃhamukhā, which is in the Treasury of Revelations.

7. See Akester 2016.

8. Diary p. 87b.

9. Diary p. 87b.

10. The second day of the tenth month of the Fire Serpent Year.

11. Diary p. 88a.

12. Diary p. 88a. There is some controversy surrounding the Karmapa prophecy, which is based on a passage in Konchok Gyurme pp. 219b–220b. See Wong 2010 for a partisan presentation of the controversy. Chokgyur Lingpa does not mention it in his autobiography when recording the revelation of the Seven Profound Cycles, but in the *Seven Profound Cycles Treasure History* (Anonymous 1982, p.7a) one finds a curious passage in which the Fourteenth Karmapa allegedly announces, on the arrival of Chokgyur Lingpa at Karma Gon: "During the life of every Karmapa there should be a great treasure revealer to repel obstacles; now, it seems, [mine] has arrived."

13. The eleventh day of the tenth month of the Fire Serpent Year.

14. The fourteenth day of the tenth month of the Fire Serpent Year.

15. The fifteenth day of the tenth month of the Fire Serpent Year.

16. Diary pp. 88a–b.

17. Diary p. 88b.

18. Diary p. 88b.

19. The tenth day of the eleventh month of the Fire Serpent Year.

20. Diary p. 88b.

21. Diary p. 89a.

22. Diary pp. 89a–90a.

23. The twenty-third day of the twelfth month of the Fire Serpent Year

24. The twenty-ninth day of the twelfth month of the Fire Serpent Year.

25. Diary p. 90a.

26. Diary p. 90a.

27. Diary p. 90b.

28. Second month of the Earth Horse Year.

29. Diary p. 90b.

30. Diary p. 91a.

31. Diary p. 91a; *One Hundred Treasure Revealers* p. 93a; *Fabulous Grove of Uḍumbara Flowers* pp. 96b–97a.

32. Diary p. 91b.

33. Diary p. 91b.

34. Diary p. 91b.

35. The twenty-second day of the fourth month of the Earth Horse Year.

36. Diary pp. 91b–92a.
37. The eighth day of the fifth month of the Earth Horse Year.
38. June 21 to the tenth day of the fifth month of the Earth Horse Year.
39. Diary p. 92a
40. Diary p. 92b.
41. Diary pp. 92b–93a.
42. Diary p. 93a.
43. Diary p. 93b.
44. The tenth day of the tenth month of the Earth Horse Year.
45. Diary p. 93b.

## 18. GOVERNMENT SERVICE, THE CONTINUED OPENING OF TSĀDRA, AND THE TENTH SITU'S ENTHRONEMENT: 1858–1860

1. Diary p. 94a.
2. *Ma yum sras*, which Barron (Autobiography p. 122) reasonably read as Chokling and his mother. However, I read the *ma yum* to mean his consort and the *sras* as his son/s. Konchok Gyurme (p. 57b) curiously drops the passage. Kongtrul below uses *ma sras* to refer to the queen and prince/s. While it is possible that Chokling's mother had come to Derge, it seems more likely that he was there with his consort and children.
3. Diary p. 94a.
4. Diary p. 94a.
5. The first day of the first month of the Earth Sheep Year.
6. Diary p. 94a.
7. Diary p. 94a.
8. Diary pp. 94a–b. On Tro Maṇḍala, see Jigme Zangcho et al. 1995, vol. 1, pp. 445–49.
9. The twelfth month of the Wood Tiger Year.
10. Diary p. 94b. Kongtrul composed thirteen of the twenty-eight texts relating to the Heart Drop of the Venerable Goddess of Immortality in the Treasury of Revelations. On this revelation see *Fabulous Grove of Udumbara Flowers* p. 112a. Chokling revealed the Mahākaruṇika cycle on December 10, 1857 (twenty-fifth day of the tenth month, Fire Serpent Year) at Khandro Bumdzong in Nangchen. Chokling had revealed the Wish-Fulfilling Jewel of the Guru's Intent at Tsike on October 17, 1858 (the tenth day of the ninth month of the Earth Horse Year). The Karmapa's liturgy is simply titled *Medical Offering*.
11. Diary p. 95a.
12. Diary pp. 95a–b.
13. Diary p. 95b.
14. *All-Pervading Melody of the Pure Lands* p. 13a.
15. Diary pp. 95b–96a.
16. The tenth day of the third month of the Earth Sheep Year.
17. On the earth rite see Gardner 2005–2006.

18. The fifteenth day of the third month of the Earth Sheep Year.
19. I have not found another mention of this man and have not been able to identify him. Kongtrul uses the term *nye du* which could also mean "close associate." *All-Pervading Melody of the Pure Lands* p. 15a.
20. Diary p. 95b. *All-Pervading Melody of the Pure Lands* p. 14a.
21. Diary p. 96a.
22. Diary p. 96a.
23. *Tsadra Gazetteer.*
24. *Breeze Requesting the Auspicious Tune.*
25. Diary p. 96a, *Breeze Requesting the Auspicious Tune* p. 8a, *Tsādra Gazetteer* p. 4b. For a translation of the *Tsādra Gazetteer*, see Ngawang Zangpo 2001, pp. 229–32. The three deities in Three Cycles of the Secret Heart Essence are Vajrasattva, Yangdak Heruka, and Vajrakīla.
26. Diary p. 96b.
27. Diary p. 96b. Kongtrul seems to have erred here. He wrote *phur pa thugs kyi thig le'i snying thig.* The cycle is actually *rdor sems.* Alternately, he erred in the name of the text. If it was Kīla, then the title is *Yang gsang thugs kyi phur gcig.*
28. The fifth day of the first month of the Iron Monkey Year.
29. Diary p. 97a.
30. See Jamgon Kongtrul 2002h, 14b ff. This work is translated in Ngawang Zangpo 1997.
31. Diary p. 97a.
32. Diary p. 97a.
33. The second day to the tenth day of the fifth month of the Iron Monkey Year.
34. The eighth day of the third month of the Iron Bird Year.
35. Diary pp. 97a–97b, *All-Pervading Melody of the Pure Lands* p. 100a.

## 19. THE FIRST THREE-YEAR RETREAT AT TSĀDRA: RIMAY PART ONE: 1860–1862

1. The fifth month of the Iron Monkey Year.
2. Diary p. 97b.
3. Diary p. 97b, Yudru Tsomo 2015, p. 93, Yeshe Dorje p. 165–66.
4. Diary p. 97b. On the Tamer of Beings see *Fabulous Grove of Udumbara Flowers* p. 88a. The Heart Essence of the Lake Born, which Khyentse had revealed at Sengchen Namdrak, is related to Dispelling All Obstacles, and for that reason Kongtrul, in *Fabulous Grove of Udumbara Flowers*, ascribes its revelation to both Khyentse and Chokgyur Lingpa. In published form, however, it is credited solely to Khyentse.
5. The sixth month of the Iron Monkey Year.
6. Diary pp. 97b–98a.
7. Kongtrul recorded the beginning and end of each cycle save for the beginning of the seventh. In Diary p. 130b he erred in noting the start of the fourth retreat, incorrectly numbering it the third.

8. For a discussion of Tibetan hermitages, see José Cabezón's studies of the Sera Hermitages available on the THL.org website.

9. For a popular study of the Tsādra retreats, see Ngawang Zangpo 1994.

10. In his diary Kongtrul uses the phrases *lo gsum mtshams rgya* and *lo gsum gyi bsnyen sgrub* to refer to the three-year, three-month schedule. He explained the time frame in the Treasury of Knowledge (Jamgon Kongtrul 2005, pp. 179–80), which is the source of the quoted passage. Translators Guarisco and McLeod (note 66 p. 445) explain that were one to calculate the year by the lunar day rather than the solar day, the 1,125 pristine awareness breaths would equal three years, two months, and a little more than two days. Because the moon is by then already in the next phase, it has become common to refer to three years and three months. Similar temporal calculations appear in other tantras, such as the *Hevajra*, and other Indian tantras have three years and three months, such as the *Āyurvedasarvasvasārasaṃgraha*. I thank José Cabezón for this reference.

11. The twenty-second day of the sixth month of the Iron Monkey Year.

12. The ninth day of the eighth month of the Iron Monkey Year.

13. Diary p. 98a.

14. The twenty-ninth day of the eighth month of the Iron Monkey Year.

15. The seventh day of the tenth month of the Iron Monkey Year.

16. Diary p. 98a.

17. Diary p. 98b.

18. Diary p. 99a. See also Ngawang Zangpo 1994.

19. Diary p. 99a. Ngawang Zangpo (1994, p. 49) points out that an eighth man, the woodsman, was also a member of the community.

20. Diary p. 99b. On the eight chariots of accomplishment, see Kapstein 1996 and Deroche 2009. Khyentse came to give a series of empowerments beginning on April 18, 1861, the eighth day of the third month of the Iron Bird Year.

21. *Illuminating Morality* pp. 6a–9b.

22. *Illuminating Morality* pp. 10a–11b.

23. *All-Pervading Melody of the Pure Lands* p. 94b.

24. *All-Pervading Melody of the Pure Lands* p. 95a.

25. *All-Pervading Melody of the Pure Lands* p. 95a.

26. *All-Pervading Melody of the Pure Lands* pp. 96a–b.

27. *Illuminating Morality* p. 20b.

28. *Illuminating Morality* pp. 4a–b.

29. *Illuminating Morality* p. 23b.

30. The twenty-fifth day of the eleventh month of the Iron Monkey Year.

31. Diary pp. 99a–b.

32. The fourteenth day of the first month of the Water Dog Year.

33. Diary p. 100b.

34. Diary p. 106a. The late third month/early fourth month of the Wood Mouse Year.

## 20. The Treasury of Knowledge: Rimay Part Two: 1861

1. Diary pp. 100b–101a. Kongtrul does not specify when Dabzang Tulku made his request. The passage comes after events dated to the second month of the Water Dog Year but begins with the phrase "Prior to this time" (*'di skabs sngar*). The second month began on March 1, 1862.

2. Spring and summer corresponds to the fourth to seventh month of the Water Pig Year, which in his diary Kongtrul recorded as the Iron Pig Year.

3. Diary pp. 105a–b.

4. On the genre of Tibetan religious history, see Vostrikov 1970. Tucci (1949, p. 139), touching briefly on the genre, wrote "Tibetans show a particular interest, if not precisely a great accuracy, in recording facts." Martin 1997 is the standard bibliography of Tibetan historical material.

5. On Kongtrul's borrowing, see Guarasco's Translator's Introduction to *Myriad Worlds*, p. 38 and Komarovski pp. 87–88. With the support of the Tsadra Foundation, the entire Treasury of Knowledge has been translated into English in ten volumes by multiple translators working at the request of Kalu Rinpoche and Bokar Rinpoche and published by Shambhala.

6. Diary p. 51a.

7. Smith 2001, p. 251.

8. *Necklace of Clear Understanding* p. 3a.

9. *Necklace of Clear Understanding* p. 5b.

10. *Necklace of Clear Understanding* p. 15a. The four seals are the core beliefs of a valid Buddhist path: All compounded things are impermanent, all emotions are painful, all phenomena are without inherent existence, and nirvāṇa is beyond description.

11. *Necklace of Clear Understanding* p. 15a. Van der Kuijp 1983, pp. 40–41 addresses this passage, but he translates the phrase *sa chen khu dbon rnams* as Sachen Kunga Nyingpo, Sakya Paṇḍita, and Pakpa Lodro Gyeltsen, who were indeed uncle and nephew but would be hard-pressed to find common ground with others on this list. I thank Jonathan Gold for help with this passage.

12. *Necklace of Clear Understanding* p. 15a. For the reconciliatory positions of Śākya Chokden, Karma Trinle, the Eighth Karmapa, and Pema Karpo, see Higgins and Draszczyk 2016.

13. Diary p. 110b. Kongtrul taught the work sometime between early June and early October 1866, which corresponds to the fifth and the eighth months of the Fire Tiger Year.

14. The seventh month of the Iron Sheep Year. Diary p. 125b.

15. Around the tenth month of the Water Bird Year. Diary p. 131b.

16. Diary p. 136b.

17. Diary pp. 132b, 135a.

18. The second sixth month of the Iron Serpent Year. Diary p. 157b.

19. The fifteenth day of the third month of the Earth Mouse Year. Diary p. 173b.

## 21. THE NYARONG WAR: 1862–1866

1. Yudru Tsomo's 2015 study is a comprehensive history of the Nyarong War, and the following narrative relies heavily on her work. Tashi Tsering 1985 is a sympathetic account. Other studies that have touched on the war are Petech 1972 and 1973; Adshead 1984; Aris 1992; Kolmaš 1968; and Shakabpa 1967. First-hand accounts by foreigners of conditions in Kham in the wake of the war are found in Baber 1882 and Teichman 1922.

2. The second or third month of the Water Dog Year.

3. Diary p. 101a.

4. Diary p. 101b.

5. The fourth month of the Water Dog Year.

6. Diary p. 101b.

7. Diary pp. 101b–102a.

8. The eighth month of the Water Dog Year.

9. The fifteenth day of the eighth month of the Water Dog Year.

10. The twenty-ninth day of the eighth month of the Water Dog Year.

11. The thirtieth day of the eighth month of the Water Dog Year.

12. Diary pp. 102a–b.

13. The ninth month of the Water Dog Year.

14. The fifteenth day of the ninth month to first half of the twelfth month of the Water Dog Year.

15. Diary p. 103a.

16. Diary p. 104b.

17. Diary p. 103b.

18. The second month of the Water Pig Year.

19. The fourteenth day of the third month of the Water Pig Year.

20. Diary p. 104b. Matthew Akester (Jamgon Kongtrul 2012, p. 221, note 278, and p. 222, note 279) cites scholar Yangling Dorje and the biography of Khyentse written by Adzom Drukpa for the date of the destruction of Dzongsar.

21. Diary p. 105a. For the story of the Fourth Dzogchen Rinpoche, see Tashi Tsering 1985, pp. 207–8.

22. There were two lines of Tongkhor Zhabdrung, the line having split in the seventeenth century. Kongtrul likely referred to the Eighth Tongkhor from Kham Tongkhor Monastery rather than the Ninth Tongkhor from Amdo Tongkhor Monastery, both of whom were his contemporaries.

23. Yudru Tsomo 2015, p. 199.

24. Diary p. 106a.

25. The eighth month of the Water Pig Year.

26. Diary p. 105b.

27. Diary p. 105b.

28. Diary p. 103b.

29. Diary p. 106a; Yudru Tsomo 2015, chapter 7.
30. The first month of the Earth Mouse Year.
31. The seventh month of the Earth Mouse Year.
32. Diary p. 105b.
33. The ninth and tenth months of the Earth Mouse Year.
34. Diary pp. 106a–b.
35. Diary p. 106b. Kongtrul used the Tibetan phrase *mgo btags zhus pa* which literally means "bind one's head."
36. Diary pp. 107a–b.
37. See the entries on Nyarong in Jigme Zangcho 1995, volume 1.
38. Petech 1973, p. 120; Baber 1882, pp. 98–99. See also Yudru Tsomo 2013 and Tashi Tsering 1985.
39. Diary p. 108a; Yudru Tsomo 2015, chapter 7.
40. The fifth month of the Water Ox Year.
41. The sixth month of the Water Ox Year.
42. Diary p. 108a.
43. Diary p. 108b.
44. Diary pp. 109a–b.

## 22. AFTERMATH OF THE WAR, PART ONE: MAKE LOVE NOT WAR: 1866–1868

1. The eighteenth day of the first month of the Fire Tiger Year
2. The twenty-fifth day of the second month of the Fire Tiger Year.
3. The thirteenth day of the third month of the Fire Tiger Year.
4. The fourth month of the Fire Tiger Year.
5. Before the fourteenth day of the ninth month of the Fire Tiger Year. Diary pp. 110a–111b. "Lymphatic" here is *gnyan rims*, which has a definition of infection and swelling.
6. The twenty-fifth day of the fifth month of the Fire Tiger Year.
7. Diary p. 110a. The transmissions including the "oral lineage" Vajrakīla and General Assembly of Mamo, both revealed at Wokmin Karma in 1858 and which Khyentse counted as Chokgyur Lingpa' twenty-second revelation. "Oral lineage" means that it was a treasure revelation that was given orally by a deity or saint in a vision, rather than physically written on a scroll or read from a text in a vision. Neither of these went into the Treasury of Revelations.
8. Konchok Gyurme pp. 69a–b.
9. Diary p. 110b.
10. Diary p. 110b. Khyentse omitted the Bon treasures from his account of Chokgyur Lingpa's treasures, but Konchok Gyurme (p. 123b) added them to the list as an "auxiliary" to the twenty-fifth revelation. Chokling's gazetteer is *Dechen Burmo Gazetteer*. Kongtrul's smoke offering text is *Smoke Offering Manual at the Supreme*

*Abode Burmo Drak.* Six of the ten texts in the United Intention of the Three Roots have colophons that identify Lhamdo Burmo as the site of revelation.

11. Diary p. 110b. On the ritual in question see Jamgön Kongtrul 1998, pp. 483–84, note 185.

12. Diary pp. 110b–111a.

13. Diary p. 111a.

14. Diary p. 111b.

15. Diary p. 111b.

16. The fourteenth day of the ninth month to the tenth day of the eleventh month of the Fire Tiger Year.

17. Diary p. 112a.

18. The twenty-fifth day of the ninth month to the twelfth day of the tenth month of the Fire Tiger Year.

19. The twenty-seventh day of the tenth month of the Fire Tiger Year.

20. The painting is no. 13434 on the Himalayan Art Resources website. See Jamgon Kongtrul 2012, facing page 142 for a reproduction of the front and back and translation. The narrative on the back of the painting is reputed to be written by Chokgyur Lingpa himself and is repeated without alteration in his short autobiography, unrelated to the section that precedes and follows it. This suggests that the narrative was written for the painting, that the painting therefore predates the autobiography, and that it was made within four years of the event. Narratives of the Rongme revelations are: *Fabulous Grove of Udumbara Flowers* pp. 90a–91a, Lodro Puntsok pp. 27–34, *Autobiography of Chokgyur Lingpa* pp. 6a–8b, *Breeze Requesting the Auspicious Tune* pp. 8b–9a, Konchok Gyurme pp. 181b–182a, and Orgyen Tobgyal pp. 14–16.

21. The twenty-ninth day of the ninth month of the Fire Tiger Year.

22. The first day of the tenth month of the Fire Tiger Year.

23. The fifth day of the tenth month of the Fire Tiger Year.

24. The ninth day of the tenth month of the Fire Tiger Year.

25. Painting and *Autobiography of Chokgyur Lingpa* p. 7b.

26. The eleventh day of the tenth month of the Fire Tiger Year.

27. Sources give many names for this lake, including Permanently Abiding Turquoise Lake and Permanently Abiding Wild Lion Turquoise Lake (*Autobiography of Chokgyur Lingpa* pp. 6b and 8a); Lion's Roar Turquoise Lake (Lodro Puntsok 2004, p. 36); Invincible Wild Lion Turquoise Lake (*Breeze Requesting the Auspicious Tune* p. 9a); and simply Lion Turquoise Lake (Painting).

28. Diary p. 112a.

29. Diary p. 112b.

30. Diary p. 112b.

31. The second month of the Fire Hare Year.

32. May 1867 corresponds to the fourth month of the Fire Hare Year.

33. The twenty-fifth day of the fourth month of the male Wood Bird Year.

34. Diary p. 112b.

35. Diary p. 113a.
36. Diary p. 113a.
37. Diary pp. 113a–b.
38. On Zhabkar, see Shabkar Tsogdruk Rangdrol pp. 32–33.
39. Diary p. 114b. The dream is repeated in *Fabulous Grove of Uḍumbara Flowers* pp. 107a–108b.
40. Diary 115a.
41. Diary pp. 115a–b.
42. Diary p. 115b.
43. Diary p. 115b.
44. The twelfth month of the Fire Hare Year.
45. Diary p. 116a.

## 23. Aftermath of the War, Part Two: Kongtrul's Kham Gazetteer, the Death of Chokgyur Lingpa, and the Treasury of Instructions: 1867–1871

1. For a translation of the gazetteer, see Gardner 2006.
2. For another view, see, for example, Samuel 1993, chapter 27, "Tibet: Gelugpa Power and Rimed Synthesis."
3. The twenty-fifth day of the twelfth month of the Fire Hare Year.
4. In *Breeze Requesting the Auspicious Tune* (p. 9a), Khyentse dates Chokling's thirty-sixth casket, which occurred above Dzogchen Monastery, to May 26, which corresponds to the twenty-third day of the fourth month of the Fire Hare Year. He dates his final revelation to August 15, 1867, which corresponds to the fifteenth day of the seventh month of the Fire Hare Year (p. 9a). Kongtrul and Konchok Gyurme do not agree on the dates of Chokling's Tibet trip. Kongtrul collapses the entire trip into a single passage in his diary, denying any sense of continuity. Konchok Gyurme (p. 283a) has him travel to Tibet in the year he turned forty and return in the Earth Serpent Year, when he turned forty-one. This would mean he left in 1868 and returned in 1869.
5. Diary p. 113b.
6. Diary p. 114a.
7. Diary p. 114a.
8. The fourth month of the Iron Horse Year. *Breeze Requesting the Auspicious Tune* p. 18a.
9. Diary p. 120a.
10. Orgyen Tobgyal p. 10.
11. Ngawang Zangpo 1994, pp. 51–52; Surya Das p. 87.
12. Diary p. 116a.
13. The twenty-fifth day of the second month of the Earth Dragon Year.
14. The tenth day of the fourth month of the Earth Dragon Year.
15. The first of the second fifteenth day of the seventh month of the Earth Dragon Year (there were two such days that month).

16. Diary p. 117a.
17. The eighth month of the Earth Dragon Year.
18. Diary p. 117a.
19. The fourth month of the Fire Snake Year. Khyentse's recent "oral tradition" revelation was Crucial Point of the Oral Lineage Action Vajrakīla. But here Kongtrul writes *lung lugs* rather than *snyan brgyud*.
20. Diary p. 117b.
21. Diary p. 118a. I thank Elizabeth Callahan for help in identifying the Tsak Darma Gyelpo reference. The commentary is of the Ngok material, making the Ram and Tsak pair representative of both Marpa and Ngok. Callahan also confirmed that Kongtrul's commentary draws from Rangjung Dorje, Zhamar Chodrak Yeshe, and Dakpo Tashi Namgyal
22. The ninth month of the Fire Serpent Year.
23. Diary p. 118b. Brunnhölzl (2014, p. 314) points out Kongtrul's appropriation of Dolpopa, as does Mathes (2008, p. 84). Kongtrul's *Uttaratantra* commentary is translated in Fuchs and Hookam.
24. Diary p. 118b.
25. Kongtrul gives three specific days of the month, but neglects to record the month.
26. Diary pp. 119a–b.
27. The fifth month of the Iron Horse Year.
28. The sixth month of the Iron Horse Year.
29. The ninth month of the Iron Horse Year.
30. Diary p. 119b.
31. I am not certain of the identity of the Tsurpu Jamyang named here.
32. Diary pp. 120a–b. Two of Kongtrul's commentaries on the Third Karmapa's treatises are translated in Brunnhölzl 2009, 203–312.
33. December 1870 corresponds to the tenth month of the Iron Horse Year.
34. Diary pp. 120a–121a.
35. *Breeze Requesting the Auspicious Tune* p. 11a.
36. Diary p. 121b.
37. Diary pp. 121b–122a.
38. Diary p. 198b.
39. Diary pp. 122a–123a. Kapstein 1996, p. 275.
40. Diary p. 123a.
41. For a translation of Kongtrul's catalog of the Treasury of Instructions, see Jamgön Kongtrul Lodrö Thayé 2013.
42. Jamgon Kongtrul 1999, p. 82a. Kongtrul uses some rare poetry here; in describing the spread of the lotus of his faith Kongtrul uses a synonym for "nonsectarian"; *ris med* for "without sectarian bias" and *phyogs med* for "without any limitations."
43. The third or fourth month of the Iron Bird Year. Diary p. 100a.
44. Sometime after the second month of the Water Dog Year.
45. Diary p. 102a.

46. The Tibetan for the phrase is *"mdzod chen lnga'i thog ma shes bya mdzod du bshag."*
47. Diary p. 101a.
48. Late 1867: Kongtrul writes the date as *rab byung bco lnga pa thog mar tshes pa me yos zla ba bcu gcig pa'i dga' ba dang po.* There were two eleventh months that year. According to the Rangjung Yeshe Dictionary, the date *"dga' ba dang po"* could mean either the first or the sixteenth of the month. Thus the date might be read as November 27, December 12, December 26, 1867, or January 10, 1868. *Fabulous Grove of Uḍumbara Flowers* p. 52a.
49. *Fabulous Grove of Uḍumbara Flowers* pp. 52a–b.

## 24. The 1870s: Revelations, Tsādra's Pilgrimage Year, and Expulsion from Pelpung: 1871–1878

1. Lodro Donyo (2005, p. 555) gives Tashi Wozer's age at ordination as twenty, while a text referenced on his BDRC page (P1373) gives the year of 1862. I have not seen this book.
2. Schapiro 2012, p. 51.
3. Diary p. 123b.
4. *Mirage of Nectar* p. 34b.
5. *Mirage of Nectar* pp. 37a–38a.
6. *Mirage of Nectar* pp. 38b–39a.
7. Surya Das pp. 213–15. "Kuntuzangpo's kingdom" is a metaphor for the dharmakāya.
8. The second month of the Iron Sheep Year.
9. Diary pp. 123b–124a.
10. The fourth month of the Iron Sheep Year.
11. Diary p. 124a. On the history of refining mercury in Tibet, see Garrett 2013. The phrase translated as "suppress the barbarians" is *kla klo'i kha gnon.*
12. The twelfth day of the second month of the Water Monkey Year.
13. Diary pp. 126b–127a.
14. The third month of the Water Monkey Year.
15. Diary pp. 127a–b.
16. The fifth month of the Water Monkey Year.
17. Diary pp. 127b–128a.
18. *Tsādra Gazetteer* p. 3a.
19. The first notice is translated in Ngawang Zangpo 2001, pp. 233–35.
20. Diary p. 123a as translated by Ngawang Zangpo (2001, p. 235).
21. The thirteenth day of the fourth month of the Iron Sheep Year.
22. Diary pp. 124a–b. The second notice, in 1883, was also sent out less than two months before the monkey month, on May 8, 1883, which corresponds to the second day of the fourth month of the Water Sheep Year; the monkey month began on July 5 that year. The second invitation is translated in Ngawang Zangpo 2001, pp. 116–19. The third invitation, translated in Ngawang Zangpo 2001, pp. 235–39, is not dated.

23. Diary p. 124b.
24. Diary p. 125a.
25. The seventh month of the Iron Sheep Year.
26. Diary pp. 125a–b.
27. Diary pp. 125b–126a.
28. Diary pp. 125b–126b.
29. The thirtieth day of the eleventh month of the Iron Sheep Year.
30. Diary p. 125b.
31. The eighth month of the Iron Sheep Year.
32. The end of the Iron Sheep Year or beginning of the Water Monkey Year.
33. The tenth day of the first month of the Water Monkey Year.
34. Diary pp. 125b–126b.
35. The fifth month of the Water Monkey Year.
36. Diary pp. 126b–128a.
37. Diary pp. 128a–b.
38. The tenth day of the seventh month to the fifteenth day of the ninth month of the Water Monkey Year.
39. Diary p. 128b.
40. Diary p. 129a.
41. The ninth month of the Water Monkey Year.
42. Diary pp. 129a–b.
43. The third day of the tenth month of the Water Monkey Year.
44. Diary p. 129a.
45. Diary p. 129b.
46. Diary p. 129b.
47. Diary p. 130a.
48. The ninth month of the Water Bird Year. Kongtrul erred in his diary, writing that the third group began.
49. Diary pp. 130a–131a.
50. The eleventh month of the Water Bird Year.
51. Diary pp. 131a–b.
52. Diary p. 130b.
53. Diary p. 130b.
54. Diary p. 131b.
55. The end of the Water Bird Year.
56. Diary p. 132a.
57. Diary p. 132a.
58. Diary p. 132a. For a translation of the first section of *Light of Wisdom*, see Padmasambhava Guru Rinpoche 1999.
59. The third month of the Wood Dog Year.
60. Diary pp. 132a–b.
61. Diary p. 132b.

62. Diary pp. 132b–133a.
63. Diary pp. 135a–b.
64. *Marvelous Gem-Like Vision* p. 4a.
65. Diary pp. 119a–b.
66. *Mirage of Nectar* p. 34a.
67. *Marvelous Gem-Like Vision* pp. 16a–b.
68. Autobiography, p. 404, note 60.
69. Diary p. 133a.
70. *Fabulous Grove of Uḍumbara Flowers* p. 99b.
71. Diary p. 189b.
72. *Marvelous Gem-Like Vision* p. 7a.
73. Diary pp. 132b–133a.

## 25. Eleven Years of Exile: Ronggyab, Retreat, the Seven-Line Guru Sādhana, and Drubchen across Derge: 1874–1886

1. Diary pp. 183a, 139b, 140a, 142a, 146b, 150b.
2. The sixth month of the Wood Dog Year.
3. Diary pp. 133b, 136b, 137a.
4. The eighth month of the Wood Dog Year.
5. Diary p. 133b.
6. Diary pp. 134b, 138b, 140b, 141a, 150b, 151b. In 1870 Chime Takpai Dorje, following his marriage, had traveled to Tibet where a member of his entourage killed a staff member of the Qing office in Shigatse. The Amban—the Qing Dynasty's representative in Lhasa—insisted that the king surrender the murderer, which he did to the outrage of the petty chieftains traveling with him. On their return to Derge, the king called a meeting of the chieftains to air grievances, but they refused to attend and went as far as having Dokhar Tsewang Norbu beaten. The chieftains henceforth largely disregarded central authority in Derge. The tension would fester until erupting as open civil war twenty-five years later. See Hartley pp. 25–26.
7. The sixth or seventh month of the Fire Mouse Year.
8. Diary p. 139a.
9. The end of the seventh month to the eleventh month of the Fire Mouse Year.
10. Diary pp. 139b–140a.
11. The seventh month of the Fire Ox Year.
12. Diary pp. 142a–b.
13. The seventh day of the tenth month of the Fire Ox Year. See also the colophon to the cycle's sādhana, titled *Blossoming Lotus*.
14. Diary 143a.
15. The twelfth month of the Fire Ox Year.
16. The third month of the Fire Ox Year.
17. The ninth month of the Earth Tiger Year.

18. Diary pp. 142b–147b.
19. Diary pp. 143b–144b.
20. Diary pp. 145a–b, 146a.
21. The tenth day of the first month of the Water Snake Year.
22. Jamgon Kongtrul 1976a, p. 171.
23. The twenty-eighth day of the first month of the Fire Ox Year. Jamgon Kongtrul 1976b, p. 448.
24. *Mirage of Nectar* pp. 33b–37a.
25. *Mirage of Nectar* p. 34b, Diary p. 135b.
26. Diary p. 135b.
27. Diary pp. 147b–148b.
28. Kongtrul's Kham Gazetteer p. 8a
29. Chokling's Kham Gazetteer p. 14b.
30. Diary p. 148b.
31. Diary p. 149a.
32. The twelfth month of the Earth Tiger Year.
33. Diary pp. 149b–150a.
34. Diary p. 150a.
35. Diary p. 152a.
36. Diary pp. 152b–153a.
37. The fourteenth day of the first month of the Iron Dragon Year.
38. The seventeenth day of the first month of the Iron Dragon Year.
39. Diary pp. 151a, 153a–b, the first of the two sixth months of the Wood Sheep Year. Diary p. 156b.
40. Diary pp. 153b, 155b.
41. Diary pp. 153b–154a.
42. *Marvelous Gem-Like Vision* pp. 17a–b.
43. The eighth month of the Iron Dragon Year.
44. Diary pp. 153b–154a.
45. Diary p. 156a.
46. The fifteenth day of the first month to the twenty-first day of the third month of the Water Horse Year.
47. The nineteenth day of the fourth month to the first day of the eighth month of the Water Horse Year. Diary pp. 157a–158b.
48. The fifteenth day of the eighth month of the Water Horse Year.
49. The fourteenth day of the tenth month of the Water Horse Year.
50. Diary p. 159a.
51. Diary p. 159a.
52. The tenth month of the Water Horse Year.
53. Diary pp. 158b, 160b.
54. Diary pp. 161a–b.
55. Diary p. 161b.
56. Around the sixth month of the Water Sheep Year.

57. Diary p. 161b.
58. The original revealer of Khyentse's Guru Cakrasaṃvara was said to be a man named Gyaton Lama.
59. Essence of Light was said to have been originally discovered by a man named Drime Kunga.
60. Diary p. 138a.
61. Khyentse credited Orgyen Lingpa with initially discovering the Oceanic Gathering of Precepts.
62. Khyentse credited the Vajrāmṛta revelation to Ramo Shelmen.
63. Diary p. 134b.
64. Diary pp. 162a–163b.
65. The twelfth month of the Water Sheep Year.
66. Diary pp. 163b–164a.
67. The third month of the Wood Monkey Year.
68. Diary p. 164a.
69. The fourth month of the Wood Monkey Year.
70. The Gathering of All Ḍākinī's Secrets is the Khyentse revelation that is credited to Jomo Menmo.
71. Liberation of All the Arrogant is credited to Drugu Yangwang Tsel.
72. Diary pp. 164a–b.
73. The twenty-fifth day of the tenth month of the Wood Monkey Year to the third day of the first month of the Wood Bird Year.
74. The eighth day of the second month of the Wood Bird Year. Diary pp. 165a–166a.
75. The fifth day of the third month of the Wood Bird Year.
76. *Mirage of Nectar* p. 36a.
77. Diary p. 166a.
78. The sixth month of the Wood Bird Year.
79. Diary p. 167a.
80. Diary pp. 167b–168a.
81. Diary p. 123b.
82. Diary p. 151a.
83. Diary pp. 166a–b.
84. Diary p. 166b.
85. Diary pp. 166b, 168a.

## 26. Transmission, Old Age, and the Death of Khyentse Wangpo: 1886–1897

1. The sixth day of the twelfth month of the Wood Bird Year.
2. Diary p. 168a.
3. Diary p. 168a.
4. The third month of the Earth Ox Year. Diary p. 175a.
5. Diary pp. 168b, 170b.
6. The eleventh month of the Fire Dog Year.

7. Diary p. 169a. I have not been able to identify to what "Five Maṇḍalas of the Karma Kagyu Oral Lineage" refers.

8. The eighth month of the Fire Dog Year.

9. Diary p. 169b.

10. Diary p. 169b.

11. The twelfth month of the Wood Dog Year.

12. Khyentse credited Sanggye Lama as the original revealer of Combined Practice of the Three Roots.

13. Diary p. 170b.

14. The first month of the Fire Pig Year.

15. The fourth month of the Fire Pig Year.

16. The seventeenth day of the third month of the Fire Pig Year.

17. The twenty-fourth day of the third month of the Fire Pig Year.

18. The fifth day of the fourth month of the Fire Pig Year.

19. The seventh day of the fourth month of the Fire Pig Year.

20. Kongtrul recorded the date as the fifteenth day of the fourth month, which according to Henning was omitted.

21. Diary pp. 170b–171b.

22. The tenth month of the Fire Pig Year.

23. Diary p. 172a.

24. The thirtieth day of the first month of the Earth Mouse Year.

25. The thirteenth day of the seventh month of the Earth Mouse Year.

26. The tenth day of the third month of the Earth Mouse Year. Victor is one of the twenty-eight lunar mansions, or *nakṣatras*. These are the divisions of the moon's orbit around the earth by lunar days, of which there are 27.3; the twenty-eighth nakṣatra is only periodically added.

27. May 17 to the sixth day of the fourth month of the Earth Mouse Year.

28. Diary pp. 173a–b.

29. Diary pp. 175b–176a.

30. Diary p. 176a.

31. Diary p. 176b.

32. Diary p. 178a.

33. Diary p. 179a.

34. Diary p. 187b.

35. The seventh month of the Iron Hare Year.

36. Diary p. 180a.

37. Diary p. 183a.

38. Diary p. 180a.

39. Diary p. 117a.

40. Diary p. 147a.

41. Diary p. 147a.

42. Diary p. 160a.

43. Diary pp. 136b–137a.

44. Diary p. 179a.

45. Diary p. 136b.
46. Diary p. 176b.
47. Diary p. 178a.
48. The second month of the Iron Hare Year.
49. The tenth month of the Iron Hare Year.
50. Diary pp. 178a–b, 180a.
51. The second month of the Water Dragon Year.
52. The twenty-first day of the second month of the Water Dragon Year.
53. Diary p. 181a.
54. The twenty-fourth day of the second month of the Water Dragon Year.
55. The twenty-seventh day of the second month of the Water Dragon Year.
56. Diary p. 181a.
57. The twenty-ninth day of the second month of the Water Dragon Year.
58. The thirteenth day of the second month of the Water Dragon Year.
59. Diary p. 181b.
60. Diary p. 181b. The Guru's Two Doctrines is a "rediscovered treasure" ascribed originally to a person named Gya Lotsāwa Dorje Zangpo.
61. The first fourth month of the Iron Hare Year.
62. Diary pp. 182a–b.
63. The sixth month of the Iron Hare Year.
64. Diary pp. 182b–183b.
65. The twenty-eighth day of the tenth month of the Water Dragon Year.
66. Diary pp. 183a–184a.
67. Diary pp. 184a–b.
68. Diary pp. 184b–185a.
69. The twenty-first day of the second month of the Water Snake Year.
70. Diary p. 185b.
71. Diary p. 186a.
72. Diary pp. 185b–186a. Khyentse's own verse autobiography is titled *Condensed Essence*.
73. *One Hundred Treasure Revealers* (pp. 80a–b), Pema Yeshe (p. 27b), and Kongchok Gyurme (p. 89a) all credit the information that Chokgyur Lingpa received this seven transmissions to a prophecy from Three Cycles of Dzogchen, which Chokling and Khyentse revealed together in 1857. On the history of the seven descents, see Schwieger 2010 and Germano 2002.
74. *Fabulous Grove of Uḍumbara Flowers* p. 56a.

## 27. THE DEATH OF KONGTRUL: RIMAY PART FIVE

1. In the more common Pukpa calendrical calculation, the female Earth Pig Year of the fifteenth sexegenary cycle had two eleventh months. This has caused some confusion regarding the month and year of Kongtrul's death; in the Pukpa system the twenty-seventh day of the first eleventh month would be December 29, 1899, but the twenty-seventh day of the second eleventh month by that calculation corresponds

to January 28, 1900. Thus, we see the year of Kongtrul's death given as either 1899 or 1900. Nesar Tashi Chopel, almost certainly following the Tsurpu system, makes no record of a second month.

2. *Marvelous Gem-Like Vision* p. 11b.

3. *Marvelous Gem-Like Vision* p. 5b.

4. *Marvelous Gem-Like Vision* pp. 8b, 9b. The supplication prayer is translated in Ngawang Zangpo 2002.

5. *Marvelous Gem-Like Vision* p. 11a.

6. *Marvelous Gem-Like Vision* p. 11b.

7. *Marvelous Gem-Like Vision* p. 13b.

8. *Marvelous Gem-Like Vision* p. 13b.

9. Ngawang Zangpo 2001, p. 92.

10. *Marvelous Gem-Like Vision* pp. 11a–b.

11. See Kolmaš 1988.

12. *Marvelous Gem-Like Vision* pp. 15a–b.

13. *Marvelous Gem-Like Vision* p. 21b.

14. Higgins and Draszczyk p. 224. On Shukden, see Batchelor and Lopez 1998 and Dreyfus 1998.

15. Jamgön Kongtrul Lodrö Thayé 1995, Foreward.

16. Smith 2001, p. 271. The same phenomenon of multiple incarnations occurred after the death of Khyentse Wangpo: he split into Dzongsar Khyentse Chokyi Lodro, Dilgo Khyentse of Zhechen Monastery, Beru Khyentse of Pelpung, Dzogchen Khyentse Guru Tsewang, and Jamyang Chokyi Wangchuk. Jamyang Chokyi Wangchuk was enthroned at Dzongsar but died young, after which Chokyi Lodro, who had initially been enthroned at Katok, was invited to Dzongsar. Chokyi Wangchuk's reincarnation was found and installed at Derge Gonchen.

17. Ngawang Zangpo 2003, p. 360.

18. Jamgon Kongtrul 2010, p. 28.

19. Campbell 1996 and *Tricycle* 1996.

20. Pang 2014, p. 29. Few writers who have touched on Kongtrul's life or writing have not at some point wrestled with Smith's undefined "movement," and I see little value in repeating the many examples of that struggle.

21. Trungpa 1981, pp. 89–90.

22. Trungpa 1981, pp. 90–91.

## Timeline

1. See BDRC person record 1392.

# LIST OF WORKS CITED

Abhidharmakośa

Abhisamayālaṃāra: *Mngon rtogs rgyan*

All-Pervading Benevolence: *Bcu gcig zhal dpal mo lugs kyi sgrub thabs smyung gnas cho ga gzhan phan kun khyab*

All-Pervading Melody of the Pure Lands: A Catalog of the Buildings and Contents of the Pelpung Hermitage Kunzang Dechen Wosel Ling: *Dpal spung sa yang khrod kun bzang bde chen 'od gsal gling rten dang brten par bcas pa'i dkar chag zhing khams kun tu khyab pa'i sgra snyan*

Amarakoṣa

Ambrosia from My Heart: *Byang gter gsol 'debs le'u bdun ma'i dmigs zin mdor bsdus bkod pa snying gi bdud rtsi*

Amulet Box of Mahāmudrā: *Phyag chen gwa'u ma*

Anāvila-tantrarāja Tantra: *Rgyud kyi rgyal po dpal rnyog pa med pa*

Ancestral Line of the Vidyādhara: *Rig 'dzin gdung sgrub*

Ascertaining the Three Vows: *Rang bzhin rdzogs pa chen po'i lam gyi cha lag sdom pa gsum rnam par nges pa zhes bya ba'i bstan bcos*

Auspiciously Curling Tune: *Bkra shis dkhil pa'i dbyangs snyan*

Avataṃsaka Sūtra: *Mdo phal po che*

Averting Untimely Death: *Dus min 'ci zlog*

Beams of Sunlight: *Dpal kye'i rdo rje zhes bya ba'i rgyal po'i 'grel pa legs bshad nyi ma'i 'od zer*

Bhadrakalpikasūtra: *Bskal pa bzang po'i mdo*

Blazing Jewel of Temporal Rule: *Mnga' dbang rin chen 'bar ba*

Blossoming Lotus: The Sādhana for Chanting the Seven-Line Prayer: *Tshig bdun 'don thabs sna tshogs pa'i sgrub thabs pad+ma rgyas pa*

Bodhipathapradīpa

Book of Kadam: *Bka' gdams glegs bam*

Breeze Requesting the Auspicious Tune: *Bkra shis dbyangs snyan bskul ba'i dri bahon*

A Brief Clarification of the List of Twenty-Five Great Abodes of Kham Together with their Auxiliaries: *Mdo khams gnas chen nyer lnga yan lag dang bcas pa'i mdo byang gi gsal byed zin thung nyung ngu*

A Brief Inventory of the Great Abodes of Tibet Composed by Padmasambhava, the Wise One of Oḍḍiyāna: *Bod kyi gnas chen rnams kyi mdo byang dkar chags o rgyan gyi mkhas pa padma 'byung gnas kyis bkod pa*

Cakrasaṃvara Tantra: *Khor lo bde mchog gi rtsa rgyud*

Candalī Swift Mother of Life: *Tshe yum mgyogs ma tsanda lI'i sgrub skor*

Candoratnākara: *Sdeb sbyor rin chen 'byung gnas*

Candravyākaraṇa: *Lung ston pa tsandra pa'i mdo*

Catalog of Drentang Panchen Kumbum: *Paṇ chen dran thang sku 'bum dkar chag*

Catalog of Tsādra: *See* All-Pervading Melody of the Pure Lands: A Catalog of the Buildings and Contents of the Pelpung Hermitage Kunzang Dechen Wosel Ling

A Celebration of the Opening of One Hundred Doors to Great Wonder; A Lecture on the Maṇḍala Offering to the Supreme Emanation of Maitreya on the Occasion of His Investiture onto the Lion Throne: *Byams mgon mchog gi sprul pa'i sku seng ge'i khrir phebs pa'i maNDala rgyas bshad ngo mtshar sgo brgya 'byed pa'i dga' ston*

Chariot for Traversing the Noble Path: *Sgrub brgyud karma kam tshang pa'i phyag chen lhan cig skyes sbyor gyi sngon 'gro bzhi sbyor kyi ngag 'don 'phags lam bgrod pa'i shing rta*

Chest of Amṛta: *Zab lam thugs kyi nor bu las /rtsa ba'i sgrub chen dang bdud rtsi sman sgrub gnyis kyi sgrub khog zung 'brel du bkod pa grub gnyis bdud rtsi'i za ma tog*

Chronicles of Padmasambhava: *Padma bka' thang*

Clearing Obstacles to the Path: *Bar chad lam sel*

A Cloud of Pleasures: *Gsur mchod 'dod yon sprin phung*

Collected Instructions on the Mantra: *Ma ni bka' 'bum*

Collected Nyingma Tantras: *Rnying ma rgyud 'bum*

Collected Works of Dolpopa: *Dol po pa'i gsung 'bum*

Collected Works of Jigme Lingpa: *Jigs med gling pa'i gsung 'bum*

Collected Works of Tāranātha: *TA ra nA tha'i gsung 'bum*

Combined Practice of the Three Roots: *Rtsa gsum dril sgrub*

Combined Practice of the Undying Three Roots of the Tathāgata: *Bde gshegs rtsa gsum 'chi med dril sgrub*

Combined Precepts of Dzogchen: *Yang gyu 'bal brag nas spyan drangs pa rdzogs pa chen po bka' 'dus las rtsa sgrub snying po don bsdus sogs gter gzhung*

Compendium of Sādhana: *Sgrub thabs kun 'dus*

Compendium of Practical Astronomy: *Rtsis kyi bstan bcos nyer mkho bum bzang las skar rtsis kyi lag len 'jug bder bsdebs pa legs bshad kun 'dus*

Complete Collection of Essentials: *Nyer bum yongs rdzogs*

A Complete Spontaneous Fulfillment of Wishes: An Invocation to the Gracious Goddess: *Bka' drin lha mo'i gsol mchod bsam don lhun grub*

Complete Union of the Intent of the Three Roots: *Rtsa gsum dgongs pa kun 'dus*. JKW treasure.

Concise Words on Mahāmudrā: *Phyag rgya chen po'i tshig bsdus pa*

Condensed Essence: *Jam dbyangs mkhyen brtse'i dbang po'i rnam thar snying po dril ba*

Conquest of Poison: *Gro lod gsang sgrub gdug pa kun 'dul*

Consummate Profundity: *Zab pa phul phyin*

Crucial Point of the Oral Lineage Action Vajrakīla: *Snyan brgyud phrin las phur pa'i gnad tig*

Cuckoo's Auspicious Song: *Rje gter chen bla ma dbus phebs skor gyi lam yig mdor bsdus bkra shis dpyid kyi rgyal mo'i dbyangs snyan*

Cycle of Dependent Origination: *Rten 'brel chos skor*

Cycle of Four and Forty: *Bzhi tshan bzhi bzhu pa'i skor*

Cycle on Red Jambhala: *Gnod sbyin dzambha la dmar po'i chos skor*

Dechen Burmo Gazetteer: *Bde chen 'bur mo'i gnas yig*

Dharma Ocean of Precepts: *Dpal bka' 'dus chos kyi rgya mtsho*

Discourse on Pulse Diagnosis and Urinalysis: *Phyi rgyud rtsa chu'i mdo*

Dispelling All Contamination of Broken Samaya: *Dam grib nyes pa kun sel*

Dispelling All Obstacles: *Bar chad kun gsal*

Ear of Divine Grain: *Lha mo dpal chen g.yang chog zur 'debs yongs 'du'i snye ma*

An Easy Introduction for the Challenged: *Blo sbyong don bdun ma'i khrid yig blo dman 'jug bde*

Eight Commands: Perfection of Secrets: *Bka' brgyad gsang ba yang rdzogs*

Eight Commands: Gathering of All Sugatas: *Sgrub chen bka' brgyad bde gshegs kun 'dus*

Eight Commands: Gathering of Sugatas: *Bka' brgyad bde gshegs 'dus pa*

Eight Cycles of the Path: *Lam skor brgyad*

Eighteen Meanings of A: *Sems sde a don bco brgyad*

Embodiment of the Guru's Secrets: *Bla ma gsang 'dus*

Embodiment of the Secret Ḍākinī: *Mkha' 'gro gsang ba kun 'dus*

Encompassing All Knowledge: *Theg pa'i sgo kun las btus pa gsung rab rin po che'i mdzod bslab pa gsum legs par ston pa'i bstan bcos shes bya kun khyab*

Enlightened Intent: Innermost Gathering: *Thugs sgrub yang 'dus*

Essence of Clear Light: *Dam chos shog sde drug pa las rdor sems thugs kyi snying po'i dbang gi cho ga 'od gsal snying po*

Essence of Light: *'Od kyi snying po*

Excellent Vase of Bounty: *Sgrub thabs 'dod 'jo bum bzang*

Expanded Treasury: *Rgya chen bka' mdzod*

Fabulous Grove of Uḍumbara Flowers: The Abbreviated Life Story of the Noble and Omniscient Jamyang Khyentse Wangpo Kunga Tenpai Gyeltsen: *Kun mkhyen bla ma rin po che'i khyad par gyi rnam thar la ched du brjod pa u dumba ra'i dga' tshal.*

Fierce Lama: The Mother Khrodhakāli: *Bla ma drag po yum bka' khros ma nag mo*

Five Books of Maitreya: *Byams chos sde lnga*

Five Chronicles: *Thang yig sde lnga*

Five Cycles of The Essence of the Noble Dharma: *Dam chos snying po skor lnga*

Five Maṇḍalas of the Karma Kagyu Oral Lineage: *Karma snyan brgyud 'khor lo lnga*

Forest of All Delights: *Lus mchod sbyin gyi zin bris mdor bsdus kun dga'i skyed tshal*

Four Dharmas of Protector of the Teachings: *Bstan srung chos bzhi*

Four Hundred Verses: *Dbu ma bzhi brgya pa*
Freedom from Fear: *Sgrol ma'i 'jigs pa kun skyab*
A Full Clarification of the Hidden Meaning: *Sbas don kun gsal*
Garland of Jewels: *Nor bu phreng ba*
Garland of Treasures: *Gter phreng*
Gathering of All Ḍākinīs' Secrets: *Mkha' 'gro gsang ba kun 'dus*
Gathering of the Great Heart: *Yang snying 'dus pa*
Gathering of Secrets: *Thugs rje chen po gsang ba 'dus pa*
Gathering of Wisdom Holders: *Rig 'dzin yongs 'dus*
General Assembly of Mamo: *Ma mo sbyi bdus*
God's Melody: *Mchog gzigs bla ma dam pa g.yung drung phun tshogs kyi gdung rten dkar chag lha'i sgra snyan*
Great Commentary on Discipline: *Dul TI ka chen po / 'dul ba nyi ma'i dkyil 'khor*
Guhyagarbha Tantra: *Rgyud gsang ba snying po*
Guhyasamāja: *Gsang ba 'dus pa*
Guide to Signs: *Lung du ston pa rtag gi 'jug pa*
Guru Sādhana: The Treasure Trove of Qualities: *Gu ru sgrub thabs yon tan gter mdzod*
Guru: Union of the Eight Commands: *Bla ma bka' brgyad bka' 'dus*
Guru's Heart Advice in Ten Chapters: *Gu ru'i zhal gdams snying gtam le'u bcu pa*
Heart Drop of the Ḍākinī: *Mkha' 'gro snying thig*
Heart Drop of the Ḍākinī Expanse: *Klong gsal mkha' 'gro snying thig*
Heart Drop of Mitra: *Mi tra snying thig*
Heart Drop of Vairocana: *Ba'i ro thugs tig sde lnga*
Heart Drop of the Venerable Goddess of Immortality: *Chi med 'phags ma'i snying thig*. Kongtrul writes *'phags ma'i thugs thig* in several places.
Heart Essence of Chetsun: *Lce btsun snying thig*
Heart Essence of the Karmapas: *karma snying thig*
Heart Essence of Mañjuśrīmitra: *'Jam dpal bshes gnyen snying thig*
Heart Essence of the Noble Deathless One: *Chi med 'phags ma snying thig*
Heart Essence of the Tamer of Beings: Mahākaruṇika Cittaviśramaṇa: *Gro 'dul 'phags pa'i thugs tig thugs rje chen po sems nyid ngal gso*
Heart Essence of the Three Classes: *Rigs gsum snying thig*
Heart Essence of Vairocana: *Rjes dran tshe sgrub bai ro'i thugs tig gsang ba'i rgya can*
Heart Essence of Vajrasattva: *Rdor sems nying thig*
Heart Essence of Vajrasattva's Enlightened Mind: *Rdor sems thugs kyi nying thig*
Heart Essence of the Vast Expanse: *Klong chen snying thig*
Heart Essence of Vimalamitra: *Bi ma nying thig*
Heart Essence of Yeshe Tsogyel: *Mtsho rgyal snying tig*
The Heart Essence of Yutok: *G.yu thog snying thig*
The Heart of the Sun: *Gter kha so bzhi ba 'chi med padma shel ri'i gnas kyi mdo byang nyi ma'i snying po*
Hevajra Tantra: *Kye rdo rje'i rgyud*

How to Clear One's Eyes Using Mahāruṇika: A Treasure of the Siddha Nyanton: *Thugs rje chen po'i sgo nas mig gi gsal byed nyang ston grub pa'i gter ma*

Illuminating Garlands of Light: *Zab mo nang don gyi rnam bshad snying po gsal bar byed pa'i nyin byed 'od kyi phreng ba*

Illuminating Morality: Regulations for the Retreats at the Pelpung Hermitage Kunzang Dechen Wosel Ling: *Dpal spungs yang khrod kun bzang bde chen 'od gsal gling gi sgrub pa rnams kyi kun spyod bcas khrims blang dor rab gsal phen bde'i 'byung gnas*

Illuminating the Profound Inner Principles: *Rnal 'byor bla na med pa'i rgyud sde mtsho'i snying po bsdus pa zab mo nang gi don nyung ngu'i tshig gis rnam par 'grol ba zab don snang nyed*

Innermost Heart Drop of the Guru: *Bla ma yang tig*

Innermost Heart of Immortality: *Chi med yang snying kun 'dus kyi sgo nas brtan bzhugs kyi cho ga bya ba'i khrigs rim 'chi med grub pa'i dga' ston*

Innermost Secret Kīla Razor: *Phur pa yang gsang spu gri*

Integration of Means and Wisdom: *Tshe sprub thabs shes kha sbyor*

Iron Hook of Subjugation: A Sādhana and Mending for the Baghavān Kurukullā: *Bcom ldan 'das rig byed ma'i skong ba dngos grub 'gugs pa'i lcags kyu*

Irrepressible Lion's Roar: *Theg pa chen po rgyud bla ma'i bslan bcos snying po'i don mngon sum lam gyi bshad srol dang sbyar ba'i rnam par 'grel pa phyir mi ldog pa seng ge nga ro*

Jamyang Khyentse Wangpo's Guide to Tibet: *Dbus gtsang gnas yig ngo mtshar lun ston me long*

Jeweled Comet's Tail: *Zab lam thugs kyi nor bu las /las bzhi mchog lnga'i sbyin sreg gi lug len 'dus du bkod pa nor bu sna tshogs mdog can*

Jewel-Like Commentary: *Dpal brtag pa gnyis pa'i 'grel pa rin chen rgyan 'dra*

Jewel Ornament of Liberation: *Dwags po thar rgyan*

Kālacakra Tantra: *Dus 'khor rtsa rgyud*

Kavyadarśa: *Snyan ngag me long*

Lake and Rock Teachings: *Rol rdor gter chos mtsho brag*

Lama Jewel Ocean: *Bla ma nor rgyal*

Lamp That Illuminates the Essence: *Dpal kye'i rdo rje'i rgyud kyi rgyal po'i snying po gsal bar byed pa'i sgron me*

A Lecture on Planting the Silken Arrow on the Occasion of the Arrival in the Kham Kingdom of Derge of the Daughter of Tibetan Minister Dokhar: *Mdo khams sde dge'i rgyal khab tu bod blon mdo mkhar pa'i btsun mo byon skabs mda' dar 'dzugs pa'i 'bel gtam yod*

Liberation of All the Arrogant: *Dregs pa kun sgrol*

Liberation Through Seeing: *Mthong grol*

Light Rays of the Stainless Vajra Moon: Guiding Instructions on the View of Great Other-Emptiness Madhyamaka: *Gzhan stong du ma chen po'i lta khrid rdo rje zla ba dri ma med pa'i 'od zer*

Light of Wisdom: *Lam rim ye shes snying po'i 'grel pa ye shes snang ba rab tu rgyas pa*

Lightning Garland of Protective Deities: Peaceful Garland, Wrathful Garland: *Zhi phreng drag phreng chos skyong glog phreng*

Lion's Roar of Brahmā: *Tshom bu tshogs su sgrub pa'i gtong thun gsal bar spros pa tshangs pa'i nga ro*

Longevity Lord Yamāntaka: *Gshin rje tshe bdag*

Lotus of Advice: A Manual for Reciting the Union of All Rare and Precious Jewels: *Yang zab dkon mchog spyi 'dus kyi bsnyen yig bklag chog tu bkod pa pad+ma'i zhal lung*

Lotus Crest: *Padma gtsug gtor*

Lotus Distillation: *Padma bcud sdud*

Lunar Crystal Mirror: The Texts and Tradition of Vajrakīla, the Conqueror of Māra: *Rdo rje phur pa bdud 'joms rol pa'i pu sta ka'i bzhugs byang dang brgyud pa'i yi ge zla shel me long*. In the Diary Kongtrul refers to the work as *Phur pa bdud 'joms rol pa'i yig cha*

Madhyamakāvatāra: *Dbu ma la 'jug pa*

Mahākaruṇika: Dredging the Pit of Cyclic Existence: *Thugs rje chen po 'khor ba dong sprugs*

Mahākaruṇika: Gathering of Sugatas: *Thugs rje chen po bde gshegs kun 'dus*

Mahākaruṇika: Guide to Beings: *Thugs chen 'gro 'dul*

Mahākaruṇika: Resting At Ease: *Thugs chen sems nyid ngal gso*

Mahākaruṇika: Spontaneous Liberator of the Lower Realms: *Thugs rje chen po ngan song rang grol*

Mahāmudrā: Eliminating the Darkness of Ignorance: *Phyag chen ma rig mun gsal*

Mañjuśrīnāma-Samgīti: *Nam dpal mtshan brjod*

Marvelous Gem-Like Vision: *Rje kun gzigs 'jam mgon ngag gi dbang phyug yon tan rgya mtsho'i zhabs kyi 'das rjes kyi rnam par thar pa ngo mtshar nor bu'i snang ba*

Māyajāla Tantra: *Sgyu 'phrul drva ba'i rgyud*

Meaningful to Behold: *Dpal dus kyi 'khor lo'i zab lam rdo rje'i rnal 'byor gyi chos skor rdzogs ldan rnal 'byor dga' tshal*

Medical Offering: *Sman mchod*

Melodious Āḍambara Drum: *Dpal gyi ri 'jam mgon bla ma gu Na'i mtshan gyi skyes rabs gsol 'debs lha yi rnga bo che'i sgra dbyangs*

Melodious Rain of White Lapis: *Bai dkar dbyangs 'char*

Melodious Supplication: An Outline of the Khyungpo Lineage: *Khyung po'i gdung rabs rags bsdus kyi gsol 'debs bkra shis dbyangs snyan*

Mirage of Nectar: *Du shes gsum ldan spong ba pa'i gzugs brnyan padma gar gyi dbang phyug phrin las 'gro 'dul rtsal gyi rtogs pa brjod pa'i dum bu smrig rgyu'i bdud rtsi*

Mirror of Faith: *Rdzong chen khams phug 'od gsal grub pa'i rtse mo'i dkar chag gter byon zur 'debs dad pa'i me long*

Mirror of Mindfulness: *Rdzong chen khams phug 'od gsal grub pa'i gnas kyi ngo sprod dran pa'i me long*

Mountain Doctrine: *Chags med ri chos*

Mountain Doctrine: Ocean of Certainty: *Ri chos nges don rgya mtsho*

Music from the Ocean of the Mind: An Account of Devīkoṭa Tsādra Rinchen Drak, the Supreme Site of Enlightened Mind: *Thugs kyi gnas mchog chen po de bI ko TI tsA 'dra rin chen brag gi rtog pa brjod pa yid kyi rgya mtsho'i rol mo*

Necklace of Clear Understanding: A Brief Nonsectarian Religious History: *Rīs med chos kyi 'byung gnas mdo tsam smos pa blo gsal Mgrin pa'i mdzes rgyon*

Ocean of Certainty: *Phyag chen nges don rgya mtsho*

Ocean of Definitive Meaning: *Phyag chen ngas don rgya mtsho*

Ocean of Deities: *Yi dam rgya mtsho'i sgrub thabs rin chen 'byung gnas*

Ocean of Dharma That Embodies All Teachings: *Bka' 'dus chos kyi rgya mtsho*

Ocean of Enumerations: *Rnam drangs rgya mtsho*

Ocean of the Supreme Bliss Ḍākinī: *Mkha' gro bde chen rgya mtsho'i sgrub skor*

Oceanic Gathering of Precepts: *Bka' 'dus chos kyi rgya mtsho*

One Hundred Gods of Nartang: *Snar thang rgya rtsa*

One Hundred Instructions of Darmo: *Dar mo bka' brgya ma*

One Hundred Instructions of the Jonang: *Jo nang khri brgya*

One Hundred Peaceful and Wrathful Deities: *Zhi khro'i lha brgya*

One Hundred Transmissions of Mitra: *Mi tra brgya rtsa*

One Hundred Treasure Revealers: *Gter ston brgya rtsa*

Opening the Eye of Discrimination: *Shu bha 'brug dgu gling sogs chos 'khor chen po rnams kyi bca' yig blang dor mig 'byed*

Opening of the Secret Invincible Vajra of Liberation: *Dpal dgyes pa rdo rje'i rgyud kyi rgyal po brtag pa gnyis pa'i tshig don rnam par 'grol ba gzhom med rdo rje'i gsang ba 'byed pa*

Openness of Realization Tantra: *Dgongs pa zang thal*

Oral Lineage of Lamdre: *Lam 'bras snyan brgyud*

Outline of the Supplication to Chokgyur Lingpa: *Gter chen mchog gyur gling pa'i rnam thar gsol 'debs kyi bsdus don bkra shis dbyangs kyi yan lag*

Peaceful and Wrathful: Compendium of Teachings: *Bka' 'dus zhi khro*

Peaceful and Wrathful Magical Display: *Sgyu 'phrul zhi khro*

Pointing Out the Dharmakāya: *Cho sku mdzub tshugs*

Prayer in Seven Chapters: *Gsol 'debs le'u bdun pa*

Prayers of Supreme Devotion: *Gsol 'debs mos gus rab byed*

Precious Garland of the Supreme Path: *Lam mchog rin chen phreng ba*

Profound Essence of Endless Ambrosia: *Bla ma dgongs pa 'dus pa las/ dpa' bo rkyang sgrub dang gsal byed thugs kyi nor bu'i bsnyen sgrub kyi yi ge bdud rtsi stong gi zab bcud*

Profound Essence of Tārā: *Dgongs gter sgrol ma'i zab tig*

Profound Essence Uniting the Families of the Three Roots: *Rtsa gsum rigs 'dus zab tig*

Profound Inner Principles: *Zab mo nang don*

Profound Meaning of Ati: *Smin gling a ti zab don*

Profound Oral Lineage of Siṃhamukhā: *Zab gsang seng gdong snyan brgyud*

Profound Path, Jewel of the Mind: *Zab lam thugs kyi nor bu*

Profound Path in Seven Sections: *Lam zab le'u bdun ma*

Quick Method for Accomplishing the Two Principles of the Maṇḍala Rite: *Dkyil 'khor gyi cho ga don gnyis myur 'grub*

Rain of Virtue: *Lhan thabs mjug gi cho ga dge legs char 'bebs*

Ratnagotravibhāga (Uttaratantra): *Rgyud bla ma*

Ratnakūṭa: *Dam chos dkon mchog brtsegs pa*

Resting at Ease Trilogy: *Sems nyid ngal gso*

Sādhana of the Guru's Intent: Wish-Fulfilling Jewel: *Bla ma'i thugs sgrub yid bzhin nor bu bsam pa lhun grub*

Sarvabuddha Samayoga: *Sangs rgyas mnyam sbyor*

Sea of Enjoyment: *Skad gnyis shan sbyar la nye bar mkho ba'i zin bris las dang po pa 'jug pa'i rol mtsho*

Secret Essence: *Gsang thig snying po*

Secret Treasury of the Ḍākinī: *Mkha' 'gro gsang mdzod*

Secret Visions of the Fifth Dalai Lama: *Lnga pa rin po che'i dag snang rgya can*

Self-Liberated Mind of the Peaceful and Wrathful Deities: *Zhi khro dgongs pa rang grol*

Seven Cycles of the Secret Essence: *Gsang thig snying po'i skor*

Seven-Line Guru Sādhana: *Bla sgrub rtsa ba tshig bdun pa*

Seven-Line Prayer: *Tshig bdun gsol 'debs*

Seven-Point Mind Training: *Blo sbyong don bdun ma*

Seven Profound Cycles: *Thugs dam zab pa skor bdun*

Seven Treasuries: *Mdzod bdun*

Short Lineage of Tangtong Gyelpo that Unites Pure Vision, Spoken Word, and Treasure: *Dag snang dang bka' gter gsum 'dus thang rgyal nye brgyud*

Six Scrolls of Profound Dharma: *Dam chos shog sde drug*

Sky Teachings: *Gnam chos*

A Sliver of Enlightened Mind: *Rta mgrin gsang ba 'dus pa las/rta mgrin nag po'i dbang chog dregs pa srog gi rgya can skur ba'i cho ga dbang chen thugs kyi tshal pa*

Smiling Powerful Vajra: *Phur ba dbang chen bzhad pa*

Smoke Offering Manual at the Supreme Abode Burmo Drak: *Gnas mchog 'bur mo brag dkar la bsang mchod 'bul ba*

Source of Jewels, the Collected Sādhanas of the Jonang Tradition: *Jo nang sgrub thabs rin 'byung*

Source That Yields Virtue and Excellence: *Dge legs 'dod 'jo*

Spacious Expanse of the View: *Lta ba klong yangs*

Sphere of Mind: *Thugs kyi thig le*

Splendid Roar That Completely Vanquishes the Gyelyang Demon: *Rgyal dbyangs bdud las rnam par rgyal ba'i rngam sgra*

Spontaneous Accomplishment of Goals: *Bsam lhun gsol 'deb*

Spontaneous Fulfillment of All Wishes: Treasure Trove of Qualities: *Bsam lhun yon tan gter mdzod*

Stages of Approach and Accomplishment of the Three Vajras: *Rdorje gsum gyi bsyan sgrub*

Stages of the Path of Secret Mantra: *Gsang sngags lam rim*
Stages of the Path of the Three Kinds of Beings: *Skyes bu gsum gyi lam rim*
Stages of the Path of the Wisdom Essence: *Lam rim ye shes snying po*
Stainless Light: An Explanation of the Two-Part Hevajra Tantra: *Brtag gnyis rnam bshad dri med 'od*
Stainless Moonlight: *Kho bo dpal karma pa bco long pa'i skyes rabs kyi rtogs pa brjod pa ngo mtshar bdud rtsi'i rlabs phrang dri med zla zer*
Stirring the Depths (Seven Profound Cycles): *Zhi khro na rak dong sprugs kyi dbang chog bdud rtsi'i gang gA*
Stirring the Depths of Saṃsāra: *Khor ba dor sprugs*
Sublime Sādhana of the Vidyādhara: *Rig 'dzin mchog sgrub*
Supplication to Chokgyur Lingpa: *Sprul pa'i gter chen mchog gyur gling pa'i rnam thar gsol 'debs bkra shis 'khyil pa'i dbyangs snyan*
Sūtra That Gathers All Intentions: *Dus mdo / dgongs pa'i 'dus pa'i mdo*
Sūtra on the Questions of the King of the Nāgas
Tambura of Goodness: *Gnas mchog rdzong chen khams phug yan lag dang bcas pa'i gsol mchod dge legs kyi tam+bu ra*
Tambura Song of Devotion: *Mkha' 'gro'i gtso mo ye shes mtsho rgyal gyi rnam thar mdor bsdus sgo nas gsol ba 'debs pa mos gus gdung ba'i tam+bu ra*
Tantra of Luminous Expanse: *Mdun nas klong gsal*
Tantric-System Vajrakīla: *Phur pa rgyud lugs / rgyud lugs phur pa*
Tārāyoginī Tantra: *Sgrol ma rnal 'byor ma.*
Ten Million Relics: *Bye ba ring bsrel*
Ten Stanzas on Suchness: *Sde kho na nyid bcu pa*
Testament of the King. *Rgyal po bka' chems.*
Thirty Verses: *Lung ston pa rtsa ba sum cu pa*
Three Cycles of the Secret Heart Essence: *Gsang thig snying po'i skor gsum*
Three Deities of Long Life: *Tshe lha rnam gsum*
Three Methods of Carrying the Path: *Lam mkhyer gsum*
Three Principal Aspects of the Path: *Lam gtso rnam gsum*
Three Sections of Dzogchen: *Rdzogs chen sde gsum*
Tincture of Molten Meteoric Iron: *Gnam lcags zhun 'dril*
Torch of Certainty: *Nges don sgron me*
Treasury of the Expansive: *Rgya chen bka' mdzod*
Treasury of Instructions: *Gdams ngag mdzod*
Treasury of Kagyu Tantra: *Bka' brgyud sngags mdzod*
Treasury of Knowledge: *Shes bya mdzod*
Treasury of Revelations: *Rin chen gter mdzod*
Treasury of the Uncommon: *Thun mong ma yin pa'i mdzod*
Treasury of Wish-Fulfilling Jewels: *Dam pa'i chos rin po che mdo sngags rig gnas dang bcas pa ji ltar thos shing de dag gang las brgyud pa'i yi ge dgos 'dod kun 'byung nor bu'i bang mdzod gsan yig*
Treatise Distinguishing Ordinary Consciousness from Primordial Awareness: *Rnam shes ye shes 'byed pa'i bstan bcos*

Treatise on Buddha-Nature: *De gshegs snying po bstan pa'i bstan chos kyi 'grel pa don gsal lung gi 'od zer*

Trilogy of the Guru's Two Doctrines: *Bla ma bstan gnyis skor gsum*

Truly Perfected King: *Mngon rdzogs rgyal po*

Turquoise-Trimmed Golden Reliquary: *Bcu gcig zhal dpal mo lugs smyung gnas sgrub pa'i lag len gser sdong g.yu'i phra tshom*

Twenty-Five Scriptural Teachings of Niguma: *Ni gu'i gzhung bka' nyer lnga*

Unified Saṃvara Buddha: *Bde mchog sangs rgyas mnyam sbyor*

Union of All Rare and Precious Jewels: *Dkon mchog spyi 'dus*

Union of the Families of the Three Immortal Kāyas: *Chi med sku gsum rigs 'dus*

United Command of the Three Roots: *Rtsa gsum bka' 'dus*

United Families of the Three Kāyas: *Sku gsum rigs 'dus*

United Intent of the Ḍākinī: *Mkha' 'gro dgongs 'dus*

United Intent of the Dharma Protectors: *Chos skyong dgongs 'dus*

United Intent of the Gurus: *Bla ma dgongs pa 'dus pa*

United Intent of Samantabhadra: *Kun bzang dgong 'dus*

United Intent of the Three Roots: *Rtsa gsum dgongs pa 'dus pa rig 'dzin mchog sgrub*

United Intent of the Three Roots: Initiation of the Vidyādhara: *Rtsa gsum dgongs 'dus zab mo gter gyi mdzod las/rig 'dzin don gyi dbang bskur*

Unsurpassed Innermost Vajrakīla: *Phur pa yang gsang bla med*

Vajra Array Great Transmission: *Lung chen rdo rje bkod pa*

Vajra of Meteoric Iron Long Life Sādhana: *Tshe sgrub gnam lcags rdo rje*

Vajra Necklace: *Gu ru'i rnam thar rdo rje'i rgyan phreng*

Vajradaṇḍa Sādhana (from Dispelling All Obstacles): *Bla ma'i thugs sgrub bar chad kun sel las gsang bdag rdo rje be con gyi sgrub thabs*

Vajrakīla Essence of Mind: *Rdor sems thugs kyi thig le*

Vajrakīla Tantra: *Rdo rje phur pa rtsa ba'i rgyud*

Vanquishing All Arrogant Ones: *Dregs pa kun 'joms*

Vimalamitra Guru Sādhana: *Bi ma'i bla sgrub lam zab snying po*

Vimalaprabhā: *Dri med 'od*

Wish-Fulfilling Essence Manual of Oral Instructions: *Zhal gdams snying byang yid bzhin nor bu*

Wish-Fulfilling Jewel of the Guru's Intent: *Bla ma thugs sgrub yid bzhin nor bu*

Wish-Fulfilling Jewel of the Guru's Unexcelled Innermost Essence: *Bla ma yang tig yid bzhin nor bu*

Wish-Fulfilling Treasury: *Yid bzhin mdzod*

# Bibliography

## Tibetan

Anonymous. 1982. *Seven Profound Cycles Treasure History* (*Gter chen Mchog gyur gling pa'i zab bdun gter mdzod bzhes ba'i tshul lo rgyus ngo tshar lnga ldan*). In *The Treasury of Revelations and Teachings of Mchog-gyur-bde-chen-gliṇ-pa*, vol. 12, 352–55. Paro, Bhutan: Lama Pema Tashi.

Chokgyur Lingpa (Mchog gyur gling pa). 1976. *Secret Path of Wisdom* (*Bi ma mi tra'i yang tig ye shes gsang lam*). In *Treasury of Revelations* (*Rin chen gter mdzod chen mo*), vol. 46, 168–97. Paro: Ngodrup and Sherab Drimay.

———. 1982 (1853). *Lotus Crest Sādhana* (*Thugs rje chen po padma gtsug tor dri ma med pa'i sgrub thabs theg dgu dang 'brel ba gter gzhung*). In *The Treasury of Revelations and Teachings of Mchog-gyur-bde-chen-gliṇ-pa*, vol. 10, 125–266. Paro, Bhutan: Lama Pema Tashi.

———. 1982 (1857). *A Brief Inventory of the Great Abodes of Tibet Composed by Padmasambhava, the Wise One of Oḍḍiyāna* (*Bod kyi gnas chen rnams kyi mdo byang dkar chags o rgyan gyi mkhas pa padma 'byung gnas kyis bkod pa*). In *The Treasury of Revelations and Teachings of Mchog-gyur-bde-chen-gliṇ-pa*, vol. 24, 95–124. Paro, Bhutan: Lama Pema Tashi.

———. 1982 (1859). *Gazetteer of the Supreme Site of Enlightened Mind, Tsādra Rinchen Drak* (*Gsang thig snying po'i skor las thugs kyi gnas mchog tsA 'dra rin chen brag gi dkar chag*). In *The Treasury of Revelations and Teachings of Mchog-gyur-bde-chen-gliṇ-pa*, vol. 30, 159–63. Paro, Bhutan: Lama Pema Tashi.

———. 1982. *Autobiography of Chokgyur Lingpa* (*Sprul pa'i gter ston chen mo'i rnam thar gyi sa bon zhal gsung ma dang gter 'byung 'ga' zhig bel gtam sna tshogs bcas phyogs bsdom rgyal bstan nyin bye 'og snang bes*). In *The Treasury of Revelations and Teachings of Mchog-gyur-bde-chen-gliṇ-pa*, vol. 36, 175–230. Paro, Bhutan: Lama Pema Tashi.

Dorje Rabten (Rdo rje rab brtan). 2000. *Biography of Zhechen Wontrol Gyurme Tutob Namgyel* (*Zhe chen dbon sprul 'gyur med mthu stobs rnam rgyal gyi rnam thar*). New Delhi: Shechen Publications.

Jamgon Kongtrul ('Jam mgon kong sprul). 1976a. *Tambura Song of Devotion* (*Mkha' 'gro'i gtso mo ye shes mtsho rgyal gyi rnam thar mdor bsdus sgo nas gsol ba 'debs pa mos gus gdung ba'i tam+bu ra*). In *Treasury of Revelations* (*Rin chen gter mdzod chen mo*), vol. 6, 161–71. Paro: Ngodrup and Sherab Drimay.

———. 1976b. *United Intent of the Three Roots: Initiation of the Vidyādhara* (*Rtsa gsum dgongs 'dus zab mo gter gyi mdzod las / rig 'dzin don gyi dbang bskur*). In *Treasury of Revelations* (*Rin chen gter mdzod chen mo*), vol. 9, 431–48. Paro: Ngodrup and Sherab Drimay.

———. 1976c. *Vajra Necklace* (*Gu ru'i rnam thar rdo rje'i rgyan phreng*). In *Treasury of Revelations* (*Rin chen gter mdzod chen mo*), vol. 97, 269–91. Paro: Ngodrup and Sherab Drimay.

———. 1982. *Auspiciously Curling Tune: A Biographical Supplication to the Treasure Revealer Chokgyur Lingpa* (*Sprul pa'i gter chen mchog gyur gling pa'i rnam thar gsol 'debs bkra shis 'khyil pa'i dbyangs snyan*). In *The Treasury of Revelations and Teachings of Mchog-gyur-bde-chen-gliṇ-pa*, vol. 39, 1–9. Paro, Bhutan: Lama Pema Tashi.

———. 1982 (1868). *A Brief Clarification of the List of Twenty-five Great Abodes of Kham Together with their Auxiliaries* (*Mdo khams gnas chen nyer lnga yan lag dang bcas pa'i mdo byang gi gsal byed zin thung nyung ngu*). In *The Treasury of Revelations and Teachings of Mchog-gyur-bde-chen-glin-pa*, vol. 24, 125–43. Paro, Bhutan: Lama Pema Tashi. A manuscript edition complete in thirteen folio sides was made available to me through the generosity of Khenpo Sonam Tendzin (Mkhan po bsod nams bstan 'dzin) of Katok Monastery.

———. 1999. *Catalog of the Treasury of Instructions* (*Sgrub brgyud shing rta chen po brgyad kyi smin grol snying po phyogs gcig bsdus pa gdams ngag rin po che'i mdzod kyi dkar chag bkra shis grags pa'i rgya mtsho*). In *Treasury of Instructions* (*Gdams ngag mdzod*), vol. 18, 381–554. Delhi: Shechen Publications.

———. 2002a. *A Gem of Many Colors: An Account of Lodro Taye, Who Pretends to Be A Mendicant at the Feet of Teachers Without Partiality or Bias* (*Phyogs med ris med kyi bstan pa la 'dun shing dge sbyong gi gzugs brnyan 'chang ba blo gros mtha' yas kyi sde'i byung ba brjod pa nor bu sna tshogs mdog can*). In *Treasury of the Expansive* (*Rgya chen bka' mdzod*), vol. 10, 237–656. Delhi: Shechen Publications.

———. 2002b. *Illuminating Morality: Regulations for the Retreats at the Pelpung Hermitage Kunzang Dechen Wosel Ling* (*Pal spungs yang khrod sgrub sde rnams kyi bca' khrims blang dor rab gsal*). In *Treasury of the Expansive* (*Rgya chen bka' mdzod*), vol. 6, 1101–163. Delhi: Shechen Publications.

———. 2002c. *All-Pervading Melody of the Pure Lands: A Catalog of the Buildings and Contents of the Pelpung Hermitage Kunzang Dechen Wosel Ling* (*Dpal spung sa yang khrod kun bzang bde chen 'od gsal gling rten dang brten par bcas pa'i dkar chag zhing khams kun tu khyab pa'i sgra snyan*). In *Treasury of the Expansive* (*Rgya chen bka' mdzod*), vol. 6, 697–949. Delhi: Shechen Publications.

———. 2002d. *Necklace of Clear Understanding: A Brief Nonsectarian Religious History* (*Ris med chos kyi 'byung gnas mdo tsam smos pa blo gsal mgrin pa'i mdzes rgyan*). In *Treasury of the Expansive* (*Rgya chen bka' mdzod*), vol. 5, 859–90. Delhi: Shechen Publications.

————. 2002e. *Fabulous Grove of Uḍumbara Flowers: The Abbreviated Life Story of the Noble and Omniscient Jamyang Khyentse Wangpo Kunga Tenpai Gyeltsen (Rje btsun bla ma thams cad mkhyen cing gzigs ba 'jam dbyang mkhyen brtse'i dbang po kun dga' bstan pa'i rgyal mtshan dpal bzang po'i rnam thar bdor bsdus ba ngo mtshar udumbara'i dga' tshal).* In *Treasury of the Expansive (Rgya chen bka' mdzod),* vol. 10, 1–236. Delhi: Shechen Publications. The Derge Printing House also preserves an edition that is nearly identical to the Pelpung print.

————. 2002f. *Mirage of Nectar: A Fragmentary Account of the Past Lives of Pema Gargyi Wangchuk Trinle Drodul Tsel, A Mere Reflection of a Renunciant with the Three Authentic Perceptions ('Du shes gsum ldan spong ba pa'i gzugs brnyan padma gar gyi dbang phyug phrin las 'gro 'dul rtsal gyi rtogs pa brjod pa'i dum bu smrig rgyu'i bdud rtsi).* In *Treasury of the Expansive (Rgya chen bka' mdzod),* vol. 10, 657–738. Delhi: Shechen Publications.

————. 2002g. *Music from the Ocean of the Mind: An Account of Devikoṭa Tsādra Rinchen Drak, the Supreme Site of Enlightened Mind (Thugs kyi gnas mchog chen po de bI ko TI tsA 'dra rin chen brag gi rtog pa brjod pa yid kyi rgya mtsho'i rol mo).* In *Treasury of the Expansive (Rgya chen bka' mdzod),* vol. 7, 159–227. Delhi: Shechen Publications.

————. 2002h. *A Celebration of the Opening of One Hundred Doors to Great Wonder: A Lecture on the Maṇḍala Offering to the Supreme Emanation of Maitreya on the Occasion of His Investiture onto the Lion Throne (Byams mgon mchog gi sprul pa'i sku seng ge'i khrir phebs pa'i maNDala rgyas bshad ngo mtshar sgo brgya 'byed pa'i dga' ston).* In *Treasury of the Expansive (Rgya chen bka' mdzod),* vol. 5, 911–68. Delhi: Shechen Publications.

————. 2007. *One Hundred Treasure Revealers (Gter ston brgya rtsa'i rnam thar).* Lhasa: Bod ljongs mi dmangs dpe skrun khang.

————. 2009. *A Commentary on the Stages of the Path of the Light of Wisdom (Lam rim ye shes snying po'i 'grel pa).* Kathmandu: Rigpe Dorje Publications.

Jamyang Khyentse Wangpo ('Jam dbyangs mkhyen brtse'i dbang po). 1982. *Breeze Requesting the Auspicious Tune (Gter chen rnam thar las 'phros pa'i dris lan bkra shis dbyangs snyan bskul ba'i dri bzhon).* In *The Treasury of Revelations and Teachings of Mchog-gyur-bde-chen-gliṅ-pa,* vol. 39, 15–52. Paro, Bhutan: Lama Pema Tashi.

Jigme Samdrub ('Jigs med bsam grub), ed. 1995. *History of the Monasteries of Kardze Prefecture (Khams phyogs dkar dzes khul gyi dgon sde so so'i lo rgyus gsal bar bshad pa nang bstan gsal ba'i me long).* 3 vols. Beijing: Zhongguo zangxue yanjiu zhongxin lishi zongjiao yanjiusuo.

Konchok Gyurme (Dkon mchog 'gyur med). 1982 (1921). *Biography of Chokgyur Lingpa (Gter chen mchog gyur bde chen gling pa'i rnam thar bkra shis dbyangs kyi yan lag gsal byed).* In *The Treasury of Revelations and Teachings of Mchog-gyur-bde-chen-gliṅ-pa,* vol. 38, 1–629. Paro, Bhutan: Lama Pema Tashi.

Lodro Donyo (Blo gros don yod). 2005. *Biography of Tashi Wozer (Bkra shis 'od zer gyi rnam thar)*. In *Indranīla Ornament: A History of the Kālacakra (Dus 'khor chos 'byung in+dra nI la'i phra tshom)*, 555–58. Mirik: 'Bo dkar nges don chos 'khor gling gi bla spyi spar bskrun zhus.

Lodro Puntsok (Blo gros phun tshogs). 2004. *The Encouraging Drum-Beat of the Gods: A Gazetteer of Mesho (Sman shod gnas yig phyogs sgrig dang bskul lha dbang rnga sgra)*. Dzongsar Monastery.

Pema Yeshe (Padma ye shes). 1982. *Melody of the Fifth Auspicious Birth (Gter chen mchog gyur gling pa'i thun mong phyi'i rnam thar bkra shis skye ba lnga pa'i dbyangs snyan)*. In *The Treasury of Revelations and Teachings of Mchog-gyur-bde-chen-gliṇ-pa*, vol. 39, 81–153. Paro, Bhutan: Lama Pema Tashi.

Tashi Chopel (Bkra shis chos 'phel). 2002. *Marvelous Gem-Like Vision (Rje kun gzigs 'jam mgon ngag gi dbang phyug yon tan rgya mtsho'i zhabs kyi 'das rjes kyi rnam par thar pa ngo mtshar nor bu'i snang ba)*. In *Treasury of the Expansive (Rgya chen bka' mdzod)*, vol. 10, 739–83. Delhi: Shechen Publications.

———. 2009. *Treasury of Wish-Fulfilling Jewels ('Jam mgon kong sprul yon tan rgya mtsho'i gsan yig dgos 'dod kun 'byung)*. Beijing: Mi rigs dpe skrun khang.

## ENGLISH

Adshead, Samuel Adrian M. 1984. *Province and Politics in Late Imperial China: Viceregal Government in Szechwan, 1898–1911*. London: Curzon Press.

Akester, Matthew. 2016. *Jamyang Kyentsé Wangpo's Guide to Central Tibet*. Chicago: Serindia Publications.

Aris, Michael. 1989. *Hidden Treasures and Secret Lives*. London: Kegan Paul International.

———. 1992. "The Tibetan Borderlands." In *Lamas, Princes, and Brigands: Joseph Rock's Photographs of the Tibetan Borderlands of China*, edited by Michael Aris, 13–19. New York: China House Gallery China Institute in America.

Baber, Edward Colborne. 1882. *Travels and Researches in Western China*. London: J. Murray.

Batchelor, Stephen, and Donald S. Lopez, Jr. 1998. "Deity or Demon: The 'Unmentionable' Feud over Tibet's Dorje Shugden." *Tricycle* 7 (3): 58–82.

Blondeau, Anne-Marie. 1998. *Tibetan Mountain Deities, Their Cults and Representations*. Vienna: Verlag der Österreichischen Akademie der Wissenschaften.

Blondeau, Anne-Marie, and Ernst Steinkellner. 1996. *Reflections of the Mountain: Essays on the History and Social Meaning of the Mountain Cult in Tibet and the Himalaya*. Vienna: Verlag der Österreichischen Akademie der Wissenschaften.

Brunnhölzl, Karl, trans. 2008. *Luminous Heart: The Third Karmapa on Consciousness, Wisdom, and Buddha Nature*. Nitartha Institute Series. Ithaca: Snow Lion Publications.

Brunnhölzl, Karl. 2014. *When the Clouds Part*. Boulder: Snow Lion Publications.

Buddhaghoṣa. 1870. *Buddhaghosha's Parables*. Translated by Henry Thomas Rogers. London: Trübner and Company.

Butters, Albion Moonlight. 2006. "The Doxographical Genius of Kun mkhyen kLong chen cab 'byams pa." PhD diss., Columbia University.

Campbell, June. 1996. *Traveller in Space: Gender, Identity and Tibetan Buddhism*. London: Continuum.

Chaix, Rémi. 2016. "Construction Work and Wages at the Dergé Printing House in the Eighteenth Century." *Cross-Currents: East Asian History and Culture Review* 19: 48–70.

Ch'en, Kenneth. 1946–1947. "The Tibetan Tripitaka." *Harvard Journal of Asiatic Studies* 9: 53–62.

Chögyam Trungpa. 1981. *Journey Without Goal: The Tantric Wisdom of the Buddha*. Boston: Shambhala Publications.

Chokling Dewey Dorje. 2008. *The Great Gate*. Kathmandu: Rangjung Yeshe Publications.

Cuevas, Bryan. 2015. *The All-Pervading Melodious Drumbeat: The Life of Ra Lotsawa*. New York: Penguin.

Dalton, Jacob. 2004. "The Development of Perfection: The Interiorization of Buddhist Ritual in the Eighth and Ninth Centuries." *Journal of Indian Philosophy* 32 (1): 1–30.

———. 2016. *The Gathering of Intentions: A History of a Tibetan Tantra*. New York: Columbia University Press.

Das, Surya. 1992. *The Snow Lion's Turquoise Mane: Wisdom Tales from Tibet*. New York: Harper Collins.

Davidson, Ronald. 2002. *Indian Esoteric Buddhism: A Social History of the Tantric Movement*. New York: Columbia University Press.

———. 2005. *Tibetan Renaissance*. New York: Columbia University Press.

Deroche, Marc-Henri. 2009. "'Phreng po gter ston Shes rab 'od zer (1518–1584) on the Eight Lineages of Attainment: Research on a *Ris med* Paradigm." In *Contemporary Visions in Tibetan Studies. Proceeding of the First International Seminar of Young Tibetologists*, edited by Brandon Dotson, Kalsang Norbu Gurung, Georgios Halkias, and Tim Myatt, 319–42. Chicago: Serindia Publications.

———. 2018. "On Being 'Impartial' (*ris med*): From Non-Sectarianism to the Great Perfection." *Revue d'Etudes Tibétaines* 44: 129–58.

Doctor, Andreas. 2005. *Tibetan Treasure Literature: Revelation, Tradition, and Accomplishment in Visionary Buddhism*. Ithaca: Snow Lion Publications.

Doctor, Andreas, and Karma Gelek. Unpublished Catalog of *The Treasury of Revelations and Teachings of Gter chen Mchog gyur bde chen gling pa*.

Dreyfus, Georges. 1998. "The Shugden Affair: Origins of a Controversy." *Journal of the International Association of Buddhist Studies* 21 (2): 227–70.

Emerson, Ralph Waldo. 1880. "An Address Delivered Before the Senior Class in Divinity College, Cambridge, Sunday Evening, July 15, 1838." In *The Works of Ralph Waldo Emerson*, vol. 5, 98–125. Boston: Houghton, Osgood and Company.

Epstein, Lawrence, ed. 2002. *Khams pa Histories: Visions of People, Place and Authority*. Leiden: Brill.

Fuchs, Rosemarie. 2000. *Buddha Nature: The Mahayana Uttaratantra Shastra with Commentary*. Ithaca: Snow Lion Publications.

Gardner, Alexander. 2003. Review of "*Khams pa Histories: Visions of People, Place and Authority*," by Lawrence Epstein. *Tibet Journal* 28 (3): 61–96.

———. 2005–2006. "The Sa Chog: Violence and Veneration in a Tibetan Soil Ritual." *Études mongoles et sibériennes, centrasiatiques et tibétaines* 36–37: 283–324.

———. 2006. *The Twenty-five Great Sites of Khams: Religious Geography, Revelation, and Nonsectarianism in Nineteenth-Century Eastern Tibet*. PhD diss., University of Michigan.

Garrett, Francis. 2009. "The Alchemy of Accomplishing Medicine (*sman sgrub*): Situating the Yuthok Heart Essence (*G.yu thog snying thig*) in Literature and History." *Journal of Indian Philosophy* 37: 207–30.

———. 2013. "Mercury, Mad Dogs, and Smallpox: Medicine in the Si tu paṇ chen Tradition." *Journal of the International Association for Tibetan Studies* 7: 277–301.

Germano, David. 2002. "The Seven Descents and the Early History of Rnying ma Transmissions." In *The Many Canons of Tibetan Buddhism: Proceedings of the Ninth Seminar of the International Association for Tibetan Studies*, edited by Helmut Eimer, 225–64. Leiden: Brill.

Greatrex, Roger. 1994. "A Brief Introduction to the First Jinchuan War (1747–1749)." In *Tibetan Studies: Proceedings of the Sixth Seminar of the International Association for Tibetan Studies, Fagernes, 1992*, edited by Per Kvaerne, vol. 1, 247–263. Oslo: Institute for Comparative Research in Human Culture.

Gros, Stéphane, ed. 2016. Introduction to "Frontier Tibet: Trade and Boundaries of Authority in Kham." *Cross-Currents: East Asian History and Culture Review* 19: 1–26.

Gyatso, Janet. 1992. "Genre, Authorship, and Transmission in Visionary Buddhism: The Literary Traditions of Thang-stong rGyal-po." In *Tibetan Buddhism: Reason and Revelation*, edited by Ronald Davidson and Steven Goodman, 95–106. Albany: State University of New York Press.

———. 1993. "The Logic of Legitimation in the Tibetan Treasure Tradition." *History of Religions* 33 (2): 97–134.

———. 1994. "Guru Chos-dbang's *gTer 'byung chen mo*: An Early Survey of the Treasure Tradition and Its Strategies in Discussing Bon Treasure." In *Tibetan Studies: Proceedings of the Sixth Seminar of the International Association for Tibetan Studies, Fagernes, 1992*, edited by Per Kvaerne, vol. 1, 275–87. Oslo: Institute for Comparative Research in Human Culture.

———. 1996. "Drawn from the Tibetan Treasury: The gTer ma Literature." In *Tibetan Literature: Studies in Genre*, edited by José Ignacio Cabezón and Roger Jackson, 147–69. Ithaca: Snow Lion Publications.

———. 1997. "From the Autobiography of a Visionary." In *Religions of Tibet in Practice*, edited by Donald S. Lopez, 369–75. Princeton: Princeton University Press.

———. 1998. *Apparitions of the Self: The Secret Autobiographies of a Tibetan Visionary*. Princeton: Princeton University Press.

Harding, Sarah. 2010. *Niguma, Lady of Illusion*. Boulder: Shambhala Publications.

Harrison, Paul. 1996. "A Brief History of the Tibetan bKa' 'gyur." In *Tibetan Literature: Studies in Genre*, edited by José Ignacio Cabezón and Roger Jackson, 217–228. Ithaca: Snow Lion Publications.

Hartley, Lauran Ruth. 1997. "A Socio-historical Study of the Kingdom of Sde-dge (Derge, Kham) in the Late Nineteenth Century: Ris-med Views of Alliance and Authority." MA thesis, Indiana University, Bloomington.

Higgins, David, and Martina Draszczyk. 2016. *Mahāmudrā and the Middle Way: Post-classical Kagyü Discourses on Mind, Emptiness and Buddha-Nature*. Vienna: Arbeitskreis für Tibetische und Buddhistische Studien.

Hillis, Gregory Alexander. 2002. "The Rhetoric of Naturalness: A Critical Study of the gNas lugs mdzod." PhD diss., University of Virginia.

Hirshberg, Daniel. 2016. *Remembering the Lotus-Born: Padmasambhava in the History of Tibet's Golden Age*. Boston: Wisdom Publications.

Hookham, S. K. 1991. *The Buddha Within: Tathāgatagarbha Doctrine According to the Shentong Interpretation of the Ratnagotravibhāga*. Albany: State University of New York Press.

Huber, Toni. 1990. "Where Exactly are Cāritra, Devikoṭa and Himavat? A Sacred Geography Controversy and the Development of Tantric Buddhist Pilgrimage Sites in Tibet." *Kailash* 16 (3–4): 121–64.

———. 1994a. "Putting the Gnas back into Gnas-skor: Rethinking Tibetan Buddhist Pilgrimage Practice." *Tibet Journal* 19 (2): 23–60. Reprinted in Huber 1999b, 77–104.

———. 1994b. "When What You See Is Not What You Get: Remarks on the Traditional Tibetan Presentation of Sacred Geography." In *Tantra and Popular Religion in Tibet*, edited by Geoffrey Samuel, Hamish Gregor, and Elisabeth Stutchbury, 39–52. New Delhi: International Academy of Indian Culture and Aditya Prakashan.

———. 1997a. "Guidebook to Lapchi." In *Religions of Tibet in Practice*, edited by Donald S. Lopez, 120–34. Princeton: Princeton University Press.

———. 1997b. "Ritual and Politics in the Eastern Himalaya: The Staging of Processions at Tsari." In *Les Habitants du Toit du Monde*, edited by Samten G. Karmay and Philippe Sagant, 221–60. Nantierre: Société d'ethnologie.

———. 1999a. *The Cult of Pure Crystal Mountain: Popular Pilgrimage and Visionary Landscape in Southeast Tibet*. New York: Oxford University Press.

———. 1999b. *Sacred Spaces and Powerful Places in Tibetan Culture*. Dharamsala: Library of Tibetan Works and Archives.

———. 2000: "Constructions of Space and Place in Tibetan and Himalayan Societies." *Asia Quarterly* 8: 13–14.

Jackson, David. 2003. *A Saint in Seattle: The Life of the Tibetan Mystic Dezhung Rinpoche.* Boston: Wisdom Publications.

———. 2006. "Situ Panchen's Paintings of the Eight Great Siddhas: A Fateful Gift to Derge and the World." In *Holy Madness: Portraits of Tantric Siddhas,* edited by Rob Linrothe, 93–107. Chicago: Serindia Publications and Rubin Museum of Art.

———, ed. 2009. *Patron and Painter: Situ Panchen and the Revival of the Encampment Style.* New York: Rubin Museum of Art.

Jacoby, Sarah H. 2014. *Love and Liberation: Autobiographical Writings of the Tibetan Buddhist Visionary Sera Khandro.* New York: Columbia University Press.

Jamgon Kongtrul. 1977. *The Torch of Certainty.* Translated by Judith Hanson. Boston: Shambhala Publications.

———. 1987. *The Great Path to Awakening.* Translated by Ken McLeod. Boston: Shambhala Publications.

Jamgön Kongtrul Lodrö Tayé. 1995. *Myriad Worlds: Buddhist Cosmology in Abhidharma, Kālacakra, and Dzog-chen.* Ithaca: Snow Lion Publications.

Jamgön Kongtrul. 1998. *Buddhist Ethics.* Translated by the International Translation Committee. Ithaca: Snow Lion Publications.

Jamgön Kongtrul Lodrö Thayé. 1999. *The Teacher-Student Relationship.* Translated by Ron Gerry. Ithaca: Snow Lion Publications.

Jamgön Kongtrul. 2002. *Creation and Completion: Essential Points of Tantric Meditation.* Translated by Sarah Harding. Boston: Wisdom Publications.

Jamgön Kongtrul Lodrö Thayé. 2003. *The Autobiography of Jamgön Kongtrul: A Gem of Many Colors.* Translated by Richard Barron. Ithaca: Snow Lion Publications.

Jamgön Kongtrul. 2005. *Systems of Buddhist Tantra.* Translated by Elio Guarisco and Ingrid McLeod. Ithaca: Snow Lion Publications.

———. 2010. *Buddhism's Journey to Tibet: The Treasury of Knowledge Books Two, Three, and Four.* Translated by the Kalu Rinpoché Translation Group. Ithaca: Snow Lion Publications.

Jamgön Kongtrül Lodrö Taye. 2011. *One Hundred Treasure Revealers.* Translated by Yeshe Gyamtso. Woodstock, New York: KTD Publications.

Jamgon Kongtrul. 2012. *The Life of Jamyang Khyentse Wangpo.* Translated by Matthew Akester. Kathmandu: Shechen.

Jamgön Kongtrul Lodrö Thayé. 2013. *The Catalog of the Treasury of Precious Instructions.* Translated by Richard Barron. New York: Tsadra Foundation.

Jampa Mackenzie Stewart. 2004. *The Life of Gampopa.* Ithaca: Snow Lion Publications.

———. 2014. *The Life of Longchenpa: The Omniscient Dharma King of the Vast Expanse.* Boulder: Snow Lion Publications.

Kano, Kazuo. 2016. *Buddha-nature and Emptiness: rNgog Blo-ldan-shes-rab and a Transmission of the Ratnagotravibhāga from India to Tibet.* Vienna: Vienna Series for Tibetan and Buddhist Studies.

Kapstein, Matthew. 1980. "The Shangs-pa bKa'-brgyud: an unknown school of Tibetan Buddhism." In *Studies in Honor of Hugh Richardson,* edited by Michael Aris and Aung San Suu Kyi, 138–44. Warminster: Aris and Phillips.

———. 1992. "Remarks on the Maṇi-bka'-'bum and the Cult of Avalokiteśvara in Tibet." In *Tibetan Buddhism: Reason and Revelation,* edited by Ronald Davidson and Steven Goodman, 79–93. Albany: State University of New York Press.

———. 1996. "gDams ngag: Tibetan Technologies of the Self." In *Tibetan Literature: Studies in Genre,* edited by José Ignacio Cabezón and Roger Jackson, 275–89. Ithaca: Snow Lion Publications.

———. 2007. "Tibetan Technologies of the Self, Part II: The Teachings of the Eight Great Conveyances." In *The Pandita and the Siddha: Tibetan Studies in Honour of E. Gene Smith,* edited by Ramon N. Prats, 110–29. Dharamsala: Amnye Machen Institute.

Karmay, Samten. 1972. *The Treasury of Good Sayings: A Tibetan History of Bon.* London: Oxford University Press.

———. 1988. *The Great Perfection: A Philosophical and Meditative Teaching of Tibetan Buddhism.* Leiden: Brill.

Karmay, Samten, and Jeff Watt, eds. 2008. *Bon: The Magic Word.* New York: Rubin Museum of Art.

Khenpo Karthar Rinpoche. 2013. *Four-Session Guru Yoga by Miky Dorje: Khenpo Karthar Rinpoche's Commentary Based on the Commentary by Karma Chakme Rinpoche.* Woodstock, New York: KTD Publications.

Kolmaš, Josef. 1968. *A Genealogy of the Kings of Derge (Sde-dge'i rgyal rabs), Dissertationes orientales, vol. 12.* Prague: Oriental Institute in Academia.

———. 1988. "Dezhung Rinpoche's Summary and Continuation of the Sde-dge'i rgyal-rabs." *Acta Orientalia (Budapest)* 42 (1): 119–53.

Komarovski, Yaroslav. 2011. *Visions of Unity: The Golden Paṇḍita Shakya Chokden's New Interpretation of Yogācāra and Madhyamaka.* Albany, New York: State University of New York Press.

Kværne, Per, and Elliot Sperling. 1993. "Preliminary study of an inscription from Rgyal-rong." *Acta Orientalia* 54.

Lama Kunsang, Lama Pemo, and Marie Aubèle. 2012. *History of the Karmapas: The Odyssey of the Tibetan Masters with the Black Crowns.* Ithaca: Snow Lion Publications.

Li An-che. 1947. "Dege: A Study of Tibetan Population." *Southwest Journal of Anthropology* 3 (4): 279–93.

Lopez, Donald S. 2009. *In the Forest of Faded Wisdom.* Chicago: University of Chicago Press.

MacDonald, Alexander. 1990. "Hindu-isation, Buddha-isation, Then Lama-isation or: What Happened at La-phyi?" In *Indo-Tibetan Studies: Papers in Honour and Appreciation of Professor David L. Snellgrove's Contribution to Indo-Tibetan studies*, edited by Tadeusz Skorupski, 199–208. Tring, U.K.: Institute of Buddhist Studies.

———. 1997. *Maṇḍala and Landscape*. New Delhi: D.K. Printworld.

Martin, Dan. 1990. "Bonpo Canons and Jesuit Cannons: On Sectarian Factors Involved in the Ch'ien-lung Emperor's Second Goldstream Expedition of 1771–1776 Based Primarily on Some Tibetan Sources." *Tibet Journal* 15 (2): 3–28.

———. 1991. "The Emergence of Bon and the Tibetan Polemical Tradition." PhD diss., Indiana University, Bloomington.

———. 1996. "Unearthing Bon Treasures: A Study of Tibetan Sources on the Earlier Years in the Life of Gshen-chen klu-dga'." *Journal of the American Oriental Society* 116 (4): 619–44.

———. 1997. *Tibetan Histories: A Bibliography of Tibetan-Language Historical Works*. London: Serindia Publications.

———. 2001. *Unearthing Bon Treasures: Life and Contested Legacy of a Tibetan Scripture Revealer, with a General Bibliography of Bon*. Leiden: Brill.

Mathes, Klaus-Dieter. 2008. *A Direct Path to the Buddha Within: Gö Lotsāwa's Mahāmudrā Interpretation of the Ratnagotravibhāga*. Boston: Wisdom Publications.

Mayer, Robert. 1997. "Were the gSar-ma-pa Polemicists Justified in Rejecting Some rNying-ma-pa Tantras?" In *Tibetan Studies*, edited by H. Krasser, M. T. Much, E. Steinkellner, and H. Tauscher, vol 2, 619–32. Vienna: Verlag der Österreichischen Akademie der Wissenschaften.

McKay, Alex. 1998. *Pilgrimage in Tibet*. Richmond: Curzon.

Ngari Panchen Pema Wangyi Gyelpo. 1996. *Perfect Conduct: Ascertaining the Three Vows*. Translated by Khenpo Gyurme Samdrub and Sangye Khandro. Boston: Wisdom Publications.

Ngawang Zangpo. 1994. *Jamgon Kongtrul's Retreat Manual*. Ithaca: Snow Lion Publications.

———. 1997. *Enthronement: The Recognition of the Reincarnate Masters of Tibet and the Himalayas*. Ithaca: Snow Lion Publications.

———. 2001. *Sacred Ground: Jamgon Kongtrul on "Pilgrimage and Sacred Geography."* Ithaca: Snow Lion Publications.

———. 2002. *Guru Rinpoche: His Life and Times*. Boulder: Snow Lion Publications.

Orgyen Tobgyal Rinpoche. 1990. *The Life and Teachings of Chokgyur Lingpa*. Translated by Tulku Jigmey Khyentse and Erik Pema Kunsang. Kathmandu: Rangjung Yeshe Publications.

Padmasambhava Guru Rinpoche. 1999. *The Light of Wisdom*. Translated by Erik Pema Kunsang. Kathmandu: Rangjung Yeshe Publications.

Pang, Rachel H. 2014. "The Rimé Activities of Shabkar Tsokdruk Rangdrol (1781–1851)." *Revue d'Etudes Tibétaines* 29: 5–30.

Patrul Rinpoche. 1994. *Words of My Perfect Teacher.* Boston: Shambhala Publications.

Petech, Luciano. 1972. *China and Tibet in the Early 18th Century: History of the Establishment of Chinese Protectorate in Tibet.* 2nd, revised Vol. Leiden: Brill.

———. 1973. *Aristocracy and Government in Tibet, 1728–1959.* Roma: Istituto Italiano per il Medio ed Estremo Oriente.

Quintman, Andrew. 2010. *Life of Milarepa.* New York: Penguin.

———. 2013. *The Yogin and the Madman.* New York: Columbia University Press.

Rangjung Dorje. 2014. *The Profound Inner Principles; With Jamgon Kongtrul Lodro Taye's Commentary Illuminating "The Profound Principles."* Translated by Elisabeth M. Callahan. Boston: Snow Lion Publications.

Ringu Tulku. 2006. *The Ri-me Philosophy of Jamgon Kongtrul the Great: A Study of the Buddhist Lineages of Tibet,* edited by Ann Helm. Boston: Shambhala Publications.

Ronis, Jann. 2011. "Powerful Women in the History of Degé: Reassessing the Eventful Reign of the Dowager Queen Tsewang Lhamo (d. 1812)." *Revue d'Etudes Tibétaines* 21: 61–81.

Samuel, Geoffrey. 1993. *Civilized Shamans: Buddhism in Tibetan Societies.* Washington: Smithsonian Institution Press.

Schapiro, Joshua. 2012. "Patrul Rinpoche on Self-Cultivation: The Rhetoric of Nineteenth-Century Tibetan Buddhist Life-Advice." PhD diss. Harvard University.

Schmidt, Erik Pema Kunsang. 2000. *The Lineage of Chokling Tersar.* Kathmandu: Rangjung Yeshe Publications.

Schopen, Gregory. 1996. *Bones, Stones, and Buddhist Monks: Collected Papers on the Archaeology, Epigraphy, and Texts of Monastic Buddhism in India.* Honolulu: University of Hawai'i Press.

Schwieger, P. 2010. "Collecting and Arranging the gTer ma Tradition: Kong sprul's Great Treasury of the Hidden Teachings." In *Edition, éditions: l'écrit au Tibet, évolution et devenir,* edited by Anne Chayet, Cristina Scherrer-Schaub, Françoise Robin & Jean-Luc Achard, 321–36. München: Indus Verlag.

Shabkar Tsogdruk Rangdrol. 1991. *The Life of Shabkar, Autobiography of a Tibetan Yogi.* Translated by Matthieu Ricard. Albany: State University of New York Press.

Shakabpa, W. D. 1967. *Tibet, A Political History.* New Haven: Yale University Press.

Smith, E. Gene. 2001. *Among Tibetan Texts: History & Literature of the Himalayan Plateau.* Boston: Wisdom Publications.

Tashi Tsering. 1985. "Ñag-roṅ Mgon-po rnam-rgyal: A 19th Century Khams-pa Warrior." In *Soundings in Tibetan Civilization,* edited by Barbara Nimri Aziz and Matthew Kapstein, 198–214. New Delhi: Manohar.

Teichman, Eric. 1922. *Travels of a Consular Officer in Eastern Tibet, Together with a History of the Relations Between China, Tibet and India.* Cambridge: The University Press.

Terchen Barway Dorje. 2005. *Precious Essence: The Inner Autobiography of Terchen Barway Dorje*. Translated by Yeshe Gyamtso. Woodstock, New York: KTD Publications.

Tricycle. 1996. "The Emperor's Tantric Robes: An Interview with June Campbell." *Tricycle* 6 (2): 38–40.

Trungram Gyatrul Rinpoche Sherpa. 2004. "Gampopa, the Monk and the Yogi: His Life and Teachings." PhD diss. Harvard University.

Tsering Wangchuk. 2017. *The Uttaratantra in the Land of Snows: Tibetan Thinkers Debate the Centrality of the Buddha-Nature Treatise*. New York: State University of New York Press.

Tucci, Giuseppe. 1940. *Travels of Tibetan Pilgrims in the Swat Valley*. Calcutta: Greater India Society.

Tulku Thondup. 1986. *Hidden Teachings of Tibet: An Explanation of the Terma Tradition of the Nyingma School of Buddhism*. London: Wisdom Publications.

Tulku Urgyen Rinpoche. 2005. *Blazing Splendor: The Memoirs of Tulku Urgyen Rinpoche*. Translated by Erik Pema Kunzang and Macia Schmidt. Kathmandu: Rangjung Yeshe Publications.

van der Kuijp, Leonard. 1983. *Contributions to the Development of Tibetan Buddhist Epistemology: From the Eleventh to the Thirteenth Century*. Hamburg: F. Steiner.

———. 1988. "Two Early Sources for the History of the House of Sde-dge." *Journal of the Tibet Society* 8: 1–20.

van Spengen, Wim, and Lama Jabb. 2009. *Studies in the History of Eastern Tibet: PIATS 2006, Tibetan Studies: Proceedings of the Eleventh Seminar of the International Association for Tibetan Studies, Königswinter 2006*. Leiden: Brill.

Vostrikov, Andrei Ivanovich. 1970. *Tibetan Historical Literature*. Calcutta: Indian Studies: Past & Present.

Wangchen Rinpoche. 2009. *Buddhist Fasting Practice: The Nyungne Method of Thousand-Armed Chenrezig*. Ithaca: Snow Lion Publications.

Wong, Sylvia. 2010. *The Karmapa Prophecies*. Delhi: Motilal Banarsidass.

Yeshe Dorje. 2013. *Cloud of Nectar*. Translated by Oriol Aguilar. Archidosso: Shangshung Publications.

Yeshe Tsogyel. 1993. *The Lotus-Born. The Life Story of Padmasambhava*. Boston: Shambhala Publications.

Yudru Tsomu. 2013. "Constructing Images of Gönpo Namgyel." *Revue d'Etudes Tibétaines* 26: 57–91.

———. 2015. *The Rise of Gönpo Namgyel in Kham: The Blind Warrior of Nyarong*. New York: Lexington Books.

# Index